KU-336-854

MARTIN GOODMAN

A History of Judaism

PENGUIN BOOKS

PENGUIN BOOKS

UK | USA | Canada | Ireland | Australia
India | New Zealand | South Africa

Penguin Books is part of the Penguin Random House group of companies
whose addresses can be found at global.penguinrandomhouse.com.

First published by Allen Lane 2017
Published in Penguin Books 2019
001

Copyright © Michael Goodman, 2017

The moral right of the author has been asserted

Set in 8.98/12.2 pt Sabon LT Std
Typeset by Jouve (UK), Milton Keynes
Printed and bound in Great Britain by Clays Ltd, Elcograf S.p.A.

A CIP catalogue record for this book is available from the British Library

ISBN: 978-0-141-03821-6

www.greenpenguin.co.uk

MIX
Paper from
responsible sources
FSC
www.fsc.org   FSC® C018179

Penguin Random House is committed to a
sustainable future for our business, our readers
and our planet. This book is made from Forest
Stewardship Council® certified paper.

Contents

PART III
The Formation of Rabbinic Judaism (70–1500 CE)

PART IV
Authority and Reaction (1500–1800)

Maps

Maps 2, 4 and 6–11 are after N. de Lange, *Atlas of the Jewish World* (Oxford and New York, 1984).

List of Illustrations

The plan of the Second Temple on p. 47 is after Th. A. Busink, *Der Tempel von Jerusalem*, 2 vols. (Leiden, 1980), vol. 2, p. 1179.

Acknowledgements

The idea for this book came from Stuart Proffitt at Penguin. When I proposed to Stuart that I might write a book encapsulating new ideas which have emerged while giving lectures in Oxford over many years on varieties of Judaism in the late Second Temple period and on the formation of rabbinic Judaism, he persuaded me that the volume should extend both before and after the periods that are at the centre of my expertise. I have enjoyed the challenge and the wider perspective it has brought.

Attempting to cover the whole history of Judaism has been daunting and has been possible only with a great deal of help. For the shape of the history in its initial planning I owe much to the expert advice of my colleagues Joanna Weinberg and Miri Freud-Kandel. Many ideas to be found throughout the volume arose in discussions in 2009–10 within the project on 'Toleration within Judaism' funded by the Leverhulme Trust, and I am very grateful to Joseph David, Corinna R. Kaiser and Simon Levis Sullam, the three research fellows who worked with me on the project during that year. The book has also benefited over the past eight years from the expertise of exceptional research assistants: Charlotte Goodman, Daniel Herskowitz, Judah Levine, Micha Perry, Deborah Rooke, Joshua Teplitsky, Benjamin Williams and Milena Zeidler. Sarah Stroumsa and Hugh Williamson both gave me invaluable advice on large sections of an early draft. Philip Alexander, Norman Solomon and Adam Ferziger read and commented on the whole text and saved me from many errors. Those that remain are my responsibility alone: I have been acutely aware of the danger of over-simplification inherent in seeking to include so much in so small a compass.

I acknowledge with gratitude the munificent grant from the Leverhulme Trust for the project on 'Toleration within Judaism' and generous grants for assistance in preparing the book for publication from the Faculty of Oriental Studies in Oxford and the Oxford Centre for Hebrew and Jewish Studies. Publication was undoubtedly delayed by my duties since 2013 as president of the Centre, which involved abandoning work on the book altogether for a while, but the final text may well have been improved by the opportunity to reconsider and recast the earlier draft, and I am grateful to colleagues at the Centre and the Leopold Muller Memorial Library, especially Sue Forteath, Martine Smith-Huvers and César Merchán-Hamann, for providing the most helpful, congenial and stimulating environment possible for writing a history of this scope.

This is not the first time I have had cause to thank Neelum Ali for her extraordinary patience and dedication in turning my handwriting into typescript. These last years have not been easy, and my gratitude is all the warmer. I am grateful also to Ben Sinyor and Richard Duguid, and all who worked on the book in its final stages. I have been much helped by Cecilia Mackay in the selection of images for illustration. The text was superbly copy-edited by Peter James. The index was expertly produced by Dave Cradduck.

Over the ten years since this book was first mooted our family home has moved from Birmingham to Oxford. I have had many discussions with Sarah about what should go into the book, and this final version should be seen as a tribute to our life together for over forty years. This book is for her and for our children, Joshua, Alexander, Daisy and Charlotte, and for the next generation, currently represented by Ezra.

Martin Goodman
Oxford
May 2017

Note

Explanatory glosses appear between round brackets in the main text and between square brackets in quotations, except in citations from the Dead Sea scrolls, which use the conventions in G. Vermes, *The Complete Dead Sea Scrolls in English* (London, 1997) (see p. 536 below). The abbreviation 'b.' is used for the Hebrew 'ben' ('son of') and the abbreviation 'R.' is used for the Hebrew title 'Rabbi'.

Glossary

ABBREVIATIONS

A   Aramaic
Arab   Arabic
G   Greek
H   Hebrew
Y   Yiddish

Amidah [H]   Lit. 'standing'. The main prayer at daily services.

amora (pl. *amoraim*) [A]   Lit. 'interpreter'. Term applied to the rabbinic sages cited in the Talmuds active from the conclusion of the Mishnah in *c.* 200 CE to the end of the fifth century CE.

etrog [H]   Citron (a fruit like a lemon) used in liturgical worship on Sukkot.

gaon (pl. *geonim*) [H]   Lit. 'excellency'. Title of the head of the main academies in Iraq from the sixth to the eleventh centuries.

genizah [H]   Lit. 'concealment'. Place for deposit of sacred texts when they are worn out.

geonic period   The sixth to eleventh centuries CE (see *gaon*).

golem [H]   In kabbalistic tradition, a man made of clay and magically brought to life.

Habad [H]   Acronym for a form of mysticism adopted by Lubavitch *hasidim*.

haftarah (pl. **haftaroth**) [H]   Reading from the Prophets following a reading from the Torah in synagogue liturgy.

Haggadah [H]   The narration of the exodus from Egypt at the Seder on Pesach.

hairesis (pl. *haireseis*) [G]   Lit. 'choice'. A school of philosophy.

hakham [H]   Lit. 'sage'. Rabbinic title.

halakhah (pl. **halakhot**) [H]   Lit. 'walking'. The legal elements in rabbinic teaching.

hallah [H]   Lit. 'dough offering'. Plaited loaf made for Sabbath and festivals.

Hallel [H]   Lit. 'praise'. Sequence of psalms sung on festival and other special days in synagogue.

Hanukkah [H]   Lit. 'dedication'. Festival commemorating the re-dedication of the Temple after the Maccabean revolt.

haredi (pl. *haredim*) [H]   Lit. 'fearful'. Name applied to modern adherents of traditional orthodox Judaism.

hasid (pl. *hasidim*) [H]   Lit. 'pious'. Self-description adopted by followers of Hasidism since the eighteenth century.

Hasidei Ashkenaz [H]   Lit. 'the pious ones of Ashkenaz'. Pietists in the Rhineland and northern France in the twelfth and thirteenth centuries CE.

havdalah [H]   Ceremony marking the end of the Sabbath.

haver (pl. *haverim*) [H]   'companion'. 1. In tannaitic sources, person punctilious with regard to tithes and ritual purity; 2. in amoraic times and later, a rabbinic sage.

havurah (pl. *havurot*) [H]   Fellowship of Jews meeting for religious purposes.

hekhalot [H]   Lit. 'halls'. The celestial realms through which the visionary ascends to the throne of God in Merkavah mysticism.

herem [H]   Lit. 'ban'. The formal exclusion of an individual from the community.

hiddush (pl. *hiddushim*) [H]   'novelties'. New legal doctrines derived from talmudic or biblical commentary.

kabbalah [H]   Lit. 'tradition'. Mystical movement started in medieval Spain and Provence.

kaddish [H]   Prayer of sanctification and praise of God, recited at breaks in synagogue liturgy and as a memorial prayer for the dead.

kalam [Arab]   Islamic scholastic theology.

kedushah [H]   Lit. 'sanctification'. Part of synagogue liturgy evoking the worship of God by the angels.

kiddush [H]   Lit. 'sanctification'. Benediction recited over wine on Sabbaths and festivals.

Kol Nidrei [H]   Prayer about release from vows, recited at the beginning of Yom Kippur.

kosher [H]   Lit. 'suitable' or 'fit'. Most often used to refer to food and drink.

maggid [H]   Lit. 'speaker'. 1. popular preacher; 2. heavenly voice speaking through a mystic.

maskil (pl. *maskilim*) [H]   Lit. 'intelligent'. In the nineteenth century, a follower of the Jewish Enlightenment (*Haskalah*).

masorah [H]   Lit. 'tradition'. Notes and signs in texts of the Hebrew Bible indicating variants, pronunciation and cantillation.

Masorti [H]   Lit. 'traditional'. Name sometimes ascribed to Conservative Judaism.

matsah (pl. *matsot*) [H]   Unleavened bread eaten on Pesach.

Mekilta [A]   Commentary on the book of Exodus.

menorah (pl. *menorot*) [H]   Seven-branched candelabrum.

midrash (pl. *midrashim*) [H]   Exegesis of scripture.

mikveh (pl. *mikvaot*) [H].   Lit. 'gathering'. A ritual bath.

min (pl. *minim*) [H]   Lit. 'kind' or 'species'. Heretic.

Mishnah [H]   Collection of rabbinic legal opinions collated in the early third century CE.

mitnagdim [H]   Lit. 'opponents'. Opponents of Hasidism in the eighteenth and nineteenth centuries.

mitzvah (pl. *mitzvot*) [H]   Lit. 'command'. A duty understood to be religiously required.

Musar [H]   Lit. 'ethics'. Ethical renewal movement which started in eastern Europe in the nineteenth century. ·

nasi [H]   Lit. 'prince'. Title given to figures in authority, in particular the Jewish patriarch in Palestine in the third and fourth centuries CE.

omer [H]   Lit. 'sheaf'. 1. A sheaf of wheat waved by the priest in the temple; 2. the period of counting the days between Pesach and Shavuot.

perushim [H]   Lit. 'separatists'. Term used in rabbinic texts to refer to Pharisees.

Pesach *Passover* [H]   1. Spring festival which commemorates the exodus of Israel from Egypt; 2. the lamb sacrificed on the eve of the festival in Temple times.

pilpul [H]   Casuistic argumentation in the study of the Talmud.

piyyut (pl. *piyyutim*) [H]   Poem used in synagogue liturgy.

Purim [H]   Early spring festival celebrating the salvation of Persian Jews as described in the biblical book of Esther.

Rosh haShanah [H]   The New Year festival.

Seder [H]   Lit. 'order'. Liturgy and banquet on the first evening of Pesach, commemorating the exodus of Israel from Egypt.

sefira (pl. *sefirot*) [H]   Lit. 'enumeration'. In kabbalah, an emanation of the Divine.

Shavuot [H]   Festival of Pentecost.

Shekhinah [H]   Divine Presence.

Shema [H]   Lit. 'hear'. Declaration of the Unity of God which introduces three biblical paragraphs which are recited twice daily.

Shemoneh Esreh [H]   Lit. 'eighteen'. A series of nineteen benedictions regularly recited in silent prayer.

shofar [H]   Ram's horn, sounded particularly on the New Year.

Sifra [A]   Commentary on the book of Leviticus.

shtetl [Y]   Lit. 'little town'. Term used for Jewish settlements in eastern Europe.

Sukkot [H]   Festival of Tabernacles or Booths.

tallit [H]   Prayer shawl, fringed at the four corners.

Talmud [H]   Commentary to the Mishnah compiled in the third to sixth centuries CE.

Tanakh [H]   Acronym for the Bible (Torah, *Neviim* (Prophets) and *Ketuvim* (writings)).

tanna (pl. *tannaim*) [H]   Lit. 'repeater'. A rabbinic teacher from before C. 200 CE.

targum (pl. *targumim*) [H]   Aramaic translation of the Bible.

tefillin [H]   Phylacteries. Square leather boxes enclosing pentateuchal texts, worn on the head and arm during prayer.

Torah [H]   Lit. 'teaching'. 1. The Pentateuch (i.e. the first five books of the Hebrew Bible); 2. the whole body of rabbinic law and practice.

tosafot [H]   Lit. 'additions'. Commentaries on Rashi's commentary on the Talmud.

Tosefta [A]   Lit. 'addition'. Compilation of rabbinic opinions similar in format to the Mishnah and generally serving as a supplement to the Mishnah.

tsaddik [H]   Lit. 'righteous'. In Hasidism, the term is used specifically to refer to a spiritual leader or rabbi.

tsitsit [H]   Fringes attached to the four corners of a small *tallit* (worn under clothing) or a large *tallit* (used as a prayer shawl).

Yahad [H]   Lit. 'community'. The self-designation of the Jewish group which produced the sectarian rules found among the Dead Sea scrolls.

yahrzeit [Y]   Lit. 'anniversary'. Yiddish word for the anniversary of the death of a close relative.

yeshivah (pl. **yeshivot**) [H]   Academy where the Torah (with special emphasis on the Babylonian Talmud) is studied.

Yizkor [H]   Lit. 'May he remember'. Synagogue liturgy with prayers in memory of the dead.

Yom Kippur [H]   Day of Atonement.

Zohar [H]   Mystical work revered by kabbalists since the fourteenth century.

Introduction: Approaching the History of Judaism

At the third new moon after the Israelites had gone out of the land of Egypt, on that very day, they came into the wilderness of Sinai ... Then Moses went up to God; the Lord called him from the mountain, saying, 'Thus you shall say to the house of Jacob, and tell the Israelites: "You have seen what I did to the Egyptians, and how I bore you on eagles' wings and brought you to myself. Now therefore, if you obey my voice and keep my covenant, you shall be my treasured possession out of all the peoples. Indeed, the whole earth is mine, but you shall be for me a priestly kingdom and a holy nation." These are the words that you shall speak to the Israelites.' ... On the morning of the third day there was thunder and lightning, as well as a thick cloud on the mountain, and a blast of a trumpet so loud that all the people who were in the camp trembled. Moses brought the people out of the camp to meet God. They took their stand at the foot of the mountain. Now Mount Sinai was wrapped in smoke, because the Lord had descended upon it in fire; the smoke went up like the smoke of a kiln, while the whole mountain shook violently. As the blast of the trumpet grew louder and louder, Moses would speak and God would answer him in thunder ...

This dramatic account of the divine revelation to Moses on Mount Sinai is preserved in the biblical book of Exodus. The history of Judaism comprises the continued and varied history of interpretation of this covenant by this 'holy nation' over some three millennia.[1]

Over a thousand years after Moses is believed to have been vouchsafed this revelation, the Jerusalem priest and historian Josephus inserted the earliest surviving theology of Judaism composed for a non-Jewish readership into his book *Against Apion*, a defence of Jewish traditions against the calumnies of gentile authors. Josephus ascribed to Moses the creation of a new and perfect constitution for humankind, asserting that this constitution was so different from all others known in his time, such as monarchy, democracy and oligarchy, that it could properly be encapsulated only by inventing a new term in Greek, *theokratia*, 'theocracy', because Moses had insisted that God should be in charge of everything: 'He did not make piety a part of virtue, but recognized and established the others as parts of it ... All practices and occupations, and all speech, have reference to our piety towards God.'[2]

By the time of Josephus, in the later first century CE, Moses was already a heroic figure shrouded in myth. Josephus reckoned Moses had actually lived some 2,000 years before his time, asserting robustly, 'I maintain that our legislator exceeds in antiquity the legislators referred to anywhere else.' Views about Moses among the non-Jews for whom Josephus wrote his theology were markedly less enthusiastic. That he was regarded by the Jews as their legislator was widely known among both Greeks and Romans, and in the late fourth century BCE Hecataeus of Abdera considered him 'outstanding both for his wisdom and for his courage'. But others attacked him as a charlatan and impostor – Josephus' contemporary Quintilian, a Roman expert on rhetoric, could even use Moses as an example of the way that 'founders of cities are detested for concentrating on a race which is a curse to others' without even needing to name the person he called 'the founder of the Jewish superstition'. The more outsiders attacked Judaism, the more a pious Jew like Josephus would claim the excellence of his tradition, which has 'made God governor of the universe'. As Josephus asked rhetorically, 'What regime could be more holy than this? What honour could be more fitting to God, where the whole mass [of people] is equipped for piety ... and the whole constitution is organised like some rite of consecration?'[3]

The contrast to other peoples was also what led Josephus to his assertion that, because all Jews are taught the laws which govern their way of life, so that 'we have them, as it were, engraved on our souls', they therefore agree in everything to do with their religion:

> It is this above all that has created our remarkable concord. For holding one and the same conception of God, and not differing at all in life-style or customs, produces a very beautiful harmony in [people's] characters. Among us alone one will hear no contradictory statements about God, such as is common among others – and not just what is spoken by ordinary people as the emotion grips them individually, but also in what has been boldly pronounced among certain philosophers, some of whom have attempted to do away with the very existence of God by their arguments,

while others eliminate his providence on behalf of humankind. Nor will one see any difference in our living-habits: we all share common practices, and all make the same affirmation about God, in harmony with the law, that he watches over everything.[4]

As will become apparent in the course of this book, the 'unity' and 'uniformity' in practice and belief which distinguished Jews from Greeks and other polytheists in the ancient world, with their multitude of deities, cults, myths and customs, left plenty of room for variety and diversity within Judaism, not only then but throughout its history.

A history of Judaism is not a history of the Jews, but Judaism is the religion of the Jewish people, and this book must therefore trace the political and cultural history of the Jews in so far as it impinged on their religious ideas and practices. At the same time, Judaism is a world religion – and not just in the sense that, through force of circumstance, the Jewish people had been widely scattered for millennia, so that their religious ideas have often reflected, by either adoption or rejection, the wider non-Jewish world within which Jews have found themselves living. Even if Judaism is not as divorced from ethnicity as some other world religions such as Christianity, Islam or Buddhism (although, within these religions also, religious identity can sometimes be an ethnic or cultural marker), Jewish identity was defined by religion as well as by birth long before Josephus wrote about the excellence of the special constitution ascribed to Moses. By the second century BCE at the latest, almost all Jews had come to accept as Jews those proselytes who wished to adopt Jewish customs and define themselves as Jews. Throughout most of the history discussed in this book, Judaism has had the potential to be a universal religion, and Jews have believed that their religion has universal significance, even if (unlike some Christians) Jews have never pursued a universal mission to convert others to their religion.[5]

Attempting to isolate, describe and explain the religious aspects of Jewish culture over some three millennia is a daunting task, and not only because of the abundance of material and the weight of scholarship. The past 2,000 years have witnessed a great variety of expressions of Judaism. It would be straightforward to define the essence of Judaism in light of the characteristics valued by one or another of its branches in the present day, and to trace the development of those characteristics over the centuries, and such histories have indeed been written in past centuries. But it is evidently unsatisfactory to assume that what now seems essential was always seen as such. In any case, it cannot be taken for granted that there was always a mainstream within Judaism and that other varieties of the religion were, and should be, seen as tributaries. The metaphors of a great river of tradition, or of a tree with numerous branches, are seductive but dangerous, for the most important aspects of Judaism now may have little connection with antiquity. It is self-evident, for instance, that the central liturgical concern of 2,000 years ago – the performance of sacrificial worship in the Jerusalem Temple – has little to do with most forms of Judaism today.[6]

One way to avoid imposing on the history of Judaism an invented narrative to justify the concerns of the present day is to describe as objectively as possible the various forms of Judaism which have flourished at specific times, allowing the family resemblance between these different forms to justify discussing them all within a single history. There is much to be said for this pluralist approach, but by itself it may seem rather unsatisfactory, since outsiders have always tended to see Judaism as a single religion, however diverse it may appear from within, and rhetoric about the virtue of unity within the Jewish community has been a commonplace of Jewish religious literature since the Bible. If all the historian could achieve was to describe the host of strange expressions of Judaism in past centuries without drawing out any connection between them, the result would be a gallery of curiosities to amuse and puzzle the reader, but there would be no story to explain why Judaism has evolved as it has, and is still now a religion with influence over the lives of millions.

The approach of this book is therefore a marriage between the unapologetically linear histories of earlier generations and the 'polythetic' descriptions favoured by contemporary scholars concerned to keep an open mind about the claims of all traditions. The book traces the different expressions of Judaism known to have flourished alongside each other at any one time and then examines – so far as evidence allows – the relations between those varieties. It tries to establish when and where different branches of Judaism competed with each other for legitimacy or for adherents, and when and where one tolerated the other, either in a spirit of open acceptance or with grudging animosity.[7]

Judaism has a rich history of rifts, sometimes over matters which may seem minor to the outsider, but, despite the rhetoric used against their opponents by religious enthusiasts, religiously motivated violence between Jews was not common. The biblical story of Pinchas, who took the law into his own hands to strike down immorality by summary execution of a licentious Israelite and the idolatress he had brought into his family, provided a model for zealotry, but it was invoked only rarely. Nothing within Judaism was quite like the Christian wars of religion in Europe in the early modern period, or the deep hostility which has sometimes scarred relations between Sunni and Shia in Islam. Exploring the extent of toleration within Judaism is one of the themes of this book.[8]

At the same time, a history must seek to trace developments within Judaism from one period to another, and I try whenever possible to show how each variety of Judaism claimed to relate to that of previous generations and to identify the particular elements of the earlier tradition which they actually chose to emphasize. Since adherents of most manifestations of Judaism have made claims about their faithfulness to the past, it might seem strange that variety has abounded to the extent that it has. Evidently conservative claims often masked change and innovation. This history will note which of these innovations were to influence the religious lives of Jews in later periods and which were to prove dead ends.

It is rarely easy in discussion of any part of this history to establish firm boundaries for who was a Jew. It is an error to imagine that Jewish identity was secure and unproblematic before the complexities of the modern world. At all periods the self-perception of those who considered themselves Jews might not align with the perceptions of others. Uncertainty about the status of a child of one Jewish parent was already a concern when Josephus wrote, since it was around the first century CE that Jews began to take the status of the mother as decisive rather than that of the father. Then, as now, the conversion to Judaism of a gentile might be recognized by one set of Jews and not by another. The practical solution adopted in this book is to include any individuals or groups prepared to identify themselves by all three of the main names used by Jews to refer to themselves throughout their history. 'Israel', 'Hebrew' and 'Jew' had quite specific referents in origin but came to be used by Jews almost interchangeably, and the decision of some groups which separated themselves from Judaism, such as Samaritans and some early Christians, to call themselves 'Israel' in opposition to 'Jew' marked a definitive break.

Even for those Jews who remained in the fold the connotations of these different names could vary greatly. In English, the term 'Hebrew' was quite polite in reference to a Jew in the nineteenth century but would be mildly offensive now. French Jews in the nineteenth century called themselves 'Israélite' and it is only recently that 'juif' has lost a derogatory overtone. Shifting terminology used by Jews in Hebrew and Greek to refer to themselves in times of political stress in the first century CE suggests that this was nothing new. All depends on context, and context will in turn explain much of the development within Judaism, so that the book touches on the general history of much of the Near East and Europe, and (for later periods) the Americas and further afield, in order to explain the religious changes which are its main concern.

The impact on Jews of events in the wider world have thus shaped the periods into which the history of Judaism is divided in this book, from the empires of the Near East, Greece and Rome to the Christianization of Europe, the huge impact of Islam and the creation of the modern world from the Renaissance through the Enlightenment to the complex Jewish world today, in which the fortunes of many diaspora Jews are intimately bound up with the nation state of Israel. Just one period is defined by an event specific to Jewish history. The destruction of the Second Temple in Jerusalem in 70 CE began a new era in the development of Judaism that has had profound effects on all the forms of Judaism which survive today. It is unlikely that any Jews appreciated at the time how much their religion was going to change as a result of the loss of the Temple, but treating 70 CE as a watershed in the history of Judaism is justified not least in order to correct Christian theological conceptions of Judaism as the religion of the Old Testament superseded and rendered redundant by the advent of Christianity. The Judaism of the rabbis which has shaped the religion of all Jews in the modern world in fact evolved over the first millennium CE in parallel with the Christian Church. Rabbinic Judaism is indeed based on the collection of texts which Christians call the Old Testament and Jews call the Hebrew Bible. In particular, the rabbis designated the Pentateuch, the first five books of the Hebrew Bible, as the Torah ('teaching'), the same term they applied more widely to all the guidance imparted to the Jewish people by divine revelation. But the rabbis did not just read the Bible literally. Through development of techniques of *midrash* ('didactic exposition'), they incorporated into halakhah ('law') their interpretations of the biblical texts in conjunction with legal rulings transmitted through custom and oral tradition. In practice, the halakhah, especially as preserved in the Babylonian Talmud, is as fundamental to rabbinic Judaism as the Bible.

Over the centuries Judaism has been expressed in a wide variety of languages, reflecting these surrounding cultures. The national language of the Jews is Hebrew, but Aramaic (the vernacular of the Near East in the first millennium BCE) is found in the Bible, most of the Jewish writings preserved from the first century CE are in Greek, and fundamental works of Jewish philosophy from the Middle Ages are in Arabic. In a book written in English it is hard to convey adequately the nuances inherent in the varied linguistic and cultural worlds from which these writings emerged, or the extent to which terminology of quite distinct origins might come to be understood by Jews as referring to the same thing. The strip of land by the eastern coast of the Mediterranean said in the Bible to have been promised to the Jewish people is identified in the earliest narratives in the Bible as Canaan but elsewhere in the biblical texts as the Land of Israel. Known in the Persian empire as the province of Yehud and under Greek rule as Judaea, the same region was designated the province of Syria Palaestina by the Roman state in 135 CE. The result can be confusing for the modern reader, but the choice of terminology was often significant, and I have allowed the sources to speak for themselves as much as possible.

My attempt to present an objective history of Judaism may strike some readers as naive. Many of the great scholars of the *Wissenschaft des Judentums*, who began the scientific study of Jewish history in nineteenth-century Europe, wrote in the hope that their attempts to evaluate the ancient Jewish sources critically, unencumbered by traditional rabbinic interpretations, would serve to strengthen claims to authenticity by one or another trend within Judaism in their time. With the establishment of Jewish studies as a recognized academic discipline in western universities, particularly from the 1960s, such links with current religious polemics have become rare. Within Europe, many professors of Jewish studies are not Jewish and can claim with some credibility to approach their subject dispassionately, although Christian or atheist assumptions will of course import their own biases. This is not my position. I was born into a family of English Jews who took their Jewish identity seriously. My father's study was full of books on Judaism inherited from his father, who had been secretary of the London congregation of the Spanish and Portuguese Jews for many years and wrote books of his own, including a history of the Jews. The family practised little beyond a Sabbath-eve dinner each Friday, an annual family Seder and occasional attendance at services in Bevis Marks synagogue. My own decision as a teenager to adopt a more observant lifestyle was a form of mild rebellion (with which the rest of the family coped with admirable patience). It is probably significant that I have found a home in the Oxford Jewish

Congregation, which is unusual in the United Kingdom for housing Progressive and Masorti as well as orthodox services within a single community. How much this background has affected my perception of what was central and what was marginal in the development of Judaism will be for readers to judge.

The distinction between a history of Jewish religion and Jewish history more broadly has not always been easy to draw. The concept of 'religion' as a separate sphere of life has been a product of western Christian culture since the Enlightenment and had no precise equivalent in the ancient world, since the relation of humans to the divine was fully integrated into the rest of life. The closest equivalent to 'religion' in the ancient Hebrew language was *torah* ('teaching'), the guidance given to Israel by divine revelation encompassing areas of life which in other societies might be considered secular, such as civil and matrimonial law. As a result, this book will include discussion of practices and customs as much as theology. Systematic theology has only sporadically featured in Judaism, generally under the influence of external stimuli such as Greek philosophy, Islam or the European Enlightenment, but this does not mean that Judaism can be defined by orthopraxy rather than orthodoxy, and one of the objectives of the book will be to assert the significance of ideas at many junctions in the history of the Jews and their religion. At root, certain religious ideas percolate through the history of Judaism and render contemporary notions such as Secular Judaism, an affiliation divorced from any belief in God, problematic. Most important of these is the notion of a covenant which binds God specifically to the Jewish people and lays special duties on them in return. Throughout its history Judaism has claimed that its universal significance is encapsulated in the relationship to God of one divinely chosen group.

This book thus discusses beliefs and ideas as much as practices, institutions and communal structures. I have tried as much as possible to describe the lived religion of the mass of ordinary Jews over the centuries alongside the accounts of innovation and exotic careers of mavericks which are encountered most often in the historical record. I have tried also to allow for the possibility that movements and ideas which can only be faintly glimpsed in the surviving sources may at the time have been far more important than appeared to the later tradition. The chance discovery in 1947 of the Dead Sea scrolls in caves near Qumran revealed types of Judaism about which all knowledge had been lost for two millennia. When the early rabbis of the first two centuries CE, whose legal teachings were preserved in the Mishnah and Tosefta in the third century, or their successors whose commentaries were incorporated into the Babylonian Talmud in *c.* 600 CE, looked back at the biblical period of the development of Judaism, the lessons which struck them most already differed greatly from the preoccupations of their ancestors.

When to begin the history? With Abraham, the patriarch, as the first to recognize that there is only one God? With Moses, receiving the law from this God on Mount Sinai? Centuries later perhaps, with the establishment by Ezra of a Jewish nation focused on the worship of the same God in the Temple in Jerusalem? Or with the completion of most books of the Bible in the second century BCE? There is something to be said for each of these options but I have chosen to start later still, in the first century CE, when Judaism was described as a distinctive form of religious life and Josephus looked back, into what he perceived as the mists of antiquity, to explain the theology, codified texts, practices and institutions of the fully fledged religion he proudly claimed as his own. We shall see that the long process through which this religion had formed over the previous centuries was sometimes faltering, and our knowledge of this process remains tantalizingly partial. At the heart of the Bible lies a story of the emergence of the distinctive religion of the Jews, but uncertainty about the dating and process of composition of key biblical texts and about the significance of archaeological evidence from the biblical period has sustained remarkably divergent interpretations of the historicity of these narratives. The rabbis inherited the biblical tradition but treated it, for the most part, ahistorically. We are therefore fortunate to have an extensive account from the first century CE, soon after the Bible had begun to be treated as sacred scripture, in which the history of the Jews and the development of their religion were explained by a learned insider versed both in the traditions of the Jews and in the most advanced techniques in his time of scientific investigation into the past. The author of that account was Josephus, and it is with his *Antiquities* that we shall start.

PART I

Origins

(*c.* 2000 BCE–70 CE)

I. The Near East in the Second Millennium BCE

Black Sea

HITTITE
EMPIRE

Mediterranean Sea

Ras Shamra

LEBANON

Damascus
Tyre

CANAAN

Jerusalem

LEV

Raamses

Kuntillet Ajrûd

SINAI

MIDIAN

EGYPT

R. Nile

Red Sea

Abraham's journey

0   100   200 miles

0   100   200   300 km

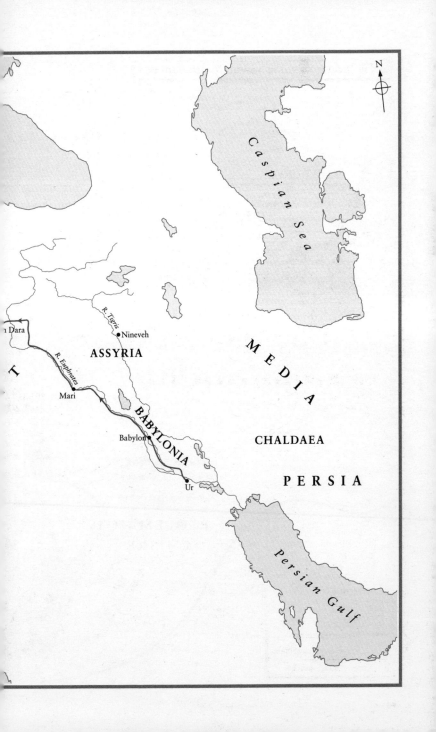

2. The Jewish World in 300 BCE

Black Sea

MACEDONIA

GREECE

Mediterranean Sea

Antioch

Sidon
Damascus
Tyre

Cyrene

Alexandria

Jerusalem

JUDAEA

PTOLEMAIC
EMPIRE

R. Nile

Red Sea

Elephantine

areas of Jewish settlement

dense

light

limit of Greek rule

0 — 100 — 200 miles
0 — 100 — 200 — 300 km

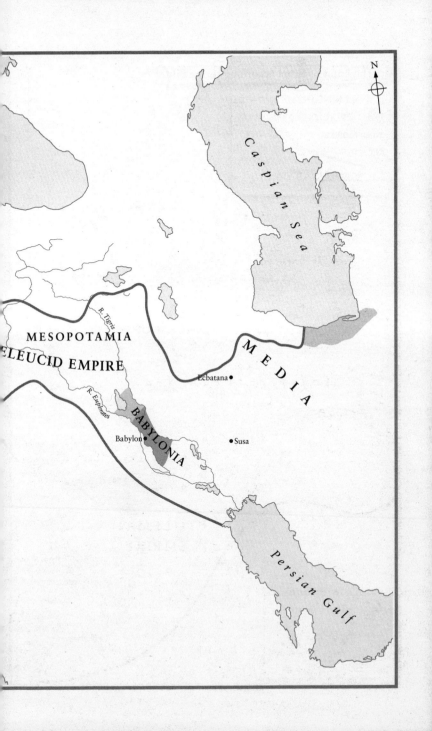

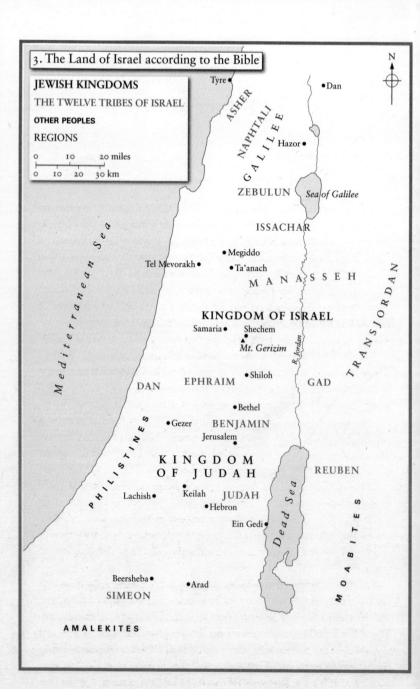

3. The Land of Israel according to the Bible

N

JEWISH KINGDOMS

THE TWELVE TRIBES OF ISRAEL

OTHER PEOPLES

REGIONS

| 0 | 10 | 20 miles |
| 0 | 10 | 20 | 30 km |

Tyre

Dan

ASHER

NAPHTALI

GALILEE

Hazor

ZEBULUN

Sea of Galilee

ISSACHAR

Mediterranean Sea

Megiddo

Tel Mevorakh

Ta'anach

MANASSEH

KINGDOM OF ISRAEL

Samaria

Shechem

Mt. Gerizim

R. Jordan

TRANSJORDAN

Shiloh

GAD

DAN

EPHRAIM

Bethel

Gezer

BENJAMIN

Jerusalem

**KINGDOM
OF JUDAH**

REUBEN

Dead Sea

Lachish

Keilah

JUDAH

Hebron

Ein Gedi

PHILISTINES

Beersheba

Arad

SIMEON

MOABITES

AMALEKITES

I

Deserts, Tribes and Empires

At the end of the first century CE Josephus looked back with pride on the antiquity of his people and the remarkable accuracy of the Hebrew records in which their history was preserved. It was true that much of this history had escaped the notice of the non-Jewish world, and that Greek writers had paid regrettably little attention to the Jews, but this could be remedied. Before composing the account of Jewish theology in *Against Apion*, Josephus set out for gentiles a continuous narrative of Jewish history from the beginning to his own day. His twenty books of *Jewish Antiquities* may have been the first such narrative ever written.[1]

Josephus was writing under the burden of a national trauma. Born in 37 CE into an aristocratic family in Jerusalem, he had served as a priest in the Temple as a young man before being caught up in 66 CE as a rebel leader in the political struggle against the imperial power of Rome which led, in 70 CE, to the destruction of the Temple. He had been captured by the Romans in 67 CE, but in recognition of a prophecy he was said to have made to the Roman general Vespasian that he would become emperor, he was granted his freedom when the prophecy came true. He composed all his writings on the fringes of the imperial court in Rome, where he seems to have made it his life's mission to persuade a sceptical Roman populace that the Jews who had just succumbed to the might of Rome were in fact a great people with a long history well worthy of the attention of their conquerors and the wider non-Jewish world.[2]

For those readers of this book who know the Hebrew Bible, which for Christians constitutes the Old Testament, the first half of Josephus' *Jewish Antiquities* will be both familiar and, on occasion, disconcerting. The Bible is full of stories about the Jewish past, but these stories are not always easy to reconcile with non-biblical evidence. Reconstructing the history of Israel in the biblical period was as difficult in the first century CE as it is now. Josephus followed the biblical account for the first ten books of his history, but with additions and omissions which reflected how the Bible was being read in his own day. His narrative is impressively coherent and often vivid, and I shall allow it to speak for itself. He was immensely proud of the authenticity of his history, but for us the significance of his version lies not in its accuracy (which can often be doubted) but in its claim to accuracy. We shall see that the Jews' understanding of their national history has played a major role in the development of their ideas and practices. Josephus provides our earliest full testimony to this historical understanding. We shall find reasons to doubt the reliability of some of the traditions he transmitted, and at the end of this chapter I shall venture some tentative proposals about what may really have happened, and when, but all religions have stories about their origins, and for the creation of the historical myths on which Judaism has been founded, what really happened matters much less than what Jews believed had happened. And for this, the best witness, writing soon after the completion of the Bible, was Josephus.

Josephus began his narrative by telling his readers about 'our law-giver Moses', on whose wisdom (as enshrined in the biblical text) almost everything in that history, so Josephus claimed, depends. Hence Jewish history for Josephus started where the Bible starts, with what Moses had said about the creation of the world and humanity, and the separation of the nations after the flood in the time of Noah. Josephus had already filled half the first book of the *Jewish Antiquities* with world history before he even began to speak of the 'Hebrews' and the genealogy of Abraham, but the reader was left in no doubt about the importance of Abraham, who was 'the first boldly to declare that God, the creator of the universe, is one', nor his significance for the story of the Jews to follow. Abraham, wrote Josephus, was originally an inhabitant of the city called Ur of the Chaldees, but his religious ideas aroused hostility among the Chaldaeans and the other people of Mesopotamia and he emigrated to the land of Canaan. There, apart from a brief period in Egypt to escape the impact of famine in Canaan, he remained until his death at the age of 175. He was buried beside his wife Sarah, in Hebron, where his son Isaac was also to be buried in the ancestral tomb.[3]

Josephus proceeds to tell at length the fortunes of some of Abraham's descendants in Egypt after Joseph, Isaac's grandson, was taken there as a slave but was raised by Pharaoh to a position of exceptional authority because of his facility in the interpretation of dreams. Joseph provided a refuge in Egypt for his father Jacob and his many brothers when they and their flocks were forced by famine to move south from Canaan in search of food. The family settled happily in Egypt, but Josephus is at pains to note that Jacob prophesied on his deathbed that his descendants would all find habitations in Canaan in due course and that the bones of both Jacob and all his sons, including in due course Joseph, would eventually be buried back in the family sepulchre in Hebron.[4]

The second half of Book 2 of Josephus' *Antiquities* turns to the story of the eventual mass exodus of Jacob's descendants from Egypt after the Egyptians grew envious of the prosperity of the Hebrews – a name for the ancestors of the Jews first used here in Josephus' narrative, and followed in the next sentence by a reference to the same people as 'the race of the Israelites'. The division of the people into tribes (named after the sons of Jacob and, in the case of the half-tribes Ephraim and Manasseh, his grandsons) is explained by Josephus as the will of Jacob shortly before his death, when he 'charged his own sons to reckon among their number Joseph's sons, Ephraim and Manasseh, and to let them share in the division of Canaan' as requital for Joseph's exceptional generosity to his brothers.

The Hebrews, wrote Josephus, were subjected to 400 years of hardship before they were rescued under the leadership of Moses, son of Amram, 'a Hebrew of noble birth', who, with his brother Aaron, led them out of Egypt and through the wilderness towards Canaan. Moses himself, despite his forty years in the desert, including the dramatic revelation on Mount Sinai when he received the laws from God and gave them to his people, was not to reach their destination. His final days were shrouded in mystery: 'A cloud of a sudden descended upon him and he disappeared in a ravine. But he has written of himself in the sacred books that he died, for fear lest they should venture to say that by reason of his surpassing virtue he has gone back to the Deity.' The gentile reader of this history, already at the end of the fourth book of this long work (and one-fifth of the way through the whole account), might reasonably have felt a bit puzzled by some aspects of the story up to now, not least the failure of Josephus to refer to any of his protagonists as Jews despite his assertion in his introduction that he would show 'who the Jews are from the beginning'. The story recounted in Book 1 about the naming of Jacob as 'Israel' by an angel did not even explain his use of the same name, 'Israel', for Jews generally.[5]

The next part of the national story fell into a pattern more familiar for Josephus' readers in a work of history, since the narrative turned to war and politics. The Hebrews, he said, had fought a series of campaigns under the command of Joshua against the Canaanites, some of whom were terrifying giants 'in no wise like to the rest of mankind', whose 'bones are shown to this day, bearing no resemblance to any that have come within man's ken'. The conquered land was parcelled out among the Hebrew nation, but agricultural success bred wealth, which in turn led to voluptuousness and neglect of the laws which Moses had transmitted to them. Divine punishment for such impiety took the form of disastrous civil wars, followed by subjection to foreigners (Assyrians, Moabites, Amalekites, Philistines) and the heroic efforts of a series of judges, granted power by the people both to rule and to lead them in battle against their enemies. In due course the people demanded kings as military leaders, and the judge Samuel, who had been divinely chosen at birth to lead the nation and had been a prophet with direct guidance from God since the age of eleven, in his old age reluctantly appointed Saul as the first king of the Jews, with a mission (amply fulfilled) to fight the neighbouring peoples.[6]

At this stage in his narrative, Josephus traces the fortunes of the people – designated as Jews, Israelites and Hebrews, apparently at random – in a series of local wars. The Amalekites, a hereditary enemy whose extirpation had been divinely ordained, continued to harass Israel because Saul was insufficiently ruthless, wishing to spare Agag, the Amalekite king, 'out of admiration for his beauty and stature'. More insistently dangerous opposition came from the Philistines, against whom the Hebrews fought a series of campaigns in the course of which a new king David made his name as a warrior, having been selected by God to receive the kingdom as a prize not 'for comeliness of body, but for virtue of soul . . . piety, justice, fortitude and obedience'. He had already been anointed secretly by Samuel while still a shepherd boy.[7]

When Saul died in battle against the Amalekites, David at first composed laments and eulogies for the dead king and his son Jonathan; these elegies, Josephus notes, 'have survived to my own time'. David was informed by God through a prophet in what city he should rule over 'the tribe called Judah' and was told to settle in Hebron, while the rest of the country was ruled by a surviving son of Saul. But the result was civil war, which lasted many years until Saul's son was murdered by the sons of his own followers and 'all the principal men of the people of the Hebrews, the captains of thousands and their leaders', came to Hebron and offered their loyalty to David, as the king chosen by God to save the Hebrews' country by conquering the Philistines. With a large combined force of troops from all the tribes and half-tribes (Judah,

Simeon, Levi, Benjamin, Ephraim, Manasseh, Issachar, Zebulun, Naphtali, Dan and Asher, and Reuben and Gad from across the Jordan), David feasted in Hebron to celebrate his confirmation as king and marched on Jerusalem. Jerusalem was inhabited at this time by Jebusites 'of the Canaanitic race'. No reason is given by Josephus for the assault, but once David had conquered the citadel and rebuilt Jerusalem he named it 'City of David' and chose it as his royal residence. Five hundred and fifteen years had elapsed between the original conquest of Canaan by Joshua and the capture of Jerusalem by David.[8]

Josephus described at length the great victories of David against the Philistines and then the subjection to his rule of the surrounding nations. They were forced to pay tribute to him, so that he amassed 'such wealth as no other king, whether of the Hebrews or other nations, ever did'. On his death there was buried with him in Jerusalem so much money that 1,300 years later a Jewish high priest raided one of the chambers in David's tomb in order to buy off a besieging army. Many years after that (just a century before Josephus was writing), King Herod opened up another chamber and extracted another large sum.[9] Despite his earlier claims about the unequalled wealth of David, Josephus asserted, illogically, that it was exceeded by his son and successor Solomon, whose wisdom far surpassed even that of the Egyptians. Undistracted by the continuous warfare which had preoccupied his father, Solomon built in Jerusalem the great temple for God which David had planned but not started. Copies of the letters written by Solomon to Hiram, king of Tyre, to request help in acquiring cedars of Lebanon for the purpose in return for grain could still be found in the public archives in Tyre – as anyone could discover, Josephus said, by enquiry with the relevant public officials. Solomon ruled for eighty years, having come to the throne at the age of fourteen, but the glories of his reign were not to last after his death, when his realm was split into two. Rehoboam, Solomon's son, was ruler only of the tribes of Judah and Benjamin in the south, in the region of Jerusalem, while the Israelites in the north, with their capital in Shechem, established their own centres for sacrificial worship in Bethel and Dan, with different religious practices, to avoid having to go to Jerusalem, 'the city of our enemies', to worship. To this innovation Josephus ascribed 'the beginning of the Hebrews' misfortunes which led to them being defeated in war by other races and to their falling captive' – even though he admits that the degeneracy of Rehoboam and his subjects in Jerusalem itself invited divine punishment.[10]

The initial agent of divine vengeance was Shishak, king of Egypt, and

the history of the following generations of the Hebrew kings is punctuated in Josephus' account by the interventions of great empires (Egypt,
Assyria and Babylonia) as well as of the lesser powers of the region,
especially the kings of Syria and Damascus, and by civil war between
the kings in Jerusalem and the kings of the Israelites with their new capital in Samaria to the north. The fate of the kingdom of the Israelites
was sealed when the king of Assyria learned that the king of Israel had
attempted to make an alliance with Egypt to oppose Assyrian expansion. After a siege of three years, the city of Samaria was taken by storm
and all the ten tribes which inhabited it were transported to Media and
Persia. Foreigners were imported to take possession of the land from
which the Israelites had been expelled. Josephus, the Jerusalem priest,
shows no sympathy: it was a just punishment for their violation of the
laws and rebellion against the dynasty of David. The imported foreigners, 'called "Cuthim" in the Hebrew tongue and "Samaritans" by the
Greeks', adopted the worship of the Most High God who was revered
by the Jews.[11]

In contrast to Samaria, Jerusalem was preserved at this time against
Assyrian attack by the piety of its king Hezekiah. But Jerusalem too was
eventually to fall victim to the overwhelming military might of a great
empire. Trapped between the expansionary ambitions of the Babylonians, the successor empire to the Assyrians, and the power of Egypt to
the south, a series of kings in Jerusalem tried to play one side against the
other, but ultimately failed to ensure security. After a horrific siege of
Jerusalem, King Sacchias (called Zedekiah in the Bible) was captured,
blinded and taken off to Babylon by the Babylonian king Nebuchadnezzar. The Temple and palace in Jerusalem were razed to the ground,
and the people were transplanted to Babylonia, leaving all of Judaea
and Jerusalem deserted for seventy years.[12]

Josephus did not have much to inform his readers about the fortunes
of the Jews in Babylonia beyond the accurate prophecy of Daniel, first
in the court of Nebuchadnezzar and then – many years later, when Babylon was under siege by Cyrus, king of Persia, and Darius, king of
Media – in the court of Belshazzar. Daniel correctly interpreted the
meaning of obscure words which had appeared on the wall of the dining hall in the midst of a feast. The words signified that God would
break up the kingdom of Babylon between the Medes and the Persians.
Daniel became a great figure in the court of Darius and built at Ecbatana
in Media a fortress 'which was a very beautiful work and wonderfully
made, and remains and is preserved to this day ... In this fortress they

bury the kings of Media, Persia and Parthia even now, and the person to whose care it is entrusted is a Jewish priest; and this custom is observed to this very day.'[13]

In the first year of the reign of Cyrus, Josephus tells his readers, the king was inspired by an ancient prophecy which he read in the book of Isaiah (which had been composed 210 years earlier) to restore the Jewish exiles to their land:

> Thus says King Cyrus. Since the Most High God has appointed me king of the habitable world, I am persuaded that he is the god whom the Israelite nation worships, for he foretold my name through the prophets and that I should build his temple in Jerusalem in the land of Judaea.

The king summoned to him the most distinguished Jews in Babylon and gave them leave to go to Jerusalem to rebuild the Temple, promising financial support from his governors in the region of Judaea. Many Jews preferred to stay in Babylon to avoid losing their possessions. But some returned to Judaea, only to find the process of reconstruction hampered by the surrounding nations, and especially by the Cuthaeans who had been settled in Samaria by the Assyrians when the ten tribes were deported many years earlier. The Cuthaeans bribed the local satraps to hinder the Jews in rebuilding their city and temple. Such opposition was so successful that Cyrus' son Cambyses, who was 'naturally wicked', gave explicit instructions that the Jews should be forbidden to rebuild their city. But then a revolution in Persia brought to power a new dynasty, whose first ruler, Darius, had long been a friend of Zerubbabel, the governor of the Jewish captives in Persia and one of the king's bodyguards. Zerubbabel used his influence to remind Darius that he had once vowed, before he became king, that if he obtained the throne he would reconstruct the Temple of God in Jerusalem and restore the Temple vessels which Nebuchadnezzar had taken as spoil to Babylon.[14]

And so the Temple was indeed rebuilt, and became the centre of government for the Jews who had returned to Jerusalem. The last king of Jerusalem from before the exile had been treated well in the Babylonian court after the death of Nebuchadnezzar, but royal rule was not restored. Instead, the Jews had 'a form of government that was both aristocratic and oligarchic', with High Priests at the head of affairs. They had the firm support of the Persian state except in the time of Artaxerxes, when machinations in the Persian royal court occasioned by the pique of the king's favourite minister Haman brought all the Jews of the empire into

mortal danger. From this they were rescued only by the heroic intervention of the king's beautiful Jewish wife Esther.[15]

The demise of the Persian empire as a result of the military conquests
of Alexander of Macedon had great implication for the Jews, who initially remained loyal to the Persian king Darius. When Alexander
himself paid a visit to Jerusalem, however, he did not plunder the city as
his followers expected but prostrated himself before the High Priest and
offered up sacrifices in the Temple. The great conqueror, according to
Josephus, recognized the power of the Jewish God. The Samaritans
decided to profess themselves Jews in order to obtain favour also for
their city of Shechem, but in vain: when Alexander pressed them as to
their identity, 'they said they were Hebrews but were called the Sidon-
ians of Shechem', and when he asked again if they were Jews, they said
they were not, as a result of which they were denied the privileges they
requested. From now on, according to Josephus, the Samaritans and
their temple became a refuge for Jews from Jerusalem accused of violating religious laws.[16]

The rest of Josephus' history of his people to his own day covered
periods and topics which will in many respects have been more familiar
to his contemporary gentile readers. (A fuller account for readers of this
book can be found in Chapter 5.) Josephus' readers will have known
how Alexander's generals divided the Near East between them in a protracted struggle over his imperial legacy after his early death, with
Seleucus ruling over Babylon and surrounding regions and Ptolemy
gaining control of Egypt. Josephus asserted that Jerusalem fell to
Ptolemy through a ruse, for the king entered the city on the Sabbath as
if coming to make a sacrifice, so that there was no opposition. Ptolemy
ruled harshly, and took many from the Judaean hill country as captives
to Egypt, but under his rule and that of his descendants Jerusalem in
due course prospered. Many Jews settled in Egypt of their own accord,
attracted by the excellence of the country, not least the new city of Alexandria, which became the Ptolemaic capital. Josephus claims that the
respect in which the Ptolemies held the Jews was revealed by the decision of Ptolemy Philadelphus to commission a translation of the Jewish
law into Greek. If the Jews suffered under Ptolemaic rule, it was only
because of the devastation of their land, along with those of surrounding regions, during the campaigns of the Seleucids to win their territory
from the Ptolemies. These campaigns ended with the victory of Antiochus the Great and the annexation of Judaea to the Seleucid state.[17]

Antiochus began his rule over Jerusalem by proclaiming the right of the Jews to continue undisturbed their ancestral worship in Jerusalem, with a proclamation published throughout the kingdom:

> It is unlawful for any foreigner to enter the enclosure of the Temple which is forbidden to the Jews, except to those of them who are accustomed to enter after purifying themselves in accordance with the law of the country. Nor shall anyone bring into the city the flesh of horses or of mules or of wild or tame asses, or of leopards, foxes or hares or, in general, of any animals forbidden to the Jews. Nor is it lawful to bring in their skins or even to breed any of these animals in the city. But only the sacrificial animals known to their ancestors and necessary for the propitiation of God shall they be permitted to use. And the person who violates any of these statutes shall pay the priests a fine of three thousand drachmas of silver.[18]

Such toleration of the special taboos of the Jews was not to last. After factional strife between the Jews for control of the high priesthood in Jerusalem, which was in the gift of the Seleucid king, some of the Jewish leaders informed Antiochus IV Epiphanes, the son of Antiochus the Great, that they wished 'to abandon their country's laws' and 'to adopt the Greek way of life'. Antiochus Epiphanes marched against Jerusalem, took the city and despoiled the Temple. His motivation was greed, because of the Temple's wealth, but he did not stop at looting. The king 'built a pagan altar upon the altar of the temple and slaughtered pigs on it' and ordered the Jews to give up the worship of their own God and to cease their practice of circumcising their sons, torturing those who refused to obey. Persecution instigated rebellion, led by an aged priest named Mattathias and his sons, notably Judah Maccabee. The success of that revolt, and the purification of the Temple, established the family as a new ruling dynasty, named 'Hasmonaean' after the great-grandfather of Mattathias. They ruled as High Priests, and in due course also as kings and in one case (Alexandra, the widow of Alexander Jannaeus) as queen.[19]

Josephus' narrative unsurprisingly became increasingly detailed closer to his own day. The Hasmonaean regime for a while revelled in independence from Seleucid control and then in conquests outside the region of Jerusalem, incorporating Galilee to the north and Idumaea (the region around Hebron) to the south into the territory of the Jews, but dissension within the Hasmonaean dynasty gave an opportunity to the great Roman general Pompey to intervene, capturing Jerusalem after an intense siege in which he took advantage of the Jews' observance of Sabbaths to build up his earthworks. Thus, as Josephus noted bitterly, 'we lost our freedom and became subject to the Romans.'[20]

Josephus went on to note in the same lament that, as a result of this miscalculation by the Hasmonaeans, 'the royal power which had formerly been bestowed on those who were High Priests by birth became the privilege of commoners.' He portrayed the accession to royal power in Judaea of the Idumaean Herod the Great as a direct product of realpolitik in the Roman senate. The vote of the senate was followed immediately by pagan sacrifices by Roman magistrates in order to ratify the decree, which was deposited in the Roman Capitol; and Herod won control of Jerusalem only with the aid of Roman forces. But despite these inauspicious beginnings, and despite political insecurities caused not least by the machinations of his own extensive family, Herod's reign was in some ways glorious, and the Jewish Temple was refashioned into a magnificence which aroused wonder far beyond the Jewish world.[21]

The fragility of Herod's rule, which was founded largely on the fear which his Jewish subjects felt for him and his secret police, became clear with the eruption of a series of revolts upon his death. The Romans sought to give authority to his descendants, and a small proportion of his territories remained under their rule through to the time when Josephus was writing. But ten years after his death Judaea itself was entrusted to a Roman governor, with a brief to impose direct rule, including a census for the extraction of the land tax. It was the census which sparked an immediate uprising.

Josephus wrote with all too much hindsight about what he had seen with his own eyes some decades later, when opposition to Roman rule culminated in an exceptionally violent siege of Jerusalem and the total destruction of Herod's Temple. He sometimes wrote about this disaster as if it had been inevitable, but in the course of his detailed narrative in the last part of his great work, he also drew attention at times to indications to the contrary. Agrippa I, grandson of Herod, enjoyed a brief but glorious reign as king of Judaea when Josephus was aged between four and seven. It is unlikely to be accidental that the narrative of Agrippa's tortuous political career dominates the whole nineteenth book of Josephus' *Antiquities*. Josephus' history was intended to demonstrate how glorious Jewish history had been – and, by implication, could be again, once the Jews could be allowed to put behind them the disastrous war, and Jerusalem, and its Temple, could be restored to their former glory.

How truthful was Josephus' account of the origins and history of the Jews? He insists at frequent intervals on his veracity and cites documents whenever he can to show the strength of his evidence, but there was, of course, a great deal that he simply could not know. Organizing the material of the Hebrew Bible, on which he based the first half of his history, into a continuous narrative was itself a major feat, more recognized in the respect paid to his *Antiquities* by Christians in the Middle Ages and the early modern period than by scholars today. The process required some silent changes to his sources, as in the substitution of the name of one Persian king for a different one in the biblical text when he recounted the heroic actions of Esther, in an attempt to bring the chronology of his Jewish narrative into line with the accepted chronology of the ancient empires familiar to his non-Jewish Greek and Roman readers. Discrepant narratives in biblical texts – when, for instance, the books of Kings are contradicted by Chronicles – were smoothed out. Occasionally he missed out material which he must have found in his source, such as the episode, described in the biblical book of Exodus, of a golden calf made by Moses' brother Aaron for the Israelites to worship, just at the time when Moses was receiving divine instruction on Mount Sinai. Presumably he wished to avoid recounting a story which reflected so badly upon his people.[22]

Josephus' narrative covered not just many centuries, which he tried hard to enumerate for his readers on the basis of the written sources at his disposal, but also a wide geographical sweep from Mesopotamia to Rome, incorporating landscapes as various as the fertile irrigation economies of Mesopotamia and Egypt, the great and terrible wilderness of the Sinai peninsula, and the coastal lands of the Mediterranean, where the regularity of annual rainfall patterns marked the difference between starvation and plenty. It is all the more striking how evidently he believed that the real focus of his history was the hill country of Judaea. Indeed, in *Against Apion*, composed a few years after the completion of the *Antiquities*, Josephus cited the landlocked isolation of his homeland as a reason for the failure of most Greek historians of earlier generations, the most trusted source of historical knowledge for Josephus' Greek and Roman readers, to make mention of the magnificent history of the Jews: 'Now we do not inhabit a country with a coast, nor are we keen on trade or on the mixing with others that results from it . . .'[23]

The problem of the silence of Greek sources about Jewish history to which Josephus was responding was real, and his heroic efforts in *Against Apion* to unearth references to Jews in obscure corners of Greek literature (including an allusion by Choerilus to Homer's mention of Solymi, taken by Josephus as a reference to Jerusalem (Greek: *Hierosolyma*)) only went to show how little there was to be found.[24] The problem remains to this day, even if modern historians can now complement the Jewish and Greek sources with evidence from other contemporary written sources, such as hieroglyphic documents from Egypt and cuneiform tablets from Mesopotamia which Josephus was unable to use. If historians now are sceptical about much of Josephus' version of the distant Jewish past, this is less because of the discovery of new texts than a result of critical study over the past two centuries of the nature and composition history of the biblical writings and the archaeological investigations of the Near East in more recent years. At its most extreme, it has been suggested that the whole history of the Jews before the third century BCE was invented at that time by the compilers of the Bible. Such invented histories for peoples who lacked knowledge of their origins can certainly be attested in this period – it was, for instance, at around this time that Romans began to adopt elements of the myth of the Trojan war in order to link the foundation of Rome to Greek theories of the origins of peoples.[25]

Such extreme scepticism is probably unwarranted. No amount of critical study can shed light on the veracity of the travel narratives of Abraham and his descendants, but there is much evidence in the Near East in the third and second millennium BCE of the nomadic lifestyle represented in these stories, with fragile relations both between tribal groupings and between them and more settled urban centres on the fringes of desert areas. It is also clear that some nomadic tribes came into close contact with the highly regimented Egyptian state towards the end of the second millennium BCE, although efforts to link Egyptian records directly to the biblical narrative of the Exodus are unconvincing. Archaeological evidence from the early Iron Age in the land of Israel does not confirm the biblical story of conquest by Israelite tribes infiltrating rapidly from the Transjordan, but the evidence is consonant with the incorporation of outsiders into a local population in this period, perhaps in a more gradual fashion.[26]

Excavation of impressive stone fortresses at Megiddo and elsewhere from the early first millennium has demonstrated the extent of urbanization in the period Josephus assigned to the united monarchy under Saul, David and Solomon, although whether these fortresses, or the monumental remains from *c.* 1000 BCE found in recent decades just south of the Temple Mount in Jerusalem, confirm the history of monarchy as described in the biblical narrative is much more debated. Impressive buildings cannot by themselves demonstrate the extent of Jewish national self-consciousness as presupposed in Josephus' narrative. Finds of

Hebrew inscriptions, the earliest agreed examples dated to the eighth century BCE, confirm the existence in Israel at this date of people using this distinctive branch of the Canaanite group of Semitic languages, but much of the extensive archaeological data from the land of Israel in the tenth to seventh centuries BCE could have been produced by ethnic groups other than Jews, and a direct link between particular archaeological sites and specific biblical stories is rarely possible. On the other hand, such links are not totally absent. Every reference from the first half of the first millennium BCE in extant non-biblical sources – Aramaic, Moabite, Assyrian and Babylonian – to a king of Israel (the northern kingdom, ruled originally from Shechem and eventually from Samaria) or to a king of Judah (the name adopted by the southern kingdom, with its capital in Jerusalem) has the same name as the biblical narrative at approximately the same date as would be expected from the Bible. The account of the reign in Jerusalem at the end of the eighth century BCE of Hezekiah, which Josephus derived from the biblical books of Kings and Chronicles, and which included attacks on Hezekiah's territory by Assyrian armies, is confirmed in very general terms by reference to victorious campaigns in Judah, including a siege of Jerusalem, in the reliefs, now in the British Museum, of the Assyrian king Sennacherib. The versions of these campaigns of 701 BCE in the Assyrian records do not exactly agree with those in the Jewish sources, but it is clear that they are referring to the same events.[27]

There can be no doubt that the historical traditions of the kingdoms of Israel and Judah and exile to Assyria and Babylon have been manipulated by later generations to teach moral lessons to their contemporaries, but they are highly unlikely to have been invented from scratch. By the fifth century BCE, and the return of some Jews from Babylonian exile to Jerusalem, coins bearing the word 'Yehud' show that the name of the Jews was in use for a political entity under Persian rule. The rest of the biblical narrative about the Temple state of Jerusalem in the Persian period is difficult to illuminate through archaeology, but an archive of documents from the Egyptian Jewish community which manned a garrison in Elephantine on the first cataract of the Nile from the late sixth to the early fourth century BCE reveals these diaspora Jews writing to the Temple authorities in Jerusalem for advice on how to keep the Jewish festivals in their own local shrine (see Chapter 3).[28]

This long history can be understood only in the light of wider political and cultural conditions in the Middle East. The urbanization of

Mesopotamia, a process dependent on both the region's fertility and development of irrigation systems, long predated the birth of Abraham in Ur, whatever date might be assigned to this event – the internal chronology of the Bible places his birth in the first half of the second millennium BCE, but this chronology is highly unlikely to have been based on any firm ground. An extensive network of trade routes across the fertile crescent in the second millennium BCE provides the background to the stories of his migration to Canaan. The stability of the kingdom of Egypt through the eighteenth and nineteenth dynasties, in the second half of the same millennium, with foreign policy dedicated to expansion to the north, explains the centrality of Egypt in the narratives of Israelite patriarchs and the exodus. The imperial ambitions of the kings of Assyria from the mid-ninth century BCE, which extended their influence to the southern Levant, and the need to placate those ambitions as well as those of Egypt to the south, explains much of the foreign policy of the kings of Israel and Judah up to the end of the seventh century BCE. The similar ambitions of the Babylonian kings who conquered the Assyrian empire in 612 BCE led to the fall of Jerusalem in 586 BCE. The return of Jews from exile in Babylon was the direct result of the capture of Babylon by Cyrus, king of Persia, in 539 BCE, and the beginning of Greek rule over Jerusalem in 332 BCE was the product of the rapid conquest of the Persian empire by Alexander the Great. In the tradition of Macedonian kingship inherited by Alexander, the legitimacy of a ruler was proved by foreign conquest, and these values were preserved by the Ptolemaic and Seleucid dynasties in their numerous wars in the third century BCE to control Judaea, less for its own sake than as a prize of empire.[29]

The location of Judaea at a strategic crossroad between the empire of Syria and Egypt explains much of the frequency of external interventions in a region with few natural resources to make it important in its own right. The fertile plain which runs from north to south along the Mediterranean provided access to maritime trade only through a small number of harbours on an inhospitable coast. The hill country which runs parallel from Galilee to the Negev desert produced only the basic products of Mediterranean agriculture (grain, wine and oil) in the valleys and on terraced hillsides. Further east, the rift valley of the Jordan, which sinks far below sea level on its way to the Dead Sea, is exceptionally fertile around the Sea of Galilee, and the oasis of Ein Gedi by the Dead Sea was famous for its balsam groves. Further east still, the grazing lands of the Transjordan steppe merge gradually into the desert from which, according to the biblical account, the Israelites had emerged in the time of Joshua to conquer the land. Invasion and warfare have been part of the history of the region ever since.

Each invading culture had left its mark on the Jews by the time that Josephus was writing his history at the end of the first century CE. Many aspects of Mesopotamian accounts of the creation of the world are similar to the stories in Genesis. Egyptian artefacts of all kinds are common in archaeological sites in the land of Israel in the second and early first millennium BCE. Aramaic, the official language of the Persian state, had become the lingua franca of all the inhabitants of the fertile crescent alongside Greek, the official language of the Macedonian kingdoms in the Near East after Alexander. The rebuilding of Jerusalem by Herod the Great had incorporated many of the most recent innovations in Roman architecture, and Agrippa, who ruled as the last king of Judaea from 41 to 44 CE, bore a Roman name.[30]

The influence of other cultures on Jews and Judaism was even greater in the diaspora than in the homeland. Already by 200 BCE there were Jewish communities in Babylonia and Egypt, and over the next two centuries many Jews were to be found in parts of Asia Minor (modern Turkey), Greece and Macedonia, in Cyrene (in modern Libya) and, from the mid-first century BCE, in the city of Rome. The origin of some of these communities, such as Babylonia and Rome, had been through deportation of war captives from Judaea, but they were swelled by economic migrants and mercenaries, and by an unknown number of proselytes from the host societies in which they lived. Josephus was able to tell only sporadic stories about some of these diaspora communities, such as the adventures of the Jewish brigands Asinaeus and Anilaeus in northern Mesopotamia in the early first century CE and the travails of the large Jewish population of Alexandria in Egypt, where political relations between Jews and Greeks under Roman rule were often fraught. Josephus reports that on occasion both Hasmonaean and Herodian rulers intervened with the Roman state on behalf of the political rights of diaspora communities. By the second century BCE Jews in all parts of the diaspora shared a concern for the welfare of the Jerusalem Temple and its cult, although individual communities were free to develop in distinctive local ways without any imposition of control from the authorities in Judaea.[31]

Modern scholars have done their best to make sense of the biblical narrative in light of other evidence in much the same way as Josephus, although he would have been horrified by the suggestion that some of the tradition was invented. Most would place the stories about Abraham and his immediate descendants in the Middle Bronze Age, between 2000 and 1800 BCE, on the basis of similarities between their semi-nomadic lifestyle and population movements in northern Syria known from documents at Mari. According to the biblical texts, there were 215 years between the arrival of Abraham in Canaan and the migration of Jacob and his family to Egypt, and a further 430 years before the exodus, but these figures were probably derived from the genealogies to which they are attached and are not reliable even within the context of the biblical narrative.

Dating the exodus to the mid-fifteenth century BCE by reference to the claim in I Kings that Solomon, who ruled in the tenth century BCE, began to build the Jerusalem Temple '480 years after the Israelites left Egypt' is similarly problematic, since the number 480 was almost certainly a literary invention based on twelve generations of forty years between Moses and Solomon. Mention in the book of Exodus of the garrison cities of Pithom and Raamses makes the reign in Egypt of the pharaoh Rameses II in the thirteenth century BCE much the most plausible context for the exodus story.

When the Bible envisages a period of forty years of wandering in the desert between Egypt and Canaan before the Israelites entered the land under the command of Joshua, the story no longer concerns family groups, as in the patriarchal period, but a nation on the move, divided into twelve tribes named after the sons (and, in the case of Ephraim and Manasseh, grandsons) of Jacob, from whom they claimed descent. It is impossible to know how much these tribal divisions in the desert were retrojected into the narrative to explain the later history of these tribes when they were settled in the land of Canaan and Transjordan. The story of the conquest itself is also impossible to verify. A more gradual assimilation with the settled inhabitants of the land after c. 1200 BCE accords better with the archaeological evidence, but there is no reason to doubt the general outline of the narrative in the books of Judges and Samuel, with stories about small tribal groups, loosely aligned with each other and frequently at war with oppressive neighbours such as Midianites, Ammonites and Philistines.

Unity came with the appointment of Saul as a king for all Israel to act as a champion against these enemies in the last quarter of the eleventh century BCE. With the advent of the regal period and a great deal of chronological data in the books of Kings and Chronicles, some of which can be correlated with external sources, biblical history takes on a much clearer definition. The united monarchy over which Saul, David and Solomon presided lasted from *c.* 1025 to *c.* 928 BCE. Once divided into two kingdoms, the kingdom of Israel in the north was ruled by twenty kings (some as co-regents) until the Assyrian conquest and its total eclipse with the capture of Samaria in 722 BCE. Forcibly transplanted to northern Mesopotamia and further east in accordance with the standard practice of the Assyrian state to transfer defeated populations to regions far from their origins, the ten tribes were lost to history.

The southern kingdom of Judah survived intact in the shadow of the Assyrian state through the seventh century BCE, and towards the end of the century King Josiah, who ruled from 639 BCE, took advantage of the decline of the Assyrian state under attack from Medes and Babylonians to expand his territory north into regions formerly part of the kingdom of Israel. The death of Josiah in the battle of Megiddo in 609 BCE marked the end of this last period of prosperity for Judah. Squeezed between the imperial ambitions of Babylonia and Egypt and riven by internal divisions, the kingdom, including Jerusalem and the Temple, was destroyed by the Babylonians in 586 BCE.

Unlike those taken into captivity from the northern kingdom nearly a century and a half earlier, those exiled from Judah did not lose their national identity. Both those who fled to Egypt and the large numbers forcibly transported to Babylonia retained an attachment to their homeland. It helped that neither the Babylonians nor the Egyptians interfered with the religious and social life of the Jewish communities in their midst. As a result, when the Persian king Cyrus conquered Babylon in 539 BCE and gave permission to the exiled Jews to return from Babylon to Judah, many declined to uproot themselves.

Those who did return to Jerusalem were thus few at first, and it was only in *c.* 515 BCE that the Temple was completed. Even then the restored community was far from the national centre it had been seventy years before. It was not until the mid-fifth century BCE that a really distinctive Jewish polity re-emerged. According to the biblical books of Ezra and Nehemiah, Ezra was sent in 458 BCE, along with a band of fellow Jews from Babylon, with a mandate from the Persian king Artaxerxes I to impose the law of the Torah on the community in Jerusalem. Nehemiah, the cupbearer of Artaxerxes, was appointed governor of Judah from 444 to 432 BCE and led a drive to repopulate the city of Jerusalem with Jews. The Persian state was content to allow the Jews of the province they called 'Yehud' to enjoy a good deal of self-government.

The sudden demise of the Persian empire in 331 BCE through the conquests of Alexander of Macedon made little change to the status of the Jews of Yehud, which the Greeks called 'Judaea'. The struggles for his territory between the generals who succeeded Alexander after his death in 323 BCE left Judaea by 301 BCE as part of the empire of the Ptolemies, which was based in Egypt. After a century of conflict, including six 'Syrian wars' in the region of Judaea between the Ptolemies and their Seleucid rivals, whose sprawling territories included Syria and Mesopotamia, Judaea was under Seleucid control by 198 BCE.

The change in regime made little difference to the Jews of Judaea until the intervention of the Seleucid king Antiochus IV Epiphanes (175–164 BCE) described so vividly by Josephus. The precise course of events, and their causes, are unclear (see Chapter 5), but by 167 BCE Antiochus had sanctioned not only the settlement of a non-Jewish population in Jerusalem but the introduction of a pagan cult into the Temple. Successful resistance led by Judah Maccabee recovered the Temple for Jewish worship by 164 BCE and in due course led to the establishment of Judah's family as a new ruling dynasty in Judaea. By 129 BCE, the government of Judaea was effectively independent of Seleucid control.

In the early first century BCE, the Hasmonaean dynasty (so called after an ancestor of Judah Maccabee) extended Jewish rule to a territory comparable in extent to the kingdom of David. But independence was temporary. With the capture of Jerusalem by Pompey in 63 BCE, Judaea came under Roman sway, exercised at first through support of individual members of the Hasmonaean family as client rulers, and from 37 BCE through the imposition of Herod as king of Judaea. Herod's rule depended entirely on Roman backing, and on his death in 4 BCE his kingdom was divided by the Romans between three of his sons. Archelaus, who had been appointed ethnarch of Judaea, was dismissed from his post in 6 CE following an appeal by his subjects to the emperor Augustus, and for the next sixty years Judaea was placed under the control of a Roman governor in the same way as other provinces, with the exception of a brief period (41 to 44 CE) when Agrippa I, Herod's grandson, ruled over a kingdom as extensive as that of his grandfather. Direct Roman rule proved to be a disaster. In 66 CE the Jews of Judaea rebelled and in 70 CE, after a brutal siege, both the Temple and the city of Jerusalem were destroyed.

Josephus' *Jewish Antiquities* ended with a reference to this destruction, which he had described in full in his earlier account of the war which led up to it. It will be evident that, although the structure and explicit purpose of Josephus' history presupposed the continuity of the Jewish people from Abraham to his own day, it is likely that the distinctive national identity he took for granted had only emerged gradually in the course of centuries under the influence of many different cultures. We have seen the variety of names by which Jews could refer to themselves by Josephus' time. Josephus called himself both *hebraios* and *ioudaios*, while the Jewish rebels in Jerusalem from 66 to 70 CE proclaimed on their own coins the freedom of Israel and of Zion (a name originally applied to a hill in Jerusalem but often treated in biblical and later Jewish usage as synonymous either with Jerusalem or with the Jewish people as a whole). The remembered past was complex, and not infrequently inglorious, and Josephus could sometimes write the story of the Jews in his own time as a litany of suffering: 'Looking over the whole sweep of history, I would say that the sufferings of the Jews have been greater than those of any other nation.'

But whatever the genuine origins of the Jewish people, Judaism was a religion rooted in historical memory, real or imagined, as we shall see, and the historical books of the Hebrew Bible, which lay at the core of the religion, gave shape both to Jewish forms of worship, many of which were specifically configured to recall events in this salvation history, and to Jewish understanding of the relationship between man and God.[32]

2

The Formation of the Bible

The Hebrew Bible, from which most of the history of the Jews discussed in the previous chapter is known, was believed by them to have been written by divine inspiration. Most of the Bible consists in a continuous historical narrative, in the Pentateuch (the five books of Moses), Joshua, Judges, Samuel, Kings, Ezra–Nehemiah and Chronicles, of the origins of Israel from the travails of Abraham and his descendants down to the return to Zion of some Babylonian exiles and their attempts to re-establish Jerusalem as a religious and national centre. The books of Ruth, Esther and Daniel contain separate narratives of significant events at various points within this national history. The books of Isaiah, Jeremiah, Ezekiel, Hosea, Joel, Amos and a number of lesser preachers from Obadiah to Malachi preserve oracular teachings ascribed to prophets whose lives and careers are in some cases also mentioned in the historical books. Wisdom teachings and theological reflection are found in the pithy apophthegms of Proverbs and Ecclesiastes and the sober narrative of Job. The book of Psalms contains a rich collection of religious lyric poetry, very different from the intense love poetry of the Song of Songs. Beginning with an explanation of the creation of the universe and humankind, and ranging in topic from national, and indeed international, concerns to the most personal and private, these books use a wide variety of literary genres and styles. Instructions for worship, and legal commands and prohibitions, feature strongly in the Pentateuch (especially Leviticus, Numbers and Deuteronomy) and were to play a major role in the later development of Judaism, but they constitute only a small part of the Bible as a whole.[1]

How had this collection come to be written? People in antiquity thought of the biblical books as each having had an author, but it is likely that many of these works were the product of several generations of writers who reworked or added to a text inherited from earlier generations, sometimes incorporating material from an oral tradition, before a final editor redacted the texts to the form in which they are now preserved. Much critical effort has been devoted to trying to establish the nature, date and purpose of these earlier components of the biblical texts. That the Bible contains some material composed, in one form or another, in the period before the Babylonian exile which began in 586 BCE is not disputed, but there is less agreement about its extent, let alone how much can be traced back to original documents, local hero-tales, story cycles, village proverbs or the traditions inherited from their teachers by the disciples of individual prophets. Only occasionally do the texts themselves give any direct hint. The Pentateuch, universally believed in antiquity to have been composed by Moses, is actually told by an anonymous, third-person narrator, with Moses appearing only as a character in the story. In the book of Psalms, occasional references to the Psalms of Asaph and the Psalms of the sons of Korach suggest that the book as we now have it contains excerpts from earlier collections. Conversely, the conclusion that the current form of the book of Isaiah must contain the sayings of a prophet who lived long after Isaiah himself had been reached in the twelfth century by Abraham ibn Ezra, the Spanish Bible commentator, who noted that references in chapters 40–66 to the Persian king Cyrus II, who ruled in the sixth century BCE, must have been composed by someone other than the prophet Isaiah son of Amoz whose career in Jerusalem in the eighth century BCE is narrated in II Kings.[2]

For Josephus and other Jews in the first century CE the nature of the raw materials out of which the biblical texts had been created was irrelevant, since they took the final form of each text at face value as if it had been composed from scratch. Different biblical books reached their final forms at different times, but the great majority were redacted at least by the fourth century BCE. It is increasingly recognized by biblical critics that this process of editing often involved a great deal of literary skill and provided an opportunity to insert the theological messages which justified the inclusion of these works among the sacred books of the Jews. Whatever the disparate prophecies found in the book of Isaiah, the beautiful scroll of the full text of Isaiah found at Qumran by the Dead Sea (see plate) demonstrates that the book was seen as a single and precious religious text in the late second century BCE when it was copied. Indeed, the evidence for the Bible as a collection of books of special sanctity comes less from the books themselves, whose contents (especially when they are devoted to long genealogies) can sometimes seem strikingly mundane, than in the attitudes to these books attested in later centuries. Philo, Josephus and the authors of the Dead Sea scrolls treated the precise wording of biblical texts as a source of spiritual enlightenment. So too did the early rabbis: the *tannaim* (the rabbinic sages whose teachings are preserved in the Mishnah) and their successors the *amoraim* (sages of the third to sixth centuries CE whose teachings are enshrined in the Talmud) produced biblical commentaries, such as the tannaitic compilations *Mekilta* on Exodus, *Sifra* on Leviticus and *Sifre* on Numbers and Deuteronomy, dedicated specifically to deriving moral and legal lessons from such close readings.[3]

The biblical text itself was the product of multiple external influences on the literary genres, religious motifs and legal formulations scattered through the biblical books. The Mesopotamia from which Abraham was alleged to have come, and to which some of his supposed descendants returned as exiles after 586 BCE when Jerusalem was conquered by the Babylonians, was by the third millennium BCE home to a highly developed civilization with efficient bureaucracies, whose operations can still be traced on hundreds of thousands of cuneiform tablets. The Babylonians espoused complex religious myths which in some cases, such as the Sumerian version of the flood story, bear striking resemblance to the stories in the Bible. Similarities have long been noted between some characteristics of the detailed law codes of the Babylonian state, such as the need to pay for medical care for an opponent one has injured in a fight in the Code of Hammurabi, and the rulings found in the law codes in the Pentateuch.[4]

The Egypt where Israel was said to have suffered in slavery before salvation under the leadership of Moses had been for millennia an equally advanced society, managing (as in Mesopotamia) an irrigation economy through a centralized state. With some notable exceptions, such as the biblical book of Proverbs, Egyptian cultural and religious influences have been less easy to detect in most of the biblical texts, perhaps reflecting the frequent expression of hostility to the Egyptian state to be found, for instance, in the prophecies of Jeremiah. Such hostility was founded both on the traditions of the exodus and on the proximity of Egypt as a great power on the borders of Israel and Judah: 'the God of Israel said: "See, I am bringing punishment upon ... Egypt and her gods and her kings, upon Pharaoh and those who trust in him ..."' It has been suggested that the intolerant monotheism attributed to Moses, with its clear divide between true and false religion, was influenced by the failed religious revolution in Egypt of the pharaoh Akhenaten, who abandoned traditional Egyptian polytheism in favour of worship of a single solar deity in the fourteenth century BCE, but easier to trace is the reverse impact of Egyptian culture, in that the most conspicuous religious practices of pagan Egypt came to be seen as the greatest sin.

Of the religious influence of the Persian state, under whose benevolent auspices Jewish exiles returned from Babylonia in the sixth century and in due course rebuilt the Jerusalem temple, perhaps most striking was the proliferation of speculation about angels as denizens of the divine realm. The impact of Greek ideas on Judaism, after the Persian state had been swept away by Alexander of Macedonia between 332 and 323 BCE and Jerusalem had been incorporated into a series of states ruled by Macedonian kings who favoured Greek culture (see Chapter 5), came too late to have more than a minimal effect on the Bible itself, although the cynicism of Ecclesiastes may be ascribed to the influence of Greek philosophy. These echoes of the wider world in which the Bible was formulated are scattered unevenly through the text and have been used, along with linguistic evidence from the Hebrew, as dating criteria for the composition of particular books. Thus, for instance, in conjunction with linguistic evidence from the Hebrew, the Greek ideas found in Ecclesiastes suggest a date in the third century BCE despite the traditional attribution of the work to King Solomon some 800 years earlier.[5]

The Bible was the product of a variety of landscapes, from the marshes, lagoons, mudflats and reed banks of Mesopotamia and the villages and pyramids huddled alongside the Nile in Egypt, to the world of nomads in the rocky, sandy wastes of the Sinai desert punctuated by occasional wells, and the peasant agriculture of the land of Israel in the Iron Age, with its regular harvests of grain, wine and oil. These landscapes were as much imagined as real – the Jordan has never been a particularly impressive river, and Judaea appears to be a 'land flowing with milk and honey' only in contrast to the aridity of the semi-desert to the east and south – but they all left profound imprints on the development of a religion which was to be practised in very different environments in the next two millennia.

By the time the Bible had been compiled in roughly its present form in the third century BCE, much the most important in the eyes of all Jews were the five books of Moses, the Pentateuch. To Josephus, the authoritative books of the Jews constituted 'the law and the prophets', a formulation he shared with his contemporaries who wrote the New Testament. Of the biblical manuscripts found among the Dead Sea scrolls, fragments of the Pentateuch, especially Deuteronomy, predominate. The figure of Moses, as author of the Pentateuch, was already exceptional in the eyes of Jews from his depiction in the Pentateuch itself, where God is portrayed as specifically distinguishing him from other prophets, to whom the Lord makes himself known in visions and dreams: 'Not so with my servant Moses ... With him I speak face to face – clearly, not in riddles; and he beholds the form of the Lord,' so that 'never since has there arisen a prophet in Israel like Moses, whom the Lord knew face to face.' Such rhetoric is all the more striking because the Pentateuch itself portrays Moses as a flawed leader, barred from entering the promised land for his lack of faith when faced by a popular uprising at Meribah. There are remarkably few references to Moses at all in the biblical prophetic books or in the Psalms, even though much of the contents of the Pentateuch is presented as the divine word mediated to the people through Moses: 'The Lord spoke to Moses, saying ...'[6]

None of the other books of the Bible presents divine revelation in such a consistently direct fashion, but those other books were nevertheless seen by the time of Josephus as sharing the same aura of divine inspiration as the Pentateuch. Josephus is the earliest witness to something like a canon of scripture, noting that, among Jews, unlike other peoples,

> it is not open to anyone to write of their own accord ... but the prophets alone learned, by inspiration from God, what had happened in the distant and most ancient past ... Among us there are ... only twenty-two books, containing the record of all time, which are rightly trusted. Five of them are the books of Moses, which contain both the laws and the tradition from the birth of humanity up to his death ... From the death of Moses until Artaxerxes, king of the Persians after Xerxes, the prophets after Moses wrote the history of what took place in their own times in thirteen books; the remaining four books contain hymns to God and instructions for people on life.[7]

It seems clear that Josephus had in mind in this passage something close to the specific shape of the Bible as it was later conceived by the rabbis and by Christians. Although his purpose in referring to these books in this passage was to insist on the veracity of Jewish traditions about their history, it was impossible to omit from his list the last four books (presumably at least Psalms and Proverbs and Ecclesiastes, although which other book came into this category is less certain), even though these did not contain history at all.[8]

The belief in the divine origin of the words recorded in the Pentateuch rendered sacred the parchments on which these words were inscribed. Josephus recorded riots when a scroll of the Torah was burned by a Roman soldier in Judaea in the mid-first century CE; when the synagogue of the Jews in Caesarea came under attack from local gentiles in 66 CE, just before the outbreak of war against Rome, the Jews abandoned the building but preserved the scrolls. Josephus recorded of himself that after the destruction of the Temple in 70 CE he begged a gift of sacred books from the Roman emperor Titus.

In early rabbinic terminology found in the Mishnah, sacred books were those that 'defile the hands'. This notion must be connected to the more general concepts of purity and impurity in biblical texts (see Chapter 4), but in this case it apparently concerned a sort of religious charge, like the force said to have killed Uzzah for touching the ark of the covenant in the time of King David, although with less deadly effect. The notion is without parallel in other pre-Christian ancient religions; in many respects Jewish reverence for scriptural texts as objects was closest in nature to pagan attitudes to the statues of their gods. Already in rabbinic texts from the early third century CE rules can be found for the copying of sacred texts; these rules were to be increasingly elaborated over ensuing centuries, with detailed instructions even for the decorative flourishes in the shape of crowns on top of certain letters in Torah scrolls. The emergence of careful rules can be observed in the biblical manuscripts from Qumran, the earliest to survive (in some cases dating back as early as the second century BCE), in practices such as the use of palaeo-Hebrew letters or dots for the divine name, probably to prevent accidental uttering of the name aloud, which, as we shall see (Chapter 4), was felt to constitute sacrilege.[9]

Such emphasis on the nature and value of the written biblical texts implied great faith in the reliability of the scribes who copied them out for study and liturgical use. It is probable that archetypes of at least some biblical texts were preserved in the Temple in Jerusalem, but whether or how often these archetypes were consulted is unknown. The biblical manuscripts from Qumran exhibit much textual variety, ranging from numerous orthographical variants in manuscripts of the Pentateuch, with Hebrew words sometimes written with the consonants to mark vowels and sometimes not, to much larger variations in the text: in a fragmentary manuscript of the books of Samuel, the version at Qumran is much closer to the account of this period in Chronicles than in Samuel in the later rabbinic Bible.

There had been a long tradition of scribes as adjuncts of administration in bureaucratic states in the Near East and Egypt, and it is possible that some of those who copied Jewish religious texts in the Persian period, such as Ezra 'the scribe' (as he is described in the biblical text itself), held such official positions in Jewish society in earlier times. The biblical texts preserve a tradition that scribes were trained within family-like guilds and that a prominent family of scribes could play a major role in political life in the period of the monarchy, when the highest scribal office was that of royal scribe, but there is no evidence of a class or guild of Jewish scribes by the end of the Second Temple period. It is possible to discern the distinctive work of numerous individual scribes in the production of the Dead Sea scrolls between the second century BCE and the first century CE, but the texts themselves make no reference to who they were, and neither Josephus nor the tannaitic rabbis of the first two centuries CE have anything to say about the qualifications or social role of a scribal guild.

Scribes were widely employed for everyday purposes, such as the copying of legal documents, as can be seen on marriage documents and deeds of sale of the first and second centuries CE found in caves by the Dead Sea. It seems likely that any such scribe who turned his hand to copying out a religious text would need to have the trust of his clients, who would generally be unable to check the accuracy of his text. One should imagine such scribes approaching their task with reverence, in the knowledge that the object they were creating became holy through their actions. For rabbinic Jews who believed that touching any biblical text, even an excerpt of just eighty-five letters, would render the hands impure, the process of writing must have been even more solemn than that of a non-Jewish sculptor creating a statue for worship, for whom (according to Cicero) the sculpture became holy only once completed and dedicated. It was perhaps because such scribes were necessarily perceived as both learned and pious that the authors of the Gospels imagined them as an identifiable section in the Galilean crowds envisaged as communing with Jesus.[10]

Somewhat at odds with the value ascribed to the Hebrew texts and its physical copies was the translation of the sacred texts into other languages, but it is evident that this was being done by Jews even before the mid-second century BCE, when the final parts of what is now the Hebrew Bible – the last prophecies in the book of Daniel, which seem to have been composed in 167 BCE – were written. The Pentateuch was translated into Greek, probably in Alexandria, already in the third century BCE, and the rest of the biblical books were translated over the next century or so. Differences in translation styles suggest that a number of translators were at work, possibly in different places. At some time in the mid-second century BCE, a Jewish author composed a romantic account, purportedly a letter to a non-Jew called Philocrates from his brother Aristeas, of how the translation of the Torah had come about at the command of the Graeco-Macedonian king Ptolemy Philadelphus a century earlier. According to this 'letter', Ptolemy summoned seventy-two sages from Jerusalem to complete a translation of the Jewish law into Greek for inclusion in the royal library, and the text is full of declarations of admiration for Jewish wisdom by the gentile king. The reliability of this account has long been questioned, but it does demonstrate the pride of the Jewish author in the Greek text which he claimed had resulted. By the mid-first century CE, this translation was being celebrated on the island of Pharos in the harbour of Alexandria with an annual festival, when 'not only Jews but multitudes of others cross the water ... to do honour to the place in which the light of that version first shone out.' The philosopher Philo (see Chapter 7), who recounted the details of the festival, added tellingly to the version of the Letter of Aristeas in his description of the translation process. According to the Letter of Aristeas, the seventy-two translators compared their versions at the end of each day in order to achieve the best possible version of the Hebrew. Philo's version was different. According to him, the translators, having chosen the island of Pharos 'where they might find peace and tranquillity and the soul could commune with the laws with none to disturb its privacy', sat there in seclusion, and, becoming 'as it were, possessed', each wrote exactly the same words 'as though dictated to each by an invisible prompter'.[11]

This Greek translation of the Bible, known as the Septuagint ('the Seventy') in (numerically slightly inaccurate) commemoration of the story of the translators of the Pentateuch, is preserved for us now almost entirely through copies made by Christians, for whom it was from the first century CE the authoritative version of the biblical text, but these comments by Philo reveal that by the first century CE some Alexandrian Jews revered the Septuagint no less. Nor was the Greek translation ignored in the land of Israel, for a full text of the Minor Prophets (the biblical books from Hosea to Malachi) was found in the Septuagint Greek in a scroll in Cave 8 at Qumran by the Dead Sea along with the rest of the Dead Sea scrolls. Occasional references in the Babylonian Talmud to 'the translation of Ptolemy' reveal awareness of the

translation much later in antiquity, in the sixth century CE, even among
Jews whose religious ideas were expressed in Aramaic, although for
such Jews the Greek translation never reached the authoritative status
ascribed to it by Philo, any more than did the Aramaic translations from
late antiquity, the *targumim*, which were treated as adjuncts to the Hebrew text to aid in its interpretation, rather than as substitutes. Already
in the first century CE some Jews, who presumably took a different view
of the Septuagint to Philo, began a process of revising the Greek text to
bring it closer to the Hebrew, and these revisions, in the names of Theodotion, Symmachus and Aquila, circulated widely among both Jews and
Christians in late antiquity.[12]

The biblical books were composed by many different authors over a
long period and it would be naive to expect a consistent theology or
worldview throughout the corpus, but they were clearly seen to share
important characteristics. We know that the demarcation of these texts
as particularly sacred involved selection from a wider corpus of Jewish
literature, excluding for example such Jewish writings as the revelations
ascribed to the antediluvian sage Enoch, mentioned in passing in Genesis, of which multiple copies have been found in fragmentary form
among the Dead Sea scrolls alongside copies of books which were to be
included in the biblical canon. The Enochic books were evidently very
popular at the time the main contours of the biblical corpus were being
defined, in the fourth and third centuries BCE, but they were never
themselves treated as scripture. Among the characteristics shared by the
books incorporated into the Bible the most important was the centrality
of the covenant with God revealed to Moses, and it may be that the
Enochic books were excluded because they claimed as the source of
their divine revelation a figure believed to have lived long before Moses,
rather than Moses himself.[13]

What makes scripture different from other writings, beyond the notion
of divine inspiration? The original authors came from very different
backgrounds and had different purposes for writing. It is likely that
many legal and historical texts in the Bible, including parts of the Pentateuch, were composed by priests from the Jerusalem Temple seeking
to reinforce the claims of the Temple as the focus of worship. The prophetic
books combine collections of sayings uttered by the prophet under
divine inspiration with autobiographical accounts of the prophet's
ministry and narratives about the prophet put together by others. The
wisdom literature, such as the book of Proverbs, commends a general

piety without specifically Jewish traits; parallels with Egyptian wisdom teachings make it likely that such collections of pithy advice were put together within scribal schools. The Psalter was probably compiled as a hymn book for use in the Temple in the Persian period, incorporating a number of much earlier song collections which in turn combined songs celebrating royal victories with hymns praising God and songs of collective and individual lament, trust and thanksgiving.

The Bible is thus an amalgam of styles and genres. Speeches, sermons, prayers and sayings are juxtaposed with contracts, letters, lists and laws, and with narratives which vary from myths, such as the story of the flood and Noah's ark, to sagas such as the career of Samson in the book of Judges. There are formal records like the account of Solomon's building of the Temple and the reforms instituted by Josiah (which are likely to come from the Temple annals), and more literary narratives – court histories like the account of the succession to King David in II Samuel and I Kings, and the rags-to-riches story of the shepherd boy David's rise to power. The Bible also contains a great deal of poetry, often woven into the narrative as victory songs (such as the song of Deborah in the book of Judges), as well as mocking songs and funeral dirges (as used by the prophet Amos to proclaim an imminent catastrophe: 'Fallen, no more to rise, is maiden Israel; forsaken on her land, with no one to raise her up'). The Song of Songs contains an anthology of lyrics celebrating love and marriage, probably edited into a unified composition containing a single love story. The book of Job also contains much poetry, but the tone of the narrative, depicting patience in the face of appalling adversity to demonstrate that the truly righteous will continue to serve God even if worship does not profit them, could not contrast more with the Song of Songs. The spirit of sceptical rationalism and resignation found in Ecclesiastes, which repeats no fewer than twenty times that 'All is vanity,' offers a similar contrast. The literal sense of the word *hevel*, conventionally translated as 'vanity', is probably 'a breath of wind', suggesting transience, uselessness or deceptiveness.[14]

Such a heterogeneous collection of writings – variously comforting, poetic, instructive, funny and dull – does not lend itself to conceptions of a unified corpus, and indeed such notions were slow to emerge. In his preface to Ecclesiasticus, the translation into Greek of the Wisdom of Ben Sira which was composed later than Ecclesiastes and in more optimistic vein, the grandson of Ben Sira wrote in the late second century BCE about the 'many great teachings' which 'have been given to us through the Law and the Prophets and the others that followed them'.

But it is not clear that he had a notion which specific writings by 'the others that followed them' shared the status of the Law and the Prophets, and since Ecclesiasticus itself was included by Greek-speaking Jews in the Septuagint, it is evident that Jews in his time had no agreed list of canonical books to which to refer. The Hebrew Ben Sira was not in the end to be included in the Hebrew Bible, even though the text (of which ancient fragments have been found at Masada and Qumran) was known and admired by the tannaitic rabbis. The reasons why the rabbis excluded Ben Sira and other writings accepted by the Greek tradition, such as Tobit and Judith, are obscure. As late as the second century CE the *tannaim* discussed whether the Song of Songs and Ecclesiastes defile the hands, and according to the Babylonian Talmud there were rabbinic debates even in the third century CE about the status of the books of Ruth and Esther.[15]

By the fourth century CE, rabbinic Jews were agreed on the special status of the twenty-four books comprising the Hebrew Bible as used today. They categorized as *Neviim* ('Prophets') both the books containing the speeches of the prophets whose names they bear and the historical accounts (Joshua to Kings) which provide the background to their prophetic careers. The rest of the Bible was defined as *Ketuvim* ('Writings'). The acronym *Tanakh* (Torah, *Neviim*, *Ketuvim*) was used to refer to the Bible as a whole.

The discrepancy between these twenty-four books included in the Hebrew Bible and the larger corpus of the Greek Bible was known at the end of the fourth century to the Christian scholar Jerome, who took the Hebrew to be more authentic despite the fact that Christians had relied on the Greek since the first century CE. Jerome placed the anomalous books found in the Greek but not the Hebrew (Tobit, Judith, Wisdom of Solomon, Ecclesiasticus, the books of Maccabees and a few others) into a separate category ('apocrypha' or 'deutero-canonical') to be considered valuable but not divinely inspired. Jerome's anxiety to distinguish the authentic biblical works from other books reflects a specifically Christian concern to define a canon of scripture in the sense of a fixed list of authoritative books of both the Old and New Testaments. This concern was linked to the need for self-definition for Christian communities in the early centuries of the Church and was not shared by Jews, although the eventual choice by the rabbis of the twenty-four books may have been in reaction to the lists which the Christians had adopted.[16]

The limits of what constituted the Bible thus long remained fluid for Jews, but the principle that some books had greater authority than others was universally accepted much earlier. It is also probable that by the end of the second century BCE both the Torah and the Prophets constituted closed corpora which it would be sacrilege to change, so that continuing uncertainty lingered only about what should be included in the Writings, the third part of the Bible. It is worth asking why Jews felt impelled to give such authority to particular writings in the third and second centuries BCE.

It is unlikely that the explanation lies in an attempt by individuals or groups to impose a specific ideology upon the Jewish community, not least because there is no evidence of any attempt to create consistency across the corpus. We have already seen the variety of tone and purpose of the different biblical books, but different theological emphases also cohabit within the corpus, with (for example) ethics based in much of the Torah on Israel's contract with God but based in the wisdom literature on universal standards of justice. There are different attempts to understand the justice of God in the face of the sufferings of humanity in the extended expressions of grief at the destruction of the First Temple in Lamentations and the contrasting views of Kings and Chronicles on whether God brings retribution for sin immediately (as in Chronicles) or only after many generations (as in Kings). The contrast between the books of Chronicles and the material, from Genesis through to the books of Kings, from which the author derived his historical account points up the degree of duplication and discrepancy allowed to coexist within the biblical corpus. The stories are essentially the same but the chronicler's reworking of his sources contains so many minor alterations that it constitutes biblical exegesis within the Bible.

In the end, the best explanation of the adoption by Jews of the notion of a specially authoritative body of texts on which they could rely for their history and laws comes back to the statement by Josephus with which we began. In claiming that 'it is not open to anyone to write of their own accord' and that 'the prophets alone learned, by inspiration from God, what had happened in the distant and most ancient past,' Josephus set up the literary traditions of the Jews in direct contrast to the myriad contradictory histories, customs and legal systems to be found among the Greeks. It was in the Greek world that Jews found their traditions at odds with the new cultural horizons which Helenization opened up, and they responded by affirming the absolute authority of the main religious texts they had inherited from previous generations (see Chapter 5).

*

Despite all their variety, common themes recur throughout the biblical books. They present the Jewish God both as creator of the world and as the only divine being with whom Israel is to have a relationship. God has guided the history of Israel, especially in the exodus from Egypt and the possession of the promised land of Canaan, but God sometimes interprets the covenant strictly, and punishes his people for disobedience. The texts are preoccupied with the limits of God's unconditional love for his people. How can a God be both just and merciful and allow suffering in the world? Whatever the answer, the Bible assumes that individual Jews have a duty to remain within the national covenant by faithfully observing the injunctions imparted through Moses. This entailed both ritual and ethical punctiliousness, with a moral code which is remarkably consistent across the biblical corpus, stressing justice and care for the poor and defenceless (especially widows and orphans), while prohibiting murder, theft, bribery, corruption and a wide variety of irregular sexual behaviours.

As we shall see in the next two chapters, the biblical texts provided more than enough guidance for Jews to try to shape their forms of worship in public and in private and for them to structure their relationships within their society in accordance with the stipulations of their God. But we shall also see, in Part II of this book, that, by the time of Josephus, interpretation of these texts had led to the development of diverse forms of Judaism which understood the texts in very different ways.

3
Worship

Interpretation of biblical injunctions had spawned by the first century CE two different but complementary forms of worship, both of them unique to Judaism in the ancient world. The sacrificial cult in the Jerusalem Temple was one of the wonders of the Roman empire, attracting non-Jewish tourists as well as masses of Jewish worshippers and boasting distinctive practices which elicited admiration from some and scorn from others. The institution of the synagogue as a place for prayer as well as for teaching the law and reading the biblical texts to a congregation was one of the most striking religious innovations in antiquity. In principle, Temple worship could exist without synagogues, and synagogues without a Temple, but in practice these two forms of worship coexisted comfortably for at least 300 years before the destruction of the Second Temple in 70 CE.

TEMPLE

The Torah stated with great clarity that the Lord wished to be worshipped with sacrifices of animals, and with drink and meal offerings and incense, laying out with some precision the procedure to be followed: 'If the offering is a burnt-offering from the herd, you shall offer a male without blemish ... the priests shall arrange the parts, with the head and the suet, on the wood that is on the fire on the altar; but its entrails and its legs shall be washed with water. Then the priest shall turn the whole into smoke on the altar ...' Such offerings might be brought either by individuals – usually to give thanks for good fortune or to seek pardon for wrongdoing – or by priests on behalf of the community. These physical acts, with the emotions and prayers that accompanied them, constituted the primary link between Israel and God as envisaged in most of the biblical books.[1]

In the Pentateuch, this sacrificial cult is described as located in a portable tabernacle which travelled with the children of Israel during their journeys across the Sinai desert. The construction and the appearance of the Tabernacle are described in fine detail in the book of Exodus, from the ark of acacia wood overlaid with gold to house the 'testimony' of the Lord (presumably a written text) to the golden 'mercy-seat' or cover, gold-winged cherubim, gold plates and dishes for incense, gold flagons and bowls for drink offerings, the table overlaid 'with pure gold' for 'the bread of the Presence', the lampstand with seven lamps 'of pure gold', and the 'ten curtains of fine twisted linen, and blue, purple and crimson yarns', with images of cherubim skilfully worked into them. The reason for their elaborate display is explicit in the biblical text: Moses is said to have been commanded by the Lord to tell the Israelites to gather an offering 'from all whose hearts prompt them to give' so that they might 'make me a sanctuary, so that I may dwell among them'.[2]

The notion that a divinity might expect his or her worshippers to provide a dwelling place as a focus for ritual worship was common to all the more complex societies which had contact with Canaan in the first millennium BCE. Animal sacrifices and other offerings were the standard form of worship throughout the region. Stone cult temples had been dedicated to gods in Egypt at least from the early third millennium BCE, and temples had been constructed from mud brick in Mesopotamia from even earlier. In Palestine and the surrounding regions a variety of Bronze Age temples from the second millennium BCE have been excavated, from fortress temples at Hazor and Megiddo to the outdoor circular altar at Nahariyah and the 'High Place' at Gezer, with ten huge standing stones in alignment, each adjacent to a large stone basin, and the temples at Lachish and Tel Mevorakh, with their rich collections of votive vessels, jewellery and other offerings. The variety of temple styles, sometimes in imitation of Egyptian structures, continued into the Iron Age, the period when, according to the biblical account, the sacrificial cult also moved, through the initiative of Solomon, from temporary tent-like structures, such as the Tabernacle described in Exodus, to a more permanent building in Jerusalem.[3]

The erection of permanent temples to house and honour divinities was a gradual process in many parts of the Near East and the eastern Mediterranean world. In Greece the worship of the gods had been organized around the royal palaces in the Mycenaean period but by the first millennium BCE, with Greek society divided into separate communities without any centralized state, each community marked off, by a wall or boundary stone, a sacred area for sacrifices and dedications without any building. It was only in the eighth century BCE that temples began to be built, perhaps reflecting influence through Greek trading contact with Egypt. In Palestine this process had begun rather earlier, and the narrative in I Kings of Solomon's decision to build the Jerusalem Temple is thus not implausible, even if its magnificence may have been exaggerated: 'Solomon overlaid the inside of the house with pure gold ... Next he overlaid the whole house with gold, in order that the whole house might be perfect; even the whole altar that belonged to the inner sanctuary he overlaid with gold.' Also plausible is the rationale for this vast expense as given by the author of I Kings: 'Now the word of the Lord came to Solomon, "Concerning this house that you are building, if you will walk in my statutes, obey my ordinances, and keep all my commandments by walking in them, then I will establish my promise with you, which I made to your father David. I will dwell among the children of Israel, and will not forsake my people Israel."' The Temple, like the ritual it housed, was designed to ensure divine favour.[4]

If the biblical chronology is correct, the Jerusalem Temple after its foundation by Solomon was the main focus for Jewish worship for a thousand years, from *c.* 1000 BCE to its razing by the Romans in 70 CE, with only a comparatively brief interruption between the destruction of Solomon's edifice in 586 BCE and the building of the Second Temple by the returned exiles in the late sixth and fifth centuries BCE. The centrality of the building in the eyes of many Jews emerges clearly in the prophecies of Haggai and Zechariah, who urged this rebuilding on Zerubbabel, the governor of Judah, and Joshua, the High Priest, rebuking those who said, 'The time has not yet come to rebuild the Lord's house.' Haggai's message was not complicated: the Lord of hosts had ensured that 'the heavens above you have withheld the dew, and the earth has withheld its produce,' because 'my house lies in ruins, while all of you hurry off to your own houses'. Even during the period between the Temples, the prophet Ezekiel, dreaming in exile in Babylonia about perfect worship of God, had an intense vision that intermingled recollections of the destroyed Temple with pure fantasy: 'water was flowing from below the threshold' of the Temple, forming a stream which became 'a river that could not be crossed' and which continued down to the Dead Sea, where it would sweeten the waters and they would swarm with fish.[5]

The actual practice of the sacrificial cult in the Temple is not accorded universal approval in the biblical texts. Critical comments are found most often in the writings of the earlier prophets, Amos, Hosea, Micah, Jeremiah and Isaiah. Many of their comments concern issues of moral priorities: as Micah complains, what is the point of burnt-offerings if you do not do what the Lord requires, 'to do justice, and to love kindness, and to walk humbly with your God'? Other prophetic passages complain bitterly about incorrect forms of sacrifice – 'When you offer blind animals in sacrifice, is that not wrong? And when you offer those that are lame and sick, is that not wrong?' – or sacrifices to divinities other than the God of Israel: 'Do not rejoice, O Israel! . . . for you have played the whore, departing from your God.' Jeremiah reports the wrath of the Lord because the people 'make cakes for the queen of heaven; and they pour out drink-offerings to other gods', recording the divine rebuff that burnt-offerings are useless because 'on the day that I brought your ancestors out of the land of Egypt, I did not speak to them or command them concerning burnt-offerings and sacrifices. But this command I gave them, "Obey my voice, and I will be your God, and you shall be my people."'

Some of these critiques of sacrifice may have been issued by prophets from within the Temple itself, but their critiques were preserved in a biblical corpus in which the Temple and its importance is frequently stressed throughout. Even the apparently clear rejection of sacrifice in Psalm 50 – 'I will not accept a bull from your house, or goats from your folds . . . If I were hungry, I would not tell you, for the world and all that is in it is mine. Do I eat the flesh of bulls, or drink the blood of goats?' – is prefaced by calling for a gathering of 'my faithful ones, who made a covenant with me by sacrifice', so that this polemic too seems most likely to be aimed at those who fail to 'offer to God a sacrifice of thanksgiving' (as prescribed in Leviticus) and to pay their vows, again with a sacrifice, to the Most High.[6]

According to the biblical account, the Temple of Solomon was a rectangle, 100 cubits (roughly 55 yards) long and 50 cubits (27 yards) wide, erected on a platform. The inner space was divided into three sections. An open doorway from the surrounding courtyard led into a porch, with two great bronze pillars, called 'Jakhin' and 'Boaz', on either side of the entrance. This porch led through double doors into a large room which was the locus of most of the rituals. A further set of doors, made of olive wood, led into the inner sanctuary, which was a cube in shape (20 cubits to each side). The floors of the central and inner rooms were set with cypress boards and the cedar wood walls were carved with floral and other images. Ritual objects in the central chamber included lampstands and a gold table for the 'bread of the Presence'. In the external courtyard were found the altar and an enormous bronze basin, called 'the sea' in the text of Kings, with lavers and other bronze objects. Within the inner sanctuary was to be found the 'ark in which is the covenant of the Lord' which had been brought to Jerusalem by David, protected by the outstretched wings of two enormous cherubim, made of olive wood and covered with gold.[7]

The building thus described is similar in plan and decoration to other temples from this region and period, in particular the Syro-Hittite temple excavated at Ain Dara, north-west of Aleppo in Syria, but it was not identical to any of them – unsurprisingly in view of the range of forms found in regional temple architecture. The Bible portrays the centralizing of cult in Jerusalem as a gradual process, with what is seen as frequent backsliding by the people into worship in other places, and the relationship between the Jerusalem Temple and other Israelite shrines in the Iron Age period is unknown. A small courtyard shrine of around the tenth century BCE at Megiddo has offering stands and a limestone altar. At Ta'anach, near Megiddo, a rather larger shrine has two terracotta stands with sun discs, sacred trees, cherubs, lions and other motifs. The massive ashlar podium of the monumental altar at Dan in northern Israel may date to a century later. Similar in design to the Temple of Solomon was a temple in Arad, which was still being rebuilt in the seventh century BCE. At Kuntillet Ajrûd, in the Sinai desert, a building of the eighth century BCE was found at the entrance to a caravanserai, with plastered benches on each side and plastered walls covered with inscriptions which invoked El, Yahweh and Baal. 'El' and 'Yahweh' were names used by Jews to refer to the Jewish God, but 'Baal' was not, and it is clear that this was a society which continued to embrace polytheistic worship. Storage jars within the fortress are decorated with scenes including sacred trees and a half-nude female seated on a throne, and an inscription referring to blessings by 'Yahweh of Samaria and his asherah', providing some context to the urging of the biblical prophets to forsake the worship of other gods. 'Asherah' was the name of a Canaanite goddess known best from the Ugaritic texts discovered at Ras Shamra on the Syrian coast, in which she is often represented as the consort of the god El.[8]

The biblical narrative has remarkably little to report about the appearance of the Second Temple built by Zerubbabel in the late sixth century BCE. Solomon's Temple was said to have undergone many changes over the years, including the plundering of its treasures by later kings, but it was still a grand building and the precise day of its destruction 'in the fifth month, on the tenth day of the month, which was the nineteenth year of King Nebuchadnezzar, king of Babylon', was bitterly recalled by the prophet Jeremiah. The pillars of bronze were removed, and the ark of the covenant disappeared (if it had not already been taken earlier, as some legends claimed). Zerubbabel's Temple thus lacked these elements that had been so important in the earlier building, but it may have included the 5,400 gold and silver vessels which, according to the book of Ezra, the Persian king Cyrus allowed the returning exiles to take from Babylon to Judah (although this tradition sits uneasily with the assertion in the Second Book of Kings that in 597 BCE Nebuchadnezzar had all the gold vessels from the Temple cut into pieces). Other references to the building in biblical texts are too allusive and symbolic to provide any clear notion of the extent to which the Temple of Solomon was replicated. The Jerusalem vision of Zechariah, with its reference to the 'Holy Mountain', is idealized, as is the overblown and wholly spurious description in the second century BCE by the author of the Letter of Aristeas of the extraordinary fertility of the countryside surrounding the glorious shrine, but both attest the importance attributed to the Temple as a building to be revered.[9]

Of changes to the building during the five centuries it remained in use, the best attested is the desecration in 168 BCE by Antiochus Epiphanes, which came close to bringing the history of Judaism to an abrupt end by transferring worship in the Temple from the Jewish God to a new divinity (probably Zeus) embodied in a statue which the books of Maccabees termed the 'abomination of desolation'. (For a more detailed discussion of these traumatic events, see Chapter 5.) Jews were required to offer sacrifices of pigs and other unclean animals at new altars and sacred precincts set up to other gods. The books of Maccabees undoubtedly exaggerate the significance of the role in saving Judaism played by Mattathias and his sons, not least because they were written at a time when Mattathias' descendants were in power in Judaea and dependent on myths about their heroic deeds against Antiochus as justification for their control of the high priesthood. But the danger was real enough – the region is littered with artefacts from local religions which did not survive past antiquity, and if worship of the Jewish God in the Jerusalem Temple had ended in the 160s BCE rather than nearly two and a half centuries later, in 70 CE, it is highly unlikely that there would have been a later history of Judaism (or, for that matter, of Christianity) to record.

Antiochus' attack on Jewish worship, however, seems to have been achieved without major alterations to the building itself. According to I Maccabees, composed probably about forty years after the events described, when Judah Maccabee re-entered the sanctuary and found 'the sanctuary desolate, the altar profaned and the gates burned', he was able to organize a rededication at some speed:

> He chose blameless priests devoted to the law, and they cleansed the sanctuary and removed the defiled stones to an unclean place. They deliberated what to do about the altar of burnt offering, which had been profaned. And they thought it best to tear it down, so that it would not be a lasting shame to them that the Gentiles had defiled it. So they tore down the altar, and stored the stones in a convenient place on the temple hill until a prophet should come to tell what to do with them. Then they took unhewn stones, as the law directs, and built a new altar like the former one. They also rebuilt the sanctuary and the interior of the temple, and consecrated the courts. They made new holy vessels, and brought the lampstand, the altar of incense, and the table into the temple. Then they offered incense on the altar and lit the lamps on the lampstand, and these gave light in the temple. They placed the bread on the table and hung up the curtains. Thus they finished all the work they had undertaken. Early in the morning on the twenty-fifth day of the ninth month, which is the month of Chislev, in the one hundred and forty-eighth year, they rose and offered sacrifice, as the law directs, on the new altar of burnt offering that they had built.[10]

A century and a half later, the same Temple no longer seemed so impressive to Herod, who, despite his comparatively humble origins, had been appointed king of Judaea by the Romans and rushed to build a monument to his remarkable political achievement. Rebuilding had to be done with great care to ensure no interruptions in the sacrificial cult and no pollution of the site. A thousand priests were trained to carry out the masonry work on the Temple itself. A much larger workforce extended the Temple platform using arches as substructure and huge retaining walls, of which parts still survive. The Temple proper and its furnishings were left untouched, but its exterior was covered with so much gold that the reflection could almost blind those who looked on it. Building began in 20 BCE and, the inner sanctuary, porticoes and outer courts were completed by 12 BCE. But, according to Josephus, a contemporary eyewitness, additions and repairs were still in operation in 66 CE, four years before the destruction of the building by Roman forces.[11]

How was worship carried out in the Temple? It is easier to provide an answer for the last century of its long existence than for earlier periods, but, even allowing for the near certainty that the surviving evidence provides an idealized picture, it is possible to reconstruct a picture of the daily Temple regime with a degree of detail not possible for any other temple in the ancient world. The reason is simple: Josephus, himself a Jerusalem priest, wrote extensively about the Temple in his narrative of the life of Herod and in his account of the war against Rome which led to the Temple's destruction, and, a hundred years after Josephus, the earliest rabbinic text, the Mishnah, discussed contentious issues in the administration of sacrifices and offerings by the Temple authorities in an attempt to clarify correct procedures. Whatever had been the case in earlier times, by this final period the Temple was unusual in the ancient world in being open for worship every day: the great gates were ceremoniously opened at dawn and closed at sunset. A large staff ensured an orderly procession of private offerings, with individuals purchasing animals and birds fit for sacrifice from a market in the porticoes on the edge of the Temple precinct. The day was punctuated by a series of public sacrifices in which the priests offered up prayers and slaughtered animals on behalf of the people as a whole. These public offerings were made on ordinary weekdays each morning, afternoon and evening, with special extra sacrifices on the Sabbath and on new moons: 'At the beginnings of your months you shall offer a burnt-offering to the Lord: two young bulls, one ram, seven male lambs a year old without blemish . . .'[12]

The main impression for a visitor on a normal day will have been of space. The daily communal ritual took place only in a restricted area around the inner court of the priests, where the animals were slaughtered, burned and (occasionally) eaten, and libations were poured. Much of the rest of the immense building was often more or less empty. Even before the great rebuilding by Herod, the size of the piazza in which worshippers could gather was noticed by outsiders. This great courtyard for the general public was almost wholly barren of the trees, votive offerings and statues standard in pagan shrines. In the first century CE the philosopher Philo remarked both on the lack of trees and on the cleanliness of the Temple area. He ascribed the absence of trees to the need to maintain an atmosphere of religious austerity in the Temple, which would be compromised by the 'easy enjoyment' which a grove would provide, noting also that the excrement needed for fertilizer was forbidden within the walls. In Philo's time what hit the eye were the bright decorations of objects dedicated by individuals and hung on the

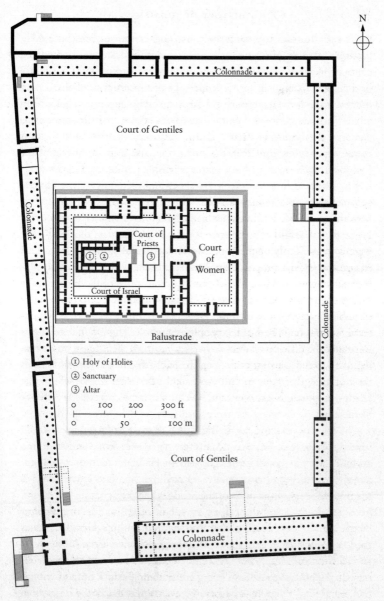

N

Court of Gentiles

Colonnade

Colonnade

Court of
Priests

Court of Israel

① ②   ③

Court
of
Women

Balustrade

Colonnade

① Holy of Holies
② Sanctuary
③ Altar

0   100   200   300 ft

0   50   100 m

Court of Gentiles

Colonnade

Plan of the Second Temple just before its destruction in 70 CE, based on a combination of the descriptions by Josephus and in the Mishnah. From the Court of Israel, from which women were excluded, male Jews could observe from close up the sacrifices carried out by the priests. The massive extension of the Court of the Gentiles to the south and east completed by Herod in 12 BCE enabled the Temple to accommodate large crowds of pilgrims.

walls and doors surrounding the court, such as the golden chain dedicated by Herod's grandson Agrippa I to commemorate his release from captivity in Rome, or the gilded gate donated (according to the Mishnah) by a certain Nicanor from Alexandria. Huge tapestries displayed a panorama of the heavens in purple, blue and scarlet. A remarkable golden vine, described in some detail by Josephus, was sufficiently famous to come to the attention of the gentile historian Tacitus. The precious metals and stones glinted in the sun, giving rise in descriptions of the building to recurrent images of intense light.[13]

The Letter of Aristeas referred to the exceptional quiet of the Temple, in which each official knew his task without instruction, but silence was broken by the herds of animals being taken to slaughter or the occasional sound of choral singing of psalms. The allocation of some of the Psalms to the Temple liturgy on specific occasions probably goes back to early times, since the relevant headings (such as 'A Song for the Sabbath Day') can be found in early Greek translations of the Hebrew; the inclusion in the great Psalms Scroll, found at Qumran, of seven compositions not preserved in the later Hebrew and Greek traditions suggests some continuing liturgical flexibility. More difficult to gauge is the impact of the different smells of the Temple, from the incense offered on the altar to the scent of roast meat from the sacrifices. These offerings took place in the open air and presumably the rising smoke would dissipate into the atmosphere: the fire of the altar, like the fire of the candelabra, was secluded from ordinary worshippers in the area reserved for priests. It is likely that some of these ordinary Jews would visit the Temple, if they could, just to be in the divine presence and address their prayers to God, as the barren Hannah did in the sanctuary at Shiloh in earlier times before there were kings in Israel, according to the biblical story of the birth of the prophet and judge Samuel. The public offerings made by the priests on behalf of the nation on the altar before the Holy of Holies – 'a lamb a year old, without blemish . . . and the grain-offering . . . and the drink-offering' or 'two loaves of bread as an elevation-offering . . . of choice flour, baked with leaven' – were out of sight of most of the worshippers in the Temple court, but individuals had numerous religious obligations, even apart from their personal offerings, to involve them in the heightened atmosphere of dedicated piety.[14]

Three times a year, on the great festivals of Pesach (Passover), Shavuot (Pentecost) and Sukkot (Tabernacles), the Temple was transformed by the arrival of great crowds of pilgrims. The obligation for every adult

Jewish male to 'appear before the Lord' three times a year is prescribed in the Torah, and it is likely that Jews who came from any distance chose to bring their private free-will, sin, thanksgiving and other offerings at the same time. The Pesach festival in the spring began on the first evening with a mass barbecue of roasted lamb. Each lamb was eaten by a small company of men, women and children, and the feast was accompanied by a narration of the exodus from Egypt. The following seven days were marked as special by abstention from leavened foods and by observance of holiday rest at the beginning and end of the Pesach period. Seven weeks later, Shavuot marked the end of the grain harvest and was celebrated, by those pilgrims who came from the land of Israel, by offering the first fruits to the priests in a ritual described vividly in the Mishnah:

> How do they take up the First-fruits . . . ? They that were near brought fresh figs and grapes, and they that were far off brought dried figs and raisins. Before them went the ox, having its horns overlaid with gold and a wreath of olive-leaves on its head. The flute was played before them until they drew nigh to Jerusalem. When they had drawn nigh to Jerusalem they sent messengers before them and bedecked their First-fruits. The rulers and the prefects and the treasurers of the Temple went forth to meet them. According to the honour due to them that came in used they to go forth. And all the craftsmen in Jerusalem used to rise up before them and greet them, saying, 'Brethren, men of such-and-such a place, you are welcome!' . . . The rich brought their First-fruits in baskets, overlaid with silver and gold, while the poor brought them in wicker baskets of peeled willow branches, and baskets and First-fruits were given to the priests.[15]

The festival of Sukkot in the early autumn marked the completion of the agricultural year, 'when you have gathered in the produce from your threshing floor and your wine press'. It was designated in the Torah as a seven-day festival of rejoicing for 'you and your sons and your daughters, your male and female slaves, as well as the Levites (see p. 53), the strangers, the orphans, and the widows resident in your towns' – that is, for the whole community. Since the main aspect of the festival involved the waving in the Temple of four agricultural species (the *lulav*, which consisted of palm, myrtle and willow branches bound together, and the etrog, a citrus fruit), and dwelling in a temporary booth rather than at home, it was easy for ordinary Jews to feel fully drawn in to the celebration. In the Mishnah, Sukkot is described simply as 'Festival', and it seems to have been the best attended of the pilgrim feasts, perhaps because, with the gathering of the harvest, it was easier for farmers to leave their fields. Attendance by pilgrims from Mesopotamia is suggested by a tradition in the Mishnah that prayer for immediate rain was postponed for fifteen days after Sukkot, to enable Babylonian pilgrims 'to reach the Euphrates'.[16]

The Herodian Temple, with its huge courtyard, was well equipped to house pilgrims not just from the land of Israel but from the wider diaspora, and many seem to have come by the land route from Babylonia and, aided by the comparative safety of travel under Roman rule, from Mediterranean communities. Hence the picture in the Acts of the Apostles of the multiple languages to be heard in Jerusalem at Pentecost, where there were 'devout Jews from every nation under heaven' living in Jerusalem – 'Parthians, Medes, Elamites, and residents of Mesopotamia, Judaea and Cappadocia, Pontus and Asia, Phrygia and Pamphylia, Egypt and the parts of Libya belonging to Cyrene, and visitors from Rome, both Jews and proselytes, Cretans and Arabs'. As Philo put it earlier in the first century CE, Moses 'judged that since God is one, there should be also only one temple', not consenting 'to those who wish to perform the rites in their houses' but bidding them 'rise up from the ends of the earth and come to this temple':

Countless multitudes from countless cities come, some over land, others over sea, from east and west and north and south at every feast. They take the temple for their port as a general haven and safe refuge from the bustle and great turmoil of life, and there they seek to find calm weather, and released from the cares whose yoke has been heavy upon them from their earliest years, to enjoy a brief breathing-space in scenes of genial cheerfulness. Thus filled with comfortable hopes they devote the leisure, as is their bounden duty, to holiness and the honouring of God. Friendships are formed between those who hitherto knew not each other, and the sacrifices and libations are the occasion of reciprocity of feeling and constitute the surest pledge that all are of one mind.[17]

Much of the excitement of pilgrimage must have come from being part of a crowd. A highlight of the festival of Sukkot was the rite of the Water-Drawing, when water was carried ceremoniously from the Pool of Siloam to the Temple and poured on to the altar from a golden ewer simultaneously with the regular wine libation, to the accompaniment of dancing and music and general rejoicing. The ritual seems to have been intended as a prayer for rains to fall in the coming winter: 'Men of piety and good works used to dance before them with burning torches in their hands, singing songs and praises. And countless Levites [played] on harps, lyres, cymbals and trumpets and instruments of music ...' According to the Mishnah, 'they have said: "He that has never seen the joy of the place of water-drawing has never in his life seen joy." '[18]

Away from the crowds and the excitement in the Temple itself, there was much to render the whole experience of pilgrimage special, since the first fruits and the second tithe of agricultural produce from the land of Israel, or their monetary equivalent, were required to be consumed within the walls of Jerusalem. It is not surprising that the economy of Jerusalem was thus geared to exploitation of mass religious tourism, with numerous animals and birds on sale for private offering in the precincts surrounding the Temple site, alongside facilities for changing money into Tyrian shekels, the currency accepted by the Temple authority for donations. Nor should it surprise that those who provided such necessary services for a profit might be charged with turning a house of prayer into 'a den of robbers', as Jesus is said to have claimed, or that, although the religious requirement to attend fell on adult males alone, the festivals apparently attracted women and children in large numbers.[19]

Such mass pilgrimage was unique in the ancient world, and had not been a feature of the Jewish Temple throughout its history; international pilgrimage may indeed have become common only after the rebuilding by Herod. According to Josephus, the Roman governor of Syria in 65 CE estimated the total number of adult male worshippers at 2,700,000, to which should be added women and children. The figure is not trustworthy, but the impression of a vast crowd such as can be seen today in Mecca is confirmed by numerous stories about the political volatility of the festivals. The main structure of the festivals was derived from the explicit stipulations in the Torah, but some at least of the ceremonial must have been introduced at later periods, such as the ox with gilded horns and the flute-players in the procession of the first fruits, which seems to have been borrowed from Greek custom. Nothing in the biblical text hints at the ceremony of the Water-Drawing and it is probable that hints of opposition to the ritual, as recorded in the Mishnah, reflect concern that this was an unwarranted innovation: 'To the priest who performed the libation they used to say, "Lift up your hand!" for once a certain one poured the libation over his feet, and all the people threw their citrons at him.' One striking element in the ceremony, the use of ritual dance, is particularly difficult to trace back into earlier Temple liturgy, despite the tradition that King David had danced ecstatically in front of the ark of the Lord on its original arrival in Jerusalem.

The impression that festival ceremonies evolved over time is reinforced by a remarkable letter found in an archive from the ancient
Jewish community of Elephantine on the island of Yeb, on the Nile near
Aswan. This document, from the late fifth century BCE, was probably
sent by the Jerusalem authorities to Egypt to instruct the Jews of Elephantine in how to observe the Pesach according to the Torah. The text
of the letter has to be reconstructed in large part from our knowledge of
the biblical texts, but the general gist is clear:

> [To my brothers Je]daniah and his colleagues the Jewish T[roop], your
> brother Hanan[i]ah. The welfare of my brothers may the gods [seek after
> at all times]. And now, this year, year 5 of Darius the king, from the king it
> has been sent to Arsa[mes . . .] . . . Now, you, thus count four[teen days of
> Nisan and on the 14th at twilight the Passover ob]serve and from day 15
> until day 21 of [Nisan the Festival of Unleavened Bread observe. Seven
> days unleavened bread eat. Now], be pure and take heed. Work [do] n[ot
> do] [on day 15 and on day 21 of Nisan. Any fermented drink] do not
> drink. And anything of leaven do not [eat and do not let it be seen in your
> houses from day 14 of Nisan at] sunset until day 21 of Nisa[n at sunset.
> And any leaven which you have in your houses b]ring into your chambers
> and seal [them] up during [these] days.

Since the Elephantine Jews worshipped in their own local temple, in this
respect at least the celebration of Pesach will have differed greatly from
that described by Philo in Egypt some 500 years later.[20]

The sacrifices and other offerings in the Jerusalem Temple were performed by a hereditary caste of priests. All priests (in Hebrew, *cohanim*)
claimed descent through the male line from Aaron, brother of Moses, to
whom, according to the Torah, this task had been assigned. The priest
had to be male, and without any physical blemish: '[no one] who is
blind or lame, or one who has a mutilated face or a limb too long, or
one who has a broken foot or a broken hand, or a hunchback, or a
dwarf, or a man with a blemish in his eyes or an itching disease or scabs
or crushed testicles' was allowed to approach the altar to perform
priestly duties. Purity of lineage was deemed of sufficient concern for
the marriage partners of priests to be limited. A priest was forbidden to
marry a divorced woman or a harlot, in case doubt was cast on the offspring of the marriage, and Josephus noted with pride the care with
which priests' family records were preserved in archives. By Josephus'
time there were many thousands of priests living both in the land of
Israel and in the diaspora (especially in Babylonia and in Alexandria in

Egypt), and the priests of Judaea and Galilee were divided into twenty-four groups or 'courses' which took turns at stints in charge of the Temple service.[21]

That service was immensely complex, and a great deal of training must have been needed to perform the stipulated actions for animal slaughter with the required precision. The animal had to be checked for imperfections which might invalidate the offering. The Bible sometimes refers to the sacrifices as God's food, but the showbread was simply put on display, and the oxen, cattle, calves, sheep and goats offered, 'from the herd or from the flock', along with doves and pigeons, were burned to make 'an offering by fire of pleasing odour to the Lord', along with meal offerings of grain and oil, libations of wine, and incense. The biblical texts in Exodus, Leviticus and Numbers, and (even more) the tannaitic rabbinic texts such as the Mishnah and Tosefta, went into great detail about the procedure to be followed in each different offering. There were precise rules for sprinkling, daubing and pouring the animals' blood, and for distributing the food between the altar, where it was burned, and the priests and the worshippers, who in the case of 'peace' offerings enjoyed what was in essence a sacred meal in which priests shared, with only certain parts of the meat burned on the altar.[22]

The primacy of the Aaronide priestly caste in the Temple by the time of Josephus had almost certainly been achieved over the centuries only after some struggle. The Pentateuch preserves a tradition that all the tribe of Levi, of which the Aaronides in the Second Temple period were a sub-group, were eligible to carry out the sacrificial service in the desert: 'the Lord set apart the tribe of Levi to carry the ark of the covenant of the Lord, to stand before the Lord to minister to him, and to bless in his name, to this day'. But by the late Second Temple period, the Levites were relegated to minor duties in the Temple as gate keepers and musicians, responsible for the psalms and instrumental accompaniment, having displaced other categories of temple servants, such as the *nethinim* who made repairs and looked after the fabric of the building in the time of Nehemiah. A struggle over status continued right to the end: as late as the 60s CE, the Levites petitioned to be allowed to wear white clothes like the priests. Josephus, as a priest, considered this disgraceful, and blamed this innovation in liturgical practice for causing the destruction of the Temple in 70 CE by provoking divine retribution.[23]

The expertise of priests, and their right to a privileged proximity to the divine service in the Temple, gave them a special status within Jewish society, even if (as the number of priests increased) a decreasing proportion of them could serve in the Temple in any year. Thus a tithe of all agricultural produce in the land of Israel was to be handed over to a priest, and a priest could hope to be a beneficiary of this pious gift from his non-priestly neighbour regardless of any service he might or might not carry out in the Temple. Unjust distribution to priests of tithed grain, through intimidation of poorer priests by the servants of richer priests at public threshing floors, was a serious grievance in the last years of the Temple, and the Levites, who had been envisaged as beneficiaries of tithes in the book of Nehemiah, no longer seem to have received a share.

Josephus' assertion, in his apologetic description of Judaism in *Against Apion*, that the 'appointed duties' of the priests included general supervision of their fellow Jews, is likely to be idealized, since he also claimed in this passage that priests were chosen for their pre-eminence in persuasion and prudence, blithely ignoring the role of inheritance in priestly status. But it is plausible enough that many priests who did serve in the Temple will have become expert in wider issues than just the mechanics of sacrifice. For instance, the biblical notion that only a priest was considered able to decide whether surface dis-colouration in fabrics, people's skin or the walls of houses should be deemed *tsara'at*, a technical term generally but inaccurately translated as 'leprosy', continued to be observed in the last years of the Temple, and some priests must have become quite good at this task. The special status of priests as mediators of divine blessing was reinforced by their recitation, enjoined by the Torah, of a special blessing in the Temple after the daily sacrifice:

> The Lord spoke to Moses, saying: 'Speak to Aaron and his sons, saying, "Thus you shall bless the Israelites: You shall say to them, 'The Lord bless you and keep you; the Lord make his face to shine upon you, and be gracious to you, the Lord lift up his countenance upon you, and give you peace.'" So they shall put my name on the Israelites, and I will bless them.'

The text of this blessing was inscribed on two tiny silver amulets, dated to the first half of the seventh century BCE, which were found in 1979 in a rock-hewn burial chamber at Ketef Hinnom in Jerusalem.[24]

Within the priesthood itself there emerged by the end of the Second Temple period a clear hierarchy of status. Out of all the priests there could only be one High Priest at any one time. To this High Priest was entrusted, most crucially, the duty on Yom Kippur (the Day of Atonement, a day in the early autumn set aside annually for ritual repentance) of seeking forgiveness for the people as a whole. The ritual, laid out in essence in Leviticus but much elaborated in the Mishnah, involved extensive purification, and confession by the High Priest of the sins committed by him, the priests and all Israel over the preceding year. Dressed in white linen, the High Priest entered the Holy of Holies to sprinkle there the blood of a sacrificed bull and goat while offering incense. He then confessed the whole community's sins over another goat, chosen by lot, which would be driven out of the Temple and away from the city, originally to die in the wilderness, although as time went on the practice developed of ensuring the goat's destruction by taking it to the top of a precipice and hurling it down. How much this ritual evolved only after the destruction of the Temple of Solomon in 586 BCE is unknown, but by the late Second Temple era selection for this role was a matter of great significance. It was bolstered in Second Temple times by the wider role often played by High Priests in the secular politics of Judaea.

It is all the more striking that for many centuries a tradition grew up that only those priests descended from Zadok, an Aaronide priest believed to have served as High Priest in the time of David and Solomon, were eligible for the high priesthood. It was only after the revolt of the Maccabees in the 160s BCE that priests from other families were appointed to these positions – in the first instance, from the family of the Maccabees themselves, and then, from the beginning of Herod's rule in 37 BCE, from priestly families who had migrated either to Babylonia or to Alexandria, who therefore could pose no political threat to Herod as ruler. It is not accidental that when the prophet Ezekiel in the sixth century BCE in Babylonia imagined an idealized Temple, he postulated that all the priests would be Zadokites, nor that the role of 'the sons of Zadok' looms large in some versions of the Community Rule found among the Dead Sea scrolls (see Chapter 6). Even though in practice the High Priests in the Temple came from other priestly families for the last two centuries before 70 CE, it is clear that Zadokites continued to be considered by many Jews more appropriate for the role than other priestly families.[25]

How much did this public service in the Temple on behalf of the people matter for non-priestly Jews? Local Jerusalemites may have dropped in to the Temple on ordinary weekdays to pray or bring offerings for thanks or repentance. The Temple courtyard will often in any case have been busy as the only public meeting place in the city – so for instance, according to Acts, Jewish Christians in the days after the crucifixion of Jesus, 'spent much time together in the Temple ... And day by day the Lord added to their number those who were being saved.' But for Jews who lived at a greater distance, physical attendance at the Temple will inevitably have been much rarer. Many will only have attended pilgrim festivals, and those from abroad can have attended even the festivals no more than a few times. Philo, from Alexandria, seems to have been to Jerusalem only once.

The significance of the Temple was therefore more symbolic than practical – but no less powerful for that. For the individual hoping that the rains would come and help the crops to grow, it was comforting to know that the daily sacrifices were being made on behalf of Israel to preserve the covenant with God. When the same individual repented of his sins on the Day of Atonement, with fasting and prayer, it helped to know that the High Priest was also praying on behalf of Israel as he performed the ritual of the scapegoat. For many, the connection of individual to Temple was reinforced by two payments. For those in the land of Israel, the payment to priests of tithes on agricultural produce reinforced the notion that the priestly service was indeed on their behalf. And for all Jews, including those in the diaspora, the annual levy of a half-shekel from all adult male Jews to pay for the regular Temple sacrifices gave a symbolic joint ownership of those sacrifices to each of them. The rule, as elaborated in the Mishnah, was that no individual could pay more or less than the half-shekel, so that no one could feel the communal sacrifices somehow served them more than others. The principle of shared ownership was derived from the injunction from Moses to the children of Israel in the desert as recorded in Exodus, that 'the rich shall not give more, and the poor shall not give less, than the half-shekel, when you bring this offering to the Lord to make atonement for your lives'. The extension of the single payment recorded in the biblical text to an annual payment seems to have occurred only in the Second Temple period. It appears from one passage in the Dead Sea scrolls that this extension encountered some opposition, but the practice was certainly widespread by the mid-first century BCE, before the rebuilding of the Temple by Herod: the Roman orator Cicero referred in the 60s BCE to the collection of gold made by the Jews of Asia Minor, in the west of modern Turkey, for transmission to the Temple in Jerusalem (and the confiscation of this gold by a Roman governor).[26]

The magnificence of the Jerusalem Temple in large part derived, of course, from this influx of wealth from all over the Jewish world. Unlike followers of other gods, by the first century CE most Jews thought it wrong to offer sacrifices in local temples or at local altars, believing instead that such cult should take place only in the place which had been divinely ordained: as Josephus put it, 'One temple of the one God – for like is always attracted to like.' This unification of the Temple worship had been hard won and remained under threat even up to 70 CE. The Jews of Elephantine in Egypt, who made sacrifices in their own temple in the fifth century BCE, wrote to the Jerusalem authorities requesting authorization to rebuild their temple after it had been destroyed through the machinations of local Egyptians. It is significant that they felt it necessary to ask permission, but they clearly saw no reason to be apologetic about their local shrine. The biblical books of Kings record the strategy adopted in the time of the Temple of Solomon by Jeroboam, the first ruler of the northern kingdom of Israel, to strengthen his kingdom by persuading the people to worship two golden calves, one set up in Bethel and another in Dan, in order to remove the need for them to worship at the Jerusalem Temple. That there was indeed a temple cult at Dan in the Iron Age has been confirmed by excavation, as we have seen, and finds of altars, often made of carved stones with a rectangular flat top and a pointed 'horn' in each of its four corners, in many sites of the first half of the first millennium BCE suggest that the centralization of sacrifice did not come naturally – unsurprisingly, in view of the ubiquity of local sacrificial cults in all other religions with whom worshippers of the Jewish God came into contact.[27]

Propaganda for the Jerusalem Temple as the only valid place on earth for the offering of sacrifices to the Lord was all the more intense because of earlier opposition to centralization, and nowhere more so than in the pious literature which recorded the purification of the Temple in the 160s BCE by Judah Maccabee after it had been desecrated by Antiochus Epiphanes (see above). The victory was celebrated on 25 Kislev 'for eight days with rejoicing, in the manner of the festival of booths' (that is, Sukkot), so that 'carrying ivy-wreathed wands and beautiful branches and also fronds of palm, they offered hymns of thanksgiving to him who had given success to the purifying of his own holy place'. This description of the origins of the festival of Hanukkah is found in the Second Book of Maccabees, composed at the latest within a century of the events it describes. The book is prefaced by a letter from 'the Jews in Jerusalem and those in the land of Judaea, to their Jewish kindred in Egypt', urging them to 'keep the festival of booths in the month of Kislev'.

It is all the more striking that in Egypt another temple for worshipping the Jewish God had in fact been built in Leontopolis just after the revolt of the Maccabees, by a group of priests in exile from the Jerusalem Temple. According to Josephus, somewhere around 140 BCE a certain Onias, son of the former Jerusalem High Priest, obtained from the Egyptian king Ptolemy and his queen Cleopatra 'authority to build a temple in Egypt similar to that at Jerusalem, and to appoint Levites and priests of his own race', in return for his 'many and great' services as a mercenary leader. The temple thus built (on the site of a previous pagan temple) was said by Josephus in one passage to be indeed similar to that of Jerusalem, 'but smaller and poorer', although elsewhere he asserted specifically that it was not like that in Jerusalem, but like 'a tower of huge stones and sixty cubits in altitude'. Onias' motives are now difficult to fathom, since Josephus claimed variously that he wished primarily to fulfil the ancient prophecy of Isaiah that 'on that day there will be an altar to the Lord in the centre of the land of Egypt', that he wanted to bring together the Jewish inhabitants of Egypt at a single shrine rather than the scattered temples they were currently using 'contrary to what is proper', or that he wished dishonestly to rival the Jews at Jerusalem, and that he hoped 'by erecting this temple to attract the multitude away from them to it'.

The history and eventual fate of the Leontopolis temple seem to reflect Jewish ambivalence towards such an enterprise. On the one hand, the temple remained in continuous operation for considerably more than two centuries, until it was closed down, and in due course despoiled, by the Romans in c. 73 CE, after the destruction of Jerusalem. The rabbis, as cited in the Mishnah, envisage a pious individual vowing to make personal offerings in 'the House of Onias' and being obliged to keep such vows: '[if he said] "I will offer the Hair-offering [as a nazirite] in the House of Onias", he should offer it in the Temple [in Jerusalem]; but if he offered it in the House of Onias he has fulfilled his obligation.' It seems that nazirites, who vowed to 'separate themselves from the Lord' by abstention from vine products and allowing hair to remain uncut, could fulfil in Leontopolis as well as in Jerusalem their duty to shave their hair at the end of their consecration at 'the entrance of the tent of meeting', as ordained in Numbers 6:18. On the other hand, neither the writings of Philo nor any other Egyptian Jewish text makes any overt reference to the Leontopolis temple, and attempts to discover covert references are not convincing.[28]

Whether or not Onias intended Leontopolis to rival Jerusalem, he certainly does not seem to have suggested that the Jerusalem cult was itself invalid. The same was not true of the Samaritans, and this vital distinction is what pushed them, both in their own eyes and in the eyes of Jews, to the fringes of Judaism or beyond. According to the Samaritan tradition, down to modern times, the Samaritans are the direct descendants of the tribes of Israel who, having survived the destruction of the northern kingdom of Israel by the Assyrians in the eighth century BCE, and avoided deportation, preserved the Torah of Moses not least by worshipping in the divinely ordained sanctuary of Shechem next to Mount Gerizim. The hostile biblical account, by contrast, asserts that the inhabitants of Samaria were descended from non-Israelite colonists, including those from Cuthah (hence 'Cuthaeans') brought to Samaria by the Assyrians, and that it was only out of fear, because 'the Lord has sent lions among them', when the king of Assyria sent an Israelite priest to 'teach them the law of the god of the land', that they began to worship the Lord.[29]

Whatever their origin, the biblical book of Ezra reports that by the time the Jerusalem Temple was being rebuilt in the late sixth century BCE the inhabitants of the land were opposed to the project. Two inscriptions from the island of Delos refer to the local Samaritan population as 'Israelites who send the temple tax to Mount Gerizim' in the mid-second century BCE. It was this allegiance to a separate shrine which all too clearly distinguished them from the Jews by the time of the Hasmonaean High Priest of Jerusalem, John Hyrcanus. Hyrcanus seems to have destroyed their sanctuary in the late second century BCE, when as Josephus recorded he defeated 'the Cuthaeans, the race inhabiting the country surrounding the temple modelled on that at Jerusalem'. Josephus alleged in the first century CE that the attitude of the Samaritans to the Jews in his time varied according to circumstance: 'Whenever, by turns, they see things going well for the Jews, they call themselves their relatives ... When, however, they see that things are going badly for them, they say that they owe nothing to them and that they have no claim to their loyalty or race.' So, for instance, at the time of the Maccabean revolt, when the Jews were being persecuted, they are said to have claimed originally both to have come from Sidon in Phoenicia and to have descended from the Medes and Persians, no longer admitting that the Jews 'were their kin or that the temple on Garizein was that of the Most Great God', despite confessing to their ancestral custom of observing 'the day which is called the Sabbath by the Jews' and their erection of 'a temple without a name in the mountain called

Garizein'. On the Jewish side, the early rabbinic attitude to Samaritans reflected the same ambivalence. When, for instance, three eat together, the Mishnah requires the saying of a communal grace after meals even '[if one that ate was] a Cuthite'. But rabbinic ambivalence did not extend to the validity of worship on Mount Gerizim which (unlike Leontopolis) was simply seen as wrong, or was ignored, by other Jews. In practice Samaritans were treated by Jews as a separate, and often hostile, ethnic group. Jews did not become Samaritans, nor did Samaritans ever become Jews.[30]

SYNAGOGUE

Josephus stressed to readers of *Against Apion* that Moses, as the best of legislators, took care to ensure that all Jews knew what the law entailed:

> He left no pretext for ignorance, but instituted the law as the finest and most essential teaching material; so that it would be heard not just once or twice or a number of times, he ordered that every seven days they should abandon their other activities and gather to hear the law, and to learn it thoroughly and in detail. That is something that all [other] legislators seem to have neglected . . . Were anyone of us to be asked about the laws, he would recount them all more easily than his own name. So, learning them thoroughly from the very first moment of consciousness, we have them, as it were, engraved on our souls . . . As for the habits of daily life: that everything should have piety as its goal, one could gather even from women and slaves.[31]

Josephus doubtless exaggerated the extent of ignorance about their own laws to be found in other nations. But it is true enough that the synagogue, as an institution for mass adult religious education, was unparalleled in the ancient world before Christianity. Philo took a characteristically philosophical stance in describing such education, noting that the Jews 'have houses of prayer and meet together in them, particularly on the sacred sabbaths when they receive as a body a training in their ancestral philosophy'. But the author of the Acts of the Apostles put the matter more directly: 'in every city, for generations past, Moses has had those who proclaim him, for he has been read aloud every sabbath in the synagogues.'[32]

An inscription from Jerusalem, dated to the first century CE, recalls the dedication of a synagogue, hostel and other installations by a certain Theodotus, son of Vettenus, described as 'priest and *archisynagogos* [ruler of the synagogue], son of the *archisynagogos*, grandson of the *archisynagogos*'. It is clear that a priest could be a ruler of a synagogue, and since the inscription states that the synagogue was built 'for the reading of the Torah and the study of the commandments', it is worth recalling the assertion by Josephus in *Against Apion* that instruction in the Torah was carried out by priests. Theodotus' inscription had been set up to record a synagogue building, but it is unknown how many synagogues were purpose built for religious use by his time. The term *synagoge* in Greek means 'assembly', and could be used to refer either to the community or to its building. There was no obvious need for a specific building. According to the biblical book of Nehemiah, the law of Moses had been read ceremonially by the scribe Ezra in the fifth century BCE in the open air: 'the priest Ezra brought the law before the assembly . . . He read from it facing the square before the Water Gate . . . So they read from the book, from the law of God, with interpretation.'[33]

Reading the Torah of Moses to the people as a whole was the main purpose of this teaching, and over time a system evolved whereby the whole Pentateuch would be read in sections on consecutive Sabbaths to ensure that the full text was completed each year. Quite when this procedure was inaugurated is uncertain, but the Mishnah implies an established order for reading the texts liturgically when it notes the instances of breaking off from that order to mark special occasions: 'on the first days of the months, at Hanukkah, at Purim, on days of fasting . . . and on the Day of Atonement'. A tradition in the Babylonian Talmud records that in Palestine the cycle of reading the Torah was devised for completion in three years rather than the annual cycle which became standard in later rabbinic Judaism, and possible traces of this triennial cycle have been noted in the medieval scribal tradition of the masoretes (see Chapter 10). But evidence of its origins, and of the annual cycle, are elusive, and it is not impossible that communities felt free to select the reading of the week as they saw fit all the way through the Second Temple period and beyond.[34]

What does seem clear is that regular readings from the other books of the Bible were also standard. The Acts of the Apostles refers to the reading of 'the law and the prophets', and according to the Gospel of Luke, Jesus encountered trouble in his home town of Nazareth when 'he went to the synagogue on the Sabbath day, as was his custom' and 'the scroll of the prophet Isaiah was given to him', whereupon he unrolled the scroll, read the passage from Isaiah proclaiming good news to the poor and oppressed, rolled up the scroll, gave it back to the attendant and sat down, and, with 'the eyes of all in the synagogue . . . fixed upon him', began the interpretation of the text which caused uproar: 'Today this scripture has been fulfilled in your hearing.' In this story at least, the choice of reading seems to have been left to the reader, and the same may be implied by disagreement in the Mishnah over the propriety of using some passages for public readings at all: 'They may not use the chapter of the Chariot as a reading from the Prophets, but R. Judah permits it.' It is paradoxical that the (minimal) information to be gleaned from the Mishnah about public readings of this kind comes from a section dedicated to more detailed discussion of the only biblical book which seems regularly to have been recited in full in one sitting. This book, neither from the Torah nor from the Prophets but from the Writings, was the book of Esther. The reading of the scroll of Esther provided the central rite for the festival of Purim, which celebrated the Jews' escape from destruction under the Persian king Ahasuerus, events which constitute its main narrative: according to the Mishnah 'the Scroll is read on the 11th, 12th, 13th, 14th, or 15th [of (the month of) Adar], never earlier and never later,' and the text goes on to define which date is correct for which community.[35]

When a passage had been read, the congregation expected an interpretation – hence the attentive (if unappreciative) audience for Jesus' interpretation of Isaiah in the synagogue of Nazareth. Such interpretation could vary greatly both in format and in contents. Most straightforward was translation into the vernacular, not just the translation of the whole text into Greek for those unfamiliar with Semitic languages, as we have seen in Chapter 2, but a *targum*, a version in Aramaic of the Hebrew of both the law and the prophets verse by verse: 'He that reads in the Law may not read less than three verses [in total]; he may not read to the interpreter more than one verse . . . They may leave out verses in the Prophets, but not in the Law. How much may they leave out? Only so much that he leaves no time for the interpreter to make a pause.' The Aramaic versions of the Pentateuch and prophets which survive from later antiquity include much which goes far beyond a straight translation of the Hebrew, as in the leading role ascribed to Isaac as a free agent in one Aramaic version of the dramatic story in Genesis 22 of Abraham's willingness to sacrifice his only son when commanded to do so by the Lord: 'Isaac spoke up and said to his father: "Tie me well lest I struggle because of the anguish of my soul, with the result that a blemish will be found in your offering, and I will be thrust into the pit of destruction." The eyes of Abraham were looking at the eyes of Isaac, and the eyes of Isaac were looking at the angels on high. Isaac saw them but Abraham did not see them.'[36]

Other forms of interpretation were probably more discursive, in the form of sermons, but their nature can only be surmised from the literary texts which preserve extended passages of such interpretation. Such is the commentary on Habakkuk from Qumran:

> 'Thou hast ordained them, [O Lord,] for judgement; Thou hast established them, O Rock, for chastisement. Their eyes are too pure to behold evil; and Thou canst not look on distress.' Interpreted, this saying means that God will not destroy His people by the hand of the nations; God will execute the judgement of the nations by the hand of His elect. And through their chastisement all the wicked of His people shall expiate their guilt who keep His commandments in their distress. For it is as he said, 'Too pure of eyes to behold evil': interpreted, this means that they have not lusted after their eyes during the age of wickedness.[37]

Early rabbinic Bible exegesis was preserved in tannaitic texts compiled in the second century CE or later, but is likely to contain much earlier material. It certainly contains some interpretations that can be traced back explicitly to the first century CE because of parallels with motifs found in the writings of Josephus or Philo, such as the legend of the extraordinary beauty of Moses as a child. In Josephus' version, 'when he had attained the age of three years God gave him wondrous increase of his stature, and no one was so indifferent to his beauty that on beholding Moses he was not astonished at his handsomeness. And it happened that many people who happened to meet him as he was borne along the road turned back at the sight of the child and left aside their serious affairs and used their time to view him. For the vast and undiluted childish charm that enveloped him captivated those who saw him.' One can see such stories about Moses woven into sermon form in rabbinic biblical commentaries of many centuries later: 'Because he was so handsome, everyone was eager to see him, and whoever saw him could not tear himself away from him. Pharaoh also used to kiss and hug him, and he [Moses] used to take the crown of Pharaoh and place it upon his own head, as he was destined to do when he became great.'[38]

It is hard from the surviving evidence to know how much Bible interpretation took place in the context of such teaching after the public reading of the texts, and how much took a more literary form. There is no evidence, for instance, of liturgical use by Jews of the book of Jubilees, which was composed, probably in the mid-second century BCE, as an account of a revelation disclosed to Moses on Mount Sinai by an 'angel of the presence' deputed to tell Moses everything 'from the beginning of creation'. Jubilees is a rewritten version of the narrative from the start of Genesis to the middle of Exodus encased in a chronology of 'jubilees', that is, units of forty-nine years ('seven weeks of years'). Some Bible interpretation seems entirely literary, like the legend, found both in Josephus' *Antiquities* and (in different form) in the work of Artapanus, an Egyptian Jewish writer of the same period as the author of Jubilees, that Moses, who was said in passing in the Pentateuch to have married a 'Cushite woman', had won this bride by virtue of his prowess as general of the Egyptian army in a campaign against the Ethiopians, in the course of which he had won the admiration and the love of Tharbis, the daughter of his adversary, the Ethiopian king. Other forms of biblical interpretation were aimed at supporting legal stances, such as the hermeneutical rules ascribed to R. Ishmael, a rabbinic sage of the second century CE, which refer, for instance, to the 'construction of a general principle from one verse and construction of a general principle from two verses' with an example:

> 'If he knocks out his slave's tooth' (Exod 21:27). I might understand this to mean even if it is only a milk tooth that the master knocked out, but Scripture also states: 'If a man strikes his slave's eye . . . and destroys it' (Exod 21:26). Just as the eye is an organ which cannot grow back again, so also the tooth must be one which cannot grow back again. So far only the tooth and the eye are specifically mentioned. How about the other chief organs? Behold, you can establish a general principle on the basis of what is common to both of these. The specific character of a tooth is not the same as that of an eye, nor is the specific character of an eye the same as that of a tooth, but what is common to both of them is that loss of them constitutes a permanent defect: they are chief organs and visible, and if the master intentionally destroys them, the slave gets his freedom in recompense.[39]

The public teaching of the laws, of which Josephus and Philo boasted, must have been accompanied at times by communal prayer, since Jews in Egypt as far back as the third century BCE referred to their communal buildings as 'prayers': the word used in Greek, *proseuche*, was a strange term to use of a building, which reinforces the notion that prayer must have been its central function. The term was not generally used of communal buildings in the land of Israel in the Second Temple period, but one exception suggests that the same notion was possible there too.

Josephus wrote in his autobiography about a general assembly in the *proseuche* in Tiberias in Galilee in 67 CE, describing it as 'a very large building and able to hold a huge crowd'. He narrated the story of a crowded meeting there on a Saturday morning, which was prevented from turning ugly, according to him, by a break for lunch; then of a second meeting, on Sunday morning, for which the people assembled in the *proseuche*, although they had no idea why they were being convened; and finally of a third meeting on the Monday, which was declared a fast day, where the community were 'performing the customary acts and turning to their prayers' until the assembly broke up in a riot.[40]

We cannot say for certain what form these prayers took, since most direct evidence from before 70 CE relates not to communal but to private prayers, such as the prayer at time of greatest danger attributed to Esther in the Greek version of her story: 'O my Lord, you only are our king; help me, who am alone and have no helper but you ... O God, whose might is over all, hear the voice of the despairing and save us from the hands of evildoers. And save me from my fear!' Many private prayer texts were found among scrolls from before 70 CE discovered in Qumran, suggesting widespread piety at least among those whose texts were hidden in the Qumran caves, but other texts found among the Dead Sea scrolls look much like prayers to be recited communally: 'We shall recount Thy marvels from generation to generation. Blessed be the Lord who has caused us to rejoice.' One of the longer scrolls contains a substantial number of thanksgiving hymns which may have been sung by the community like the psalms: 'Blessed art Thou, O Lord, Maker [of all things and mighty in] deeds: all things are thy work! Behold, Thou art pleased to favour [thy servant], and hast graced me with Thy spirit of mercy and [with the radiance] of Thy glory ...' Philo wrote about a group of contemplative Jews in his day, the Therapeutae (see Chapter 6), who had a mixed choir of men and women which imitated the singing of Moses and Miriam after the crossing of the Red Sea: 'the choir of the Therapeutae of either sex, note in response to note and voice to voice, the treble of the women blending with the bass of the men, create an harmonious concert, music in the truest sense.' But we do not know whether such liturgical practice, picked out for praise by Philo probably with a non-Jewish readership in mind, was normal in Jewish liturgy or (as is perhaps more likely) the exception.[41]

By contrast to the scarcity of direct evidence from before 70 CE, the Mishnah provides a good deal of insight into standard liturgical patterns by the end of the second century CE. It is possible that many of those patterns should be traced back centuries to long before the end of Temple worship in Jerusalem, but it is worth noting that none of the Qumran prayer texts is obviously related to the liturgy underlying the Mishnah. The basic structure of the communal prayers in the early rabbinic texts is the blessing formula: 'Blessed are you, O Lord our God, King of the universe, who . . .'. The very first section of the Mishnah discusses the rules for reciting the relevant blessings before and after the Shema, the first of a group of three passages from the Pentateuch recited in the morning and the evening, beginning '*Shema Yisrael*': ' Hear O Israel, the Lord our God, the Lord is one . . . You shall love the Lord your God with all your heart, with all your soul and with all your strength.' The Nash Papyrus, from the second century BCE, containing on a single sheet a Hebrew text of the Shema along with the Ten Commandments, suggests that the Decalogue was also recited liturgically by some Jews. The Mishnah records such recitation, before the Shema, by the priests in the Temple during the procedures for the daily sacrifices, but liturgical recitation of the Ten Commandments by other Jews is not assumed in the Mishnah, and later rabbinic tradition recorded specific prohibition of such recitation in case it encouraged the heretical notion that only these commandments were divinely ordained.

The Mishnah does, however, assume regular recitation alongside the Shema of a standard form of prayer which by the end of the first century CE was known to Rabban Gamaliel II and R. Joshua as 'the Eighteen' (Shemoneh Esreh), which survived in various recensions to become the standard form of Jewish prayer. Already in the versions known to the rabbis in the second century CE, the Shemoneh Esreh actually includes not eighteen but nineteen benedictions, suggesting either an earlier use of eighteen specified blessings before the addition of the nineteenth blessing at some time after 70 CE or a compromise between conflicting versions of what the eighteen blessings should be. In any case, although the division of the Shemoneh Esreh, to be recited three times a day, into three sections (praise, petition and thanksgiving) probably reflects the structure of general communal prayer in late Second Temple times, the eventual acceptance that there should be nineteen blessings in itself provides evidence of a certain fluidity in the liturgical tradition, as do references to the destruction of the Temple in 70 CE in the versions of the blessings found in the Mishnah.[42]

Both the Shema and the Shemoneh Esreh could be recited either privately or communally. Communal prayer is assumed by rules for dealing with, for instance, one who 'went before the Ark and fell into error'; in such a case, 'another must take his place ... Where does he begin? At the beginning of the Benediction in which the other fell into error.' On the other hand, most early rabbinic rules apply more to private prayer. There were debates in the first century CE about posture in the saying of the Shema – is it right to recline in the evening, reflecting the biblical injunction to talk of the commandments 'when you lie down and when you rise up'? The Shemoneh Esreh was to be said standing up unless circumstances, such as when riding an ass and unable to dismount, make this physically impossible. Hence these blessings were sometimes known as the Amidah, or 'standing'. Such prayer required concentration, according to the Mishnah: 'None may stand up to say the prayer save in a sober mood ... Even if the king salutes a man he may not return the greeting; and even if a snake was twisted around his heel he may not interrupt his prayer.' Prostration in prayer, with both feet and hands outstretched, is said in the Mishnah to have been practised in the Temple when the High Priest pronounced the divine name during the service on the Day of Atonement, but neither the Mishnah nor earlier Jewish texts have anything to say about this form of reverence, or about kneeling or bowing, during normal prayer elsewhere.[43]

Notwithstanding the assumed power of private prayers, and (as we shall see in Chapter 8) the possibility of pious individuals living as solitary ascetics, Jews, like others in the ancient world, took for granted that worship should usually be communal. Inscriptions from the countryside in Egypt refer to the prayer house as the main institution of these diaspora Jewish communities. For all Jews, the eve of Pesach, when, as Philo put it in Alexandria in the first century CE, 'the whole nation performs the sacred rites and acts as priest with pure hands and complete immunity' to eat the roast lamb which marked the feast, so that 'on this day every dwelling house is invested with the outward semblance and dignity of a temple', involved a ceremony at which 'the guests assembled for the banquet have been cleansed by purificatory lustrations ... to fulfil with prayers and hymns the custom handed down by their fathers'. The purpose was to give thanks for the miracle of deliverance from Egypt at the time of the exodus, both by telling the story and (in part) by re-enacting it. Unleavened bread was eaten ceremoniously to recall the hurry with which the Israelites had been required to leave Egypt after the tenth plague brought upon Egypt had involved the death of the first-born sons of the Egyptians. It is not now possible to know how much the wording of the narration of the exodus resembled in Temple times the Seder service, a domestic banquet accompanied by the retelling of the exodus story, as it developed after 70 CE, but the ceremony itself must have been very similar for those many Jews unable to participate in the pilgrimage festival in Jerusalem.

This use of communal liturgy to reinforce national memories was the explicit purpose of the reading of the book of Esther in synagogues on the festival of Purim (see p. 62) and of the domestic lighting of candles on the festival of Hanukkah which commemorated the victory of the Maccabees over Antiochus Epiphanes. This latter deliverance, unlike Esther's, seems to have been celebrated liturgically not by telling the story, but primarily by exhibiting lights for eight days on what, as we have seen, II Maccabees called 'the festival of booths in the month of Kislev'. R. Judah in the second century CE noted that a shopkeeper who left his light outside a shop so that the flax carried by a passing camel caught fire and burned the shop was not liable for damage to the flax or the camel if the light was a Hanukkah light. The only liturgical issue for Hanukkah discussed in the Mishnah is the reading from the Pentateuch during the festival: the Mishnah stipulates that the section in Numbers is to be read which describes the offerings to be brought to the sanctuary in the desert by the princes of the tribes, thus implicitly linking the original dedication of the sanctuary to the rededication of the altar in the time of the Maccabees.[44]

In view of the role of synagogues as teaching institutions, the choice of synagogue leaders and administrators must have been of importance to Jews in antiquity just as in more recent periods of Jewish history. One would expect the role of the public reader of the Torah to have been of great significance, since he had the onerous task of reading out sacred scripture accurately despite the lack of vowels and other punctuation in the text, and he would need to know by heart traditional readings which seemed to contradict the manuscript text (what the later scribes called the 'read' text rather than the 'written'), but there is remarkably little evidence for such individuals being held in high esteem. The Acts of the Apostles refers to 'rulers of the synagogue' in diaspora communities as responsible for the preservation of communal discipline in places like Corinth, where they are said to have attempted (unsuccessfully) to control the apostle Paul. Honorific and funerary inscriptions bearing in Greek the same titles, or similar titles such as 'fathers of the synagogue' or 'elders', have been found in many sites in the eastern Mediterranean where Jews were settled in late Hellenistic and early Roman times.

A number of square or rectangular public buildings in late Second

Temple period sites in the Judaean desert (at Masada and Herodium), in Gamala on the Golan and in the Judaean hills (at Kiryat Sefer and Modiin) have been identified quite plausibly as synagogues, but in light of the multiple purposes attested for the complex of buildings erected by Theodotus, and the use of the 'prayer house' in Tiberias in Galilee for political meetings in 67 CE noted by Josephus, it is likely that such buildings were essentially communal rather than religious. On the other hand, the Gospels mention healings and miracles being performed in synagogues in Galilee, and Josephus described problems at the synagogue of Caesarea in 66 CE which came to a head, during a dispute with a non-Jewish landowner who tried to build workshops blocking the way to the synagogue, when local gentiles sacrificed some birds just outside the synagogue entrance. In the view of the local Jews, this action caused 'their site [to be] polluted', which suggests that they attributed sanctity to the synagogue edifice.[45]

Ascription of sanctity to synagogues while the Temple was still standing seems to have been more common in the diaspora than in the land of Israel. Thus Philo noted that in Alexandria in his time there was uproar when hostile Greeks installed images of the emperor Gaius in the Jews' prayer houses in the city, including 'in the largest and most notable a bronze statue of a man mounted on a chariot and four', which Philo and the other Jews took to be idols. The synagogue in Antioch in Syria, adorned with brass offerings and attracting to its religious services many local Greeks, was even described by Josephus in one passage as a 'temple'. Philo writing about the Essenes (on whom see Chapter 6), probably for non-Jewish readers, in his treatise *That Every Good Man is Free*, referred to the instruction they received on every seventh day in the 'holy places which are called synagogues'. But such sanctity was of a quite different level to the sanctity of the Jerusalem Temple. Thus when the synagogue in Caesarea came under attack in 66 CE, the Jews there 'snatched up the laws and retreated to Narbata', a district at some distance from Caesarea, leaving the synagogue to its fate, whereas four years later many of the priests and lay people of Jerusalem defended the Temple to the death.[46]

The synagogue had developed as an institution in the final centuries of the Second Temple period quite separately from the development of the Jerusalem Temple itself. There is no reason to imagine that synagogue architecture, organization or liturgy in this period were shaped by the Temple with its ritual, nor (conversely) that the synagogue represented a type of Judaism different from that in the Temple.[47] In the eyes of most Jews, wherever they were, nothing that went on in a synagogue, whether teaching or prayer, could rival the central role of worship through sacrifices and offerings in the Temple. That communal prayer in synagogues was valuable was taken for granted, and doubtless such liturgy was increasingly appreciated at greater distances from Jerusalem, but, unlike the sacrifices, prayer had not been decreed in any clear fashion in the law of Moses. No one seemed yet to think that such prayer might substitute for sacrifice.

4

The Torah of Moses: Judaism in the Bible

Who is the God to whom Jews offered their sacrifices and prayers? In the polytheistic world of antiquity most worshippers placed much emphasis on ensuring that they named correctly the deity with whom they wished to establish relations. By contrast, the God of the Jews was sometimes seen as mysteriously hard to pin down, so that the philosopher Plutarch in the first century CE wrote a treatise on the subject (in which he concluded, from the nature of Jewish worship, that it was most likely that the Jewish God was Dionysus, the Greek god of wine). For Jews themselves, identifying God in prayer was simple: he was the God of Abraham, Isaac and Jacob, whose story is told in the Bible.[1]

'In the beginning God created the heavens and the earth.' God is portrayed in the Bible as the supreme ruler of the universe, creator of all things through his words, judge and lawgiver of all mankind, subject to no constraints from natural laws or competing cosmic forces. In contrast to the myths of other peoples in the Near East and classical world, the Jews did not tell cosmological stories to explain the origins of the divinity they worshipped. His power is simply assumed. God is often stated to be intangible and too holy for humans to view, but this does not prevent him being imagined as father, shepherd, judge or king: 'the Lord sits enthroned over the flood; the Lord sits enthroned as king forever.' Anthropomorphic imagery was encouraged by the notion in the early chapters of Genesis that man and woman were created in the image of God, but other images are also found, most notably God as the sun, shining forth with bright light: the Psalmist called his God 'a sun and shield'.[2]

God was referred to by a number of names, titles and epithets which are likely to have accreted gradually, as different notions about God were consolidated. In the prayer ascribed to Solomon on the dedication of the First Temple, he asks whether God (*elohim* in Hebrew) will indeed dwell on earth, since 'even heaven and the highest heaven cannot contain you, much less this house that I have built', but he goes on to appeal directly to 'YHVH, my God' to open his eyes towards 'the place of which you said, "My name shall be there"'. The special significance accorded to the divine name YHVH (conventionally pronounced 'Yahweh' in English with the letter *vav* transliterated as 'w') lies in the tradition, well established by the end of the Second Temple period, that the name was too holy to be said aloud except by the High Priest in the Holy of Holies. We have noted the scribal conventions attested in early manuscripts among the Dead Sea scrolls of writing the name in distinctive palaeo-Hebrew script or substituting for it with dots or strokes. The origins of the Tetragrammaton ('four-letter' name, that is the four Hebrew letters – *yod, hay, vav, hay* – transliterated as YHVH) are associated with the biblical story that Moses enquired of God, when God spoke to him before the exodus out of a bush which blazed with fire but was not burned up, 'if I come to the Israelites and say to them, "the God of your ancestors has sent me to you", and they ask me "What is his name?", what shall I say to them? God said to Moses, "I am who I am"' (in Hebrew, 'I am' is AHYH, pronounced 'ehyeh'). But the processes of transmutation are obscure, and the Jews of Elephantine referred to the God they worshipped as YHV, with only three consonants. The names 'El' and 'Elohim' seem to have been used more generically in the Near East to refer to divinities more precisely by adding something about their qualities or the place where they were worshipped; in the case of the almighty God of Israel, he could be described as El-Elyon, 'God most High', since he was creator of heaven and earth.[3]

The Bible often assumes that God operates in an environment replete with other supernatural beings, even if the nature of those beings is in general left vague. The Israelites are portrayed as praising the Lord after their salvation from Egypt by exclaiming 'Who is like you, O Lord, among the gods?' On arrival in Canaan, they are shown abandoning the Lord to worship the Baals, following 'other gods, from among the gods of the peoples who were all around them'. This is a world full of gods, at variance with the radical monotheism expressed in the book of Isaiah: 'I am the Lord, and there is no other; besides me there is no god.' The divine court includes 'sons of God', who act as a sort of heavenly council and as messengers of the Lord who do his bidding. They are sometimes envisaged as 'myriads of holy ones', that is, a 'heavenly host' or 'the army of the Lord'. In later biblical texts, such figures are portrayed as angels who might speak up for the interests of individual humans, while others, notably Satan, had been granted by God the role of accusing those whose devotion to God might be questioned: 'Then he showed me the high priest Joshua standing before the angel of the Lord, and Satan standing at his right hand to accuse him. And the Lord said to Satan, "The Lord rebuke you, O Satan!"' In the book of Job, Satan's role, while still clearly subservient to that of God, is widened into a thorough test of Job's piety, to see if he will retain his faith in God's justice despite the undeserved depths of agony and despair into which he is plunged. But the whole experiment takes place only with the permission of God: 'The Lord said to Satan, "Very well, he is in your power; only spare his life." Then Satan went out from the presence of the Lord, and inflicted loathsome sores on Job.' Rather different, in the biblical conception, from these denizens of the divine court is the personification of divine attributes, most notably Wisdom. Wisdom is imagined in the book of Proverbs as a female human figure begotten by the Lord before the creation: 'The Lord created me at the beginning of his work ... when he marked out the foundations of the earth, then I was beside him, like a master worker; and I was daily his delight, rejoicing before him always, rejoicing in his inhabited world and delighting in the human race.'[4]

Much of the Bible is concerned with the relation of this omnipotent God to humankind. Less is said about relations to the rest of the creation, beyond insistence that everything, including natural bodies like the sun which were worshipped by the less discerning, was entirely under God's control, so that he could order the sun not to rise, or to stand still, or to move backwards. God is portrayed as majestic and just in his treatment of humankind, transcendent so that in his eyes the earth's inhabitants are 'like grasshoppers'. But he is also kind, compassionate and quick to forgive. These different attributes are hard to combine into a coherent depiction, even in the brief proclamation of his own qualities attributed in Exodus to the Lord himself as he passed before Moses:

> The Lord, the Lord, a God merciful and gracious, slow to anger, and abounding in steadfast love and faithfulness, keeping steadfast love for the thousandth generation, forgiving iniquity and transgression and sin, yet by no means clearing the guilty, but visiting the iniquity of the parents upon the children and the children's children, to the third and fourth generation.[5]

In the Psalms, God is frequently described as a fount of loving kindness – in the words of Psalm 136, 'his kindness endures forever' – but he is also the warrior Lord who 'crushed the heads of Leviathan' (a mythical sea monster) and who 'goes forth like a soldier, like a warrior he stirs up his fury; he cries out, he shouts aloud, he shows himself mighty against his foes'. In the biblical book of Proverbs, fear of the Lord is true wisdom.[6]

For Israel, it was both comforting and terrifying to believe that the nation had been singled out for a special covenant by such a majestic power. On Mount Sinai, according to the Torah, God had revealed to Moses the laws by which all Israel should live, and the people had accepted their special status and the responsibility it laid upon them: 'Moses ... set before them all these words that the Lord had commanded him. The people all answered as one: "Everything that the Lord has spoken we will do."' In the biblical narrative, acceptance had been followed almost immediately by disobedience, when Moses' return from the mountain was delayed and the people persuaded Aaron to produce a golden calf for them to worship, saying to him, 'Make us gods, who shall go before us; as for this Moses, the man who brought us up out of the land of Egypt, we do not know what has become of him'; this disobedience was followed rapidly by punishment through plague. In the fifth book of the Pentateuch Moses is portrayed as laying out in stark terms the implications of the covenant: 'If you obey the commandments of the Lord your God . . . then you shall live and become numerous, and the Lord your God will bless you . . . But if your heart turns away and you do not hear, but are led astray . . . I declare to you today that you shall perish.' Moses tells them to 'choose life so that you and your descendants may live'. The curses that will come on Israel for not observing all the Lord's commandments and decrees are laid out in chilling detail: 'The Lord will send upon you disaster, panic, and frustration in everything you attempt to do, until you are destroyed and perish quickly, on account of the evil of your deeds, because you have forsaken me.' There was no excuse for disobedience: 'Surely, this commandment that I am commanding you today is not too hard for you, nor is it too far away. It is not in heaven, that you should say, "Who will go up to heaven for us, and get it for us so that we may hear it and observe it?" No, the word is very near to you; it is in your mouth and in your heart for you to observe.'[7]

The power of this special relationship between God and Israel dominates the biblical worldview. The idea of a special covenant found in the Pentateuch seems to reflect both the form of international treaties in the Late Bronze Age (c. 1200–1000 BCE) and loyalty oaths in the Assyrian empire in the time of the kings of Israel and Judah, which focused on the penalties for disobedience. God is shown intervening at other times in history, but the fortunes of the great empires of Egypt, Assyria, Babylon and Persia are of interest to the authors of the prophetic and historical books of the Bible only in so far as they impact on Israel. It is taken for granted that God will continue to communicate with his people, in order to warn them of the consequences of transgressions, although such messages are transmitted in less direct form than the revelation on Mount Sinai when God spoke directly to Moses. The assumed authority of the prophets presupposed that any individual might be divinely inspired, whether by the spirit of the Lord impelling to frenzied, ecstatic behaviour, or by the word of the Lord imparting a message which its recipient felt impelled to speak, or by visions containing divine messages. The idea that all might have such prophetic gifts is a feature of the eschaton, the end of time, in the imagination of one biblical writer: 'Your sons and your daughters shall prophesy, your old men shall dream dreams, and your young men shall see visions.'

In addition to such divinely inspired individuals, priests were believed in early times to provide a direct link to God through the oracular Urim and Tummim, probably small stones which were cast as lots to discover the divine response to a direct question for which there could be an answer either 'yes' or 'no', as when David asked the Lord about Saul: 'David said, "O Lord, the God of Israel, your servant has heard that Saul seeks to come to Keilah, to destroy the city on my account. And now, will Saul come down as your servant has heard? O Lord, the God of Israel, I beseech you, tell your servant." The Lord said, "He will come down."' But such methods of discovering the divine will had fallen out of use well before the end of the Second Temple. Josephus believed that the oracular stones 'ceased to shine two hundred years before I composed this work, because of God's displeasure at the transgression of the laws', although the Mishnah records a tradition that the Urim and Tummim had ceased earlier, 'at the death of the first prophets'.[8]

The divine promise to Israel as reward for keeping the covenant with God was the peace and prosperity of Israel and numerous descendants in the land of Canaan far into the future. The biblical narrative of repeated descent into sin followed by national tragedy at the hands of outside powers is explained by the theological emphasis of the Bible on this covenant relationship. Forged, it was believed, in the experience of enslavement and liberation from Egypt, it was periodically honed by exile and suffering. It was assumed that exile to Assyria and Babylon was both a result of divine judgement and a recalling of Israel to faithfulness.

Such preoccupation left little space for speculation on God's relation to the rest of humankind. The God of Israel was also Lord of the Universe, but what, in the eyes of Jews, this meant for the behaviour of non-Jews was left unclear. In the exodus from Egypt, the suffering of the Egyptians is simply background to God's demonstration of his care for his people. God is said to harden Pharaoh's heart again and again in order to make this demonstration more impressive; the narrative has no interest in the spiritual wellbeing of Pharaoh himself. But the lack of a coherent universalist theology did not prevent the inclusion in the biblical corpus of many stories and notions with universalist implications, from the rainbow which signalled God's promise to humankind never again to flood the world as in the time of Noah to the notion of Israel as a 'light to the nations', teaching God's morality to other peoples. The Bible contained hopes for a gathering of the nations in Jerusalem in the last days to worship the God of Israel, and celebrated the successful preaching of the prophet Jonah to the gentile inhabitants of Nineveh which led them to repent. The development of a clear set of moral and religious rules for non-Jews was complicated by the assumption that the most moral gentiles could demonstrate their virtue by worshipping the God of Israel, as in the story of the Moabitess Ruth, whose reward for her faithfulness to her mother-in-law Naomi was to become the great-grandmother of King David. Such was the power of Ruth's affirmation that 'your people shall be my people, and your God my God'. Acceptance of the potential of non-Jews for religious perfection cohabits in the Bible alongside the suspicion of gentiles which spurred Ezra to insist that those who had returned to Israel from Babylon and married foreign women from the peoples of the land should send those wives away with their children, demonstrating that the primary concern at least of this narrative was Israel and the covenant: 'We have broken faith with our God.'[9]

Six of the Ten Commandments given to Moses by God on Mount Sinai relate to human behaviour in relation not to God but to other humans: 'Honour your father and your mother ... You shall not murder. You shall not commit adultery. You shall not steal. You shall not bear false witness against your neighbour. You shall not covet your neighbour's house ... or anything that belongs to your neighbour.' The biblical laws, expanded at considerable length elsewhere in the Pentateuch, cover civil and criminal law, laying down penalties for theft or murder and rules for deciding property disputes, but they also legislate in many areas that in other societies would be considered more matters of private morality. Prime among such moral rulings are the extensive teachings on charity and the treatment of the poor: 'You shall open your hand wide to your brother, to the needy and to the poor in the land.'

Care for others is cast in powerful but general terms by the prophets, who urge the duty 'to share your bread with the hungry, and bring the homeless poor into your house; when you see the naked, to cover them, and not to hide yourself from your own kin'. But it also involved more formal means for wealth distribution at the margins, such as the requirements for the owner of a field when harvesting grain to leave for the poor the corners of fields, loose grains dropped by the harvesters and forgotten sheaves, as well as all grapes on the vines that grow scattered rather than in clusters. The plot of the book of Ruth hinges on the ability of Ruth, a Moabite stranger, to glean freely day by day in the fields belonging to Boaz, who in due course becomes her husband. The essence of such moral injunctions is that they go beyond family and social ties to care for anyone who is vulnerable, and the obligation to support widows, orphans and outsiders within Israelite society is a pervasive biblical theme: 'You shall not deprive a foreigner resident among you or an orphan of justice; you shall not take a widow's garment in pledge . . . When you beat your olive trees, do not strip what is left; it shall be for the alien, the orphan, and the widow.' The reason for caring for the vulnerable lies, according to the biblical text, in the historical experience of the Israelites: 'Remember that you were a slave in the land of Egypt; therefore I am commanding you to do this.'[10]

The divine law as mediated through Moses in the Pentateuch contained quite precise rulings for the good ordering of society. Crime was to be punished, or the injured party compensated by appropriate penalties, sometimes expressed in stark terms: 'life for life, eye for eye, tooth for tooth, hand for hand, foot for foot, burn for burn, wound for wound, stripe for stripe'. Biblical law enjoined precise judicial punishments for quite specific acts deemed contrary to social order, such as the intervention of a woman in a fight between her husband and another man by seizing the genitalia of her husband's opponent, unauthorized sexual intercourse with an unmarried girl, an adulterous union with a married woman, persistent disobedience to parents, kidnapping or theft (distinguished from burglary at night). In both expression and content these laws show many similarities to law codes of the ancient Near East known from cuneiform texts. But the biblical codes differ in detail both from these earlier codes and in the various biblical versions – the codes in Exodus and Deuteronomy are not the same, and both lack provisions found in the priestly regulations scattered through Leviticus and Numbers. Without parallel in the other law codes of antiquity are the biblical regulations to forbid the taking of interest on loans 'if any of your kin fall into difficulty and become dependent on you' – the need to distinguish such social lending from loans made to foreigners for profit is explicit in Deuteronomy – and legislation for the restoration of ancestral property rights to each family at a jubilee, when 'you shall have the trumpet sounded throughout all your land and you shall hallow the fiftieth year and you shall proclaim liberty throughout the land to all its inhabitants'.[11]

Pentateuchal law betrays traces of earlier assumptions of social structures based on tribal groups and extended families, so that, for instance, the brother of a man who dies without children is required to marry the widow in order that the 'first-born will succeed in the name of the dead brother, and his name will not be blotted out of Israel', although the biblical law also contains provision for a brother to refuse the duty, albeit with social disgrace: 'if he persists, saying, "I have no desire to marry her", then his brother's wife shall go up to him in the presence of the elders, pull his sandal off his foot, spit in his face, and declare, "This is what is done to the man who does not build up his brother's house."' But much family law relates to the nuclear family, covering such issues as betrothal, marriage and divorce (which is permitted for a man if he has found something 'objectionable' about his wife, in which case all he is required to do to send her out of the house is to write and give her a certificate of divorce). If 'a spirit of jealousy' comes on a man and he suspects his wife of unfaithfulness, 'then the man shall bring his wife to the priest' with 'a grain-offering of jealousy', and the wife shall drink the 'water of bitterness'. If she has been unfaithful, 'the water that brings the curse shall enter into her and cause bitter pain, and her womb shall discharge, her uterus drop, and the woman shall become an execration among her people. But if the woman has not defiled herself and is clean, then she shall be immune ... The man shall be free from iniquity, but the woman shall bear her iniquity.' Procreation, seen as a blessing, was also considered a divine commandment since the first humans were instructed to 'be fruitful and multiply and fill the earth and subdue it'. But the family unit could also rely on the work of outsiders, including not only hired workers but slaves. As in the rest of the ancient world, slaves could be treated simply as moveable property for disposal by their masters at whim, although biblical law introduced restrictions which reflected awareness of the slave's humanity. Striking a slave hard enough to cause death was treated as a crime if the slave died immediately. If a master put out the eye or tooth of a slave, the slave was to be set free, and a fugitive slave who sought asylum from his master was not to be handed over. The interdiction against slaves working on the Sabbath, and the expectation that male slaves, if circumcised, could participate in eating the Passover lamb like free Israelites, suggest that slaves could sometimes be seen as part of the family rather than simply as chattels.[12]

All these laws governing human relations were presented in the Bible as divinely ordained through Moses with precisely the same authority as the laws which shaped the relation of individual Jews to God. We have seen that Josephus noted that, for Jews, justice, moderation, endurance and harmony with the community were 'parts of religion'. Josephus claimed that the head of the ideal Jewish polity was the High Priest, and that it was through him that divine laws were transmitted to the people: 'What could be finer or more just than a structure that has made God governor of the universe, that commits to the priests in concert the management of the most important matters, and, in turn, has entrusted to the High Priest of all the governance of the other priests?' But we have seen that the Bible also envisaged other forms of authority, from inspired prophets to wise scribes and the kings descended from David, who had been chosen to rule by God. The Bible sometimes portrays these sources of authority as in conflict, most notably in the critique of sinful kings by prophets, such as the warnings of Elijah to King Ahab to turn away from the idolatrous worship of Baal.

The Pentateuch recorded in detail how God required individuals to behave in order to sanctify their lives: 'You shall be holy, for I the Lord your God am holy.' The underlying assumption of these laws is that all life, including human life, belongs to God and that a pious life must be structured so as to acknowledge this subservience. So, for instance, the first born of the flocks and herds were sacrificed in the Temple as peace offerings, and the first-born male of the Israelites themselves was to be redeemed from a priest by payment of a ransom of 5 shekels. To be holy required a Jew to take special care in the treatment of his or her body, especially in eating food. Animals could be eaten, but only if they were of specific species – essentially, all birds apart from birds of prey; most ordinary fish (defined as having fins and scales); and most mammals of a domesticated type in the Near East, although the biblical categorization excluded both pigs and camels. The biblical text gives no reason for the list of prohibited animals, and attempts to explain them on health or other scientific grounds are not convincing. It is probable that these taboos applied originally only to priests and that they were extended to ordinary Jews only quite late in the composition of the Bible. The religious significance of the distinction between permitted and forbidden animals seems to lie in the distinction itself and the requirement it imposed upon Jews to avoid foodstuffs, such as pig products, quite widely available in the societies in which they lived. The slaughter of the mammals had to be carried out in such a way as to remove most of the blood, because 'the blood is the life'. The notion of kosher food (*kasher* means 'fit', for consumption) has a firm biblical base, even if the details of what is prohibited were to evolve considerably.[13]

Care for preserving the body in a notional state of purity extended beyond prohibition of the ingestion of certain food to a series of taboos with regard to emissions related to sexual activity or skin disease. The law treated such emissions not as wrong but as precluding some activities, most notably entry into the sanctuary of the Temple, until the trace of impurity was deemed eradicated by the passage of time and (in some cases) ritual ablutions. Menstruation and similar flows of blood were considered to render a woman ritually impure for a period, and the biblical text lays down the procedure for her return to purity through bringing bird offerings:

> If a woman has a discharge of blood for many days, not at the time of her impurity, or if she has a discharge beyond the time of her impurity, for all the days of the discharge she shall continue in uncleanness; as in the days of her impurity, she shall be unclean. Every bed on which she lies during all the days of her discharge shall be treated as the bed of her impurity; and everything on which she sits shall be unclean, as in the uncleanness of her impurity. Whoever touches these things shall be unclean, and shall wash his clothes, and bathe in water, and be unclean until the evening. If she is cleansed of her discharge, she shall count seven days, and after that she shall be clean. On the eighth day she shall take two turtle-doves or two pigeons and bring them to the priest at the entrance of the tent of meeting. The priest shall offer one for a sin-offering and the other for a burnt-offering; and the priest shall make atonement on her behalf before the Lord for her unclean discharge.

The main focus of the biblical author was the effect of female impurity on the adult males to whom the laws are essentially addressed – 'you [meaning an adult male Israelite] shall not approach a woman to uncover her nakedness while she is in her menstrual uncleanness' – rather than its impact on the woman herself.[14]

It was also necessary to demonstrate piety by taking care of physical appearance in a prescribed fashion. The Lord commanded that dress should signify obedience through the wearing of blue fringes on the corners of garments 'to remember all the commandments of the Lord, that you go not astray'. Clothing should not be made of specific mixed types of material, although the prohibition on combining wool and linen in one garment is left as unexplained in the biblical texts as the food taboos. Israelites should take care not to 'round off the hair on your temples or mar the edges of your beard ... [or] make any gashes in your flesh for the dead or tattoo any marks upon you'. Only one reason is given: 'I am the Lord.'[15]

The ultimate physical reminder (for males) of the covenant was kept hidden, since modesty in clothing was considered a virtue. As a result, the sign of the circumcision, performed on all male Jews through removal of the foreskin of the penis, was generally invisible to others. The origins of circumcision within the Jewish tradition lay, according to Genesis, as a sign of the promise made by God to Abraham that he would be the father of 'a multitude of nations', and that he would establish an everlasting covenant with Abraham and his descendants 'to be a God to you':

> God said to Abraham, 'As for you, you shall keep my covenant, you and your offspring after you throughout their generations. This is my covenant, which you shall keep, between me and you and your offspring after you: Every male after you shall be circumcised. You shall circumcise the flesh of your foreskins, and it shall be a sign of the covenant between me and you. Throughout your generations every male among you shall be circumcised when he is eight days old, including the slave born in your house and the one bought with your money from any foreigner who is not of your offspring ... So shall my covenant be in your flesh an everlasting covenant. Any uncircumcised male who is not circumcised in the flesh of his foreskin shall be cut off from his people; he has broken my covenant.

It would be difficult to overstate the importance attributed by the biblical texts to male circumcision as a mark of Jewish identity. The practice had become widespread in the ancient Near East among other peoples as well as Jews, for reasons we do not know, and some biblical stories suggest a number of other elements to its significance for the Israelites, from encouragement of marriage and fertility to deliverance from evil. But the sense that circumcision is a requirement for holiness permeates the frequent metaphorical uses of the notion, with references to circum-cision of the heart, lips and ears to make them acceptable to God. Even the fruit of a newly planted tree could be described as forbidden because it is 'uncircumcised'.[16]

For both men and women sex was intended for procreation, and the prohibition of some other sexual practices was unequivocal: 'You shall not lie with a male as with a woman; it is an abomination. You shall not have sexual relations with any animal and defile yourself with it, nor shall any woman give herself to an animal to have sexual relations with it: it is perversion.' More positively, the command to both men and women in the first chapter of Genesis to 'be fruitful and multiply' can be taken to assume that procreation is a duty as well as a blessing. Many biblical stories about barren women longing for a child take for granted the desir-ability of numerous offspring. There is no clear biblical teaching about the permissibility of contraception: later Jewish interpreters considered the death of Onan, who 'spilled his semen onto the ground whenever he went in to his brother's wife', to constitute divine punishment for inten-tionally destroying male seed, but in the context of the original biblical passage it appears that Onan's sin was neither masturbation nor the adoption of a method of contraception but, more specifically, his reluc-tance to make Tamar pregnant because any offspring would be accounted not his child but the child of his dead brother.[17]

Such constraints contrived to make the home a locus of sanctity both in sexual relations and in the preparation and consumption of meals (in both cases providing women with a larger religious role in practice than might appear from the male focus of the biblical texts). The biblical text of the Shema enjoined the writing of 'these words that I am command-ing you today' on 'the doorposts of your house and on your gates', an injunction which may have been taken literally by the late Second Temple period, if some of the biblical manuscripts from Qumran were written for that purpose. But the greatest sign of sanctity in the home was the cessation of work on the Sabbath. The Israelites were required to observe a weekly rest day even before the revelation at Sinai had been given because it was 'a holy Sabbath to the Lord'. The significance of the Sabbath was said to have been emphasized to Moses while he was still on the mountain:

The Lord said to Moses: You yourself are to speak to the Israelites: 'You shall keep my sabbaths, for this is a sign between me and you throughout your generations, given in order that you may know that I, the Lord,

sanctify you. You shall keep the sabbath, because it is holy for you; everyone who profanes it shall be put to death; whoever does any work on it
shall be cut off from among the people . . . It is a sign for ever between me
and the people of Israel that in six days the Lord made heaven and earth,
and on the seventh day he rested, and was refreshed.'

The requirement for the whole household to rest on the Sabbath is
asserted in the Ten Commandments: 'Remember the Sabbath day, and
keep it holy . . . The seventh day is a sabbath to the Lord your God; you
shall not do any work – you, your son or your daughter, your male or
female slave, your livestock, or the alien resident in your towns.' This
weekly domestic dedication to God was to be one of the most distinctive characteristics of Judaism.[18]

'You shall keep all my statutes and all my ordinances, and observe
them,' God states in Leviticus, 'so that the land to which I bring you to
settle in may not vomit you out.' The land, quite often personified in this
way, is to be kept pure of idolatry: 'you shall not follow the practices of
the nation that I am driving out before you. Because they did all these
things, I abhorred them.' The land is to be allowed to rest at regular
intervals: 'For six years you shall sow your field . . . but in the seventh
year there shall be a sabbath of complete rest for the land.' The land of
Canaan had been promised to Abraham and his descendants as an everlasting possession:

> The word of the Lord came to Abram in a vision . . . He brought him out-
> side and said 'Look towards heaven and count the stars, if you are able to
> count them.' Then he said to him, 'So shall your descendants be' . . . Then
> he said to him, 'I am the Lord who brought you from Ur of the Chaldeans,
> to give you this land to possess' . . . On that day the Lord made a covenant
> with Abram, saying, 'To your descendants I give this land, from the river
> of Egypt to the great river, the river Euphrates, the land of the Kenites, the
> Kenizzites, the Kadmonites, the Hittites, the Perizzites, the Rephaim, the
> Amorites, the Canaanites, the Girgashites, and the Jebusites.'[19]

But the land was still essentially God's, and we have seen that the first
fruits were to be offered in the Temple in gratitude. Explicit references
to the land itself as holy are hard to find beyond an elusive reference in
Zechariah to the glorious eschatological future when 'the Lord will
inherit Judah as his portion in the holy land', but the underlying notion
is evident: this was the land 'which the Lord your God cares for'. It is of
course an odd fact that (as we have seen) this promised land is known

in much of the Bible not as the Land of Israel but as the Land of Canaan, and that many of the Jews for whom the Bible provided religious guidance were living outside the land, in communities in Mesopotamia and Babylon. Also odd is the lack of clarity in biblical texts about the precise boundaries of this promised land, which vary from the maximal definition in the passage just cited from Genesis ('from the river of Egypt to the great river, the river Euphrates') to the more modest formula of the land to be subjected to a census by King David according to II Samuel ('from Dan to Beersheba') and the enumeration in Numbers – starting at the Dead Sea and defining the border points to the south, west, north and east before returning to the Dead Sea – of the territory promised to Moses on the eve of the conquest begun by Joshua.[20]

Equally strange was the use by many of these Jews of languages other than Hebrew, even in prayer. Hebrew was the special language not just of Jews but also of God, since according to Genesis God had used Hebrew words to name the world. Hebrew was the language of the Temple. But the use of Aramaic in parts of some biblical books, such as the book of Daniel, and the enthusiasm of Alexandrian Jews for the Greek Septuagint according to Philo, suggest that Hebrew was not reckoned essential for communication with the divine.[21]

The biblical message for Jews wishing to live righteously was that holiness, and justice, combined with an obedience to God that was reinforced by both love and fear, would lead to prosperity, long life and many children on the land promised to their fathers. To rejoice in the festivals divinely ordained was a religious duty: 'you shall rejoice before the Lord your God.' On the other hand, fasting, with temporary abstention from food accompanied by self-affliction of other kinds (from the avoidance of washing to the wearing of sackcloth and ashes), was both customary in mourning and practised liturgically at special times of penance, of which much the most significant was the national fast on the Day of Atonement: 'The Lord spoke to Moses, saying, "Now, the tenth day of this seventh month is the day of atonement . . . You shall do no work during that entire day; for it is a day of atonement, to make atonement on your behalf before the Lord your God."'

Crucial for the relationship between God and Israel was this assumption that atonement for sin was possible and would be accepted: 'As I live, says the Lord God, I have no pleasure in the death of the wicked, but that the wicked turn from their ways and live.' Despite biblical hints that children are fated to pay for the sins of their fathers to the third and fourth generation (see above) or (as in Daniel) that rewards and punishments come after death, when 'many of those who sleep in the dust of the earth shall awake, some to everlasting life, and some to shame and everlasting contempt,' the annual ritual of the Day of Atonement enshrined the notion that the Jewish people, even if inevitably over the year they would fail to keep correctly the covenant that had been agreed by Israel, could nonetheless be confident that, after due confession of their iniquities and transgressions, they could hope to be forgiven by a merciful God and enabled to look forward again to a prosperous and peaceful year.[22]

The biblical rite for the Day of Atonement is envisaged as communal, crowned by the sacrifices and petitions of the High Priest in the Holy of Holies (see Chapter 3). Similarly communal was the ritual atonement prescribed in Deuteronomy for an unresolved murder: the elders of the town closest to the body were commanded to take a heifer 'that has never been worked, one that has not pulled in the yoke' and to break its neck 'in a wadi with running water, which is neither ploughed nor sown', reciting the formula 'Our hands did not shed this blood, nor were we witnesses to it. Absolve, O Lord, your people Israel, whom you redeemed; do not let the guilt of innocent blood remain in the midst of your people Israel.' But many references in the Psalms assume that the individual Israelite in contrite prayer can hope for forgiveness from a merciful God: 'If you, O Lord, should mark iniquities, Lord, who could stand? But there is forgiveness with you, so that you may be revered.' The repentance of 'a broken and contrite heart' will be treated by God as a sacrifice, and not despised.[23]

Judaism as expressed in the biblical texts takes for granted the role of God in bringing salvation now both to the individual and to the community as a whole. Salvation is understood in concrete terms in both cases. The individual is saved from trouble, enemies, suffering or death. The people of Israel are saved from the hostility of other nations, famine or slavery (as in the exodus from Egypt). Occasionally a biblical text reveals hope for the salvation also of other nations, as in the vision of Isaiah that 'Many peoples shall come and say, "Come, let us go up to the mountain of the Lord, to the house of the God of Jacob" ... Nation shall not lift up sword against nation, neither shall they learn war any more.' The covenant with Noah after the flood, indicated by the rainbow, encompassed not just his descendants, comprising all humankind, but also 'every living creature that is with you, the birds, the domestic animals, and every animal of the earth'. Occasionally salvation is imagined in the Bible as postponed to a future time in which the whole world order is changed, as in the prophecies of Joel, probably occasioned by the devastation caused by a locust swarm, about 'the great and terrible day of the Lord' when 'everyone who calls on the name of the Lord shall be saved . . .'[24]

Such notions of salvation have little to say about life after death. There are occasional hints of the concept of resurrection, as in the book of Daniel. But, more often, humans are depicted as consisting of bodies into which life comes for just a brief period. Death is nothingness. Some texts refer to Sheol, the realm of death under the ground in which the dead were thought to lead a shadowy existence, but with no indication of the nature of this place except that no one in Sheol has access to God. The prophet Jeremiah claimed that God had told him that 'before I formed you in the womb I knew you, and before you were born I consecrated you.' But a fully developed notion of a pre-existent soul which exists separately from the body, and therefore can survive after death, is not to be found within the Bible. Only after the completion of the biblical texts in the third century BCE, and under the influence of Greek, and especially Platonic, thought, was the concept implanted into Jewish thought of individual souls as pre-existing the physical bodies into which they enter. Once adopted, the idea was to have a powerful influence on the development of Jewish (and Christian) teachings over more than two millennia about the role of the individual and his or her relation to God.[25]

PART II

Interpreting the Torah

(200 BCE–70 CE)

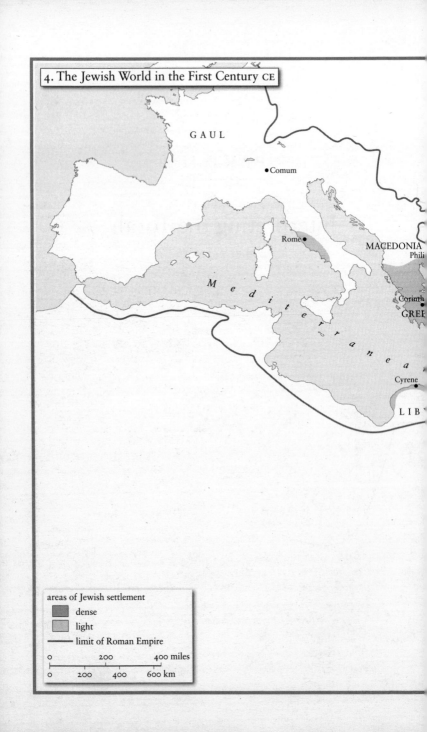

4. The Jewish World in the First Century CE

GAUL

•Comum

Rome•

MACEDONIA
Phili

Mediterranea

Corinth•

GREE

Cyrene
•

LIB

areas of Jewish settlement

[dense] dense

[light] light

—— limit of Roman Empire

| 0 | 200 | 400 miles |

| 0 | 200 | 400 | 600 km |

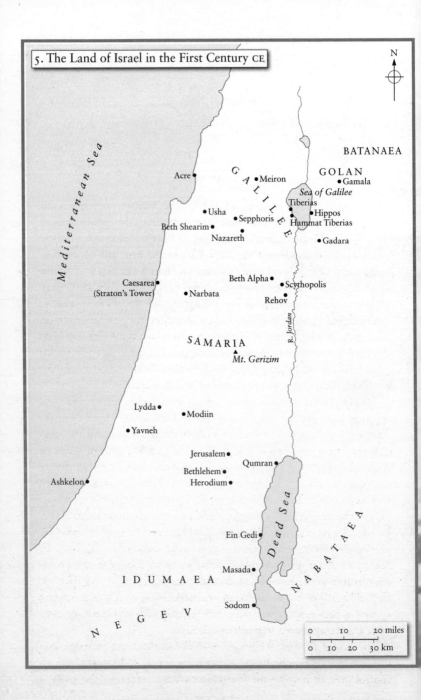

5. The Land of Israel in the First Century CE

N

BATANAEA

GOLAN

Mediterranean Sea

GALILEE

Acre ● ● Meiron ● Gamala

Sea of Galilee

Tiberias

● Usha ● Sepphoris Hippos ●

Beth Shearim ● Hammat Tiberias

Nazareth ●

● Gadara

Caesarea
(Straton's Tower) ● Beth Alpha ● ● Scythopolis

● Narbata Rehov ●

R. Jordan

SAMARIA

▲ Mt. Gerizim

Lydda ● ● Modiin

● Yavneh

Jerusalem ●

● Qumran

Bethlehem ●

Ashkelon ● Herodium ●

Dead Sea

Ein Gedi ●

NABATAEA

Masada ●

IDUMAEA

Sodom ●

NEGEV

0   10   20 miles

0   10   20   30 km

5

Jews in a Graeco-Roman World

The Bible took shape at a time when Jews and Judaism, nurtured in the world of the Near East, first came into the orbit of the civilizations of the northern Mediterranean. The power of Assyria, Babylonia and Persia, which had dominated the Near East in the first half of the first millennium BCE, was eclipsed from the late fourth century BCE by the Graeco-Macedonian empire of Alexander the Great and his successors, and, from the last century of the millennium, by Rome. Responses to Greek culture, from syncretism or acculturation to rejection or opposition, help to explain much of the variegated history of Judaism from the third century BCE to the end of antiquity. The response to Rome led most fatally to the destruction of the Jerusalem Temple in 70 CE and the end of sacrifice as the primary focus of Jewish worship.

Greeks had for centuries made contact with the Levant for trade, but the immediate impetus for the influence of Hellenistic culture throughout the Near East from the late fourth century BCE was political and military. As we have seen in Josephus' narrative (Chapter 1), in 332 BCE Alexander the Great, king of Macedon, embarked on an extraordinary campaign which ended in the conquest of the Persian empire and territory as far east as India. After Alexander's premature death in 323 BCE, his generals fought each other for more than two decades before establishing a longer-term division of the Near East in 301 BCE. Ptolemy and his descendants became rulers of Egypt, and the dynasty established by Seleucus ruled a territory which stretched from Turkey in the northwest to Iran in the east. These dynasties retained power over the next two and a half centuries, although internal conflict within each dynasty as well as between the Ptolemaic and Seleucid monarchs seeking glory through victory caused frequent instability.

The power of these kingdoms was eventually brought to an end through intervention by Rome. A city state in origin, Rome had gained control over all Italy by the fourth century BCE and over the western

Mediterranean by the end of the third century. From 200 BCE Roman power spread rapidly east, using a combination of military force and diplomacy to weaken Hellenistic rulers first in Macedon and then in Asia Minor. By the early first century BCE Rome was intervening frequently in the Levant. In 31 BCE, with the defeat of the Ptolemaic queen Cleopatra VII of Egypt, the last of the kingdoms founded by Alexander's generals passed into Roman control.

This expansion of Roman power was not through chance. From the late sixth to the first century BCE, the constitution of the Roman Republic required power to be shared between aristocrats who competed for popular favour primarily by appeal to their military achievements. Each new conquest encouraged rival politicians to seek further regions to bring under Roman domination. At precisely the point that Roman expansion reached Judaea in the mid-first century BCE, the success of the Roman state was nearly the cause of its own undoing. The glory and wealth accumulated by individual generals in foreign wars encouraged their ambitions to retain power beyond the terms of the commands to which they had been appointed by the Roman people. The civil war between Pompey the Great and Julius Caesar which began in 49 BCE started a protracted military struggle between competing Roman aristocrats into which the whole Mediterranean world was drawn. In 32 BCE Octavian, Caesar's great-nephew and heir, emerged victorious, taking the name Augustus, 'Revered', in 27 BCE. The formal constitution of the Roman state remained largely unaltered, but Augustus was in effect an autocrat and Rome became an empire.

It took time for these geopolitical changes after Alexander's conquests to have an impact on the Jews. The Persian empire had shown no interest in interfering in the local customs of the peoples it ruled, and we have seen (Chapter 1) that Josephus recorded a tradition that Alexander visited Jerusalem during his campaign and expressed his admiration for the Jewish God and his Temple. But Alexander had conquered an empire far too extensive to control simply with his Macedonian followers, and both he and the rulers who succeeded him chose to create a new ruling elite unified not only by obedience to the ruler but also by common allegiance to Greek language and culture. Many new cities were founded with Greek colonists, often based on existing Greek trading settlements, and numerous Greek cities, such as Scythopolis, Hippos and Gadara, are attested in the neighbourhood of Judaea by the end of the third century BCE. But Alexander and his successors also encouraged native elites to seek political power by adoption of Greek culture, and this was what led to the crisis of the Maccabean revolt of the 160s BCE.

So long as Judaea remained under the control of the Ptolemaic dynasty throughout the third century BCE, Jews were effectively ruled from Egypt as an overseas territory of the highly regulated Ptolemaic state. But power was much more diffused in the sprawling Seleucid empire into which Judaea was incorporated in 198 BCE after the victory of Antiochus the Great over Ptolemy V at the battle of Panium, and the opportunity arose for members of the priestly Jewish elite in Jerusalem to acquire status and authority in the eyes of their Seleucid masters through the promotion of Hellenism by reinterpreting Judaism in Greek terms. In 175 BCE, when Antiochus IV Epiphanes became the Seleucid king, a coup to depose the High Priest Onias was led by Onias' brother Jesus, who had adopted the Greek name Jason and offered to erect a gymnasium for Greek athletics and 'to enrol the people of Jerusalem as citizens of Antioch'.[1]

Quite how much these proposals by Jason changed Judaism has been much debated, since there was nothing intrinsically contrary to the Torah in physical exercise which 'induced the noblest of the young men to wear the Greek hat', and all accounts of Jason's period as High Priest derive from hostile sources which conceived of his reforms as the sinful behaviour which brought down on Israel the divine punishment which was soon to follow. From the point of view of Antiochus, the main incentive to replace Onias with Jason was probably Jason's offer to pay him a very large sum of money, since three years later, probably in 171 BCE, Jason was in turn deposed from the post of High Priest by Antiochus to make way for a certain Menelaus, who offered an even larger bribe.[2]

The detailed narratives of the dramatic events of the next decade in the two books of Maccabees, now preserved in the Apocrypha, are confused in their chronology and in their accounts of the motivation of the leading personalities of the political struggle in Jerusalem, but the outline of events is clear. During the campaign of Antiochus against Egypt in 170 to 169 BCE, Jason seized Jerusalem, forcing Menelaus to seek the protection of the Seleucid garrison in the city's citadel. Antiochus retaliated on his return from Egypt in the autumn of 169 BCE, capturing the city on behalf of Menelaus and looting the most valuable Temple artefacts, including the altar of incense and the *menorah* (the Temple's distinctive ornamental candelabrum).[3]

The author of the Second Book of Maccabees asserted specifically that this despoliation of the Temple was guided by Menelaus, 'who had become a traitor both to the laws and to his country', but Menelaus was not accused of connivance in the far worse persecution which was to come. When Antiochus invaded Egypt again in 168 BCE, he was confronted by the Roman senator Popillius Laenas, who transmitted to him the demands of the senate that he must withdraw from Egypt if he wished to avoid being at war with Rome. In a purported prophecy composed shortly after these events and incorporated in the biblical book of Daniel, the author appears to trace a direct connection between the humbling of Antiochus in Egypt and the abolition of the Temple worship and its replacement by a pagan cult:

> At the time appointed he shall return and come into the south, but this time it shall not be as it was before. For ships of Kittim [Rome] shall come against him, and he shall lose heart and withdraw. He shall be enraged and take action against the holy covenant. He shall turn back and pay heed to those who forsake the holy covenant. Forces sent by him shall occupy and profane the Temple and fortress. They shall abolish the regular burnt-offering and set up the abomination that makes desolate.

Behind the actions described by the author with such outrage lay the need of Antiochus for further income from the Jerusalem Temple now that Roman intervention had deprived him of the Egyptian booty with which he would in normal times have expected to be able to reward his successful troops.[4]

According to the First Book of Maccabees, Antiochus had addressed his whole kingdom, declaring 'that all should be one people, and that they should give up their particular customs', and the appeal was largely successful: 'All the gentiles accepted the command of the king. Many even from Israel gladly adopted his religion: they sacrificed to idols and profaned the Sabbath.' How many Jews in fact supported the abolition of their religion has been much debated. Josephus recorded that the Samaritans made a request to Antiochus to have their temple dedicated to Zeus, but the books of Maccabees give the impression, despite their hostility to the Hellenizers, that the attack on the Jewish cult was primarily an external initiative of the Seleucid state. Antiochus was an eccentric ruler who had just suffered an appalling loss of face, and he may well have had little interest in the ambitions of the Hellenizing Jewish priests. The priests in turn were unlikely to support a policy which abolished the Temple cult that they had intrigued to control.[5]

At any rate, the assault on Jewish worship and customs was carried out with rigour. The Seleucid state sent officers throughout Judaea to ensure that observance of the Sabbath and the circumcision of sons ceased and that Jews offered sacrifices to pagan gods. According to the Second Book of Maccabees, composed at the latest within a century after these events, 'when a festival of Dionysus was celebrated, they were compelled to wear wreaths of ivy and to walk in the procession in honour of Dionysus,' and when two women were brought in for having circumcised their children, 'they publicly paraded them around the city, with their babies hanging at their breasts, and then hurled them down headlong from the wall.'[6]

The veracity of such atrocity stories cannot be ascertained, but it seems clear that the violence of this repression, in marked contrast to the gradual syncretism which had been so successful in spreading Hellenism throughout much of the Near East, was responsible for inciting the armed resistance of the Maccabees – the only known case of the adherents of an eastern religion opposing by force the encroachment of Greek culture in their native land. The rebellion began in Modiin, a small town north-west of Jerusalem, under the leadership of a priest called Mattathias and his five sons. Ostentatiously refusing to worship a pagan god when an emissary of the Seleucid state arrived in Modiin to impose the king's decree, Mattathias killed a Jew about to offer sacrifice at the altar, killed the king's officer and took refuge in the mountains, where he rapidly gathered together a guerrilla force of fighters committed to destroy the pagan altars and encourage resistance by the wider Jewish population, if necessary by force. In the words of I Maccabees, 'They ... struck down sinners in their anger and renegades in their wrath.'[7]

Within a year of the start of the uprising, Mattathias was dead of old age, and his place as leader of the rebels was taken by his son Judah, whose personal name, 'the Maccabee' (of uncertain etymology but probably with the meaning 'hammer'), came to be transferred to the rebellion as a whole. The history of Judah's campaigns is portrayed differently in the glowing narratives in I Maccabees and II Maccabees, and is now impossible to discern precisely, but such hagiography of the great general certainly reflected impressive victories against considerable odds, culminating in the recapture of Jerusalem. In December 164 BCE, on 25 Kislev, the Temple was rededicated with a new altar and sacred vessels, three years after it had been profaned. Neither I Maccabees nor II Maccabees makes mention of the miracle of the oil which was to loom large in later rabbinic commemoration of this momentous occasion (see Chapter 10), but I Maccabees records that 'Judas and his brothers and all the assembly of Israel determined that every year at that season the days of dedication of the altar should be observed with joy and gladness for eight days,' marking the origins of the celebration of Hanukkah.[8]

The significance of Judah's victories for the future of Judaism is hard to overestimate. Other native cults in the regions around Judaea lost their distinctive local characteristics as they were reinterpreted in Greek fashion, but the Maccabean revolt set up a powerful notion of opposition between Judaism and Hellenism. The notion, which was to reappear at different times in the later history of Judaism, was in part the product of the propaganda of Judah's family in their efforts to establish themselves in power in Judaea in the decades following the death of Judah in battle in the autumn of 161 BCE.

By the time the First Book of Maccabees was written, probably in the 120s BCE, Judaea was being ruled by John Hyrcanus, a grandson of Mattathias and nephew of Judah Maccabee, and Hyrcanus was in firm control of an independent Judaea, with the status of High Priest. This state of pre-eminence had not been easily won by the dynasty of the Hasmonaeans (as they called themselves, in deference to an ancestor of Mattathias). Judah had succeeded in restoring the ancestral cult in Jerusalem in 164 BCE, but a Seleucid garrison remained in the city's citadel, and the military forces at the disposal of the Jewish insurgents would have proved quite incapable of retaining control of the Temple if Antiochus IV had not died while on an eastern campaign in 163 BCE and if the attentions of the Seleucid state had not been distracted by internal strife. The rival pretenders to the Seleucid throne sought political support against each other from wherever it might arise, and Judah's brothers – first Jonathan and then Simon – cleverly exploited the opportunities to extort concessions from one pretender or the other.[9]

The Hasmonaeans were priests, but, since they did not belong to the Zadokite line which had provided the High Priests in the Temple since the time of Solomon's Temple up to the deposition of Jason by Menelaus in 171 BCE, they did not immediately seize the high priesthood upon their assumption of political control. After the rededication of the Temple by Judah Maccabee, the High Priest was a certain Alcimus, from the party of the Hellenizers. Despite later traditions to the contrary in Josephus, there is no hint in the First Book of Maccabees that Judah ever became High Priest, and Josephus explicitly stated that the Temple was without a High Priest for seven years after the death of Alcimus in 159 BCE.[10]

It was only in 152 BCE that Judah's brother Jonathan, after complex negotiations with the rival Seleucid rulers Demetrius and Alexander Balas, accepted the post from Alexander Balas. I Maccabees recorded the letter sent to Jonathan by the king and Jonathan's subsequent elevation to supreme authority in the Temple:

'King Alexander to his brother Jonathan, greetings. We have heard that you are a mighty warrior and worthy to be our friend. And so we have appointed you today to be the high priest of your nation; you are to be the King's friend and you are to take our side and keep friendship with us.' [The king] also sent him a purple robe and a golden crown. So Jonathan put on the sacred vestments in the seventh month of the one hundred and sixtieth year, at the festival of booths.

Once installed in the high priesthood, the Hasmonaean dynasty was not to be dislodged for over a century – the last scion of the family to preside in the Jerusalem Temple was Aristobulus III, who died in 35 BCE – but their lack of confidence in their right to hold the most prestigious position in representing the nation to God emerged on 18 Elul (September) 140 BCE, when Jonathan's brother and successor Simon convened a 'great assembly of the priests and the people and the rulers and the elders of the country'. The assembly declared that, because of 'Simon's faithfulness and the glory that he had resolved to win for his nation', they had made him their leader and High Priest, adding that 'the Jews and their priests have resolved that Simon should be their leader and high priest for ever, until a trustworthy prophet should arise.' The selection of High Priest was no longer to be left to the decision of the gentile suzerain. It was to be decided by the Jewish nation – or (if a prophet arose) by God. The decree of the assembly was engraved on bronze tablets, put up 'in a conspicuous place in the precincts of the sanctuary', with copies in the treasury.[11]

Simon and two of his sons were assassinated in 135 BCE, and Simon's surviving son John Hyrcanus faced great obstacles in establishing himself in power until the death in 129 BCE of the Seleucid king Antiochus VII on campaign against the Parthians on the eastern edge of his empire. Antiochus' successor, Demetrius II, was distracted by internal conflict elsewhere within his kingdom, and John Hyrcanus began a campaign of conquest which incorporated under his rule the Samaritans to the north and the Idumaeans to the south. The Samaritan temple on Mount Gerizim was destroyed. According to Josephus, after subduing all the Idumaeans, Hyrcanus 'permitted them to remain in their country so long as they had the males circumcised and were willing to observe the laws of the Jews. And so, out of attachment to the land of their fathers, they submitted to circumcision and to making their manner of life conform in all other respects to that of the Jews. And from that time on they have continued to be Jews.'[12]

This policy of forcible conversion reflects the distinctively Jewish ethos of the Hasmonaean dynasty once it was established. John Hyrcanus issued coins proclaiming in Hebrew 'Yehohanan the High Priest and the *hever* [Congregation] of the Jews'. But in the reign of John Hyrcanus the dynasty was already beginning to imitate the practices of other Hellenistic states, not least in the use of mercenary troops to fight aggressive wars for territory. The First Book of Maccabees, a product of Hasmonaean propaganda about the origins of the dynasty, portrays the Hasmonaeans as champions of Judaism against Hellenism, but the more vociferous the hostility to Greek culture, the easier it proved to adopt aspects of Hellenism at will.

In the political sphere, the Hellenization of the dynasty was already apparent on the death of John Hyrcanus in 104 BCE. Hyrcanus as ruler had been content with the position of High Priest, but according to Josephus his eldest son Aristobulus 'saw fit to transform the government into a kingdom . . . and he was the first to put a diadem on his head'. Both he and his younger brother Alexander Jannaeus, who succeeded him as king after only a year, pursued a policy of territorial expansion. Aristobulus incorporated into the Jewish polity the Ituraean nation in Galilee 'whom he joined to them by the bond of circumcision', and Alexander conquered the Greek cities of the maritime plain. Josephus portrays the power behind the throne as Alexandra Salome, the widow of Aristobulus. It was Alexandra who released Alexander Jannaeus from prison on Aristobulus' death and appointed him king, and when Jannaeus died in 76 BCE she became queen in her own right.[13]

For a female member of the dynasty to rule was not uncommon in Hellenistic kingdoms – notably in Egypt, where Cleopatra VII, the paramour of Julius Caesar and Mark Antony in the second half of the first century BCE, was only the last of a series of powerful Ptolemaic queens – but it was a major break with Jewish tradition. Since a woman could not be High Priest, Alexandra appointed to that post her eldest son, Hyrcanus. Both Josephus and the rabbis (who refer to her as Shelomzion) preserve very favourable evaluations of the reign of Alexandra, in which she is said to have 'permitted the Pharisees to do as they liked in all matters, and also commanded the people to obey them; and whatever regulations, introduced by the Pharisees in accordance with ancestral tradition, had been abolished by her father-in-law Hyrcanus, these she again restored'. (On the significance of the support of the Pharisees, see Chapter 6.) But Hyrcanus as High Priest emerged as weak in the shadow of his powerful mother – indeed, Josephus asserts that she selected him for the role precisely because of his lack of energy, presumably so that he would not challenge her rule – and on her death in 67 BCE at the age of seventy-three Hyrcanus' claim to the throne was challenged by his younger brother, Aristobulus II. Within four years the conflict between the two brothers had provided an opportunity for the Romans to intervene and the independence of the Hasmonaean state came to an end.[14]

Already in 104 BCE Aristobulus I had taken the title of 'philhellene', according to Josephus, and the foundation myth of the Hasmonaean dynasty as the saviours of Judaism from Greek culture did not prevent pious Jews, in the land of Israel as well as in the diaspora, adopting those aspects of Hellenism which they felt compatible with their religion. It is ironic that the books of Maccabees themselves, with their tales of opposition to Greek values, are preserved only in the Greek language. There are many other Jewish writings in Greek preserved from the late Second Temple period, mostly only in fragmentary form. Many adopted Greek literary forms to express Jewish ideas, most remarkably in the epic poem of a certain Philo (otherwise unknown) entitled *About Jerusalem*, and the *Exagoge* ('Exodus'), composed as a Greek drama in the style of Euripides, by Ezekiel the Tragedian, with a striking portrayal of the voice of God speaking from the burning bush and an unexpected introduction, into the messenger speech of a scout sent to find a camping place for the Israelites, of a mighty bird – a phoenix – that is followed by the other birds as their king.[15]

The discovery of a fragment of Ezekiel's *Exagoge* among the papyri recovered from the Egyptian town of Oxyrhynchus reveals that the text was read in Egypt in antiquity and it is likely that Egypt was also where it was composed. But the place of composition of many other Jewish Greek texts, like the colourful rewriting of scripture in Eupolemus' work *About the Kings in Judaea*, is unknown, and it is not implausible that Eupolemus, who added to the biblical narrative material from Greek sources such as Herodotus and Ctesias in order to demonstrate the magnificence of the Jewish kings of antiquity, should be identified with the Judaean Jew of the same name who was selected by Judah Maccabee in the 160s BCE as one of the ambassadors sent to Rome to establish an alliance between Rome and the Jews. That Judaean Jews were capable of thinking and writing in Greek by the end of the Second Temple period is of course clear from the compositions of the historian Josephus at the end of the first century CE. Josephus was certainly not alone, since he devoted a portion of his autobiography to a polemic against the contemporary history composed by a rival, Justus of Tiberias, whom he described specifically as a man of good Greek education.[16]

Jewish responses to Greek culture were evidently complex. Much of the worldview revealed in the Dead Sea scrolls (see Chapter 6) can be categorized as a rejection of Hellenism, but the preservation of some Greek biblical scrolls in the Qumran caves suggests knowledge and use of Greek among at least some Jews down by the Dead Sea. It is more complex to discern elements of Greek thought in the Hebrew and Aramaic texts among the Dead Sea scrolls, but a search for parallels between motifs in, for instance, Hebrew wisdom writings and Greek philosophy is not unreasonable, since the production in this period of a large quantity of Jewish texts translated from Hebrew into Greek provides clear evidence that some Jews at least were fluent in both languages.[17]

The capture of Jerusalem by Pompey the Great on the Day of Atonement in 63 BCE – 'in the third month, on the Fast Day, in the hundred and seventy-ninth Olympiad, in the consulship of Gaius Antonius and Marcus Tullius Cicero' – was only a minor victory in the glorious campaigns of the Roman general which consolidated Roman control of the territories bordering the eastern littoral of the Mediterranean, but for the Jews this difficult beginning of a difficult relationship with the new superpower was to transform the fortunes of the nation and, in due course, their religion.[18]

Pompey's excuse for intervention in the politics of Judaea was the struggle for power between Hyrcanus II and Aristobulus II, the two sons of Alexandra Jannaea. Both sought to elicit Roman backing with massive bribes – Aristobulus sent Pompey a grape-vine made out of gold which was worth the fabulous sum of 500 talents and was later exhibited in the temple of Jupiter Capitolinus in Rome. Josephus records that neither Hasmonaean had much popular support and that 'the nation was against them both and asked not to be ruled by a king, saying that it was the custom of their country to obey the priests of the god who was venerated by them, but that these two, who were descended from the priests, were seeking to change their form of government in order that they might become a nation of slaves.' If Josephus recorded such sentiments correctly, Pompey ignored these pleas and chose to support the claims of Hyrcanus, entering Jerusalem easily with the aid of Hyrcanus' supporters but breaking into the Temple Mount only after a long siege. Josephus reported with admiration that 'during the siege the priests were not hindered from performing any of the sacred ceremonies through fear, but twice a day, in the morning and at the ninth hour, they performed the sacred ceremonies at the altar,' and that these offerings continued even once the wall was breached and the Roman soldiers rushed in and began their slaughter.[19]

With Pompey's victory, Judaea came under Roman jurisdiction exercised through Hyrcanus II, who was in turn subject to control by the Roman governor of Syria. Hyrcanus fulfilled this role for twenty-three years, from 63 to 40 BCE, but his position was always precarious. Danger lurked both in continued opposition by his brother Aristobulus and Aristobulus' son, Antigonus, and in the volatile state of the Roman world in general during these years which culminated in the outbreak of civil war between Pompey and Julius Caesar in 49 BCE.

A dependent ruler like Hyrcanus had no stake in the elite aristocratic power struggle which thrust the Roman world into turmoil. Bribes and negotiations conducted through his chief minister Antipater, father of the future king Herod, enabled Hyrcanus to retain his position by supporting first Julius Caesar, then (after the Ides of March 44 BCE) his assassins, and, finally, his political heirs, Mark Antony and Octavian, when the assassins had been defeated at Philippi in autumn 42 BCE. But all these negotiations with powerful Romans were of no avail when in 40 BCE the Parthians, who had taken advantage of Roman disarray to occupy northern Syria from the east, were persuaded by Antigonus, the son of Hyrcanus' brother Aristobulus, to invade Judaea and to install him as the new ruler. Hyrcanus was taken back to Parthia as a captive, and, since any physical defect would render him unable to serve again as a High Priest, his ears were mutilated.[20]

The coins of Antigonus from 40 to 37 BCE have the title 'King Antigonus' in Greek on one side and 'Mattathias the High Priest' in Hebrew on the other. It is clear that the new High Priest had high hopes for a restoration of Hasmonaean independence as in the time of his grandparents Alexander Jannaeus and Alexandra. Such hopes did not allow for the continuing ambitions of Rome. The senate saw this loss of territory as an affront to Roman majesty and took for granted the need to restore Judaea to the Roman sphere of influence. Lacking access to any member of the Hasmonaean dynasty to impose as a ruler in place of

Antigonus, the senate turned to Herod, the son of Antipater, whose machinations on behalf of Hyrcanus through the 40s BCE had brought both him and his sons to the attention of powerful Romans, including Mark Antony, who in 40 BCE was the de facto ruler of much of the eastern Mediterranean.

The senate's decision in the autumn of 40 BCE to appoint someone like Herod to rule Judaea was as anomalous in terms of normal Roman policy as it was for Jewish tradition, and it would have been impossible if the Roman world had not been in crisis. Herod was from Idumaea, the region south of Judaea converted to Judaism only some seventy years previously. His mother was a Nabataean Arab. He was not related to the royal family of the Hasmonaeans, and, since he was not a priest, he could not preside in the Jerusalem Temple. It took three years for him to gain control of his kingdom, aided first by Roman defeat of the Parthian forces in Syria in 39 and 38 BCE and finally, in spring 37 BCE, by Roman help in besieging Antigonus in Jerusalem. On the capture of the city Antigonus was taken in chains to the Roman general Sosius. Sosius sent him to Mark Antony, who had him beheaded at Herod's behest. Antigonus had protested that Herod was unsuitable to be king of Judaea because he was only an Idumaean, 'that is, a half-Jew' – all the more reason for Herod to want him out of the way.[21]

For the next century all Jewish rulers in Judaea depended entirely on Roman favour to maintain their power. Herod himself navigated with skill through the treacherous shoals of the final decade of the Roman civil war. Finding himself on the wrong side in 32 BCE after the defeat of Mark Antony by Octavian Caesar (the future emperor Augustus), he pledged to the victor that he would be as faithful in his allegiance to the new master of the eastern Mediterranean world as he had been to his predecessor. By the time of Herod's death in 4 BCE, he had become a major figure in the Roman world – a friend of the emperor, a major benefactor of Greek cities, a remarkable builder and by far the best-known Jew among ordinary Romans.

To those Romans, Herod was indeed an archetypal Jew: the Sabbath was 'the day of Herod'. The judgement of other Jews will have been more equivocal. In Judaea, Herod married Mariamme, the grand-daughter of the former Hasmonaean High Priest Hyrcanus II, but was believed to have engineered the accidental death by drowning of Mariamme's young brother in case he proved a magnet for disaffection, and his lavish expenditure on the rebuilding of the Jerusalem Temple (see Chapter 3) was balanced by the erection of a temple in honour of Rome and Augustus in the new city of Caesarea which he founded on the Mediterranean coast and by his pride in presenting himself as patron of the Olympic games in Greece. He even tried briefly to introduce both Greek games and Roman wild-beast shows to the Jewish public in Jerusalem, but was persuaded to desist by public displays of opposition.[22]

The impact of Herod's reign on the religious lives of his Jewish subjects was thus ambiguous. The magnificence of the rebuilt Temple in Jerusalem, with its greatly expanded main courtyard erected over arches built according to the latest Roman architectural techniques, encouraged a much enhanced pilgrimage industry which benefited also from the comparative security of travel across the Mediterranean in a world unified under Rome. But the High Priests appointed to preside over the sacrifices were from obscure families from Babylonia and Egypt, carefully selected by Herod to ensure that they would prove no threat to his own power. Any priest who had once held the highest office inevitably retained a certain aura from so illustrious a role, but it would take time for a new high priestly elite to emerge, and no new priestly families ever matched the authority and prestige of the Hasmonaeans, or of the descendants of Zadok who had held the high priesthood before them.

The years immediately before Herod's death in 4 BCE were marked by intense struggles for power within his large family. Herod frequently changed his will in his last years. His son Archelaus eventually succeeded him as ruler of Judaea, but with the less prestigious title of ethnarch ('ruler of the nation') rather than king, and parts of Herod's territory were placed under the separate control of his brothers Antipas and Philip. The ethnarch lasted only ten years in power – in 6 CE Augustus sent him into exile in Gaul and placed Judaea under the direct control of a Roman governor.

The establishment of direct Roman rule required military intervention by Quirinius, the governor of Syria, in order to impose a census on the inhabitants of the new province, but, once this had been carried out, the emperor decided that Judaea could be safely entrusted to a junior Roman governor with minimal forces at his disposal. The Roman state expected order to be maintained primarily through the cooperation of local leaders, whose authority within the subject population was in turn reinforced by Rome. Members of the Herodian family were to continue to play an occasional role for this purpose in the internal politics of Judaea over the next sixty years, but after the removal of Archelaus in 6 CE the main representative of the Jews in the eyes of the Roman governor became the High Priest in the Temple, and the high priestly families from whose ranks the High Priest was appointed became a new ruling elite in Jerusalem.[23]

The Romans arrogated to themselves the selection of the High Priest, reverting to the system of appointment by the suzerain power which had been standard until the rise of the Hasmonaean dynasty. Some of the priests selected came from the families which had been favoured by Herod, but the family of Ananus son of Sethi, appointed in 6 CE by Quirinius to replace the incumbent Joazar son of Boethus who had proved unable to suppress opposition to the census, owed their position entirely to Roman patronage. Of the seventeen High Priests who served in the Temple between 6 CE and 66 CE, five were sons of Ananus, and one (Caiaphas, the High Priest who condemned Jesus according to the Gospel accounts) was Ananus' son-in-law.

Roman rule through such carefully selected High Priests was thrown into turmoil in 40 CE by the megalomaniac plans of the emperor Gaius Caligula. Prompted by hostile Greeks who drew his attention to the failure of Jews to worship the emperor as a god as they themselves did, and unimpressed by Jewish claims that praying to the Jewish God on behalf of the emperor was just as good, Caligula ordered Petronius, the governor of Syria, to place a cult statue of himself in the Jerusalem Temple. On his arrival at Ptolemais on his way to Jerusalem, Petronius was met by mass demonstrations and hesitated to carry out his orders. What would eventually have happened if the statue had been erected can only be guessed at, since Caligula was assassinated in 41 CE before his plan was put into action.

Chief among those who pleaded with Caligula not to desecrate the Jerusalem Temple was his friend Agrippa I, the grandson of Herod, and Agrippa I also played a crucial role in ensuring the accession of Claudius as emperor following Caligula's assassination. As a reward from Claudius, the selection of the High Priest was deputed by the Roman state to Agrippa I from 41 to 44 CE, along with rule over a kingdom as extensive as his grandfather's. On Agrippa's sudden death in 44 CE, 'eaten up by worms' according to the Acts of the Apostles, his kingdom was again divided and Judaea returned to rule by a Roman governor, but curatorship of the Temple was transferred to his brother, Herod of Chalcis. Following a short hiatus after Herod of Chalcis himself died in 48 CE, oversight of the Temple was exercised by Agrippa's son, Agrippa II, from c. 50 CE to the outbreak of revolt against Rome in 66 CE.[24]

The start of the revolt was marked in spring 66 CE by the symbolic refusal of the Jerusalem priests to continue to offer up the traditional sacrifices for the wellbeing of the emperor in Rome, and the Temple remained the focal point of rebellion throughout the four years of independence which ended in August 70 CE with the destruction of Jerusalem by Roman forces. The Jewish state, released from the shackles of Roman and Herodian domination, issued a series of remarkable coins which reverted to the Hasmonaean use of palaeo-Hebrew lettering and celebrated a new era. The coins refer to the new state as 'Israel', apparently in deliberate contrast to Roman use of 'Judaea'. Along with numerous bronze coins which proclaimed the 'freedom of Zion' and 'the redemption of Zion', the rebels minted shekels, half-shekels and quarter-shekels of exceptionally pure silver, with inscriptions referring to 'Jerusalem the holy'.[25]

The insistence on pure silver even under the constraints of war indicated that the mint authorities were concerned primarily for the pious use of these coins as offerings in the Temple. In late 67 or early 68 CE the revolutionary government selected a new High Priest by lot, eschewing the priestly families which had been favoured by Rome, much to the disgust of Josephus:

> The random result of the draw showed up the full depravity of their operation. The lot fell to one Phanni, the son of Samuel from the village of Aphthia, a man not only innocent of any high-priestly descent, but such a country bumpkin that he had no clear idea of what 'high priest' actually meant. Anyway, they dragged this poor man from his rural home and kitted him out for this alien part like an actor on the stage, robing him in the sacred vestments and prompting him to do what was required on any occasion. To them this blatant impiety was a hilarious piece of fun, but the other priests, watching from a distance this parody of the law, could only shed tears of anguish at the desecration of the holy offices.[26]

The reasons for the outbreak of revolt in 66 CE after some sixty years of direct Roman rule remain much debated despite (or because of) the detailed narrative of Josephus. Josephus was at pains to point out the times when tactless Roman governors had provoked disturbances in the years before the revolt. But he also pointed to various other causes, from a class struggle between rich and poor (exacerbated by the unequal distribution of an increasingly wealthy society) to prickly relations between the Jewish and gentile populations of the cities surrounding Judaea, such as Caesarea, and tensions between the generations within the Judaean elite, with the younger generation at the forefront of the rebellion against Rome.[27]

Among the causes of the rebellion singled out by Josephus was a distinctive philosophy preached in 66 CE, at the time of the first Roman census, by two teachers called Judas and Saddok who encouraged Jews to believe that 'God alone should be their leader and master,' so that they were quite prepared to face death 'if only they may avoid calling any man master'. Josephus described this doctrine in his *Antiquities* as 'an intrusive fourth school of philosophy', and an innovation in contrast to the three ancient philosophies of the Pharisees, Sadducees and Essenes (see Chapter 6), but it is worth noting here that Josephus' detailed narrative of the five decades immediately preceding the outbreak of war in 66 CE singularly fails to identify any of the individuals and groups involved in insurrection as subscribing to this Fourth Philosophy. Similarly, Josephus' reference in the *Jewish War* to widespread belief in 'an ambiguous oracle . . . found in their sacred scriptures, to the effect that at that time one from their country would become ruler of the world' is not reflected in descriptions of the leaders of the revolt as messianic figures. The one exception may be Simon son of Gioras, who served eventually in 70 CE as the commander-in-chief of the rebels and was accordingly given the dubious distinction of ritual execution at the culmination of the triumph in Rome of Vespasian and Titus. When Simon surrendered to Roman soldiers during the sack of Jerusalem, he was dressed in white tunics and a purple mantle. Josephus wrote that this was intended to frighten the Romans, but it is possible Simon thought such imperial clothing reflected his status as a messianic ruler.[28]

The seriousness of the revolt became clear to the Romans in 66 CE only after the unexpected defeat of the forces of Cestius Gallus, governor of Syria, who marched south to sort out the disturbances in Judaea and reached Jerusalem with an impressive show of strength but failed to protect his baggage-train sufficiently during his return to the Mediterranean coast. It is quite possible that the leaders of the provisional government, of whom many came from the high priestly families which had been favoured by Rome over half a century, imagined that they might be allowed independence of a Roman governor while remaining within the Roman empire. After all, Agrippa I had been appointed king of Judaea by the emperor Claudius only a quarter of a century before.[29]

In the event, Rome responded to the loss of Cestius' troops, the heaviest defeat to befall a Roman army within a pacified province in the history of the early Roman empire, by mobilizing a huge army to enforce the total surrender of the rebels. The campaign was slow, in part because of the caution of the elderly general Vespasian entrusted with the recapture of Jerusalem and in part because the Roman world was distracted, from late 68 CE, by the death of the emperor Nero and bids for the imperial power by a series of four senators, of whom the last (and most successful) was Vespasian himself. When Vespasian's son Titus, appointed by his father in 69 CE to complete the Judaean campaign, finally invested Jerusalem in spring 70 CE, he did so as heir apparent to the imperial power. The ferocity of the direct assault on the walls of the city over the ensuing months, with its willingness to countenance Roman casualties in the service of a speedy victory, was fired by the need to present the new imperial regime to the Roman public as heroic conquerors of a barbarian foe.

Josephus claimed, probably correctly, that Titus would have preferred not to destroy the Temple, but once the building had been set alight in the dry August heat of Jerusalem, it was impossible to save. The public sacrifices on behalf of the emperor, to ensure which Rome had gone to war in 66 CE, were now impossible, but Vespasian and Titus took the politic decision that it would reflect better on the new dynasty to revel in the destruction rather than mourn it and admit that it had been an error. The accoutrements of the Temple, as carried through the streets of Rome in triumph in 71 CE, can still be seen depicted on the Arch of Titus near the Roman Forum.[30]

It will be clear that the history of the Temple and its leadership was intimately bound up with the politics of Rome in the six decades before the Temple was reduced to rubble. Roman governors treated the High Priest as the representative of the Jews of Judaea and trusted him to keep order. For important decisions, such as a trial on a capital charge, the High Priest was expected to consult a *synhedrion*, 'council'. The Greek term was used by Josephus also to refer to the ad hoc *consilium* of advisers customarily convened by Roman magistrates, and was transliterated into Hebrew in the Mishnah as Sanhedrin, to refer to a supreme court of seventy-one judges competent to try the most difficult cases. If the High Priest's Sanhedrin operated like a Roman magistrate's council, its composition will have varied to suit the topic under discussion. Thus Jews of very different religious complexions could sit on a Sanhedrin at the same time – Pharisees and Sadducees on the Sanhedrin are said by the author of Acts to have fallen out with each other during the trial of St Paul.[31]

Until the revolt broke out in 66 CE this system of government worked well. There were disturbances, of course, over the course of sixty years, and presented cumulatively in retrospect, as in Josephus' narrative, they may appear to reflect a society on the edge of breakdown. But this perspective, informed by hindsight after Jerusalem had been destroyed, is highly misleading. Jews had lived peacefully for many years in many parts of the Roman world, and diaspora communities in Asia Minor, Syria, Egypt and indeed Rome itself had long been permitted by the Roman state to observe their own customs, such as the Sabbath, on the grounds of their venerable antiquity. Diaspora Jews were allowed to send offerings to the Jerusalem Temple, and Herodian kings intervened on behalf of Jews in Asia Minor and Alexandria when their relations with local gentiles became difficult. The Romans recognized the whole Jewish world as a single community of Jews, as (according to Josephus) the emperor Claudius noted in an edict specifically extending the privileges of the Jews in Alexandria to all the Jews 'throughout the empire under the Romans'. When the Jerusalem Temple came under threat from Gaius Caligula (see above), the Alexandrian Jew Philo abandoned the mission of his embassy on behalf of the Alexandrian Jews in order to devote himself to trying to prevent the desecration of the national shrine.[32]

Judaea itself was only lightly governed, with a small number of auxiliary troops and a quite junior governor who was not of senatorial rank, and it seems unlikely that the province was viewed by the Romans as potentially dangerous. Remarkable among the unique privileges permitted to the Jews were the pilgrimage festivals held three times a year in Jerusalem (see Chapter 3), at which enormous numbers gathered in a fashion not permitted elsewhere in the Roman world. The Roman governor stationed a second cohort in Jerusalem at the time of the festivals to help with the management of the crowds, and it was evidently known that these mass gatherings could be a time for trouble, but, as transpired in 66 CE, a few thousand troops were of little use when faced by a densely packed mass of people in the narrow streets of the city. If the 50s and 60s CE were really a time of growing tension in the province, the Roman state was impressively sanguine in its response and made no attempt to increase its military presence. It would be quite wrong to imagine first-century CE Judaea as an occupied country with a Roman soldier on every street corner. For most Jews, most of the time, Roman rule was more or less invisible.[33]

Josephus claimed specifically that four years before the outbreak of war, the city was in a state of 'peace and prosperity'. A prophecy of doom preached at the time was treated as a symptom of insanity. Both Jerusalem and the Temple were more glorious and prosperous than they had ever been before. Doubtless Jews could look back with nostalgia to a fabled past when Solomon's Temple was thought to have been even more impressive and God conversed more readily with the prophets among his people. Life is never perfect, and it is always possible to imagine a brighter future at the end of days. The notion, sometimes mooted by scholars of early Christianity, that Jews in the first century CE felt themselves to be in exile from God and longing for messianic salvation is unwarranted. The varied trends within Judaism to be examined in the next three chapters were the product not of despair but of confidence. Jews could all agree that the Torah provided them with the best possible guide to a pious life. The question was how to live that life in practice.[34]

6

'Jewish Doctrine
Takes Three Forms'

Josephus affirmed that 'Jewish doctrine takes three forms. The followers of the first *hairesis* [school] are called Pharisees, of the second Sadducees, of the third Essenes.' He made quite frequent references to these schools within Judaism in the course of his histories, introducing them first into his narrative of the different groups which sought influence over John Hyrcanus, the Hasmonaean High Priest from 135 to 104 BCE. In later Christian usage, the term *hairesis* was to denote 'heresy', but its literal meaning is 'choice', and it is clear that Josephus saw nothing untoward about the existence of these separate streams within Judaism. Indeed, he went out of his way to claim that these three philosophies had existed among the Jews 'from the most ancient times', in contrast to the novel (and, in Josephus' view, wicked) Fourth Philosophy which was invented at the start of direct Roman rule in Judaea in 6 CE. It cannot be certain whether these groups were indeed ancient or originated only when first mentioned by Josephus in the second half of the second century BCE, but it can be said that they flourished in this period, and that the ethos of the Hellenistic world, in which there co-existed competing philosophies of life such as Stoicism, Epicureanism and Pythagoreanism (to some of which Josephus on occasion explicitly compared these Jewish schools), provided the environment in which this could occur.[1]

By the beginning of the second century BCE, when almost all the Bible had been composed and much had already been translated into Greek, the common core of all later forms of Judaism – until the emergence of Humanistic and Secular Judaism in the modern era – was in place. Jews worshipped and obeyed the God of Abraham, Isaac and Jacob, whose actions in the world were recorded in the sacred histories and who was worshipped in the Temple in Jerusalem. Jews believed themselves bound to obey the commandments of God, especially as laid down in the first five books of the Bible, through the covenant sealed through Moses on Mount Sinai centuries earlier. These commandments laid down precise rules for the conduct of life from birth to death. What, then, explains the emergence in the last centuries of the Second Temple, between 200 BCE and 70 CE, of many different types of Judaism, by no means all compatible?

Part of the answer is that the Bible contained such a rich collection of ideas that decisions about which to emphasize differed in antiquity just as they do now. Choices varied enormously, and some biblical ideas, such as the Jubilee, seem never to have been adopted in practice. But of no less importance than selective interpretations of the Bible was the emergence of practices and ideas within Jewish society over the generations until, through force of custom, they were accorded the respect due to ancient tradition and came to be seen by some as normative. All Jews might claim to be following faithfully the laws as handed down in the Bible, and those laws provided precise details about behaviour in every aspect of life. As a result, the majority of Jews saw it as a religious duty to refrain from work on the Sabbath, to circumcise their sons, to avoid forbidden foods and to bring offerings, when they could, to the Jerusalem Temple. Such were the characteristics of Judaism as remarked by Greek and Latin pagan writers of the first century BCE and the first century CE. For most Jews, simply keeping the Torah as they believed that their ancestors had done will have sufficed.[2]

Probably only a minority adopted any particular philosophy. For those who did so, it seems to have been a matter of personal choice. Josephus described in his autobiography his own spiritual odyssey through the Jewish schools in his teenage years: 'At about the age of sixteen I determined to gain personal experience of the several sects into which our nation is divided.' Non-Jews who converted to Judaism out of personal conviction (rather than to facilitate marriage to a Jew) may have been attracted to specific Jewish philosophies more than native Jews. Thus the author of the Gospel of Matthew seems to have attributed to Jesus an attack on Pharisees for instilling proselytes with Pharisaic teachings: 'Woe to you, scribes and Pharisees, hypocrites! For you cross sea and land to make a single convert, and you make the new convert twice as much a child of hell as yourselves.'

This passage in Matthew was for a long time the basis of a notion that conversion to Judaism was encouraged in the late Second Temple period by Jewish missionary activity which was both a precursor to, and a rival of, mission by the first Christian generation. But the Christian mission was an exception in the religious history of the ancient world, and conversion to Judaism, when it occurred, was generally on the initiative of the proselyte. We do not know how many such converts there were. We do not even know how many Jews there were in the first century CE: the claim, common since the mid-nineteenth century, that by the mid-first century CE a tenth of the fifty million or so people living in the Roman empire were Jews is an error which originated with Bar Hebraeus, a Syriac Christian author of the thirteenth century CE. Bar Hebraeus claimed that the emperor Claudius ordered a census of the Jews and came up with a precise figure of 6,944,000 men. But Bar Hebraeus had evidently failed to understand his source. Jerome in the late fourth century CE noted that precisely the same figure was reported by Eusebius as the number of Roman citizens recorded by Claudius in a census. A census of citizens was standard practice in the Roman empire; a census of Jews would be bizarre.

In the one extended conversion narrative which survives from the first century CE, the shift made by a gentile from the status of an outsider interested in aspects of Jewish practice to that of a full convert was clearly on the initiative of the convert himself. According to a folkloric narrative preserved in Josephus' *Antiquities*, Izates, king of Adiabene, learned about Judaism from a passing Jew named Ananias and took on many Jewish customs, but it was only when he was visited by a second visitor called Eleazar that he decided to undergo circumcision in order to follow the law fully. By the time that Izates underwent the operation, presumably by the court doctor, neither of these Jews was around. There does not seem to have been a recognized conversion ceremony in the first century CE to correspond to baptism in early Christianity and conversion in rabbinic Judaism from the third century CE onwards. Nor was there any local Jewish community to confirm the new status of the king as a full member of the Jewish people. It seems that Izates decided for himself that he was now a Jew and therefore bound by the covenant between God and Israel encapsulated in the Torah. In due course he discovered that his mother, Queen Helena, had been similarly converted. She was to settle in Jerusalem, where she became a major benefactress of the city in time of famine. Her status as a prominent proselyte was known not only to Josephus in the late first century but to the compilers of the Mishnah in the early third.[3]

Evidence for the great variety of interpretations of the Torah that abounded within Jewish society already in the first three centuries after the completion of the Bible survives in such plenty because of its preservation through both rabbinic Judaism and Christianity, two religious traditions continuous to the present day. But it is striking that the evidence preserved for religious purposes by later Christians is very different from the material transmitted by the rabbis. In part, this is a matter of language: Christians passed down to later generations only those Jewish texts written in Greek (although what now survives is often a later Christian translation from the Greek into another language, such as Syriac, Ethiopic or Latin); rabbis kept texts only in Hebrew or Aramaic. Some literary genres to be found in one tradition, such as the philosophical discourses of Philo preserved by Christians or the legal disputes preserved by the rabbis, are completely unknown in the other. In each case, preservation was naturally for the purpose of religious edification in later ages. The discovery in 1947 of the Dead Sea scrolls provides some perspective, since they were preserved by chance rather than selected by the rabbis or by Christians. They reveal that some expressions of Judaism were preserved by neither of the later traditions, and they raise the suspicion that Judaism may have been even more varied in this period than one might have gathered from the material that does survive.

Among the Jewish writings preserved only through Christian use in late antiquity are the histories of Josephus, on which depends our knowledge of the post-biblical political history which had such a profound effect on religious developments. It is sobering to consider what would be known about events between the founding and the destruction of the Second Temple if only the rabbinic texts survived. Rabbinic liturgy preserved a memory of the Maccabees, but in a historical vacuum only marginally filled by obscure references in the *Seder Olam*, a work edited in the second century CE summarizing the history of the world and, in particular, of the Jews. A chronicle of anniversaries of glorious deeds and joyous events in the Second Temple period was preserved in *Megillat Ta'anit* in order to forbid public fasting on these days, but the allusive references to historical events are often impossible to interpret. In the Mishnaic tractate *Avot*, compiled probably at the end of the third century CE, the chain of tradition jumps at alarming speed from the fourth century BCE to the end of the first, from 'Simeon the Just' in the third century BCE via five generations of sages about whom almost nothing is known to Hillel and Shammai in the time of Herod. It is on Josephus that the historian of late Second Temple Judaism must primarily rely, and it is with his account of the Jewish schools that we shall start.[4]

*

We have seen that Josephus wrote about the three philosophies of Pharisees, Sadducees and Essenes in contrast to what he termed an 'intrusive fourth school of philosophy'. He claimed that this Fourth Philosophy had brought disaster on Judaea in the first century CE and had led to the destruction of Jerusalem by the Romans. The contrast on which Josephus insisted explicitly portrayed the other three philosophies as valid expressions of Judaism despite their differences. Those differences, as we shall see, were considerable.

PHARISEES

'Woe to you, scribes and Pharisees, hypocrites! For you lock people out of the kingdom of heaven ... Woe, to you, blind guides ... You blind fools! ... You snakes, you brood of vipers! How can you escape being sentenced to hell?' The words of Jesus to 'the crowds and his disciples', as reported in the Gospel of Matthew, have coloured all later images of the Pharisees in Christian culture. The accusation against Pharisees, who 'sit on Moses' seat', was that they were only acting piety: 'You are like whitewashed tombs, which on the outside look beautiful, but inside they are full of the bones of the dead and of all kinds of filth.' In European languages, 'Pharisaism' has come to mean self-righteous religious formalism, a charge that can be, and has been, turned on co-religionists within Christian society at periodic intervals, not least because an accusation of hypocrisy and lack of the genuine spirit of piety is more or less impossible for any religious person to refute – hence, for instance, Edward Pusey, in the campaign of the Oxford Movement to reinvigorate the Church of England in the nineteenth century, with his assertion that 'of all the Pharisaism of the day, our church-going seems to be the masterpiece.' On the other hand, identification of Pharisaism with the rabbinic tradition by later rabbinic Jews has engendered in the popular Jewish imagination a sanitized version of the Pharisees in which they are envisaged as early rabbinic sages, despite the evidence, as we shall see, that such identification is mistaken.[5]

It is rather odd in any case to start an account of the Pharisees either with the hostile Gospel evidence or with the retrojection of later rabbis, since the source more likely to be able to tell us about Pharisaism in the late Second Temple period was the contemporary Jew Josephus, who asserted explicitly in his autobiography that he wrote about Pharisaism as an insider: after submitting himself as a teenager to 'hard training

1. A tiny silver scroll from around 600 BCE inscribed with a portion of the priestly blessing in Num. 6:24–6. It was found in a burial chamber at Ketef Hinnom in Jerusalem and probably used as an amulet. The writing on it constitutes the oldest surviving text from the Hebrew Bible.

2. Interior of head *tefillin* capsule of the first century CE, probably from Qumran. Made of calf leather, it measures only 13mm × 22mm. The four folded strips in the lower compartments contain passages from the Pentateuch written in minuscule script.

3. An almost complete scroll of the biblical book of Isaiah in 54 columns, discovered in Qumran in 1947. Columns 8–10, reproduced here, contain Isaiah 8:8–11:12. Dated to *c.* 125 BCE, the text in the Isaiah scroll disagrees only in minor details with the traditional text found in the medieval manuscripts which form the basis of modern bibles.

4. Warning inscription in Greek from the balustrade in the Temple between the Court of Gentiles and the Court of Israel, dated to the first century CE and reading 'No foreigner is to enter the enclosure around the sanctuary. Whoever is caught will have himself to blame for the death which follows.'

5. The Temple Mount (Haram al-Sharif) in Jerusalem, viewed from the Mount of Olives. The Dome of the Rock, with its golden roof, was built in the seventh century CE as a mosque on the platform constructed by Herod.

6. The Western Wall of the exterior of the Temple Mount has been a site of Jewish prayer since the destruction of the Second Temple in 70 CE. The huge stones now visible at ground level were the foundations of the original wall.

7. The façade of the Jerusalem Temple depicted on a tetradrachm minted by Jewish rebels in Judaea in 132 CE. The memory of the Temple remained an enormously important element in Judaism long after the Temple itself had been destroyed.

8. Carved stone block from Migdal in Galilee, with the earliest-known image of the Temple *menorah* found in a synagogue. The stone, which is 24 inches long, 20 inches wide and 18 inches high and supported on stone legs, was located in the centre of the building, which dates from the first century CE.

9. Masada, the great fortress and site of the mass suicide of *sicarii* in 74 CE. Herod's palace is at the northern end of the rock in the foreground. The Dead Sea is visible on the left.

10. Part of the book of Ben Sira (Ecclesiasticus) found at Masada. This fragment, containing portions of Ecclesiasticus 39:27–43.30, was copied in the first century BCE, within a century and a half of the book's composition.

11. Qumran by the Dead Sea, showing the settlement site occupied in the first centuries BCE and CE and some of the caves in which the Dead Sea scrolls were found.

12. Columns 16 and 17 of the Great Psalms Scroll, containing parts of Psalms 136, 108 and 145. The scroll, dated to the first half of the first century CE, was found in Cave 11 at Qumran. The divine name, which appears in the middle of the first line of the right column and recurs frequently in the text, is marked out by the use of distinctive palaeo-Hebrew letters.

13. Stone vessels from Jerusalem in the late Second Temple period. Such receptacles were popular in Judaea and Galilee in the first century CE, probably in part because stone, unlike pottery, was regarded as unsusceptible to ritual impurity.

14. (*below*) *Mikveh* at Qumran from the first century CE. Many such baths for ensuring ritual purity have been found on archaeological sites in Roman Palestine.

15. The base of a glass vessel, which was to be affixed near a burial niche as a tomb marker, from fourth-century Rome. The gold-leaf design, fixed between two layers of translucent glass, shows a Torah ark with three layers of scrolls, above a *menorah*.

16. One of many biblical scenes found on the walls of the mid-third century synagogue at Dura-Europos in Syria when the building was uncovered in 1932. Moses is shown leading the children of Israel out of Egypt and across the Red Sea, aided by the strong right arm of God.

and laborious exercises' in order to gain personal experience of Pharisaism, Sadduceanism and Essenism, 'in my nineteenth year I began to govern my life by the rule of the Pharisees.' Nor was Josephus alone in claiming personal acquaintance with Pharisaism, since Paul described himself before he 'gained Christ', as having been, 'as to the law, a Pharisee'. According to the author of Acts of the Apostles, Paul had been educated in Jerusalem 'at the feet of Gamaliel', who is himself described elsewhere by the same author as having been a Pharisee. Paul is described as defending himself before Agrippa against a charge of stirring up agitation among the Jews and profaning the Temple by stating that 'all the Jews know my way of life from my youth, a life spent from the beginning among my own people and in Jerusalem. They have known for a long time, if they are willing to testify, that I have belonged to the strictest sect of our religion and lived as a Pharisee.' The dissension between Sadducees and Pharisees on the Sanhedrin during his trial arose when Paul announced, 'Brothers, I am a Pharisee, a son of Pharisees. I am on trial concerning the hope of resurrection of the dead.'[6]

It is evident from these passages that the name 'Pharisee' could be used with some pride as a self-designation (and therefore clearly lacked the abusive connotations derived in later usage from the Gospel polemic). *Pharisaios* in Greek means nothing, and it must be a transliteration of an Aramaic word derived from the root *prsh*, which means 'separate': Pharisees were those who separated something from something else (quite what is separated left unstated). Early rabbinic texts which refer in Hebrew to *perushim* ('separated ones', in the passive) presumably had the same group in mind, since these *perushim* are described as disputing with *tsedukim* or Sadducees (see below), but the name they used was probably an insulting play on the Pharisees' real name – such value-laden nicknames crop up elsewhere in early rabbinic Judaism, as in reference to the rebel leader Simon bar Kosiba as either Bar Kokhba ('son of a star') or Bar Koziba ('son of a lie'), and the designation *perushim* as 'separatist' was certainly intended to express disapproval in some rabbinic texts.[7]

One can assume, then, that both Josephus and Paul were in a position to tell their readers about the nature of Pharisee doctrines and the Pharisees' role in society, but not necessarily that they therefore did so. It is obvious enough that Paul would hardly present an objective record of what he called his 'earlier life in Judaism', but more notable than any bias is his silence – nothing in his self-description gives a hint of what Pharisaism entailed beyond 'blameless' in respect of 'righteousness under the law'. Josephus, by contrast, had much to say about Pharisees as a group, and rather less about individual Pharisees, in his *Jewish War* and *Jewish Antiquities* as well as in his autobiography. But he was writing for non-Jewish readers with a desire to demonstrate the excellence of this Jewish philosophy, so it may be that he chose to depict Pharisees in idealized Greek garb: he stated explicitly in his *Life* that the Pharisees 'have points of resemblance to what is called Stoicism among the Greeks'. A particular problem arises with his description of the Pharisees acting as a political party in the Hasmonaean period, since his narrative of these political events was derived from the historical writings of the Greek intellectual Nicolaus of Damascus, who, lacking sympathy for or knowledge of Jewish religion, seems to have described Pharisees and Sadducees as if they were political parties on the Greek model.[8]

The characteristic doctrines of Pharisees according to Josephus were their insistence on 'attributing everything to Fate and to God: they hold that to act rightly or otherwise rests, indeed, for the most part with men, but that in each act fate co-operates', and their belief that 'every soul is imperishable, but the soul of the good alone passes into another body, while the souls of the wicked suffer eternal punishment.' Elsewhere, Josephus states that Pharisees believe that the rewards and punishments of souls after death occur 'under the earth', that eternal imprisonment is the lot of evil souls and that good souls receive an easy passage to a new life (perhaps a reference to metempsychosis). Such notions of reincarnation lacked any biblical base and probably reflect Greek influence. They were not the only new ideas about life after death which engendered controversy among Jews in the first century CE (see Chapter 8).

But what distinguishes the Pharisees above all is their presentation of themselves as accurate interpreters of the law. Josephus states explicitly of Simon son of Gamaliel that he was 'of the *hairesis* of the Pharisees, who have the reputation of being exceptional in their accuracy concerning the ancestral laws', and the same self-description is found in Paul's reference to his Pharisee background according to the author of Acts, in his claim to have been 'educated strictly according to our ancestral law, being zealous for God, just as all of you are today'.[9]

Strikingly absent from this list of distinctive Pharisaic doctrines are any of the specific religious issues about which Jesus took the Pharisees to task according to the Gospels. The vehemence of Jesus' polemic in the Gospels seems to reflect competition with Pharisees on the part either of Jesus himself or (more likely) of the Christian communities later in the first century CE in which the Gospels circulated. According to the Gospel of Matthew, Jesus exclaimed, 'Woe to you, scribes and Pharisees, hypocrites! For you clean the outside of the cup and the plate, but inside you are full of greed and self-indulgence,' but Josephus did not attribute any special concern for purity to the Pharisees (although he ascribed such a concern to the Essenes). According to Matthew, Jesus said, 'Woe to you ... for you tithe mint, dill, and cumin, and have neglected the weightier matters of the law'; but Josephus (who wrote a good deal about the giving of tithes) said nothing about this as a specifically Pharisee concern. In the Gospel of Mark, Jesus responds to a complaint by Pharisees that his disciples were plucking heads of grain as they made their way through the cornfields with the bon mot that 'the sabbath was made for humankind, and not humankind for the sabbath', but a special concern for Sabbath observance was treated by Josephus as a characteristic not of Pharisees but of Essenes. The early rabbinic texts did indeed preserve evidence, as we shall see (Chapter 7) of groups in the first century CE which were distinguished by their devotion to scrupulous purity and tithing, and they also preserved evidence of much discussion on Sabbath observance in the same period by the sages whom they saw as their spiritual forebears and teachers. But they did not ascribe any particular fascination with these issues to the Pharisees, except as a topic on which to express their differences with Sadducees (see below).[10]

What mattered to Pharisees was their approach to the Torah as a whole. Characteristic of their approach as it is attacked by Jesus in the Gospels is its scrupulousness. Pharisees insisted that oaths must be correctly formulated if they are to be binding. In the time of Herod a group of Pharisees refused to take an oath of loyalty to the king (presumably out of a concern that they might have to break such an oath, though Josephus notes only that they were 'a group of Jews priding itself on its adherence to ancestral custom and claiming to observe the laws of which the Deity approves'). It is to this self-professed scrupulousness that can be attributed the remarkable influence of the Pharisees, since it gave authority to their endorsement of a deeply conservative interpretation of the Torah.

Josephus referred in a number of passages to this influence. The Pharisees 'are extremely influential among the townsfolk', and 'all prayers and sacred rites of divine worship are performed according to their exposition.' They 'have the masses as ally', in contrast to the Sadducees, who persuade only the wealthy. What he fails to explain is why this intense group of self-appointed legal experts should have carried such weight with the rest of the population of Judaea. We do not know how many Pharisees there were. The best we can provide is a minimum figure of 6,000 in the time of Herod, since that was the number of Pharisees who refused to take the oath of loyalty to the king but were forgiven after the wife of Pheroras, one of Herod's relatives, paid a fine for them – Josephus noted specifically that the women of Herod's court were ruled by the Pharisees. Neither this figure nor any other evidence about the Pharisees suggests they constituted more than a small proportion of the overall population of Judaea. In one passage Josephus stated that the Pharisees were careful to simplify their lifestyle and avoid luxury, though that is not incompatible with the accusation of Jesus in Matthew that Pharisees 'love to have the place of honour at banquets and the best seats in the synagogue and to be greeted with respect in the marketplaces and to have people call them "rabbi" ["my master" or "my teacher"]'. But it is hard to see why such self-promotion as dedicated ascetic experts in the law would bring popularity unless the interpretation of the law was itself welcomed by the wider population.[11]

In fact Josephus, in stating quite explicitly the basis of Pharisaic interpretation of the Torah, provides more than enough reason for their popularity. The Pharisees 'passed on to the people certain regulations received from the fathers which had not been written down in the law of Moses', insisting that it is right to observe 'the things from the traditions of the fathers'. A similar term is used by the Pharisees in the Gospel of Mark when they tackle Jesus for allowing his followers to eat without first washing their hands: 'Why do your disciples not walk according to the tradition of the elders?' The Christian heresiologist Hippolytus, writing in the second century CE, described the Pharisees as accepting 'ancient tradition'. As to how this tradition was handed down through the generations, the sources on the Pharisees are silent apart from stating that they were not written down, but Philo asserted with some passion that traditions of virtuous living are taught to children not through writing or words but by example:

> Another commandment of general value is 'You shall not remove your neighbour's landmarks which your forebears have set up.' Now this law, we may consider, applies not merely to allotments and boundaries of land in order to eliminate covetousness but also to the safeguarding of ancient customs. For customs are unwritten laws, the decisions approved by men of old, not inscribed on monuments nor on leaves of paper which the moth destroys, but on the souls of those who are partners in the same citizenship.

For children ought to inherit from their parents, besides their property, ancestral customs which they were reared in and have lived with even from the cradle, and not despise them because they have been handed down without written record. Praise cannot be duly given to one who obeys the written law, since he acts under the admonition of restraint and the fear of punishment. But he who faithfully observes the unwritten deserves commendation, since the virtue which he displays is freely willed.

Religion is caught, not taught.[12]

The influence of the Pharisees is thus easily explained, for as self-proclaimed religious experts they endorsed to a wider Jewish population the traditional modes of living according to the Torah. An individual Jew who (for instance) saw handwashing before eating bread as an integral part of the tradition because this was what his grandparents had done may not have been able to say whether his behaviour was influenced by a Pharisee confirming the validity of this interpretation of the law, but the Pharisee's endorsement will have been welcomed, and the Pharisee himself popular.[13]

Becoming a Pharisee seems, from Josephus' description of his teenage spiritual journey, to have been a matter of personal choice. There does not seem to have been any Pharisee organization or group to which it was necessary to pledge allegiance, although Josephus noted that 'the Pharisees are affectionate to each other,' while they 'cultivate harmonious relations with the community', and that 'they show respect and deference to their elders.' We have seen Josephus' explicit assertion that the Pharisees had wide influence, but they remained distinctive, not least (according to the standard version of Matthew) because they ensured that they should be so: 'They do all their deeds to be seen by others; for they make their phylacteries broad and their fringes long.' (Phylacteries, or *tefillin*, are the small leather boxes containing biblical texts, worn on the head and arm during prayer.) Since they endorsed the religious status quo, which included extra-biblical practices, their relations to other groups were defined largely by the attitudes of others to the normal interpretation of the Torah. Thus we are told the Pharisees had frequent 'controversies and serious differences' with the Sadducees from the mid-second century BCE to the destruction of the Temple in 70 CE because the Sadducees denied the validity of non-written traditions. The early rabbinic texts consistently describe the relationship between the two groups as antagonistic: 'The Sadducees say "We cry out against you, Pharisees, for you declare clean an unbroken stream of liquid [that is, a liquid poured from a pure vessel into an impure one]." The Pharisees say, "We cry out against you, O you Sadducees, for you declare clean a channel of water that flows from a burial ground."' It is all the more remarkable that Pharisees and Sadducees were willing to share the common religious space of the Temple.[14]

Relations between Pharisaism and other types of Judaism were more complicated. It would presumably be possible to hold to Pharisee doctrines as a Christian, since, despite the vituperation about Pharisees attributed to Jesus in the Gospel of Matthew, he is quoted as instructing the crowd that, because the scribes and the Pharisees sit on Moses' seat, 'therefore do whatever they teach you and follow it.' Jesus' objection, according to the Gospel, was not to Pharisaic teaching but to hypocritical Pharisaic practice, 'for they do not practise what they teach'. It was presumably possible also to be both a Pharisee and a nazirite, provided that you took the nazirite vow very seriously, since, according to the Gospels, Pharisees were adamant on the sanctity of oaths, even if Jesus is portrayed as claiming that this could result in a contravention of one of the Ten Commandments:

> Then he said to them [the Pharisees], 'You have a fine way of rejecting the commandment of God in order to keep your tradition! For Moses said, "Honour your mother and father"; and, "Whoever speaks evil of father or mother must surely die." But you say that if anyone tells father or mother, "Whatever support you might have had from me is Corban" (that is, an offering to God) – then you no longer permit doing anything for a father or mother, thus making void the word of God through your tradition that you have handed on. And you do many things like this.'

It would certainly be possible as a Pharisee to be dedicated to scrupulous observance of the laws of purity and tithing like the *haverim* ('fellows') known from the rabbinic texts (see Chapter 7), although there is no reason to suppose that dedication to such observance indicated that someone was a Pharisee.[15]

That it would also be possible to be both a Pharisee and a rabbinic-type sage is evident from the career of Rabban Gamaliel. According to Acts, Gamaliel was the teacher of St Paul and a leading Pharisee in the Sanhedrin in Jerusalem, 'a teacher of the law, respected by all the people': his influence was sufficient to persuade the council to release the apostles with a flogging on the grounds that the nascent Christian movement was bound to fail in any case if it was not 'of God'. The same Gamaliel is mentioned in the Mishnah as giving rulings as a rabbinic sage for the procedure in drawing up a bill of divorce and for allowing witnesses to the new moon to leave the large courtyard where they assembled to go for a stroll on the Sabbath: 'Beforetime they might not stir thence the whole day; but Rabban Gamaliel the Elder ordained that they might walk within two thousand cubits in any direction.' Gamaliel's influence and reputation within the rabbinic movement of the first century CE can be gauged from the statement in the Mishnah that 'when Rabban Gamaliel the elder died, the glory of the law ceased and purity and abstinence died.' His son, Simon, who was sent in 67 CE by the revolutionary government in Jerusalem to remove Josephus from his command in Galilee, and was described in Josephus' autobiography as 'a native of Jerusalem, of a very illustrious family, and of the *hairesis* of the Pharisees', is mentioned in the Mishnah as making a ruling which dramatically altered the price of doves:

> Once in Jerusalem a pair of doves cost a golden *denar*. Rabbi Simeon b. Gamaliel said: by this Temple! I will not suffer the night to pass by before they cost but a [silver] *denar*. He went into the court and taught: 'If a woman suffered five miscarriages that were not in doubt or five issues that were not in doubt, she need bring but one offering, and she may then eat of the animal-offerings; and she is not bound to offer the other offerings.' And the same day the price of a pair of doves stood at a quarter-*denar* each.[16]

Compatibility was not the same as identity, and the early rabbis treated the *perushim* as a group separate from themselves: 'Rabban Yohanan ben Zakkai said: "Have we nothing else against the *perushim* beyond this? For they also say, 'The bones of an ass are clean or the bones of Yohanan the High Priest are unclean.'" They said to him, "As is our love for them, so is their uncleanness – that no man make spoons of the bones of his father or mother."' The term used by rabbis for their own group – *talmidei hakhamim* ('sages'), on whom see Chapter 7 – was quite different, and it is simply wrong to think of the Pharisees as rabbis, or vice versa. All the more striking is the apparent rabbinization of Pharisaic history by the time of the compilation of the Babylonian Talmud in the sixth century CE. During the reign of the Hasmonaean Alexander Jannaeus, from 103 to 76 BCE, the Pharisees led a popular rebellion to protest at his unworthiness to offer sacrifices as High Priest. The revolt, which broke out in the Temple at the festival of Sukkot with a mass demonstration through pelting him with etrogs, led to six years of civil war and huge losses, including mass executions. Josephus claimed that 800 prisoners were crucified in Jerusalem while

Alexander caroused with his mistresses. Later rabbinic reminiscences about the same episode, involving the sage Simeon b. Shetah, are rather milder: 'King Jannai and his queen were taking a meal together. Now after he had put the Rabbis to death, there was no one to say grace for them.'[17]

Although the rabbis never described themselves as Pharisees, and never asserted that their movement had arisen out of Pharisaism, they had a natural affinity to the Pharisaic interpretation of the Torah because they, like the Pharisees, accepted the validity of ancestral traditions. Many of those traditions were to continue, with rabbinic endorsement, down to the modern day – but because they were traditional, not because they were Pharisaic. Thus when Christian authors in late antiquity referred to the Jewish leaders of their time as Pharisees, reflecting the usage of the Gospels, any rabbis of their acquaintance may have been puzzled but they will not have been upset.[18]

SADDUCEES

Josephus had also been a Sadducee, so he wrote, but by the time he was composing his histories and autobiography he had lost sympathy with them. To an extent remarkable for an author who wished to include this type of Judaism in the category of the legitimate, in contrast to the Fourth Philosophy, he presented the Sadducees in deeply unflattering terms: they are boorish and rude in their behaviour, accomplishing almost nothing, noted for savagery in judgement, with no following among the masses. No Sadducee literature survives to counter this picture – the Gospels and Acts and early rabbis express similar hostility – or indeed to fill in the gaps in Sadducee doctrine. These are less easy to establish from the ancient evidence than might be surmised from the confident statements of scholars, both Jewish and Christian, who have asserted since the nineteenth century that Sadducees were secular, Hellenistic, wealthy aristocrats of priestly origin, with links to the High Priests and the Roman administration and a conservative attitude to the interpretation of the Torah. Almost all this traditional image proves on examination to be either untrue or unprovable, although the real Sadducees that emerge from closer investigation are no less interesting.[19]

The name 'Sadducee' gives little away: the Greek *Saddoukaios* must have an Aramaic origin like *Pharisaios*, and the rabbinic Hebrew equivalent *tsedukim* cannot be assumed to be a literal translation. A connection to the name of David's High Priest Zadok is plausible since we have seen the prestige accorded to this priestly family (and we shall see more when we look at references to the 'Sons of Zadok' in the Dead Sea scrolls), but that does not account for the double delta in the Greek name. Conversely, a reference to *tsaddik*, 'righteous', would make sense for the self-designation of a religious group, but that does not account for the *-ou-* in *Saddoukaios* in its spelling both in Josephus' writings and in the New Testament. Early rabbinic mentions of Boethusians (*baitusin*) probably also referred to the Sadducees, since this group is found, like the Sadducees, in debate with Pharisees and early rabbis in the Herodian period, and the views that the rabbis attribute to the Boethusians are ascribed to the Sadducees elsewhere in the rabbinic corpus. The name is probably connected to Boethus, one of the High Priests appointed by Herod. Group names may, of course, bear little relation in any case to the concerns of the group itself as it developed over centuries. Josephus refers to Sadducees first in the time of John Hyrcanus, so they had a history of at least two centuries, and quite possibly much more.[20]

In the early 60s CE, the Jewish king Agrippa II, great-grandson of Herod the Great, exercised the right devolved on him by the Roman authorities to appoint the High Priest in the Jerusalem Temple by deposing the current incumbent and bestowing the office on a certain Ananus, one of five sons of another Ananus who, most unusually, had all become High Priest in turn. The younger Ananus was, according to Josephus, 'rash in his temper and unusually daring'. He was also, wrote Josephus, notable in that he 'followed the school of the Sadducees', whose 'heartless' approach in judgement had a decisive effect on his brief tenure of this high religious office. In the absence of the Roman governor, Ananus took action against a series of alleged malefactors:

And so he convened the judges of a sanhedrin and brought before them a man named James, the brother of Jesus who was called the Christ, and certain others. He accused them of having transgressed the law and delivered them up to be stoned. Those of the inhabitants of the city who were considered the most fair-minded and who were strict in observance of the law were offended at this. They therefore secretly send to King Agrippa urging him, for Ananus had not even been correct in his first step, to order him to desist from any further such actions. Certain of them even went to meet [the governor] Albinus, who was on his way from Alexandria, and informed him that Ananus had no authority to convene a sanhedrin without his consent. Convinced by these words, Albinus angrily wrote to Ananus threatening to take vengeance upon him. King Agrippa, because of Ananus' action, deposed him from the high priesthood which he had held for three months and replaced him . . .[21]

This Ananus is, remarkably, the only individual Sadducee named as such in the ancient sources, although (as we have seen) Josephus said he had tasted Sadducee doctrine, and the Hasmonaean John Hyrcanus is said to have favoured the Sadducees when he fell out with the Pharisees for refusing to punish with sufficient vigour a certain Eleazar who slandered him by alleging falsely that his mother had been a captive. Ananus was to have an illustrious and tumultuous later career. In October 66 he became one of two commanders-in-chief of the Jewish rebels against Rome, presiding over a coalition which included at least one Pharisee and at least one Essene among his fellow commanders. It was a role that, according to Josephus (who was one such ally), he performed with distinction and diplomatic skill until hounded to death by his political opponents:

A man on every ground revered and of the highest integrity, Ananus, with all the distinction of his birth, his rank and the honours to which he had attained, yet delighted to treat the very humblest as his equals. Unique in his love of liberty and an enthusiast for democracy, he on all occasions put the public welfare above his private interests. To maintain peace was his supreme object.[22]

What characterized Ananus as a Sadducee apart from his attitude to judgement? The Sadducee doctrine of greatest interest to the New Testament authors was their denial of life after death: 'the Sadducees say that there is no resurrection, neither angel, nor spirit.' Josephus noted similarly that they would have none of such notions as 'the persistence of the soul after death, penalties in the underworld, and rewards', although he mentioned nothing about a denial of angels. As we have seen (p. 120), tannaitic texts record Sadducee legal interpretations at odds with Pharisees or rabbinic sages over specific purity issues such as whether impurity can climb up an unbroken stream of liquid. Most important was their view that a priest who burned the red heifer (whose ashes alone could remove corpse contamination) must wait till sunset after immersion before carrying out the ritual: 'they had [first] rendered unclean the priest that should burn the heifer, because of the Sadducees: that they should not be able to say, "It must be performed only by them on whom the sun has set."' Such doctrines might lead to disputes of considerable significance for the validity of Temple worship carried out by priests deemed incorrectly purified from pollution.[23]

Underlying these specific areas of practical disagreement lay a fundamentally distinctive interpretation of the Torah. Sadducees, wrote Josephus, 'hold that only those regulations should be considered valid which were written down, and that those which had been handed down from the tradition of the fathers need not be observed'. Such biblical fundamentalism was revolutionary, overturning the practices of generations, and it had consequences. It led, for instance, to a different interpretation from other Jews of the biblical injunctions in relation to the *omer*, the sheaf of barley offered in the Temple in Jerusalem just after Pesach. It affected also the counting of seven weeks from then to Shavuot, when two loaves of wheat were offered in the Temple to mark the start of the wheat harvest. The biblical text requires this counting (known as 'counting the *omer*') to start on the day after the Sabbath after Pesach, which most Jews took to refer to the second day of Pesach (taking 'Sabbath' to mean the festival itself). But the Sadducees (in rabbinic texts, 'Boethusians') took 'the day after the Sabbath' to refer to the Sunday after Pesach (taking 'Sabbath' literally). The issue was probably in part a desire to avoid violating the Sabbath by harvesting the *omer* sheaf on a Saturday if the first day of Pesach fell on a Friday. But the result was momentous: Sadducees will have found themselves celebrating Shavuot, the fiftieth day of the *omer* counting, on a day different from other Jews.[24]

It is very hard to know how reliance on the biblical text alone could be possible. Like later fundamentalists, such as the Karaites (see Chapter 12), Sadducees must have developed their own systems of interpretation, whatever they claimed about their attitude to tradition.[25] Of greatest difficulty for readers of the Bible might be thought the view of the role of God in human affairs ascribed to the Sadducees by Josephus:

Sadducees ... do away with Fate altogether and place God beyond both the committing and the contemplating of evil: they claim that both the honourable and the despicable reside in the choice of human beings, and that it is according to the judgement of each person to embrace either of these. The survival of the soul, the punishments and rewards in Hades – they do away with them. And whereas Pharisees are mutually affectionate and cultivate concord in relation to the community, Sadducees have a rather harsh disposition even towards one another.[26]

This insistence on human responsibility for everything is reiterated by Josephus elsewhere as a characteristic of the Sadducees – 'all things lie within our own power, so that we ourselves are responsible for our well-being, while we suffer misfortune through our own thoughtlessness.' It is hard to see how this view could be reconciled with any reading of the narrative of divine interventions in the Bible, or how Josephus could include, as he did, Sadducees with such beliefs in the category of respectable Jewish philosophies. The doctrine he ascribed to the Sadducees was not far distant from the belief that he attacked as both Epicurean and profoundly mistaken in his description of the accuracy of the prophecies of Daniel, where he noted that the Epicureans:

cast aside providence from life and do not think that God administers its affairs, and hold that it is not steered by the blessed and incorruptible Being towards perseverance of the whole; but they say that the world is borne along automatically without a driver and without a care. If it was without a protector in this way, then when the world was crushed by an unforeseen misfortune it would have been destroyed and ruined, in just the same way that we also see ships without helmsmen being sunk by winds or chariots being turned around when they have no one holding the reins. Therefore, on the basis of the things predicted by Daniel, it seems to me that they go very much astray from the true opinion who hold the view that God exercises no providence at all over human affairs; for we would not be seeing all things coming about according to his prophecy if the world went along by some automatic process.[27]

Rejection of ancestral tradition might suffice to explain why the Sadducees lacked a popular following: 'This doctrine has come only to few men' and 'there is achieved by them nothing, so to speak.' Crucially, they are unable to enforce their views, for 'whenever they assume some office, though they submit unwillingly and perforce, yet submit they do to the formulas of the Pharisees, since otherwise the masses would not tolerate them.' Josephus may appear here to be a fairly hostile witness, but it is worth recalling that he wished his readers to accept the Sadducaic philosophy as a valid form of Judaism in contrast to the Fourth Philosophy. Josephus does not specify in this passage on which matters the views of the Pharisees dominate, but it is a fair guess that he had in mind the 'prayers and sacrifices' – that is, the ritual of the Jerusalem Temple – on which, as we have seen, Josephus asserted that the teachings of the Pharisees prevailed.[28]

What kind of person became a Sadducee? The philosophy was one it was evidently possible both to adopt and reject at will, since (as we have seen) Josephus claimed to have done just that as a teenager. He described the Sadducees as 'men first in estimation', and as 'persuading only the well-to-do', but this seems to have been a sociological observation rather than a reflection of any entry requirement for the group – the rabbinic references to *tsedukim* give no hint that they came from a different social standing to the *perushim*. It is worth noting that Rabban Gamaliel, whom we have seen as part of a family of leading Pharisees, assumed that Pharisees and Sadducees were neighbours, since he referred to a ruling by his father about managing relations with a Sadducee who once lived in the same alley as his family in Jerusalem. The Pharisee Simon b. Gamaliel was a close political ally of the Sadducee Ananus b. Ananus in 66–7 CE during the first two years of the war against Rome.[29]

As Josephus notes in the passage just quoted, Sadducees do not seem to have shown much group solidarity or even respect for each other. They 'own no observance of any sort apart from the laws; in fact, they reckon it a virtue to dispute with the teachers of the path of wisdom that they pursue' and they are 'even among themselves rude'. These were fierce individualists: each Sadducee relied on his reading of the sacred text alone. It is therefore rather surprising that in the Hasmonaean period they are described by Josephus as a quasi-political group in their assertion of authority over John Hyrcanus, who (as we have seen) is said to have deserted the Pharisees to join the Sadducees. We have seen in the name of the Boethusians a possible connection to one of the High Priests appointed by Herod, but there is nothing in any of our sources to suggest that Sadducees were normally priests (let alone that priests were normally Sadducees). The fact that Ananus was explicitly described by Josephus as a Sadducee suggests that affiliation to the Sadducees could not be taken for granted for High Priests, although the author of Acts referred to a group of Sadducees as hangers-on with the High Priest in Jerusalem when Peter and John were spreading the Gospel in the Temple.[30]

It is probably right to think of the Sadducees as a marginal group in the wider history of late Second Temple Judaism. That their philosophy was incompatible with Pharisaism is obvious in light of the extensive evidence for the disputes between these groups, but their views on the lack of a life after death, and their doctrine that God does not influence the world, will also have made it hard to combine their philosophy with most other branches of Judaism. On the other hand, there is no strong reason to believe that their approach to the Bible could not continue long past the Second Temple period, since nothing in the views ascribed to them required the continued existence of the Temple (and Josephus, writing in the 80s and 90s CE, gave every impression that Sadducaism was still a philosophy which Jews could adopt in his day). Hence the Karaite movement of the end of the first millennium CE was to be seen by the rabbis as a revival of Sadducaism. Indeed, since to be a Sadducee was an individual choice and required joining no community, in principle it would be possible to become a Sadducee now.[31]

ESSENES AND THERAPEUTAE

In marked contrast to the individualist Sadducees were the Essenes, whose communal life was the subject of a number of idealizing portraits by writers of the first century CE who agreed in their enthusiasm for these 'athletes of virtue' and the perfection of their communal regime, despite some stark differences in their descriptions of what the Essene life entailed. For the Platonizing philosopher Philo, the Essenes were devoted to the study of philosophical ethics. For Josephus, intent on telling his gentile readers about the best to be found in Judaism, the Essenes were a pious group dedicated to a regime like that of the Pythagoreans, a religious society founded by the Greek philosopher Pythagoras in Italy in the fifth century BCE and dedicated to purity, self-examination, distinctive taboos and explicit ethical principles. Such propaganda evidently had its success, for the Essenes were the only Jewish group to come to the notice of non-Jewish writers. The elder Pliny, a Roman polymath from Comum in north Italy who compiled an immense amount of heterogeneous information in his *Natural History* in the mid-first century CE, wrote with admiration about the Essenes:

> They are a people unique of its kind and admirable beyond all others in the whole world, without women and renouncing love entirely, without money, and having for company only the palm trees. Owing to the throng of newcomers, this people is daily re-born in equal number; indeed, those whom, wearied by the fluctuations of fortune, life leads to adopt their customs, stream in in great numbers. Thus, unbelievable though this may seem, for thousands of centuries a race has existed which is eternal yet into which no one is born: so fruitful for them is the repentance which others feel for their past lives!

A younger contemporary of Pliny, the Greek orator Dio Chrysostom, who came from Bithynia in modern Turkey, is said by his biographer to have praised the Essenes 'who form an entire and prosperous city near the Dead Sea, in the centre of Palestine, not far from Sodom'. It is probably significant, in view of the state-inspired antipathy towards Jews to be found in much of the Roman empire following the suppression of the Jewish revolt in 70 CE (see Chapter 9), that neither Pliny nor Dio described these Essenes as Jews.[32]

The name of the Essenes is given in variant forms in these texts. Both Philo and Josephus haver between *essaios* and *essen*, and both versions appear also in later writers such as Hegesippus, a Christian author of the second century CE, apparently a converted Jew, who was cited by Eusebius in the fourth century. Philo is puzzled by the name *esseni*, noting that 'although the word is not strictly speaking Greek, I think it may be related to the word *hosiotes* ["holiness"]'. But the falseness of the etymology, which leads him to gloss *essaioi* as *hosioi* ('saints') later in the same treatise, is patent. More plausible would be a Semitic name which could be adopted with pride as a self-description, perhaps related to the Aramaic *asya* ('healer') or *hasayya* ('pious'), but no suggested etymology makes real sense of the *essen* form of the name, which is the most common in Greek and the only form attested in Latin.[33]

What was so special about these religious enthusiasts? All our sources stress their lifestyle more than their specific doctrines – but since these are all descriptions by outsiders, this may not reflect accurately the Essenes' own evaluation of themselves. Philo described an exclusively masculine community engaged in agriculture and crafts when not occupied in communal meals, accustomed to asceticism in clothing (which they hold in common – 'And not only do they have a common table, but common clothes also'). Their wealth was held communally too: 'None of them can endure to possess anything of his own; neither house, slave, field, nor flocks, nor anything which feeds and procures wealth. But they set down everything in a heap in their midst, and enjoy in common the resources of them all. They live together in brotherhoods, having adopted the form of associations and the custom of eating in common. They employ their whole activity for the common good.'

Philo gave a different version elsewhere of the same community of goods and care:

Firstly, no house belongs to any one man; indeed, there is no house which does not belong to them all, for as well as living in communities, their homes are open to members of the sect arriving from elsewhere. Secondly, there is but one purse for them all and a common expenditure. Their clothes and food are also held in common, for they have adopted the practice of eating together. In vain would one search elsewhere for a more effective sharing of the same roof, the same way of life and the same table. This is the reason: whatever they receive as salary for their day's work is not kept to themselves, but it is deposited before them all, in their midst, to be put to the common employment of those who wish to make use of it. As for the sick, they are not neglected on the pretext that they can produce nothing, for, thanks to the common purse, they have whatever is needed to treat them, so there is no fear of great expense on their behalf. The aged, for their part, are surrounded with respect and care: they are like parents whose children lend them a helping hand in their old age with perfect generosity and surround them with a thousand attentions.

The refusal to own slaves was particularly unusual in the ancient world, and even more unusual was the reason. According to Philo, the Essenes 'condemn slave-owners, not only as unjust in that they offend against equality, but still more as ungodly, in that they transgress the law of nature which, having given birth to all men equally and nourished them like a mother, makes of them true brothers, not in name but in reality. But for its own greater enjoyment crafty avarice has dealt mortal blows at this human kinship, putting hostility in the place of affection, and hatred in the place of friendship.' Josephus states more succinctly in the *Antiquities* simply that the Essenes 'consider slavery an injustice'.[34]

The general agreement between Philo's description of the Essenes and that given by Josephus in the *Antiquities* suggests either that Josephus had read Philo or that the two relied on a common source (which also happened to give precisely the same number for the group, 'more than four thousand'). Their emphasis on renunciation of both women and money fits well with the account given by Pliny.[35]

Rather different was the long account of Essene life given by Josephus in the second book of his *Jewish War*. It is a remarkably full ethnographic account, aimed clearly at non-Jewish readers, and a set-piece to which Josephus referred his readers on a number of occasions elsewhere in his work:

The third [school], who certainly are reputed to cultivate seriousness, are called Essenes; although Judeans by ancestry, they are even more mutually affectionate than the others. Whereas these men shun the pleasures as vice, they consider self-control and not succumbing to the passions virtue. And although there is among them a disdain for marriage, adopting the children of outsiders while they are still malleable enough for the lessons they regard them as family and instil in them their principles of character: without doing away with marriage or the succession resulting from it, they nevertheless protect themselves from the wanton ways of women, having been persuaded that none of them preserves her faithfulness to one man. Since [they are] despisers of wealth – their communal stock is astonishing –, one cannot find a person among them who has more in terms of possessions. For by a law, those coming into the school must yield up their funds to the order, with the result that in all [their ranks] neither the humiliation of poverty nor the superiority of wealth is desirable, but the assets of each one have been mixed in together, as if they were brothers, to create one fund for all.

According to this account, Essenes were to be found in many places:

No one city is theirs, but they settle amply in each. And for those school-members who arrive from elsewhere, all that the community has is laid out for them in the same way as if they were their own things, and they go in and stay with those they have never even seen before as if they were the most intimate friends. For this reason they make trips without carrying any baggage at all – though armed on account of the bandits. In each city a steward of the order appointed specially for the visitors is designated quartermaster for clothing and the other amenities . . . They replace neither clothes nor footwear until the old set is ripped all over or worn through with age. Among themselves, they neither shop for nor sell anything; but each one, after giving the things that he has to the one in need, takes in exchange anything useful that the other has.[36]

Josephus went on to describe the peculiar nature of the worship and communal meals of the Essenes:

Before the sun rises, they utter nothing of the mundane things, but only certain ancestral prayers to him, as if begging him to come up. After these things, they are dismissed by the curators to the various crafts that they have each come to know, and after they have worked strenuously until the fifth hour they are again assembled in one area, where they belt on linen covers and wash their bodies in frigid water. After this purification they gather in a private hall, into which none of those who hold different views may enter: now pure themselves, they approach the dining room as if it were some [kind of] sanctuary . . . The priest offers a prayer before the food, and it is forbidden to taste anything before the prayer; when he has had his breakfast he offers another concluding prayer . . . And to those from outside, the silence of those inside appears as a kind of shiver-inducing mystery. The reason for this is their continuous sobriety and the rationing of food and drink among them – to the point of fullness.

Josephus informs his readers in some detail about the initiation procedures of the Essenes:

> To those who are eager for their school, the entry-way is not a direct one, but they prescribe a regimen for the person who remains outside for a year, giving him a little hatchet as well as the aforementioned waist-covering and white clothing. Whenever he should give proof of his self-control during this period, he approaches nearer to the regimen and indeed shares in the purer waters for purification, though he is not yet received into the functions of communal life. For after this demonstration of endurance, the character is tested for two further years, and after he has thus been shown worthy he is reckoned into the group. Before he may touch the communal food, however, he swears dreadful oaths . . .

These oaths included a dedication to communal solidarity, 'that he will neither conceal anything from the school-members nor disclose anything of theirs to others, even if one should apply force to the point of death'. Equally rigorous were the Essene rules for internal discipline and trials, which are 'just and extremely precise: they render judgement after having assembled no fewer than a hundred, and something that has been determined by them is non-negotiable. There is a great reverence among them for – next to God – the name of the law-giver, and if anyone insults him he is punished by death. They make it a point of honour to submit to the elders and to a majority. So if ten were seated together, one person would not speak if the nine were unwilling.' So too the procedures for expulsion: 'Those they have convicted of sufficiently serious errors they expel from the order. And the one who has been reckoned out often perishes by a most pitiable fate. For, constrained by the oaths and customs, he is unable to partake of food from others. Eating grass and in hunger, his body wastes away and perishes. That is why they have actually shown mercy and taken back many in their final gasps, regarding as sufficient for their errors this ordeal . . .'[37]

Interspersed within this account of the rigours of communal discipline, Josephus dropped some surprising statements about Essene theology (and not only the unvarnished assertion we have seen, that 'before the sun rises, they utter . . . ancestral prayers to him'). The Essenes 'are extraordinarily keen about the compositions of the ancients, selecting especially those [oriented] toward the benefit of soul and body. On the basis of these and for the treatment of diseases, roots, apotropaic materials, and the special properties of stones are investigated.' They keep the Sabbath 'more rigorously than any other Jews', for 'not only do they prepare their own food one day before, so that they might not kindle a fire on that day, but they do not even dare to transport a container – or go to relieve themselves'. Their concern for purity included both numerous cold baths (as we have seen) and avoidance of oil – 'they consider olive oil a stain, and should anyone be accidentally smeared with it he scrubs his body.' They took exceptional care to deal with excrement: 'digging a hole of a foot's depth with a trowel – this is what that small hatchet given by them to the neophytes is for – and wrapping their cloak around them completely, so as not to outrage the rays of God, they relieve themselves into it [the hole]. After that, they haul back the excavated earth into the hole ... Even though the secretion of excrement is certainly a natural function, it is customary to wash themselves off after it as if they have become polluted.'[38]

Josephus asserted that expertise 'in the holy books and the different sorts of purification and the sayings of the prophets' led to expertise in foreseeing the future. This is a skill which Josephus elsewhere ascribed to specific Essenes, most notably a certain Judas, 'an Essene who had never misled or lied in his prophecies'. In 104 BCE, when the Hasmonaean king Aristobulus I inherited power from his father, John Hyrcanus, and had his younger brother Antigonus murdered, the Essene Judas 'saw Antigonus passing by the Temple, [and] cried out to his companions and disciples, who were together with him for the purpose of receiving instruction in foretelling the future, that it would be well for him to die as one who had spoken falsely, since Antigonus was still alive, although he had foretold that he would die at the place called Straton's Tower, and now he saw him alive ... But as he was saying this and lamenting, the news came that Antigonus had been killed [in another place given the same name].' Another Essene, by name Manaemus, was said by Josephus successfully to have predicted the rise of Herod to power: 'This man had (once) observed Herod, then still a boy, going to his teacher, and greeted him as "King of the Jews". Thereupon Herod, who thought that the man either did not know who he was, or was teasing him, reminded him that he was only a private citizen. Manaemus, however, gently smiled and slapped him on the backside, saying, "Nevertheless, you will be king and you will rule the realm happily, for you have been found worthy of this by God ..."'[39]

The pride with which Josephus referred in his other works to the excursus on the three philosophies of which the long description of the Essenes constituted much the largest part suggests that this description was his own composition rather than culled from another source. It is therefore remarkable that he appended to his description a note about a second order of Essenes which, 'though agreeing with the others about regimen and customs and legal matters', was said to have 'separated in its opinion about marriage'. Josephus goes on to insist on the reluctance with which these marrying Essenes have sexual relations with their wives. They ensure that they 'do not marry for pleasure but because it is necessary to have children', avoiding intercourse once their wives are pregnant. It is disconcerting to find that the absence of women in Essene communities so emphasized by Philo in his *Hypothetica*, and by Pliny, is here claimed unnecessary for these other Essenes. There was evidently variety within groups as well as within Judaism as a whole.[40]

None of these sources is explicit about Essene methods in interpreting 'the holy books'. Philo states that 'most of the time, and in accordance with an ancient method of inquiry, they philosophise among themselves through symbols', but Philo may have emphasized this allegorical method to suit his own preference for allegory, and the strictness of Essene Sabbath observance we have noted may suggest quite a literal approach to the text of the Bible. In a passage particularly suspect for Hellenizing his subject to make it sound attractive to his Greek readers, Josephus asserted that the Essenes have a firm belief in the immortality of the soul. This belief is not ascribed to the Essenes by other authors, even though Josephus places great emphasis on it as a lure for other Jews to join the Essenes: 'For the good become even better in the hope of a reward after death, whereas the impulses of the bad are impeded by anxiety ... These matters, then, the Essenes theologize with respect to the soul, laying down an irresistible bait for those who have once tasted of their wisdom.' Josephus' claim elsewhere in the *Antiquities* that 'the sect of Essenes' (in contrast to Pharisees or Sadducees) 'declares that Fate is mistress of all things, and that nothing befalls men unless it be in accordance with her decree' is not mentioned by him in the accounts in the *Jewish War* and is presented slightly differently elsewhere in the *Antiquities*, where he writes that 'the Essenes like to teach that in all things one should rely on God'.[41]

It should be evident that the ancient accounts of the Essenes do not entirely agree, and that simply conflating them is misleading. One possibility is that they were a wide movement with different branches, but that hypothesis runs counter to the figure of 'more than four thousand' Essenes given explicitly by both Philo and Josephus. For Pliny, who emphasized the great numbers who thronged to the Essenes, this was a group to be found in one quite specific place to the west of the Dead Sea, at a distance from the 'insalubrious shore'. Dio's 'entire and prosperous city near the Dead Sea' could also refer to a sizeable number, but the regimented communities described by the Jewish sources seem likely to have been a good deal smaller than Pliny or Dio suggested. As to where Essenes were to be found, the evidence is very confused, for Philo suggests in one work that they live 'in a number of towns in Judaea and also in many villages and large groups', despite his insistence in another work that 'fleeing the cities because of the ungodliness customary among town-dwellers, they live in villages'. Josephus not only says that they are found 'not in one town only, but in every town several of them form a colony' but he explains (as we have seen) that travellers are looked after by other Essenes when on their journeys. Evidently Essenes were integrated into wider Judaean society despite the holiness of their lives. Hence, of course, their apparent participation, albeit on the margins, in political life in the Hasmonaean and Herodian periods. Hence too, perhaps, the existence in Jerusalem of a 'gate of the Essenes', which suggests a sizeable colony in the holy city.[42]

Nothing in Josephus' long description in the *Jewish War* of the pious Essenes suggests that they did not worship with sacrifices in the Jerusalem Temple. It is therefore likely that they did so. There are, however, reasons to suppose that their views on how the sacrifices should be carried out gave them a rather a different attitude to the Temple cult than was to be found among other Jews (even though, as we have seen, Pharisees and Sadducees will have had to tolerate their differences in the shared shrine). According to the Greek manuscripts of *Antiquities*, Josephus wrote that the Essenes 'send offerings to the Temple but perform their sacrifices using different customary purifications. For this reason they are barred from entering into the common enclosure, but offer sacrifices among themselves.' Quite how they were thought to conduct themselves in Jerusalem as a result is obscure, although it does suggest some sort of participation in the cult in obedience to the explicit injunction of the Torah. The Latin translation of Josephus, dated to the fifth century CE, asserts that the Essenes offered no sacrifices because of their disagreement about purifications, but this was probably a retrojection from a time when both Jews and Christians had become accustomed to worship without sacrifice. When Philo wrote of the Essenes that to be special worshippers of God they thought it right to make their minds truly holy, rather than to sacrifice living beings, he did not thereby imply that sacrifices were seen by them as undesirable, just that they had a different route to particular piety.[43]

The term used by Philo for the Essenes as special worshippers was *therapeutae* ('healers'), and in a separate work, *On the Contemplative Life*, he wrote about a contemplative sort of Essene, to whom he gave the specific name of 'Therapeutae' or, for female devotees, 'Therapeutridae'. What distinguished these Therapeutae from the Essenes, according to Philo (our only testimony to their existence), was their devotion to the life of contemplation rather than action. They are said to have left their homes in the cities for an idyllic life 'above the Mareotic lake on a somewhat low-lying hill very happily placed both because of its security and the pleasantly tempered air. Their safety is secured by the farm buildings and villages round about and the pleasantness of the air by the continuous breezes which arise both from the lake which debouches into the sea and from the open sea hard by. For the sea breezes are light, the lake breezes close and the two combining together produce a most healthy condition of climate.'

The Mareotic lake in the Egyptian delta lay south-west of the city of Alexandria, separated by a narrow isthmus from the Mediterranean Sea. Here the men and women of the community lived a dedicated life:

> They are accustomed to pray twice every day, at sunrise and sunset. When the sun rises they ask for a 'fine day', the 'fine day' being [that] their minds will be filled with a heavenly light. In the second instance they pray that the soul, being entirely relieved from the disturbance of the senses and being in its own council and court, may follow the way of truth. The entire interval from morning until evening is for them an exercise, for they philosophize by reading the sacred writings and interpreting allegorically the ancestral philosophy. They consider the words of the literal text to be symbols of Nature which has been hidden, and which is revealed in the underlying meaning.

They relied on 'writing drawn up by the men of a former age' and they used the allegorical writings as exemplars. Hence 'they do not confine themselves to contemplation but also compose hymns and psalms to God in all kinds of metres and melodies which they write down with the rhythms necessarily made more solemn.'[44]

There has, unsurprisingly, been much suspicion that these ascetic philosophers were an invention of Philo, the dedicated philosopher who was himself unable to escape as much as he would have liked from the world of action, as we shall see (Chapter 7). The life of the Therapeutae seems too intense to be real. Each individual is said to live in isolation (in contrast to the communal life of the Essenes) except on the Sabbath, when they meet for improving talk. They eat and drink only after sunset, and as little as possible, some accustoming themselves 'as they say the grasshoppers have, to live upon air', and restricting themselves to cheap bread and salt (or hyssop for the dainty) and spring water. They are said to celebrate in particular the festival of Shavuot, to which the number fifty has been assigned as being 'the most sacred of numbers and the most deeply rooted in nature'. On this occasion, after praying with hands outstretched and eyes turned up to heaven, they enjoy a vegetarian, teetotal banquet, each lying in order on couches, men on the right and women on the left, while their leader examines something in the holy writings, 'unfolding the meaning hidden in allegories', and they sing hymns in perfect harmony:

> The choir of the Therapeutae of either sex . . . create an harmonious concert, music in the truest sense . . . Thus they continue till dawn, drunk with this drunkenness in which there is no shame, then not with heavy heads or drowsy eyes but more alert and wakeful than when they came to the banquet, they stand with their faces and whole body turned to the east.[45]

Of the details in Philo's description which encourage confidence that he was describing a real group of Jews, the most telling is his inclusion of women as full members, in contrast to the womenfolk of the married Essenes described by Josephus, whose role was only to procreate, and whose only recorded religious act was to bathe 'wrapped in linen' when their menfolk wore a loincloth. Since Philo was elsewhere strikingly antagonistic to women as 'selfish, excessively jealous, skilful in ensuring the morals of a spouse and in seducing him by endless charms', his particularizing the full role of women among the Therapeutae is unlikely to have come from his imagination, let alone his description of the practicalities in allowing men and women to worship together in chaste fashion:

> This common sanctuary in which they meet every seventh day is a double enclosure, one portion set apart for the use of men, the other for the women. For women too regularly make part of the audience with the same ardour and the same sense of their calling. The wall between the two chambers rises up from the ground to two or three or four cubits built in the form of a breast work, while the space above up to the roof is left open. This

> arrangement serves two purposes; the modesty becoming to the female sex is preserved, while the women sitting within ear-shot can easily follow what is said since there is nothing to obstruct the voice of the speaker.

More probably the product of ascetic invention is Philo's note that most of the women are 'aged virgins, who have kept their chastity not under compulsion, like some of the Greek priestesses, but of their own free will in their ardent yearning for wisdom. Eager to have her [wisdom] for their life mate they have spurned the pleasures of the body and desire no mortal offspring but those immortal children which only the soul that is dear to God can bring to birth unaided because the Father has sown in her spiritual rays, enabling her to behold the verities of wisdom.'[46]

Philo noted that the contemplative life was to be found 'in many parts of the world', and that it is 'abundant in Egypt . . . and most of all in the neighbourhood of Alexandria' (his home city), but whether he meant that communities of Therapeutae were to be found in these places as well as by the Mareotic lake is unclear. From his description it is in any case evident that religious groups like, but not identical to, the Essenes in Judaea were to be found elsewhere in the Jewish world in the first century CE, and we shall have more to say about other such Jews when we look at the communities who produced the Dead Sea scrolls. Communal living was the essence of each of these groups, and we hear little about individual Essenes in Jewish society except as prophets (see above). One notable exception was a certain John the Essene who in October 66 CE was appointed by the revolutionary government in Jerusalem to take command of the defence of areas in the north and west of Judaea. Described by Josephus as a man 'of exceptional strength and intelligence', John will have found himself in alliance with the Sadducee Ananus and the Pharisee Simon son of Gamaliel, as well as with Josephus himself. John died in an assault on Ascalon in early 67, and Josephus notes explicitly the involvement of Essenes in the war and their willingness to face martyrdom:

> The war against the Romans proved their souls in every way: during it, while being twisted and also bent, burned and also broken, and passing through all the torture-chamber instruments, with the aim that they might insult the lawgiver or eat something not customary, they did not put up with suffering either one: not once gratifying those who were tormenting [them], or crying. But smiling in their agonies and making fun of those who were inflicting their tortures, they would cheerfully dismiss their souls, [knowing] that they would get them back again.[47]

Providing for continuity in a celibate community is not easy, as Christian monastic orders have sometimes found. Pliny noted it as admirable that the Essenes had survived so long by recruiting penitents to their number. Philo asserted that only 'men of ripe years already inclining to old age' became Essenes, in direct contradiction to Josephus' statement that the celibate Essenes 'adopted the children of others at a tender age in order to instruct them', and his reference to the 'other order of Essenes who accepted the necessity of marriage specifically for a propagation of the species', since otherwise 'the race would very quickly disappear'. At any rate even someone born as an Essene would be hard put to live an Essene life without a community to join. There was of course no need for the Temple in Jerusalem to continue to function for Jews to choose to adopt the lifestyle of the Essenes. But if they did so in later antiquity they left no trace in the Jewish sources from after 70 CE which were preserved by the rabbis.[48]

THE 'FOURTH PHILOSOPHY'

The origins of the Essenes is shrouded in mystery; Josephus simply stated that in the time of the Hasmonaean High Priest Jonathan in the mid-second century BCE the Essenes were already one of three *haireseis* of the Jews, and if we are to believe Pliny (as we probably should not) the Essenes had existed for 'thousands of centuries' before his time. By contrast, the origin of what Josephus referred to as the 'fourth philosophy' (in comparison to the Pharisees, Sadducees and Essenes, the three standard Jewish doctrines) was pinpointed by him precisely to 6 CE, the year when the Romans imposed a census on Judaea to prepare for the direct taxation on land which accompanied the imposition of rule by a Roman government. It was then that 'a certain Galilean man by the name of Judas incited the locals to rebellion, lambasting them if they were going to put up with paying tribute to the Romans and tolerate masters after God. This man was a sophist of his own peculiar school, which had nothing in common with the others.' In his parallel (and fuller) account of the history of the same year in his *Antiquities*, written some years later, Josephus emphasized specifically the new-fangled nature of this philosophy as the reason to consider it pernicious: 'Here is a lesson that an innovation and reform in ancestral traditions weighs heavily in the scale in leading to the destruction of the congregation of the people.' The troubles which overtook the body politic all came about because of the 'previously unaccustomed nature of this philosophy'.[49]

The novelty in this Fourth Philosophy lay entirely in its teachings about authority. The followers of this doctrine, according to Josephus, 'have a passion for liberty that is almost unconquerable, since they are convinced that God alone is their leader and master'. The immediate impact of the philosophy, since it coincided with the imposition of Roman rule, was to foment anti-Roman feeling, but the implications of the philosophy as described by Josephus went much wider. The objections of these Jews had nothing specifically to do with Roman or foreign rule, for they could have been expected to oppose equally a continuation of rule by a Jew. Archelaus, the son of Herod who in 6 CE was sent by the Romans into exile in southern Gaul, was just as much a 'mortal master' as the Roman emperor. Since Josephus objected so vehemently to this new philosophy, it cannot be identified with the notion of theocracy which, as we have seen (Introduction, p. xx), Josephus described in *Against Apion* as the crowning glory of the Jewish constitution, with the divine will mediated through the High Priest. Nor, since it is stated specifically to be new, can it be identified with the objection to the appointment of a king over Israel, rather than relying on judges to mediate the word of God, which formed an important theme of the biblical books of Samuel (see Chapter 1). Josephus seems to have envisaged a form of anarchic Judaism in which each Jew claimed a direct line to God, perhaps through individual reading of the biblical texts (although he says nothing about the relationship of this group to scripture).[50]

No name is given by Josephus to this philosophy in any of the three short passages in which he describes it, and even within these brief descriptions he contradicts himself. According to the *Jewish War*, and one of the passages in the *Antiquities*, the leader was a Galilean named Judas, but in the other passage in the *Antiquities* Judas is said to have come from Gamala on the Golan (east of the Sea of Galilee) and to have been in alliance with a certain Saddok, a Pharisee. The explicit assertion in one passage that this group had nothing in common with the other three philosophies is directly contradicted by the statement in another passage that 'this school agrees in all other respects with the opinions of the Pharisees', except with regard to their passion for liberty. There is perhaps also something incongruous in the notion that Judas 'set himself as a leader' of the fourth of the philosophies, despite his opposition to mortal rule of any kind.[51]

It seems that this type of Judaism was something very different from the Pharisees, Sadducees and Essenes, and not just in respect of Josephus' disapproval. The lack of a name is telling: this was not a group with a clear identity or programme (perhaps inevitably, in view of its anarchic core). We have seen (Chapter 5) that, despite his generic claim that this school of Judaism led to the 'folly' which followed the outbreak of revolt in 66 CE (sixty years after its origin), Josephus did not attribute this philosophy directly to any individual Jew in all his detailed history of the events which ended with rebellion and the destruction of the Temple. It is perhaps better to think of this *hairesis* more as a tendency to political anarchy on religious grounds, provoked by heavy-handed Roman government, than as a really distinct type of Judaism. In that case, agreement with Pharisees will have been the product of acceptance of ancestral tradition (apart from the 'love of liberty'), and Josephus' exaggerated claim in the *Jewish War* that Judas and his followers shared nothing at all with other movements within Judaism marks an attempt to highlight the exceptional nature of the principle of opposition to Rome which arose from this radical devotion to God alone as master.[52]

Any attempt to categorize anti-Roman feelings within Jewish society as marginal in this way was hard to sustain after the Jews of Judaea had just fought and lost a major war against Rome, and in practice Josephus referred to other Jewish groups between 6 and 70 CE who were ranged against Rome. Of these, one group, the *sicarii*, were explicitly linked by Josephus to the Fourth Philosophy when he described the defence of the fortress of Masada by the Dead Sea against Roman forces in 74 CE by a band of *sicarii* who had occupied it in 66 CE:

> This fortress was called Masada; and the *sicarii* who occupied it had at their head a man of influence named Eleazar. He was a descendant of the Judas who, as we have previously stated, induced multitudes of Jews to refuse to enrol themselves, when Quirinius was sent as censor to Judaea. For in those days the *sicarii* came together against those who consented to submit to Rome and in every way treated them as enemies, plundering their property, rounding up their cattle, and setting fire to their habitations.

This passage implies that the *sicarii* followed the Fourth Philosophy, and, in describing the fortitude under torture by the Romans of those *sicarii* who escaped to Egypt after the fall of Judaea, Josephus stressed their refusal, in line with the teachings of Judas the Galilean, to utter the crucial words which would have acknowledged the lordship of Caesar. But elsewhere in his history Josephus discussed the *sicarii* as a group known not for their ideology but for their tactics. The *sicarii* were notorious for urban terrorism, creeping up on victims in crowds and stabbing them with their short daggers (*sicae*) before melting away into the mêlée. Josephus asserted specifically that the group first appeared in the early 50s CE in the time of the procurator Felix.

Since Josephus failed to call the followers of the Fourth Philosophy '*sicarii*' when he described the philosophy in either of his historical works, and since he disliked heartily both the *sicarii* and the Fourth Philosophy, there would be no reason for him not to give this name to this form of illegitimate Judaism if that was a name they gave themselves. It is probable that the link between the *sicarii* and Judas of Galilee was essentially just a family one. Eleazar b. Yair, who led the defenders of Masada, was only one of a number of Judas' descendants to cause trouble for the Roman authorities in the first century CE. How many of these descendants subscribed to the Fourth Philosophy is unknown.[53]

ZEALOTS

Among the other types of Judaism described in Josephus' histories was another group opposed to Rome, separate from the *sicarii* and with a clearer group identity than the adherents of the Fourth Philosophy. The Zealots, we are told by Josephus in disgust, were a group of brigands who took on this name in the spring of 68 CE when they invaded the Temple in Jerusalem: 'for so they called themselves, as though they were zealots in the cause of virtue and not vice in its basest and most extravagant form'. These Zealots were to play a major role first in the ensuing civil war between the factions in Jerusalem over the next two years, and then in the final defence of the city against the assault of Roman forces. In 68 CE they took control of the Temple from the government led by the Sadducee Ananus b. Ananus, whom they accused, with some justification, of insufficient vigour in prosecuting the war. Opposition by Ananus led to open warfare around the Temple site:

> The people too now clamoured for him to lead them against the foe whom
> he urged them to attack, each man fully ready to brave the first danger. But
> while Ananus was enlisting and marshalling efficient recruits, the Zealots
> hearing of the projected attack ... were furious, and dashed out of the
> Temple, in regiments and smaller units, and spared none who fell in their

way. Ananus promptly collected his citizen force, which, though superior
in numbers, in arms and through lack of training was no match for the
Zealots. Ardour, however, supplied either party's deficiencies ... Thus,
swayed by their passions, they met in conflict ... Any Zealot who was
struck climbed up into the Temple, staining with his blood the sacred
pavement, and it might be said that no blood but theirs defiled the
sanctuary.

Within weeks the strife led to the dramatic murder of Ananus, and from
then to the spring of 70 the Zealots were de facto in charge of the inner
Temple and the performance of the sacrifices. Only when the Roman
forces under Titus began their siege of the city just before Passover in 70
CE did the Zealots agree to cooperate with the other Jewish forces
against the common enemy.[54]

Josephus, who produced our only account of the actions of the Zealots during these years, was hardly an objective observer. By 68 CE he
had himself surrendered to the Romans, in response, he said, to a divine
instruction. The only Jewish rebels to whom he was inclined to accord
any legitimacy were the faction led by his old ally Ananus. It is thus
hard to know how much credence to give to his description of the
excesses of the Zealots at the height of the revolt:

With an insatiable lust for loot, they ransacked the houses of the wealthy;
the murder of men and the violation of women were their sport; they
caroused on their spoils, with blood to wash them down, and from mere
satiety unscrupulously indulged in effeminate practices, plaiting their hair
and attiring themselves in women's apparel, drenching themselves with
perfumes and painting their eyelids to enhance their beauty. And not only
did they imitate the dress, but also the passions of women, devising in their
excess of lasciviousness unlawful pleasures and wallowing as in a brothel
in the city, which they polluted from end to end with their foul deeds. Yet,
while they wore women's faces, their hands were murderous, and
approaching with mincing steps they would suddenly become warriors
and whipping out their swords from under their dyed mantles transfix
whomever they met.

It is unlikely that Josephus would provide his readers with a clear notion
of the religious ideology of Jews whom he despised so intensely, and as
a result their religious views have to be deduced essentially from their
adherents and their actions rather than Josephus' evaluation.[55]

Josephus described the Zealots as brigands, but their leaders appear to have been priests. Most notable was Eleazar b. Simon (or Gion), a priest who two years earlier, in October 66, had been cold-shouldered by the national assembly in the appointment of generals notwithstanding his control of a great part of the public treasure, because 'they observed his tyrannical nature and that the zealots with him conducted themselves like a bodyguard'. Josephus ascribed Simon's eventual rise to power to a combination of his trickery and his control of these financial resources, but the priestly origin of the Zealot leaders and their passion for protecting the Temple suggests a more religious motivation. Their trust in divine intervention emerged at the very start of their control of the Temple in their decision, noted above in Chapter 5, to appoint a new High Priest by lot. Josephus, deploring their decision, stated that the Zealots asserted 'that in old days the high priesthood had been determined by lot; but in reality their action was the abrogation of established practice and a trick to make themselves supreme by getting these appointments into their own hands'. In all this vituperation, it is worth noting that the Zealots are said to have claimed ancient custom as their justification. By using the lot, of course, choice was transferred from humans to God.[56]

The name 'Zealot' seems to have carried particular resonance in the late Second Temple period, and the same terminology is used of others who seem to have had no connection with the party of Eleazar b. Simon which played so central a role in the life of Jerusalem in the last years before its destruction. One of the followers of Jesus was called 'Simon the Zealot' according to the Gospel of Luke. There was much fascination with the story of the prototype of Zealots, Pinchas ('Phineas' in Greek), the grandson of Aaron the priest. According to Numbers, Pinchas killed a certain Zimri with a single spearthrust when he found him in the act of sexual intercourse with a Midianite woman, because he (Pinchas) was 'zealous for his God'. Ben Sira called Pinchas 'third in renown' after Moses and Aaron for being zealous in this way. The author of I Maccabees depicted Mattathias (father of Judah Maccabee) as showing zeal 'as Phineas had done', and later rabbinic texts expand on the excellence of his enthusiasm for righteousness. Such intense devotion, lifting the pious out of ordinary obedience to a higher plane, could be claimed by Jews of all kinds without suggesting membership of any philosophical school or political party. According to the Gospel of John, Jesus acted out of zeal in clearing the Temple. Paul identified himself as a former zealot: 'I advanced in Judaism beyond many among my people of the same age, for I was far more zealous for the traditions of my ancestors.' The Mishnah lays down that 'if a man stole a sacred vessel, zealots [*kanaim*, the Hebrew equivalent of the Greek *zelotai*] may fall upon him.'[57]

Extreme religious enthusiasm could clearly take many forms, including licensed violence on behalf of perceived morality, and evidently in 68–70 CE it was harnessed by one group of Jews to channel opposition to the Roman state. Nothing connects these Zealots to the followers of the Fourth Philosophy preached in 6 CE by Judas and Saddok, apart from Josephus' ascription to both groups of blame for the disaster that had overtaken Jerusalem. Josephus was generous in apportioning blame to more or less all the actors in the drama he described, apart from himself. But there might seem rather stronger grounds for connecting the Zealots to the *sicarii*. We are told that in 66 CE *sicarii* led by a certain Menachem, 'son of Judas called Galilean, that most clever sophist who once upon a time in the days of Quirinius had upbraided the Jews for recognising the Romans as masters after God', seized weapons from Herod's armoury in Masada. He then returned 'like a veritable king' to Jerusalem, becoming 'an insufferable tyrant', and went in state to the Temple 'decked in royal dress and attended by armed zealots', before being crushed and killed by the priestly aristocrats who had begun the revolt against Rome and had no intention of losing control to this intruder and his gang. But Josephus recorded in this same passage that among Menachem's *sicarii* was Eleazar b. Yair, 'a relation of Menachem, and subsequently despot of Masada', and in his account of the eventual siege of Masada, Josephus went out of his way to distinguish Zealots as a group separate from the *sicarii*.[58]

Little thus suggests that the radical anarchic philosophy preached by Judas in 66 CE ever became a movement within Judaism in its own right. We have seen in Chapter 5 that, despite claiming that Judas' preaching had been responsible for the destruction of Jerusalem, in all his descriptions of specific anti-Roman uprisings between 6 CE and the outbreak of revolt in 66 CE Josephus ascribed none to Judas' followers. The author of Acts put into the mouth of the Pharisee Gamaliel the explicit statement that 'Judas the Galilean rose up at the time of the census and got people to follow him; he also perished, and all who followed him were scattered.'[59]

The hostile account of Josephus does not disguise the common concern of all these anti-Roman groups for worship in the Temple, misguided though they may have been in their attempts to preserve it. In the case of the Zealots their willingness to allow other Jews to worship in the Temple at Passover in 70 CE led to the end of their independence as a political group in control of the inner Temple while Jerusalem was under siege:

> When the day of unleavened bread came round ... Eleazar and his men partly opened the gates and admitted citizens desiring to worship within the building. But John [of Gischala, leader of a rival faction], making the festival a cloak for his treacherous designs, armed with concealed weapons the less conspicuous of his followers, most of whom were unpurified, and by his earnest endeavours got them stealthily passed into the temple to take prior possession of it. Once within, they cast off their garments and were suddenly revealed as armed men ... Being now in possession of the inner court of the temple and all the stores which it contained, they could bid defiance to Simon.

The Fourth Philosophy and the Zealots left no direct legacy in later forms of Judaism. The rabbinic sages as recorded in the Babylonian Talmud were to recall the Temple's destruction as a product of the 'causeless hatred' of the Jews of that time. The rabbis preserved a deep hatred of Rome as the wicked kingdom that had brought the Temple worship to an end, but they did not advocate rebellion. Nor did they claim that Jews should seek political freedom on religious grounds.[60]

THE YAHAD IN THE DEAD SEA SCROLLS

The discovery and eventual publication since 1947 of some 900 ancient texts which had been hidden in caves near Qumran by the Dead Sea have brought to light types of Judaism in the late Second Temple period to which neither Josephus nor any other source preserved by the late Jewish and Christian traditions referred. Historians have tried over the past sixty years or so to identify the authors of some of these texts with previously known groups, including all four of the philosophies described by Josephus, but, although the forms of Judaism revealed in these texts exhibit some characteristics in common with each of these groups (unsurprisingly in view of their origin in the same traditions of post-biblical Judaism), they do not appear identical to any of them. Josephus was composing military and political history rather than ethnography or theology, and there are no reasons to suppose that he intended to include all current forms of Judaism when he described the four philosophies of Judaism. Since, on the contrary, he wrote elsewhere about John the Baptist, Jesus and Philo, he must have been well aware that other types of Judaism existed in his day. Hence, rather than interpret the Dead Sea scrolls through the lens of what Josephus tells us about other groups (most often, the Essenes), the nature of the community (or communities) of these distinctive sectarians must be examined in its own right.[61]

Many of the scrolls contain biblical texts, hymns, wisdom writings and other material which could have been used by any branch of Judaism in this period. The scrolls include fragments of every book of the Hebrew Bible apart from Esther, with multiple copies particularly of the Pentateuch and Psalms, texts of Bible interpretation (like the Aramaic Genesis Apocryphon, which smooths out the stories of Genesis) and liturgical works like the Songs of the Sabbath Sacrifice, depicting angelic worship, which could have been uplifting for any Jew engaged in devout prayer:

> For the Master. Song of the holocaust of the seventh Sabbath on the six-teenth of the month. Praise the most high God, O you high among all the gods of knowledge. Let the holy ones of the 'gods' sanctify the King of glory, who sanctifies by his holiness all his holy ones. O Princes of the praises of all the 'gods', praise the God of majestic praises, for in the splendour of praises is the glory of His kingship. In it are (contained) the praises of all the 'gods' together with the splendour of all [His] king[ship]. Exalt His exaltation on high, O 'gods', above the gods on high, and His glorious divinity above all the highest heights. For He [is the God of gods], of all the Princes on high, and the King of king[s] of all the eternal councils . . .[62]

But alongside remnants of a more general Judaism, the caves also housed copies of rules which presuppose a sectarian community or communities, and of distinctive forms of Bible interpretation which claim that the real meaning of some parts of scripture is related to the history of this community. How the rest of the scrolls relate to the sect-arian texts has proved difficult to establish. The scrolls were found in eleven natural caves scattered in the hills above the settlement at Qum-ran. Most are parchment, but some are made from papyrus, and one enigmatic text, which lists hiding places of treasure, is written (for rea-sons unknown) on copper.

Scientific investigation has confirmed the dating of these objects to approximately 2,000 years ago, and painstaking scholarship has now pieced together and deciphered almost all the fragments. But major problems of interpretation remain in relating the scrolls to each other and to the settlement site at Qumran, which was excavated primarily in the 1950s but continues to reveal new information. Were the scrolls written in Qumran or brought from elsewhere, perhaps from Jerusalem? Should the finds in some of the caves, like the Greek documents found in Cave 7, be treated as separate caches, or should all the scrolls be understood as the 'library' of a single group? Would the archaeology of the Qumran site suggest its use by pious Jews even if its occupation was unrelated to the find of the scrolls near by? Amid all this uncertainty, one fact seems indisputable. At some time in the late first century CE these scrolls were deposited in jars in the caves, for safekeeping, by pious Jews. Something went wrong, since these Jews never came back, probably because of intervention by Roman forces, and the scrolls were undisturbed for nearly 1,900 years.[63]

The clearest indication of the existence of a distinctive separate community as the origins of at least some of the scrolls can be found in the wording of part of the Community Rule:

> The Master shall teach the saints to live(?) {according to the book} of the Community [Rul]e, that they may seek God with a whole heart and soul, and do what is good and right before Him as He commanded by the hand of Moses and all His servants the Prophets ... He shall admit into the Covenant of Grace all those who have freely devoted themselves to the observance of God's precepts, that they may be joined to the counsel of God and may live perfectly before Him in accordance with all that has been revealed concerning their appointed times, and that they may love all the sons of light, each according to his lot in God's design, and hate all the sons of darkness, each according to his guilt in God's vengeance ... All those who embrace the Community Rule shall enter into the Covenant before God to obey all His commandments so that they may not abandon Him during the dominion of Belial because of fear, terror or affliction. On entering the Covenant, the Priests and Levites shall bless the God of salvation and all His faithfulness, and all those entering the Covenant shall say after them, 'Amen, Amen!'

The Community Rule, which seems to have been intended for the Master of the community, provides instruction on entry into the Covenant of the Community, statutes for the community's Council and 'rules of conduct for the Master in these times with respect to his loving and hating'. The text is known from some twelve manuscripts, of which one (from Cave 1) preserves eleven columns, and the others (from Caves 4 and 5) are fragmentary. The number of the manuscripts, and the differences between them not least with regard to the leadership of the 'Sons of Zadok' (see below), suggest strongly that the Rule was put into practice (although that in turn raises the question why copies of the Rule were preserved once they had become out of date).[64]

The Community in the Rule is called the 'Yahad', which seems to be a semi-formal self-designation, although elsewhere the initiates are referred to as the *Rabbim* ('the many'). The group is also called by other Hebrew terms for a congregation, such as *edah* or *kahal*. It seems likely that they saw no need for a special term, since they saw themselves as the true Israel, divided into priests and laity:

> The Council of the Community shall be established in truth. It shall be an Everlasting Plantation, a House of Holiness for Israel, an Assembly of Supreme Holiness for Aaron. They shall be witnesses to the truth at the Judgement, and shall be the elect of Goodwill who shall atone for the Land and pay to the wicked their reward. It shall be that tried wall, that precious corner-stone, whose foundations shall neither rock nor sway in their place. It shall be a Most Holy Dwelling for Aaron, with everlasting knowledge of the Covenant of Justice, and shall offer up sweet fragrance. It shall be a House of Perfection and Truth in Israel that they may establish a Covenant according to the everlasting precepts.[65]

The sectarian life as envisaged in the Community Rule took a form which was to become common among Christian monks much later in antiquity. It was centred on communal meals eaten in purity in much the same fashion as the Essenes and Therapeutae. Priestly authority was emphasized, and study of the law: 'And the Congregation shall watch in community for a third of every night of the year, to read the Book and to study the Law and to bless together. Each man shall sit in his place: the Priests shall sit first, and the elders second, and all the rest of the people according to their rank. And thus shall they be questioned concerning the Law, and concerning any counsel or matter coming before the Congregation, each man bringing his knowledge to the Council of the Community.' Rules within this community were to be enforced with great precision:

> If one of them has lied deliberately in matters of property, he shall be excluded from the pure Meal of the Congregation for one year and shall do penance with respect to one quarter of his food. Whoever has answered

to his companion with obstinacy, or has addressed him impatiently, going so far as to take no account of the dignity of his fellow by disobeying the order of a brother inscribed before him, he has taken the law into his own hand; therefore he shall do penance for one year [and shall be excluded].[66]

It is not possible fully to reconcile this lifestyle with the rather different communal life attested in the so-called Damascus Document, of which fragments were found in three of the Qumran caves. This document was already known before 1947 from two incomplete medieval copies of the tenth and twelfth centuries discovered in 1896–7 in the *genizah* (store-house) of a medieval synagogue in Cairo (on which more in Chapter 9). The rule book, which gets its name from its frequent references to 'the New Covenant in the Land of Damascus', lays down instructions for members of a community evidently involved in the wider life of Israel, including (for instance) rules 'concerning the oath of a woman', laws to do with property, treatment of manservants and maidservants, sexual relations between a man and a woman, and relations with gentiles: 'No man shall stretch out his hand to shed the blood of a Gentile for the sake of riches and gain. Nor shall he carry off anything of theirs, lest they blaspheme, unless so advised by the company of Israel. No man shall sell clean beasts or birds to the Gentiles lest they offer them in sacrifice. He shall refuse, with all his power, to sell them anything from his granary or wine-press, and he shall not sell them his manservant or maidservant inasmuch as they have been brought by him into the Covenant of Abraham.' It is taken for granted that members of the community might engage in commerce albeit under controlled conditions: 'No man shall form any association for buying and selling without informing the Guardian of the camp.'[67]

The fragments of the Damascus Document found in Cave 4 at Qumran include rules about relations with women, so there is no reason to suspect these passages in the Cairo copies to be medieval additions to the original documents: 'Whoever has approached his wife not according to the rules, fornicating, he shall leave and shall not return again. (If he has murmured) against the Fathers he shall leave and shall not return. (But if he has murmured) against the Mothers, he shall do penance for ten days.' As we shall see below, some relationship between the group which lived by this Rule and those who lived according to the Community Rule is suggested by their allusions to distinctive characters in a shared sectarian history. The precise nature of their relationship is beyond recall, but twelve fragments of a manuscript which included material from both the Sabbath law in the Damascus Document and the penal code in the Community Rule suggest strongly that the two groups were connected in some way.[68]

Both groups envisaged authority as lying in the hands of priests. So, for instance, a priest would recite the blessing for each group of them gathered for a communal meal, and 'where the ten are, there shall never be lacking a priest learned in the Book of Meditation, they shall all be ruled by him' (although, according to the Damascus Document, one of the Levites could replace a priest if he is more experienced). For both groups, an official described as the 'Guardian' was in charge of admitting neophytes, and of both instructing and examining them: 'He shall love them as a father loves his children, and shall carry them in all their distress like a shepherd his sheep.' In both groups, initiation into the sect was marked by an oath for entry into the covenant, and there were yearly meetings to decide whether the behaviour of each individual required that his position within the community be altered. It has been suggested that both communities celebrated this annual covenant ceremony on Shavuot, since we have seen that the Therapeutae gave special prominence to this day. The book of Jubilees, of which a number of fragments have been found at Qumran, considers Shavuot the most important of the festivals because renewing the covenant between God and Israel was a central part of its observance, and asserts that it had fulfilled this function since the time of Noah, even before Moses.[69]

Among the other scrolls found at Qumran which are likely to have been composed by or for one or other of the sectarian communities are the War Scroll, which describes the symbolic struggle between the Sons of Light and the Sons of Darkness, in which the sectarians imagine themselves fighting a series of stylized battles until God will destroy Belial and his kingdom, and probably the Temple Scroll. The Temple Scroll is a very long text dealing with biblical law mostly relating to the Temple, sacrifices and festivals, but also law courts, purity regulations, vows and many other topics. It presents the harmonization of different biblical texts as if it was a new revelation spoken by God in the first person: 'Justice and justice alone shall you pursue that you may live and come to inherit the land that I give you to inhabit for all days.' Frequent reference to Belial in the moving Thanksgiving Hymns, which are similar to the biblical Psalms, suggest a sectarian origin. But for many other scrolls it is impossible to ascertain whether they are sectarian or not.[70]

Of the distinctive doctrines of these sectarians, most significant were their notions of a new covenant and of the role in their history of a

Teacher of Righteousness. Most evidence about the career of this Teacher is found in the remarkable interpretations of the prophecies of Habakkuk found in a single, but well-preserved, scroll from Cave 1. The interpretation, which in each case follows a citation from the biblical text, assumes knowledge of the story, so that historians now have to piece together a narrative of the origins of the Yahad from a series of allusions, such as the following on the phrase in the text of Habakkuk 'Behold the nations and see, marvel and be astonished; for I accomplish a deed in your days, but you will not believe it when told':

> [Interpreted, this concerns] those who were unfaithful together with the Liar, in that they [did] not [listen to the word received by] the Teacher of Righteousness from the mouth of God. And it concerns the unfaithful of the New [Covenant] in that they have not believed in the Covenant of God [and have profaned] His holy Name. And likewise, this saying is to be interpreted [as concerning those who] will be unfaithful at the end of days. They, the men of violence and the breakers of the Covenant, will not believe when they hear all that [is to happen to] the final generation from the Priest [in whose heart] God set [understanding] that he might interpret all the words of His servants the Prophets, through whom He foretold all that would happen to His people and [His land].

In another passage, the biblical phrase 'O traitors, why do you stare and stay silent when the wicked swallows up one more righteous than he?' is interpreted as 'This concerns the House of Absalom and the members of its council who were silent at the time of the chastisement of the Teacher of Righteousness and gave him no help against the Liar who flouted the Law in the midst of their whole [congregation].' At some point, it seems, a Teacher had proclaimed new teachings to these sectarians, through which they believed themselves elect so long as they remained faithful, and all others damned:

> None of the men who enter the New Covenant in the land of Damascus, and who again betray it and depart from the fountain of living waters, shall be reckoned with the Council of the people or inscribed in its Book from the day of the gathering in of the Teacher of the Community until the coming of the Messiah out of Aaron and Israel. And thus shall it be for every man who enters the congregation of men of perfect holiness but faints in performing the duties of the upright. He is a man who has melted in the furnace; when his deeds are revealed he shall be expelled from the congregation as though his lot had never fallen among the disciples of

God. The men of knowledge shall rebuke him in accordance with his sin
against the time when he shall stand again before the Assembly of the men
of perfect holiness. But when his deeds are revealed, according to the interpretation of the Law in which the men of perfect holiness walk, let no man
defer to him with regard to money or work, for all the Holy Ones of the
Most High have cursed him.[71]

The group evidently harboured deep grudges against those who had
betrayed the community in the past:

And thus shall it be for all among the first and the last who reject (the precepts), who set idols upon their hearts and walk in the stubbornness of their
hearts; they shall have no share in the house of the Law. They shall be
judged in the same manner as their companions were judged who deserted
to the Scoffer. For they have spoken wrongly against the precepts of righteousness, and have despised the Covenant and the Pact – the New
Covenant – which they made in the land of Damascus. Neither they nor
their kin shall have any part in the house of the Law. From the day of the
gathering in of the Teacher of the Community until the end of all the men
of war who deserted to the Liar there shall pass about forty years. And during that age the wrath of God shall be kindled against Israel; as He said,
'There shall be no king, no prince, no judge, no man to rebuke with justice.'
But those who turn from the sin of Jacob, who keep the Covenant of God,
shall then speak each man to his fellow, to justify each man his brother, that
their step may take the way of God. And God will heed their words.

The texts do not name either the Scoffer or the Liar. Presumably their
identity was obvious to the sectarians themselves.[72]

The contents of the new covenant embraced by the sect can only be
deduced from the concerns evidenced in the sectarian scrolls. It had
little in common with the new covenant adopted by early Christians
some generations later. Presumably a large part consisted in instructions
for the ascetic lifestyle, ritual ablutions and sacred meals, which set
these Jews apart from others. Numerous wisdom writings confirm an
emphasis on both ethics and knowledge: 'You are a poor man. Do not
say: Since I am poor, I will not seek knowledge. Shoulder every discipline, and ... refine your heart, and your thoughts with a multitude of
understanding.' Running through a great deal of sectarian literature is a
concern for the end of days, in which (as envisaged in the War Scroll)
the members of the Yahad were expected to take a leading role and the
Sons of Light could expect eternal life: 'God has given them to His

chosen ones as an everlasting possession, and has caused them to inherit the lot of the Holy Ones. He has joined their assembly to the Sons of Heaven to be a Council of the Community, a foundation of the Building of Holiness, an eternal Plantation throughout all ages to come.' Numerous references suggest a belief that there would be more than one Messiah, both the Messiah of David and the Messiah of Aaron.[73]

What distinguished the group more immediately was their use of a calendar different from that used in the Temple. The survival among the scrolls (albeit in fragmentary form) of numerous calendars suggests that the use by the sectarians of a solar calendar required much dedication. It is probably significant that one such calendar was copied on the same scroll as the sectarian tractate *Miksat Ma'asei haTorah* ('Some Observances of the Law'), a text generally known nowadays as 4QMMT, which pontificated on disputed issues of law, not least with regard to purity and the Jerusalem Temple. It is not however obvious how this different calendrical system will have affected the relationship of these sectarians to the Temple. It has often been suggested that members of the Yahad turned their backs on the Temple and constructed for themselves a new Judaism in which the life and prayers and sacred meals of the community took the place of the sacrifices performed by the priests, and that this separation was reinforced by the sect's distinctive calendar. But we have seen that Pharisees and Sadducees shared the Temple despite calendric disagreements, and no text found among the scrolls asserts any link between the calendar and the decision of the sectarians to separate themselves from other Jews, even though the Habakkuk commentary does indeed refer to a time in the past when the (or a) community, or its leader (the Teacher of Righteousness), broke with a wicked priest, and to a time in the future when a corrupt priest or priests will suffer for their sins:

> This saying concerns the Wicked Priest, inasmuch as he shall be paid the reward which he himself tendered to the Poor. For 'Lebanon' is the Council of the Community; and the 'beasts' are the simple of Judah who keep the Law. As he himself plotted the destruction of the Poor, so will God condemn him to destruction. And as for that which He said, 'Because of the blood of the city and the violence done to the land': interpreted, 'the city' is Jerusalem where the Wicked Priest committed abominable deeds and defiled the Temple of God. 'The violence done to the land': these are the cities of Judah where he robbed the Poor of their possessions.[74]

The community imagined itself as in some sense constituting a sacrifice offered to God in atonement for sin, and plenty of sectarian texts hint at dissatisfaction with the way that the Temple is run. The Temple Scroll envisages a building which differed markedly from the Temple as remodelled in the time of Herod, suggesting a belief that the current Temple had not been built according to the divine archetype. But there is no direct evidence that the sectarians cut themselves off from the actual Temple in their own day, which was, as we have seen, the main locus for Jewish worship as mandated in the biblical texts which the sectarians held dear in the same way as other Jews.

In later centuries Jews and Christians were to learn to worship without a Temple, but, in a world in which sacrifices and offerings were normal in all religious systems, it would be extraordinary for these sectarians to turn their back on the cult in Jerusalem. And in fact the scrolls are full of references to its centrality. Prescriptions for sacrifices and references to the Temple are scattered widely through the biblical texts from Qumran, and there are also to be found no fewer than sixty-three references to Jerusalem in the non-biblical texts (and few to other cities). There are detailed rules in the Temple Scroll for the Temple cult, building and furnishings, frequent references to priests and to Aaron, and calendars for the operation of the priestly courses in the sanctuary. The advice on how to run the Temple found in the sectarian document MMT, which survives in a number of fragmentary copies, reflected dispute among Jews about how this was to be done but does not read like the polemic of a group which had cut itself off from the Temple altogether.[75]

It had of course proved perfectly possible for Jews in earlier generations to criticize reliance on sacrifices by those who did not keep the rest of God's commandments, without thereby advocating abstention from the sacrificial cult. Sectarian attitudes to the Temple may well have varied over time, without requiring withdrawal from the worship of God according to the explicit injunction of the Torah. The Damascus Document itself prescribed rules for bringing offerings: 'No man shall send to the altar any burnt-offering, or cereal offering, or incense, or wood, by the hand of one smitten with any uncleanness, permitting him thus to defile the altar. For it is written, "The sacrifice of the wicked is an abomination, but the prayer of the just is an agreeable offering."' Quite what participation in the Temple cult might entail for individual sectarians is more difficult to say. One text suggests an objection to paying annually the Temple tax of half a shekel on the basis of an ingenious interpretation of a biblical ruling. For sectarian priests, a decision not to serve in the Temple would presumably be a big issue, but for non-priests actual attendance did not in any case have to be frequent, as we have seen.[76]

The number of sectarians in the Yahad at any one time is unknown, and attempts to make an estimate, on the basis of the size of the Qumran settlement and the number of skeletons in the adjoining cemetery, are too hypothetical to be of any value, since it is not known how many (if any) of the sect lived at Qumran and it is not certain how the cemetery, which included female and child skeletons as well as adult males, related to the settlement. The Rules themselves divide the community into tens, fifties, hundreds and thousands, but these numbers may be fanciful. Whatever the size of the community or communities, it is clear that these Jews cut themselves off in some psychological way from the rest of Israel: 'We have separated from the mass of the people.' Unlike the *haireseis* described by Josephus, the members of the Yahad seem to have viewed their interpretation of the Torah as the only valid one, leaving in ambiguity the status of those Jews – the majority – who did not share their views. Sometimes, as in the War Scroll, the sectarian writings categorize Jews who sin as Sons of Darkness, condemned along with gentiles to damnation after defeat by the Sons of Light.

The writings of the Yahad, especially some of the biblical commentaries, contain many references to the events which had formed the background to their separation, but they are couched often in obscure and allusive terms, such as 'the Wicked Priest', 'the Men of Lies', 'the Scoffers', 'the furious young Lion'. It is thus easier to recover the constructed memory of their past shared by the sectarians than what really happened. On the other hand, there are enough clear references to known political figures ('King Jonathan', 'Aemilius' and a few others) to render plausible a history of the Yahad which began during the Maccabean crisis of the 160s BCE but which first took shape (perhaps under the leadership of the Teacher of Righteousness) after a quarrel with the Hasmonaean High Priest Jonathan (the 'Wicked Priest'?) in the mid-second century BCE. It is possible that the issue which divided the sectarians from Jonathan was his presumption in assuming the high priesthood despite not being of the Zadokite line, which would explain the prominence of the 'sons of Zadok' in the Damascus Document and in the text of the Community Rule from Cave 1, and why the sect by contrast emphasized their own Zadokite credentials. If so, Zadokite influence may have died away, since the 'sons of Zadok' are conspicuously absent from the parallel passages of the Community Rule in the copies found in Cave 4.[77]

The Community recalled with venom the hostility of these past opponents: 'This concerns the Wicked Priest who pursued the Teacher of Righteousness to the house of his exile that he might confuse him with his venomous fury. And at the time appointed for rest, for the Day of Atonement, he appeared before them to confuse them, and to cause them to stumble on the Day of Fasting, their Sabbath of repose.' Exactly what happened on this (evidently memorable) occasion is now obscure. It seems likely that the Wicked Priest was taking advantage of the difference between his own calendar and that of the sect, although whether the calendar itself was the cause of disagreement is not stated. In any case, the Yahad looked forward to the destruction of its enemies:

> 'By cutting off many peoples you have forfeited your own soul': interpreted this concerns the condemned House whose judgement God will pronounce in the midst of many peoples. He will bring him hence for judgement and will declare him guilty in the midst of them, and will chastise him with fire of brimstone.

In fact, their future hopes, as expressed in the War Scroll, encompassed eschatological violence which would affect many more than their own immediate enemies.[78]

For themselves, the sectarians expected a re-enactment of their communal meals in the presence of the Priestly Messiah and the Messiah of Israel, when 'the Messiah of Israel shall extend his hand over the bread, and all the congregation of the Community shall utter a blessing, each man of his dignity', according to 'the Rule for all the congregation of Israel in the last days, when they shall join [the Community to wa]lk according to the law of the sons of Zadok the priests and of the men of their Covenant who have turned aside from the way of the people, the men of his Council who keep his covenant in the midst of iniquity'.[79]

The Dead Sea sectarians expressed high hopes for the lives they made for themselves separate from the rest of Israel:

> They shall separate from the congregation of the men of injustice and shall unite, with respect to the Law and possessions, under the authority of the sons of Zadok, the Priests who keep the Covenant, and of the multitude of the men of the Community who hold fast to the Covenant. Every decision concerning doctrine, property, and justice shall be determined by them. They shall practise truth and humility in common, and justice and uprightness and charity and modesty in all their ways. No man shall walk in the stubbornness of his heart so that he strays after his heart and eyes and evil inclination, but he shall circumcise in the Community the foreskin of evil inclination and of stiffness of neck that they may lay a foundation of truth for Israel, for the Community of the everlasting Covenant.[80]

Unfortunately for them, the legacy of these hopes was negligible. The settlement site at Qumran was destroyed violently by Roman forces at some time between 68 and 73 CE and those who hid the scrolls were unable to retrieve them from their hiding places. It would have been possible to recreate the Yahad elsewhere if Jews had been so inclined, but if any such groups survived they left no trace in the rabbinic and early Christian sources or the archaeological evidence which tell us about Judaism in the ensuing centuries, apart from the intriguing medieval copies of the Damascus Document which were found in Cairo in the tenth and twelfth centuries CE.

It is clear that by the first century CE numerous Jewish groups with strikingly different understandings of their shared religious tradition coexisted in Judaean society. For most Jews, the Jerusalem Temple provided a unifying force, and there can be no doubt that Pharisees and Sadducees shared in the Temple services both as priests and as lay people despite their different ideas about fundamental tenets of theology and about practical issues of how the Temple should be run. This was a society in which Jews of dramatically different theological complexions argued and bickered, but ultimately tolerated each other. However, the members of the sectarian Yahad who treated other Jews with disdain as 'sinners of Israel' must have lived more or less separately from other Jews, and, as we shall see, at least one variety of Judaism which arose in the first century CE was in due course to leave the fold of Judaism altogether.

7

The Limits of Variety

There are some who, regarding laws in their literal sense in the light of symbols of matters belonging to the intellect, are overpunctilious about the latter, while treating the former with easy-going neglect. Such men I for my part should blame . . . It is quite true that the Seventh Day is meant to teach the power of the Unoriginate and the non-action of created beings. But let us not for this reason abrogate the laws laid down for its observance . . . It is true that receiving circumcision does indeed portray the excision of pleasures and all passions, and the putting away of impious conceit . . . but let us not on this account repeal the law laid down for circumcising. Why, we shall be ignoring the sanctity of the Temple and a thousand other things, if we are going to pay heed to nothing except what is shown us by the inner meaning of things.

With this powerful assault on Jews who interpreted the Torah only allegorically and saw no value in keeping the laws in their literal sense, the Jewish philosopher Philo, whose own allegoricizing form of Judaism will be discussed later in this chapter, revealed that there was no limit to variety in understanding the teachings of Moses. Allegorical readings of the Bible could impose any meaning whatever on the text both then and now. This brief mention by Philo in his commentary on Abraham's wanderings as described in chapter 12 of Genesis constitutes the only reference to these extreme allegorists known from antiquity, and there is no evidence that a purely symbolic interpretation of the injunctions of the Torah was widespread. But it is clear that Philo knew about at least two such Jews (since he wrote about them in the plural). Philo believed that the failure of these Jews to keep the law literally as well as symbolically was reprehensible, but in attacking them he revealed that their interpretation was possible.[1]

Evidently Josephus' typology of Judaism as divided into just three kosher philosophies provided only a partial picture of Judaism in his day and many other varieties flourished alongside the Pharisees, Sadduces and Essenes. Josephus might have responded that none of these other varieties was of much importance because none of them attracted large numbers of adherents in his time. If so, he was to be proved wrong in the case of two branches of first-century Judaism which were to have a huge impact on the religious developments of the next 2,000 years. The rabbinic sages constituted only a small fringe movement in Judaea in the first century CE but they laid the foundations of mainstream Judaism down to the present. The Christian movement inspired by Jesus, which began as just one more variety of Judaism, started by the end of the first century CE to evolve outside Judaism altogether.

SAGES

'Sage' (*hakham*) or 'pupil of a sage' (*talmid hakham*) was the name by which members of the rabbinic movement in the first century CE referred to themselves. What distinguished them from other Jews was their confident belief that they were part of a select group of learned scholars who had preserved an unbroken chain of transmission of oral teachings. These teachings had been passed on from teacher to pupil since the time of Moses up to the present, as expressed succinctly in tractate *Avot* in the Mishnah:

> Moses received the Law from Sinai and committed it to Joshua, and Joshua to the elders, and the elders to the Prophets; and the Prophets committed it to the men of the Great Synagogue. They said three things: Be deliberate in judgement, raise up many disciples, and make a fence around the Law. Simeon the Just was of the remnants of the Great Synagogue. Antigonus of Soko received [the Law] from Simeon the Just ... Jose b. Joezer of Zeredah and Jose b. Johanan of Jerusalem received [the Law] from them ... Joshua b. Perahyah and Nittai the Arbelite received [the Law] from them. Judah b. Tabbai and Simeon b. Shetah received [the Law] from them ... Hillel and Shammai received [the Law] from them. Hillel said: Be of the disciples of Aaron, loving peace and pursuing peace, loving mankind and bringing them nigh to the Law ... Rabban Gamaliel said: Provide thyself with a teacher.

Whether there had really been such an oral tradition dating back many centuries before the first century CE cannot now be known – the Mishnah, dating to the early third century CE, provides the earliest testimony to the notion, and neither the Bible nor Josephus preserves any record of such traditions. But reality matters less than perceptions. It is clear that rabbinic sages believed in the existence of this oral tradition, and that they also believed that through this tradition they received authority ultimately from Moses himself.[2]

The history of this early rabbinic movement is known only from sources preserved by later rabbis, for whom the teachers of the first century BCE and the first century CE, such as Hillel, Shammai and Gamaliel, were revered predecessors. Legends about these sages in due course accumulated much as they did for the leading personalities in the biblical narratives. For a sound understanding of the movement before the destruction of the Jerusalem Temple in 70 CE, it is therefore wise to discount the testimony of any rabbinic sources later than the traditions enshrined in the Mishnah and other tannaitic sources in the third century CE.

We learn from these tannaitic sources that study groups of sages were well established at least a century before the destruction of the Temple in 70 CE. Mishnaic tradition goes back, as we have seen, to Moses himself, but provides hardly any more information about the early links in the chain than wisdom sayings, such as the maxim attributed to Nittai the Arbelite some time in the Hasmonaean period: 'Keep yourself far from an evil neighbour and consort not with the wicked and lose not belief in retribution.' Traditions from the end of the first century BCE attributed to Hillel and Shammai and to their followers are less vague, but even then the 200 years between Hillel and the compilation of the Mishnah reduced knowledge of these early sages to very schematic form. The Torah scholars were recalled as a series of pairs in each generation, with traditions on how each of the pair ruled on issues of the day, such as whether hands should be laid on an offering in the Temple before it is slaughtered, although the records of their disputes were not always very illuminating:

Jose b. Joezer says: '[On a festival-day a man] may not lay [his hands on the offering before it is slaughtered].' Joseph b. Johanan says, 'He may.' Joshua b. Perahyah says, 'He may not.' Nittai the Arbelite says, 'He may.' Judah b. Tabbai says, 'He may not.' Simeon b. Shetah says, 'He may.' Shemaiah says, 'He may.' Abtalion says, 'He may not.' Hillel and Menahem did not differ, but Menahem went forth and Shammai entered in. Shammai says, 'He may not lay on his hands.' Hillel says, 'He may.'[3]

As this passage illustrates, the dispute form was characteristic of this type of Judaism. The role of the pupil in the *beth midrash* ('house of study') was to puzzle out the intricacies of the Torah by applying logic to the teachings he has received – a tricky task if they simply disagreed with each other, as here. The effect was a more dynamic tradition than the simple reliance on authority to be found in the Qumran sects, if a less anarchic system than the scriptural fundamentalism of the Sadducees. But above all it was a religious society in which study and debate, so long as the subject was elucidation of the holy law of Moses, were valued for their own sake. No pupil would learn from the passage just cited whether to lay hands on an offering before slaughter, but they would certainly learn that this was an issue about which debate was reasonable.

Of the series of disputes among the sages while the Temple still stood, the best preserved are those of the Houses of Hillel and Shammai, which could take in almost any aspect of life. This included, for instance, how to say a blessing after a meal:

> These are the things wherein the House of Shammai and the House of Hillel differ in what concerns a meal. The House of Shammai say: '[On a Sabbath or a Festival-day] they say the Benediction first over the day and then over the wine.' And the House of Hillel say, 'They say the Benediction first over the wine and then over the day.' The House of Shammai say, 'They wash the hands and then mix the cup.' And the House of Hillel say, 'They mix the cup and then wash the hands.' The House of Shammai say, 'A man wipes his hands with a napkin and lays it on the table.' And the House of Hillel say, '[He lays it] on the cushion.' The House of Shammai say, 'They sweep up the room and then wash the hands.' And the House of Hillel say, 'They wash the hands and then sweep up the room . . .' If a man ate and forgot to say the Benediction, the House of Shammai say, 'He must return to his place and say it.' And the House of Hillel say, 'He may say it in the place where he remembers [his error].' Until what time may he say the Benediction? Until the food in his bowels is digested.

Why these schools of interpretation were described as 'Houses' is unknown – the term evidently means 'school', but it is not a usage to be found elsewhere either in Second Temple times or in the following period. That the numerous divergences between them failed to prevent the Houses cooperating in precisely the areas of greatest concern to them should be taken as evidence of respect for disagreement based on honest attempts to expound the law:

> Notwithstanding that these declare ineligible whom the others declare eligible, yet [the men of] the House of Shammai did not refrain from marrying

women from [the families of] the House of Hillel, nor [the men of] the House of Hillel from marrying women from [the families of] the House of Shammai; and despite all the disputes about what is clean and unclean, wherein these declare clean what the others declare unclean, neither scrupled to use aught that pertained to the others in matters concerned with cleanness.[4]

Each House could, and evidently did, try to change the mind of the others, occasionally with success – the Mishnah records a series of issues on which 'the House of Hillel changed their opinion and taught according to the opinion of the House of Shammai'. The differing opinions of the Houses somehow coexisted with the notion that the opinion of the majority is to be followed, so that the real intention of the Torah can be decided by a vote of scholars. It was quite possible for that vote to agree with neither Shammai nor Hillel, as in determining the time from which women may be deemed unclean from a menstrual flow:

Shammai says, 'For all women it is enough for them [that they be deemed unclean only from] their time [of suffering a flow].' Hillel says, '[A woman is deemed to have been unclean] from [the previous] examination to [the present] examination, even if [the interval is of] many days.' And the Sages say, 'It is not according to the opinion of either.'

In much later centuries rabbis were to be troubled by the apparent tolerance by these sages of views with which they disagreed, culminating in a tradition in the Palestinian Talmud, which dates to the fourth century CE or later, that eventually a divine utterance (*bat kol*) fixed that 'practice always follows the school of Hillel, and everyone who transgresses the rulings of the school of Hillel merits death.' But this clarity contrasts all the more strikingly with the apparent acceptance of difference by the Houses themselves.[5]

The disputes between the Houses mentioned in the tannaitic sources relate mainly to religious dues, the keeping of the Sabbath and festivals, marriage laws and laws of purity. But the Houses may have had other interests too – we do not know whether the anonymous editor of the Mishnah in *c.* 200 CE – traditionally reckoned to be R. Judah haNasi – could, or wished to, record everything taught by sages from two centuries earlier. What made the sages different was not their focus on any specific issues, since these were all topics discussed widely by Jews in the last years of the Second Temple, but their devotion to discussion and debate about the minutiae of such issues in fraternities in which the study of the Torah was valued for its own sake. The process of learning by the pupils was through question and answer and logical reasoning by the teacher. The duty of the student was to remember faithfully what he had heard, and powers of memory were much prized.[6]

The Mishnah preserves the names (or nicknames, such as Ben Bag-Bag or Ben He-He) of fifty or so sages whose teaching can be dated between c. 200 BCE and 70 CE, but about many of these sages no more is known than a maxim; for instance, to Ben He-He is attributed the saying that 'according to the suffering, so is the reward.' Since, as we have seen in the disputes of the Houses, authority does not appear to have rested automatically with one teacher rather than another, there seems to have been no interest in the tannaitic period in the biographies of sages (in marked contrast to early Christian focus on the life of Jesus), and very little can be said with any certainty about their lives. Scrupulous ascription of a teaching to a particular teacher, which in turn can be contrasted with the anonymity of the legal rulings in the Community Rule and the Damascus Document used by the Qumran Yahad, seems to have fulfilled a more general function in explaining the process of transmission from teacher to pupil on which the sages based their tradition as a whole.[7]

Within the community of sages, the greeting 'rabbi' ('my lord' or 'my master') was widely found as a term of respect. By the end of the first century CE it was being used also as a title attached to the names of individual sages. The title 'Rabban' ('our teacher') is rare in the tannaitic sources and is employed primarily to designate either Rabban Gamaliel or his descendants, evidently as a mark of honour. We have seen in the last chapter that Gamaliel was a leading Pharisee, and his special title demonstrates that it was possible to be at the forefront of the scholarly community of sages while also being a Pharisee. But the differences between the sages and the Pharisees are clear. The Pharisees, it will be recalled, interpreted the Torah in light of ancestral custom as observed in practice. The sages were equally conservative, accepting such notions as the Sabbath limit for travel, or the sharing of a courtyard space on a Sabbath through the legal fiction of temporary shared ownership, but they did so on the basis of spoken traditions handed down from teacher to pupil.[8]

We do not know how many sages were to be found in the century before 70 CE but everything points to a small elite group. They seem to have been concentrated in Jerusalem, or at least Judaea. Stories about their discussions suggest quite a small group, and it is significant that they apparently did not come to the attention either of Josephus or of the authors of the New Testament. Their influence over the wider community may have been greater before 70 CE if, as the tannaitic rabbis asserted in the early third century CE, they taught at times in the Temple, in the 'Chamber of Hewn Stone', from which, according to the Mishnah, 'Torah goes forth to all Israel'. But we should not imagine, as rabbis many centuries later were to do, that the sages before 70 CE controlled the religious institutions of Jerusalem, from the Temple service to the Sanhedrin. They were just one group of religious enthusiasts among many. What made them special was their dedication to working out precisely how they, and other religious enthusiasts, should live according to the law of Moses.[9]

NAZIRITES AND *HAVERIM*

Among the enthusiasts whose supererogatory piety the sages discussed were nazirites, to whose special vow a whole section of the Mishnah was dedicated. The nature of the nazirite vow, involving abstention from wine, strong drink and grapes, while letting the hair grow and (except for lifelong nazirites) avoiding contact with corpse impurity even for the burial of a close relative, is laid out clearly in the Bible in the book of Numbers (see above, p. 58). Other biblical texts describe the vow in action, particularly in stories about Samuel and Samson, who were both dedicated to lifelong naziritism from before birth. Most nazirite vows were taken for a brief period by an individual seeking to consecrate himself or herself to God for a month or so for a special reason, such as thanksgiving for benefits received or in hope of divine aid when in trouble.[10]

The nazirite vow was evidently common both in the diaspora and in Judaea in the late Second Temple period. The Septuagint translation of the relevant chapter of Numbers denotes the nazirite vow as the 'great vow'. The apostle Paul is probably described in Acts as taking a nazirite vow, and the Jewish princess Berenice, when in 66 CE she intervened to try to avert rebellion against Rome, was in Jerusalem to complete her days as a nazirite. This vow was perhaps particularly attractive for supererogatory piety for rich and powerful women like Berenice who wished to demonstrate their devotion. A story is told also of Queen Helena of Adiabene as a nazirite. According to the Mishnah:

It once happened that the son of Queen Helena went to war and she said, 'If my son returns in safety from the war I will be a nazirite for seven years,' and her son returned from the war, and she was a nazirite for seven years. At the end of the seven years she came up to the Land [of Israel], and the House of Hillel taught her that she must be a nazirite for yet another seven years; and at the end of this seven years she contracted uncleanness. Thus she continued a nazirite for twenty-one years.[11]

About the religiosity of *haverim*, or 'fellows', we learn only from the tannaitic texts. A definition of what it is to be a 'fellow' was inserted, without explanation, into a section of the Tosefta which concerns the treatment of agricultural products about which there is some doubt whether they have been properly tithed: 'He who takes upon himself four things, they accept him as a *haver* – not to give heave-offering and [not to give] tithes to [a priest who is] an ordinary person [*am haarets* – that is, not a *haver*], and not to prepare foodstuffs requiring conditions of cleanness for . . . an ordinary person, and to eat unconsecrated food in a state of cleanness.'[12]

Both this passage and others in the Tosefta assume that some Jews dedicated themselves to particular care with regard to purity and tithing. Not only did they insist that any tithes they gave to a priest must be consumed by him in the required state of purity after ritual ablutions, but they took upon themselves the non-biblical requirement to ensure that everything they themselves ate – including unconsecrated food – should be eaten in a state of purity. We have already seen that many Jews, such as Essenes, Therapeutae and the Yahad, took purity very seriously in the last century before the Temple was destroyed in 70 CE, but the *haverim* were apparently distinctive in treating their purity and tithing undertakings as the main focus of their groups and in living their dedicated lives within the wider Jewish community despite the constant threat this posed to their piety.

According to the biblical injunctions, the heave-offerings and tithes taken so seriously by these Jews were dues given to the priests and to the poor. We have seen the significance of such offerings to the income of the priests and hence the upkeep of the Temple worship. But the concerns of the *haverim* seem to have been more with the operation of giving than with the effects of the gift. The biblical rules were complex and confusing. The Bible does not prescribe the proper proportion of agricultural produce to be set aside for a heave-offering, but the Mishnah records that 'The proper measure of heave-offering, if a man is liberal, is one-fortieth part (the House of Shammai say: one-thirtieth); if he is liberal in medium degree, one-fiftieth part; if he is mean, one-sixtieth part.' Biblical law referred to giving tithes only of corn, wine and oil, but some Jews evidently widened the application greatly: 'A general rule have they laid down about tithes: whatsoever is used for food and so kept watch over and grows from the soil is liable to tithes.'

The definition of produce which required tithing left plenty of room for uncertainty about when a crop had ripened sufficiently to become a food: 'When do fruits become liable to tithes? Figs – after their earliest ripening; grapes and wild grapes – after their stones become visible; sumach and mulberries – after they become red (and all red fruits [are liable] after they become red); pomegranates – after they soften; dates – after they begin to swell; peaches – after they begin to show red veins; walnuts – after their cells take shape.' Scrupulous observance of such rules could be a matter for self-dedication by itself, without necessarily a particular concern for purity laws:

> 'He who undertakes to be trustworthy – tithes what he eats and what he sells and what he purchases. And he does not accept the hospitality of an ordinary person,' the words of R. Meir. And the sages say, 'One who accepts the hospitality of an ordinary person is trustworthy.' Said to them R. Meir, '[If] he is not trustworthy concerning himself, should he be trustworthy concerning me?' They said to him, 'Householders have never refrained from eating with one another, nonetheless the produce in their own homes [that is, the homes of those who have undertaken to be trustworthy] is properly tithed.'[13]

Dedication to life as a *haver* seems to have involved some kind of formal statement before a *havurah* ('fellowship'). This was not apparently a vow like the dedication vow of a nazirite. A dispute is recorded in the name of rabbinic sages from the mid-second century CE over the possibility of a *haver* who has reneged on his obligation to be accepted back into the fellowship: '"And [as for] all those who reneged [after having been accepted as *haverim*], they never accept them again," the words of R. Meir. R. Judah says, "If they reneged in public, they accept them [again]; in secret, they do not accept them." R. Simeon and R. Joshua b. Qorha say, "In either case they accept them, as it is written, 'Return O faithless children.'"' Part of the explanation for such leniency may be the apparent incompatibility of some occupations with the undertaking of a *haver*: 'At first they would say, "A *haver* who becomes a tax-collector – they expel him from his *havurah*." They changed their minds to say, "As long as he is a tax-collector, he is not reliable. [If] he withdrew from the office of tax-collector, behold, this one is [again] reliable." [14]

Much of the evidence for stipulations about the life of these *haverim* is preserved for us, as we have seen, in the names of rabbinic sages from some time after the destruction of the Temple in 70 CE. But traditions of a dispute between the Houses of Hillel and Shammai on the length of probation for a prospective *haver* – the period of thirty days proposed by the House of Hillel contrasts markedly with the much longer probation of would-be Essenes – suggest that fellowships of this kind were already a phenomenon of the first century CE or even earlier.

Self-dedication by an individual could cause much tension within a family. The Tosefta worries about what should happen if the son of a *haver* went to the home of his maternal grandfather, an ordinary Jew. The compiler of the Tosefta rules leniently that 'his father does not worry lest he [the grandfather] feed him foodstuffs requiring conditions of cleanness' – unless he knows that this will happen, in which case it is forbidden. Trading in foodstuffs with ordinary Jews, or lending or giving food, created all sorts of moral dilemmas, but the rabbinic texts which report such dilemmas presuppose that such contacts take place and simply have to be overcome:

> An ordinary person who served in a store [owned by a *haver*] – even though the *haver* comes and goes – behold, this is permissible, and he [the *haver*] does not worry lest he [the ordinary person] have substituted [untithed produce of his own for the *haver*'s tithed merchandise]. If he [the husband] was trustworthy [in the matter of tithing] and his wife was not trustworthy, they purchase [produce] from him but do not accept his hospitality.

Such *haverim* are never described in any source as acting as a group, as did Pharisees, Sadducees or Essenes, and even nazirites. They did not, so far as is known, engage other Jews in disputes over purity and tithing. This was a purely personal dedication. It had implications for the social reality of their religious lives only because of practicalities: scrupulous concern for the preparation of food was possible only within households and groups of the similarly dedicated. [15]

What was the relationship of such *haverim* to the rabbinic sages who recorded all these rules about how *haverim* should conduct themselves? The act of recording does not in itself imply anything about identity: as we have seen, the editors of the Mishnah and Tosefta each devoted a tractate to correct fulfilment of the nazirite vow without suggesting that they thought that sages like themselves should become nazirites. One passage in the Tosefta may suggest an increasing assumption among rabbinic sages in the aftermath of the destruction of the Temple in the late first century CE that scrupulous observance of purity and tithing laws could be taken for granted of a rabbinic sage, even if in earlier times he had been required to make a formal, public declaration of his desire to join a fellowship:

> He who comes to take upon himself [the obligations of being a *haver*] – even [if he is] a disciple of the sages – must take upon himself [that is, must make a formal, public declaration]. But a sage who sits in session [on the court] does not have to take upon himself [formally and publicly], for he has already taken upon himself from the moment that he entered the session [in the court]. Abba Saul says, 'Even a disciple of the sages does not have to take upon himself [formally and publicly] and furthermore others take upon themselves before him.'[16]

The focus of the tannaitic texts on the religious issues faced by adult rabbinic males masks the significant opening for personal religiosity that being a *haver* provided for both women and slaves:

> The daughter of a *haver* who married an ordinary person, the wife of a *haver* who [subsequently] married an ordinary person, the servant of a *haver* who was sold to an ordinary person – behold, these remain in their presumed status [as a *haver*] until they are suspected. R. Simeon b. Eleazar says, 'They must take upon themselves [the obligations of being a *haver*] afresh.' . . . It happened that a certain woman was married to a *haver* and she fastened tefillin straps for him. [Then] she married a customs-collector and knotted customs seals for him.

Just as a woman could become a nazirite, so too could she take upon herself the obligations of scrupulous observance of purity and tithing. But in this case her willingness to do so will have dramatically affected the religious life of the whole household. As the Tosefta noted, if a man is trustworthy with regard to tithing but his wife is not trustworthy, 'it is as if he dwells in the same cage with a serpent.' The text states negatively the remarkable fact that these *haverim* – male and female – focused their religious efforts on the production and consumption of meals in a domestic setting in which women were assumed to play the major role. Hence the alleged stipulation by Rabban Gamaliel, on behalf of his daughter in the mid-first century CE: 'Rabban Gamaliel married off his daughter to Simeon b. Natanel the priest and made an agreement with him that this was done on condition that she not prepare foods requiring conditions of cleanness under the supervision of an ordinary person.'[17]

The enthusiasm for scrupulous tithing which distinguished these *haverim* had lost its appeal by the medieval period. In part this was because the medieval rabbis decreed that the duty to set aside tithes did not apply in the diaspora, on the basis of a ruling in the Mishnah that 'every precept dependent on the Land [of Israel] is in force only in that land.' A preoccupation with purity remained, but by the sixth century CE within rabbinic circles the term *haver* came to be transferred to the rabbinic sages themselves, so that it was said that 'the *haverim* are none other than the scholars.' But one powerful legacy of the original *haverim* that remained throughout the history of Judaism was the centrality of the home, and especially the kitchen, as a locus of piety. It was there that kosher dietary laws could and should be observed with scrupulous care.[18]

ALLEGORIZERS

The philosopher Philo, a contemporary of Rabban Gamaliel, would have agreed with these *haverim* on the importance of the purity and tithing laws in the Torah. He noted with approval that Moses 'ordains that first-fruits should be paid of every other possession; wine from every winepress, wheat and barley from every threshing-floor, similarly oil from olives, and fruits from the other orchard-trees, so that the priests may not have merely bare necessities, just keeping themselves alive in comparatively squalid conditions, but enjoy the abundance of the luxuries of life and pass their days amid cheerful and unstinted comfort in the style which befits their position.' But for Philo the significance of keeping the Torah as scrupulously as possible lay not just in the act itself but in its deeper meaning. He devoted much of his life, and many treatises, to elucidating what that meaning might be.[19]

Enough is known about Philo's life from his writings to establish quite precisely the cultural and social milieu he inhabited, even if the details of his own career are elusive. He was born in *c.* 10 BCE into a leading family in the long-established Jewish community of Alexandria, soon after the Roman conquest of Egypt had demoted the city from a royal capital dedicated to conspicuous consumption to a teeming entrepot in which a disgruntled population witnessed the power and wealth of the hinterland exported to Rome.

The city, founded by Alexander the Great himself three and a half centuries earlier, was built on a grid plan on a narrow strip of land bounded by the Mediterranean to the north and Lake Mareotis to the south, and was equalled only by Rome in size and magnificence. At its heart were the royal or Greek quarters, with colonnaded streets flanked by numerous spectacular public buildings in a mixture of Greek and Egyptian styles. It was dominated by the palace of the Ptolemies, and the great centre of learning in the Museum, where the famous library of the city had been housed until it was burned accidentally by Julius Caesar in 48 BCE and replaced by another in the Temple of Serapis in the Egyptian quarter. This was an international city, linked to the rest of the Mediterranean from the harbour guarded by the Pharos lighthouse, one of the wonders of the world. Greek Alexandrians retained the sense of entitlement which derived from the origins of the city as an island of superior Greek culture deliberately distinguished from the Egyptian society which surrounded them (and by which they were supported through fabled wealth).

But by Philo's time the world of these sophisticated Greeks was under threat both from the influx of non-Greeks – primarily Egyptians and Jews, who had long had their own quarters of the city – and from the apparently arbitrary interventions of Roman governors whose interests lay less in the welfare of the city than in that of Rome, and indeed themselves. The assumptions of Greek Alexandrians about the superiority of Hellenism were adopted to a considerable extent by at least some of the Jews of the city. Philo was a full Alexandrian citizen and had enjoyed a classic Greek education in grammar, mathematics and music as well as literature, drama and athletics. He moved in the highest Jewish social circles. One nephew, Marcus Julius Alexander, married the Herodian princess Berenice who was afterwards to become mistress of the Roman emperor Titus. Another, Marcus' brother Tiberius, became, first, governor of Judaea on behalf of Rome in 46–8 CE and then, in the 60s CE, prefect of Egypt. Tiberius notoriously abandoned his ancestral traditions in the course of this spectacular political career, in marked contrast to his uncle Philo. Philo himself was unambiguously committed to his people and his religion: on at least one occasion he made a pilgrimage to the Jerusalem Temple, and in the autumn of 39 CE he travelled to Rome to plead with the emperor Gaius Caligula on behalf of the civil rights of the Alexandrian Jewish community.[20]

At some point in his education, Philo became acquainted not just with Greek rhetoric and the standard Stoic philosophical views of his day but with some of the major works of Plato, in particular the *Timaeus* and the *Phaedrus*. Quite how he gained this expertise is unknown. His family would have been rich enough for him to have a tutor, but the abstruse philosophy of Plato, who had written back in the fourth century BCE, was not popular in the first century CE, and Philo's predilection for his writings was idiosyncratic. Even more idiosyncratic was to be Philo's use of his philosophical learning. For he was to assert, at considerable length and with much ingenuity, that the law of Moses, when construed properly through allegory, must be understood as a version of Plato's philosophy – or, more precisely, that Plato and Moses had both seen the same truths.

Philo wrote a great deal, and a great deal of what he wrote survives. His works were preserved, mostly in their original Greek but in some cases in a sixth-century Armenian translation and in Latin, through the efforts of Christian copyists, for whom his interpretation of the Jewish law proved useful. In the late second century CE, Clement of Alexandria was the first Christian writer to cite Philo's allegorical readings of the Greek version of the Jewish Bible, the Septuagint, which was now also the Christian Old Testament. A generation earlier, in the mid-second century CE, mainstream gentile Christians had come under attack from the influential and charismatic Christian teacher Marcion, who urged them to discard the Old Testament altogether, since they no longer wished to keep its injunctions literally as the Jews did. In response, Clement, unwilling to jettison altogether the scriptures which earlier Christians had cited as fulfilled in Christ, inaugurated a new way of reading the Old Testament through Platonizing allegory. In this endeavour, the writings of Philo proved invaluable. By the mid-fourth century, the Church historian Eusebius referred to Philo as 'widely known to very many people, a man of the greatest distinction not only among those of our own tradition, but also among those who set out from the tradition of profane learning'.[21]

Philo's allegorical interpretation of the Torah was intended to provide his readers with a true interpretation of the teachings of Moses, who had 'both attained the very summit of philosophy and ... been divinely instructed in the great and essential part of Nature's love'. So, for instance, the dietary laws restricting which animals can be eaten symbolize the way to acquire knowledge and hence choose virtue:

Of all the numbers from the unit upwards ten is the most perfect, and, as Moses says, most holy and sacred, and with this he seals his list of the clean kinds of animals when he wishes to appoint them for the use of members of his commonwealth. He adds a general method for proving and testing the ten kinds, based on two signs, the parted hoof and the chewing of cud. Any kind which lacks both or one of these is unclean. Now both these two are symbols to teacher and learner of the method best suited for acquiring knowledge, the method by which the better is distinguished from the worse, and thus confusion is avoided. For just as a cud-chewing animal after biting through the food keeps it at rest in the gullet, again after a bit draws it up and masticates it and then passes it on to the belly, so the pupil after receiving from the teacher through his ears the principles and love of wisdom prolongs the process of learning, as he cannot at once apprehend and grasp them securely, till by using memory to call up each thing that he has heard by constant exercises which act as the cement of conceptions, he stamps a firm impression of them on his soul. But the firm apprehension of conceptions is clearly useless unless we discriminate and distinguish them so that we can choose what we should choose and avoid the contrary, and this distinguishing is symbolized by the parted hoof. For the way of life is twofold, one branch leading to vice, the other to virtue and we must turn away from the one and never forsake the other. Therefore all creatures whose hooves are uniform or multiform are unclean, the one because they signify the idea that good and bad have one and the same nature, which is like confusing concave and convex or uphill and downhill in a road; the multiform because they set before our life many roads, which are rather no roads, to cheat us, for where there is a multitude to choose from it is not easy to find the best and most serviceable path.[22]

The Moses thus revealed by Philo was a Platonized teacher. What better evidence could there be for the existence of the Platonic forms than the vision of the Tabernacle vouchsafed to Moses before its construction:

It was determined, therefore, to fashion a tabernacle, a work of the highest sanctity, the construction of which was set forth to Moses on the mount by divine pronouncements. He saw with the soul's eye the immaterial forms of the material objects about to be made, and these forms had to be reproduced in copies perceived by the senses, taken from the original draught, so to speak, and from patterns conceived in the mind ... So the shape of the model was stamped upon the mind of the prophet, a secretly painted or moulded prototype, produced by immaterial and invisible forms; and then the resulting work was built in accordance with that shape by the artist impressing the stampings upon the material substances required in each case.

Plato's *Timaeus* was often called in by Philo to illustrate the veracity of Moses' insights, which did not mean that Plato alone had seen the truth, for Philo also drew on Stoic arguments in his discussion of providence, and his fascination with arithmology was adopted from Neopythagoreans as in his discussion of the Ten Commandments:

> Our admiration is at once aroused by their number, which is neither more nor less than is the supremely perfect, Ten. Ten contains all different kinds of numbers, even as 2, odd as 3, and even–odd as 6, and all ratios, whether of a number to its multiples or fractional, when a number is either increased or diminished by some part of itself.[23]

In keeping with his Platonic bent, Philo separated the world into two realms. Only in the upper, intelligible realm can truth be found, and the aim of life must be to lift up the soul to 'see God', although God is sometimes described by him as inhabiting a sphere above even the world of ideas, and thus 'ineffable, inconceivable and incomprehensible'. This extreme transcendentalism led Philo to the somewhat contradictory assertions that, although God is the only object worth knowing, he is without quality and therefore unknowable.[24]

Philo frequently stressed the unity of God, identifying the divine name as pronounced to Moses in Exodus with the Form of Forms as defined by Plato. How could a God so exalted have any relation to the bodily world of 'opinion' in which humans live, without compromising the perfection of the divine? The problem was not unique to Philo, hence the plethora of divine intermediaries presupposed in other Jewish writings of the late Second Temple period. But Philo's solution, which was central to his thought, was distinctive and powerful. Many Greek philosophers had discussed the role in human life of *logos*, meaning 'speech' or 'rational order', and *logos* is found in Wisdom of Solomon as the agent of God: 'it was your word [*logos*], O Lord, that heals all people'. For Philo, the Logos is the chief power of God which brings God to man and man to God. The notion was not wholly consistent. The Logos is a copy of God, and human intelligence is a copy of the Logos. There are two Logoi:

> One is the archetypal reason above us, the other the copy of it which we possess. Moses calls the first the 'image of God', the second the cast of that image. For God, he says, made man not 'the image of God' but 'after the

image'. And thus the mind in each of us, which in the true and full sense is the 'man', is an expression at third hand from the Maker, while between them is the Reason which serves as model for our reason, but itself is the effigies or presentment of God.

Sometimes Philo identified the Logos with the mind of God. At other times, the Logos was reckoned 'midway between man and God'. And indeed Philo often dropped into language which assumed the working of divine powers within the human soul as envisaged in Stoic thought. But consistency was less important than Philo's implication that through the Logos, and with the help of a true understanding of the biblical texts, man can ascend to the divine realm.[25]

This view of the nature of reality had an impact on Philo's understanding of ethics. Since man is composed of body and soul, his body connecting him to matter and his soul to the divine, he is in a constant struggle to control his passions through reason. Hence Philo's version of the real meaning of the migration of Abraham from Mesopotamia as recounted in Genesis:

'And the Lord said unto Abraham, Depart out of your land, and out of your kindred, and out of your father's house, into the land which I shall show you; and I will make you a great nation and will bless you and will make your name great, and you shalt be blessed. And I will bless them that bless you, and them that curse you I will curse, and in you shall all the tribes of the earth be blessed' (Gen 12:1–3). God begins the carrying out of His will to cleanse man's soul by giving it a starting-point for full salvation in its removal out of three localities, namely, body, sensation, and speech. 'Land' or 'country' is a symbol of body, 'kindred' of sensation, 'father's house' of speech. How so? Because the body took its substance out of earth (or land) and is again resolved into earth ... Sensation, again, is of one kin and family with understanding, the irrational with the rational, for both these are parts of one soul. And speech is our 'father's house', 'father's' because Mind is our father.[26]

The allegorical technique used by Philo in this passage is typical of his procedure in the thirty-one treatises of his *Allegorical Commentary*, which was evidently addressed to highly educated Jewish readers with an interest in very detailed analysis of the inner meaning of the book of Genesis. Philo's *Questions and Answers on Genesis*, which for the most part survives only in Armenian translation, provides similar interpretations of the text for a less sophisticated readership, distinguishing explicitly in each case between the literal meaning and the deeper meaning:

> Why does (Scripture) say, 'Every reptile that lives shall be to you for food'? The nature of reptiles is twofold. One is poisonous, and the other is tame. Poisonous are those serpents which in place of feet use the belly and breast to crawl along; and tame are those which have legs above their feet. This is the literal meaning. But as for the deeper meaning, the passions resemble unclean reptiles, while joy (resembles) clean (reptiles). For alongside sensual pleasures there is the passion of joy.

This exegetical method, combining close examination of the literal meaning of the text and the etymology of words with assertion of a deeper significance, was borrowed from contemporary Stoic scholarship, not least in the study of Homer, when the technique was often used to save Homer from a charge of impiety. In Philo's very different case, the allegorical meaning of the biblical text generally added something to a straightforward understanding and was used only rarely to dismiss the literal meaning:

> 'And God brought a trance upon Adam, and he fell asleep; and He took one of his sides' and what follows. These words in their literal sense are of the nature of a myth. For how could anyone admit that a woman, or a human being at all, came into existence out of a man's side? And what was there to hinder the First Cause from creating woman, as He created man, out of the earth? For not only was the Maker the same Being, but the material too, out of which every particular kind was fashioned, was practically unlimited. And why, when there were so many parts to choose from, did He form the woman not from some other part but from the side? And which side did he take? For we may assume that only two are indicated, as there is in fact nothing to suggest a large number of them. Did he take the left or the right side? If He filled up with flesh (the place of) the one which He took, are we to suppose that the one which He left was *not* made of flesh? Truly our sides are twin in all their parts and are made of flesh. What then are we to say? 'Sides' is a term of ordinary life for 'strength' . . . Having said this, we must go on to remark that the mind when as yet unclothed and unconfined by the body (and it is of the mind when not so confined that he is speaking) has many powers.

One option favoured by the scholars of Homer was to amend any text which they found unsatisfactory, but Philo could not allow himself to do this with the Septuagint text, since he believed it had been produced by translators who should be regarded as 'prophets and priests of the mysteries, whose sincerity and singleness of thought has enabled them to go hand in hand with the purest of spirits, the spirit of Moses'.[27]

Philo was not the first or last Jew to base an idiosyncratic interpretation of the Torah on explicit allegorizing. We have seen that the Yahad sectarians, who asserted that the 'real meaning' of passages in Habakkuk or Nahum related to the history of their community, were doing something very similar. We shall find a similar procedure occasionally in early rabbinic Bible interpretation which may go back to the Second Temple period (see Chapter 11). Nothing suggests that Philo was aware either of the Jewish groups which produced these commentaries on scripture or of the commentaries themselves. A few specific interpretations of some texts did come through both to Philo and to the rabbis from a common tradition. But Philo did not deal with specific legal issues as the rabbis did. He showed rather a concern to demonstrate the rationality of the laws and the excellence of their moral implications.

It would have been more likely for Philo to come into contact with the writings of Aristobulus, a predecessor in Alexandria. Aristobulus wrote philosophical interpretations of Moses' teachings in the mid-second century BCE, asserting that 'Plato followed the tradition of the law that we use ... just as Pythagoras, having borrowed many of the things in our traditions, found room for them in his own doctrinal system.' Aristobulus was at pains to insist that anthropomorphic references to God in the biblical text must be read allegorically: 'for what our lawgiver Moses wishes to say, he does so at many levels, using words that appear to have other referents (I mean to things that can be seen); yet in doing so he actually speaks about "natural" conditions and structures of a higher order ...'. Thus Aristobulus reassured his readers that the Sabbath refers to the 'sevenfold principle ... through which we have knowledge of things both human and divine'. He appealed in support of his interpretation to verses alleged to come from the Greek poets Hesiod, Homer and Linus, although some of these at least were pious Jewish forgeries.[28]

Aristobulus' use of allegory seems to have differed from Philo's only in his lack of sophistication, and the two Jewish philosophers can be seen to react to the same cultural milieu in Alexandria (albeit over a chronological gap of a couple of centuries). But there is no strong reason to view them as part of a distinctive school or tradition in the city, for Philo did not apparently cite or refer to Aristobulus' philosophy anywhere in his voluminous works. On the other hand, allegorizing was evidently a popular mode of exegesis among Alexandrian Jews, since Philo remarks not infrequently on customary interpretation of specific texts, as in the interpretation of one of the passages in Genesis, in which Abraham and Sarah went to Egypt and the king of Egypt was overcome with plague because of his lust for Abraham's wife Sarah:

> I have also heard some natural philosophers who took the passage alle-gorically, not without good reason. They said that the husband was a figure for the good mind, judging by the meaning given for the interpret-ation of this name that it stood for a good disposition of soul. The wife, they said, was virtue, her name being in Chaldean Sarah but in our lan-guage a sovereign lady, because nothing is more sovereign or dominant than virtue.

Elsewhere, Philo refers to contemporary allegorists with whom he dis-agrees; we have seen above the vehemence of his opposition to extreme allegorists who treated the literal interpretation of the laws 'with easy-going neglect' because they thought only the symbolic meanings of importance.[29]

If any of these other allegorists in Philo's day wrote down any of their interpretations of the biblical texts, none now survives. The works of Aristobulus are known only through the citation of fragments by Chris-tian writers of the third and fourth centuries, principally Clement and Eusebius. The preservation of so large a body of Philo's allegorizing biblical exegesis by these Christian authors, in contrast to the scraps of Aristobulus, and the complete absence in their works of other allegoriz-ing Jewish biblical commentaries suggest that Philo's work was either unique in its formation or (just as probable) unique in its preservation in manuscript form over the century and a half between the death of the author and the first definite Christian citation of his work.

In favour of Philo's Judaism as somewhat exceptional in his day is the reference to him by Josephus, who mentioned him just once in con-nection with the embassy of the Alexandrian Jews to Caligula but specifically noted that he was 'not inexpert in philosophy', an accolade he accorded to no other contemporary Jew in his narrative. The descrip-tion was earned perhaps less by Philo's religious works than by his philosophical treatises, such as the two dialogues *On Providence* and *On Animals*, which cite Greek sources rather than the Bible, assume a readership conversant with Hellenistic philosophy and are presented as dialogues with a certain Alexander, who is almost certainly to be iden-tified with Philo's nephew, the apostate Tiberius Julius Alexander.

There seems no doubt that Philo tried to reach out to a readership much wider than the insiders who might be able to appreciate the dense argument of the allegorical commentary, for the series of works in his *Exposition of the Law*, which included his treatise on the creation of the world, his lives of the patriarchs, his commentaries on the Decalogue and the Special Laws, and his discussions *On Virtues* and *On Rewards and Punishments*, are far more accessible, explaining for the wider Jewish community the principles of the law and paraphrasing the biblical material alongside allegorical interpretations. Whether Philo had partly in mind a non-Jewish audience for the *Exposition* is uncertain, but he explicitly reached out to non-Jews in the two books which constitute the *Life of Moses*, a sort of companion piece to the *Exposition*:

> I purpose to write the life of Moses, whom some describe as the legislator of the Jews, others as the interpreter of the Holy Laws. I hope to bring the story of this greatest and most perfect of men to the knowledge of such as deserve not to remain in ignorance of it; for, while the fame of the laws which he left behind him has travelled throughout the civilized world and reached the ends of the earth, the man himself as he really was is known to few. Greek men of letters have refused to treat him as worthy of memory, possibly through envy, and also because in many cases the ordinances of the legislators of the different states are opposed to his.

We have no idea who in fact read Philo's voluminous works before they were raided by Christians from the late second century CE for reasons of which he would have strongly disapproved: Clement was attracted to allegory as a way to avoid a literal interpretation of the legal sections of the biblical text, so his sympathies will have been precisely with the extreme allegorists singled out by Philo for disapproval. Back in the first century CE, Josephus may have drawn on Philo's philosophical treatise *That Every Good Man is Free* for his brief account in the *Antiquities* of the Essenes, but if so, the result was somewhat garbled. In other parts of Josephus' history where Philo's works would have illuminated his narrative, such as his account of events in Rome in the time of Caligula, he shows no sign of having read Philo's version.[30]

Even if Philo's allegorizing writings were largely ignored by his fellow Jews, this does not imply that he was marginal within the Judaism of his day, since he was evidently deeply immersed in the religious life of his own community in Alexandria. He never suggested that a literal understanding of the Torah was wrong, just that it was insufficient. He was as downcast as the other Jewish ambassadors to Caligula when the emperor responded to their pleas for the Temple in Jerusalem and the Jews of Alexandria by asking quizzically 'Why do you refuse to eat pork?' Philo wrote that 'We answered, "Different people have different customs" . . .' He did not give the philosophical answer he had offered to his Jewish readers in the *Exposition*, that pork was forbidden to Jews precisely because it is the most delicious of meats, so that abstention might encourage self-control. Such a philosophical answer might have sounded plausible enough in Rome in the mid-first century CE, when many philosophers subscribed to vaguely Cynic notions of abstinence. But it is probable that Philo was seen by the emperor less as a philosopher than as a Jew.[31]

No certain trace survives of any continuation of Philo's Judaism in the centuries immediately after 70 CE. The biblical scenes on the frescoes from the third-century synagogue at Dura-Europos in modern Syria (see Chapter 12) have been interpreted as references to the mystical allegories of Philo, but the interpretation is dubious. Possible traces of Philonic influence have been traced in the opening of *Bereshit Rabbah*, a rabbinic commentary on Genesis from the fourth to sixth century CE, in which R. Oshaiah Rabbah is said to have stated that the Torah declares: 'I was the working tool of the Holy One, blessed be He. In human practice, when a mortal king builds a palace, he builds it not with his own skill but with the skill of an architect. The architect moreover does not build it out of his head, but employs plans and diagrams to know how to arrange the chambers and the wicket doors. Thus God consulted the Torah and created the world.' The formulation looks rather similar to Philo's comment in his *De Opificio Mundi* that:

> God, being God, assumed that a beautiful copy would never be produced apart from a beautiful pattern, and that no object of perception would be faultless which was not made in the likeness of an original discerned only by the intellect. So when He willed to create this visible world He first fully formed the intelligible world, in order that He might have the use of a pattern wholly God-like and incorporeal in producing the material world, as a later creation, the very image of an earlier, to embrace in itself objects of perception of as many kinds as the other contained objects of intelligence.

But if this was influenced by Philo, it was unacknowledged, and for a millennium and a half Philo's variety of Judaism became invisible to Jews, with occasional exceptions such as the individual who wrote down the manuscript of the *Midrash Tadshe* in (probably) eleventh-century Provence. The great Italian scholar Azariah de' Rossi reintroduced Philo, under the name Yedidiah, to an astonished Jewish world in the sixteenth century. In the nineteenth century his allegorizing was to strike a chord with Reform and Liberal Jews. But only in the twenty-first century have some of his writings, translated into Hebrew, been introduced into the liturgy of some Reform congregations.[32]

JESUS AND PAUL

In his narrative of political events when Pontius Pilate was governor of Judaea in the time of the emperor Tiberius, Josephus followed an account of a riot in opposition to the building of an aqueduct using money from the sacred treasury with a description of a disturbance of a different kind. In the medieval manuscripts of his *Antiquities*, this description is transmitted in a remarkable form:

> About this time there lived Jesus, a wise man, if indeed one ought to call him a man. For he was one who wrought surprising feats and was a teacher of such people as accept the truth gladly. He won over many Jews and many of the Greeks. He was the Messiah [Christos]. When Pilate, upon hearing him accused by men of the highest standing amongst us, had condemned him to be crucified, those who had in the first place come to love him did not give up their affection for him. On the third day, he appeared to them restored to life, for the prophets of God had prophesied these and countless other marvellous things about him. And the tribe of the Christians, so called after him, has still to this day not disappeared.[33]

More was written in antiquity about this one younger contemporary of Philo, Jesus of Nazareth, than about any other Jew in the last centuries of the Second Temple. It may therefore seem rather surprising that for much of the twentieth century historians declared that it was impossible to say anything at all about his life and teachings. This failure of nerve was caused directly by the plethora of information: since so much of that information is contradictory and patently designed to present Jesus in a specific light, it seemed impossible to derive from any of it a clear picture of what really happened. The New Testament, compiled in *c.* 120 CE from documents composed by a variety of authors shortly after the crucifixion of Jesus, contains in its four Gospels four biographies of Jesus which, despite their many agreements (derived in part from use of common sources), give somewhat different accounts of some important aspects of Jesus' career. The differences are explained by the theological focus of the genre. 'Gospel' translates the Greek word *evangelion*, which means 'good news' and was already understood in the earliest writings in the New Testament as a reference to the news of the salvation of humanity through the death and resurrection of Jesus Christ.

The four canonical Gospels were believed in the early second century to have been transmitted by the apostles of Jesus. They were clearly reckoned by the compilers of the New Testament canon to have enough in common to be adopted as authoritative in preference to the derivative narratives found in the many 'apocryphal' gospels known from citation in later Christian writings or from the discovery of papyrus codices in Nag Hammadi in Egypt. It is disconcerting to note that the earliest Christian evidence, the writings of Paul, which date to the midfirst century CE, is almost totally silent about the career and teachings of Jesus, apart from the crucifixion. Roman sources revealed nothing about Jesus until the early second century, when they show awareness of his origins in Judaea and the name 'Christus'. The polemical stories preserved in the rabbinic literature about Yeshu or 'that man', known in the medieval tradition as Toledot Yeshu, are all hostile versions of the stories told by Christians. They may go back to a Jewish counternarrative to the Gospels circulating from the first century CE among Jews who rejected Jesus.[34]

The explicit account of Jesus' career cited above is found in all the extant manuscripts of the *Antiquities* of Josephus. It has the appearance of objective history. But since the seventeenth century its authenticity has been doubted – on good grounds, for Josephus, who was not a Christian, could hardly have said of Jesus 'this was the Messiah'. It seems almost certain that Josephus wrote something about Jesus, and it may even be possible to identify in the passage as found in the manuscripts those words which a Christian interpolator is unlikely to have added. But this would not leave much more information than that Jesus lived around this time, that he was crucified by Pilate and that the 'tribe of the Christians, so called after him, has to this day still not disappeared'.[35]

In more recent years it has become clear that historical despair was premature and unnecessary. Doubtless some pieces of ancient information about Jesus are more suspect than others, but it is reasonable to suppose that those elements of the tradition about his life and teaching which fitted least well with the outlook of the Christian communities that preserved them are likely to have survived in the tradition simply because they were true. Such criteria would permit us to state firmly quite a number of nearly certain facts about Jesus. Jesus was born into a village family in Galilee, quite low on the social scale. He came into contact with John the Baptist, a charismatic Jewish teacher active at least from *c.* 28 CE, who challenged Jews to repent their sins and mark their repentance by immersion in the cleansing waters of the River Jordan. Jesus preached only to Jews, showing little interest in gentiles. He was crucified horribly and shamefully as a political threat by Pontius Pilatus, the Roman governor. Some other stories told about Jesus, such as his birth in a manger in Bethlehem, are more likely to be patent fictions (in this case designed to associate Jesus with the royal city of David). In between the probable details and the clearly fictitious are many stories that are entirely plausible but less certain because they accord well with the priorities of the early Christians who preserved them, such as Jesus' preaching of repentance 'for the kingdom of heaven is at hand' and his miraculous acts of healing and exorcism. But 'less certain' does not mean 'not true', and it is plausible enough, despite the apparent disjunction between Jesus and Paul, that other parts of the Jesus movement after his death declared themselves as his followers precisely because they felt themselves to be subscribing to the same ideals.[36]

Of all the aspects of Jesus' life that mark him out from other Jewish religious figures, the survival after his death of a group named after him is the most remarkable. The closest parallel would be the Teacher of Righteousness at Qumran, since his influence too continued down to later generations, but the sectarian scrolls do not name the Teacher, and in fact the surviving scrolls refer to him only rarely. As the Pharisee Gamaliel is made to note by the author of Acts, other groups had faded away once their leader was no more. In most other respects, Jesus himself is portrayed in the Gospels as being like any other Jew, from his circumcision soon after birth through his observance of the Sabbath, attendance at synagogue services to hear the Torah read, the observance of festivals, and pilgrimage to the Temple. Despite later Christian doubts about the efficacy of sacrifices, Jesus is portrayed in the Gospels as accepting such offerings as normal, urging only that 'when you are offering your gift at the altar, if you remember that your brother or sister has something against you, leave your gift there before the altar and go; first be reconciled to your brother or sister, and then come and offer your gift.'[37]

Jesus restricted his diet to kosher food. The declaration by the author of the Gospel of Mark, after a comparison between 'what goes into the mouth' and 'what comes out of the mouth', that Jesus 'declared all foods clean' is omitted from the parallel passage in the Gospel of Matthew. It must be a later gloss, since it makes no sense of Luke's account, in Acts, of Peter's vision, in which he is portrayed as astonished to be instructed to eat unclean things:

> About noon the next day, as they were on their journey and approaching the city, Peter went up on the roof to pray. He became hungry and wanted something to eat; and while it was being prepared, he fell into a trance. He saw the heaven opened and something like a large sheet coming down, being lowered to the ground by its four corners. In it were all kinds of four-footed creatures and reptiles and birds of the air. Then he heard a voice saying, 'Get up, Peter; kill and eat.' But Peter said, 'By no means, Lord; for I have never eaten anything that is profane or unclean.' The voice said to him again, a second time, 'What God has made clean, you must not call profane.'

The objections recorded in the Gospels are not to what Jesus ate but to the company in which he had his meals. In a society in which exceptional piety was marked for some, such as Essenes, members of the Qumran Yahad and *haverim*, by table fellowship with like-minded enthusiasts, it was remarkable that Jesus was believed deliberately to have sought prostitutes, tax-gatherers and other sinners as his dining companions.[38]

What was it about Jesus that attracted followers? Crowds could be accounted for by the public miracles and exorcisms, but crowds could (and did) melt away under pressure. For his close devotees, his evident charisma and the eschatological language of an imminent kingdom of heaven aroused enthusiasm and loyalty, reinforced by such symbolic actions as the 'cleansing of the Temple':

> And he entered the Temple and began to drive out those who were selling and those who were buying in the Temple, and he overturned the tables of the money-changers and the seats of those who sold doves; and he would not allow anyone to carry anything through the Temple. He was teaching and saying 'Is it not written, "My house shall be called a house of prayer for all the nations"? But you have made it a den of robbers.'

A minor disturbance of this kind on the edges of the Temple site will have had little impact on the smooth running of this huge institution, but its symbolism had a lasting effect on his admirers, not least some years after his death when his prophecy that the great building of Herod would in due course be destroyed like its predecessor came to pass:

> As he came out of the Temple, one of his disciples said to him, 'Look, Teacher, what large stones and what large buildings!' Then Jesus asked him, 'Do you see these great buildings? Not one stone will be left here upon another; all will be thrown down.' When he was sitting on the Mount of Olives opposite the temple, Peter, James, John and Andrew asked him privately, 'Tell us, when will this be, and what will be the sign that all these things are about to be accomplished?'[39]

A prophetic call to repentance and more intense adherence to the inner core of the teachings of scripture, as in the Sermon on the Mount, with its formula, 'You have heard it said to those of ancient times ... but I say to you', combined with eschatological hope, might be enough to explain the impact of Jesus on his fellow Jews during his lifetime. The debate between Jesus and the 'scribes and Pharisees' over the minutiae of keeping the Torah are similar in style and content to the debates between Pharisees and Sadducees or the discussions recorded in the sectarian texts from Qumran. The stance ascribed to Jesus varies from the lenient to the stringent interpretation that Moses allowed divorce only 'because of your hardness of heart': 'But from the beginning of creation, "God made them male and female." For this reason a man shall leave his father and mother and be joined with his wife, and the two shall become one flesh. So they are no longer two, but one flesh. Therefore what God has joined together, let no one separate.'[40]

Nothing in these debates suggests a fundamental rift between Jesus and his fellow Jews that might lead to a charge of blasphemy. According to the first three Gospels (Matthew, Mark and Luke), it was not the scribes and Pharisees, but rather the High Priest Caiaphas and his advisers, who handed over Jesus to the Roman authorities for punishment. According to the narrative in the Gospel of Mark, the accusation of blasphemy came late in the proceedings:

> Now the chief priests and the whole council were looking for testimony against Jesus to put him to death; but they found none. For many gave false testimonies against him, and their testimonies did not agree. Some stood up and gave false testimony against him, saying, 'We heard him say, "I will destroy this Temple that is made with hands, and in three days I will build another, not made with hands."' But even on this point their testimony did

not agree. Then the high priest stood up before them and asked Jesus, 'Have you no answer? What is it that they testify against you?' But he was silent and did not answer. Again the high priest asked him, 'Are you the Messiah, the Son of the Blessed One?' Jesus said, 'I am' and 'you will see the Son of Man seated at the right hand of the Power,' and 'coming with the cloud of heaven'. Then the high priest tore his clothes and said, 'Why do we still need witnesses? You have heard his blasphemy! What is your decision?' All of them condemned him as deserving death.

Whatever the truth of the details of this narrative, the reason for which Jesus was eventually crucified by order of Pontius Pilate was evidently political, since the inscription on the cross stating the charge against him read 'The King of the Jews'. It is likely that the concern of Caiaphas was similarly political. It was dangerous for the Jewish authorities to have a large crowd gathering in Jerusalem in a state of eschatological fervour on the eve of one of the great pilgrim festivals, regardless of the content of Jesus' preaching.[41]

Whether Jesus actually claimed of himself to be the Messiah as reported in Mark cannot now be known, but the frequent references to him by the name Christ in the letters of Paul show clearly that this status was ascribed to him by his followers after his death. What the name implied is harder to pin down since, as we shall see (Chapter 8), Jewish notions about the origins and functions of the predicted Messiah varied greatly in this period. The word *Christos* conveyed no particular connotations at all in the epistles 'of one called to be an apostle of Christ Jesus by the will of God'.

Paul preached that 'the Lord Jesus Christ' was the Son of God, 'the Father of mercies and the God of all consolation'. The expression 'Son of God' has many different meanings in Paul's writings. It refers (as in many parts of the Hebrew Bible) to Israel as a people, or to Christian believers, as well as to Jesus. But the Gospels of Matthew and Luke link Jesus' sonship more specifically to his conception and birth, and the Gospel of John goes further by describing his sonship as a relationship which has existed from eternity, through which God has given his son 'authority over all people, to give eternal life to all whom you have given him'. Ideas about the relationship of Jesus to God developed rapidly within the early Christian movement, culminating in the notion of his divinity. But it is striking that for Paul, whose letters constitute the earliest evidence for Christian thought, the most remarkable part of Jesus' career had come at the end, when he was 'declared to be Son of

God with power according to the spirit of holiness by resurrection from the dead'.[42]

The resurrection is key to the continuation of his movement after Jesus had suffered a shameful and agonizing death through crucifixion. Nothing in the earlier history of Judaism had prepared for this. Even in the stories about Jesus' own career, the raising of Lazarus from the dead had not been believed to imply anything special about Lazarus. It was believed of some select biblical figures, notably Enoch and Elijah, that they had never really died, but the notion at the heart of Paul's message, of the central significance of death and resurrection, was new within Judaism.[43]

This was not the only novelty in the new movement which sprang up within weeks of Jesus' death around the year 30 CE. Jesus' followers began to proclaim that Jesus had been sent by God to redeem all humankind, that his death had been a necessary part of the inauguration of the Kingdom of God, and that, crucially, a belief in the power of Jesus, now exalted to God's right hand, would prepare any who turned to him for salvation in the judgement to come and for eternal life. Jesus had lived among peasants and craftsmen and taught in the small village communities of the hills of western Galilee. These were modest settlements with olive and wine presses and storage facilities for grain hollowed out in the limestone. Jesus had eschewed (it seems) even the small Greek cities of Galilee such as Sepphoris, which lies only a few miles to the south of Nazareth. He had reached out to a wider Jewish following only in the context of infrequent visits to the holy city of Jerusalem. But within a very few years after his death teachings about him, and inspired by him, were to reach to the other end of the Mediterranean.

Disentangling the beliefs of these early followers of Jesus in the surviving Christian texts from the overlay of later doctrines is not always easy. In the eyes of later gentile Christians who had passed through a process of shedding Jewish practices, the Jewishness of Jewish Christians was often suspect. Any Christian who was believed to take the Torah too literally was vulnerable to a charge of being a Jew. Since most of our evidence comes from gentile Christian sources, it is hard to know how much their ethnic origins mattered to the Christians who had been born Jews and wished to combine their new faith with the old.[44]

It is probable that some of Jesus' followers gathered after the crucifixion of their leader in Galilee, where a 'young man, dressed in a white robe' told them that the risen Jesus would be sighted. But for the first decades after 30 CE both Paul's letters and the narrative in the Acts of the Apostles refer mostly to the 'assembly' (*ekklesia*) in Jerusalem. The account of the early Church in Acts has been doubted by some scholars as the product of a distinctive salvation history and treated with as much scepticism as evidence for the historical Jesus. With respect to the career of Paul this scepticism has some justification. But there is no reason to doubt the account in Acts of communal meetings for table fellowship and prayer much in the same fashion as the Yahad, Essenes and *haverim*, but with a distinctive emphasis in their teaching on the crucial role of Jesus in bringing salvation. Hence the oration attributed to Peter, one of Jesus' closest disciples and a dominant figure in the Christian community in Jerusalem, at Shavuot (Pentecost):

> Fellow Israelites, I may say to you confidently of our ancestor David that he both died and was buried, and his tomb is with us to this day. Since he was a prophet, he knew that God had sworn with an oath to him that he would put one of his descendants on the throne. Foreseeing this, David spoke of the resurrection of the Messiah, saying 'He was not abandoned to Hades, nor did his flesh experience corruption.' This Jesus God raised up, and of that all of us are witnesses. Being therefore exalted at the right hand of God, and having received from the Father the promise of the Holy Spirit, he has poured out this that you both see and hear. For David did not ascend into the heavens, but he himself says, 'The Lord said to my Lord, "Sit at my right hand, until I make your enemies your footstool."' Therefore let the entire house of Israel know with certainty that God has made him both Lord and Messiah, this Jesus whom you crucified.

The international population of Jerusalem at festival time, when, according to Acts, 'there were devout Jews from every nation under heaven living in Jerusalem', led to the rapid spread of the message of these enthusiasts to Jewish synagogues in the eastern Mediterranean diaspora by apostles who were in many cases, such as Philip, Barnabas, Prisca, Aquila and Apollos, as well as Paul, themselves diaspora Jews.[45]

One impulse to this diaspora mission was persecution in Jerusalem, and notably the martyrdom of the diaspora Jew Stephen. Stephen had been attacked by a mob who 'with a loud shout all rushed in to gather against him ... [and] dragged him out of the city and began to stone him' until he died. In the narrative of Acts, this mob action was provoked by a long speech by Stephen in the style of the biblical prophets, highly critical of the spiritual blindness of Israel throughout history. The historicity of this account is now unknowable. But although we are told that in the immediate aftermath of Stephen's death 'a severe persecution began against the Church in Jerusalem, and all except the apostles were scattered throughout the countryside of Judaea and Samaria', the continuation of a Christian community in the city down to the outbreak of revolt in 66 CE suggests that non-Christian Jews in general treated those who preached salvation in Christ as mavericks rather than dangerous. Despite occasional persecution, there was still a community in Jerusalem throughout the 50s and early 60s CE, and they continued to preach and pray in the Temple. That is how Paul was to end up being arrested there by the crowd some years after Stephen's martyrdom. The execution of James the brother of Jesus in Jerusalem by the Sadducee High Priest Ananus, discussed above (Chapter 6), took place in 62 CE. Christian Jews were no odder in first-century Jerusalem than others, such as the prophet Jesus son of Ananias who proclaimed woe in Jerusalem from the year after James' death to the eventual destruction of the city in 70 CE, about whom more will be said in Chapter 8.[46]

Paul himself could not have been clearer in his letter to the Philippians about his own status as a Jew:

> If anyone else has reason to be confident in the flesh, I have more: circumcised on the eighth day, a member of the people of Israel, of the tribe of Benjamin, a Hebrew born of Hebrews; as to the law, a Pharisee; as to zeal, a persecutor of the church; as to righteousness under the law, blameless.

Similarly in his letter to the Romans, towards the end of his life: 'I ask, then, has God rejected his people? By no means! I myself am an Israelite, a descendant of Abraham, a member of the tribe of Benjamin.' When in his second letter to the Corinthians he boasted in replying to his critics that he was as much a Hebrew, Israelite and descendant of Abraham as them, he went on, while demonstrating his devotion to Christ by the floggings he had undergone for the sake of his mission, to indicate in passing the lengths to which he would go to maintain his membership of the Jewish community, claiming: 'Five times I have received from the Jews the forty lashes minus one.' Punishment by a Jewish court implied inclusion. The judges in a Jewish court in a city of the eastern Roman provinces in the mid-first century CE could try, convict and punish only fellow Jews. And since Paul could have stopped the punishment at any time by claiming no longer to be part of the Jewish community (like for instance, his younger contemporary Tiberius Julius Alexander), his willingness to undergo such a lashing demonstrates powerfully the importance to him of continuing to belong within Judaism.[47]

If Paul was a Roman citizen, his submission to a Jewish court will have been all the more remarkable, but our evidence that he held this status comes not from his own letters but from the less reliable narrative of his career to be found in the Acts of the Apostles, when his citizenship proves crucial in enabling him to escape a flogging:

> The tribune directed that he was to be brought into the barracks, and ordered him to be examined by flogging, to find out the reason for this outcry against him. But when they had tied him up with thongs, Paul said to the centurion who was standing by, 'Is it legal for you to flog a Roman citizen who is uncondemned?' When the centurion heard that, he went to the tribune and said to him, 'What are you about to do? This man is a Roman citizen.' The tribune came and asked Paul, 'Tell me, are you a Roman citizen?' And he said, 'Yes.' The tribune answered, 'It cost me a large sum of money to get my citizenship.' Paul said, 'But I was born a citizen.' Immediately those who were about to examine him drew back from him; and the tribune also was afraid, for he realized that Paul was a Roman citizen and that he had bound him.

The fact that this episode provides the author of Acts with the crucial link in his narrative of the shift of Christian mission from Jews in Jerusalem to gentiles in Rome has been taken as reason either to believe it true or to judge it to be fabricated. What is certain is that the author of Acts looked back at Paul's career from the perspective of a gentile Christian community, and that his narrative included much that is not to be found in Paul's own letters. This does not imply that everything not in the letters must be untrue, since there was no reason for the letters to include everything about Paul's life. But in principle it would be good to understand Paul, as an undoubtedly complex Jew, primarily from what he himself wrote. Even this procedure is not without difficulty, since six of the thirteen letters in the New Testament attributed to him appear to have been written not by him but by his followers in the decades following his death. And it is in the nature of letters composed for a specific audience or a specific occasion to be indirect and allusive in a fashion which would have been entirely comprehensible to their original recipients even if they are baffling to us.[48]

Despite such problems, we know a great deal more about Paul than about most other Jews of his time. Born with the name Saul, in Tarsus in Cilicia (in south-western Turkey), he was brought up a Pharisee and, according to Acts, 'sat at the feet of Gamaliel'. We have already noted his claim in his letter to the Galatians that as a youth he had been a zealot for ancestral traditions. As a diaspora Jew, he wrote in Greek, with competence in Greek rhetoric, and he probably knew the Bible mainly from its Greek translation. Soon after the crucifixion of Jesus, when he first came into contact in Judaea with the followers of Jesus, he 'persecuted the Church of God', as he told the Corinthians. Why he was 'trying to destroy' the Church he did not explain in any of his own epistles. The book of Acts represents his having taken the initiative to get authority for this persecution from the High Priest in Jerusalem: 'Saul, still breathing threats and murder against the disciples of the Lord, went to the high priest and asked him for letters to the synagogues at Damascus, so that if he found any who belonged to the Way, men or women, he might bring them bound to Jerusalem.' This journey to Damascus, in 33 CE, was to change everything, for as he was travelling he had a vision of 'Jesus, our Lord' on which he was later to base his claim to be an apostle of Christ.[49]

Paul's vision is narrated with great drama more than once by the author of Acts, and it became the central pillar of his own understanding of his mission in life:

> Now as he was going along and approaching Damascus, suddenly a light from heaven flashed around him. He fell to the ground and heard a voice saying to him, 'Saul, Saul, why do you persecute me?' He asked, 'Who are you, Lord?' The reply came, 'I am Jesus, whom you are persecuting. But get up and enter the city, and you will be told what you are to do.' The men who were travelling with him stood speechless because they heard the voice but saw no one. Saul got up from the ground, and though his eyes were open, he could see nothing; so they led him by the hand and brought him into Damascus. For three days he was without sight, and neither ate nor drank.

He had been, so he wrote to the Corinthians, 'caught up to the third heaven – whether in the body, or out of the body, God knows . . . caught up into Paradise', where he 'heard things that are not to be told, that no mortal is permitted to repeat'. The vision shares much with the apocalypses described in other Jewish texts (on which more in Chapter 8), but in this case Paul was happy to declare it as his own rather than shelter behind a pseudonym – and to use it as the basis of his authority.[50]

Paul declared himself to have been called by God, through the revelation of his Son, 'so that I might proclaim him among the gentiles'. His extensive journeys around the eastern Mediterranean world from c. 33 CE to c. 60 CE were aimed primarily at bringing non-Jews to seek salvation through faith in Christ without first becoming Jews. Members of the new communities he founded were not expected to think of themselves as part of Judaism. He himself, however, was prepared to become 'as a Jew to Jews', and he visited the assembly of Jewish believers in Jesus in Jerusalem to discuss with them in 49–50 CE 'the gospel that I proclaim among the gentiles, in order to make sure that I was not running, or had not run, in vain'.[51]

In the version in Acts of Paul's meeting with Peter, James and others of the Jerusalem Church, the discussion was all about the minimum moral standards to be expected from gentile converts. Paul is portrayed as himself behaving as an ordinary Jew, having his hair cut to fulfil a vow, offering sacrifices in the Temple, undergoing ritual purification, paying the expenses of a nazirite ceremony for others, and stating in the Sanhedrin that he is a Pharisee. Paul's own references to his attitude to Judaism are rather more ambivalent, perhaps reflecting either changes in his own beliefs from time to time or the rhetoric of a particular letter, or both. Thus in his last letter, to the Christian community in Rome, Paul affirmed that to the Israelites, his 'kindred according to the flesh', belong 'the adoption, the glory, the covenants, the giving of the law, the worship, and the promises; to them belong the patriarchs, and from them, according to the flesh, comes the Messiah'. Later in the epistle he urged his gentile Christian readers to recognize that although 'a hardening had come upon part of Israel' (in their failure to recognize Christ), 'all Israel will be saved; as it is written, "Out of Zion will come the Deliverer; he will banish ungodliness from Jacob."' According to Paul in this passage, 'as regards election they [Israel] are beloved, for the sake of their ancestors, for the gift, and the calling of God are irrevocable.' But, in contrast, Paul had written earlier to the Galatians about the insufficiency of the Torah to bring salvation – 'no one will be justified by the works of the law' – and he had specifically noted that 'we ourselves are Jews by birth and not gentile sinners; yet we know that a person is justified not by the works of the law but through faith in Jesus Christ.'

It seems likely that when the main aim of a letter was to persuade gentile Christians of the unimportance of observing the Torah for them, Paul played down the importance of the Torah for him. The letter to the Galatians reflects the conundrum as experienced by Paul's fellow missionaries in his accusation against Cephas (another name for the apostle Peter):

But when Cephas came to Antioch, I opposed him to his face, because he stood self-condemned; for until certain people came from James, he used to eat with the Gentiles. But after they came, he drew back and kept himself separate for fear of the circumcision faction. And the other Jews joined him in this hypocrisy, so that even Barnabas was led astray by their hypocrisy. But when I saw that they were not acting consistently with the truth of the gospel, I said to Cephas before them all, 'If you, though a Jew, live like a gentile and not like a Jew, how can you compel the gentiles to live like Jews?'

Only in addressing a Jewish readership was Paul likely to affirm that 'the law is holy, and the commandment is holy and just and good', and to emphasize that his doctrine that 'God is one; and he will justify the circumcision on the grounds of faith and the uncircumcised through that same faith' does not 'overthrow' the law: 'By no means! On the contrary, we uphold the law.'[52]

Who was it that Paul believed he had seen in his vision? His letters are full of striking images:

Let the same mind be in you that was in Christ Jesus, who, though he was in the form of God, did not regard equality with God as something to be exploited, but emptied himself, taking the form of a slave, being born in human likeness. And being found in human form, he humbled himself and became obedient to the point of death – even death on a cross. Therefore God also highly exalted him and gave him the name that is above every name, so that at the name of Jesus every knee should bend, in heaven and on earth and under the earth, and every tongue should confess that Jesus Christ is Lord, to the glory of God the Father.

This poetic description of Christ as Lord was probably adopted by Paul from a pre-existing hymn. It casts Christ's pre-existence, before incarnation as Jesus, in a role similar to Wisdom in earlier Jewish texts or the Logos in Philo. It is notable how little Paul refers to earlier texts about the notion of the expected Messiah. His image of Christ has more in common with the veneration of mediator figures like exalted angels in the mystical texts from Qumran and elsewhere.

Paul's powerful rhetoric produced a number of metaphors about the nature and role of Christ which are difficult to condense into a single coherent theology. Of most importance to Paul was the belief that the death of 'Jesus Christ our Lord' had been a sacrifice, and that his resurrection was the beginning of a general resurrection for a new age. It is all part of a divine plan of which Christ is an instrument: 'God sent his Son, born of a woman, born under the law, in order to redeem those

who were under the law, so that we might receive adoption as children.'
But, despite this divine origin, the believer in Christ is said to be 'baptized into Christ', suggesting a unity of believers with Christ, and the
believers themselves as 'one body in Christ'. Elsewhere he talks of 'putting on' Christ like a garment. The relation between God and Christ as
his son is no more resolved for Paul than for other early Christians (its
working out would take many centuries and give rise to many disputes),
although he comes close to asserting their identity in his eagerness to
counter the polytheism of his gentile Christian congregations:

> Indeed, even though there may be so-called gods in heaven or on earth – as
> in fact there are many gods and many lords – yet for us there is one God,
> the Father, from whom are all things and for whom we exist, and one
> Lord, Jesus Christ, through whom are all things and through whom we
> exist.[53]

Paul was evidently a highly unusual Jew even in a period in which
variety flourished, and we shall see that his teachings led in due course
to a parting of the ways between Judaism and Christianity. But it seems
unlikely that it was his theology that led to the persecution by Jewish
communities in the 50s CE about which he boasted in II Corinthians.
Imposition of the 'forty lashes minus one' was dangerous for Jewish
community leaders and the threat posed by Paul must therefore have
been severe. Nothing either in his own letters or in the account in Acts
suggests a substantial movement of diaspora Jews to join his movement.
On the contrary, according to Acts he complained with some vehemence
that he had been rejected by them and had therefore turned to the gentiles. It was a matter of importance for him that his new gentile Christian
communities were precisely not to think of themselves as Jews, since
faith in Christ was alone sufficient for salvation. Those most likely to be
upset by his mission to gentiles to come to faith in Christ and stop worshipping their ancestral gods were not his fellow Jews but the gentile
city authorities and the representatives of pagan cults, such as the silversmiths in Ephesus who made statues of the local goddess Artemis and
who could see the customary worship of the civic community under
threat. The concern of the 'rulers of the synagogue' was more probably
that an attack on the religious customs of local gentile society by a visiting Jew such as Paul might throw into doubt the delicate position of
the local Jews as a minority who were tolerated only so long as they did
not infringe the good order of the wider gentile community and the relationship of that community to its gods.[54]

Paul the Jew regarded faith in Christ as the fulfilment of God's covenant with Israel. He saw his own mission to the gentiles as a divinely ordained task akin to that of the prophets, who had themselves foretold that the nations would worship the God of Israel in the last days. It is clear from his own account that even his fellow Jews who believed in Jesus took some persuading of the validity of his 'gospel for the uncircumcised'. His letters contain much polemic against those who required gentiles to convert to Judaism as well as faith in Christ in order to achieve salvation, and his relationship with the Jewish Christian community in Jerusalem led by Peter and James (see above) was at times difficult. For those Jews in whose eyes Jesus was just another religious enthusiast who had come to a sad end through the actions of the Roman authorities in Judaea, Paul's mission was irrelevant. The Christians in the communities he set up did not think of themselves as Jews, and Jews generally responded by treating gentile Christians as irrelevant to them. Paul himself lamented the failure of most of his fellow Jews to be enlightened by his message: 'Moses ... put a veil over his face to keep the people of Israel from gazing at the end of the glory that was being set aside. But their minds were hardened. Indeed, to this very day, when they hear the reading of the old covenant, that same veil is still there, since only in Christ is it set aside.'[55]

By the end of the first century CE, most Christians were gentile in origin and saw their faith as distinct from Judaism. But throughout the second and third centuries CE the doctrines espoused by different groups professing Christianity were just as varied as those of first-century Judaism. Among these groups were small coteries of Christians who professed themselves as Jews either because this was their ethnic origin or as a statement of adherence to the Torah alongside their faith in Jesus as saviour. Most of what we are told about these Jewish Christians comes from hostile and unreliable witnesses within what became the mainstream of the Church. So, for instance, it is from the attacks of heresiologists such as Irenaeus, Hippolytus and Epiphanius that we learn about the Ebionites, Jewish Christians who kept the Torah, rejected the epistles of Paul and believed that Jesus was the human son of Joseph and Mary, and that the Holy Spirit came on him only when he was baptized. The Ebionites are said to have flourished in the second to fourth centuries CE and are sometimes by these ancient sources located specifically to the east of the River Jordan. Their name comes probably from the Hebrew *evyon*, 'poor', which may reflect the severe asceticism they are alleged to have adopted. That they portrayed themselves as Christians can be presumed from the polemic of other Christians. Whether they also portrayed themselves as Jews, or were just described polemically as Jews by their opponents because of their attitudes to the Torah, is unknown.[56]

In the fourth century both the great Christian theologian Jerome and the heresiologist Epiphanius noted the existence of a gospel in Aramaic in use among a group in Syria called Nazoraeans. These Nazoraeans were said to be Christians of Jewish origin who continued to obey much of the Torah but were 'orthodox' Christians in other respects. The relation between this group and the Ebionites is debated, but 'Nazoraean' probably referred to Nazareth as the place of Jesus' residence and is related to the term *notsrim* found, in reference to Christians, in rabbinic texts. Later attempts to bring Jews to Christian beliefs, down to the modern phenomenon of Jews for Jesus, have all begun not as movements from within Judaism but as missions to the Jews from the gentile Christian mainstream. Many of these Hebrew Christian groups – some, like Beth Sar Shalom, dating back to the nineteenth century – preach vehemently to non-Christian Jews that acceptance of Jesus as Messiah is not a rejection of Judaism but, on the contrary, its fulfilment. In order to encourage this mission, they themselves sometimes observe Jewish religious rituals such as the Seder and regard themselves as fully Jewish.

Quite different in origin are the Judaizing groups which have broken away from mainstream Christianity over the centuries, such as the Szombatos ('Sabbatarians') in seventeenth-century Transylvania, who insisted that literal observance of the laws in the Old Testament should be an integral part of the religion of all Christians, not just those born as Jews. The Subbotniki, a sect which emerged in Russia at the end of the eighteenth century, advocated observance of the Jewish Sabbath, circumcision, avoidance of unclean animals, and strict monotheism. Exiled to Siberia in 1826, the Subbotniki maintained a distinct identity into the twentieth century, when some of them adopted non-Christian Judaism and settled in Palestine as Jews.[57]

The attitude of many Christians to Judaism over much of the past two millennia has been more hostile, but the extreme views expressed by Marcion (see above, in the discussion of Philo), who claimed that the God of the Old Testament is an inferior creator of the material world to be distinguished from the saviour God proclaimed in the New Testament, were roundly rejected by what became the mainstream Church. Marcion's theology would have required a total break between Judaism and Christianity, but he was denounced by his fellow Christians and eventually excommunicated. For Christians who aligned themselves against Marcion over the following centuries, a total disjunction of their faith from Judaism was impossible so long as they continued to appeal to their own interpretations of biblical prophecies found in the Septuagint.

But the need of scripture-based Christians to relate their new creed to Judaism was not balanced by any religious requirement for Jews to relate themselves to Pauline Christianity. Not even the name Paul is to be found in any surviving Jewish writings from late antiquity. Unlike Jesus, against whom the rabbis, as we have seen, devised a coded polemic, Paul and later Christians were apparently simply ignored.

Within the broad church of Judaism in the first century CE it was possible to combine different interpretations of the Mosaic law with a variety of enthusiasms for supererogatory piety without any conflict. Thus Rabban Gamaliel, the teacher of Paul before Paul became a follower of Jesus, was both a Pharisee and a rabbinic sage. It was possible to be either a Pharisee or a Sadducee or a rabbinic sage and also to be a *haver* or nazirite. It was possible in principle to interpret the Torah allegorically as Philo did and to belong to any of the three philosophies of Judaism singled out by Josephus and discussed in Chapter 6.

All the more curious, then, is the eventual parting of the ways between Christianity and Judaism which marked the limits of variety within Judaism. Defining and dating the parting has proved contentious, since Judaism and Christianity have continued to share the common heritage of the Hebrew Bible down to the present. As we have seen, the only element of early Christianity which seems to have been without parallel elsewhere in first-century Judaism was the founding of a new religious movement in the name of a leader after his death.

Much of the disagreement about the nature and date of the split between Christianity and Judaism derives from difference of perspective. Someone considered Jewish by a Christian might not consider himself or herself Jewish. He or she might or might not be considered a Jew by non-Christian Jews. Contact and conflict between members of distinct groups, and their sharing of theological notions or liturgical practices, might or might not imply a lack of clarity for the ancient participants of each group about the differences between them.

Modern scholars sometimes find themselves at a loss to decide whether surviving texts written even as late as the fourth century CE were Jewish or Christian. But for most Christians the break with Judaism had begun in the time of Paul, with the growth of a gentile Church which saw itself as the true Israel in contrast to the Jews of the old covenant. Ultimately, the cause of the split lay less in any perceived incompatibility of Christian theology within the variegated religious landscape of contemporary Judaism than in the self-definition of Christians, for whom the urgings of Paul to see their faith in Christ as novel and all-encompassing were reinforced by the tendency of the wider Roman world to treat Christianity as the religion of gentiles who had forsaken their ancestral gods rather than as a branch of Judaism.[58]

8

Preoccupations and Expectations

It will have become apparent in the course of the last two chapters that even Jews who disagreed on fundamental matters during the late Second Temple period shared a common concern for issues on which they focused their enthusiasm. Jews of many different religious persuasions, it seems, had views on purity and how to observe the Sabbath. There was considerable discussion about the correct computation of the calendar and the validity of oaths. There was much speculation about demons and angels. There was wide concern for prophecy about the immediate and eschatological future, and debate about the value of martyrdom and expectation for life after death. None of these concerns was the sole property of any one group or philosophy within Judaism in the first century CE. On the contrary, these preoccupations were widely shared and constituted the main topics for innovation and argument across the whole spectrum of late Second Temple Judaism.

PURITY, SABBATH AND CALENDAR

The laws of purity were laid out in considerable detail in the Pentateuch, as we have seen (Chapter 4), but in the late Second Temple period many Jews discussed intensively both the relation of pollution to sin and the mechanics of acquiring pollution and of cleansing. Biblical notions of impurity applied both to ritual pollution which came from natural processes such as death, sex and disease and were reckoned physically contagious, causing impurity to a lesser degree, and to moral pollution. Thus the language of ritual impurity applied metaphorically to sin, so that the Psalmist pleaded 'Purge me with hyssop, and I shall be clean' and Isaiah looked forward to the time when 'the Lord has washed away the filth of the daughters of Zion and cleaned the bloodstains of Jerusalem from its midst by a spirit of judgement and a spirit of burning'.

The allusive language of the Torah left unclear precisely what constituted pollution. The book of Leviticus uses the word *tame* ('unclean') to refer within a few chapters first to animals unfit for comsumption and then to a woman after childbirth and a man with a skin disease. The same word (*tame*) was used to condemn an illegitimate marriage union: 'If a man shall take his brother's wife, it is an unclean thing.' The biblical text left space for intense disputes over very precise issues. Hence the debate whether an unbroken stream of liquid transfers pollution upstream, which we have seen (Chapter 6) was discussed both by Pharisees and Sadducees and in the sectarian missive MMT sent from the Dead Sea Yahad to (probably) the High Priest in Jerusalem: 'And furthermore concerning the pouring (of liquids), we say that it contains no purity. And furthermore the pouring does not separate the impure {from the pure}, for the poured liquid and that in the receptacle are alike, one liquid.'[1]

Many Jews in this period seem to have taken purity notions far beyond the biblical base. The rationale of food laws in Leviticus was that 'you shall not defile yourselves . . . you shall be holy, for I am holy.' They had been for many Jews a symbol also of separation from the gentile world. In Jubilees, composed in the second century BCE, eating with gentiles is itself seen as defiling. A taboo on the use of gentile olive oil was widespread among Jews from at least the second century BCE, so that sale to the Jews of Syria of Jewish oil from Galilee was a lucrative trade during the first year of the independent Jewish state of 66–70 CE. In Jerusalem, Galilee and at Qumran many fragments have been found of stone vessels, used for food and drink probably because stone was not considered susceptible to impurity. The Mishnah attributes to the Houses of Hillel and Shammai in the first century CE an assumption that there should be a general prohibition on eating meat and milk together on the basis of the biblical injunction not to seethe a kid in its mother's milk. The wider prohibition, which has had substantial impact on Jewish cuisine down to modern times, was apparently unknown to Philo in Alexandria, since he took the biblical text literally and saw nothing wrong with mixing meat and milk so long as the milk of the mother animal was not used, and the taboo may originally have been confined to the circles of the rabbinic sages, but it was probably more widespread: the prohibition is not singled out for emphasis in the Mishnah and the first-century sages are portrayed as in debate over its extension to the avoidance of placing fowl on the same dining table as cheese.

We have seen that the language of purity and pollution permeates the sectarian texts found among the Dead Sea scrolls, where the members of the community required purity of body as well as spirit for a life of perfect holiness: 'They shall not enter the water to partake of the pure Meal of the men of holiness, for they shall not be cleansed unless they turn from their wickedness: for all who transgress His word are unclean.' We have seen also that Essenes extended the notion of pollution to defecation. The *haverim* ate ordinary food in the same state of purity as was required for priests eating tithed produce. The Gospels report Jesus as taking Pharisees to task for hypocrisy in their concern for purity: 'You blind Pharisee! First clean the inside of the cup, so that the outside also may become clean.'[2]

Ritual pollution could be ritually purified by bathing, and among some Jews such bathing took on new significance. Identifying ritual baths in the many structures found by archaeologists that may have been used for this purpose is not always easy, since stepped pools did not necessarily have a ritual function, but the number of possible pools found in Jewish sites suggests their use was common. The Essenes practised daily ablutions, as did presumably the Hemerobaptists ('Daily Bathers'), a Jewish group in the first century known only from references in later Christian texts. Most striking of all was the use of bathing to mark forgiveness of sins by John the Baptist, as described by Josephus. John 'had exhorted the Jews ... to join in baptism ... They must not employ it to gain pardon for whatever sins they committed, but as a consecration of the body implying that the soul was already thoroughly cleansed by right behaviour.'[3]

The biblical regulations for the observance of the Sabbath proved equally susceptible to multiple interpretations. The habit of Jews of stopping work once a week was one of their characteristics most widely known in the broader Mediterranean world, in part perhaps because some Greek cities gave Jews special privileges not to appear in court cases on the Sabbath – as we have seen, extreme allegorists were attacked by Philo precisely for not observing this taboo. The Essenes interpreted Sabbath restrictions with great strictness, refusing to go outside their camps even to defecate until the end of the day, whereas the *tannaim* adopted the notion of a 'sabbath limit' as a distance of 2,000 cubits which did not count as forbidden travel on the day of rest. The custom endorsed by the *tannaim* of cordoning off a courtyard between two houses for the purpose of the Sabbath to allow objects to be carried into what would otherwise be public space was an innovation not recognized by Sadducees, whose lack of cooperation might prove an obstacle if they were neighbours.

The extent of change in Sabbath observance was recognized explicitly in the books of Maccabees with regard to warfare on Saturdays. Profanation of the Sabbath had been one of the first elements in the persecution of Judaism by Antiochus, so the pious rebels were unwilling originally to commit such profanation in pursuit of their cause. As a result, they died horrifically, holed up in hiding-places in the wilderness: 'Then the enemy quickly attacked them. But they did not answer them or hurl a stone at them or block up their hiding places, for they said, "Let us all die in our innocence . . ." So they attacked them on the sabbath, and they died.' In response, Mattathias (father of Judah Maccabee) and his colleagues decided that defensive warfare must be justified:

> And all said to their neighbours: 'If we all do as our kindred have done and refuse to fight with the gentiles for our lives and for our ordinances, they will quickly destroy us from the earth.' So they made this decision that day: 'Let us fight against anyone who comes to attack us on the sabbath day; let us not all die as our kindred died in their hiding-places.'[4]

For Josephus, this interpretation of the Sabbath laws had become standard – 'the law permits us to defend ourselves against those who begin a battle and strike us, but it does not allow us to fight against an enemy that does anything else' – but he himself presented evidence that this understanding had failed to reach some other parts of the Jewish world two centuries after Mattathias. In telling a story about some Jewish brigands in Mesopotamia in the mid-first century CE, Josephus noted that one of them, a weaver called Asinaeus from Nehardea, when told by one of his scouts that Parthian horsemen were about to attack his camp, and reminded that 'our hands are tied because the commandment of our ancestral law orders us to do no work,' had to decide for himself to fight on the Sabbath day: 'He thought it better observance of the law, instead of gladdening the foe by a death without anything accomplished, to take his courage in his hands, let the straits into which he had fallen excuse violation of the law, and die, if he must, exacting a just vengeance.'[5]

The strictest interpretation of the Sabbath is that enjoined in the book of Jubilees, which presented the Sabbath as the basic unit of God's time, adding to the biblical prohibitions of work a number of new restrictions, including lifting a load, drawing water, sexual intercourse and fasting. For Jubilees, the Sabbath was the basis of the 364-day calendar to which the author ascribed immense importance. This schematic calendar, in which the year was divided precisely into four quarters of ninety-one days, and incorporated all sorts of regularities around the numbers 4, 7 and 13, was in quite widespread use in the last centuries BCE. It is also found in a section of I Enoch, composed probably in the third century BCE, which calls itself 'the Book about the Motion of the Heavenly Luminaries' and contains revelation of astronomical wisdom to the patriarch Enoch by the angel Uriel:

> This is the first law of the luminaries: the luminary (called) the sun has its emergence through the heavenly gates in the east and its setting through the western gates of the sky. I saw six gates through which the sun emerges and six gates through which the sun sets. The moon rises and sets in those gates and the leaders of the stars with the ones they lead, six in the east and six in the west, all of them – one directly after the other. There were many windows on the right and left of those gates.

Fragments of this Enoch text, or something similar, were found among the Dead Sea scrolls, and some of the sectarian scrolls treat the 364-day year as a divinely ordained system reflecting the true order of the world.

Unlike this calendar, which followed a roughly solar pattern, lunar time reckoning was more common among Jews: 'From the moon comes the sign for Festal days, a light that wanes when it completes its course.' Both Josephus and Philo presupposed a calendar that operated according to the moon, and the early rabbis took it for granted that a month would start only when the new moon had been observed and confirmed by appropriate human authorities. Calendrical discrepancies even between those operating lunar calendars could raise very practical issues, as we have seen in the differences between Pharisees and Sadducees about the date of festival offerings in the Temple.[6]

VOWS, OATHS AND ASCETICISM

Speculation about the calendar may perhaps be ascribed to the lack of clarity on the calendar in biblical texts. The opposite is the case with vows and oaths, of which the Bible has many examples, while warning strongly against swearing falsely in God's name and requiring sacrifices for failure to uphold an oath, even if the oath was made in error. Even the biblical discussion of the right of an adult male sometimes to annul vows and oaths made by his wife or daughter assumes the strength of such binding utterances. Hence the imprecations of Ben Sira in the second century BCE against oaths of any kind: 'Do not accustom your mouth to oaths, nor habitually utter the name of the Holy One; for as a servant who is constantly under scrutiny will not lack bruises, so also the person who always swears and utters the Name will never be cleansed from sin. One who swears many oaths is full of iniquity.' Philo urged avoidance of oaths and vows wherever possible. Josephus states that the Essenes avoided oaths altogether (although he also notes that their initiation rite included 'tremendous oaths', so they were not perhaps consistent).

Jesus is portrayed in the Gospel of Matthew as taking the same stance:

> Again, you have heard that it was said to those of ancient times, 'You shall not swear falsely, but carry out the vows you have made to the Lord.' But I say to you, Do not swear at all, either by heaven, for it is the throne of God, or by the earth, for it is his footstool, or by Jerusalem, for it is the city of the great King ... Let your word be 'Yes, Yes' or 'No, No'; anything more than this comes from the evil one.

By contrast, both the Pharisees and the early rabbis assumed that vows and oaths would be made (as envisaged in the Bible) and that what mattered was scrupulous observance – hence the vehement accusation attributed to Jesus:

> Woe to you, blind guides, who say, 'Whoever swears by the sanctuary is bound by nothing, but whoever swears by the gold of the sanctuary is bound by the oath.' You blind fools! For which is greater, the gold or the sanctuary that has made the gold sacred? And you say, 'Whoever swears by the altar is bound by nothing, but whoever swears by the gift that is on the altar is bound by the oath.' How blind you are! For which is greater, the gift or the altar that makes the gift sacred? So whoever swears by the altar, swears by it and by everything on it; and whoever swears by heaven, swears by the throne of God and by the one who is seated upon it.

Against this background it is notable that the nazirite vow was evidently common both in the diaspora and in Judaea throughout this period, as we have seen in Chapter 7.[7]

Some Jews in this period ascribed religious value to asceticism, of which the nazirite vow was just one example, in its own right. The clearest expression of this attitude may be found in Josephus' description of a teacher named Bannus with whom he claimed to have lived for three years as a teenager. Josephus wrote that he had discovered Bannus living in the desert 'wearing clothes [made] from trees, scavenging food that grew by itself, and washing frequently for purification – with frigid water, day and night'. It is hard to tell how much of the piety that Josephus evidently ascribed to this teacher derived from the harshness of his life and how much from his avoidance of pollution by manufactured clothes and food. In many respects John the Baptist is portrayed in the Gospels as similar to Bannus in his insistence on purity, since (apart from ablutions) he wore camel-hair clothing and a skin tied around his loins, and ate only locusts and wild honey, eating no bread and drinking no wine, but in at least one passage in the Gospel of Matthew he is portrayed as remarkable not only for the purity of his food but for his abstinence: in comparison to Jesus, who 'came eating and drinking, and they say, "Look, a glutton and drunkard"', 'John came neither eating nor drinking, and they say, "He has a demon."'[8]

We have seen (in Chapter 4) that the use of fasts for repentance was well established in the Bible, but fasting seems to have become much more common among Jews in the late Second Temple period. The Roman historian Tacitus wrote that Jews 'by frequent fasts . . . bear witness to the long hunger with which they were once distressed', and Josephus singled out fasts as among the characteristics of Judaism (along with the Sabbath and food taboos) which have spread to the gentile masses: 'there is not one city, Greek or barbarian, nor a single nation, where the fasts . . . are not observed.' Lack of rain or other natural disasters could prompt a public fast, as described (or perhaps just imagined) in the Mishnah:

> On the first three days of fasting, the priests of the course fasted but not the whole day; and they of the father's house did not fast at all. On the second three days, the priests of the course fasted throughout the whole day, and they of the father's house fasted but not the whole day. But on the last seven days, both of them fasted throughout the whole day. So R. Joshua. But the Sages say: On the first three days of fasting neither fasted at all. On the second three days the priests of the course fasted but not the whole day, and they of the father's house did not fast at all. On the last seven days, the priests of the course fasted throughout the whole day, and they of the father's house fasted but not the whole day.[9]

Such fasting for rain could take highly ritualistic form, as in stories about the fasts and prayers of the pious Honi the circle-maker, who seems to have lived in the first half of the first century BCE:

> Once they said to Honi the Circle-maker, 'Pray that rain may fall.' He answered, 'Go out and bring in Passover ovens that they be not softened.'

He prayed, but the rain did not fall. What did he do? He drew a circle and
stood within it and said before God, 'O Lord of the world, your children
have turned their faces to me, for that I am like a son of the house before
thee. I swear by your great name that I will not stir hence until you have
pity on your children.'

The rain came, although achieving the right level of precipitation to
satisfy the public – neither too light nor too violent – required further prayer. In due course the rain fell in such abundance that Honi
had to pray for the 'rain of goodwill, blessing and graciousness' to go
away.

Private fasting might be expected to bring the individual closer to
God to experience apocalyptic visions (see below), but it could also be
a simple mark of humble piety, as of the beautiful widow Judith who
'fasted all the days of her widowhood, except . . . the festivals and days
of rejoicing of the house of Israel . . . No one spoke ill of her, for she
feared God with great devotion.' This image of Judith's piety at home is
portrayed in the book in the Apocrypha which bears her name as
entirely private until a national emergency draws her into very public
action, striking off the head of Holofernes, the commander of the Assyrian army, to public praise from the whole community. Such an image is
typical of a number of heroines of Second Temple literature: Esther was
the virtuous woman prepared to infiltrate the Persian court to save her
people, and Susanna, the story of whose failed seduction formed a novella within the Greek version of the book of Daniel, was a virtuous wife
willing to die rather than succumb.[10]

MAGIC, DEMONS AND ANGELS

Ezekiel had reported women 'who sew magic bands upon all wrists and
make veils for the head of persons of every stature, in the hunt for
souls', and the book of Exodus specifically singles out the sorceress as a
danger ('you shall not permit a female sorcerer to live'), but post-biblical
Jewish magic was developed (as far as is known) by male practitioners,
and their actions could be treated as pious if carried out in the right
spirit. We have already seen the power of Honi the circle-maker to bring
rain. Early rabbinic sources attributed similar miracles to the pious
Hanina b. Dosa, who is known in the Mishnah as 'a man of deed' able
to predict the fate of the ill:

Once the son of R. Gamaliel fell ill. He sent two scholars to R. Hanina b. Dosa to ask him to pray for him. When he saw them he went up to an upper chamber and prayed for him. When he came down he said to them: 'Go, the fever has left him.' They said to him: 'Are you a prophet?' He replied: 'I am neither a prophet nor the son of a prophet, but I learnt this from experience. If my prayer is fluent in my mouth, I know that he is accepted: but if not, I know that he is rejected.' They sat down and made a note of the exact moment. When they came to R. Gamaliel, he said to them: 'By the temple service! You have not been a moment too soon or too late, but so it happened: at that very moment the fever left him and he asked for water to drink.'

Opposition to magic remained frequent and vehement. One story attributes the cause of Israel's slavery at the hands of the Midianites in biblical times to the belief of the people of Israel in the Midianite magician Aod (who 'worked with his magic tricks . . . and the people of Israel were deceived . . . And God said "I will deliver them into the hands of the Midianites, because they have been deceived by them"'). But the lines between legitimate prayer and magic, and between medicine and magic, were thin, and Josephus traced back to Solomon the healing incantations which still exorcised demons in his day:

God also enabled him to learn the technique against demons for the benefit and healing of humans. He composed incantations by which illnesses are relieved, and left behind exorcistic practices with which those binding demons expel them so that they return no more. And this same form of healing remains quite strong among us until today. For I became acquainted with a certain Eleazar of my own people, who in the presence of Vespasian and his sons, along with their tribunes and a crowd of soldiers, delivered those possessed by demons.

The New Testament describes many such exorcisms both by Jesus and by others, although some such healing is recounted with approval, some with scorn:

God did extraordinary miracles through Paul, so that when the handkerchiefs or aprons that had touched his skin were brought to the sick, their diseases left them, and the evil spirits came out of them. Then some itinerant Jewish exorcists tried to use the name of the Lord Jesus over those who had evil spirits, saying, 'I adjure you by the Jesus whom Paul proclaims.' Seven sons of a Jewish high priest named Sceva were doing this. But the evil spirit said to them in reply, 'Jesus I know, and Paul I know; but who are you?' Then the man with the evil spirit leapt on them, mastered them all, and so overpowered them that they fled out of the house naked and wounded.[11]

Exorcisms presuppose a world containing unseen evil forces which can operate against the interests of humans unless God intervenes. The Hebrew Bible has little to say about the nature of demons and evil spirits (although their existence is presumed), but in the late third century BCE the Book of the Watchers, preserved in I Enoch, attributed the origins of evil spirits to forbidden intercourse between fallen angels (or 'watchers') and human women. These evil spirits are envisaged in some texts from Qumran as ranged (as the Sons of Darkness) against the Sons of Light; in the last days, according to the War Scroll (composed probably in the first century BCE), 'in three lots shall the sons of light brace themselves in battle to strike down iniquity, and in three lots shall Belial brace itself to thrust back the company of God.' The role of Belial (and other figures, such as Mastema, who is sometimes identified with Belial) as leader of these 'spirits of the angel of destruction' reflects a moderately dualistic view of the cosmos in which, despite the overwhelming power of God as creator, the state of the present world is governed by the tensions of conflicting powers, with the world and humanity divided into two opposing but not coeternal forces as described in the book of Jubilees:

> During the third week of this jubilee impure demons began to mislead Noah's grandchildren, to make them act foolishly, and to destroy them. Then Noah's sons came to their father Noah and told him about the demons who were misleading, blinding, and killing his grandchildren. He prayed before the Lord his God and said: 'God of the spirits which are in all animate beings . . . because your mercy for me has been large and your kindness to me has been great: may your mercy be lifted over the children of your children; and may the wicked spirits not rule them in order to destroy them from the earth. Now you bless me and my children so that we may increase, become numerous, and fill the earth. You know how your Watchers, the fathers of these spirits, have acted during my lifetime. As for these spirits who have remained alive, imprison them and hold them captive in the place of judgement. May they not cause destruction among your servant's sons, my God, for they are savage and were created for the purpose of destroying.[12]

Such notions may have helped to explain how the supreme benevolent deity allows evil to flourish in the world, but they coexisted with the Deuteronomistic concept of divine punishment for sin which allowed for human free will. As Josephus observed, lamenting the failure of the Jews to recognize the divine signs warning of the disastrous destruction of the Temple if they did not change their ways, 'reflecting on these things one will find that God has a care for men, and by all kinds of premonitory signs shows His people the way of salvation, while they owe their destruction to folly and calamities of their own choosing.' It is remarkable however that even this balance, which might seem implicit in the whole biblical narrative of God's relation to Israel, was disputed in Josephus' day by the Sadducees, as we have seen in Chapter 6. According to the Mishnah, R. Akiva was to say in the second century CE that 'all is foreseen, but freedom of choice is given.'[13]

The problem of linking the human to the divine sphere was in part tackled by speculation on the role of angels, which had been ill defined in the Bible but became increasingly precise in the last centuries of the Second Temple, expanding into speculation on the nature of a whole divine world, replete with angels of different orders. We have seen in Chapter 6 that such angels are envisaged in the Songs of the Sabbath Sacrifice found among the Dead Sea scrolls as intensively engaged in worship: 'The [cheru]bim prostrate themselves before him and bless. As they rise, a whispered divine voice [is heard], and there is a roar of praise. When they drop their wings, there is a [whispere]d divine voice. The cherubim bless the image of the throne-chariot above the firmament, [and] they praise [the majes]ty of the luminous firmament beneath His seat of glory.'[14]

Angels are active in the eschatological battle alongside the Sons of Light against the Sons of Darkness in the War Scroll. They are envisaged as organized in hierarchies, led by the archangels Michael, Gabriel, Raphael and Uriel, and functioning as priests in the heavenly temple: 'He gave us the sabbath day as a great sign so that we should perform work for six days and that we should keep sabbath from all work on the seventh day. He told us – all the angels of the presence and all the angels of holiness (these two great kinds) – to keep sabbath with him in heaven and on earth.' But angels also played an important role in bringing before the Lord the prayers of the righteous, and in intervening on their behalf in the world. Hence the extraordinary story found in III Maccabees, with a fictional setting in the third century BCE, of the foiling of an attempt by the king Ptolemy Philopater to have Jews trampled to death in the hippodrome by elephants:

Just as Eleazar was ending his prayer, the king arrived at the hippodrome with the animals and all the arrogance of his forces. And when the Jews

observed this they raised great cries to heaven so that even the nearby valleys resounded with them and brought an uncontrollable terror upon the
army. Then the most glorious, almighty, and true God revealed his holy
face and opened the heavenly gates, from which two glorious angels of
fearful aspect descended, visible to all but the Jews. They opposed the
forces of the enemy and filled them with confusion and terror, binding
them with immovable shackles. Even the king began to shudder bodily,
and he forgot his sullen insolence. The animals turned back upon the
armed forces following them and began trampling and destroying them.

Such notions about angels existed alongside other speculation
about intermediaries between God and humankind. We have seen
(Chapter 7) the role of the Logos in the philosophy of Philo. The author
of Wisdom of Solomon, composed probably in the second century BCE,
built on the biblical wisdom tradition to portray the personified figure
of Wisdom herself as a companion of God (although, in the rather
breathless description, the precise relationship is left unclear, perhaps
deliberately):

> For wisdom is more mobile than any motion; because of her pureness she
> pervades and penetrates all things. For she is a breath of the power of God,
> and a pure emanation of the glory of the Almighty; therefore nothing
> defiled gains entrance into her. For she is a reflection of eternal light, a
> spotless mirror of the working of God, and an image of his goodness ...
> She reaches mightily from one end of the earth to the other, and she orders
> all things well. I loved her and sought her from my youth; I desired to take
> her for my bride, and became enamoured of her beauty. She glorifies her
> noble birth by living with God, and the Lord of all loves her. For she is an
> initiate in the knowledge of God, and an associate in his works.[15]

VISIONS AND PROPHECY

Both the figure of Wisdom and angels might bring divine messages to
humans. Angels played this role particularly in the narrative of apocalyptic texts, of which a great variety survives from this period, mostly
because of their popularity among later Christians. So, for instance, the
Apocalypse of Abraham, preserved only in Slavonic, contains the instruction of the patriarch by the angel Yaoel: 'The angel he sent to me in the
likeness of a man came, and he took me by my right hand and stood me
on my feet.' In these apocalyptic texts theological understanding comes

to the sage from outside, by divine initiative through a vision, as in the biblical book of Daniel:

> In the third year of King Cyrus of Persia a word was revealed to Daniel, who was named Belteshazzar. The word was true, and it concerned a great conflict. He understood the word, having received understanding in the vision. At that time I, Daniel, had been mourning for three weeks ... On the twenty-fourth day of the first month, as I was standing on the bank of the great river (that is, the Tigris), I looked up and saw a man clothed in linen, with a belt of gold from Uphaz around his waist. His body was like beryl, his face like lightning, his eyes like flaming torches, his arms and legs like the gleam of burnished bronze, and the sound of his words like the roar of a multitude. I, Daniel, alone saw the vision; the people who were with me did not see the vision, though a great trembling fell upon them, and they fled and hid themselves. So I was left alone to see this great vision. My strength left me, and my complexion grew deathly pale, and I retained no strength. Then I heard the sound of his words; and when I heard the sound of his words, I fell into a trance, face to the ground.

How such experiences as narrated in the texts related to lived experience is unknown. Daniel in this account stated that he 'had eaten no rich food, no meat or wine had entered my mouth, and I had not anointed myself at all, for the full three weeks' (of mourning) before the wisdom came, which may suggest that these narratives reflect ascetic practices resulting in trance-like dreams and automatic writing. Such behaviour is attested in other societies and is exemplified in the mystical vision of the (probably Jewish) author of the book of Revelation in the New Testament:

> I was in the spirit on the Lord's day, and I heard behind me a loud voice like a trumpet saying, 'Write in a book what you see and send it to the seven churches ...' Then I turned to see whose voice it was that spoke to me, and on turning I saw seven gold lampstands, and in the midst of the lampstands I saw one like the Son of Man, clothed with a long robe and with a golden sash across his chest. His head and his hair were white as white wool, white as snow; his eyes were like burnished bronze, refined as in a furnace, and his voice was like the sound of many waters. In his right hand he held seven stars, and from his mouth came a sharp, two-edged sword, and his face was like the sun shining with full force.[16]

Such revelations should perhaps not surprise in a religious system that is founded on the revelation to Moses on Mount Sinai. But there are numerous traditions from the end of the Second Temple that prophecy had ceased some centuries earlier. Such traditions reflect an apparent failure of religious nerve, which may also account for the attribution of many of the apocalyptic texts that survive from this period to ancient sages of the biblical past, such as Enoch, Abraham, Daniel and Ezra. Josephus suggested obscurely that the 'exact succession of the prophets' had been broken in the time of Artaxerxes five centuries before he wrote. A similar tradition was recorded by the early rabbis that 'when the last of the biblical prophets died, the holy spirit ceased in Israel'; from then onwards, 'they were informed by means of a heavenly voice.'

The tradition that true prophecy had come to an end some time in the past was somewhat at odds with the activities, described by Josephus himself, of numerous prophets. Of these, the most evidently accurate was Jesus son of Ananias (see Chapter 5), 'a rude peasant', who stood in the Temple from the festival of Tabernacles in 62 CE to the destruction in 70 CE predicting its downfall: 'A voice from the east, a voice from the west, a voice from the four winds; a voice against Jerusalem and the sanctuary, a voice against the bridegroom and the bride, a voice against all the people'. It seems however to be significant that, even though Josephus could proudly boast about his own ability to interpret dreams and his skill 'in divining the meaning of ambiguous utterances of the Deity' – a skill, attributed to his priestly descent, which meant that he was 'not ignorant of the prophecy of the sacred books' – he never calls himself a prophet any more than he calls Jesus son of Ananias a prophet. On the contrary, he labelled numerous religious leaders 'pseudo-prophets' who led the people astray. Evidently contemporaries who claimed divine inspiration might expect scorn. 'No prophet is accepted in the prophet's home town,' as Jesus is said to have noted ruefully, and pseudonymity or anonymity were safer. Most of the sectarian Dead Sea scrolls are in fact anonymous, and the practice of pseudepigraphy for revelation was aided by its common use in other genres. Wisdom was commonly assigned to Solomon, psalms to David and legal interpretations to Moses, simply because such developments of thought were regarded essentially as elaborations of the paradigms created by the biblical founder figures.[17]

ESCHATOLOGY AND MESSIANISM

The messages conveyed to the pseudonymous sages in these apocalypses after they had ascended to heaven sometimes concerned the fate of individuals. In the Testament of Abraham, a remarkable text from the fifth century CE preserved by Christians in various languages but probably originally composed in Greek by an Egyptian Jew in the first or early second century CE, the author imagined, with some humour, the last days of Abraham and portrayed the patriarch learning from the archangel Michael about the inevitability of death and the operation of divine judgement. But most apocalypses known from the late Second Temple period concern revelations of a new age or world order which will overwhelm the present age with its glory.

The prevalence of these eschatological notions in the major Jewish apocalypses preserved by Christians, such as I Enoch and IV Ezra, may reflect Christian concerns for insight into the mysteries of the cosmos and its future. But the discovery of some of these apocalyptic texts, such as I Enoch, at Qumran, along with fragments of previously unknown apocalyptic writings, shows that eschatological speculation was also found among other Jews. The Qumran sectarians looked forward like other Jews to 'the end of days'. Even Philo speculated on the nature of the end time, when all who return to the law of God will assemble in the holy land:

> For even though they dwell in the uttermost parts of the earth, in slavery to those who led them away captive, one signal, as it were, one day will bring liberty to all. This conversion in a body to virtue will strike awe into their masters, who will set them free, ashamed to rule over men better than themselves. When they have gained this unexpected liberty, those who but now were scattered in Greece and the outside world over islands and continents will arise and post from every side with one impulse to the once appointed place, guided in their pilgrimage by a vision divine and superhuman unseen by others but manifest to them as they pass from exile to their home ... When they have arrived the cities which but now lay in ruins will be cities once more; the desolate land will be inhabited; the barren will change into fruitfulness; all the prosperity of their fathers and ancestors will seem a tiny fragment, so lavish will be the abundant riches in their possession, which flowing from the gracious bounties of God as from a perennial fountain will bring to each individually and to all in

common a deep stream of wealth leaving no room for envy. Everything
will suddenly be reversed . . .

Other expectations, found scattered through texts from the Qumran
War Scroll to the apocalypses and early rabbinic literature, speculate on
the confusion before the last days, the great battles against hostile powers, and the eventual renewal of Jerusalem, the gathering of the dispersed
and a kingdom of glory in the holy land: 'You, O Lord, you chose David
king over Israel, and you swore to him concerning his offspring forever,
that his palace would never fail before you . . . And he shall gather a
holy people whom he shall lead in righteousness, and he shall judge the
tribes of the people that has been sanctified by the Lord, his God.'[18]

There are no good reasons to believe that such speculation about the
eventual fate of Israel, however common it may have been, played a
dominant role in the religious life of many Jews in the late Second
Temple period. Philo at least, despite his interest in the end time, was
content to wait for the divine timetable. Early Christians (who preserved
many of these texts) were unusual in defining their world outlook through
the prism of the last days which they believed had already arrived. On the
other hand, the behaviour of some other Jewish groups in first-century
Judaea suggests similar urgent expectations. A certain Theudas in the
mid-40s CE gathered a crowd of followers and persuaded them to take
up their possessions and to follow him down to the Jordan, claiming
'that he was a prophet and that at his command the river would be
parted and would provide them with an easy passage'. The effort was
thwarted by Roman cavalry and the capture and execution of Theudas,
but the enthusiasm generated implies expectations of a miraculous
change, even if, as the Pharisee Gamaliel is alleged to have said to the
Sanhedrin in Jerusalem, the uprising came to nothing because the undertaking was of human origin and not 'of God'. A decade later, a Jew from
Egypt, similarly declaring himself a prophet, gathered a large number of
supporters in the desert, intending to lead them to the Mount of Olives,
asserting 'that he wished to demonstrate from there that on his command the wall of Jerusalem would fall down, through which he promised
them an entrance into the city'. Once again the Roman authorities intervened before the claim was put to the test.[19]

Neither Theudas nor the Egyptian was said by Josephus to have presented himself as a messiah, and it is clear that messianism in the narrow
sense, involving identification of an individual as a messiah, was much
less common than a general belief in eschatological redemption. This is

not because Josephus tried to suppress information about Jewish hopes for a messianic leader, for, as we have seen in Chapter 5, in fact he emphasized in his narration of the destruction of Jerusalem that 'what more than all else incited them to the war was an ambiguous oracle ... to the effect that at that time one from their country would become ruler of the world'. This oracle was indeed of particular significance for Josephus, since what he took as its correct meaning, 'the sovereignty of Vespasian, who was proclaimed emperor on Jewish soil', had first been recognized by Josephus himself through divine grace and had led to the dramatic reversal of his fortunes which accounted for his freedom to write about these events in comfort in Rome. Josephus was well aware of the Greek term *Christos*, 'anointed one', as a translation of the Hebrew *mashiah*, but he used it only in reference to Christians, and not for any of the other religious enthusiasts whose role in first-century Judaea he documented.[20]

According to Acts, the name *Christianoi* was first accorded to Christians – by others – in Antioch in the mid-first century, to mean 'followers of *Christos*'. Christians are the only group known to have been characterized by messianic beliefs in this way. Eschatological hope did not require expectation of a role for a messianic figure. It is striking that the fullest depiction in any of the Dead Sea scrolls of the battles of the last days, laid out with graphic detail in the War Scroll, envisages the Sons of Light under the leadership of a Prince and a priest and God himself:

And when [Belial] girds himself to come to the aid of the sons of darkness, and when the slain among the foot-soldiers begin to fall by the mysteries of God, and when all the men appointed for battle are put to ordeal by them, the Priests shall sound the trumpets of Summons for another formation of the reserve to advance into battle; and they shall take up their stand between the formations. And for those engaged [in battle] they shall sound the 'Retreat'. Then the High Priest shall draw near, and standing before the formation, he shall strengthen by the power of God their hearts [and hands] in His battle. Speaking he shall say ... the slain, for you have heard from ancient times through the mysteries of God ... This is the day appointed by Him for the defeat and overthrow of the Prince of the kingdom of wickedness, and he will send eternal succour to the company of His redeemed by the might of the princely Angel of the kingdom of Michael. With everlasting light He will enlighten with joy [the children] of Israel ... He will raise up the kingdom of Michael in the midst of the gods, and the realm of Israel

in the midst of all flesh. Righteousness shall rejoice on high, and all the
children of His truth shall jubilate in eternal knowledge. And you, the sons
of His Covenant, be strong in the ordeal of God! His mysteries shall uphold
you until He moves His hand for His trials to come to an end.[21]

Speculation about the nature of the Messiah in any case took wildly
different forms in the late Second Temple period. The role of Elijah as a
messenger from God 'before the great and terrible day of the Lord' was
stated explicitly by the prophet Malachi: 'he will turn the hearts of the
parents to their children and the hearts of children to their parents, so
that I will not come and strike the land with a curse.' The Qumran
Community Rule referred more generically to 'the Prophet', alluding to
the future prophet like Moses promised in the book of Deuteronomy.
The author of the Gospel of John assumed that the obvious questions to
John the Baptist when he appeared in the millennium, once he had
denied being the Messiah, were 'Are you Elijah?' and 'Are you the
prophet?'[22]

The Messiah himself was sometimes thought of as an earthly king
and ruler from the house of David, endowed by God with special powers: 'And he shall lead all of them in equity, and there shall be no
arrogance among them, that any one of them should be oppressed. This
is the majesty of the king of Israel, which God knew, to raise him up
over the house of Israel to discipline it.' At other times he was envisaged
as a supernatural figure, a 'son of man' whose name was uttered 'before
the Lord of the Spirit before the stars of the heaven were made', with
outstanding qualities:

For he is mighty in all the secrets of righteousness; and unrighteousness
will vanish like a shadow, and will have no place to stand. For the Chosen
One has taken his stand in the presence of the Lord of Spirits; and his glory
is forever and ever, and his might, to all generations. In him dwell the spirit
of wisdom and the spirit of insight, and the spirit of instruction and might,
and the spirit of those who have fallen asleep in righteousness. He will
judge the things that are secret, and a lying word none will be able to
speak in his presence; for he is the Chosen One . . .

Some of the more supernatural depictions of the Messiah in Jewish
writings have been influenced by the Christian copyists of the manuscripts in which they are found, but certainly free from Christian influence
are the remarkable references in the sectarian Dead Sea scrolls to a great
variety of messianic images. The scrolls sometimes refer to the priestly

'Messiah of Aaron', sometimes to the 'king Messiah', and sometimes to both together, as in the injunction to the members of the community in the Community Rule: 'They shall depart from none of the counsels of the Law to walk in all the stubbornness of their hearts, but shall be ruled by the primitive precepts in which the men of the Community were first instructed until there shall come the Prophet and the Messiahs of Aaron and Israel.'

We have seen (Chapter 5) that Simon son of Gioras, commander-in-chief of the Jewish rebels in the last days of the war against Rome, may have believed himself a messiah, but no one really knew what the Messiah would be like. When in the mid-first century CE Paul preached to his non-Jewish Christian congregation as an 'apostle of Christ Jesus', the word 'Christ' acted as a proper name, with no descriptive content. It is hard to know why any of his readers would have interpreted the appellation 'Anointed' as implying anything whatever about the last days of the world. Millenarianism was in the air, but there is no reason to think it was gathering force at the end of the Second Temple period.[23]

LIFE AFTER DEATH AND MARTYRDOM

Eschatological speculation often included a general resurrection and judgement of the dead. According to I Enoch, departed souls are held in pens, 'three dark and one light' (with the light reserved for the good), 'until the great day of judgement'. This notion of souls as sleeping until the end of history was widespread. But many Jews also now began to hope for individual resurrection after death before the last days, although they differed in their expectations of the nature of this life. The heroic mother of seven brothers put to death in the Maccabean persecution is portrayed by the author of II Maccabees as encouraging them with an expectation of a return to physical life through God's grace: 'Therefore the Creator of the world, who shaped the beginning of humankind and devised the origin of all things, will in his mercy give life and breath back to you again, since you now forget yourselves for the sake of his laws.' The story ends with the death of the mother too. The author of Jubilees, also probably writing in the second century BCE, said of the righteous that 'their bodies will rest in the earth and their spirits will have much joy.' The author of Daniel imagined that the wise shall shine 'like the brightness of the sky, and those who lead many to righteousness, like the stars for ever and ever'. Both the author of

Wisdom of Solomon and Philo adopted the Platonic notion that the soul is immortal, 'weighed down by the perishable body': 'these mortals who were made of earth a short time before and after a little while go to the earth from where all mortals are taken, when the time comes to return the souls that were borrowed.'[24]

Jewish epitaphs from this period only occasionally refer to an afterlife, although some from Egypt mention 'hopeful expectation', and one states that the soul of the dead has gone to join the holy ones. It seems that most Jews, like many gentile contemporaries, were willing to remain vague about their doctrine in this area. Josephus records the very different notions about life after death to be found among Pharisees, Sadducees and Essenes, from a Jewish version of the Greek notion of the Isles of the Blessed for the souls of the righteous (attributed to Essenes) to resurrection or reincarnation (attributed to the Pharisees) to a denial of any sort of life after death, attributed to the Sadducees. The Gospels describe this Sadducee denial of an afterlife as a matter for public disputations with Pharisees, in which the Sadducees confront the Pharisees with the implication of resurrection for a widow of seven brothers: 'in the resurrection, whose wife will she be of the seven?' According to Acts, Paul broke up a meeting of the High Priest's Council by crying out that, as a Pharisee, a son of Pharisees, 'of the hope and resurrection of the dead I am being judged'.[25]

Attribution of such importance to this particular theological issue was, so far as we know, rare, not least because the Sadducee denial of life after death seems to have become a fringe view by the first century CE. Apocalyptic texts imagine the souls of the righteous ascending to heaven and speculate on the levels of the heavenly world, picking up on Greek notions of the ascent of souls from the physical body to the highest part of the cosmos. That the garden of Eden, the primordial home of humankind, is also the home of the deceased righteous is attested first in the Gospel of Luke, when Jesus reassures one of the robbers crucified with him that 'today you will be with me in the *paradeisos*.' This presumably reflected an existing Jewish idea, since it is found also in the *targumim* (paraphrastic Aramaic translations of the Bible which are hard to date but contain many traditions of the first centuries CE), and in the Testament of Abraham, in which God says, 'Take my friend Abraham to Paradise, where are the tents of the righteous ones ... There is no toil there, no grief, no sighing, but peace and rejoicing, and endless life.'[26]

The ubiquity of such expectation is cited by Josephus in his summary of Judaism in *Against Apion*: 'each individual . . . has come to believe – as the legislator prophesied and as God provided firm assurance – that to those who keep the laws and, should it be necessary to die for them, meet death eagerly, God has granted renewed existence and receipt of a better life at the turn [of the ages].' For Josephus, this future hope was closely bound up with the willingness of Jews to die for their beliefs. He noted that he would have hesitated to write about this devotion 'had not the facts made all men aware that many of our countrymen have on many occasions even now preferred to brave all manner of suffering rather than to utter a single word against the Law'. A universal willingness to face death was placed by Josephus as the culmination of his description of the constitution bequeathed to the Jewish people by Moses:

> As for us, then, has anyone known – not to pitch the number so high – even two or three who have been traitors to the laws or afraid of death, and I mean not that easiest of deaths, which comes to those in battle, but that accompanied by physical torture, which seems to be the most hideous of all? I myself think that some of our conquerors have applied this to those in their power not out of hatred but because they wanted to see, as an amazing spectacle, if there were any people who believed that the only evil they faced was to be forced either to do something contrary to their laws or to say a word in contravention of them.

In his account of the significance of the biblical books to the Jews, Josephus claimed that 'time and again ere now the sight has been witnessed of prisoners enduring torture and death in every form in the theatres rather than utter a single word against the laws and the allied documents.'[27]

This veneration for martyrdom can be traced back to the description just noted in the Second Book of Maccabees of the heroic deaths of a mother and her seven sons on the orders of Antiochus IV Epiphanes during the persecution which led to the Maccabean revolt. The deaths of the martyrs are narrated in vivid and grisly detail, encouraging the reader to imagine the scene and empathize with the sufferer:

> It happened also that seven brothers and their mother were arrested and were being compelled by the king, under torture with whips and thongs, to partake of unlawful swine's flesh. One of them, acting as their spokesman, said, 'What do you intend to ask and learn from us? For we are ready to die rather than transgress the laws of our ancestors.' The king fell into

a rage, and gave orders to have pans and cauldrons heated. These were heated immediately, and he commanded that the tongue of their spokesman be cut out and that they scalp him and cut off his hands and feet, while the rest of the brothers and the mother looked on. When he was utterly helpless, the king ordered them to take him to the fire, still breathing, and fry him in a pan. The smoke from the pan spread widely, but the brothers and their mother encouraged one another to die nobly.[28]

A cult of martyrdom, in which the spread of stories about heroic resistance was as crucial as the resistance itself, can be found in many strands of later Judaism, as we saw in Chapter 6 in Josephus' description of the Essenes. A hope for resurrection strengthened the resolve both of these Essenes and of early Christian martyrs, who looked explicitly to the Maccabean heroes as their models. In due course rabbis in late antiquity, from the third century onwards, were to devise their own martyrdom stories in competition, with grisly but uplifting tales of the torture to death of R. Akiva by the Romans (see Chapter 10). Already in the first century the story of the binding of Isaac, which in the original version in Genesis constituted a test of Abraham's willingness to sacrifice his son at God's behest, had been altered to emphasize the willingness of Isaac to undergo martyrdom. In Josephus' rewriting of the story in the *Antiquities*, Isaac is said to have been twenty-five years old when he went up to Mount Moriah with his father, only to be told by Abraham that he was to be the sacrifice. Isaac responded with appropriate piety:

And Isaac, for it was necessary for one who had chanced upon such a father to be noble in his attitude, received these words with joy; and saying that it was not even right for him to have been born in the first place, if he were about to spurn the decision of God and his father and not readily offer himself to the wishes of both, when if even his father alone were choosing this it would have been unjust to disobey, he rushed to the altar and the slaughter.

This tradition of Isaac as willing victim is widespread in Jewish literature in late antiquity, not least the *targumim*, where its later popularity may owe something to rivalry with the Christian image of the willing submission of Jesus to the awful suffering of death by crucifixion.[29]

The Judaism for which it was worth dying in the eyes of those martyrs was the covenant between God and Israel enshrined in the law of Moses, and it is worth emphasizing, after this examination of such a plethora of interpretations of that law, the centrality before 70 CE of worship in the Temple in Jerusalem. Josephus described graphically the willingness of massed crowds of Jews to sacrifice their lives to protect the Temple from desecration by the Roman emperor Gaius when he attempted to set up a statue of himself there in 40 CE:

> When the Jews appealed to their law and the custom of their ancestors, and pleaded that they were forbidden to place an image of God, much more of a man, not only in their sanctuary but even in any unconsecrated spot throughout the country the Roman governor asked, 'Will you then go to war with Caesar?', to which the Jews replied that they offered sacrifice twice daily for Caesar and the Roman people, but that if he wished to set up these statues, he must first sacrifice the entire Jewish nation; and that they presented themselves, their wives and their children, ready for the slaughter.[30]

What was to be the religious reaction of Jews when, just thirty years later, their sanctuary was reduced to rubble by a later Caesar, the future emperor Titus?

PART III

The Formation of Rabbinic Judaism

(70–1500 CE)

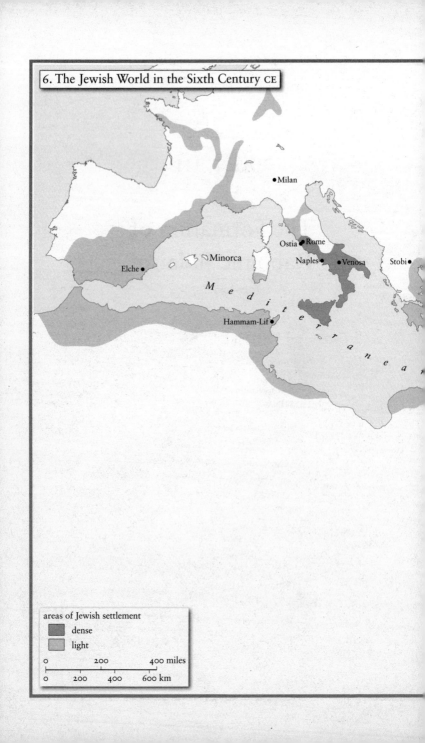

6. The Jewish World in the Sixth Century CE

Milan

Ostia ● Rome
Minorca
Elche ●
Naples ● ● Venosa
Stobi ●

M e d i t e r r a n e a n

Hammam-Lif ●

areas of Jewish settlement
dense
light

0   200   400 miles

0   200   400   600 km

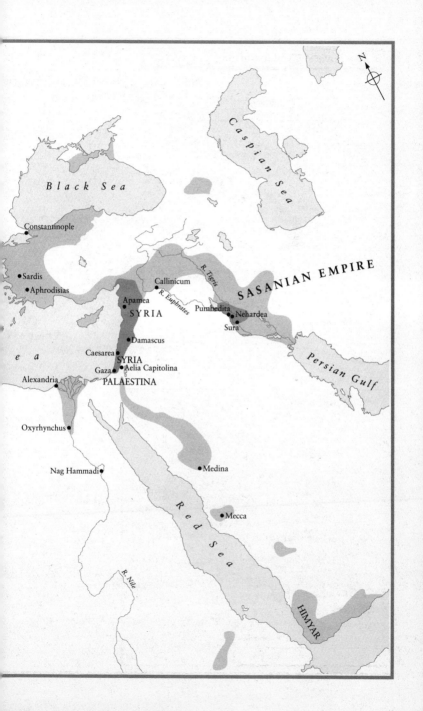

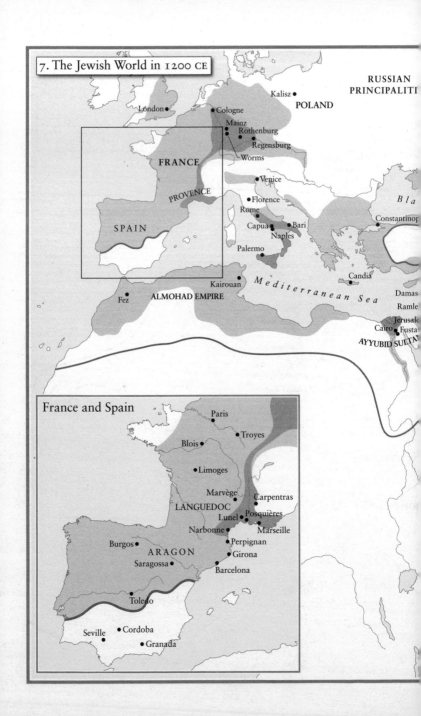

7. The Jewish World in 1200 CE

RUSSIAN PRINCIPALITI

Kalisz
POLAND
London
Cologne
Mainz
Rothenburg
Regensburg
FRANCE
Worms
PROVENCE
Venice
Florence
Rome
Constantinop
Bla
SPAIN
Capua Bari
Naples
Palermo
Candia
Kairouan
Mediterranean Sea
Damas
Fez
ALMOHAD EMPIRE
Ramle
Jerusale
Cairo Fusta
AYYUBID SULTA

France and Spain

Paris
Troyes
Blois
Limoges
Marvège
Carpentras
LANGUEDOC
Posquières
Lunel
Narbonne
Marseille
Burgos
Perpignan
ARAGON
Girona
Saragossa
Barcelona
Toledo
Seville Cordoba
Granada

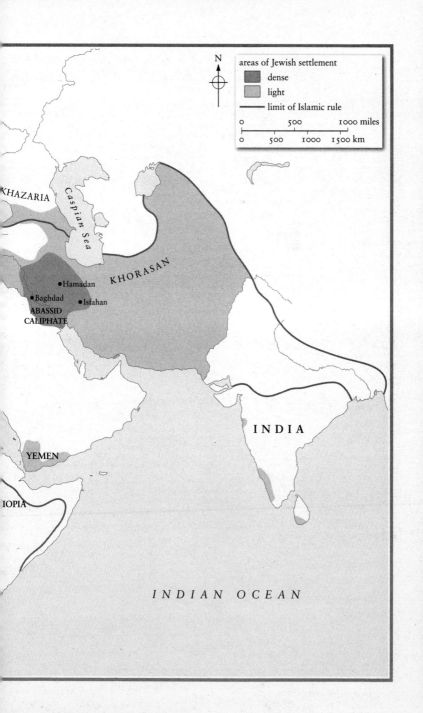

9

From Pagan Rome to Islam and Medieval Christendom

The capture of Jerusalem in 70 CE changed irrevocably the relations between the Roman state and the Jews. Whether or not the Temple had been destroyed on purpose, once it had happened the new imperial dynasty headed by Vespasian treated its destruction as a boon to the imperial peace. In the triumph through the streets of Rome in 71 CE in which the appurtenances of the Temple were carried in procession, at the culmination was a copy of the Jewish law. Jews were no longer to be allowed by Rome to worship with sacrifices and offerings in Jerusalem. All Jews in the empire were required instead to pay to the imperial treasury a special tax, originally designated for the rebuilding of the temple of Jupiter Capitolinus in Rome. Of the ancient privileges they had once enjoyed for the celebration of their ancestral religion, Jews could now boast only the scant comfort of a negative right to decline participation in religious rites directed to other gods.[1]

Josephus, writing in the aftermath of destruction, seems to have believed that the real meaning of the dream of Nebuchadnezzar revealed centuries earlier by the prophet Daniel about the eventual destruction of successive empires of gold, silver, bronze and iron by a great stone was that Roman power too would come to an end in time through the intervention of the God of the Jews, but despite Jewish hopes for retribution on the 'wicked kingdom', it was to be many years before this part of the divine plan was fulfilled. Imperial Rome flourished, expanding its frontiers in the second century not least in the Near East. There were setbacks on the northern and eastern frontiers in the third century, but the state emerged intact and prosperous in the early fourth, only to undergo a remarkable transformation, with the conversion of Constantine to faith in Christ and the gradual Christianization of wider Roman society, particularly from the end of the century. As Roman power in the north of Europe and the western Mediterranean crumbled under assault from Germanic invasions during the fifth century, the successor states established their own Christian societies (albeit not always of the same type of Christianity as the Roman emperors). The old religions did not disappear everywhere immediately, but most inhabitants of Europe through the Dark Ages to the high medieval period lived in Christian societies of one kind or another.[2]

Of all the great empires faced by Rome during its rise to power, only the Parthian dynasty in Mesopotamia never succumbed fully to Roman might, but in the 220s CE the Parthian state was taken over from within by an Iranian dynasty. The Sasanians claimed a spurious continuity with the Achaemenids, such as Cyrus and Xerxes, of half a millennium earlier and, already in the third century CE, championed Zoroastrianism as a state religion. The Greek-speaking Roman empire in the eastern Mediterranean and Syria, based from the early fourth century CE in Constantine's second capital in Byzantium (now renamed 'Constantinople'), found itself in frequent conflict with the Sasanian Persian state, which harboured expansionary ambitions as great as those of Rome, until the Sasanians were swept away, quite suddenly, in the seventh century by the rise of Islam – a political movement which, founded in the Arabian peninsula, led to conquests as rapid as those of Alexander a millennium earlier. Palestine fell under Muslim control, as did Egypt and, a little later, the Mediterranean coast of North Africa. Byzantium itself held out as the centre of a rump of Greek Christianity to 1453, but for the most part Christian political influence in the Levant was limited to periodic attempts at the reconquest of Palestine by Crusaders from the Latin west from the late eleventh century to the thirteenth. At the other end of the Mediterranean, parts of Spain remained under Muslim rule from the Umayyad conquest in the eighth century to 1491, when the emir of Granada relinquished the last Muslim-controlled city in the peninsula to the Christian monarchs of Castile and Aragon.

Jews – already widely scattered before 70 CE with diaspora settlements in many coastal regions of the eastern Mediterranean as well as established in large numbers in Egypt, Babylonia and the city of Rome, and even more dispersed after the devastation of the homeland – were affected by all these changes in the wider world. Within the Roman empire, Jewish settlement is attested between the second and fifth centuries CE as far west as Spain and as far north as Gaul and Germany. These areas were to become great centres of Jewish life by the beginning of the second millennium CE.

In the land of Israel, a much reduced population in Judaea after the disaster of 70 CE was deprived of all political self-government. But the

Jewish population itself did not disappear. In 132 CE the Jews of Judaea erupted into a second revolt against Rome under the leadership of Simon bar Kosiba, a charismatic and ruthless rebel commander known in some of the later traditions as Bar Kokhba, 'son of a star'. After the bloody failure of the revolt, Jews were banned from living in the area of Jerusalem. Jewish settlement was concentrated primarily in the Galilee, a region sufficiently obscure in Roman eyes for the Jewish village population to be left to its own devices. In Byzantine Palestine of the fourth to sixth centuries, when imperial wealth was pumped into the Christian Holy Land, a number of Jewish settlements in Upper Galilee fell into disuse, but elsewhere fine mosaic floors attest to the number, wealth and religious concentration of Jews in Lower Galilee and further south, both on the Mediterranean coast and by the Dead Sea in places like Ein Gedi.

Economic prosperity did not encourage love of a Byzantine state that treated Jews, like all those it considered religious deviants, as second-class citizens, and when Sasanian Persia attacked the Byzantine state in the early seventh century, the Persians were seen by Jews as potential harbingers of a messianic age. After Persian forces had conquered Jerusalem from the Byzantines in May 614 they handed over control of the city to the Jews; within three years such local Jewish autonomy was brought to an end by the Persians themselves, and in 627 a revived Byzantine army under the emperor Heraclius regained control of Palestine, entering Jerusalem on 21 March 629 in magnificent procession. Under pressure from the local Christian clergy, the Jews were expelled again from Jerusalem and its vicinity. Many converted to Christianity, or fled to other countries.[3]

Byzantine rule over Palestine gave way within ten years, in 637 or 638, to Arab invaders inspired by the new faith of Muhammad, who died in 632. According to early Islamic traditions, Muhammad had much sympathy with Judaism at the start of his mission in Arabia. The city of Medina, to which he migrated from his home in Mecca, was itself home to a number of Jewish tribes. Muhammad made agreements with these local Jews, but, according to the later Muslim traditions, he turned violently against them when they failed to accept his call, massacring some and expelling others from the peninsula as his power grew, leaving in the Koran and his sayings a complex legacy which could support both tolerance and intolerance of the 'People of the Book'.

Jews from southern Palestine are said in Islamic sources to have negotiated with Muhammad himself, and Arab conquest certainly brought relief from Byzantine persecution. But the Jewish population of the land of Israel was not to grow again to any great extent for many centuries, although the Jewish community prospered for the first half-century of Arab rule, protected by the founder of the Umayyad dynasty, Caliph Mu'awiya. Conditions worsened in the eighth century, with the introduction of restrictions on the public conduct and religious obser-vances of non-Muslims by Omar II. The level of such restrictions on Jews and Christians as the protected non-Muslim population (the *dhimmi*) varied over ensuing centuries, and some Jews at least must have accepted the invitation to convert to Islam. Those Jews who remained in the land were generally to be found in trading towns, such as Ramleh. There was a slightly larger concentration up to the ninth century in Tiberias in Galilee, after which Jerusalem again became the main centre of Jewish population in Palestine for two centuries until the turmoil brought by the Crusaders from the end of the eleventh century. Over the following centuries the surviving smaller communities were reinforced occasionally by settlers from Europe, with new centres of population in Acre and Ashkelon. The return of Muslim rule in 1291 under the Mamluks brought some respite and, from the beginning of the fifteenth century, a resurgence of Jewish settlement in Jerusalem.

The Jews of the Mediterranean diaspora were affected by the same upheavals in the wider world. Ructions in Egypt and Cyrene (modern Libya) following the destruction of Jerusalem in 70 CE were rapidly quashed by the Roman state, only to burst out again in a huge uprising, from 115 to 117 CE, by the Jews in the south-eastern corner of the Mediterranean. This revolt in the last years of the emperor Trajan resulted in the disappearance of the whole of the powerful Jewish com-munity of Egypt and Alexandria. A hundred years later, Cassius Dio recorded that any Jew who set foot on the island of Cyprus was still to be put to death. The Jews of Asia Minor and Greece seem to have remained more at peace, flourishing at least to the sixth century CE but often subjected to restrictions by Christian emperors after Constantine. At times they came under direct physical pressure from Christian clergy: when a synagogue in Callinicum (modern Raqqa) in Mesopotamia was burned down by a mob in 388, the emperor Theodosius I, keen to pre-serve imperial order, tried to punish the perpetrators and require them to reconstruct the building at their own expense, only to be thwarted by Ambrose, bishop of Milan, who viewed such a rebuilding as sacrilegious.

The severity of the restrictions placed upon Jews by the Christian state, and the efficiency with which they were enforced, naturally varied greatly over the ensuing millennium to the fall of Byzantium in 1453. After the Islamic conquest of the land of Israel and of Egypt, Jews were found in the major cities still ruled by Byzantium (which included, after its reconquest by Justinian in the mid-sixth century, much of southern Italy). The emperor Justinian II in 692 CE prohibited Jews and Christians from bathing together in public places. Decrees were issued by Basil I (in 873–4) and Romanos I (in 930) ordering the forcible conversion of the Jews. It is evident that those Jews in the empire who remained in their faith did so only on sufferance. But there was a Jewish quarter, Pera, in Constantinople, at the time of the Fourth Crusade in 1204, and still enough Jews in Greece and the Balkans in the thirteenth century to attract the attention of local Byzantine rulers such as Theodore I Angelus, who between 1214 and 1230 proscribed Judaism in the region of Epirus and Salonica under his control.[4]

Some Jews from these lands fled to Khazaria, a Turkish kingdom to the north-east of the Black Sea in the lower Volga region, which flourished (at times extending a good deal to the west) from the eighth to the tenth century. Khazaria was ruled over by a dynasty which in c. 730 adopted Judaism as the state religion, probably in part as a ruse in their complex diplomatic relations with neighbouring Christian Byzantines and Muslim Arabs. They were not the first to see the advantages of Judaism as a religion which would preserve independence from the imperialist Christian ambitions of Byzantium. Already in the late fourth century CE the king of the Himyarite tribe in south Arabia had protected his power in Yemen against Christian Byzantium in the north and the Christian kingdom of Aksum in Ethiopia on the other side of the Red Sea by conversion to Judaism. The Khazars were generally known to their Muslim neighbours as Jews, but how much of the population adopted the religion of the Khazar kings is unknown. Muslims, Christians and pagans formed the majority of the population and were granted internal autonomy, and accounts of the origin of Khazarian Judaism refer to some 4,000 nobles adopting the Jewish faith alongside their king Bulan. The twelfth-century Jewish traveller Benjamin of Tudela made no mention of Khazaria as a Jewish kingdom, but he did refer to Khazars in Constantinople and Alexandria, and there is evidence that at least some documents of Khazar Jews were to be found in the following centuries also in the Ukraine and Poland.[5]

The fate of the Jews in Babylonia was very different to that of their co-religionists under Roman and Christian rule. Little is known about the

Babylonian community in the last centuries of the Second Temple, although there were close contacts with Judaea through pilgrimage to Jerusalem. Herod made use of Babylonians to garrison part of Batanaea on the pilgrimage route, and he appointed a Babylonian to the position of High Priest at the beginning of his rule. Unlike their fellow Jews in Adiabene, further north in Mesopotamia, the Babylonians do not seem to have participated in the war to defend the Temple in Jerusalem, although they may have been caught up in the diaspora revolt of 115 to 117, which broke out as the emperor Trajan extended Roman military power perilously close during his campaigns to the east. Left in peace by the Parthian state, they were also generally tolerated by the Sasanians after the mid-220s, despite the prominence of Zoroastrian magi within the regime and despite occasional attempts by the state to extirpate non-Zoroastrian religions, as recorded in an inscription from the late third century set up on the Ka'ba-yi Zardusht by the High Priest Kartir:

> And in kingdom after kingdom, and place after place throughout the whole empire, the services of Ohrmazd and the gods became superior ... And Jews and Buddhist Sramans and Brahmins ... and Nasoreans and Christians and Maktak and Zandiks in the empire became smitten.[6]

As Kartir's inscription indicated, Jews were not the only religious minority within the state. The political leader of the Jewish community, styled *resh galuta* ('exilarch') in the rabbinic texts, was entrusted by the state with considerable authority from the third century down into the Islamic period. He had the right to appoint judges in both civil and criminal cases when Jews were involved; in return, the Jews recognized the authority of the Sasanian state in a fashion quite different from their opposition to the 'wicked kingdom' of Rome. Jews seemed to have fared much better under the Sasanians than their Christian neighbours, whose religious affiliation suggested too much sympathy with the Roman enemy. Nonetheless, there is evidence of a drastic deterioration in the condition of the Jews in the sixth century, and persecutions were sufficient for the Jews of Babylonia to embrace with enthusiasm the Islamic conquest of the seventh century.

Under the Arab caliphate, and a revival of the secular authority of the Jewish exilarch under Islamic rule, the Jews of what was now known as Iraq flourished, despite occasional discrimination against Jews along with other *dhimmis*. Inevitably affected by the vagaries of the political fortunes of different Islamic dynasties, so that to Benjamin of Tudela the Baghdad community in the twelfth century seemed to be in decline, they remained nonetheless numerous and retained considerable influence even after the Mongol conquest in the mid-thirteenth century. Only after the conquest of Iraq in 1393 by Tamerlane, who destroyed much of Baghdad and other towns, was there a considerable exodus, with Jews not returning until the end of the fifteenth century.[7]

Babylonian Jewry was already in the eighth century at the heart of an Islamic civilization which stretched far to the west. As Arab influence grew, so too did the influence of the Jews of Baghdad over the communities in Syria, Palestine, Egypt, North Africa and Spain. Baghdad had been founded in the eighth century as a distinctively Islamic city alongside ancient Babylon, but by its heyday in the tenth and eleventh centuries it had expanded far beyond its original circular fortifications into a rich urban culture which integrated Christians and Zoroastrians as well as Jews, with a series of palaces, courtyards, ponds and gardens watered by the canals linking the Tigris and Euphrates, six great mosques, a reported 1,500 bath houses and city markets so opulent that they inspired the stories in *One Thousand and One Nights*. The Jews who lived there must have felt they were at the centre of the civilized world.

In later centuries, other Islamic cities with large Jewish populations were also to reach similar levels of prosperity and sophistication, not least Cairo, where the lucrative spice trade between the Indian Ocean and the Mediterranean added to the income from the crops of the fertile Nile valley. The locus of Jewish authority shifted to match. By the time of the Jewish thinker Maimonides in the twelfth century, Cairo eclipsed Baghdad as a centre of Jewish intellectual life. Cairo's greatest period was in the thirteenth and fourteenth centuries under the Mamluk sultanate, when sultans and emirs competed in the erection of mosques, colleges and monasteries, with an ever-growing population, intensive commerce, gardens and pavilions. R. Meshulam of Volterra, visiting on Sunday 17 June 1481, swore that 'if it were possible to put Rome, Venice, Milan, Padua, Florence and four more cities together, they would not equal in wealth and population half that of Cairo.' Further to the west, many Jews lived also in Kairouan in modern Tunisia, which had been founded in 670 by Uqba ibn Nafi, the conqueror of North Africa, and which flourished until the sack of the city in 1057 by Arabs from Egypt.[8]

The decline of Babylonian hegemony over the religious development of Judaism was linked to the break-up of the Islamic world into independent caliphates from the eleventh century, and in particular the influence of the Jewish community in Islamic Spain. Jews had been settled in Spain by at least the early fourth century, since the Council of Elvira in 305 attempted to impose restrictions on Jewish social relations with Christians, forbidding Christians to live in the house of Jews, or to eat in their company, or to bless the produce of their fields, and in 417 or 418 the community in Minorca was converted en masse by force following a riot vividly described in a letter celebrating the event composed by a local bishop. They fared little better under the Visigothic kings who supplanted the Roman state in the Hispanic peninsula as the empire weakened. When in 613 King Sisebut, ruler of Hispania and Septimania (in south-west France), ordered all Jews to be baptized or leave the kingdom, many went into exile. Those who remained, or returned in ensuing years under more lenient regimes, became in many cases crypto-Jews. They or their descendants were among those who welcomed the arrival of Muslim invaders in 711 – according to Arabic accounts, the invaders handed over major towns such as Cordoba, Granada, Toledo and Seville for Jews to garrison.[9]

It would be wrong to characterize the following centuries of Jewish life in Islamic Spain as idyllic, not least because Jews (like Christians) were subject to heavy taxes in the Islamic state. But Jews prospered particularly under the tolerant regime of the Umayyads, with their capital in Cordoba, which itself became a major Jewish centre. Several Jewish dignitaries served in the administration and armies of these Islamic rulers, becoming drawn into the complex dynastic politics following the Berber conquest of Cordoba in 1013. The rise of such dignitaries did not always have positive consequences for the wider Jewish population – it was, for instance, the cause of a dramatic massacre of Jews in Granada in 1066 – but in general Jewish life flourished in Islamic Spain until the mid-twelfth century, when the Almohad dynasty from Morocco invaded and enforced a flurry of forced conversions to Islam.

Already from the early eleventh century Jews' position within Muslim society was complicated by the start of Christian reconquest from the north, and the periodic willingness of Christian kings, mindful of the advantages of Jewish political and economic support, to grant their Jewish subjects many more rights than they had enjoyed under earlier Christian regimes. Such tolerance did not last: in 1235 the Council of Tarragona attempted to control the influence of the Jews by both financial and political restrictions and in 1250 a more systematic attack on the local Jews was launched in Saragossa. The attitudes of the Catholic monarchs to the Jews varied throughout the fourteenth century, with tension between the kings (who needed income from taxes levied from the Jews), the clergy and the merchant class. On 4 June 1391 anti-Jewish riots broke out in Seville instigated by the violent sermons of a cleric named Ferrand Martinez, and the disorder spread throughout the peninsula, with the royal authorities powerless to protect the Jews, of whom many, if they survived, converted.

The number of such conversions in the fifteenth century proved a problem for Christians as much as Jews, since there was much doubt, real or imagined, about the genuine Christian faith of these 'new Christians'. A desire to purify the state persuaded Isabella and Ferdinand, monarchs from 1479 of a united kingdom of Castile and Aragon, to invite the Dominicans to begin an inquisition into 'Judaizing' among such 'conversos'. The inquisitors seem to have found it impossible to find such hidden Jews while Jews who openly confessed their faith were still around. In 1483 Jews were expelled from Andalusia, and in the autumn of the same year, Tomás de Torquemada was appointed inquisitor general. When Granada, the last Muslim stronghold in Spain, fell to Ferdinand and Isabella in January 1492, the time seemed right to remove Jews altogether from Spain, and on 31 March 1492 the edict of expulsion was signed in Granada.[10]

Some of the intolerance of Jews had seeped into Catholic Spain from the Christian communities further north in parts of Europe where Jews lived in small communities throughout the medieval period. Some Jews probably settled in northern Catalonia and southern France soon after 70 CE, but evidence for Jewish settlement in France is mostly found from the fifth century and after, under Frankish and Merovingian kings, when numbers were increased by refugees from Visigothic Spain. Jews flourished particularly under Carolingian rule, in the eighth and ninth centuries, with the establishment in the eleventh century of important centres of Jewish learning in Limoges, Narbonne and Troyes. The arrival of Jews in Germany was probably later. There must have been some Jews in Cologne in 321 CE, when the Roman emperor ruled that they could be required to serve on the city council. But further Jewish settlement was only gradual, primarily through the arrival of merchants from Italy and France, like the Kalonymus family from Lucca in Italy, which settled in Mainz in the tenth century. The peace of both French and German communities was shattered during the Crusades. The Crusaders turned on the Jews of the Rhine valley on the way to the Holy Land from April to June 1096 in the First Crusade, and more violence followed in later Crusades. In 1215 the Fourth Lateran Council decreed that Jews had to wear a special badge to distinguish them from Christians, and a wave of persecutions can be traced through the annals of these communities down to the end of the Middle Ages.[11]

The source of one frequent spark of violence against the Jews was the blood libel, first known in France (in Blois) in 1171, in Spain (in Saragossa) in 1182 and in Germany (in Fulda) in 1235. But before any of these it appeared in England, where in 1144 it was claimed that the Jews had bought the 'boy-martyr' William before Easter 'and tortured him with all the tortures wherewith our Lord was tortured, and on a Long Friday hanged him on a rood in hatred of our Lord'. Jews had settled in England only in the wake of the Norman conquest in 1066. Most had come from northern France and had close links to the monarchy, providing financial services to the Crown, and thus settled in many of the bigger cities, with the most important settlement in London. The role of financial intermediary between people and king may explain some of the strength of anti-Jewish feeling, exacerbated by the crusading zeal of Richard the Lionheart. Hostility to the Jews culminated in September 1189 with the looting of the Jewish quarter of London and in 1190 the mass suicide of the Jews of York in Clifford's Tower in York Castle. The English Jews remained subdued for the next century, until on 18 July 1290 Edward I issued an edict for their banishment – the first general expulsion of Jews from any country in the Middle Ages.[12]

Whether from such expulsions, or for trade or other reasons, the demography of Jewish settlement shifted constantly throughout the Middle Ages. Some Jews from Germany moved east, settling in Poland, Lithuania and Russia, taking with them a distinctive Jewish German dialect which was to develop into Yiddish. Many Italian Jews emigrated in the last centuries of the first millennium CE, with some choosing to go north and others across the Mediterranean to North Africa. Charlemagne settled Italian Jews in Mainz in the eighth century. And Italian scholars took their learning to the rabbinic schools in Fustat (south of Cairo) and in Kairouan in the same period. Italian Jews themselves were in close contact with Palestine, acting as a conduit for the transfer of Palestinian religious traditions into northern Europe.

It is clear that a simple 'lachrymose' account of Jewish history over these centuries would be misleading. There were periods and places, particularly under Islamic rule in Egypt, North Africa and Spain, which witnessed Jewish communities flourishing in peace. An emphasis on disasters is a product of the evidence produced by Jews in commemoration and lament, and the history of some Jewish communities is impossible to reconstruct with any clarity. Something can be gleaned, for example, about the history of the Jews of Yemen from local inscriptions on stone and from fragmentary texts preserved in Cairo, but these only occasionally come fully into focus. So, for instance, their leader Jacob b. Nathanel al-Fayyumi sought guidance in *c.* 1170 about a local messianic movement, eliciting from Maimonides in Egypt his *Epistle to Yemen*. Much less can be said about life in the Jewish settlements on the south-west coast of India beyond the fact that they were granted privileges, preserved by the community in Cochin, from the Hindu ruler of Malabar in the late tenth or early eleventh century CE and are mentioned by travellers and geographers from the twelfth century on. Nor can much be said about the Kaifeng Jews of China who settled in Henan Province probably in the ninth or tenth century, or about the history of the Beta Israel in Ethiopia, known to others as Falashas (which means 'exiles' in Amharic), who believed themselves descended from Menelik, the son of King Solomon and the queen of Sheba. Whatever the truth of these beliefs, it is certain that at least some Jews were settled in Ethiopia before the conversion to Christianity of the Axum dynasty under the influence of the Roman empire in the fourth century CE, and that Jewish captives from Himyar in southern Arabia were settled in Ethiopia in the sixth century.[13]

Much of the evidence for Jewish life in all these varied regions comes from archaeological remains of synagogues, from funerary inscriptions, from comments by Christian and Muslim writers, and from the pious literature of religious Jews themselves preserved in manuscripts from the eleventh century and after. But a particular bright light is shone on one corner of this Jewish world by analysis of some 200,000 fragments discovered in the *genizah* of the synagogue of Fustat in Cairo. These writings, deposited in the *genizah* from *c.* 882 to the late nineteenth century to avoid sacrilege through their destruction if they contained the divine name, include large numbers of secular documents and letters as well as biblical and other religious works. They reveal contacts between the Jews of Egypt and many other parts of the Jewish world throughout these centuries, and demonstrate how partial our knowledge must be of those areas of Jewish settlement for which evidence like that in the *genizah* does not survive.[14]

The geographical dispersion of Jews in itself created variation in the Judaism of different regions. Jerusalem was lost as a religious centre after 70, and Jews puzzled out their religious ideas not just in Hebrew, Aramaic and Greek but in Arabic, which for a few centuries became the lingua franca across most of the Jewish world, and more local languages. We shall see in the chapters that follow how individual Jews moved from one community to another – from Palestine to Babylonia or in the opposite direction in late antiquity, or from Spain to France to Germany or England, or east to Poland or Russia – bringing with them religious ideas and customs. A plethora of letters in the Cairo Genizah reveals a desire for formal contact for religious advice as well as trade and more mundane matters.

Despite such contacts, Jewish communities developed at separate speeds and in divergent ways. We shall see that the end of 'medieval' Judaism came much later in parts of eastern Europe than in Germany. The separate treatment in this book of the history of Judaism in the early modern period from 1500 will be more valuable in illuminating religious change in Italy and Holland than in, for instance, Yemen (see Part IV). But we shall also see the frequent evidence of contacts between Jews encouraging unity despite the recognition of difference.

Judaism without a Temple

The destruction of Jerusalem by Roman troops in 70 CE demanded a religious explanation. If God, the supreme ruler of the universe, had allowed such a disaster to be visited on his people, it must be as part of a divine plan. The author of an apocalyptic text which purports to describe the prophetic visions of Ezra, the priest and scribe of the fifth century BCE, but which must in fact have been composed in the last decades of the first century CE, envisaged divine vengeance on the Roman empire. He pictured Rome as a three-headed eagle destined for destruction during the last days which had now come upon the earth:

> The Most High has looked at his times; now they have ended, and his ages have reached completion. Therefore you, eagle, will surely disappear, you and your terrifying wings, your most evil little wings, your malicious heads, your most evil talons, and your whole worthless body, so that the whole earth, freed from your violence, may be refreshed and relieved, and may hope for the judgement and mercy of him who made it.

But we have no idea how many other Jews shared in this eschatological hope. IV Ezra is preserved only through copies and translations made by Christians, among whom the text proved immensely popular, presumably in part because of their strong interest in the imminent end times, but it is not known whether the text held similar appeal for non-Christian Jews.[1]

For ordinary Jews, such as Josephus, the obvious explanation for disaster was already predicted in biblical texts about the curses which awaited Israel for failing to keep to the covenant with God, and in the numerous promises of redemption when Israel repents of her sins. The current abyss of misery was simply part of a regular cycle of sin, punishment, repentance, forgiveness and restoration traced through numerous generations in the biblical books of Kings. By implication, a reformed Israel was guaranteed divine aid, and exile from the holy city of Jerusalem would in due course come to an end.

This optimistic note of confidence in the power of the God of Israel permeates the writings of Josephus, all of which were composed in the aftermath of the war. The Roman readers of his *Jewish War* and *Jewish Antiquities* might have been surprised to learn from his passionate narratives that the events which had culminated in the destruction of the capital city of the Jews had been orchestrated by the same Jewish God whose sanctuary had been ransacked, but this was precisely the message which Josephus wished to convey. The corollary was that Jews needed only to return to the path of piety for God again to look after his chastened people.

Presumably not all Jews were equally sanguine about the future under the care of the Jewish God. Some, like Tiberius Julius Alexander, Philo's nephew, are known to have left Judaism altogether as they moved into the ranks of the Roman imperial elite. In the early second century CE the names of descendants of Herod the Great can be found on inscriptions which show no awareness of their Jewish connections. Other Jews will simply have become unidentifiable in the evidence for the mixed populations of Roman cities in which ethnic groups can be observed only when they made an effort to preserve their distinctive cultures.[2]

But if most Jews understood the divine plan in the same biblical light as Josephus, the theological implication was not change but continuity, or, more precisely, a renewed commitment to the covenant of the Torah which alone could ensure a reversal of fortunes through divine grace. It is therefore reasonable to assume that understanding of the Torah will have remained as varied after 70 CE as before. The version of Judaism to which Pharisees reaffirmed their loyalty will have been Pharisaic. The same, *mutatis mutandis*, for Sadducees and Essenes. It is noticed surprisingly rarely that when Josephus writes in the 70s, 80s and 90s of the first century CE about these different philosophies of the Jews, he did so in the present tense, with no hint that any of them had ceased to exist since the disaster of 70 CE. It was quite possible that Judaism would become more and not less varied with the demise of the Temple as the communal institution in which differences in theology and practice were provided with a public platform.

The common claim by historians of Judaism that 70 CE marked an end to such variety, and even to explain this change as a product of solidarity in the face of disaster, is based on an illusion caused by a change not in the diversity of Judaism but in the diversity of the evidence for that Judaism. The Christian tradition, which preserved Jewish Greek writings such as the works of Josephus composed before 100 CE, lost interest in the preservation of non-Christian Jewish writings after *c.* 100 CE because Christians were creating an extensive literature of their own. As a result, the nature of Judaism from the end of the first century to the end of the first millennium CE has to be divined primarily from the great mass of religious traditions preserved by rabbis who had little or no interest in non-rabbinic forms of Judaism (see Chapter 11), although (as we shall see in Chapter 12) traces of these other forms of Judaism can still be discovered in the archaeological and epigraphic record.

We have seen that, according to Josephus, who was an eyewitness from the Roman camp, the destruction of the Temple in August 70 CE was not intended by the Roman high command. In the chaos of the siege a fire started by a lighted brand flung into the sanctuary by a Roman soldier spread rapidly out of control and attempts by Titus to save the building were in vain. Josephus was clear that Titus had been the instrument of the Jewish God in punishing his people for their sins. It was equally clear that, just as God had brought about in due course the rebuilding of the Temple after its destruction by the Babylonians in 586 BCE, so too its rebuilding could be expected now. The Torah contained explicit injunctions to Jews to bring sacrifices and offerings, so to decide that this was no longer possible was hardly an obvious option. The Jerusalem Temple was not the only religious building to burn down by accident in the Roman empire – indeed, the temple of Jupiter Capitolinus in Rome had burned down the previous year. The obvious option for Jews was to hope and pray for a rapid rebuilding of their shrine, and for them to strain every sinew to bring it about.[3]

Josephus, writing in the mid-90s CE, took it for granted that Jews were expected still to worship in the Temple, boasting in *Against Apion* about its excellence:

> One temple of the one God – for like is always attracted to like – common to all people as belonging to the common God of all. The priests will continuously offer worship to him, and the one who is first by descent will always be at their head. He, together with the other priests, will sacrifice to God, will safeguard their laws, will adjudicate in disputes, and will punish those who are convicted . . . We offer sacrifices not for our gratification or drunkenness – for that is undesirable to God and would be a pretext for violence and lavish expenditure – but such as are sober, orderly,

well-behaved, so that, especially when sacrificing, we may act in sober moderation. And at the sacrifices we must first offer prayers for the common welfare, and then for ourselves; for we were born for communal fellowship, and the person who sets greater store by this than by his own personal concerns would be especially pleasing to God.

Nothing in this paean of praise for the Temple hints at the fact, which will have been as blatant to his readers as to him, that it had been destroyed a quarter of a century earlier.[4]

Josephus was wrong in his expectation that the Jerusalem Temple would be rebuilt. Once it was in ruins, Vespasian and Titus invested too much political capital in propaganda about the defeat of the Jews as justification for their seizure of imperial power in Rome to permit any suggestion that its destruction should be regretted, let alone that a new building should arise in its place. The dedication of the Jews who had defended the sanctuary during the siege, and the defensive advantages of the site, discouraged their immediate successors from permitting rebuilding. The founding by Hadrian of the Roman colony of Aelia Capitolina on the site of Jerusalem in 130 CE put paid to the possibility of a new Jewish Temple for the remaining centuries of Roman rule. An abortive attempt by the pagan emperor Julian to rebuild the Temple in 364 CE in order to annoy Christians was prevented by Julian's premature death on campaign. The Temple Mount lay desolate until the late seventh century CE, when the Umayyad caliph Abd al-Malik constructed on the site the magnificent Islamic shrine of the Dome of the Rock which still stands there today.[5]

It is however probable that Josephus was not alone among Jews in expecting the rebuilding of the Temple. A hundred years after him, the compiler of the Mishnah in c. 200 CE included discussion of the detailed practice of Temple worship – not just the set feasts (Sabbath, the pilgrim festivals, the Day of Atonement) but the general treatment of 'hallowed things' (animal-offerings, meal-offerings, sacrilege) and the dimensions of the Temple building and its constituent parts. At least some non-Jews, for whom worship with sacrifice, libations and other offerings was among the most normal characteristics of Judaism, seem to have shared the assumption that in due course the Jerusalem Temple would again house crowds of pilgrims. Late in the third century, 200 years after the destruction, the pagan orator Menander of Laodicea (in Asia Minor) was still pointing to the pilgrim festivals in Jerusalem as the most impressive example of mass pilgrimage. He noted that 'the glory of [a religious] festival is enhanced when those who assemble are either very great in number or of the highest repute. An example of high repute . . . is Olympia, where renowned people meet,' but, he noted, 'the largest multitudes are to be found at the festival of the Hebrews living in Syria Palestine, as they are gathered in very large numbers from most nations.'[6]

In due course Jews were to develop new expressions of Judaism which came to terms with the loss of the Temple, but it is not clear how long it took for the yearning for a rebuilt Temple to subside. Some of the coins of the rebels led by Bar Kokhba in 132–5 CE carried images of the Temple and the legend 'For Jerusalem'. The attempted rebuilding by Julian in the mid-fourth century passes almost unremarked in the extant rabbinic writings from Palestine in this period, but this may be because, being at the instigation of a pagan ruler rather than through the efforts of Jewish priests, it was deemed invalid. Temple imagery and reference to the priestly 'courses' in many mosaic inscriptions on synagogue floors of the fifth and sixth centuries CE have encouraged speculation that Jews in this period harboured hopes for an imminent rebuilding, but this may be an over-interpretation. In any case, rebuilding was not a practical possibility under Christian rulers intent on turning Palestine into a Christian holy land in which Jesus' prediction of the destruction of the Temple could be witnessed as fulfilled. It would not be until the twelfth century, in an Islamic world where sacrifice was no longer part of the wider culture, that Maimonides would assert that God had encouraged sacrificial cult in the first place only in order to wean Jews away from the human sacrifice to be found among surrounding peoples.[7]

Even Maimonides believed that in the last days the Temple would be restored by God, as assumed in the daily prayer which had been in regular use, at least among rabbinic Jews, since soon after 70 CE:

> To Jerusalem, your city, may you return in compassion, and may you dwell in it as you promised. May you rebuild it rapidly in our days as an ever-lasting structure, and instal within it soon the throne of David. Blessed are you, Lord, who builds Jerusalem . . . Find favour, Lord our God, in your people Israel and their prayer. Restore the service to your most holy house, and accept in love and favour the fire-offerings of Israel and their prayer. May the service of your people Israel always find favour with you.[8]

In the meantime, the response of rabbinic sages back in 70 CE to the Temple destruction was severely practical:

> If a Festival-day of the New Year fell on a Sabbath they might blow the

ram's horn in the Holy City but not in the provinces. After the Temple was destroyed Rabban Yohanan b. Zakkai ordained that they might blow it wheresoever there was a court. R. Eliezer said, 'Rabban Yohanan b. Zakkai ordained it so only for Yavneh.' They replied, 'It is all one whether it was Yavneh or any other place wherein was a court.' ... Beforetime the *lulav* was carried seven days in the Temple, but in the provinces one day only. After the Temple was destroyed, Rabban Yohanan b. Zakkai ordained that in the provinces it should be carried seven days in memory of the Temple ... Beforetime they used to admit evidence about the new moon throughout the day. Once the witnesses tarried so long in coming that the levites were disordered in their singing; so it was ordained that evidence could be admitted only until the afternoon offering ... After the Temple was destroyed Rabban Yohanan b. Zakkai ordained that they might admit evidence about the new moon throughout the day.[9]

The emphasis on ensuring liturgical continuity is significant. In the centuries after 70 CE synagogue buildings gradually began to take on an aura of sanctity, albeit at a level below that of the Temple. Synagogue mosaic inscriptions in Aramaic and Greek record the gifts of pious Jews to 'this sacred place' in numerous sites in Galilee in the fifth and sixth centuries. Considerable expenditure on such mosaics, many of them elaborately depicting biblical scenes such as the binding of Isaac by Abraham, in itself attests the new veneration accorded to these buildings.

Archaeologists in the early 1930s found in Dura-Europos on the Euphrates a synagogue of the third century CE embellished with a remarkable series of paintings illustrating a variety of biblical stories, from Miriam rescuing Moses from the Nile to the vision of Ezekiel of the resurrection of the valley of dry bones (see p. 293). At the centre of the main wall in the Dura-Europos frescoes is a niche on which was depicted the Jewish Temple and some of its appurtenances. The same image is to be found on many of the mosaics in Palestine in late antiquity, along with stylized versions of palm branches, rams' horns and other items associated with the great festivals. The synagogue had become, by late antiquity, what the rabbis described sometimes as a 'small sanctuary', in allusion to God's words in the book of Ezekiel: 'Though I removed them far away among the nations, and though I scattered them among the countries, yet I have been a sanctuary to them for a little while in the countries where they have gone.'

In ensuing centuries, synagogues were to be increasingly embellished.

Many were extensively decorated internally in accordance with local styles, as in the Islamic artistic motifs incorporated into the magnificent stucco which still survives on the walls of the fourteenth-century El Transito synagogue in Toledo. That stained glass was used in windows in the synagogue of Mainz is known to us from the objections raised by a rabbi in the twelfth century who ordered their removal. Evidently Jews had come to assume that conspicuous expenditure on embellishing synagogue worship was an act of piety. Hence also the many fine examples of Jewish liturgical art, generally executed by Christian artists to designs presumably agreed with their Jewish patrons, found in the illumination of Hebrew prayer books. Such illustrated manuscripts reached a peak of sophistication in northern Europe, Italy and Christian Spain in the fourteenth century in such masterpieces as the Sarajevo Haggadah.[10]

Communal prayer was adapted to suit. Whatever the original wording of the Amidah prayer (on which see Chapter 3), it is certain that it was adapted after 70 CE by the addition of prayers for the rebuilding of the Temple. The Sabbath and festival prayers evolved specific wording in which a description of the sacrifices substitutes for the sacrifice itself:

> May it be your will, Lord our God and God of our ancestors, to lead us back in joy to our land and to plant us within our borders. There we will prepare for you our obligatory offerings . . . And the additional offering of this Sabbath day we will prepare and offer before You in love, in accord with Your will's commandment, as You wrote for us in Your Torah through Your servant Moses, by Your own word, as it is said: 'On the Sabbath day, make an offering of two lambs a year old, without blemish, together with two-tenths of an ephah of fine flour mixed with oil as a meal-offering, and its appropriate libation. This is the burnt-offering for every Sabbath, in addition to the regular daily burnt-offering and its libation.'

Quite when such wording became common among Jews is uncertain, but the tradition in the Babylonian Talmud that the order, general content and benediction formulas were standardized at Yavneh by Rabban Gamaliel II and his colleagues in the late first century CE shows that these elements were fairly constant at least in Babylon by the sixth century. In the following centuries versions of the Amidah were committed to writing. The *kedushah*, a prayer which describes the sanctification of God by the angels in heaven as found in Isaiah and the imitation of such sanctification by Israel on earth, was already interwoven into the repetition of the Amidah in late antiquity. It reflects an early desire to instil a mystical element into the most solemn portions of this communal prayer: 'Holy, holy, holy is the Lord of Hosts! The whole earth is full of his glory.'[11]

In course of time this liturgy became greatly embellished. Around the fifth century Jews in Palestine began to compose hymns for insertion into the regular prayers. These *piyyutim* (poems) were often works of considerable complexity and beauty, and many were attributed to specific authors – in Byzantine Palestine from the fifth to seventh centuries, notably Yosi b. Yosi, Yannai and Eleazar Kallir. Schools of *paytanim* (poets) were found in Byzantine southern Italy in the ninth century and further north in Italy in the tenth century. A series of great *paytanim* were to be found in Germany and Spain from around the same period. Liturgical music seems to have developed less extensively in this period, with no use of musical instruments in synagogue worship. But the dispersion of Jewish communities led to the gradual development of distinctive regional melodies for chanting both the reading of the Torah and the communal prayers. Worship involved the whole body, and posture remained an important element in prayer, with developing customs about standing and bowing at particular times, although dance had less of a role in worship than in other religious traditions – the *Tanzhaus* in medieval Jewish communities in Germany was primarily for communal celebrations of weddings.[12]

At the centre of Sabbath and festival liturgy was the regular reading of the Torah which had been established long before the Temple was destroyed (see Chapter 3), and an immense amount of effort was invested in safeguarding the integrity of the biblical text and in encouraging its study. The multiplicity of readings in many biblical books which seems to have been standard at the end of the Second Temple period, as in the biblical manuscripts found at Qumran, had given way a thousand years later to a consolidated text in which divisions into words, sentences and paragraphs, and (crucially) the vocalization of the consonantal text, standardized its meaning. The scholars responsible for the production of what became the *masorah*, or 'traditional text', worked mostly in the second half of the first millennium CE and mostly in the land of Israel, culminating in the biblical text determined in the school of Tiberias in the tenth century. Their critical notes included marking each place where what is read in the text (*keri*) is to be different from what is written (*ketiv*). This process could completely change the apparent meaning of a passage, reading (for instance) *lo* (with a *vav*) to mean 'for him' instead of *lo* (with an *aleph*) to mean 'not' in Isa

63:9. Instead of reading that 'it was no messenger or angel but his presence that saved them,' the text was understood by the masoretes to say 'He was their saviour. In all their distress he was distressed,' with the important implication that God suffers with the suffering of Israel. The impulse to such clarification of the texts, along with the careful enumeration of the number of words, the uses of particular letters and other such minutiae, reflects an increasing veneration of the text in its own right. This veneration had its own momentum, but the concerns of Karaites as biblical fundamentalists (see Chapter 12) may have played a part in its later stages.

The liturgical interpretation of the Torah continued to be enhanced in some congregations, as in Second Temple times, by consecutive translation of the Hebrew text into Aramaic. The Aramaic *targumim*, some of which incorporate a great deal of commentary into their versions of the original, were still in use in much of the first millennium CE, until particular versions were put into their final form in around the fifth century CE and adopted by different communities: Targum Onkelos was used in Babylonia and a number of different *targumim* are known from Palestine, of which one, found in just one manuscript, was discovered only in 1956 in the Vatican.

Exegesis of the text was the role of the *darshan*, or 'expounder', who is envisaged in the Babylonian Talmud as a preacher tasked with delivering a sermon on Sabbaths and festival days. At least some of the works of biblical exegesis preserved through the rabbinic tradition from late antiquity seem to have originated in this synagogue setting. So, for instance, the Pesikta (literally 'section') cycle of Palestinian *midrashim*, which deals with selected passages from the Pentateuch and the Prophets and exists in two versions, one apparently mostly from the fifth century and the other mostly from the ninth century, follows the cycle of the calendar from Rosh haShanah. The exposition branches off into law as well as narrative for homiletic purposes, usually by placing one biblical verse in apposition to another:

'Yet the righteous holds on his way, and he that has clean hands enhances strength' (Job 17:9). 'The righteous' is the Holy One, of whom it is said 'The Lord is righteous, He loves righteousness' (Ps 11:7); 'and he that has clean hands' is also the Holy One, to whom it is said 'You who are of eyes too clean to behold evil' (Hab 1:13); 'he ... enhances strength' is again the Holy One who enhances the strength of the righteous to enable them to do His will. Another comment: 'The righteous holds on his way' applies to

Moses, of whom it is said 'He persisted in executing the righteousness of the Lord and His ordinances with Israel' (Deut 33:21) . . . Rabbi Azariah, citing Rabbi Judah bar Rabbi Simon, said, 'Whenever righteous men do the Holy One's will, they enhance the strength of the Almighty.'[13]

The community for whom all this public liturgy existed was primarily male, and whether women attended synagogues at all in late antiquity is uncertain. But a woman's courtyard, partitioned from the men's section by a formal divider (*mehitsah*), was not uncommon in medieval synagogues. In Provence, in the late Middle Ages, women listened to the service through a grille in the ceiling of a room underneath the synagogue. In Germany, women prayed in separate rooms parallel to the men's synagogue. In communities in Muslim lands, women generally had no separate space reserved to them but might listen to the service through a window from outside the synagogue building.[14]

The communities which erected these buildings for public prayer often took on also the provision of shared facilities for other religious needs, such as purification after ritual pollution. There is no way to tell who owned and constructed the numerous ritual baths (*mikvaot*) which were to be found in Jewish settlements in Palestine in the fourth to sixth centuries CE. Many, perhaps most, may have been private. But in many parts of medieval Europe such ritual baths were communal property and were treated as an essential prerequisite for the religious life, especially for the purification of women after menstruation and childbirth. In some European communities, such as Speyer in the twelfth century, considerable funds were expended to provide a grand architectural setting for the ritual bath.[15]

By the early medieval period communities also came to see the purchase and upkeep of a Jewish cemetery as a religious duty. The Mishnah in third-century Palestine envisages the community as responsible for marking graves to avoid accidental defilement. But it is in the Babylonian Talmud that the principle is first found enunciated that burial next to a righteous person, and therefore a fellow Jew, is desirable:

For R. Aha b. Hanina said, 'Whence is it inferred that a wicked man may not be buried beside a righteous one?' – From the verse, 'And it came to pass as they were burying a man that behold they spied a band and they cast the man into the sepulchre of Elishah, and as soon as the man touched the bones of Elishah, he revived and stood up on his feet.' . . . And just as a wicked person is not buried beside a righteous one, so is a grossly wicked person not to be buried beside one moderately wicked. Then should there not have been four graveyards? It is a tradition that there should be but two.

A similar notion must lie behind the custom exhibited from the third to the sixth century at Beth Shearim, in Lower Galilee, of bringing corpses from afar in ossuaries for burial in the proximity of learned rabbis. For other diaspora Jews, a desire to be buried next to fellow Jews led at times to the purchase by individual Jewish families of specific locations for the purpose, such as the Jewish catacombs of Rome (used from the third to the fifth century) and the catacombs from Venosa, further south in Italy in Apulia (used from the fourth to the eighth century). A cemetery was not in itself hallowed, but by the early medieval period Jewish communities in both Christian and Muslim lands purchased plots for communal burial. Among the earliest known is the cemetery at Worms, which dates back to the tenth century.[16]

In contrast to their partial exclusion from the public religious life of the community, women and children were fully integrated into the development of religious liturgy within the family group at home. Already in the Mishnah it is taken for granted that responsibility for the religious life of the household falls (with severe consequences) in some crucial matters on the householder's wife: 'For these transgressions, women die in childbirth: because they have been negligent in regard to their periods of separation [after menstruation], in respect to the consecration of the first cake of the dough, and in the lighting of the Sabbath lamp.' According to the Mishnah, 'light the lamp' is one of the crucial commands a man must give to his household when darkness is falling on the eve of Sabbath. The lighting of Sabbath candles on Friday evenings remains pervasive in most forms of Judaism to the present.[17]

Preparing for the Sabbath was thus not without anxiety for the women of the household, but they were full participants in the pleasures of the celebration itself when, on a Friday evening, the Sabbath day was blessed by the man of the house over wine and bread:

Blessed are You, Lord our God, King of the Universe, who has made us holy though His commandments, who has favoured us, and in love and favour gave us His holy Sabbath as a heritage, a remembrance of the work of creation. It is the first among the holy days of assembly, a remembrance of the exodus from Egypt. For You chose us and sanctified us from all the peoples, and in love and favour gave us Your holy Sabbath as a heritage. Blessed are You, Lord, who sanctifies the Sabbath.

As the Sabbath came to an end, a similar form of words marked, over wine, spices and lighted candle, the passage into the working week in the ceremony of havdalah ('separation'):

> Blessed are You, Lord our God, King of the Universe, who distinguishes between sacred and secular, between light and darkness, between Israel and the nations, between the seventh day and the six days of work. Blessed are You, Lord, who distinguishes between sacred and secular.

In several versions of the havdalah services from the later Middle Ages, mention is made of the imminent coming of Elijah, as harbinger of the Messiah, following a belief, which seems to have originated in northern Europe after the Crusades (presumably as a reflection of eschatological longing in a time of deep suffering), that Elijah's arrival would be on a Saturday evening.[18]

Observance of the Sabbath was unaffected by the demise of the Temple, but the rest of the liturgical year evolved greatly now that thrice-yearly pilgrimage was no longer possible as the focus of worship and created the rhythm of the annual round of festivals and fasts which lasts to the present day. The essence of Pesach became the recitation of the Haggadah at the Seder meal on the eve of Pesach (in the spring), in which the basic narration of the exodus was augmented by customs, stories and songs which accrued gradually over the centuries after 70 CE:

> Why is this night different from all other nights? On all other nights we eat either *hametz* [leavened bread] or *matzah* [unleavened bread], but on this night only *matzah*. On all other nights we eat all kinds of herbs, but on this night only bitter herbs. On all other nights we do not dip even once, but on this night twice. On all other nights we can eat either sitting or reclining, but on this night we all recline.

The rest of Pesach was celebrated by the avoidance of leavened food, as prescribed in the Bible, for seven days, with the first and last days marked by abstention from work. Calendrical uncertainty in the diaspora, based on the notion that it took time to transmit the announcement of a new moon in the land of Israel, led to the development of a tradition that each of these full holidays should be observed on two days rather than one, so that Pesach lasted for eight days rather than seven.[19]

Shavuot itself came to be seen less as a harvest festival than as a time to celebrate the giving of the Torah, although the reading of the biblical book of Ruth in the synagogue on Shavuot may reflect both the theme of the barley harvest and Ruth's acceptance of the Torah. It is more difficult to discern why some of the other *megillot* (scrolls) were assigned their liturgical places in the annual cycle of reading – the Song of Songs is read on Pesach and Ecclesiastes during Sukkot – although the public reading of Lamentations on the Fast of 9 Av in late July or early August, which commemorates the destruction of the Temple both in 586 BCE and in 70 CE, has a clear rationale. The Fast of Av is the only fast for twenty-four hours, from nightfall to nightfall, apart from Yom Kippur. All other fasts begin only at daybreak, including the fast of Tammuz, which commemorates the breach of the walls of Jerusalem before the fall of the city in 586 BCE and marks the start of three weeks of mourning which become more intense in the nine days from 1 Av and culminates in the fast on the 9th.

The early autumn was marked by ten days of reflection and repentance between Rosh haShanah (the New Year) and Yom Kippur. The Bible had little to say about Rosh haShanah, 1 Tishri, beyond a requirement that it be 'a day of solemn rest, a memorial proclaimed with the blowing of horns, a holy convocation', but the Mishnah already considers this day the start of penitence, since on Rosh haShanah 'all who have entered into the world pass before him [for judgement] like a flock of sheep'. The synagogue liturgy, combining a focus on the sounding of the shofar (ram's horn) with confession and petition, was well established by the sixth century CE and became increasingly elaborate with the addition of numerous hymns in the early Middle Ages. Since this festival fell on the first of the month, not even those in the land of Israel could be told in good time when the month started, and Rosh haShanah was (and is) celebrated for two days in Israel as well as in the diaspora.[20]

The culmination of penitence on the fast of Yom Kippur began with Kol Nidrei, a public statement in Aramaic on behalf of all the congregation that all kinds of vows made before God and unintentionally unfulfilled should be considered null and void. Well established by the end of the first millennium CE, despite the strong opposition of rabbinic authorities both at that time and in succeeding generations, the declaration refers in some communities to the year just passed, in others to the year ahead, and, in some communities, to both. The liturgy during the fast day contains numerous allusions to the Temple ritual, but the primary focus is private repentance, with frequent assertion of the need for full confession and an intention to avoid repeating the same offences in the year to come.

Sukkot, which comes only five days after Yom Kippur, retained its character as primarily a harvest festival, with the waving of the four species (palm, etrog, myrtle and willow) in synagogues and meals taken in the *sukkah*, a booth with cut vegetation for the roof that let in some sunlight. Observance was more difficult in some of the less clement climates in the diaspora than in the land of Israel, and rules developed about the degree of discomfort from cold or wet which made use of the *sukkah* inappropriate.

During late antiquity the custom gradually grew that the four species should be carried in procession round the synagogue each day to the chant of *hoshana* in recollection of circuits round the altar in Temple times. On the seventh day there were seven circuits, and this day came to be known as Hoshana Rabba, 'The Great Hoshana', which was also the occasion for beating willow branches. *Hoshana* means 'O deliver', and *hoshanot* prayers, addressing God by different epithets and beseeching his aid, were much elaborated in the sixth to seventh century CE by poets like Elazar Kallir. Originally prayers for rain, in keeping with the timing of the Sukkot festival, they became quite general in the liturgy as it developed.

The end of Sukkot was marked by a final eighth day (Shemini Atseret) on which no work was to be undertaken. In the diaspora, where two days of the festival were observed, the second day in due course took on a character of its own in celebration of the completion of the annual cycle of reading the Torah and the start of the new cycle with the book of Genesis. This celebration, known as Simhat Torah, is not attested until the beginning of the second millennium CE, but it has become a major festival for diaspora Jews, with much singing and dancing by the congregation.

The month of Heshvan which follows all these festivals has no special festivals or fasts, so the next festival is Hanukkah which begins near the end of the month of Kislev (usually in December). The festival celebrates the rededication of the Temple by Judah Maccabee (see Chapter 5), but rabbinic Jews did not read the full account in the books of Maccabees, which survived only in Greek, and the Babylonian Talmud explained the lighting of lamps for eight days as a memorial of a miracle at the time of Judah's victory: only enough pure oil for one day was found in the Temple when it was rededicated, but the oil kept burning for eight days until fresh supplies of pure oil could be brought.

The festival of Purim in Adar (usually March) also purports to commemorate an event of divine salvation, in this case recorded in the biblical book of Esther (see Chapter 2). The reading of the scroll of Esther was evidently an established part of synagogue liturgy as known already to the rabbis in the early third century CE, since a whole tractate of the Mishnah was devoted to its regulation. The tradition of accompanying the reading with carnival seems to go back to late antiquity. According to the Babylonian Talmud, hearing the scroll read out is a duty incumbent on women as well as men, and people are encouraged to get so drunk that they can no longer distinguish the hero of the tale, Mordecai, from the villain Haman.

The focus of some of these festival liturgies was with the rest of the community in synagogue, but much – from the Pesach Seder to the Hanukkah lamps – took place primarily in the home, and a desire to beautify such liturgical practices encouraged production of distinctive domestic ceremonial objects, such as Sabbath lamps and candlesticks, silver *kiddush* cups for wine to sanctify the Sabbath and plates for *hallah* (a plaited loaf of special Sabbath bread), spice containers for havdalah, eight-branched lamps for the Hanukkah lights and decorative vessels for the special foods of the Passover Seders. Such objects, with the *mezuzah* on the doorposts, would mark the religious affiliation of a Jewish home as clearly as a picture of Christ might signify a Christian home, or a verse from the Koran might indicate Islam.[21]

The impact of the prevailing religious cultures which surrounded Jewish communities was as much through Jewish opposition as through imitation and adoption. In the first centuries after 70 CE, when Jews everywhere were compelled to respond in some way to what they considered to be pagan idolaters, the rabbis proved adept at simplifying and caricaturing much of the pagan life around them, confining their concern to Jewish avoidance of anything which might smack of idolatry: 'For three days before the festivals of the gentiles it is forbidden to have business with them ... And these are the festivals of the gentiles: the calends, the saturnalia, the commemoration of empire, the anniversaries of kings, and the day of birth and the day of death.' The Jews of Dura-Europos commissioned from a local painter a depiction for their synagogue of the destruction of the idol Dagon and seem to have come close to polemic against the numerous pagan cults in their vicinity. But numerous synagogue mosaics from late Roman Palestine depict the sun god Helios on his four-horsed chariot surrounded by the signs of the zodiac, and a synagogue floor from sixth-century Gaza portrays King David as an Orpheus figure with his lyre, without any apparent concern that such pagan imagery might dilute the Judaism of worshippers.[22]

The religious response of Jews to Christianity was similarly varied. Some Jews seem to have contrived to ignore Christianity altogether even at times and places where its influence might have been expected to be particularly strong. Thus the rabbis who compiled the Palestinian Talmud in the fourth century exhibit no awareness whatsoever, when discussing the religious customs of non-Jews, that since the 320s the province of Palestine had been endowed with state funds by emperors from Constantine onwards intent on creating a new Christian Holy Land. On the other hand, it has been reasonably surmised that Jewish Bible interpretation in late antiquity was at least sometimes engaged in a covert dispute with Christian understanding of the same scriptural passages. This is particularly likely in interpretations of the proof texts used by Christians to bolster their own faith, although most explicit evidence for such disputes comes from Christian sources such as Justin Martyr's *Dialogue with the Jew Trypho*, in which Trypho is portrayed as taking issue with Justin's interpretation of the prophecy in Isaiah that 'the young woman is with child and shall bear a son.' Justin, in accordance with the Gospel of Matthew, took the passage to refer to Christ and Mary, but Trypho insisted that the son mentioned in the passage was Hezekiah and that Justin was wrong to understand the word for 'young woman' (*alma* in Hebrew) as 'virgin'. Elsewhere in Justin's *Dialogue*, Trypho objects to the claim of Christians to be Israel, and it is probably the same Christian claim to be the true Israel which is confronted polemically in *Song of Songs Rabbah*, a *midrash* redacted around the beginning of the seventh century in Palestine:

The straw, the chaff and the stubble engaged in a controversy. This one says: 'For my sake was the land sown' and that one says: 'For my sake was the land sown.' Said the wheat to them: 'Wait until the harvest comes and we shall see for whom the field was sown.' When harvest time came and all go to the threshing floor, the landowner went out to thresh, the chaff was scattered to the wind; he took the straw and threw it to the ground; he took the stubble and burnt it; he took the wheat and piled it into a stack and everybody kissed it. In like manner the nations, these say: 'We are Israel and for our sake was the world created.' And these say: 'We are Israel and for our sake was the world created.' Says Israel to them: 'Wait until the day of the Holy One, blessed be He, and we shall know for whom was the world created, as it is written 'For, behold, that day is coming; it burns like a furnace.' (Malachi 3:19)[23]

It would be wrong to read every biblical interpretation by Jews in a Christian world in the light of such anti-Christian polemic, since (as we have seen) rabbis had good reason to ponder the significance of scripture without any such incentive, but there can be no doubting the real engagement with Christian thought required for the formal disputations imposed on Jews in parts of medieval Europe from the thirteenth century. In the Disputation of Paris in 1240, which arose from a papal order that Jewish books be examined, the Jewish delegation failed to prevent the condemnation of the Talmud and cartloads of Jewish books were burned in what is now the Place de l'Hôtel de Ville. In 1263 the great rabbi Moses Nahmanides of Girona (see Chapter 13) confronted an attempt by the friar Paul Christian, an apostate from Judaism, to demonstrate that the rabbinic texts themselves revealed the truth of Christianity, by rejecting the miraculous as contrary to reason:

> The doctrine in which you believe, and which is the foundation of your faith, cannot be accepted by reason, and nature affords no ground for it, nor have the prophets ever expressed it. Nor can even the miraculous stretch as far as this, as I shall explain with full proofs in the right time and place, that the Creator of Heaven and earth resorted to the womb of a certain Jewess and grew there for nine months and was born as an infant, and afterwards grew up and was betrayed into the hands of his enemies who sentenced him to death and executed him, and that afterwards, as you say, he came to life and returned to his original place. The mind of a Jew, or any other person, cannot tolerate this; and you speak your words entirely in vain, for this is the root of our controversy.

Away from the gaze of Christians, the tone of Jewish polemic against Christianity was less cerebral. It is clear from the number of surviving manuscripts that the scurrilous versions of the life of Jesus in the Toledot Yeshu (see Chapter 7) were popular reading among Jews in the late Middle Ages.[24]

But, away from such confrontations, Jews also adopted religious ideas and practices from their Christian neighbours. The structure of Jewish communities in late antique Palestine as religious congregations clustered around a synagogue may owe much to the tendency of the late Roman Christian state to characterize its subjects in religious terms, even if this form of Jewish life was not altogether modelled on Christian

communities clustered around churches. The prohibition of bigamy by
rabbis in Germany in the tenth century must reflect the surrounding
Christian culture, since the rabbis made no attempt to ban polygamy
for Jews living in Islamic lands where polygamy was common. Somewhere between imitation and competition lies the adoption by Jews of
martyrologies similar to those which proved so powerful in the provision of narratives about saints to inspire early Christians, which in turn
were modelled on the martyr narratives of the Maccabees (see Chapter
8). For the rabbis, Akiva's death became an archetypical story of noble
suffering 'to sanctify the name of God':

> When R. Akiba was taken out for execution, it was the hour for the recital
> of the Shema, and while they combed his flesh with iron combs, he was
> accepting upon himself the kingship of heaven. His disciples said to him,
> 'Our teacher, even to this point?' He said to them, 'All my days I have been
> troubled by this verse, "with all your soul", [which I interpret,] "even if
> He takes thy soul". I said, "When shall I have the opportunity of fulfilling
> this?" Now that I have the opportunity shall I not fulfil it?' He prolonged the
> word 'one' [the last word of the Shema] until he expired while saying it.[25]

The vogue for such stories of martyrdom increased greatly in Germany during the time of the Crusades, as in the *Chronicles* of Solomon
bar Simson of the self-sacrifice of martyrs in Mainz in 1096:

> When the people of the Sacred Covenant saw that the Heavenly decree had
> been issued and that the enemy had defeated them and were entering the court-
> yard, they all cried out together – old and young, maidens and children,
> menservants and maids – to their Father in Heaven. They wept for themselves
> and for their lives and proclaimed the justness of the Heavenly judgement, and
> they said to one another: 'Let us be of good courage and bear the yoke of the
> Holy Creed, for now the enemy can only slay us by the sword, and death by
> the sword is the lightest of the four deaths. We shall then merit eternal life, and
> our souls will abide in the Garden of Eden in the presence of the great lumi-
> nous speculum forever.' ... Then in a great voice they all cried out as one, 'We
> need tarry no longer, for the enemy is already upon us. Let us hasten and offer
> ourselves as a sacrifice before God. Anyone possessing a knife should examine
> it to see that it is not defective, and let him then proceed to slaughter us in
> sanctification of the Unique and Eternal One, then slaying himself – either cut-
> ting his throat or thrusting the knife into his stomach.'[26]

The influence of Islam on Judaism was to be very different, and hard
to overestimate. Rabbinic theology, poetry, law and even biblical

interpretation reflect contemporary trends within Islam from the last centuries of the first millennium CE through to the high Middle Ages. The disputations in Baghdad in the tenth century summarized in the *Book of Beliefs and Opinions* of Saadiah Gaon took place in a relatively open and philosophical atmosphere, although the Muslim accusation that the Jews had falsified the text of the Bible in the time of Ezra, imagining God in anthropomorphic terms, led Maimonides to forbid such debates because of 'their belief that this Torah was not given from Heaven'. On the crucial issue of monotheism Jews and Muslims shared a common approach in opposition to Christian belief in the Trinity. Many Jewish thinkers were much attracted by the teachings of Islamic scholasticism (*kalam*), which began in the eighth century, about the absolute unity and incorporeality of God, to whom no attributes may be ascribed, and the perfection of divine justice. The vigour of Islamic philosophy, which incorporated much from the philosophy and natural sciences of the Greeks, especially Aristotle, was adopted by many Jewish thinkers writing in Arabic in the Muslim world, not least in Muslim Spain. Many of their works were in turn transmitted to the Jews of the rest of Europe by extensive translations in the twelfth century from Arabic to Hebrew by Abraham ibn Ezra, himself a great biblical commentator, poet, grammarian, philosopher and astronomer. Over four generations in southern France in the twelfth and thirteenth centuries, the ibn Tibbon family translated into Hebrew numerous Arabic works on philosophy, medicine, mathematics and astronomy as well as commentaries on scripture.[27]

Through such means Islamic philosophy was to transform much of the theological discourse of Judaism in Christian Europe as well as in the Islamic world in the first half of the second millennium CE, as we shall see in Chapter 13. As Islam developed, so did Jewish adoption of Islamic religious ideas. Hence, for instance, the influence of Sufism, the mystical tradition within Islam which aimed at mystical union with God through abstinence and incorporated many notions from Greek Neoplatonism, on the pietistic *Duties of the Heart* of Bahya ibn Pakuda, who wrote in Spain in the second half of the eleventh century and quoted liberally from Sufi authors:

> How is special abstinence to be defined and what need have followers of the Torah for it? As to its definition, scholars are divided. One says that special abstinence is the renunciation of everything that disturbs one [and draws him away] from [service of] God. Another says that it means

holding this world in abhorrence and curtailing desires. Another says that abstinence is quietude of the soul and curbing its musings from everything which only gratified the idle imagination. Another says that abstinence is trust in God. Another says that it means limiting oneself to the minimum of clothing required for decency, taking of food only as much as is needed to still hunger, and rejecting everything else. Another says that it means abandonment of affection for human beings and loving solitude. Another says that abstinence is gratitude for benefits received and bearing trials patiently. Another says that abstinence means denying oneself all relaxation and physical pleasure, limiting oneself to mere satisfaction of natural needs without which one could not exist, and excluding everything else from the mind. This last definition befits the abstinence taught in our Torah better than any of the other definitions above set forth.

A similar sharing of religious outlook emerged in the celebration by both Jews and Muslims of festivities surrounding pilgrimage to the alleged tomb of the prophet Ezekiel on the anniversary of his death:

A lamp burns day and night over the sepulchre of Ezekiel; the light thereof has been kept burning from the day that he lighted it himself, and they continually renew the wick thereof, and replenish the oil unto the present day. A large house belonging to the sanctuary is filled with books, some of them from the time of the first temple ... The Jews that come thither to pray from the land of Persia and Media bring the money which their countrymen have offered to the Synagogue of Ezekiel the Prophet ... Distinguished Mohammedans also come hither to pray, so great is their love for Ezekiel the Prophet ...[28]

But the impact of Islam, Christianity and any other faith was still far away in the unimagined future when Rabban Yohanan b. Zakkai and a group of rabbinic sages met in Yavneh, a small town on the Mediterranean coastal plain of Judaea, in the aftermath of the destruction of Jerusalem in 70 CE.

Rabbis in the East (70 to 1000 CE)

Rab Judah said in the name of Rav, 'When Moses ascended on high he found the Holy One, blessed be He, engaged in affixing coronets to the letters.' Said Moses, 'Lord of the Universe, Who stays Thy hand?' He answered, 'There will arise a man, at the end of many generations, Akiba b. Joseph by name, who will expound upon each tittle heaps and heaps of laws.' 'Lord of the Universe,' said Moses, 'permit me to see him.' He replied, 'Turn thee round.' Moses went and sat down behind eight rows [and listened to the discourses upon the law]. Not being able to follow their arguments he was ill at ease, but when they came to a certain subject and the disciples said to the master 'Whence do you know it?' and the latter replied 'It is a law given unto Moses at Sinai' he was comforted. Thereupon he returned to the Holy One, blessed be He, and said, 'Lord of the Universe, Thou hast such a man and Thou givest the Torah by me!' He replied, 'Be silent, for such is My decree.' Then said Moses, 'Lord of the Universe, Thou hast shown me his Torah, show me his reward.' 'Turn thee round,' said He; and Moses turned round and saw them weighing out his flesh at the market-stalls. 'Lord of the Universe,' cried Moses, 'such Torah, and such a reward!' He replied, 'Be silent, for such is My decree.'

As this legend from the Babylonian Talmud illustrates, rabbis in sixth-century Mesopotamia were well aware of the extent to which the Judaism they practised and taught had evolved from the scriptures they believed had been handed down from Moses, and they gloried in the devotion to the Torah which, in the case of Akiva, had led him, centuries before, to a grisly martyr's death. It is not accidental that the setting for the story is an academy staffed with students seated in rows. Rabbinic Judaism was created by and for sages whose special characteristic, already before 70, was, as we have seen in Chapter 7, their devotion to learning for its own sake.[1]

This devotion to learning stimulated the production of a huge corpus of rabbinic works in the course of the first millennium CE. We have already made considerable use of the rabbinic compilations of the tannaitic period compiled in the third century, notably the Mishnah and Tosefta, and the exegetical commentaries on Exodus, Leviticus and Deuteronomy, because they contain important information about the period before 70 CE (see Chapter 2). The Mishnah is divided into six *sedarim* (orders), which between them contain sixty-three tractates: *zeraim* ('seeds'), on agricultural law; *mo'ed* ('set feasts'), on laws of festivals; *nashim* ('women'), on the status of women as it affects men (betrothal, marriage and divorce law); *nezikin* ('damages'), on civil and criminal law; *kodashim* ('sacred things'), covering primarily the rules for offerings in the Temple; *tohorot* ('purities'), dealing with pollution and how it is transmitted. Most tractates begin by considering the implications of a biblical law. Thus, for instance, the first tractate, *berachot* ('blessings'), described when and how the Shema should be recited in the morning and the evening, but the form is not biblical exegesis: the relevant biblical text is assumed rather than cited at the start of each tractate, and some tractates, such as *ketubot* ('marriage contracts'), deal with topics for which there is no biblical base. The Tosefta ('Addition') is very similar to the Mishnah in structure, tone, content and size, but (unlike the Mishnah) it lacks signs of any clear editing. The Tosefta contains tannaitic material not in the Mishnah, sometimes just independently preserved and sometimes as a complement to the corresponding Mishnaic discussion.

These works are dwarfed in size and scope by the Babylonian Talmud, a massive compilation of legal enactments, ethical statements, biblical exegesis, ritual injunctions, liturgical rules, social commentary, narratives and homilies, and many other disparate elements, from astronomy to astrology and from magic to medicine. Structured as an expansive commentary (termed *gemara*, 'completion') on the greater part of the Mishnah, the Babylonian Talmud comprises primarily sayings of *amoraim* ('speakers' or 'interpreters'), Babylonian and Palestinian rabbis who taught between *c.* 200 and *c.* 500 CE, although it also contains tannaitic sayings found neither in the Mishnah nor in the Tosefta. Compiled in *c.* 600 CE, the commentary attempts to show how all apparently redundant statements in the Mishnah can be understood as necessary if properly interpreted. At times this leads to somewhat implausible explanations of these statements, particularly since any opinion attributed to a specific rabbi must be consistent with every other opinion attributed to that rabbi elsewhere. The Babylonian

Talmud is the longest literary work produced in late antiquity: the most commonly used modern edition, first published in Vilna in Lithuania in the nineteenth century, is printed on more than 6,200 pages.

Among the other rabbinic compilations from this period, the Palestinian Talmud (probably from the fourth century) has content and structure similar to the Babylonian Talmud but in less polished form and with less dialectic. Some of the discursive biblical commentaries (*midrashim*), from Palestine in the fourth and sixth centuries, were probably designed for synagogue sermons. The rabbis also preserved a number of mystical texts. The Hekhalot ('heavenly Temple') literature contains accounts of the ascent of mystics through the seven heavens and heavenly places to God's throne. The *Alphabet of Akiva*, a midrashic work from the seventh to ninth centuries, contains mystical and eschatological speculation on the letters of the Hebrew alphabet. Different versions of the *Shiur Komah* ('The Measure of the Body'), probably from the same period as the *Alphabet of Akiva*, try to convey the majesty of God by describing his dimensions in impossible hyperbole: 'The soles of His feet fill the entire universe, as it is stated [in scripture]: "Thus said the Lord . . . the earth is My footstool." The height . . . of His soles is 30,000,000 [parasangs].'[2]

From the last centuries of the millennium are preserved also collections of responsa by the heads of the Babylonian rabbinic academies and a collection of homiletic questions and answers attributed to Rav Aha' of Shabha in the eighth century. *Halakhot Gedolot*, a compilation of legal responsa by a wide range of rabbis from the mid-sixth century up to the time of the compiler, dates to the ninth century. The prayer book of Amram bar Sheshna, containing both liturgical texts and halakhic (that is, legal) instructions, belongs to the same period. The works of Sherira Gaon a century later include a remarkable letter which he sent in 986–7 to the Jews of Kairouan to explain the origins of the numerous rabbinic texts to which his contemporaries across the Jewish world had come to turn for authoritative teaching.[3]

By the time Sherira Gaon wrote this letter to the Jews of Kairouan, the works to which he referred all existed in written form, but in the third century CE rabbis referred explicitly to their teachings as 'Torah of the mouth' in contrast to the written Torah of scripture, and this strong tradition of oral transmission within the rabbinic movement discouraged the writing down of texts for many centuries. As a result, almost all our knowledge of these works survives now through manuscripts copied in Europe after 1000 CE. The earliest complete manuscripts of the

Babylonian Talmud come from the twelfth century, and of the Palestinian Talmud from the thirteenth century. Fragmentary texts from earlier periods, such as a section of Sifre to Deuteronomy on the boundaries of the land of Israel found in mosaic on the floor of the sixth-century synagogue at Rehov, near Beth Shean in Palestine, or the numerous fragments, some from as early as the eighth century, of both the Talmuds found in the Cairo Genizah, demonstrate that these parts of the larger texts certainly had an earlier existence. But they cannot remove all doubt about the possibility of medieval alterations to the surviving full manuscripts, which were, after all, copied as religious texts of continuing significance within a vibrant medieval rabbinic culture. Thus, for instance, some of the texts which purport to refer to mystical experiences of rabbis in the tannaitic period up to c. 200 CE may be pseudepigraphic and evidence only for the mystical imaginations of the rabbinic circles who copied the texts in medieval Germany.

By Sherira's time, the discussions of the rabbis were taking place in formal scholarly institutions which operated within what had become a traditional structure based on a hierarchy of knowledge and authority, attracting the enthusiastic support and admiration even of those Jews who were unable to attend the academies full time and were forced to undertake most of their study by themselves. The tenth-century chronicler Nathan the Babylonian described special periodic communal study sessions (called, for reasons unknown, *kallah* or 'bride'), for such home students:

> They gather together and come from everywhere in the *kallah* month, which is the month of Elul in the summer and Adar in the winter. And during the five months [since the previous *kallah*] each one of the disciples had been diligently studying at home the tractate announced to them by the head of the academy when they left him. In Adar he would say, 'We will study tractate such and such in Elul.' Likewise, in Elul he would announce to them, 'We will study tractate such and such in Adar.' And they all come and sit before the head of the yeshivas in Adar and Elul, and the head of the academy supervises their study and tests them. And this is the order in which they sit . . .

By Nathan's time, the heads of the academies of Sura and Pumbedita in Babylonia had long been recognized by Jews across the rabbinic world as the highest authority. Since at least the seventh century, they were accorded the formal title *gaon*, 'excellency'. These scholars were often, by the time of their appointment, quite elderly: possession of outstanding knowledge of the Talmud was prerequisite for the role, and most reached this position only after a lifetime moving up through a series of lower positions in the academies. They wielded considerable secular power among Babylonian Jews generally as well as religious authority over rabbinic Jews worldwide. For those like Sherira who believed that they belonged to a tradition which stretched back centuries in an unbroken line, it was tempting to imagine that the academies at the end of the first century had been much the same as the great institutions of their own time. In fact much had changed over the intervening 900 years.[4]

Sherira himself was aware that the tradition he had inherited had been the product of change over the centuries, if only in the sense that he and his contemporaries assumed that rabbis of earlier generations had greater authority than those of more recent times. Thus the teachers of the tannaitic period who had produced the Mishnah were accorded higher status than the *amoraim* whose discussions between the early third century and the sixth century make up the bulk of the teachings recorded in the two Talmuds. As for the *savoraim* ('expositors') believed (at least by the eighth century) to have been responsible for the final editing of the talmudic text, they were accorded so little status by Sherira's time that most of their teachings were preserved anonymously. The *savoraim* remain shadowy figures for modern scholars, even though it is certain that the discussions of earlier rabbis recorded within the Babylonian Talmud were edited by some person or persons with considerable authority, not least because many discussions conclude with comment by an anonymous voice (the *stam*) either deciding the issue raised in the talmudic argument or, not infrequently, declaring *teyku* ('let it stand'), to denote that the problem remains unresolved. It is rather odd, in light of the immense prestige of the Babylonian Talmud in later rabbinic Judaism, that this voice is unidentified in the talmudic text itself and was apparently unknown to succeeding rabbinic generations.[5]

Sherira was also aware that the centres of the rabbinic tradition he recorded were all located in Jewish populations either in Mesopotamia or in the eastern Mediterranean, especially Palestine. The rabbinic texts produced in the first half of the first millennium refer to Jewish life within only a limited geographical compass (essentially the land of Israel, Babylonia and 'Syria', conceived as an ill-defined region north of Palestine). The rabbis expressed no interest in the Mediterranean Greek-speaking Jewish communities (see Chapter 12), let alone the more distant diaspora in Ethiopia or India. Babylonian rabbis succumbed on occasion to local patriotism about the religious aura acquired by their homeland through their devout scholarship, but for these rabbis, as for all Jews, biblical notions about the special role in Judaism of the land of Israel (see Chapter 4) retained their force.

The Temple might no longer be standing, but the rabbis still imagined a world in which the most sacred place on earth was the Holy of Holies. The rest of the land of Israel might be less holy than the Temple or the city of Jerusalem, but the land of Israel nonetheless far exceeded the rest of the world in sanctity, not least because many religious duties, such as the tithing of agricultural produce, were incurred only there. Rabbis debated whether there was a religious duty to reside in the land (although Babylonian rabbis self-evidently decided for themselves that any such duty could be outweighed by other considerations, such as the learning to be gained in the Babylonian academies).

The rabbis also debated the land's precise boundaries, which were unclear in the biblical texts, as we have seen (Chapter 4). Defining the frontier was of considerable importance to those, like the inhabitants of Rehov, who lived close to the eastern border and needed to know, for instance, which local fields could in good conscience be farmed in a sabbatical year. The rabbis only gradually between the second and fifth centuries CE settled on a boundary formula. Their chosen formula was based partly on the description of the land in Numbers and partly on contemporary demographics, so that regions on the borders with a mixed population, like Caesarea, were deemed to be part of the land of Israel only if the majority of the population was Jewish.[6]

In the aftermath of 70, a group of rabbinic sages who had survived the war settled in Yavneh, a small town on the coastal plain of Judaea south of the provincial capital Caesarea, to continue their studies under the leadership of Rabban Yohanan b. Zakkai. The small study group around Yohanan, meeting in the upper storey of a house or in a vineyard near a pigeon house, arrogated to themselves the attributes of a court of law. We do not know how many other Jews paid any attention to its deliberations, but it is likely that it increased in influence over the following decades with the rise to authority within the movement of Rabban Gamaliel II, the grandson of the Gamaliel who had taught St Paul.

These early rabbinic academies were more like a circle of disciples around a master than a formal institution, but it is probable that for legal decisions the sages organized themselves as they imagined the proceedings of the Sanhedrin in Jerusalem had operated when the Temple still stood:

> The Sanhedrin was arranged like the half of a round threshing-floor so that they all might see one another. Before them stood the two scribes of the judges, one to the right and one to the left, and they wrote down the words of them that favoured acquittal and the words of them that favoured conviction. R. Judah says, 'There were three: one wrote down the words of them that favoured acquittal, and one wrote down the words of them that favoured conviction, and the third wrote down the words both of them that favoured acquittal and of them that favoured conviction. Before them sat three rows of disciples of the Sages, and each knew his proper place.'

It was taken for granted that, as in the schools of the sages before 70, difficult issues within these small academies could be decided by votes:

> They vote only in a large place. And they vote only on the basis of a tradition which someone has heard. [If] one speaks in the name of a tradition which he has heard, and the rest of them say, 'We have not heard it' – in such a case, they do not take a standing vote. But if one prohibits and one permits, one declares unclean and one declares clean, and all of them declare, 'We have not heard a tradition on the matter – in such a case they rise and take a vote.[7]

From Yavneh groups of sages moved in the early second century CE the small distance to Lydda, and after the Bar Kokhba war of 132–5 to Usha in Lower Galilee and then to Tiberias and Sepphoris further east. The relationship between sages can be deduced from the early traditions about which rabbis transmitted the teachings of which teachers, and occasionally by stories such as the narrative from the Mishnah which eventually found its way into the Passover Haggadah: 'It is related of Rabbi Eliezer, Rabbi Joshua, Rabbi Elazar ben Azariah, Rabbi Akiva, and Rabbi Tarfon that they once met for the Seder in Bnei Brak and spoke about the Exodus from Egypt all night long, until their disciples came and said to them: "Masters! The time has come to say the morning Shema!"'[8]

It is probable that in Palestine rabbinic teaching and learning remained situated within such small disciple groups down to at least the fourth century, when the Palestinian Talmud reached its final form. The disciple circle was the standard form of a philosophical school in antiquity and such informality allowed for the emergence of local centres of rabbinic learning in Byzantine Palestine. Such, for instance, was the cluster of pupils around R. Hoshaiah in third-century Caesarea, where the sages were more exposed to the influence of the non-Jewish population of Palestine than in Galilee, which was almost entirely settled by Jews. Hoshaiah lived in Caesarea at the same time as the Christian theologian Origen, with whom he may indeed have had contact, but by whose ideas he does not seem to have been directly affected.[9]

As we have seen in Chapter 7, in the second to fifth centuries CE Christians were much more affected by their relations to Judaism, as they worked out their basic theology and puzzled out the role of the Old Testament within it, than Jews were affected by Christianity. But Christianity may have affected Palestinian rabbis in more subtle ways. It is possible that the lack of references in the Palestinian Talmud to any discussions of Palestinian *amoraim* after the mid-fourth century, almost two centuries before the last amoraic teachers attested in the Babylonian Talmud, and the apparent lack of editing of the text may relate to the strains of rabbinic academies operating within a Christian Roman empire, but it is hard to reconcile such an explanation with the apparent prosperity of the Jewish communities which commissioned and financed the fine Palestinian synagogue mosaic floors dated to the fifth and sixth centuries, of which a good number have been excavated over recent decades (see Chapter 10). More plausibly assigned to relations with the majority Christian culture in the fifth and sixth centuries is the greater engagement of Palestinian rabbis than their Babylonian counterparts with the biblical text. Such engagement led, in the fifth and (probably) the sixth centuries, to the production of many rabbinic commentaries (*midrashim*) on narrative sections of biblical books, such as Genesis Rabbah (completed probably in the fifth century CE) and Leviticus Rabbah. The *midrashim* to Song of Songs, Ruth, Lamentations, Ecclesiastes and Esther seem all to have been compiled in Palestine between the fifth and seventh centuries.

By the early third century the rabbinic movement in Palestine recognized the leadership of one of their number as a quasi-monarchical ruler within the Jewish community. R. Judah haNasi, the compiler of the Mishnah, is the first sage to whose name the later tradition affixed the permanent title *nasi*, 'prince'. It is uncertain whether earlier figures of authority within the movement, such as Rabban Gamaliel II, held either the title or the same role within Jewish society, but the rabbis recorded a series of *nesi'im* through the third century, and Roman legal sources, which refer to the *nasi* as *ethnarches* in Greek and *patriarcha* in Latin, know about such religious figures in Jewish society down to the first quarter of the fifth century.

A remarkable mosaic in the synagogue of Hammat Tiberias in Galilee, depicting the sun god surrounded by the signs of the zodiac, was set up (according to the mosaic inscription) by a member of the household of the *patriarcha* in the late fourth century. By that time the patriarch was a figure of considerable standing within the wider community, both Jewish and imperial. But by the fourth century the rabbinic sources are silent about the *nasi*, and it is therefore possible that the holders of the position were no longer closely aligned to the rabbinic movement, preferring instead to stress their (possibly fictitious) descent from Hillel and their (definitely fictitious) descent from David. The Hammat Tiberias synagogue reflects a city of some sophistication in the fourth century, distinguished only by its comparatively small size and lack of pagan shrines from the huge site of Scythopolis (known to the rabbis as Beit She'an) to the south of the lake, with its theatre and odeon, or from the great provincial capital of Caesarea on the coast, with its hippodrome, amphitheatre and governor's palace. The rabbinic texts preserve stories of Palestinian rabbis operating in these cities also, but the rabbinic movement in Galilee always retained a certain rural tinge. In the fifth and sixth centuries much of the epigraphic evidence for rabbis likewise comes from the Galilean countryside, or from places like Dabburra on the Golan.[10]

In the account of the Palestinian rabbinic movement of the century after 70 which emerges from the Babylonian Talmud, of central significance in the survival of Judaism after the Bar Kokhba rebellion was the transmission of authority through *semikha*, 'ordination', of his disciples by a sage named R. Judah b. Baba, who was himself martyred by the Romans:

> Cannot one man alone ordain? Did not Rab Judah say in Rab's name, 'May this man indeed be remembered for blessing – his name is R. Judah b. Baba . . . What did R. Judah b. Baba do? He went and sat between two great mountains, [that lay] between two large cities; between the Sabbath boundaries of the cities of Usha and Shefaram and there ordained five elders: viz., R. Meir, R. Judah, R. Simeon, R. Jose and R. Eliezer b. Shamua.'

The Babylonian Talmud also transmitted the notion that during the time of Judah haNasi (in the early third century) it was decreed that only those properly authorized in this fashion could give decisions relating to religious law, including purely ceremonial law, but, although the Palestinian Talmud preserves traditions about the appointment of judges in Palestine by patriarchs and the insistence of rabbis in the third century that this must be done in conjunction with a court, such a clear-cut notion of rabbinic authority is much harder to discern in the Palestinian sources themselves. Even in Babylonia, the earliest disciple circles, which formed around Abba bar Aivu (known as Rav) and Samuel in the third century, seem to have been very informal. The view in the Babylonian Talmud probably reflects the development in later centuries of the influence of the Babylonian exilarch, whose authority became necessary for the appointment of judges: 'Said Rav, "Whosoever wishes to decide monetary cases by himself and be free from liability in case of an erroneous decision, should obtain sanction from the Exilarch."'[11]

Already in the Sasanian period, before the completion of the Talmud in c. 600 CE, the exilarch in Babylonia, as political authority, was sometimes at variance with the heads of the academies as their institutions grew in size and distinction. Rav founded the academy at Sura which survived in one form or another for almost 800 years to the mid-eleventh century. Samuel's academy at Nehardea was forced to move in the middle of the third century, but the Pumbedita academy, which saw itself as its successor, continued to exist alongside Sura for the rest of the first millennium, albeit with a move to Baghdad in c. 900 CE. The sages of this school in the fourth century – especially Rabbah bar Nahmani, Yosef b. Hiyya, Abbaye and Rava – are frequently mentioned in the Babylonian Talmud as sources of the teachings and discussion which make up the work. Most of what we know about Jewish life in the cities where those academies were found is derived from the Babylonian Talmud itself. Pumbedita, on the bank of the River Euphrates in northern Babylonia and traversed by canals, had an excellent climate for agriculture, especially dates and flax, and good connections to the caravan route to Syria which gave the city an international commercial dimension, while Sura, further to the south, was known for its production of grapes, wheat and barley, and its own busy world of craftsmen and small traders.

These academies exercised great influence way beyond their own confines, as we have already seen from the letter of Rav Sherira Gaon, Gaon of Pumbedita in the tenth century. But their success as educational institutions and producers of texts led in the final centuries of the first millennium to the undercutting of their authority, as new centres of rabbinic scholarship sprang up elsewhere, founded on this work. Within the Islamic world from the mid-seventh century, Jews could and did travel extensively, and outstanding scholars from Babylonia had settled in Kairouan in Tunisia by the eighth century. By the tenth century, the Kairouan academy was in close contact with scholars also in Egypt, Italy and Palestine. We know little about the academy in Lucena mentioned by Natronai, Gaon of Sura in the ninth century, but in the tenth century Moses b. Hanokh, who came originally from southern Italy, was appointed rabbi of Cordoba in Spain. Under the patronage of a Jewish politician, Hisdai ibn Shaprut, who had much influence over the Umayyad caliph, Moses b. Hanokh helped to break the dependence of Spanish scholars too on the authority of Babylonian teachers.

Two centuries later the Spanish philosopher Abraham ibn Daud preserved in his *Sefer haKabbalah*, which related the chain of rabbinic tradition from the biblical Moses to his own time, a legend in which Moses b. Hanokh featured as one of four rabbis who had sailed from Bari in Italy during the tenth century, been captured by Muslims and been ransomed by the Jewish communities in which they established great academies:

> The commander of a fleet, whose name was Ibn Rumahis, left Cordova, having been sent by the Muslim king of Spain ... This commander of a mighty fleet set out to capture the ships of the Christians and the towns that were close to the coast. They sailed as far as the coast of Palestine and swung about to the Greek sea and the islands therein. [Here] they encountered a ship carrying four great scholars, who were travelling from the city of Bari to a city called Sefastin, and who were on their way to a Kallah convention. Ibn Rumahis captured the ship and took the sages prisoner ... These sages did not tell a soul about themselves or their wisdom. The commander sold R. Shemariah in Alexandria of Egypt; [R. Shemariah] proceeded to Fustat where he became head [of the academy]. Then he sold R. Hushiel on the coast of Ifriqiya. From there the latter proceeded to the city of Qairawan, which at that time was the mightiest of all Muslim cities in the land of the Maghreb, where he became the head [of the academy] and where he begot his son Rabbenu Hananel. Then the commander arrived at Cordova where he sold R. Moses along with R. Hanok.

The legend is a fiction, but its invention reflects the need of Jews in later centuries to explain the increasing importance of the academies in Africa and Spain as the authority of the Babylonian centres declined.[12]

The authority of academies in Palestine as centres of rabbinic learning was far weaker than that of the Babylonian schools in the last three centuries of the first millennium, although we have noted (Chapter 10) the specialized role of the masoretes in Tiberias in establishing the final shape of the biblical texts through their acknowledged expertise in preserving traditions about vocalization, accents, divisions, spelling and scribal conventions. These masoretes were engaged in such scholarly work, primarily in Palestine, for about five centuries from the middle of the first millennium, and the prominence of the Tiberias school owed much to the influence of one family of scholars. Aharon b. Moshe b. Asher produced in the tenth century CE what was to become the standard biblical text, using a system of vowels and accents for cantillation (ritual chanting) which became normative first in manuscripts and later in printed editions. He was the fifth generation of a family dedicated to the same work. It is clear that they did more than simply record the views of their predecessors, for the text of a biblical codex containing the Prophets, copied in Tiberias by Aharon's father Moshe in 897 CE and preserved in the Karaite synagogue in Cairo, frequently disagrees with the vocalization and accents preferred by Aharon himself.

At some time after the sixth century, and possibly as late as the ninth century, Jerusalem and Ramleh became centres of rabbinic scholarship in place of Tiberias, although the link with the earlier academy was evidently precious. Daniel b. Azariah, who headed the Jerusalem academy from 1051 to 1062, signed himself '*nasi* and *gaon* of Tiberias' in a letter found in the Cairo Genizah. Daniel himself was a descendant of a Babylonian exilarch, and was therefore believed to be from the house of David. But the honour in which he was held as 'the Light of Israel, the Great Prince and Head of the Academy of the Majesty of Jacob', as he was called in the synagogue of the Palestinian Jewish community in Old Cairo, owed more to his birth than to the rabbinic learning and authority of his academy.[13]

The spread of rabbinic learning from Palestine to Italy and further north into Europe took place mostly after the end of the first millennium, but a story found in several medieval German Jewish sources, that in 917 CE a certain 'King Karl' (presumably a reference to Charlemagne, although by this date he was dead) brought the Kalonymus family, who were experts on rabbinic literature, to Mainz from Lucca in northern Italy, presupposes knowledge of rabbinic scholarship in Lucca itself at this period. Before settling in Lucca in the eleventh century, R. Kalonymus b. Moses was said to have taught in Rome, presumably in the local yeshivah which is first mentioned as a centre for talmudic scholarship in Rome at this time. At least in rabbinic circles, study of Judaism in Rome was evidently now carried out in Hebrew and Aramaic rather than in Greek. By contrast, the great academies of Germany and France, which were to prove so influential in the development of rabbinic Judaism from the eleventh century, were still in the tenth century embryonic, until the influence of R. Gershom b. Judah, who died in 1028 CE, placed the Mainz academy at the centre of the study of talmudic thought in northern Europe.[14]

Rabbinic society by the end of the first millennium had well-established rules of social control, not least the *herem* ('excommunication'). In its original biblical meaning, to condemn someone to *herem* was to invoke destruction, but within rabbinic Judaism the *herem* was a mechanism through which a rabbinic court could ordain the ostracizing or shunning of those deemed to have violated the norms of the community. As rabbinic Judaism spread, and with it the authority of rabbis from distant places, so did the possibility of a ban on those whose share in the community was essentially a notional belonging to the whole of Israel. Two such bans attributed to Rabbenu Gershom b. Judah illustrate the fracturing of rabbinic authority by the end of the first millennium. On the one hand, the *herem bet din* ('ban of the court') gave authority to local courts over all those who passed through a community: 'If a man passes through a community where there is a ban of the court and he is summoned to court under the ban in the presence of proper witnesses, even if he be in the market place, the ban is upon him until he repairs to the court to plead his case.' On the other hand, we have noted (Chapter 10) that the ban which prohibited polygamy (conventionally, but probably incorrectly, also attributed to Rabbenu Gershom) was taken as authoritative throughout the Jewish world in Germany and France but ignored by the Jews of Islamic lands.[15]

Both the subjects and the mode of rabbinic discourse had developed greatly in the thousand years between the time of Yohanan b. Zakkai and Rabbenu Gershom. Within the academies, immense effort was expended on teasing out the minutiae of legal rulings derived originally both from the Bible and from custom. Tracing the development of this halakhic discourse over the generations is bedevilled by the practice, common in the talmudic texts, of ascribing to an earlier rabbinic teacher a view which – so the compiler imagined in light of that teacher's known views on other subjects – he would have adopted when faced with an issue raised in a later generation. Nonetheless it is possible to discern at least the outline of debates in particular periods, and to see that for the most part the topics for discussion were generated within the academies themselves by a passion for logic and precision rather than a need to respond to pressures from outside.

The hermeneutical methods employed by rabbinic scholars in teasing out the law followed principles which could be, and were, systematized by the third century CE at the latest. They were highly complex:

> Anything which is included in the general statement and which is specified in order to teach [something] teaches not only about itself but also teaches about everything included in the general statement ... Anything that is included in the general statement and which is specified as a requirement concerning another requirement which is in keeping with the general statement is specified in order to make [the second requirement] less stringent and not more stringent ... Anything that is included in the general statement and which is specified as a requirement in the general statement and which is specified as a requirement concerning another requirement which is not in keeping with the general statement is specified either to make less or more stringent ... Hillel the Elder expounded seven methods before the Elders of Bethyra. A fortiori, and analogy, and two verses, and a general statement and a particular statement, and something similar to it in another place, and a thing is explained from its context.

Lists like this one (from Sifra) were refined and expanded many times in rabbinic circles in antiquity, reflecting both a high degree of methodological self-awareness among rabbinic interpreters and the willingness of individual sages to seek exact means to reach what seemed to them the best religious outcome for living practice. The lists reflected rather than shaped the actual process of formulating the law. The relationship of the lists to interpretation practice was complex. Some principles found in all the lists are rarely found in actual use, and there seems to have been tacit acceptance that some of the more imaginative methods deemed appropriate for interpreting narrative should be eschewed when it came to interpretation of legal texts.

Recourse to biblical prooftexts was generally in support of a legal opinion already reached by other means. Thus the *midrashim* of the tannaitic period (Mekhilta on Exodus, Sifra on Leviticus, and Sifre on Numbers and Deuteronomy) can be best understood as attempts to align a separate discourse based on legal reasoning with the biblical text:

'If Fire Break Out', etc. Why is this said? Even if it had not been said I could have reasoned: Since he is liable for damage done by what is owned by him, shall he not be liable for damage done by himself? If, then, I succeed in proving it by logical reasoning, what need is there of saying: 'If fire break out?' Simply this: Scripture comes to declare that in all cases of liability for damage mentioned in the Torah one acting under duress is regarded as one acting of his own free will, one acting unintentionally is regarded as one acting intentionally, and the woman is regarded like the man.

For this purpose it was taken as entirely legitimate to wrest the meaning of a word away from its original biblical context:

Does the Divine Law not say 'Eye for eye'? Why not take this literally to mean [putting out] the eye [of the offender]? – Let not this enter your mind, since it has been taught: You might think that where he put out his eye, the offender's eye should be put out, or where he cut off his arm, the offender's arm should be cut off, or again where he broke his leg, the offender's leg should be broken. [Not so; for] it is laid down, 'He that smiteth any man . . .' 'And he that smiteth a beast . . .' just as in the case of smiting a beast compensation is to be paid, so also in the case of smiting a man compensation is to be paid.

Such search for the 'real' meaning of the biblical text sometimes prompted the rabbis to resort to deciphering the code of scripture to establish the desired meaning through anagrams and abbreviations of biblical words. At other times they appealed to *gematria* (from the Greek *geometria*, 'geometry'), which involved adding up the numerical values of the letters in a word (since in Hebrew 'aleph' stands for 'one', 'beth' for 'two', and so on):

R. Simlai when preaching said: Six hundred and thirteen precepts were communicated to Moses, three hundred and sixty-five negative precepts, corresponding to the number of solar days [in the year], and two hundred and forty-eight positive precepts, corresponding to the number of the members of man's body. Said R. Hamnuna: What is the text for this? It is, 'Moses commanded us torah, an inheritance of the congregation of Jacob,' 'torah' being in letter-value, equal to six hundred and eleven; 'I am' and 'Thou shalt have no [other Gods]' [have to be added, because] we heard them direct from the mouth of the Almighty [in the Ten Commandments].[16]

By the use of such methods and intense scholarly debate over generations, the rabbis created a huge body of interpretation. When real cases for discussion did not present themselves, they invented imaginary scenarios. These could sometimes reach levels of implausibility unacceptable even to the rabbis themselves, as indicated by the occasional comments of the editors of the text, that a matter is beyond resolution, as in the following discussion of evidence that leavened bread, which should be excluded from a dwelling on Passover, may have been brought into the house by a mouse:

> Raba asked, 'What if a mouse enters with a loaf in its mouth, and a mouse goes out with a loaf in its mouth: do we say, the same which went in went out; or perhaps it is a different one? Should you answer, the same which went in went out, – what if a white mouse entered with a loaf in its mouth, and a black mouse went out with a loaf in its mouth? now this is certainly a different one; or perhaps it did indeed seize it from the other? And should you say, mice do not seize from each other, – what if a mouse enters with a loaf in its mouth and a weasel goes out with a loaf in its mouth? now the weasel certainly does take from a mouse; or perhaps it is a different one, for had it snatched it from the mouse, the mouse would have [now] been found in its mouth? And should you say, had it snatched it from the mouse, the mouse would have been found in its mouth, what if a mouse enters with a loaf in its mouth, and then a weasel comes out with a loaf and a mouse in the weasel's mouth? Here it is certainly the same; or perhaps, if it were the same, the loaf should indeed have been found in the mouse's mouth; or perhaps it fell out [of the mouse's mouth] on account of [its] terror, and it [the weasel] took it?'

Beneath the humour lies a serious concern to establish the limits of responsibility to search for evidence to ensure a life lived in accordance with the prescriptions of the Torah. In contrast to the high level of abstraction in contemporary treatises of Christians such as Origen (in the third century) or Augustine (in the late fourth and early fifth), who pondered theological issues about the nature of the divine under the influence of Greek philosophy, the talmudic rabbis were engaged in practical means to achieve sanctity at a human level. Greek philosophy did not enter into the rabbinic tradition until Saadiah, long after the talmudic period, when its adoption was under the influence of Islam (see below).[17]

Usually the rabbis relied on argument and logic, only occasionally resorting to reliance on biblical authority alone. But there were exceptions, as in a story about Yohanan b. Zakkai found in the amoraic compilation *Pesikta de-Rab Kahana*:

A heathen questioned Rabban Yohanan ben Zakkai, saying, 'The things you Jews do appear to be a kind of sorcery. A heifer is brought, it is burned, is pounded into ash, and its ash is gathered up. Then when one of you gets defiled by contact with a corpse, two or three drops of the ash mixed with water are sprinkled upon him, and he is told, "You are cleansed!"' Rabban Yohanan asked the heathen: 'Has the spirit of madness ever possessed you?' He replied, 'No.' 'Have you ever seen a man whom the spirit of madness has possessed?' The heathen replied: 'Yes.' 'And what do you do for such a man?' 'Roots are brought, the smoke of their burning is made to rise about him, and water is sprinkled upon him until the spirit of madness flees.' Rabban Yohanan then said: 'Do not your ears hear what your mouth is saying? It is the same with a man who is defiled by contact with a corpse – he, too, is possessed by a spirit, the spirit of uncleanness, and, [as of madness], Scripture says, "I will cause [false] prophets as well as the spirit of uncleanness to flee from the Land"' (Zech 13:2). Now when the heathen left, Rabban Yohanan's disciples said: 'Our master, you put off that heathen with a mere reed of an answer, but what answer will you give us?' Rabban Yohanan answered: 'By your lives, I swear: the corpse does not have the power by itself to defile, nor does the mixture of ash and water have the power by itself to cleanse. The truth is that the purifying power of the Red Heifer is a decree of the Holy One. The Holy One said: "I have set it down as a statute, I have issued it as a decree. You are not permitted to transgress My decree. 'This is the statute of the Torah'"' (Num 19:1).

Nor was it only the divine word that could be authoritative without argument, for the rabbis also ascribed to themselves, or at least to their leading figures, the power to issue *takkanot*, 'decrees', to supplement the law of the Torah. Such, for instance, was the decree, attributed in the Babylonian Talmud to authorities of the tannaitic period and by no means always followed, that education must be provided for all boys from the age of six.[18]

It is noteworthy, however, that such reliance on authority is unusual in talmudic arguments and that decisions were not generally ascribed to direct divine intervention. Indeed, supernatural revelation as a solution to legal conundrums is especially ruled out in a striking story in the Babylonian Talmud:

On that day R. Eliezer brought forward every imaginable argument, but they did not accept them. Said he to them: 'If the law agrees with me, let this carob-tree prove it!' Thereupon the carob-tree was torn a hundred cubits out of its place – others affirm, four hundred cubits. 'No proof can be brought from a carob-tree,' they retorted. Again he said to them: 'If the law agrees with me, let the stream of water prove it!' Whereupon the stream of water flowed backwards – 'No proof can be brought from a stream of water,' they rejoined . . . he said to them: 'If the law agrees with me, let it be proved from Heaven!' Whereupon a Heavenly Voice cried out: 'Why do ye dispute with R. Eliezer, seeing that in all matters the law agrees with him!' But R. Joshua arose and exclaimed: 'It is not in heaven.' What did he mean by this? – Said R. Jeremiah, 'That the Torah had already been given at Mount Sinai; we pay no attention to a Heavenly Voice, because you have long since written in the Torah at Mount Sinai, "After the majority must one incline."' R. Nathan met Elijah and asked him, 'What did the Holy One, Blessed be He, do in that hour?' – He laughed [with joy], he replied, saying, 'My sons have defeated Me, My sons have defeated Me.'

The general lack of appeal by sages to individual revelation in talmudic arguments suggests strongly that the refusal of the majority in this story to allow such an appeal by R. Eliezer was the standard approach, even though there is found in one passage in the Babylonian Talmud a remarkable assertion that the disputes between the Houses of Hillel and Shammai, which in the Mishnah are explicitly stated to have been left unresolved, were decided once and for all in favour of the House of Hillel by just such a 'heavenly voice':

R. Abba stated in the name of Samuel: For three years there was a dispute between the House of Shammai and the House of Hillel, the former asserting, 'The law is in agreement with our views' and the latter contending, 'The law is in agreement with our views.' Then a heavenly voice issued announcing, '[The utterances of] both are the words of the living God, but the law is in agreement with the rulings of the House of Hillel.'

By contrast elsewhere the rabbis invoke strong limitations on their own ability to bring about change. They assert in one passage in the Jerusalem Talmud that not even a miraculous intervention by Elijah could change the way that a ritual enjoined in the Bible is performed, since the custom followed by the people 'overrides the law'.[19]

The talmudic rabbis did not lack interest in theology and ethics, but such notions as the providence of God and the centrality of Israel and the Torah in the divine plan for the world were generally assumed in stories and apophthegms rather than argued. But the ethical teachings enshrined in the Mishnaic tractate *Avot*, 'the sayings of the fathers', were more explicit. *Avot* is a collection of proverbs uncharacteristic in its literary form both of the Mishnah and of rabbinic literature in general. Its teachings are grouped loosely into mnemonic forms often based on numeration:

> They [each] said three things. R. Eliezer said, 'Let the honour of thy fellow be dear to thee as thine own, and be not easily provoked, and repent one day before thy death; and warm yourself before the fire of the Sages, but be heedful of their glowing coals lest you be burned, for their bite is the bite of a jackal and their sting the sting of a scorpion and their hiss the hiss of a serpent, and all their words are like coals of fire . . . If love depends on some [transitory] thing, and the [transitory] thing passes away, the love passes away too; but if it does not depend on some [transitory] thing it will never pass away. Which love depended on some [transitory] thing? This was the love of Amnon and Tamar. And which did not depend on some [transitory] thing? This was the love of David and Jonathan.

As a compilation of wisdom traditions, *Avot* has most in common with biblical wisdom texts such as the book of Proverbs, but occasionally it seems to have had in mind the specific scholarly environment of the rabbinic academies:

> There are four types among them that sit in the presence of the Sages: the sponge, the funnel, the strainer, and the sifter. 'The sponge' – which soaks up everything; 'the funnel' – which takes in at this end and lets out at the other; 'the strainer' – which lets out the wine and collects the lees; 'the sifter' – which extracts the coarsely-ground flour and collects the fine flour.

On the other hand, a stress on charitable giving as a religious obligation was of much wider relevance to all Jews, and reflects a frequent ethical theme:

> There are four types of almsgivers: he that is minded to give but not that others should give – he begrudges what belongs to others; he that is minded that others should give but not that he should give – he begrudges what belongs to himself; he that is minded to give and also that others should give – he is a saintly man; he that is minded not to give himself and that others should not give – he is a wicked man.

Avot is unusual in the rabbinic corpus in its focus specifically on ethics, but both Talmuds have much to say in passing about the importance of *hesed* ('loving-kindness') and *teshuvah* ('repentance for sin'), as well as the main topics inherited from the Bible, such as the covenant between God and Israel. Ethical teachings are presented in less organized fashion in most of the rest of rabbinic literature from this period until the emergence of a distinctive ethical genre in the Geonic era (between the sixth and eleventh centuries CE) under the influence of Islamic thought. The earliest known rabbinic treatise devoted solely to ethics is the final chapter, on 'Man's Conduct', of Saadiah's *Book of Beliefs and Opinions* (see above, p. 258).[20]

Wide-ranging rabbinic discussions of law as it affected all parts of life in due course shaped rituals which took on new forms in light of their rulings. So, for instance, the Kaddish prayer, which may have originated as a marker of the conclusion of learning sessions in the academy, became by the end of the first millennium a doxology used, in various formulations, to separate each section of the synagogue service:

> Magnified and sanctified may His great name be, in the world He created by His will. May He establish His kingdom in your lifetime and in your days, and in the lifetime of all the House of Israel, swiftly and soon – and say: Amen. May His great name be blessed for ever and all time. Blessed and praised, glorified and exalted, raised and honoured, uplifted and lauded be the name of the Holy One, blessed be He, beyond any blessing, song, praise and consolation uttered in the world – and say: Amen. May there be great peace from heaven, and life for us and all Israel – and say: Amen. May He who makes peace in His high places, make peace for us and all Israel – and say: Amen.

Of new rituals which originated entirely from within the rabbinic academies, the most striking may be the celebration of Lag BaOmer. The period of counting the *omer* in its biblical formulation involved nothing more than a ritual means to celebrate the passage from Passover to Pentecost, but it was decreed in rabbinic texts of late antiquity to be a period of mourning because of a legend that in one year in the mid-second century a dreadful plague took place in the *omer* days in which 24,000 disciples of R. Akiva died of plague because 'they did not sufficiently honour one another.' Because the plague was thought to have come to an end on the thirty-third day, the anniversary was celebrated thereafter.[21]

It is clear that the main concerns of the rabbinic academies in these centuries lay in the development of law and the interpretation of the Bible. But the texts also reveal other religious interests (perhaps at a less formal level) which related to developments within other forms of Judaism either before or after this period. Within rabbinic tradition were preserved eschatological texts like *Sefer Zerubbabel*, a Hebrew apocalypse originally composed in the seventh century CE somewhere in the Byzantine empire, in which visions are attributed to Zerubbabel, who had been governor of Judah in the Persian period. According to the revelation, one messiah, 'son of Joseph', is to be killed, but a second messiah, 'son of David', will prevail over his enemies, inaugurating the erection of a new Temple. Such eschatological fervour fits well the expectations of seventh-century Jews as they witnessed first the conquest of Palestine by Persians and then the Islamic invasions (see Chapter 10). A number of apocalyptic texts composed in this period survive, some ascribed to biblical figures like Zerubbabel and Elijah and others to tannaitic rabbis such as Shimon bar Yohai. It is unlikely that these apocalypses derived originally from rabbinic authors, but it is significant that they continued to be copied within rabbinic circles in different recensions in later generations.[22]

Difficult to relate to mainstream rabbinic culture are the mystical streams which surface occasionally in rabbinic texts. The Mishnah forbids in obscure terms the teaching of particular subjects and specific passages of the Bible, notably the beginning of Genesis and first chapter of Ezekiel, with its vision of the divine chariot or throne: 'The forbidden degrees may not be expounded before three persons, nor the Story of Creation before two, nor [the chapter of] the Chariot before one alone, unless he is a sage that understands of his own knowledge.' It is clear that these passages were seen as potentially dangerous in various ways. The 'forbidden degrees' are the rules prohibiting sexual relations between close relatives, and the inhibition on study of such a topic presumably relates to the possibility that too close an analysis of forbidden sex might be titillating. A similar reason probably explains the apparently strange selection in the medieval period of this passage for public recitation, but not exposition, on the afternoon service in the synagogue on the Day of Atonement, one of the most solemn and serious times in the liturgical year. The story of creation and the vision of Ezekiel were believed to contain hidden mysteries which should be studied only by those capable of comprehending them responsibly.

By the twelfth century CE speculation on these passages was to spawn a full-scale mystical tradition, but whether we are to believe that such interpretations, and (even more) mystical practices, were already to be found among rabbis in late antiquity depends on our own understanding of a small number of obscure tales in amoraic compilations about tannaitic sages:

Four entered the Garden. One cast a look and died. One cast a look and was stricken. One cast a look and cut among the shoots. One entered safely and departed safely. Ben Azzai cast a look and was stricken. Of him scripture says: 'If you have found honey, eat only enough for you' (Prov 25:16). Ben Zoma cast a look and died. Of him Scripture says, 'Precious in the sight of the Lord is the death of his saints' (Ps 116:15). Aher cast a look and cut among the shoots . . . R. Akiva entered safely, and departed safely.[23]

At least some of the mystical stories arose from a natural desire to attribute superhuman qualities to sages from the past, like the heroic Shimon bar Yohai who was believed to have lived in a cave for twelve years at the time of the Bar Kokhba revolt in the second century CE in order to preserve the Torah, fortified by a miraculous carob tree and well of water and visited by the prophet Elijah. A strange cosmological writing, *Sefer Yetsirah*, 'The Book of Creation', presents a systematic view of the creation of the world through 'thirty-two paths of wisdom' made up of the first ten numbers and the twenty-two letters of the Hebrew alphabet. It seems to have had its origin in the third or fourth centuries CE. It was to be treated in the medieval period as a source of much mystical speculation, but whether this was already true at the time of its composition is uncertain. The obscure contents of the text are of little help:

> The ten *sefirot* are the basis; their measure is ten for they have no limit: dimension of beginning and dimension of end, dimension of good and dimension of evil, dimension of above and dimension of below, dimension of east and dimension of west, dimension of north and dimension of south. And the unique Lord, a trustworthy divine king, rules over them all from his holy abode for ever and ever.

The term *sefirah*, which means literally 'enumeration' and was to acquire great importance in later Jewish mysticism (see below, p. 347), evidently had some mystical significance for the author of this text, but the style of the book is so allusive that it is hard to know exactly what he intended to convey. The obscurantism may have been deliberate. It certainly did not prevent the text becoming popular.

Equally embedded in rabbinic discourse was astrology, with frequent references in the Talmuds to the *mazal*, 'planet' or 'luck', of individuals, despite the hostility of those, like R. Yohanan in the third century, who asserted that 'Israel has no planet'. Also deeply embedded, despite similarly strong opposition by some rabbis, were magic and dream interpretation:

R. Hisda also said, 'A dream which is not interpreted is like a letter which is not read.' R. Hisda also said, 'Neither a good dream nor a bad dream is ever wholly fulfilled.' R. Hisda also said, 'A bad dream is better than a good dream.' R. Hisda also said, 'The sadness caused by a bad dream is sufficient for it and the joy which a good dream gives is sufficient for it.' ... Ben Dama, the son of R. Ishmael's sister, asked R. Ishmael, 'I dreamt that both my jaws fell out; [what does it mean]?' – He replied to him, 'Two Roman counsellors have made a plot against you, but they have died.' Bar Kappara said to Rabbi, 'I dreamt that my nose fell off.' He replied to him, 'Fierce anger has been removed from you.' He said to him, 'I dreamt that both my hands were cut off.' He replied, 'You will not require the labour of your hands.'[24]

Rabbinic interest in astrology reflects, even if it did not lead, the incorporation of astrological notions into worship by the wider Jewish community at least in Palestine from the fourth to sixth centuries. Depictions of the signs of the zodiac were a common feature in the decoration of synagogue floors, from the charmingly rustic representation at Beth Alpha to a more sophisticated version found more recently at Sepphoris. The ascription of responsibility on the mosaic itself for the zodiac image at Hammat Tiberias, one of the finest such depictions, to a donation by a certain Severus from the household of 'the illustrious patriarchs', makes it hard to argue (as archaeologists were initially inclined to do) that such zodiacs were evidence of a type of Judaism of which the rabbis disapproved. For the magical practices reflected in the Babylonian Talmud, confirmation has emerged from Iraq in the form of thousands of bowls on which magic spells were painted in order to trap demons and prevent harm to the inhabitants of the houses where they were placed. The bowls use distinctively Jewish Aramaic terminology and seem to have operated in exactly the same way as those produced by contemporary Christians and Zoroastrians. In this respect, at least, the Jews of Babylonia, including the local rabbis, adopted local customs in the last centuries before Islam.[25]

Such variation in the surrounding cultures may be responsible for the acknowledgement within rabbinic circles that local practices in some important areas of Jewish life varied, and that such variety should be respected and upheld. The Mishnah already recognized the different betrothal customs of Judaea and Galilee, and laid down a general rule that 'in order to prevent conflicts, no one should depart from local custom.' A Jew should observe the strict custom of both his place of origin and the place he is visiting. But such toleration within the rabbinic community was not universal. So, for instance, a certain Pirkoi b. Baboi, a Babylonian scholar, in *c.* 800 CE composed in Hebrew a polemical letter to the Jews of North Africa and Spain in which he mounted an intense attack on the customs of Palestinian rabbinic Jews. He decried their practices, when he believed them contrary to halakhah, because they lacked authority as a result of Palestinian tradition being disrupted by Christian persecution.[26]

By the time of Pirkoi the number of Jews engaged in rabbinic study must have risen into the thousands, in contrast to the handful of sages who had clustered around Yohanan b. Zakkai in 70 CE. Their impact on the wider Jewish community had correspondingly greatly increased. The somewhat solipsistic concerns of rabbinic authors were with the religious lives of adult male rabbinic Jews like themselves, for whom study in the academy was an integral part of piety. For the most part other Jews, characterized as *ammei ha'arets*, 'people of the land', meaning essentially 'lax' or 'lay', were simply ignored. In Babylonia, where the large rabbinic academies seem to have operated in a self-sufficient bubble in the amoraic period, indifference could sometimes express itself as antagonism (often in exaggerated rhetoric):

> Our Rabbis taught, 'Let a man always sell all he has and marry the daughter of a scholar, for if he dies or goes into exile, he is assured that his children will be scholars. But let him not marry the daughter of an *am ha'arets*, for if he dies or goes into exile, his children will be *ammei ha'arets*.' ... R. Eleazar said, 'An *am ha'arets*, it is permitted to stab him [even] on the Day of Atonement which falls on the Sabbath.' Said his disciples to him, 'Master, say to slaughter him [ritually]?' He replied, 'This [ritual slaughter] requires a benediction, whereas that [stabbing] does not require a benediction ... Greater is the hatred wherewith the *ammei ha'arets* hate the scholar than the hatred wherewith the heathens hate Israel, and their wives [hate even] more than they ...' Our Rabbis taught, 'Six things were said of the *ammei ha'arets*: We do not commit testimony to them; we do not accept testimony from them; we do not reveal a secret to them; we do not appoint them as guardians for orphans; we do not appoint them stewards over charity funds; and we must not join their company on the road.'

It is hard to know how much of this vituperation was intended to be taken seriously.[27]

*

In the Mediterranean world, a closer relationship between rabbis and other Jews in the same centuries may have been in part a product of intervention by the Christian Roman state from the end of the fourth century CE, when emperors, intent on the imposition of Christian orthodoxy, began to categorize all their subjects in religious terms. Having decided that Jews, unlike pagans, should be allowed to continue in their 'error', they devolved authority to the Jewish patriarch (*nasi*) in Palestine to control the synagogue communities of the diaspora as well as the homeland, as in a law promulgated by the emperors Arcadius and Honorius on 1 July 397:

> The Jews shall be bound to their rites; while we shall imitate the ancients in conserving their privileges, for it was established in their laws and confirmed by our divinity, that those who are subject to the rule of the Illustrious Patriarchs, that is the Archisynagogues, the patriarchs, the presbyters and the others who are occupied in the rite of that religion, shall persevere in keeping the same privileges that are reverently bestowed on the first clerics of the venerable Christian law.

The patriarch may well have intervened in the affairs of non-rabbinic communities in the eastern Mediterranean a century earlier, for an enigmatic inscription from a synagogue in Stobi in Macedonia dated probably to the third century stipulates an enormous fine to be paid to the patriarch by anyone found to have violated the financial terms agreed between the donor of the synagogue site and the community. But it is only from the fifth century that it is possible to trace an increased use of Hebrew rather than Greek in funerary inscriptions as far west as Italy, and a scattering of individuals named on inscriptions specifically as 'rabbi' or 'ribbi', as in an epitaph of the fourth or fifth century CE from Brusciano in Campania which proclaims 'Peace. Here lies the rabbi Abba Maris, the honoured one.' It is of course possible that the term 'rabbi' was being used, even in the fifth century, simply as a mark of honour for a Jewish teacher, as it had been for Jesus in the first century, regardless of his relationship to the sages in the academy of Palestine or Babylonia, but, as more and more such inscriptions are published, such scepticism has come to seem less plausible.[28]

Already in the first century, the sages were faced with the need to deal with fellow Jews who were not just outside the rabbinic fold but, in rabbinic eyes, heretics. How, for instance, were the sages after 70 to relate to Sadducees or Essenes, to say nothing of Jewish Christians? It is striking, as we have noted (Chapter 7), that the *tannaim* as recorded in the

Mishnah and Tosefta do not pay much attention to these groups at all, let alone describe their views and practices as part of a polemic in the fashion of the Christian heresiologists who were their contemporaries. Ignoring the existence of those deemed deviant may be seen as in itself a distinctive form of opposition, and a corollary of the rabbinic quasi-solipsism already noted. On the other hand, the *tannaim* made extensive use of a new term, *min*, 'heretic', which (so far as is known) they invented. This term (derived from *min*, 'kind' or 'species') became so much part of their worldview that they also invented the noun *minut* to designate 'heresy' as an abstract noun. To the rabbis these *minim* belonged to a single category in that they were all erring Jews, even though the nature of their alleged errors differed greatly, from denying the world to come (as Sadducees were known to do) to healing in the name of Jesus b. Pantera (presumably a reference to Jewish Christians):

> R. Eleazar b. Dama was bitten by a snake. And Jacob of Kefar Sama came to heal him in the name of Jesus son of Pantera. And R. Ishmael did not allow him [to accept the healing]. They said to him, 'You are not permitted [to accept healing from him], Ben Dama.' He said to him, 'I shall bring you proof that he may heal me.' But he did not have time to bring the [promised] proof before he dropped dead. Said R. Ishmael, 'Happy are you, Ben Dama, for you have expired in peace, but you did not break down the hedge erected by the sages. For whoever breaks down the hedge erected by sages eventually suffers punishment, as it is said, "He who breaks down a hedge is bitten by a snake."'

According to talmudic traditions, at some time in the decades after 70 CE these heretics were seen by some rabbis as sufficiently threatening for them to introduce into their daily prayers a nineteenth blessing, to be added to the eighteen inherited from Second Temple times (see Chapter 4), through which God is blessed for cursing the *minim*: 'Our rabbis taught, "Simeon ha Pakuli arranged the eighteen benedictions in order before Rabban Gamaliel in Yavneh. Said Rabban Gamaliel to the Sages, 'Can any one among you frame a benediction relating to the *Minim*?' Samuel the Lesser arose and composed it."' Whether this blessing was aimed at any specific heretics is unknown. A complaint in Justin Martyr's *Dialogue with the Jew Trypho*, composed in the middle of the second century CE, may suggest that some Jewish Christians believed it to be directed at them: 'For you have murdered the Just One, and his prophets before him; now to the utmost of your power you dishonour and curse in your synagogues all those who believe in Christ.' But it is possible only to speculate quite how the curse on the *minim* might have worked in practice, since *min* was not a self-description of any Jew (including Jewish Christians). In the late fourth century, Jerome reckoned that the synagogue curse was aimed specifically at a group of Jewish Christians whom he differentiated from the mainstream Church.[29]

In any case, within earlier rabbinic theology unacceptable views were indicated clearly enough by the assertion that certain groups would not inherit the world to come:

> All Israelites have a share in the world to come, for it is written, 'Your people also shall be all righteous, they shall inherit the land for ever; the branch of my planting, the work of my hands that I may be glorified.' And these are they that have no share in the world to come: he that says that there is no resurrection of the dead prescribed in the Law, and [he that says] that the Law is not from Heaven, and an Epicurean. R. Akiva says, 'Also he that reads the heretical books, or that utters charms over a wound.'

Assertions by specific rabbis in the second century of other behaviour deemed to merit the same divine punishment suggests considerable interest in such limits. But perhaps this was an academic exercise more than a way of dealing with a real threat of heresy:

> They added to the list of those [who have no portion in the world to come] he who breaks the yoke, violates the covenant, misinterprets the Torah, pronounces the Divine Name as it is spelled out . . . R. Akiva says, 'He who warbles the Song of Songs in a banquet-hall and makes it into a kind of love-song has no portion in the world to come.'[30]

Similarly academic are the early rabbinic discussions of Samaritans, who were treated at times as if they were Jews (for example, for inclusion in a group of three gathered for grace after meals) but at other times as gentiles, so that Samaritan bread is forbidden by R. Eliezer in the strongest terms: 'Whoever eats the bread of a Samaritan, it is as if he had eaten swine's flesh.' Such ambivalence, sometimes resolved by the assertion that Samaritans are simply to be treated as gentiles (as decreed by third-century rabbis in Palestine, according to the Babylonian Talmud), shows oddly little awareness of the existence, revealed to us by their political activities against the Roman state, of a real and powerful Samaritan community in Palestine in the fourth to sixth centuries.[31]

By contrast, rabbinic responses to Karaites (see Chapter 12) were specific and direct. They tackled Karaite theology head on, reflecting the serious threat posed by Karaism, which set itself in direct opposition to the rabbis. The Babylonian *gaon* Saadiah, who played a major role in the tenth century in stemming Karaism in the east, also wrote for the benefit of his rabbinic flock a deeply polemical treatise against the 'two hundred critical comments on the Bible' that had been composed in Persia in the ninth century by a certain Hiwi al-Balkhi. Al-Balkhi's polemic, drawing on sceptical comments from many earlier sources (some of them Christian and some of them dualist), attacked the Bible in ways that were abhorrent to Karaites and rabbis alike.[32]

The legacy of the religious system crafted by the rabbinic schools over the thousand years after 70 CE has been fundamental to most later forms of Judaism, with the production by the end of the first millennium of a definitive biblical text by the masoretes and the establishment of formalized prayer in fixed forms encapsulated in the liturgical works of the *geonim*, especially Amram and Saadiah. Above all, the Mishnah and Talmuds (and especially the Babylonian Talmud) became the base texts for the development of rabbinic law from the sixth century to the present. Rabbinic forms of study, in educational institutions which matured from small study groups to large academies, spread out from insignificant beginnings in Yavneh to encompass Babylonia to the east and Spain to the west.

As a result, by 1000 CE much of the Jewish world was touched by the rabbis. But some forms of Judaism developed in quite different directions during the first millennium CE, and these will be the subjects of the next chapter.

Judaism beyond the Rabbis

GREEK JUDAISM

The bright light shone by the writings of Josephus and Philo on the world of Greek-speaking Jews in the Mediterranean diaspora in the last century of the Second Temple is dimmed after *c.* 100 CE, since for the next thousand years and more almost no literary source composed by a Greek-speaking Jew survives. As we have already noted in Chapter 10, the cessation of such evidence should be taken to reflect not the end of distinctive forms of Greek-speaking Judaism during these centuries, but simply a change in the mechanics of survival of Jewish religious writings: the rabbis preserved Jewish works only in Hebrew and Aramaic, and because from the early second century Christians had a literature of their own, they ceased to use and preserve the writings of non-Christian Jews, so that anything written in Greek by Jews after that date was not preserved in the medieval manuscript traditions.

Despite the lack of such literary remains, survival of numerous Greek Jewish inscriptions from the second to seventh centuries CE confirms the existence of Greek-speaking communities around the Mediterranean rim throughout late antiquity. Excavation of synagogues at a number of sites confirms the commitment of these communities to Judaism, although there has inevitably been much debate about the precise religious significance of the wording of the inscriptions (mostly funerary or honorific) and of the style and decoration of the synagogue buildings. As we shall see, something can be learned from comments about Jewish religious life in the Roman law codes. Comments by Christian writers about Jews frequently reflect the image of Jews in the New Testament rather than the Jews of their own time, but there are exceptions, such as the attacks by John Chrysostom in Antioch in the late fourth century on the Jews who were (so he asserted) luring his Christian congregation into their synagogues. Only a small number of Greek Jewish papyri survive from Egypt after the destruction of most of the Jewish community in 117 CE, but a continuous Greek liturgical tradition can be inferred from the survival of Greek documents (sometimes in Hebrew script) dating to the end of the first millennium in the Cairo Genizah.[1]

That Greek remained the religious language of choice for many Mediterranean Jews at least for the first half of the first millennium CE can be surmised less from the choice of Greek by Jews for inscriptions in regions such as Asia Minor and Syria, where Greek was the language of the general population, than from the use of Greek in the city of Rome, where a preference for Greek over Latin marked out Jews as a distinctive sub-group within the main body of the urban plebs. These inscriptions also provide our best evidence for the organization of these Jews into synagogue communities led by officials named as 'father of the synagogue', 'ruler of the synagogue', 'gerousiarch', 'presbyter' and similar titles. Quite how, and by whom, these leaders were appointed is uncertain, but frequent references to those who have been *disarchon* ('twice ruler') suggest some process of election.

These communities almost certainly showed the same devotion to a Greek version of the biblical text that we have seen in the circles of Philo and that transferred from Greek Judaism to Christians in the first century CE. It will have been for the benefit of such Jews that revised versions of the Septuagint were made in the second century CE in order to bring the Greek text of scripture closer to the meaning of the current Hebrew text. We have seen that this process had already begun in the late Second Temple period, but the efforts of Theodotion, Symmachus and especially Aquila (see Chapter 2) went much further than the minor changes to be seen in some of the Greek biblical texts found in Qumran. For Aquila, it was essential to represent not only the meaning of the Hebrew but also the structure of the Hebrew sentences, so that he was prepared to invent new Greek words, and to create a very idiosyncratic Greek style, in order to give the flavour of the original: his insertion of the Greek word *syn* twice in the first sentence of Genesis to represent the Hebrew *et*, which functions simply to indicate that 'heaven' and 'earth' are objects of the verb 'create', was ridiculed by Jerome at the end of the fourth century.[2]

Aquila himself may have operated within a rabbinic milieu in Palestine, but his translation certainly had a wider circulation down at least to the sixth century, as emerges from an intervention by the emperor Justinian on 8 February 553 in response (so the emperor claimed) to

serious disputes between Jews concerning the use of languages in synagogal worship:

> It was right and proper that the Hebrews, when listening to the Holy
> Books, should not adhere to the literal writings but look for the prophecies
> contained in them, through which they announce the Great God and the
> Saviour of the human race, Jesus Christ. However, although they have
> erred from the right doctrine till today, given as they are to senseless inter-
> pretations, when we learnt that they dispute among themselves we could
> not bear to leave them with an unresolved controversy. We have learnt
> from their petitions, which they have addressed to us, that while some
> maintain the Hebrew language only and want to use it in reading the Holy
> Books, others consider it right to admit Greek as well, and they have
> already been quarrelling among themselves about this for a long time.
> Having therefore studied this matter we decided that the better case is that
> of those who want to use also Greek in reading the Holy Books, and gen-
> erally in any language that is the more suited and the better known to the
> hearers in each locality . . . Furthermore, those who read in Greek shall use
> the Septuagint tradition, which is more accurate than all the others . . . Let
> all use mainly this translation; but in order that we shall not appear to
> prohibit them all the other translations, we give permission to use also
> Akilas' translation, although he was gentile and in some readings differs
> not a little from the Septuagint. What they call Mishnah, on the other
> hand, we prohibit entirely, for it is not included among the Holy Books,
> nor was it handed down from above by the prophets, but it is an invention
> of men in their chatter, exclusively of earthly origin and having in it noth-
> ing of the divine.[3]

Justinian's assertion that Aquila was a gentile picks up a Christian
tradition, first found in Irenaeus in the second century CE, that Aquila
was a Jewish proselyte; the same tradition is found in the Palestinian
Talmud: 'Aquila the proselyte translated the Law before R. Eliezer and
R. Joshua; and they praised him and said to him, "You are the most
beautiful among the children of men."' There is every reason to suppose
that at least some Greek-speaking Jews continued to use one or other of
the Greek versions of scripture throughout the Middle Ages. The majority of the Greek texts transliterated into Hebrew script found in
the Cairo Genizah are biblical texts or Bible commentaries, and as late
as 1547 a polyglot columnar edition of the Pentateuch was published
in Constantinople with the text presented in transliterated Greek, as
well as Hebrew and Aramaic and transliterated Spanish.[4]

There is no reason to believe that the types of Judaism which flourished in the Greek diaspora over these centuries all developed in identical ways. Without the central institution of the Jerusalem Temple to provide a common focus for their religious devotions, each Jewish community will have been shaped by distinctive local influences, as in Sardis in Asia Minor, where a huge building, probably a synagogue, containing Jewish symbols such as *menorot* (candelabra), has been excavated. Erected on the site of a former bath and gymnasium complex, this building was in use probably by the fourth century CE and possibly earlier, and continued in use at least to the sixth century. A forecourt with a marble fountain has a colourful mosaic floor in which inscriptions by donors are incorporated into the geometric patterns. The main hall, which is estimated to have held a thousand people, has a circular apse at the west end lined with marble benches and a mosaic with images of peacocks. Statues of lions (a common artistic motif in the region of Sardis) and a large marble table decorated with an eagle were placed in the centre of this hall, and the walls, inlaid with marble, were covered with some eighty inscriptions, almost all in Greek, recording donations by individuals variously identified by their secular status in the city or wider empire, by their occupations (for example, as goldsmiths, marble sculptors and mosaicists) and by their piety: six of the donor inscriptions describe the individual concerned as *theosebes* ('god-reverer').

The accoutrements of this building in Sardis suggest a very grand and impressive liturgy. But whether this liturgy always included teaching and the reading of the law, as in other synagogues, is less certain since the size of the building must have made it hard to hear the Torah being read. It is not impossible that the building, which is far bigger and more impressively decked out than other buildings identified as synagogues, was originally created not by Jews but by gentile worshippers of the Jewish God who appropriated the symbols of the Jewish divinity in the eclectic fashion common in the Roman world particularly in the fourth century CE. If so, the synagogue seems to have been adapted for use as a synagogue by Jews in the fifth and sixth centuries, when the name of 'Samoe, priest and wise teacher' was inserted into the mosaic floor of the hall of the building.

That the liturgy was sometimes experienced by much of the congregation only from a distance is recorded specifically for the great synagogue of Alexandria in which, according to a legendary description in the Tosefta, an official was required to wave a cloth to give a visual signal at the end of blessings, so that the congregation would know when to respond 'Amen':

> Said R. Judah, 'Whoever has never seen the double colonnade [the basilica-synagogue] of Alexandria in Egypt has never seen Israel's glory in his entire life. It was a kind of large basilica, one colonnade inside another. Sometimes there were twice as many people there as those who went forth from Egypt. Now there were seventy-one golden thrones set up there, one for each of the seventy-one elders, each one worth twenty-five talents of gold, with a wooden platform in the middle. The minister of the synagogue stands on it, with flags in his hand. When one began to read, the other would wave the flags so the people would answer, "Amen".'[5]

Both the Alexandrian synagogue (which must have disappeared with the demise of the community in 117 CE) and the Sardis synagogue were were much more substantial buildings than the other diaspora synagogues of which remains have been found, from Elche in Spain at the western edge of the Mediterranean to Dura-Europos on the Euphrates in the east. Identified primarily by inscriptions and Jewish images – above all, the *menorah* – they share an orientation towards Jerusalem and, in almost every case, a Torah shrine as a prominent fixture in their main halls, but in most other respects they vary hugely in size, design and decoration.[6]

We have already mentioned with reference to the possible later influence of Philo (Chapter 7) the rich iconography of the synagogue discovered in 1932 in Dura-Europos in Syria which was used from the late second century to the mid-third, when it was destroyed during the siege of the city by the Sasanians in 256. The synagogue, originally constructed inside a private house, was expanded by incorporation of a second building just a decade before its destruction. It was adorned with frescoes depicting biblical scenes. The very richness of the iconography in the building of a small community in a small town on the eastern fringes of the Roman empire suggests strongly that the artists drew on a wider tradition of synagogue art of this time, but nothing comparable has as yet been found either in the diaspora or in Palestine. On the other hand, the Dura images reflect in part the local environment, with, for instance, a Torah shrine similar in construction and appearance to the *aediculae* in local pagan temples.[7]

When the frescoes were uncovered in Dura-Europos in the 1930s it was widely assumed that adoption of Greek artistic norms must reflect a Hellenized form of Judaism comparable to the Judaism of Philo, but we have seen (Chapter 11) that pagan imagery such as the depiction of the sun god Helios could be used on synagogue mosaics even in the most rabbinic areas of Palestine, such as Hammat Tiberias. Some of the motifs in the Dura paintings, such as the depictions of the infant Moses in the River Nile with his eyes first shut and then opened, seem to pick up motifs found in later rabbinic *midrashim*, and finds of Aramaic and Hebrew inscriptions alongside the Greek suggest a community that could have participated in the evolving religious culture of the rabbis in nearby Babylonia. But nothing in the material unearthed at Dura indicates any direct relation with rabbis.[8]

One aspect of Judaism evidently shared by the Jews of Sardis and Dura was a willingness to expend large amounts of money on their local place of worship. In Apamea in Syria in the late fourth century, in a synagogue located in the heart of the city, a group of wealthy donors commemorated their gifts of sections of the mosaic floor with its complex geometric patterns and *menorah*: 'Thaumasis with her spouse Hesychius and [their] children and his [or her] mother-in-law Eustathia made 100 feet [of mosaic].' Most of the inscriptions commemorate donations by, or in honour of, a family, and nine of the donors are women. The synagogue was perhaps of more than just local concern, since much of the floor was donated by a certain Iliasos, '*archisynagogos* of the Antiochians'. Antioch was not far from Apamea, and presumably the two communities had close relations, so that it was diplomatic for Iliasos to pray for 'peace and mercy upon all your holy congregation'. The grand synagogue does not seem to have lasted long; by the early fifth century, it had been destroyed and converted into a church.[9]

No synagogue building from antiquity has been found in Rome, but funerary inscriptions from the communal catacombs, which were in use from the late second to the fifth century CE, refer to somewhere between ten and sixteen synagogues in the city, most of which were probably situated in Trastevere, on the right bank of the Tiber, where Jews had already settled in the time of Augustus. The practice of burial in catacombs may itself reflect absorption by Roman Jews of many aspects of local culture, despite their obstinate preference in most cases for Greek as a religious language rather than Latin even down to the fifth century. Their fondness for including in the catacombs glass objects with gold inlay portraying Jewish images such as the *menorah* reflects their adaptation of a local fashion for their own religious purpose.

Of the possible appearance of at least some of the Roman synagogues we get a glimpse from the excavation of the monumental synagogue located outside the city wall at Ostia, with its fine tripartite entrance way leading to a columned *propylaeum* over 15 feet in height, and a large main hall with a raised podium and an apse, presumably for housing the Torah scrolls. Among the decorations found in the synagogue were images of a *menorah*, ram's horn, *lulav* and etrog, and (on the floor of the main hall) a small fragment of a stone lion. The original date when the building became a synagogue is much disputed. There can be no doubt that its main function, by its final phase in the fourth to the fifth centuries CE, was for the reading of the Torah as envisaged in an earlier inscription (part in Latin, part in Greek) found reused in the vestibule outside the building entrance: 'For the safety of the Emperor, Mindius Faustus with his family built and made [it] from his own gifts, and set up the ark for the holy law.' But the design of the building follows local practices, as in Dura, and it is similar to other buildings in Ostia erected to house religious guilds.[10]

The decorative images found in these synagogues (as also in synagogues in late Roman Palestine) presumably carried symbolic religious meanings for people at the time, although it is hard for us now to go far beyond their significance as assertions of Jewish identity and, in some cases, such as the *menorah* (which became the most ubiquitous of Jewish symbols) and the incense shovel, a reminder of the Jerusalem Temple. The same images are found in the Roman catacombs, along with the totemic use of occasional words in Hebrew (most often *shalom*). But there are obvious problems in deducing from these uses the contours of the religious lives of Roman Jews, for Jewish symbols could be used by non-Jews (as was indeed often the case with the use of Hebrew and Jewish divine names in magical papyri). Conversely, Jews could appropriate pagan images: hence, for instance, as we have seen, the depiction of Orpheus playing his lyre, which a Hebrew label in the synagogue at Gaza of the sixth century informed worshippers was meant to represent David.

A remarkable late fourth-century Jewish inscription found in Aphrodisias (in modern Turkey) which honours fifty-three *theosebeis* ('god-reverers') with non-Jewish names alongside a number of Jews and three individuals specifically designated as *proselytai* suggests that, at least in this locality and at this time, Jews accepted converts to their community but that they were also prepared to accord recognition for their piety to a large number of gentile supporters of the Jewish community. This raises the possibility that such gentiles might adopt Jewish symbols for their own use without thinking of themselves, or being considered by Jews, to be Jewish. Since we have seen in Chapter 10 that it is by no means clear that before the end of the first millennium CE all Jews believed it necessary to be buried only in the company of other Jews, the labelling as 'Jewish' of specific catacombs in Rome at Monteverde or Vigna Randanini, just because their epitaphs reveal that some of the deceased buried there were certainly Jews, may be misleading. Some of the apparently liberal Jews who included what look to us like pagan images at their burial site may not have been Jews at all. And it is of course impossible now to discern the religious outlook of those Jews whose epitaphs contained no Jewish images at all.[11]

The relationship of all these Jews to the wider world of the Roman empire was affected by the Christianization of the empire after Constantine not just because the state inaugurated a policy, as we have seen, of restricting but protecting the practice of Judaism within the empire, but also because the state came to assume that Jewish communities would be organized along lines similar to Christians. In the pagan empire of the first three centuries CE Jewish communal leaders adopted titles and received honours in a fashion similar to the elites of the cities in which they lived, organizing themselves on the model of the voluntary associations. They were often established as mutual burial societies, which were a common feature of Greek and Roman urban life. But the Christian state treated Jews simply as a religious community along the same lines as local Christian churches, referring to a 'synagogue of the Jewish law' as a 'place of religion'. In 330 CE the emperor Constantine even exempted from burdensome duties on behalf of the state 'those who have dedicated themselves with complete devotion to the synagogues of the Jews'. Such treatment of Jewish communities as essentially religious did not always operate to their advantage as the Rome elite became more enthusiastic from the late fourth century in imposing Christian orthodoxy and jealous of the protection of Christian worship. The emperor Justinian in the mid-sixth century required, for instance, that the Jews alter the date of Passover so that it did not fall before the Catholic Easter, as Procopius recorded in his *Secret History*:

> Constant and daily interference with the laws of the Romans was not all
> that the Emperor did: he also did his best to abolish the laws reverenced
> by the Hebrews. Whenever the returning months happened to bring the
> Passover feast before that kept by the Christians, he would not permit the
> Jews to celebrate this at the proper time, nor to offer anything to God at

this feast, nor to perform any of their customary ceremonies. Many of them were brought to trial by those appointed governors and charged with an offence against the laws of the state, in that they had eaten lamb at this period. They were then sentenced to pay heavy fines.[12]

The cultural integration of many Mediterranean Jews into the surrounding society, even as they maintained their ethnic and religious identities, led in due course in the western Mediterranean to the adoption by some communities of Latin for synagogue inscriptions as well as local artistic motifs. In the synagogue found in 1883 at Naro (Hammam-Lif) in Tunisia by French soldiers, the main hall had an elaborate mosaic pavement featuring images of fish, ducks, pelicans, a bull, a lion and two peacocks and a series of other motifs very similar to those found in local churches in the fourth to sixth centuries. A prominent inscription records in Latin 'your servant, Juliana, who from her own funds paved with mosaic the holy synagogue of Naro for her salvation'. However, the Jews of the city of Rome seem to have been slow to abandon the use of Greek for religious purposes, and the Jews of Elche, on the east coast of Spain near Alicante, preferred to use Greek rather than Latin to refer to the 'place of prayer of the people'. There is no evidence that Latin-speaking Jews were ever tempted to devise a Latin liturgy in antiquity, although the biblical citations in the curious *Collatio Legum Mosaicum et Romanarum* ('Collation of Mosaic and Roman Laws'), a fourth-century composition which juxtaposes excerpts of Jewish law from Exodus with Roman legal rulings, may suggest that a Jewish version of the Pentateuch in Latin existed by that time.[13]

We have seen in Chapter 11 the limited geographical reach of the rabbinic movement in the first half of the first millennium CE, doubtless in part because Greek-speaking Jews would have required linguistic instruction to participate in rabbinic discourse conducted entirely in Hebrew and Aramaic (although, in view of the esoteric nature of this discourse, which will have precluded proper understanding of rabbinic discussions even by many Jews familiar with the Semitic languages, this linguistic issue should not be exaggerated). But by the reign of Justinian in the mid-sixth century, it is likely that many of the Jewish communities of the Mediterranean had come, to some extent at least, into contact with rabbis in Palestine and Babylonia. Stories in rabbinic texts about journeys by rabbis to Rome to spread their teachings in the second century CE should probably be treated as fanciful – the image of the city of Rome in ancient rabbinic texts is wholly unreal – and there is no evidence of the intensive epistolary contact between communities which bound together scattered Christian groups from the very beginnings of Christianity. But it is possible that rabbinic influence was spread in the fourth and early fifth centuries through authority delegated by the Roman state to the rabbinic patriarch in Palestine. As we noted in Chapter 11, inscriptions from the synagogue of Stobi in Macedonia record in (probably) the third century CE a threat by the donor of the buildings of an enormous fine to be paid to the patriarch by anyone who infringed the financial arrangements stipulated for the donation:

> The year 311[?], Claudius Tiberius Polycharmos, also named Acyrios, father of the synagogue at Stobi, having lived my whole life according to Judaism, have, in fulfilment of a vow, [given] the buildings to the holy place, and the *triclinium*, together with the *tetrastoon*, with my own means, without in the least touching the sacred [funds]. But the ownership and disposition of all the upper chambers shall be retained by me, Claudius Tiberius Polycharmos, and my heirs for life. Whoever seeks in any way to alter any of these dispositions of mine shall pay the Patriarch 250,000 denarii.

If this patriarch is to be identified with the *nasi* in Palestine, as is probable, it constitutes the earliest evidence for the extension of the patriarch's power into the Mediterranean diaspora.[14]

We saw in Chapter 11 that by the late fourth century the Christian Roman state was treating the Palestinian patriarch as responsible for the appointment of religious leaders for communities of Jews throughout the empire. On 3 February 398 the patriarchs were given the right, like Christian clerics within their own communities, to decide civil cases between Jews and to have those decisions upheld by the state. At the peak of its influence, in the late fourth and early fifth centuries, the office of the patriarch brought with it high Roman rank and protection of dignity by the state – 'if anyone shall dare to make in public an insulting mention of the illustrious patriarchs, he shall be subjected to a vindicatory sentence' – and the right to raise taxes from Jews in all the empire. But by 415 the patriarch Gamaliel had fallen into disfavour because (so the emperor Theodosius alleged) he 'supposed that he could transgress the law with impunity all the more because he was elevated to the pinnacle of dignities'. A law of 30 May 429 confiscated to the imperial treasury the taxes which had previously come to the 'primates' of the Jews in Palestine and other provinces, referring to the 'ending of the patriarchs' and their custom in earlier times of exacting such taxes 'in the name of crown gold'. Evidently by 429 state backing for the patriarchs as a unifying force for Judaism within the Roman world had come to an end. But by that time the state's initiative had at least enabled the leaders of Palestinian Jewry to ensure that their form of Judaism was brought to the attention of the Greek-speaking diaspora.[15]

The rabbis in Palestine in the fourth and fifth centuries knew Greek, as we have seen not least from the evidence of numerous Palestinian Greek inscriptions. But their religious discourse was in Hebrew and Aramaic, and it is plausible to connect the gradual spread of Hebrew into the western Mediterranean world from the fifth century CE with the growing influence of rabbis in these Greek-speaking communities. If so, the process of influence was gradual, as can be seen in the case of the family of a certain Faustinus in Venosa in Italy. One inscription painted in red proclaims in Greek, 'Tomb of Faustinus the father', with 'Peace to Israel. Amen' appended in Hebrew; a sign, on the left side of the gallery where the grave was found, notes in Latin: 'The niche where Faustinus the father rests.' Hebrew letters are found in funerary inscriptions in Venosa from the fifth century in far greater amounts than in the isolated use of *shalom* characteristic of the Jewish catacombs of Rome. Sometimes the Hebrew letters express Greek in transliteration, but in other cases they spell out Hebrew words, using biblical phrases, sometimes in conjunction with a Latin (rather than a Greek) translation.[16]

The spread of Hebrew may have been slow, but it was inexorable, and by the end of the first millennium the religious life of those who remained faithful to Judaism in the western Mediterranean was rarely expressed in Greek. Thus by the ninth century Jewish inscriptions from a separate cemetery discovered in Venosa are entirely in Hebrew. The reasons for the disappearance of Greek Judaism in places such as Rome where the Greek language had been such a clear cultural marker are not evident. The diminution in evidence for Greek-speaking Jews in many regions of western Europe coincides with a diminution in evidence for the lives of Jews in these regions as a whole in the eighth to tenth centuries. The number and size of Jewish communities may well have shrunk during this period in part because of the attraction or threat of conversion to Christianity (see Chapter 9).

In any case, by the time these communities became again visible in the evidence at the end of the first millennium, their religious language was Hebrew rather than Greek and their outlook essentially rabbinic. Thus in southern Italy in the mid-tenth century, the anonymous author, known to later Jewish tradition as Yosippon, of a narrative in Hebrew of the history of the Jews in the Second Temple period derived his information on the period from Josephus' *Jewish Antiquities* and *Jewish War*; but, although he came from a part of Italy which was within the Byzantine empire where the official language was Greek, he knew Josephus only through a Latin version written by a Christian called Hegesippus in the second half of the fourth century. A century later, a chronicler and poet from Capua in Italy, Ahimaaz b. Paltiel, whose rhymed account in Hebrew of the achievements of his family since the ninth century was discovered in the library of Toledo cathedral in 1895, claimed that he was descended from those who had been brought as captives to Jerusalem by Titus, but he showed little knowledge of Greek. In the eastern Mediterranean, by contrast, Jews continued to use Greek, albeit in Hebrew letters, in religious documents such as marriage contracts and biblical exegesis. In Constantinople, the Balkans and Asia Minor, Romaniot Jews, whose name refers to the origins of their liturgical rite in the Byzantine empire, continued to use such Judaeo-Greek throughout the Middle Ages, especially for reading the book of Jonah on the Day of Atonement. But, apart from such occasional use of Greek in liturgy, only a few other Jewish Greek customs survived into early modern times, such as the recitation of the seven wedding blessings at the betrothal ceremony rather than the marriage.[17]

Quite why the rabbinic movement was eventually so much more successful than the Greek Judaism it replaced in much of the Mediterranean world is not easy to explain, because we have seen that religious teachings promulgated by rabbinic Judaism itself were neither easily accessible (since few Mediterranean Jews at the end of the first millennium will have known how to read and understand Hebrew or Aramaic) nor readily comprehensible (since a religious discourse based on interpretations of talmudic discussions was essentially esoteric). But the effective transmission of religious authority among Jews to a learned rabbinic elite schooled in a special scholarly language mirrored the authority of Christian clerics schooled in Latin within wider European society.

It seems that Greek Jews faced with the prestige of rabbis armed with such knowledge felt unable to defend their own traditions. The Jews of Candia in Crete, who copied in the late fourteenth century a Greek text of Jonah now in the Bodleian Library, felt impelled in the first half of the sixteenth century to write to Meir Katzenellenbogen, the Ashkenazi rabbi of Padua, to seek (successfully) his explicit authority for their liturgical use of Greek. It was evidently now not enough for them simply to continue with the Greek Judaism of their ancestors.[18]

KARAITES

As Greek Judaism was gradually subsumed in much of the Christian Mediterranean world by the intellectual vigour and self-confidence of rabbinic interpreters of the Torah, the rabbis provoked in Islamic lands a rejectionist movement which by the end of the first millennium crystallized into the distinctive and powerful denomination of Karaites who refused to accept rabbinic traditions in the interpretation of biblical law and denied altogether the authority of the oral traditions preserved in the Talmud and the value of rabbinic discourse about the interpretation of the Talmud itself.

The foundation myths about their separation from rabbinism espoused by Karaites themselves, in a rich and well-preserved literary tradition down to the present day, and the equally suspect slurs on the motivations and doctrines of early Karaite teachers put about by the rabbis both in retrospect and at the time of the emergence of Karaism, need to be interpreted in light of the considerable evidence from the Cairo Genizah of complex relations between Karaites and followers of the rabbinical tradition (designated 'Rabbanites' by their Karaite opponents) throughout the early centuries of the new movement. Karaism was integral to the history of medieval Judaism both in what it contributed to the development of the religion as a whole and in the reactions that Karaites elicited from the rabbinic movement.[19]

Where did it all start? According to a Rabbanite account composed at some time between the tenth and twelfth century, it began with the pique of a certain Anan b. David, a rabbinic sage probably from Baghdad, who was passed over, at some time in the eighth century, for the post of exilarch in Babylon:

Anan had a younger brother named Hananiah. Although Anan exceeded this brother in both learning and age, the contemporary Rabbanite scholars refused to appoint him exilarch, because of his great lawlessness and lack of piety. They therefore turned to his brother Hananiah, for the sake of the latter's great modesty, retiring disposition, and fear of Heaven, and they set him up as exilarch. Thereupon Anan was seized with a wicked zeal – he and with him all manner of evil and worthless men from among the remnants of the sect of Zadok and Boethus; they set up a dissident sect – in secret, for fear of the Moslem government which was then in power – and they appointed Anan their own exilarch.

The story of Anan's high birth and supplanting by his brother appears, however, to have been unknown to earlier authors, both Rabbanite and Karaite, and the version of the great Karaite scholar al-Kirkisani in the second quarter of the tenth century records only Anan's Rabbanite wisdom and the hostility that his teachings aroused:

> Anan's appearance occurred in the days of the Caliph Abu Ga'far al-Mansur. He was the first to make clear a great deal of the truth about the divine ordinances. He was learned in the lore of the Rabbanites, and not one of them could gainsay his erudition. It is reported that Hai, the president of the Rabbanite Academy, together with his father, translated the book of Anan from the Aramaic into Hebrew and encountered nothing in it of which they could not discover the source in Rabbanite lore . . . The Rabbanites tried their utmost to assassinate Anan, but God prevented them from doing so.[20]

In both traditions, the attribution of a religious movement to a single founder may be a commonplace which disguises the extent to which Anan fitted into a wider movement of dissent within the world of Babylonian Judaism during the decades following the rise of Islam. The Islamic conquests of Persia and Babylonia in the mid-seventh century opened up new regions for settlement by Jews as well as others, and loosened the grip on Jewish communities distant from Baghdad both of the Babylonian exilarch and of the religious authorities in the Babylonian rabbinic academies. Already at the start of the eighth century, a certain Abu 'Isa, originally called Yitzhak b. Yaakov but known by his followers as Obadiah ('Servant of the Lord'), led a considerable armed rebellion of the Jews of Isfahan, a major centre of Jewish settlement, against the Abassid state. He claimed to be the last of five messengers (after Abraham, Moses, Jesus and Muhammad) who would precede the coming of the Messiah. Abu 'Isa himself was killed in the fighting, but he left a distinctive ascetic and mystical legacy, nurtured by Islamic notions, to his surviving followers, and these Isawites, as they were known, were still to be found, albeit in small numbers, in the tenth century in Damascus.

Among the pupils of Abu 'Isa, a certain Yudghan, who came from Hamadan in Persia, moved a great deal further from rabbinic norms by claiming to be a prophet of those followers of Abu 'Isa who believed that he was the Messiah. The Karaite historian al-Kirkisani wrote in the mid-tenth century of the Yudghanites that they 'prohibit meat and intoxicating drinks, observe many prayers and fasts, and assert that the

Sabbath and holidays are at present no longer obligatory'. By the tenth century Karaites were appalled by the extent of Yudghan's religious revolution, and al-Kirkisani was wholly opposed to the small group of Yudghanites still living in Isfahan in his time. But it was from the ferment which gave rise to these movements – and others from the same source, such as the Shadganites and Mushkanites, about whom nothing reliable can be gleaned from the hostile sources which mention only their names and wild speculation about their heretical ideas – that Anan's teachings took hold.[21]

Anan's own doctrines, as expressed in his *Sefer haMitzvot* ('Book of Precepts'), written in Aramaic, seem to have been far less radical than those of these other non-rabbinic leaders, and he does not seem to have rejected the Rabbanite method of using oral tradition altogether, but he retained the emphasis on asceticism in commemoration of the destruction of the Temple, remodelling synagogue liturgy in light of Temple worship and insisting on strict biblical interpretation even when – or perhaps especially when – it led to ascetic observance. Thus by a process of restrictive scriptural interpretation Anan laid down that no fires should be allowed on the Sabbath even if they have been lit in advance:

> One might perhaps say that it is only the kindling of fire on the Sabbath which is forbidden, and that if the fire had been kindled on the preceding weekday it is to be considered lawful to let it remain over the Sabbath. Now the Merciful One has written here: 'Ye shall not kindle fire,' and elsewhere: 'thou shalt not perform any work' (Exod 20:10), and both prohibitions begin with the letter taw. In the case of labour, of which it is written: 'Thou shalt not perform any work,' it is evident that even if the work was begun on a weekday, before the arrival of the Sabbath, it is necessary to desist from it with the arrival of the Sabbath. The same rule must therefore apply also to the kindling of fire, of which it is written: 'Ye shall not kindle,' meaning that even if the fire has been kindled on a weekday, prior to the arrival of the Sabbath, it must be extinguished.[22]

Such ascetic interpretations of the biblical texts have something in common with aspects of the Judaism of some of the Jewish groups of the late Second Temple period, most notably the Sadducees, the Qumran Yahad and the Essenes, but it is not possible to demonstrate any direct genealogical link between Anan and any of these groups, nor between Anan and priestly movements back in Second Temple times with whom he also had something in common. Equally impossible to demonstrate is any direct influence from Shiism, although Anan's rejection of rabbinic teachings parallels the rejection of Sunni teachings by Persian Shiites in the Islam of his time, and Anan's descendants were revered by his followers just as the sons of Ali were revered by Shia Muslims.[23]

Anan appears to have taught between 762 and 767. His immediate followers were never numerous, and few Jews identified themselves as Ananites by the tenth century, but he came to be seen by the Rabbanites as the single founding figure of Karaism. Karaites in later generations attributed their origins both to Anan and to another Persian teacher, Benjamin b. Moses al-Nahawandi who, according to al-Kirkisani, had in the ninth century also been steeped in rabbinic learning before elucidating a distinctive theology and adopting the name *Kara'i*, which probably referred to his distinctive emphasis on *mikra* (scripture). In the conclusion to his *Book of Rules*, which was written not in Aramaic (like the Talmud) or Arabic (like most later Karaite teachings) but in Hebrew, Benjamin's attitude to those aspects of Judaism for which no scriptural injunction can be identified is relaxed:

> Let there be abundant peace to all the Exiled [that is, Jews outside the land of Israel], from me, Benjamin son of Moses – may his memory be blessed together with that of all the righteous. I, who am dust and ashes beneath the soles of your feet, have written this Book of Rules for you Karaites, so that you might pass judgments according to it upon your brethren and friends. For every rule I have indicated the pertinent verse of Scripture. As for other rules, which are observed and recorded by the Rabbanites and for which I could find no pertinent biblical verse, I have written them down also, so that you might observe them likewise if you so desire.

Emphasis on the authority of scripture rendered Benjamin's teachings, like those of Anan, suitable for their later reputation as the founders of Karaism, but in other respects the doctrines of both were either dropped or rejected. Benjamin espoused a distinctive notion of the divine as unsullied by intervention in the world, advocating a theology similar to the Logos theory propounded 800 years earlier by Philo of Alexandria, according to which the world had been made by an angel as intermediary between the divine and created worlds. Whether Benjamin was directly influenced by Philo through a translation of Philo's work in Arabic is unknown.[24]

In any case such notions were vigorously denied by later Karaites, including, at the end of the ninth century, in Jerusalem, by the strongest influence on later Karaite doctrine, Daniel b. Moses al-Kumisi, who by contrast interpreted all biblical references to angels as indicating natural forces under divine control. Emphasis on a reliance on scripture gave space for a great deal of variety in independent interpretation of the biblical texts, which Benjamin may indeed have welcomed. Al-Kumisi was one of the first to offer rationalist readings of the biblical texts. His Karaite successors quite rapidly built up their own traditions, justified as the 'yoke of inheritance' endorsed by communal consensus and thereby distinguished from the Rabbanite claim that their oral Torah had an authority equal to that of the written text. Hence the Karaite historian al-Kirkisani in the tenth century attributed to Anan (probably fictitiously) the injunction to 'search thoroughly in the Torah' and 'not rely on my opinion'. A multiplicity of ideas was not a matter for regret:

> For this accusation ... attaches to them [the Rabbanites] only since they claim that all their teachings come by tradition from the Prophets. If things are so, there should be no disagreement; the fact that disagreement has arisen is a criticism of what they claim. We on the other hand arrive at knowledge by means of our intellects, and where this is the case, it is undeniable that disagreement will arise.[25]

Information about other dissenting forms of Judaism which may be seen as forerunners of Karaism from before the time of al-Kirkisani can be picked up only from brief remarks in his history. The Ukbarites (from near Baghdad), a short-lived movement in the second half of the ninth century, are said (among other distinctive practices) to have begun their Sabbaths on Saturday mornings at dawn rather than on the Friday evening like other Jews. In Ramleh in the land of Israel in the same period, Malik al-Ramli struck a blow for kosher cuisine by taking an oath on the site of the Temple that chickens had been used as Temple sacrifices and could therefore be eaten – thus contradicting the view of Anan that the chicken should be identified with the *dukhifat* in Leviticus 11:19 which was prohibited, and the view of al-Kumisi that 'he who fears God must not use any bird for food except turtledoves and young pigeons, also wild pigeons, "until such time as the teacher of righteousness shall have come", forasmuch as all those who eat forbidden fowl or fish shall perish and be reduced to nothing on the Day of Judgement.'[26]

By the time of al-Kirkisani in the mid-tenth century a distinctive set of Karaite doctrines was beginning to emerge, and by the twelfth century the other dissident groups disappeared or merged into the Karaite movement, with a gradual suppression of the individualism which had characterized the movement in its early period. The principle that all religious teaching should depend on the Bible alone was modified by acceptance of arguments by analogy and (for most, but not all, Karaites) human reason. New months were fixed meticulously by visual observation of the new moon, ignoring the mathematical calculation of the Rabbanites, and Rabbanite postponement of the New Year in specific cases (as, for instance, when it might cause the Day of Atonement to be followed by the Sabbath), so that Karaites might quite often celebrate festivals on a day different from other Jews. Hanukkah, as a non-biblical festival, was not observed at all. Observance of both Sabbath and dietary laws was stricter in many cases than that of the Rabbanites, rejecting the talmudic notion that a minimum quantity of a forbidden substance is required for food to be invalidated. Rabbanite rules about menstrual impurity were also rejected. A distinctive synagogue liturgy was adopted, with two prayer services a day on weekdays (instead of three), consisting mostly of passages from the Bible (especially the psalms) and references to the Temple rite, and no use of the Amidah prayer which formed such a central element in Rabbanite liturgy. By the time of Elijah b. Moses Basyatchi in the late fifteenth century, Karaite principles could even be codified, as follows:

> All physical creation, that is, the planets and all that is upon them, has been created. It has been created by a Creator who did not create Himself, but is eternal. The Creator has no likeness and is unique in all respects. He sent the Prophet Moses. He sent, along with Moses, His Law, which is perfect. It is the duty of the believer to know the language of the Law and its interpretation. God inspired also the other true prophets after Moses. God will resurrect all mankind on the Day of Judgement. God requites each person according to his ways and the fruits of his deeds. God has not forsaken the people of the Dispersion; rather are they suffering the Lord's just punishment, and they must hope every day for His salvation at the hands of the Messiah, the descendant of King David.

The sixth principle, that Karaites have a duty to know the language of the Law, led to a great deal of Karaite scholarship on the biblical text: 'This being so, every person of the holy seed of Israel must himself study the holy tongue and must teach his children to know the language of our Law and of the words of the Prophets in a proper and fitting manner, with special conditions which would facilitate its study.'[27]

In the tenth century Jerusalem became a centre for intensive Karaite study of the biblical text, with an outpouring of scholarly works, particularly Bible commentaries, lexicographies and studies of Hebrew

7. Floor mosaic from the fourth-century synagogue at Hammat Tiberias in Galilee. The main panel depicts the signs of the zodiac (identified in Hebrew), with the sun god in the central roundel and the seasons in the four corners. The panel above shows the Temple flanked by images of a *menorah*, *lulav*, shofar and incense shovel; the one below names donors in Greek, including Severos, a member of the household of 'the illustrious patriarchs'.

18. Floor mosaic, dated to the sixth century, from a synagogue in Gaza. The portrayal of the figure playing the lyre follows standard iconography in the depiction of Orpheus but the Hebrew inscription here identifies him as David.

19. Bronze magic bowl from Babylonia (fifth–sixth century CE). Such bowls, with the interior covered in protective spells, were placed upside down at entrances to trap demons and prevent them from entering the home.

20. Halakhic floor mosaic from the sixth-century synagogue at Rehov, near the border of the land of Israel as defined by the rabbis. The inscription, which deals with the implementation of the sabbatical year in the area around Rehov, is the oldest-surviving written version of a rabbinic text.

21. Marble table in the monumental synagogue (130 by 20 yards) in Sardis from the fourth century. Converted from an earlier public building probably in the late third century and in use at least to the sixth century, it could hold a thousand worshippers.

22. Lid of the sarcophagus of Faustina, a woman buried in Rome, probably in the late third century. Faustina's name is in Greek, but the shofar, *menorah* and *lulav* indicate her Jewish origin, as does the Hebrew word *shalom*. Theatre masks are a common feature on sarcophagi.

23. Maimonides' autograph draft, written in cursive Hebrew script in *c.* 1180, of a section of his *Mishneh Torah*, the first systematic code of Jewish law, found in the Cairo Genizah.

24. Part of a *ketubah* (marriage contract) in Hebrew, Aramaic and Judaeo-Arabic, between a Karaite woman and a Rabbanite man, written in 1082 CE, probably in Cairo. Special clauses state that the groom will not force the bride to compromise her Karaite principles and that the bride will observe Rabbanite festivals with her husband.

25. The synagogue of El Transito built in Toledo in the fourteenth century. Its height and prominence are unusual and reflect the political influence in Castile of its founder, Samuel haLevi Abulafia. The cathedral behind was constructed in the previous century on the site of a mosque next to the Jewish quarter. Jews, Christians and Muslims lived in close proximity in the city.

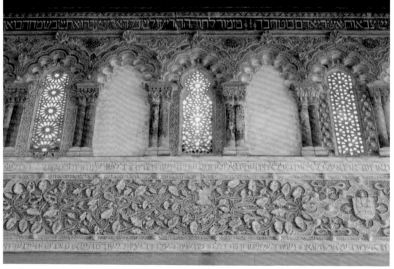

26. Stucco work in the interior of the El Transito synagogue, with monumental Hebrew inscriptions. The elaborate interior decoration is strongly influenced by Islamic artistic styles.

27. (*above*) The Altneuschul in Prague, built in 1270 in Gothic style, and still in use today. Its impressive exterior is testimony to the importance of the Jewish community in the city.

28. (*right*) The new synagogue in Oranienburger Strasse in central Berlin by Emile Pierre Joseph de Cauwer (1828–73). Designed in Moorish style and large enough to seat 3,000 people, the building was inaugurated in the presence of Otto von Bismarck in 1866.

29. The Portuguese Esnoga in Amsterdam by an unknown Dutch painter. Completed in 1675, the synagogue was one of the largest buildings in the city.

30. Bevis Marks synagogue in the city of London, built in 1701 for the Spanish and Portuguese community in a style influenced both by the recently completed Amsterdam Esnoga and by contemporary non-conformist chapels in England.

31. (*right*) Illustration of the Pesach Seder from the Sarajevo Haggadah, a magnificently illuminated manuscript dated to the mid-fourteenth century.

32. (*below*) Text of b. Meilah 20a-21a in the Baylonian Talmud printed by Daniel Bomberg in Venice in 1519. The central panels, in which the Mishnah is followed by the *gemara* (the amoraic discussion), are surrounded by medieval commentaries in a less formal ('Rashi') script. This format, established by Bomberg, has remained standard in later printings of the Talmud.

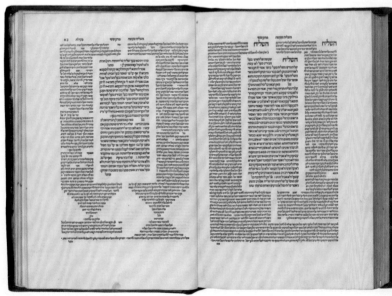

grammar. If Karaites were to be found increasingly here, as also in Damascus, Cairo and North Africa, this was in part the product of a deliberate mission to persuade Rabbanites of their folly, not least by attacking the anthropomorphism to be found in the rabbinic bible interpretation. Karaites had their own synagogues and academies, but their leaders tended to seek influence through writings and legal decisions rather than in any formal hierarchy, and they lacked institutional authority to impose their views other than by persuasion.[28]

All the more remarkable is the extent of Karaite influence on Rabbanites at the peak of Karaism in the tenth to eleventh centuries. In part this was because Rabbanites and Karaites operated in the same religious world: so, for instance, Yefet b. Eli, a Karaite scholar in Jerusalem in the second half of the tenth century, provided a literal translation of scripture into Arabic soon after Saadiah had composed for Rabbanites his immensely influential version of scripture in Judaeo-Arabic (Arabic in Hebrew script). There is no evidence that Rabbanites ever converted to Karaism en masse as a result of Karaite propaganda, but the threat of Karaism elicited a rich Rabbanite response, of which the earliest was by Saadiah himself: at the age of twenty-three, Saadiah published an attack (in Arabic) on Anan, and he has been credited with stemming the tide of Karaism through his energy and adamant opposition.

On the other hand, we have seen (p. 288) that Saadiah and Karaite scholars could and did unite in their opposition to the much more dangerous ideas of Hiwi al-Balkhi (from Khorasan, which was then in Persia), whose criticisms of the Bible in the second half of the ninth century questioned (among other things) the justice, omniscience, omnipotence, constancy and uniqueness of God, and the coherence and rationality of the biblical accounts. Thus Saadiah berated Hiwi al-Balkhi:

> Thou has asked further concerning the kinds of suffering; hunger and sickness, fear and desolation and destruction, and heat and cold, why they are not kept from men ... Know thou and understand, that God chastiseth His creatures for their good ... Thou hast complained: 'Why hath He left a remnant of the seed of evildoers?' But wherefore should He not have left Noah since he hath not sinned. Had He destroyed him, thou wouldst have said, 'Doth He consume in flame the righteous together with the wicked!'[29]

Karaites would happily agree with the Rabbanite Saadiah in this defence of the biblical tradition, and despite a literary war of words over centuries, and Saadiah's treatment of Karaites as *minim* (heretics), the two groups coexisted throughout the Near East as members of a single, albeit fractious, Jewish community down at least to the twelfth century. As leader of the Jewish community in Cairo, Maimonides was to find himself a spokesman to the Muslims for Karaites as much as for Rabbanites, and he urged his flock to show respect to Karaites:

> These Karaites, who live here in Alexandria, Cairo, Damascus, and other places of the Land of Ishmael [Islam] and outside, should be treated with respect and approached with honesty. One should conduct oneself with them with modesty and in the way of truth and peace, as long as they conduct themselves with us with integrity, avoiding crooked speech and devious talk and preaching disloyalty toward the Rabbanite Sages of the generation; all the more that they avoid mocking the words of our holy Sages (peace upon them), the Tannaim, the Sages of the Mishnah and the Talmud, whose words and customs we follow, which they established for us from Moses and the Almighty. Therefore, we should honour them and greet them, even in their houses, and circumcise their sons, even on the Sabbath, bury their dead, and comfort their mourners.

Similarly, although Karaites varied in their attitude to Rabbanite teachings, social contacts were often close, as is apparent in the marriages between Karaites and Rabbanites recorded in a series of documents from the Cairo Genizah, with surprisingly modern-sounding arrangements to allow for different customs in the keeping of festivals and other domestic arrangements:

> He shall not light the Sabbath candles against her, and not force her in her food and drink ... And this Rayyisa accepted in favour of her aforementioned husband that she shall not profane against him the festivals of our brethren the Rabbanites all the time she is with him ... They both took upon themselves to be together with full resolve, willingness and honesty, and to behave according to the custom of the Karaites who observe the holy festivals according to the sighting of the Moon.

Relations over discrepant timings of festivals were not always so tolerant: a Rabbanite in Byzantium in the eleventh century wrote to his brother in Egypt that 'the Karaites assaulted us again last year and desecrated the festivals of the Lord ... Now a violent enmity has developed between us and great quarrels have taken place.' But in the thirteenth century Sa'ad ibn Kammuna, a Rabbanite philosopher living in Iraq who described the mutual accusations of the two camps and the responses proffered in each case, implied that their disputes were not worth continuation. In Crete in the fourteenth century, the Rabbanite Shemariah b. Elijah urged that the two sides should agree, so that 'all Israel might once more become one union of brethren'.[30]

It is plausible, but has proven impossible to demonstrate, that the whole Karaite movement took much of its impulse from trends within Islam. Parallels between Karaite attitudes to the Bible and the rejection of hadith by some Muslim theologians intent on preserving the authority of the Koran are discernible only in sources nearly two centuries apart. Anan had rejected secular knowledge, but later Karaites embraced Arabic science with enthusiasm, and in the eleventh century both the Karaite philosopher Joseph b. Abraham haKohen haRo'eh al-Basir (that is, 'the Blind'), who came from Iran to Jerusalem, and his pupil Yeshua b. Judah (both writing in Judaeo-Arabic) were influenced, even more than Saadiah had been, by the Islamic scholastic theology of the Mu'tazilites, with their emphasis on the unity of God and the createdness of the world.[31]

Half a century after al-Basir the centre of Karaite life was to move away from Islamic lands (apart from Egypt), and to lose the vitality stimulated by the surrounding Muslim culture. The Karaite community of Jerusalem seems to have been wiped out in 1099 by the First Crusade along with the rest of the Jews of the city, and from the twelfth to the sixteenth century most Karaites were to be found in the Byzantine empire, with a considerable religious Karaite literature composed in Constantinople. From c. 1600, many Karaites moved north first into the Crimea and then up to Lithuania and Poland, where their relationship to Rabbanites was decisively affected by the incorporation into Russia first of Crimea in 1783 and then of Lithuania in 1795. When the Russian state under Catherine the Great in 1795 imposed different taxes on Karaites and Rabbanite Jews, and allowed Karaites to acquire land, it became possible for the 2,000 or so Karaites, who were in many cases middle-class landowners, to argue that, since they did not accept the Talmud, they were not Jews at all, and in 1835 they were redesignated as 'Russian Karaites of the Old Testament Faith'. In 1840 they were allowed to set themselves up as an independent religion of equal status to Muslims. Among the most prosperous Karaite leaders, and most keen to establish the independence of Karaites from rabbinic Judaism, was the curious figure of Abraham Firkovich, originally from Lutsk in Volhynia, whose search in the nineteenth century for old manuscripts and archaeological relics as well as tombstones in extensive travels from the Crimea and the Caucasus to Jerusalem and Constantinople was intended to demonstrate the history of the Karaites in converting the Khazars to Judaism. His legacy was the astonishing collection of Hebrew manuscripts in the St Petersburg Library, which remains of huge significance today.[32]

By the early twentieth century, there were around 13,000 Karaites officially recorded in Russia, with smaller numbers in Poland, Constantinople, Cairo, Jerusalem and a few other places. In eastern Europe, separation from Judaism served Karaites well during the Holocaust in the middle of the twentieth century, so that they were saved from Nazi persecution, in some cases with the active help of Rabbanite Jews. After 1945, relations of these European Karaites with Rabbanite Judaism remained distant, but after 1948 a number of Egyptian Karaites migrated to Israel, and they have become part of the variegated Jewish religious life of contemporary Israel. The Jewish state has welcomed them, issuing (for instance) in 2001 a stamp proclaiming (in English) 'The Karaite Jews', in honour of those Karaites who had fought for Israel. Many rabbis in Israel have also returned to the attitude of Maimonides that Karaites are Jews, albeit mistaken in their ideas. There are around 40,000 Karaites in Israel in the twenty-first century, primarily in Ramleh, Ashdod and Be'er Sheva. Another 4,000 live in the United States, where the biggest concentration is in the San Francisco area, and there are smaller communities in Istanbul and France. In recent years Karaites have begun increasingly to seek to spread their ideas, particularly through outreach on the internet. Karaites can claim, as they have since the time of al-Kumisi in Jerusalem at the end of the ninth century, to have turned to the law of Moses from which other Jews have strayed: for al-Kumisi, the Rabbanites 'have not taught me to bear the yoke of the ordinances as set forth in the Law of Moses, but rather have led me astray with "an ordinance of men learned by rote", and it is time to repent'.[33]

Why has Greek Judaism petered out and Karaism survived up to now? One reason may be the roots of the Karaite movement in principled opposition to the rabbinic mainstream, which has often left them in uncomfortable isolation but has provided them with a distinctive identity. Greek Jews, by contrast, inherited a worldview compatible with that of the rabbis, and in time their distinctiveness merged into that of rabbis trained in more vigorous traditions elsewhere in the Jewish world. We shall see more cases of the elimination of difference by such processes in later periods in the history of Judaism down to the present day.

Rabbis in the West (1000–1500 CE)

The last of the Babylonian *geonim* to exercise influence across the Jewish world was Hai Gaon. Following his death in 1038, authority within rabbinic Judaism was dispersed to a number of new centres in the Mediterranean world and northern Europe, where Jews came under the hegemony not just of Islamic rulers in Palestine, Egypt, North Africa and Spain but also of a multiplicity of Christian states united by recognition of papal jurisdiction in religious matters from Rome. In Spain, France and Germany, rabbis with a shared respect for, and deep learning in, the Babylonian Talmud as well as the biblical texts consolidated the expression of the law as guidance for everyday life while evolving, through mystical speculation as well as philosophical analysis, novel theologies about the relation of God to his creation.

The connection of intellectual talmudic scholarship to the practical concerns of European Jews was facilitated by a new role for individual rabbis as local communal arbitrators in Jewish communities in the Rhineland and in France from the eleventh century. As commercial practices grew more complex in new settlements of Jews in urban centres along the great trade routes of northern Europe, communal legislation by appointed or elected representatives and the authority of rich merchants as lay communal leaders sometimes proved insufficient for the resolution of internal disputes between Jews, and communities turned instead to rabbis as experts in Jewish law. The selection of a *rav*, the title used from the second part of the eleventh century to refer to the rabbi of a city, seems to have been by consensus of lay leaders rather than any formal procedure. The ability of local rabbis to exert control over a community depended on the support of such leaders not least because, if they wished to contest one of his decisions, they could in the last resort appeal to the state authorities.

The extent to which in European countries or North Africa a local rabbi controlled his community thus varied greatly. By the thirteenth century he was regularly expected to take responsibility for the procedures of local slaughterers and butchers in the preparation of kosher meat, for the correct preparation of the *mikveh* (ritual bath) and the granting of a divorce. Occasionally other members of the community were able to lead the prayers and read from the Torah, but often the rabbi would be expected to take a leading role in synagogue ritual. In return he received honour and respect, but no guarantee of lifetime tenure. Nor did he receive any direct salary (since payment for pronouncing on the Torah was seen as sacrilege), although communities desiring to keep their rabbis found other ways to reward their services through gifts and privileges. Ultimately, the prestige of the rabbi depended on his reputation for learning, much enhanced if he could attract students from elsewhere to travel to his town for Talmud study in his yeshivah. More ambivalent as a source of moral authority was recognition of a rabbinic appointment by the Christian state, as in the appointment in 1270 by the king of Naples and Sicily of 'Maborach Fadalchassem the Jew, inhabitant of Palermo, our faithful who has been elected by you in order to exercise the priestship in your synagogue, to slaughter in your butchery and to hold the notary's seal among you'.[1]

Diversity encouraged by such local rabbinic jurisdiction was counterbalanced by thriving interregional contacts along trade routes across the Mediterranean and along the great rivers and old Roman roads of Europe. Local rabbis sought advice in difficult cases from more learned colleagues. In any one region there was often just one rabbinic sage widely recognized as the 'leader of his generation'. Books travelled through the copying of manuscripts, of which increasing numbers have been preserved in European collections amassed from the twelfth century onwards. The number of copies made, and the number of citations of one work in another, provide an insight into the comparative influence of ideas within rabbinic circles.

RASHI AND THE DEVELOPMENT
OF HALAKHAH

One consequence of powerful Karaite denigration in the tenth to eleventh centuries of the rabbinic project to promote the elucidation of oral Torah as a valid expression of the law of Moses was the consolidation of rabbinic affirmation of their understanding of the dual Torah. In the ensuing centuries the halakhah (law), firmly based on the authority of the rabbinic discussions recorded in the Babylonian Talmud which the Karaites so vehemently denied, was to expand hugely in its reach, profundity, complexity and variety. The process can be traced in much of its bewildering detail because, despite the emphasis on the orality of the Torah, a large proportion of halakhic discussion found its way into texts written down for the benefit of Jews in distant places. As a result, halakhic developments often took a quasi-epistolary form through the transmission of responsa in much the same way as the development of Christian theology by correspondence between churches in the early centuries of Christianity. Some of these texts survive in their original form in fragments in the Cairo Genizah. Others were copied and kept for use by Jewish communities throughout the Middle Ages, ending up in the collections of humanist scholars now deposited in the libraries of universities. Yet others were preserved in the archives of monasteries and cathedrals, where the ambivalent attitude of Christian librarians to such Jewish learning led sometimes to the accidental preservation of Hebrew texts in the bindings of other works. The complex process of disengaging such texts and identifying their nature in libraries across southern Europe, especially Italy and Spain, is a task only recently begun.[2]

What kind of work was written by rabbis in these centuries? The Karaites had specifically rejected the authority of the Talmud, and rabbinic scholars were to respond with commentaries on the talmudic text, building on the exegetical culture which had begun in the ninth century with the biblical commentaries of Saadiah. Already in the first half of the eleventh century Hananel b. Hushiel in Kairouan produced a succinct summary in Hebrew of the halakhah to be found in each page of the Talmud, clarifying difficult sections of the argument. His contemporary in Kairouan, Nissim b. Yaakov b. Nissim ibn Shahin, produced in Arabic commentaries on many talmudic themes. But their efforts were to be dwarfed in influence by the line-by-line talmudic commentary of the great rabbinic scholar R. Shlomo Yitzhaki, better known as Rashi, in Troyes later in the century, and by the supplements to his work by numerous Tosafists (authors of *tosafot*, 'additions') from the twelfth to late fourteenth centuries who sought to improve Rashi's work and solve apparent contradictions both in his commentary and within the text of the Talmud itself (see below).[3]

Commentaries on the Talmud emerged from study of the halakhah for its own sake, but the processes involved in living according to the halakhah also provoked a large literature in the form of responsa. We have already seen how the responsa of the *geonim* in Babylonia established their authority among Jews in the Islamic world in the last centuries of the first millennium. Correspondents asked *geonim* for clarification of all sorts of issues relating to doctrine, liturgy and other legal questions. Many responsa were very brief (just 'forbidden' or 'permitted'), but others were more extended. The *geonim* could express irritation, as in the complaint sent from Sura by Nahshon Gaon to the scholars of Kairouan in the ninth century about the practice of sending an identical query to the two academies of Sura and Pumbedita: 'Is this not a profanation of the Divine Name . . . that you will say, "They argue with each other?" . . . Now we . . . warn you, that if you address a single query [both] to us and to Pum[bedita], nothing [by way of answer] will be sent to you either from Pum or from us.'

Towards the end of the tenth century scholars in other centres of rabbinic learning (such as Cordoba, Kairouan and Lucca) began to take on this role as deciders of case law often involving personal status, communal authority or religious custom. Many of the responsa survive of Moshe b. Hanokh, who was reputed to have brought talmudic knowledge in the tenth century to Spain, where he founded a yeshivah; according to the *Book of Tradition*, 'all questions which had formerly been addressed to the academies were now directed to him.' Responsa often used examples from the Talmud as precedents for deciding contemporary problems, or, in Islamic countries, precedents in the responsa of the *geonim*. But in Christian countries rabbis generally relied on their own reasoning (including casuistry from biblical or talmudic texts) in order to provide clear answers to questions. The corpus of responsa from any individual rabbi could be very large, and the decisions of such individuals were increasingly collected into volumes for the benefit of later generations. Thus R. Meir b. Baruch of Rothenburg, who died in prison in Alsace in 1293, himself a notable *posek* ('decider') for the Jews of France and Germany, began in his academy the collection of responsa by Ashkenazi rabbis from the whole preceding 300 years. The resulting volumes, frequently copied in the later medieval period, became a major source of Jewish law.[4]

The dual stimuli of talmudic study and the need to apply the Torah to real life combined to produce two further types of halakhic literature intended to clarify the law in difficult cases for ordinary individuals unable to get to grips with the esoteric dialectic of the Talmud, either through their own study of this new literature or (more commonly) through the advice of a local rabbi with access to the scholarly texts. On the one hand, the rabbis in twelfth-century Germany and France produced volumes of *hiddushim* ('novelties'), which apply sophisticated dialectic derived from the Talmud to legal issues not addressed in the talmudic text itself in order to extend the reach of the halakhah into contemporary life. At the same time a number of rabbinic authorities sought to codify this burgeoning legal literature into manageable form for those not sufficiently steeped in the talmudic commentaries to find their way without such guidance. In the eleventh century Yitzhak Alfasi (known as the Rif), who compiled his *Sefer haHalakhot* in Fez and, towards the end of his life, in Spain, presented a digest of the legal conclusions in the talmudic text with authoritative summaries of the legislation of the *geonim*. In some cases, he put forward his own rules for determining the law when the Talmud left an issue unclear. The Arabic *Sefer haMitzvot* ('Book of the Precepts') of Hefets b. Yatsliah, a contemporary of the Rif and one of the last scholars from Babylonia to have a lasting influence on rabbis in the west, divided the commandments into thirty-six chapters arranged by theme, each with the positive and negative commandments presented separately and citation of relevant biblical and rabbinic proof texts.[5]

Both codes were extensively used by Maimonides in his *Mishneh Torah* ('Repetition of the Torah'), which was written in Egypt in the second part of the twelfth century. Maimonides aimed specifically to overcome what he perceived as the decline in knowledge in his time by laying out every aspect of Jewish law in a superbly clear Mishnaic Hebrew without muddying the text by adding either justification or sources for the rulings laid down. This revolutionary work went far beyond the compendium form of Hefets b. Yatsliah, since Maimonides was concerned to produce not an aid to Talmudic learning – his work did not refer to the writings of Rashi even once – but instructions for living in the real world. The search for clarity and finality in codifying the law undertaken by Maimonides and his younger contemporary Eleazar b. Yehudah, who wrote a straightforward halakhic code in Worms for the benefit of Jews in Germany and northern France, was in tension with the originality and innovativeness of those rabbis who devoted themselves to *hiddushim* which constantly expanded the halakhah.

The codifiers did not hide their frustration at what they saw as the obscurantism of their rabbinical colleagues who delighted in complicating the law under which Jews did their best to live in piety. Yaakov b. Asher complained in the first half of the fourteenth century that 'there is no law that does not have difference of opinions.' His own father, Asher b. Yehiel, known as the Rosh, had produced an influential halakhic compendium which covered all halakhic practice of the time both for

Germany (where the Rosh had studied) and in Toledo in Spain, where he became head of the rabbinic academy in 1305, but in the view of Yaakov too much uncertainty remained. The solution adopted by Yaakov was to organize the halakhah in his *Arba'ah Turim* according to a novel arrangement of four 'rows' (in memory of the four rows of precious stones in the breastplate of the High Priest): *Orah Hayyim*, for daily duties such as blessings; *Yoreh De'ah* for ritual law such as dietary regulations; *Even haEzer* for family law; and *Hoshen Mishpat* for civil law. In marked contrast to Maimonides in the *Mishneh Torah*, Yaakov cited the authorities on which his decisions had been based. His was a severely practical code which left out all the law which had no longer been applied since the destruction of the Temple some twelve and a half centuries before. Its influence was to be considerable.[6]

For all these methods in the development of the halakhah, authority derived from the learning or intellectual acumen of the sages concerned, as recognized by their fellow rabbis. Some of these authorities, such as Yaakov b. Asher himself, declined to accept any rabbinic appointment. He preferred to devote himself to legal study despite living in poverty. Some halakhists were said to be of exemplary piety, but such a reputation was not necessary for acceptance of the legal rulings if the rulings themselves were deemed to deserve respect. Quite exceptional were the techniques used by a certain Jacob, from Marvège in south-central France, who wrote down in his *Responsa from Heaven* the halakhah revealed to him in dreams as a reply to his queries to God:

> I asked, on the night of the third day, the nineteenth day of Kislev, if this had come to me from the Lord or if not. This is how I asked it: O Supernal King, The Great, Mighty and Awesome God, Who keeps His covenant of mercy to those who love Him, keep Thy covenant of mercy with us. Command Thy holy angels appointed to give replies to questions put in dreams to reply to me that which I ask from before Thy glorious Throne. Let it be a true and correct reply, each thing in its place, clearly defined, whether in connection with Scripture or with legal rulings, so that no further doubt will be possible. Behold, I ask: All those things that came into my mouth as a result of the questions I asked concerning the immersion of those who have had a seminal emission, did these things come to me by the holy spirit? Is it advantageous and correct to reveal them to my son-in-law, Rabbi Joseph, and to instruct him to inform the sages of the land of them, or did they come to me by another spirit so that they have no advantage and it is better for me to conceal and hide them? They replied: They were

truly the word of the Lord and the words are ancient, the Ancient of Days said them.

It is all the more striking that the replies that Jacob claimed to have received in his dreams – none of which diverged from the teachings of other French rabbis in his time – were cited as halakhic rulings by later authorities.[7]

The centres in which halakhic developments were thrashed out had become very geographically dispersed by the eleventh century, and such dispersion increased through the rest of the Middle Ages. Between 900 and 1100 the pre-eminence of the Babylonian academies in Sura and Pumbedita was challenged within the Islamic world by Tiberias in Palestine, Kairouan in North Africa and Cordoba in Spain, and in northern Europe by the academies of Troyes in France and Worms in Germany. From 1100 new academies in Provence and what are now Austria and the Czech Republic became centres, as did academies in Poland from the early fourteenth century. With no central institution to control developments, it is not surprising that regional variations in law and liturgy emerged, despite the attempts at codification, but even within this diffuse culture the authority of a few individuals seems to have achieved recognition throughout the rabbinic world. One such individual was R. Shlomo Yitzhaki (Rashi), whose extraordinary career in the second half of the eleventh century was responsible for turning northern France and Germany into centres for biblical and talmudic studies. Like other great scholars of this period (including, as we have seen, the Rif and the Rosh), Shlomo Yitzhaki was generally referred to within rabbinic circles by an acronym of his name.[8]

Rashi was born in Troyes, a town of some importance on the bank of the River Seine, south-east of Paris. This was no provincial backwater: there had been a city on the site since Roman times, with a bishop since the fourth century and a cathedral since the ninth. By Rashi's time Troyes had developed as the hub of an important trading route, which may explain the settlement of Jews there a generation before Rashi was born. In any case, it was in Troyes that Rashi eventually set up an academy after studying with scholars in a number of other places, especially Worms. About his life it is hard to distinguish fact from legend, apart from his occupation in viticulture and the knowledge of French which surfaces in the many places in his writings when he explained difficult Hebrew words by reference to the French equivalent. But his influence, both in his own day and on later generations, can unquestionably be attributed directly to the impressive clarity and thoroughness of his exposition of the two primary texts for rabbinic education in his time, the Bible and the Babylonian Talmud.

In his Bible commentary, which covered every scripture book apart from Chronicles (and possibly Ezra and Nehemiah), Rashi emphasized far more than the commentators before him the importance of establishing the plain meaning of the text (the *peshat*), using reason and philology, and occasionally confessing ignorance when he could provide no explanation. This did not mean Rashi rejected the homiletic meanings ascribed to the biblical text by earlier rabbis, only that he claimed to subordinate such interpretations to the plain meaning. So, for instance, in his exposition of a passage in Genesis, 'And they heard the voice of the Eternal God walking about in the garden in the heat of the day,' he noted that 'There are many midrashic explanations and our teachers have already collected them in their appropriate places in Bereshith Rabbah and in other midrashim. I, however, am only concerned with the plain sense of scripture and with such teachings as explain the words of scripture in a manner that fits in with them.' This emphasis on the need to clarify the plain meaning of the scriptural text was to be followed by medieval Bible commentators in the twelfth century such as Abraham ibn Ezra in Spain and Yosef Kimhi in Provence.[9]

To some extent Rashi's claim to prefer the plain meaning acted as a rhetorical device for the inclusion of much earlier midrashic material, as in his interpretation of the revelation to Moses on Mount Sinai, in which he made use of the tannaitic midrashic compilation in the Mekhilta, with its prohibition against using an iron tool in the making of the altar:

> Thus you may learn that if thou liftest up thy iron tool above it thou profanest it. The reason of this is, because the altar is created to lengthen man's days and iron has been created to shorten man's days, it is not right that an object which shortens man's life should be lifted up above that which lengthens it ... And a further reason is: because the altar makes peace between Israel and their Father in Heaven, and therefore there should not come upon it anything that cuts and destroys.

The transmission of such moral teachings in the guise of a simple interpretation of a biblical text may be considered an exceptionally effective method of preaching in disguise.[10]

Rashi's commentary was to be much used by the Christian biblical exegete Nicholas of Lyre in the fourteenth century and there is plentiful evidence, not least in Latin–Hebrew bilingual manuscripts, for Christian interest in Jewish biblical scholarship in northern Europe in the high and late Middle Ages. Influence in the reverse direction is more difficult to show, although the mnemonic PaRDeS, which became popular in rabbinic circles from the late thirteenth century as a means of referring to four different ways to interpret the Bible (*peshat*, 'plain meaning'; *remez*, 'allusion'; *drash*, 'homiletical interpretation'; *sod*, 'mystical meaning'), may well have some connection to the medieval Christian notion of the fourfold senses of scripture. But Rashi himself, despite his integration into the secular world of Troyes and his knowledge of industry, agriculture and trade, seems not to have known Latin and to have worked without demonstrable influence from the non-Jewish intellectual world of his day.

Rashi's motivation in explicating the scriptures for a wide Jewish readership of moderate education – he assumes a basic knowledge of the biblical text, so was not concerned to reach out to the totally ignorant – seems to have been the same as that which led to his detailed commentary on almost the whole of the Babylonian Talmud. His commentary lays out the arguments found in the Talmud with great clarity, making no attempt to go beyond the talmudic text into the later developments of the halakhah, in marked contrast (as we have seen) to those who used the Talmud as the base for their own halakhic innovations. What ensured that Rashi's commentary superseded all those before it was his unique ability to clarify the methodology of the Talmud, unravelling the construction of complex passages, explaining unusual terms, providing quasi-historical background and realistic descriptions to illuminate talmudic stories and generally bringing the text alive. It was an extraordinary achievement, and has ensured that his commentary remains the standard accompaniment to talmudic study after nearly a thousand years despite the numerous disagreements with his specific interpretations raised by his pupils and successors. Rashi's writings touch frequently on such favourite themes as the unique relationship of Israel with God and the value of prayer, Torah study and modesty. But his aim and legacy are encapsulated less in what he himself said than in the educational revolution he facilitated, especially through his Talmud commentary, by bringing the esoteric world of the Talmud within the reach of a far greater range of readers than had been possible in previous generations.[11]

Among Rashi's most impressive students and trenchant critics were a number of his grandsons, the offspring of his three daughters, who carried on his tradition of Talmud study under the shadow of the First Crusade (1095-6) and the Rhineland persecutions of the following century. To some extent these scholars built on an existing movement in Worms and Mainz in the late eleventh century to synthesize varied talmudic texts in order to clarify practical decisions, but from the twelfth century their critique took the form of *tosafot*, additions to the commentary of Rashi. These additions, presented often in the form of an oral discussion within an academy – 'and if you were to say' and 'and it is possible to say' are common formulas – often questioned Rashi's comments on the basis of his statements elsewhere or new information not adduced by Rashi himself, such as manuscript readings from new copies of the Talmud from North Africa or material from the Palestinian Talmud, which was generally less studied. The most influential of these early Tosafists, through notes of his teachings incorporated into manuscripts of the Talmud by his pupils, was Jacob b. Meir Tam, a grandson of Rashi generally known as Rabbenu Tam. There are clear similarities between the Tosafists' academies and the new cathedral schools in northern Europe in the twelfth century, and there are parallels between the activities of the Tosafists and the activities of Christian glossators of this period, but whether there were direct intellectual connections between Jews and Christians at this level remains unknown.[12]

Rabbenu Tam was not afraid to advocate quite drastic revisions to traditional interpretations of the Torah if his reading of talmudic texts suggested that this was necessary. Thus, for instance, he advocated, against the view of his grandfather, Rashi, that the contents of the *tefillin* (phylacteries) should be altered so that the biblical texts they contain be written in a different order – the arguments between the two men are so finely balanced that some pious Jews nowadays put on two sets of *tefillin*, one set in accordance with the rulings of each rabbinic teacher. Such intense readings of the Talmud could lead to uncomfortable discussions of talmudic dicta such as the procedure, put forward in the name of the *tanna* R. Ilai, for dealing with uncontrollable urges to sin and the importance of keeping up appearances and avoiding being seen to sin: 'If a man sees that his [evil] desire is conquering him, let him go to a place where he is unknown, don black and cover himself with black, and do what his heart desires, but let him not publicly profane God's name.' This particular teaching the Tosafists were (unsurprisingly) unwilling to take literally.[13]

On the other hand, legal theory was often used by the Tosafists to justify existing practice when it conflicted with the law as laid down in the Talmud. Sometimes they argued from a minority opinion in the Talmud. Sometimes they claimed that existing practice safeguards other values which justify ignoring the talmudic rules. Most frequently they asserted that the conditions presupposed in the Talmud no longer apply. So, for instance, the Tosafists claimed that contemporary neglect in France of the role of washing hands after meals as required in the Talmud was justified: the Talmud had required such washing to remove 'Salt of Sodom', which was used in food and could cause blindness if it came into contact with the eyes, but such salt was no longer in use. The Talmud had defended the ruling of the Mishnah that dancing and clapping are forbidden on a festival day by proposing that such activities might encourage the repairing of a musical instrument, which would definitely be forbidden, but, since in fact French Jews enjoyed such dancing and clapping, the Tosafists claimed, not very plausibly, that the skill in fashioning or repairing musical instruments had been lost, so the original prohibition no longer applied. R. Asher b. Yehiel, the Rosh, wrote in the early fourteenth century about his own change of mind on leaving Germany for Spain about rules regarding garments made of mixed materials which might lead to an appearance of breaking the biblical law which forbids wearing wool and linen together in one garment (see Chapter 4):

> When I was in Germany I forbade the stitching of a garment of canvas underneath a garment of wool because garments of canvas are not often found in Germany and people will imagine it to be a garment of linen. Nowadays, too, silken garments are often found among us so that everyone recognizes these for what they are. Consequently, it is now permitted to stitch a garment of silk underneath a garment of wool and strands of silk are also permitted in a garment of wool.

In exceptional cases where common custom among religious Jews had diverged entirely from the rules of the Talmud, the prominent fifteenth-century German rabbi Israel b. Petahyah Isserlein condoned simply ignoring the Talmud on pragmatic grounds. Hence his ruling on the recitation of the night-time Shema while it was still light, as was standard in northern climes during the summer when the days are long:

> There is no defence for the practice according to the theory and reasoning of the Talmud. But one must surmise that the habit was adopted as a result of the weakness that has descended into the world so that the majority of the folk are hungry and wish to have their meal while it is still full daylight in the long days. If they were to have their meal before the afternoon prayers they would spend so much time over it that they would not come to the synagogue at all ... Because of this the scholars were unable to prevent the people from saying their prayers and reciting the Shema while it is still full daylight.

Such rulings from common custom did not always result in leniency: Maimonides noted in his *Yad* that 'the Evening Service is not obligatory like the Morning and Afternoon Services. Nevertheless all Israelites, wherever they have settled, have adopted the practice of the Evening Service and have accepted it as obligatory.'[14]

The journeys of rabbis such as the Rosh between different communities elicited awareness of variation in halakhah between the Jews of different regions. This was nothing new – we have seen that the rabbis in the time of the Talmud were well aware of differences between Babylonia and Palestine – but the right to differ was upheld by local rabbinic authorities with increasing vehemence as halakhic complexity increased. In Egypt, Maimonides held that anyone who broke the Mishnaic prohibition on drinking liquid that had been left exposed, in case a snake had poisoned it, should be flogged, but in France the prohibition was deemed by the Tosafists inoperative on the grounds that there were no poisonous snakes in the country. Already by the early thirteenth century the existence of different local customs which had solidified into the status of binding law was celebrated by Avraham b. Natan of Lunel, who travelled extensively in Provence, northern France, Germany, England and Spain, and described such customs, particularly with regard to prayer and synagogue rituals, in his *Manhig Olam* (often called *Sefer haManhig*, 'The Guide'). The book became a useful guide for other Jews on their travels.

Liturgical variations became particularly marked during this period, with differences between the Palestinian, Romaniot, northern French, western Ashkenazi, eastern Ashkenazi, Babylonian, Persian and Spanish rites, some of which have continued to modern times. But the clearest divide to emerge in the late Middle Ages was between Sephardim and Ashkenazim. The Jews of France, Germany and Bohemia, whose communities traced their origin from the Rhineland in the tenth century (hence 'Ashkenazi', from the Hebrew for Germany), shared sufficient traditions by the sixteenth century in language, Hebrew pronunciation, prayers and poems added to the shared basic structures of the liturgy that they came to see themselves as distinct from the Sephardim of the Iberian peninsula ('Sepharad' being taken to mean Spain in Hebrew), who in turn hung on to their traditions with vehemence. When customs spread from one group to another, they took time to be accepted. So, for instance, the practice of *tashlich*, the folk custom of reciting scriptural verses about repentance and forgiveness of sins on the afternoon of Rosh haShanah by a river or some other body of water, symbolizing the casting of sins into the sea (as in Micah 7:19), which is first attested in the early fifteenth-century writings of the German rabbi Yaakov b. Moshe haLevi Molin, known as the Maharil, a renowned exponent of Ashkenazi custom, is not mentioned in any Sephardic source until well over a century later.[15]

Some festivals were very local indeed, such as the local 'Purims' of Narbonne (instituted in 1236) and of Cairo (instituted in 1524) to commemorate local deliverance from danger with celebrations analogous to Purim. In Narbonne, a brawl between a Jew and a fisherman, which ended in homicide, had set off an anti-Jewish riot which was suppressed by the Viscount Amauri, and the event was remembered annually on 29 Adar. Such local liturgy was more formalized than the folk custom of revering the tombs of saints, which in much of the medieval Near East Jews shared with their Muslim neighbours. The objections of the Karaite theologian Sahl b. Matzliah, a resident of Jerusalem, in the tenth century, to Jews who 'visit the graves, perfume them with incense, believe in spirits and request fulfilment of their needs from the dead and spend the night at the tomb' were not successful in suppressing such customs: we have seen (Chapter 10) that the alleged gravesite of the prophet Ezekiel, for instance, located inside a synagogue in Iraq, attracted pilgrims from afar, Muslim as well as Jewish.

A custom which gradually assumed the force of law in some communities but not others in the medieval period was the requirement for men to cover their heads. There is no evidence that this practice was widespread in the talmudic period, but covering the head during prayer became common in Babylonia in later centuries and spread particularly among Jews in Islamic countries. The justification for the practice was the claim of R. Huna b. Yehoshua, as reported in the Babylonian Talmud, that he would never walk 4 cubits without his head covered because 'the Divine Presence is above my head'. Covering the head became a sign of pious acknowledgement that God is everywhere, and the practice was strengthened by the common use of head coverings during prayer by Muslims. Yitzhak Alfasi in eleventh-century Fez considered male head-covering mandatory. But in the thirteenth century there were still some male Jews in France who read the Torah bare-headed, eliciting the disapproval from Vienna of Yitzhak b. Moshe, author of *Or Zarua*, an account of halakhah and religious customs and observances in France and Germany: 'The custom of our rabbis in France of reciting blessings with uncovered head does not meet with my approval.'[16]

Many variations in custom and practice, such as veneration of tombs, had clearly been influenced by the different surrounding cultures among which Jews found themselves in their dispersion, but in some communities a distinctive ideology underpinned their attitude to halakhah. This was perhaps most evident among the Hasidei Ashkenaz, circles of pietists in the Rhineland from the mid-twelfth century to the early fourteenth, led primarily by members of the Kalonymus family in Mainz and Worms (see Chapter 9). Their asceticism and ethical devotion, encapsulated in the *Sefer Hasidim* ('Book of the Pious') written in the early thirteenth century by R. Yehudah b. Shmuel haHasid of Regensburg, was predicated on a mystical theology all of their own. The *Sefer Hasidim* outlines the norms of rabbinic life, with sections dedicated to ritual, teaching and studying Torah, and social and family life, but it also includes many exemplary stories to demonstrate correct behaviour:

> Once there was a man who did not want to release his deceased brother's wife from the obligation to marry him, and his foot began to hurt, whereupon he was told: 'The very wrong of not removing your shoe is causing your foot to hurt.' So he removed his shoe and the foot was cured. A story is told about a man who used to go from town to town for sustenance. He was poor but rich in knowledge and good deeds, and he did not want to tell his name or how much he knew. People would give him a pittance. He would then converse about the Law with the town's wise scholars, and when they saw how much he knew, people came to add to what they had given him, but he refused to take it. He said, 'You already gave me the alms of a poor man, but what you want to give me now for my knowledge I shall not accept.'

Many other narratives describe miracles and demons, reflecting popular beliefs in Germany in the twelfth century. It was among the Hasidei Ashkenaz in the twelfth and thirteenth centuries that the notion of the creation of a golem (an artificial living being) by magic through the employment of holy names, a popular myth in the folk tradition of Jews in eastern Europe in later centuries (see Chapter 15 on legends about the Maharal of Prague), is first found as the culmination of a ritual study of mystical texts. Underlying the whole approach of the Hasidei Ashkenaz to the halakhah was the notion that 'the root of saintliness is for a man to go beyond the letter of the Law', and that this should lead to asceticism.

We have seen (Chapter 10) that, a century earlier, in Muslim Spain, Bahya ibn Pakuda relied on a different tradition, based in Islamic mysticism or Sufism, in his *Duties of the Heart*, which preached the duty of showing gratitude to God at all times and adopting a moderate attitude to asceticism. Bahya taught that withdrawal from society would be wrong for any human, not least for a Jew who has been chosen by God:

Individuals who live in accordance with the definition of the highest type of asceticism, so that they resemble the spiritual beings ... renounce everything that distracts them from the thought of God. They flee from inhabited places to the deserts or high mountains, where there is no company, no society ... The love of God delights them so much that they do not think of the love of human beings ... Of all classes, this class is furthest removed from the 'mean' which our religion teaches, because they renounce worldly interests completely. And our religion does not bid us to give up social life altogether, as we have previously quoted: 'He created it not a waste; He formed it to be inhabited ...'[17]

It would be wrong to deduce from this variety that innovation and change went unchallenged over these centuries. Variant Jewish customs practised by co-religionists at a safe distance could be tolerated more easily than those within the local community. When in the ninth century a certain Eldad arrived in Kairouan to announce to the local community his origins in an independent Jewish kingdom in Africa made up from a number of the lost tribes (including Dan, to which he claimed he himself belonged), the Kairouan Jews were disturbed by the dubious form of ritual slaughter (*shehitah*) that Eldad used, only to be reassured by a letter from the great rabbi Tsemach Gaon, in Baghdad, that such diversity was not heretical because it was only to be expected in the diaspora. The Rosh, who had fled from Germany to Spain (as we have seen above) in 1306, claimed less legal justification when he endorsed the decision of rabbis in Cordoba to execute a blasphemer: even though this was not in his view permitted by halakhah, he gave his approval in order to prevent greater bloodshed and the Islamic authorities depriving the Jewish community of self-jurisdiction.[18]

The principle behind rabbinic decisions implicit in the Mishnah and Talmud had been, as we have seen (Chapter 11), that legislation according to the majority of sages should be binding on all, but with the dispersal of rabbis to numerous different countries the principle was no longer easy to follow. Rashi's grandson Rabbenu Tam tried in the twelfth century to insist instead on unanimous consent, but this was if anything even less practical, and it conflicted somewhat with his own controversies with contemporaries, such as his argument with the Provençal scholar Meshullam b. Yaakov of Lunel over the precise rules for the lighting of candles for the Sabbath and other customs. Criticism of the halakhic rulings of others even became a distinct literary genre in the writings of a younger contemporary of Rabbenu Tam, Avraham b. David, known as Rabad, who headed his own academy in Posquières in south-ern France. Rabad devoted tractates to critical notes (*hassagot*) on the works of codifiers both in the distant past (such as Yitzhak Alfasi) and in his own time, notably his bête noire, Zerahyah b. Yitzhak b. Levi Gerondi (who had himself criticized Alfasi's code). His attack on Mai-monides' *Mishneh Torah* was fierce:

> He intended to improve but did not improve, for he forsook the way of all authors who preceded him. They always adduced proof for their state-ments and cited the proper authority for each statement; this was very useful, for sometimes the judge would be inclined to forbid or permit something and his proof was based on some other authority. Had he known that there was a greater authority who interpreted the law differ-ently, he might have retracted. Now, therefore, I do not know why I should reverse my tradition or my corroborative views because of the compen-dium of this author. If the one who differs with me is greater than I – fine; and, if I am greater than he, why should I annul my opinion in deference to his? Moreover, there are matters concerning which the Geonim disagree and this author has selected the opinion of one and incorporated it in his compendium. Why should I rely upon his choice when it is not acceptable to me and I do not know whether the contending authority is competent to differ or not? It can only be that 'an overbearing spirit is in him.'[19]

Halakhic developments in the later Middle Ages had a decisive impact on the shape of rabbinic Judaism in the following centuries. The divide between Sephardim and Ashkenazim widened and was acknowledged, while all streams of rabbinic Jewry embraced with enthusiasm the com-mentaries of Rashi and his successors in the study of the Talmud. But the relations between the rabbinical academies in which the halakhah developed and the individual sages who dominated these developments were much complicated by the intrusion into the same rabbinic circles of new ideas about philosophy and mysticism, to which we now turn.

MAIMONIDES: FAITH AND PHILOSOPHY

Of the various ways in which Islam shaped the development of Judaism in the Near East, North Africa and Spain from the ninth century to the fifteenth, much the most radical was in the practice of philosophy as a bulwark for religious doctrine through rational argument. We have seen that Philo in the last century of the Second Temple had adopted Platonic notions to this purpose, and that philosophical argument at a high level of abstraction was characteristic of the development of Christian theology from the third century, but that talmudic discourse was focused on other concerns. The reintroduction of philosophy into Judaism reflected the challenge of Islamic (and, later, Christian) claims to their own versions of ultimate truth, but many of the longest-lasting philosophical notions to be adopted by all three religions were in origin the arguments of pagan Greeks, notably Plato and Aristotle. Philosophical speculation was not deemed by all Jews to be without its own dangers, as we shall see. A search for rational explanation of religion might seem to undermine the authority of revelation.

In Babylonia in the first half of the tenth century, the authority of Saadiah Gaon, whose role as leader of the rabbinic academy in Sura and vehement opposition to Karaites we have noted, integrated into Rabbanite Judaism the earlier adoption by the Babylonian philosopher David ibn Marwan Mukammis (also known as David haBavli) of the approach of the *kalam* within Islam. *Kalam* was a form of scholasticism which since the mid-eighth century had tackled issues of free will, physics (often in the form of atomistic theories), the impossibility of ascribing attributes to God and the perfection of divine justice. One doctrine of the Mu'tazilah, as the first school of the *kalam* was known, that the Koran has not existed eternally but was created along with the rest of the universe, was even declared official by the caliph al-Mamun in 833, only to be denied by his successor al-Mutawakkil in 847. By the time of Saadiah the kalamic approach was thus both well established and controversial in the surrounding Islamic culture. But the reasons for following the methods of rational interpretation of scripture used by the *kalam* given by the Gaon in his *Book of Beliefs and Opinions*, written in Judaeo-Arabic, was unapologetic:

> The reader of this book should know that we inquire into and speculate on the teachings of our religion for two reasons: first, to find out for ourselves what we have learned as imparted knowledge from the prophets of God; and secondly, to be able to refute anyone who argues against us concerning anything to do with our religion ... In this way we engage in speculation and inquiry, so as to make our own what our Lord has taught us by way of imparted knowledge. This inevitably raises a point which we must now consider. It may be asked: 'If the teachings of religion can be discovered by correct inquiry and speculation, as our Lord has informed us, what prompted his wisdom to transmit them to us through prophecy

and to confirm them by visible, miraculous proofs, rather than by rational demonstrations?' To this question, with God's help, we will give a complete answer ... Thus we were obliged at once to accept the teachings of religion, together with all that they implied, because they had been verified by the testimony of the senses. (We are also obliged to accept them on the grounds that they have been passed on to us fully authenticated by reliable tradition, as we shall explain later.) But God commanded us to take our time with our rational inquiries till we should arrive by argument at the truth of religion, and not to abandon our quest till we have found convincing arguments in favour of it and are compelled to believe God's revelation by what our eyes have seen and our ears heard. In the case of some of us our inquiries may take a long time before they are completed, but that should not worry us; no one prevented by any hindrance from pursuing his investigations is left without religious guidance.

Like the practitioners of the *kalam*, Saadiah claimed that creation had been from nothing and that God's existence can be inferred from creation. He described the Torah as revealed reason, and the purpose of creation to be happiness, which is attained through the commandments of the Torah. Saadiah's philosophy thus underpinned his halakhic works in that he distinguished between ethical commandments, which would be observed without revelation since they conform to reason, and the ceremonial commandments, which depend on revelation alone.[20]

The influence of Saadiah on later rabbinic religious philosophy was to be immense, but more through his introduction of Greek thought into the rabbinic world than through the *kalam*. His contemporary in Babylonia, David ibn Marwan Mukammis, followed *kalam* doctrine in his proofs for the existence of God, in which he stressed that since divine attributes differ from human, God's attributions cannot affect his unity:

The Maker of the world is in every aspect unlike the world. This being so, and since the world is composite, its Maker is not composite; since the world contains a variety of things, there is no diversity in its Maker; since the world is finite, its Maker is infinite; since the world is substance and accident, its Maker is neither substance nor accident.

Such rationalist thinking was brought by Saadiah into the mainstream rabbinic world, along with Aristotelian and Neoplatonic ideas which Mukammis had taken from Christianity. Saadiah and Mukammis were also cited by the moralist Bahya ibn Pakuda, whose ethical teachings we have already noted, in eleventh-century Spain. But most of the philosophical theory which underlay Bahya's pious guide to spirituality was derived from the Neoplatonic tradition: for Bahya, the soul of each individual had been placed in the body by divine decree, and it is the task of a spiritual life to enable the soul to grow, despite the temptations of the body, through the inspiration of both reason and the Torah.[21]

The penetration of Neoplatonic notions into Jewish thought reached a peak with the philosophical musings of Bahya's contemporary in Spain, Shlomo ibn Gabirol, whose literary output in a short and obscure life was astonishing. Ibn Gabirol's main work of philosophy, the *Fons Vitae* ('The Fount of Life'), was originally composed in Arabic but, apart from a few passages of the original Arabic quoted by Moses ibn Ezra, it is preserved only in a Latin translation and a few passages translated into Hebrew in later centuries. Its contents are so purely concerned with metaphysics that, despite (or perhaps because of) widespread use of the Latin version by Christians under the name 'Avicebron', it was identified as a Jewish text only in the nineteenth century. Ibn Gabirol tackled the existence of the material world despite the entirely spiritual nature of God by postulating that the world had been created by a chain of emanations in which the initial divine will still has some presence. The notion of man as a microcosm, in whom part of the intelligible world subsists alongside the corporeal, enabled ibn Gabirol to argue that men have the ability to grasp spiritual forms by their own power.

Neither ibn Gabirol's metaphysical philosophy nor his secular Hebrew poetry on wine and friendship was closely connected to previous Jewish traditions, and it is perhaps therefore unsurprising that his treatise on 'the improvement of moral qualities' argued for an ethical system which would be valid for all religious traditions:

> We have named our work, 'The Improvement of the Qualities', for the benefit largely of the masses, in order that they may gain a knowledge of the nature of the noble, and understand this matter through various methods of expression. We have introduced in the following whatever logical and demonstrable arguments have occurred to us; and, furthermore, as far as we are able, have adduced Scriptural verses. Nor, after first giving these, do I see any harm in briefly citing some utterances of the wise; and I shall follow this by adorning (what I have said) with verses of litterateurs, and some verses from the poets, and anything uncommon that occurs to me, and whatever else I can recall, so that my book may be complete in all its parts.

Such ethical literature, in the same genre as Saadiah's ethical treatise a century earlier (see p. 280), sought to define not just correct behaviour, as in halakhah, but the philosophical underpinnings of such behaviour. It was to become popular among Jews in ensuing centuries, especially after the translation of the Arabic ethical writings of Saadiah into Hebrew in the second half of the twelfth century.

Notwithstanding the abstract nature of his philosophy and his secular verse which treated the standard themes of wine, friendship, love and despair, ibn Gabirol's religious poetry showed a deep spiritual sensibility in hymns of penitence and glorification of the majesty of God, as in his poem on *The Kingly Crown*, which entered some liturgical traditions for private recitation and contemplation on Yom Kippur:

> Mysterious are Thy works, my soul well knows:
> Thine, Lord, is majesty, all pomp and power,
> Kingship whose splendour yet more splendid grows
> O'ertopping all in glory and wealth's dower.
> To Thee celestial creatures, and the seed
> Of earth-sprung kind concede
> They all must perish, Thou alone remain,
> The secret of whose strength doth quite exceed
> Our thought, as Thou transcendest our frail plane.[22]

Over seventy years after ibn Gabirol's death, Judah Halevi, another contributor to what had become a golden age for the composition of Hebrew religious poetry in Spain, wrote in Arabic between 1140 and 1170 a very different sort of philosophical treatise. His *Kuzari*, cast in the form of a dramatic dialogue like the dialogues composed by Plato, imagined a discussion between the king of the Khazars and a rabbi about the place of Judaism within world history. The Khazars had indeed adopted Judaism some 400 years before (see Chapter 9), but the significant historical background to Judah Halevi's great work was the struggle between Muslims and Christians for control of his home town of Toledo and the precarious destiny of Jews between these two powers.[23]

The aim of the *Kuzari* was to demonstrate the inadequacy of philosophy and the supremacy of revelation – and specifically the superior revelation vouchsafed by God to the Jews. Halevi insisted that God is known through experience, and especially the history of Israel, and not by abstract speculation about the First Cause. He asserted that the ancient philosophers could justify their preference for rational arguments on the grounds 'that they did not have the benefit of prophecy or of the light of revelation' and that for this they were not to blame: 'Rather, they deserve our praise for what they managed to achieve simply through the force of rational argument. Their intentions were good, they established the laws of thought, and they rejected the pleasures of this world. They may, in any case, be granted superiority, since they were not obliged to accept our opinions. We, however, are obliged to accept whatever we see with our own eyes, or any well-founded tradition, which is tantamount to seeing for oneself.' Halevi's assertion of the glorious place of Israel in history may have been composed in Arabic, but it was written in Hebrew characters and peppered with Hebrew citations. It was never likely to be mistaken for the work of a Christian as ibn Gabirol's *Fons Vitae* had been.[24]

Halevi's attack on the philosophers recognized the fundamental role that philosophy now played within the intellectual circles of Spanish Jewry in his time, and especially the upper stratum of court Jews to which he himself belonged. In these circles wealthy individuals of different religious connections shared a cultured lifestyle of poetry, music and literature and a common education in an Aristotelian philosophical curriculum which had developed in the Islamic school curriculum in Alexandria, Baghdad and Islamic Spain. The degree of tolerance to be found in the *convivencia*, in which the three cultures of Islam, Christianity and Judaism flourished symbiotically, should not be exaggerated, but what was remarkable about the religious life of this mixed society was its intellectual openness, as much for the Jewish and Christian minorities as for the Muslims who ruled over them.[25]

The culmination within Judaism of the impact of this Islamic culture on the Mediterranean world was the career and astonishing influence, during and after the twelfth century, of Moses b. Maimon. Maimonides' prolific output in the codification of halakhah, already noted in respect of the *Mishneh Torah* (p. 315), was allied to a determination to reconcile philosophy with the Jewish tradition. Both gave him exceptional influence among Jews from the western to the eastern ends of the Mediterranean Sea and ignited a controversy, which was to rage for centuries after his death, over the role of reason within Judaism. The extent of his influence on later generations was summed up by a sentence which began to circulate in rabbinic circles a century after his death: 'From Moses to Moses there was none like to Moses.'[26]

The influence of Maimonides owes something to the travels imposed upon him both by his personal circumstances and by the considerable changes in the Islamic world in his lifetime. Cordoba had already been the capital of al-Andalus, the Arabic name for Muslim Spain, for some 400 years when Maimonides was born there in 1138, and the great

Mezquita (mosque) had long dominated the urban landscape. With a huge population of Arabs, Berbers, Vandals, Visigoths and Jews, the city had been established under the rule of the Caliphate as a cultural beacon for science, medicine, philosophy, poetry and art. The Islamic library of Hakam II was said to hold over 400,000 books, and, although it was dispersed after his death, both the book market and scholarship continued to flourish in Maimonides' time – the great philosopher and polymath ibn Rushd, known to Christian Europe as Averroes, was an older contemporary in the city.

Maimonides grew up here under the Berber Almoravid dynasty, which gave relative protection to its religious minorities, including the Jews, in the fashion standard in Islamic law. But when he was ten the city was captured by the Almohads, a new dynasty, also of Berber origin, whose interpretation of Islamic Sunni law was far less liberal and may have compelled Maimonides' family to convert nominally to Islam. The change of regime was to alter Maimonides' life completely. The family left Cordoba either for Christian Spain in the north or for Seville. But in 1160, when Maimonides was twenty-two, he moved to Fez, close to the Almohad capital, before travelling east in c. 1165 towards Palestine, at that time under Crusader control. Maimonides did not reach Palestine but settled in Egypt, where in due course he became doctor to the Ayyubid court in Cairo, until his death in 1204. Nor were his personal peregrinations the only basis for his international outlook. In a central period of his life in Egypt Maimonides was engaged in trade in precious stones, which involved contacts far to the east – his brother David was drowned in the Indian Ocean on a trading expedition. And Maimonides was also much in contact with the Jewish communities both of Provence (which included the Pyrenees) and of northern France and the Rhineland, whose independence from Jewish authorities in the Islamic world was increasingly affirmed precisely in Maimonides' lifetime, not least because Christian Europe was itself asserting its power against the spread of Islam in the slow Reconquista of Spain.[27]

Maimonides' *Guide for the Perplexed* was intended for those who wished to follow both the Torah and philosophy. He insisted that the two were perfectly compatible. Aristotelian notions, which Maimonides knew from translations into Arabic by Muslim scholars in the ninth and tenth centuries, were placed in defence of the Torah on the assumption that Aristotle's philosophy was true – in all aspects apart from his theory of the eternity of the universe, which Maimonides believed conflicted with the Bible and therefore must be wrong:

There are three opinions of human beings, namely, of all those who believe that there is an existent deity, with regard to the eternity of the world or its production in time. The first opinion, which is the opinion of all who believe in the Law of Moses our Master, peace be on him, is that the world as a whole – I mean to say, every existent other than God, may He be exalted – was brought into existence by God after having been purely and absolutely non-existent, and that God, may He be exalted, had existed alone, and nothing else – neither an angel nor a sphere nor what subsists within the sphere. Afterwards, through His will and His volition, He brought into existence out of nothing all the beings as they are, time itself being one of the created things. For time is consequent upon motion, and motion is an accident in what is moved.

Maimonides' *Guide* was to have immense impact on his Jewish contemporaries, but less for his technical discussion of specific issues (such as his proofs for the existence, incorporeality and unity of God, and his interpretation of the nature of providence which claims that free will is not affected by God's omniscience and foreknowledge) than for his general justification for using philosophy as a guide to religion and a way to understanding the apparently irrational parts of the Bible. The *Guide* tackled how to speak about God in human language. It squared the anthropomorphism in the Bible with a philosophical understanding of the nature of the divine, and demonstrated that the commandments of the Torah have a rational purpose, to develop the moral and intellectual potential of men. Maimonides' role in bringing Aristotle to Jews was to be paralleled in the next century among Christians by Aquinas.[28]

Philosophy underlay all of Maimonides' contributions to the history of Judaism, despite their great variety. Before the age of twenty-three he had written a treatise on logic. His codification of halakhah in the *Mishneh Torah*, discussed above, insisted that 'a man should never cast his reason behind him, for the eyes are set in front, not in back'. His insistence on clarity of ideas as the base of Judaism was encapsulated in his *Commentary on the Mishnah*, which he had completed by the age of thirty, soon after his arrival in Egypt. It was within this *Commentary*, in a discussion of a brief portion of the Mishnaic tractate *Sanhedrin* which categorized sinners who will not inherit a portion of the world to come, that Maimonides first laid out thirteen fundamental principles of the Torah, which he enumerated as follows:

1. The existence of the Creator: There is a being who exists in the most perfect mode of existence, and he is the cause of the existence of all other

beings. 2. The unity of God: His oneness is not like that of a simple body which is numerically one . . . Rather he is one with a oneness that is absolutely unique . . . 3. The denial of corporeality to God: none of the accidents of bodies, such as motion and rest, appertain to him either by essence or by accident. 4. God's pre-existence. 5. God is the one who should be worshipped and exalted. 6. Prophecy. 7. The prophecy of Moses our Teacher: we should believe that Moses was the father of all the prophets. 8. The Torah is from heaven: we should believe that the whole Torah which is in our possession today is the same Torah as was handed down to Moses, and that in its entirety it is from the mouth of the Almighty. That is to say, that the whole Torah came to him from God in a manner which is metaphorically called 'speaking', though no one knows the real nature of that communication save Moses to whom it came. He fulfilled the function of a scribe receiving dictation. 9. Abrogation: this Torah of Moses will not be abrogated, nor shall another Torah come from God. 10. God has knowledge of the deeds of men and does not disregard them. 11. God rewards him who obeys the commands of the Torah and punishes him who transgresses its prohibitions. 12. The Messianic Age: we should believe and affirm that the Messiah will come. 13. The resurrection of the dead.

The thirteen principles were effectively a creed. They have generated both enthusiastic endorsement and strong dissent down to the present day.[29]

Some of Maimonides' stances in his philosophical Judaism seem to have been inspired by opposition to the claims of Islam, but the relationship between his thought and Islam was complex not least because he came into contact with Muslims of very different kinds. The Sunni Almoravids under whose rule he had been born were generally opposed to rational speculation altogether, whereas the Shiite Fatimids who were in control of Egypt when Maimonides first arrived there developed an Ismaili theology based on Neoplatonism. The Sunni Ayyubids in whose circles he ended his days adopted the distinctive speculative theology associated with the Persian philosopher and mystic Ghazali, whose books had been publicly burned in the Maghreb by the Almoravids in 1109. In adopting one element of Islamic theology, then, Maimonides might implicitly decry the approach of a different branch of Islam, and there is evidence from his letters that he was aware of the need to be careful about the impact his work might have in relation to his Muslim patrons. But one distinctive example of his inheritance from Almohad Islam, which had so dominated Maimonides' life as an exile from

Cordoba in his teenage years and as a young man living outwardly as a Muslim, may be the insistence on God's unity and the wish to ground it in a definition of right belief to root out heresy – hence the need for a creed. Maimonides' thirteen principles were to be enshrined in the synagogue liturgy in the form of the hymn *Yigdal*, composed in Rome probably in the fourteenth century and in widespread use since then at the conclusion of the evening services of Sabbaths and festivals:

> Great is the living God and praised.
> He exists, and His existence is beyond time.
> He is One, and there is no unity like His.
> Unfathomable, His oneness is infinite . . .
> At the end of days He will send our Messiah,
> to redeem those who await His final salvation.
> God will revive the dead in His great lovingkindness.
> Blessed for evermore is His glorious name![30]

Maimonides wrote primarily in Judaeo-Arabic, but in his forties he wrote the *Mishneh Torah* in Mishnaic Hebrew, and he later cooperated with the translation into Hebrew by Shmuel ibn Tibbon, a rabbi in Lunel in Provence, of his philosophical *Guide*. He seems to have become increasingly aware of the need to use Hebrew in order to reach a Jewish readership in Christian Europe for whom Arabic, even in Hebrew characters, was inaccessible. The wide distribution of Maimonides' prolific correspondence has become clear with the discovery of numerous letters in his hand from the Cairo Genizah. It is hard to fathom how he found the time to compose his medical treatises, or to fulfil his duties as the leader of a fractious and fractured Jewish community in Cairo.[31]

The exceptional influence of Maimonides as communal leader and halakhist during his lifetime – one of the titles ascribed to him was that of 'the Great Eagle', from the biblical book of Ezekiel, signifying his quasi-royal status within the Jewish community – both lent authority to his philosophical treatises and rendered them vulnerable to attack. Polemic against his halakhic writings was already fierce in Maimonides' lifetime, as we have seen, but the attack on his philosophy gathered momentum only in the decades after his death. The strongest polemics were by some of the rabbis in Provence most involved in mystical circles (see p. 352), with objections specifically to Maimonides' belief that resurrection (which he, like his opponents, reckoned a fundamental tenet of Judaism) would be of the soul rather than the body (although Maimonides himself, in his *Treatise on Resurrection*, argued that a spiritual concept need not conflict with the notion that the soul might return to the body). The hardening of positions between rationalists and mystics was encouraged by upheavals in the wider world, both Jewish and Christian. The Maimonidean controversy in the twelfth century was parallel to the conflict in Christian circles between Peter Abelard and Bernard of Clairvaux, but with the added stimulus for Jews of Crusader armies passing through the Rhineland and the Reconquista in the Iberian peninsula, with the dread that rational religion would not work.[32]

Meir b. Todros haLevi Abulafia, originally from Castile but teaching in Toledo, precipitated the attack, noting that if there is no bodily resurrection, 'to what end did the bodies stand watch for their God, did they go in darkness for the sake of their God? If the bodies are not resurrected, where is their hope and where are they to look for it?' Opponents of Maimonides attacked all attempts to explain miracles rationally. Maimonides' supporters responded by allegorizing all the more, with miraculous tales in the Talmud providing much suitable material. Opponents of Maimonides in Spain and Provence called for support from the rabbis of northern France, whose admired expertise in the Talmud and halakhah had never been sullied with knowledge of Aristotle. Their support was encouraged by distaste for the luxurious way of life enjoyed by the philosophically educated Jews of Islamic Spain. Philosophy did not in itself lead to hedonism, but it must have looked that way to the impoverished Jews of northern Europe. Such prejudices were acknowledged in the thirteenth century by the only rabbinic leader from Spain with sufficient stature to mediate between the parties, Moshe b. Nahman, also known as Nahmanides or Ramban.[33]

Nahmanides' own halakhic works synthesized the traditions of talmudic analysis in northern France with the analytical methods of Maimonides, and he was sufficiently involved in mystical and messianic speculation to receive a sympathetic hearing from the kabbalists of Provence in the 1230s, not least because his search for the deeper meaning of the biblical text led him to oppose Maimonides' search for rational explanation for miracles. But he was horrified by the *herem* (ban) imposed in 1232 by the rabbis of Provence on the study of Maimonides' philosophy, and by the attempts of the Provençal rabbis to persuade the talmudists of northern France to enforce a similar ban. Nahmanides' letter to the rabbis of northern France arguing against the ban asserted not that philosophy was good in itself, but that in the hands of Maimonides it had been an important weapon in the fight to keep from more profound error the upper-class Jews of Spain, who 'have filled their bellies with the food . . . of the Greeks', so that if it were not for the writings of Maimonides 'they would have lapsed almost entirely'.[34]

Such mediation was in vain in light of the passions on both sides and the clarity of the arguments both for and against the deployment of philosophy for better understanding the Torah. As each side banned the other, with a welter of letters, sermons and polemical commentaries circulating widely and rabbis travelling from one camp to the other to gain supporters, the battle came to the attention of the Christian authorities. In 1232 the Dominicans in Provence intervened by burning books of Maimonides as heretical. The shock to all involved in the controversy was immense. It was said that Jonah b. Avraham Gerondi, a leading partisan in Provence and Spain among the opponents of Maimonides, repented so deeply his involvement in the struggle that he planned a pilgrimage to Maimonides' tomb in Tiberias in Palestine, where Maimonides' body had been carried after his death.

These differences between rationalist and non-rationalist Jews within rabbinic Judaism paled beside events in Paris, where a certain Nicholas Donin, a Jew who had been excommunicated by his teacher, R. Yehiel b. Joseph, for his heretical views in repudiating the oral Torah in a fashion similar to Karaites, apostatized to Christianity, joined the Franciscans and attacked the Talmud as an obscene text full of blasphemies against Jesus, Mary and Christianity. In the ensuing disputation, held in Paris in 1240 with papal support, the Talmud was condemned, and twenty-four wagonloads of talmudic works were burned in 1242. Both sides of the Maimonidean controversy would have agreed with the desperate arguments presented by R. Yehiel to Queen Blanche against the desecration of what was, for philosophers and mystics as much as halakhists, the basis of their faith:

> The Talmud is very ancient and no one has complained about it before. Your learned Jerome knew all Jewish knowledge, including the Talmud, and he would have said something if there had been anything wrong with it. Why should we have to stand for our life against this sinner, who denied the authority of the Talmud and refused to believe in anything except the Torah of Moses without interpretation? But you all know that everything requires interpretation. It was for that reason that we excommunicated him, and from that time he has plotted against us. But we will die rather than give up the Talmud, which is the apple of our eye. Even if you should decide to burn the Talmud in France, it will continue to be studied in the

rest of the world, for we Jews are dispersed throughout the world. Our bodies, but not our souls, are in your hands.[35]

The issues which had caused such strife were too deeply based to disappear altogether, and by the end of the century passions were aroused by the extent to which allegorizing was adopted by the rationalists. In Barcelona in the late thirteenth century, Shlomo b. Avraham Adret, known as Rashba, sought a compromise. Despite his opposition to extreme allegorizing, he himself had studied philosophy, and he defended Maimonides' philosophical writings. But he was concerned that philosophy and other secular studies would distract young students from the Torah 'which is above these sciences' and issued a ban on 26 July 1305, stating that 'we have decreed for ourselves, for our children and for all those that join us, that for the next fifty years and under threat of being banned from the community, no one among us under the age of twenty-five shall study either in the original or in translation books written by the Greeks on religious philosophy or natural science ... Excluded, however, from this general ban are books on the science of medicine.'

For many rationalist rabbis by this date, such a ban was not acceptable, even if they did not themselves indulge in philosophy, and Menahem Meiri, a great talmudist from Perpignan in Provence, wrote explicitly to Adret in opposition, pointing to the (by now) many talmudic scholars who had been philosophers. A younger contemporary from Provence, Yosef b. Abba Mari Caspi, who wrote a commentary on Maimonides' *Guide* and indeed went further than Maimonides in accepting Aristotelian arguments by arguing for the eternity of the universe, left in a testamentary letter to his son an outline of the educational curriculum he believed most suitable for the young. It included, alongside practical sciences and ethics, the study of logic, theology, Aristotle's *Metaphysics* and (of course) Maimonides' *Guide*:

> There are, my son, two dispositions among contemporary Jews which must be firmly avoided by thee. The first class consists of those of superficial knowledge, whose studies have not gone far enough. They are destroyers and rebels, scoff at the words of the Rabbis of blessed memory, treat the practical precepts as of little account, and accept unseemly interpretations of biblical narratives. They betray unmistakably their inadequate acquaintance with the philosophical writings of Aristotle and his disciples ... The second class referred to above includes those of our people who hold in contempt genuine philosophy as presented in the works of Aristotle and

his like. Now, my son, I do not blame this class because they devote all their time to the Talmudic argumentation . . . My son! When thou meetest such men, address them thus: My masters! What sin did your fathers detect in the study of logic and philosophy? Is it a terrible crime to use words with accuracy? And then, what say ye of the work of Aristotle and Maimonides? Have you examined the inside of their books? If ye know more than their covers, ye know of a surety that the books are an exposition and justification of our precious precepts. If you are advanced in years, and have not yet read the words of the philosophers . . . then open your ears before the sun be darkened![36]

Assertion of the value of Aristotle's *Metaphysics*, and acceptance of Aristotelian arguments for the eternity of the world, aligned Caspi with his Provençal contemporary, Levi b. Gershon, known also as Gersonides or Ralbag, the last Jewish theologian to make extensive use of Aristotelian philosophy. Gersonides' *Wars of the Lord* covered in six books the immortality of the soul, prophecy, divine knowledge, divine providence, astronomy and mathematics, and the creation of the world. These were the major philosophical issues of the time, and, despite his great Jewish learning as Bible commentator and talmudist, Gersonides (in contrast to Maimonides, whose work he often subjected to criticism) placed Aristotle's arguments on these topics to the fore rather than the revelations of the Jewish tradition, turning for his understanding of Aristotle to the works of Maimonides' contemporary in twelfth-century Spain, the Islamic philosopher Averroes (ibn Rushd), on whose works he wrote commentaries.[37]

By the mid-fourteenth century, after the death of Gersonides, Aristotelian rationality was to lose its appeal for many Jewish thinkers in Spain, as other approaches to Torah, and especially mysticism, grew in popularity and Islamic influence waned with the retreat of Muslim control from southern Spain. Hasdai b. Abraham Crescas, who came from Barcelona and was appointed by the Christian Kingdom of Aragon from 1387 as crown rabbi to represent the Jewish community to the government, wrote at the end of his life in 1410 a fierce critique of the Aristotelian tradition within Judaism. He attacked Gersonides as heretical and advocated replacing the views of Maimonides (whom he called 'the Master') with what he presented as a more Jewish form of Judaism. In Crescas' writings, what was left of the philosophical approach was to be found less in specific doctrines than in rationalist methods. Crescas, as much as those scholastics he criticized, wrote about proofs, propositions, principles and reason, even though he claimed that (for instance) authority for the existence of God must be attributed only to the Bible. For Crescas, like Maimonides primarily a communal leader and close to the ruling powers of the time, Aristotelianism was dangerous because it had been used by Jewish intellectuals to justify deserting Judaism. It is of course ironic that Crescas' own polemic showed an intimate knowledge of the tradition he attacked. His attacks on Aristotle's philosophy should be seen alongside his *Refutation of the Principles of the Christians*, published in Catalan in 1397–8, which contained a fiercely logical critique of major Christian doctrines such as original sin, the Trinity, incarnation and the virgin birth in an effort to win back Jewish apostates to Christianity.[38]

A similar impulse to respond to the threat of Christianity lay behind the *Book of Principles* of Crescas' pupil Yosef Albo. Albo was one of the spokesmen for the Jews in a very public and protracted forced disputation in Tortosa from January 1413 to April 1414, as a result of which many Jews converted to Christianity, encouraged undoubtedly also by memories of the communal violence suffered by the Jews of Aragon in 1391 during which the son of Crescas himself had been a victim of murder. Albo's book, with its focus on law as the basis of salvation, contains an implicit anti-Christian message in the relegation of belief in a messiah to a level below that of a principle in Judaism. According to Albo, a failure to believe that a messiah would come might be a sin but it would not constitute heresy. Albo knew the works of Christian scholastics such as Thomas Aquinas, and in disputes with Christians he was acutely aware of the weaknesses of Maimonides' formulation of thirteen principles of faith, including the hope in a future messiah. Crescas had proposed a shorter list of six principles, which Albo in turn whittled down to three: the existence of God, divine revelation, and reward and punishment. It is ironic that this list of three principles, which Albo probably borrowed from his older contemporary Shimon b. Tsemach Duran (who taught in Algiers after an anti-Jewish outbreak in his native Majorca in 1391), was taken originally from the Islamic Aristotelian Averroes, who had asserted that anyone denying any one of these principles is an unbeliever in Islam. Albo's *Book of Principles* was to be immensely popular in later generations, helped by the availability of a printed edition from 1485.[39]

By the fifteenth century a philosophical approach to religious ideas had thus come to seem natural to many Jews, even while the balance of authority between reason and revelation remained a constant point of dispute. Thus Yitzhak Arama, a Spanish rabbi of the second half of the fifteenth century, adopted from Christian sermons the practice of presenting philosophical ideas in weekly addresses in the synagogue in light of the Torah reading for that Sabbath. He used appropriate rabbinic texts and a skilful use of allegory to popularize philosophical ideas for a wide audience. So, for instance, 'In the beginning God created the heavens and the earth' was to be explained by stating that 'in the very beginning God brought the heavens and the earth out of absolute non-existence. The word "Heavens" points to the two elements, the spiritual world (intelligences) which had to be created first and also the matter of the spheres that was closest to God in the order of creation.'

But Arama's own confidence in human reason was limited, since he knew from the biblical text that the tree of knowledge as described in the Garden of Eden was a tree of knowledge of evil as well as good, and that human reason, which could do so much good if tempered with faith, would veer towards evil if allowed to overflow the boundaries of faith. The 'true science' for Arama was not philosophy but kabbalah. He was one of the first commentators on the Torah to use as a classical source the Zohar, the most influential text produced by the mystics of medieval Judaism who had led so much of the opposition to the rationalism of philosophy.[40]

THE ZOHAR AND KABBALAH

Where in the minutiae of living according to the halakhah, the rationalization of philosophy and the scholastic arguments of the talmudists were medieval Jews to find a sense of the transcendence of the divine? The ethereal architecture of the Cordoba Mezquita in Islamic Spain and the great cathedrals of northern Europe which instilled religious awe in their Muslim and Christian contemporaries had no architectural counterpart in the religious lives of Jews, both because medieval Jewish communities were small and had no need for synagogues on a grand scale and, in many cases, because of restrictions placed by Christian authorities on the height of Jewish buildings, which were not to exceed that of neighbouring churches. Those Jews with wealth to expend on religious architecture lavished it on the interior decorations. The synagogue of Worms, founded in 1034 for a merchant community which flourished under royal protection and was home to a series of rabbinic scholars expert in halakhah, remained a plain rectangle even after its internal space was rearranged at the end of the twelfth century, with a double nave formed by Romanesque columns similar to those used in the contemporary construction of Worms cathedral. These were buildings designed to provide a sense of solemnity to communal gatherings, which increasingly in medieval communities were centred on the synagogue even when the subject for meeting was not itself religious, but they did not lift the spirit. Exceptional was the remarkable Altneuschul of Prague, an impressive Gothic building with a double nave modelled on contemporary Christian architecture; built in 1270, it is still in use today.[41]

For some medieval Jews – as for some medieval Christians – a sense of transcendence was found in mystical speculation, although as we shall see the circles in which such mysticism flourished remained restricted throughout the Middle Ages. Mystics had already speculated on the nature of the divine realm in the talmudic period, as we saw in our discussion of Hekhalot mysticism (Chapter 11), but mysticism only really began to take a more central role in common liturgy and prayers, and to find its way into all other areas of Jewish religious life (including halakhah), with the promulgation of the extraordinary work called the Zohar ('Splendour') in the last decades of the thirteenth century. The Zohar, a disorganized collection of twenty or so separate treatises in a stilted form of Aramaic invented with a partial knowledge of the language in order to sound impressive and exalted (see below), brought into the mainstream of Jewish religious thinking a mystical theology which took the biblical narratives as symbolic of the divine world and explained the world through the divine attributes that emanate from the hidden God.

If one takes the Zohar at its own estimation, this mystical theology constitutes a higher knowledge than halakhah and comes straight from scripture through the interpretation of the second-century rabbinic sage Shimon bar Yohai. Shimon, who had lived in Palestine at the time of the Bar Kokhba war in the second century CE and was believed to have hidden in a cave for seven years in order to escape the Romans, was thought to have composed the Zohar under the inspiration of the prophet Elijah, thus uncovering sublime truths:

> Rabbi Shimon said, 'Woe to the man who says that the Torah intends to set
> forth mere tales and common talk! If that were so, then we could at once
> compose a torah out of common talk, one of much greater worth. If the
> Torah intends to disclose everyday matters, then the princes of the world

possess books of greater excellence. Let us seek those out and make a torah of them. However, all the words of Torah are sublime and supernal mysteries. Observe: the upper world and the lower world are in perfect balance – Israel below corresponding to the angels above ... The Torah has a body ... the commandments of the Torah which are called "bodies", i.e. main principles, "of the Torah". This body is clothed in garments made up of earthly tales. Foolish people look only at those garments, the tales of the Torah: they know nothing more and do not look at what is beneath the garment. Those who are wiser look not at the garment, but at the body beneath. But the true Sages, the servants of the Most High King, those who stood at Mount Sinai, look only at the soul of the Torah, which is the root principle of all, the true Torah, and in the world to come they are destined to look at the soul of the soul of the Torah.'

But the Zohar was in fact very much a reflection of Jewish life in a medieval Christian world – hence, for instance, the frequent references in the Zohar to God as a three-fold unity, apparently deliberately promulgating an anti-Christian version of the Christian Trinity.[42]

We shall have more to say below (p. 349) on the Zohar itself, but the Zohar was the heir of a well-established mystical tradition. We have seen above how pietists in the Rhineland and northern France from the second half of the twelfth century to the thirteenth century developed an intense form of ethics encapsulated in the immensely popular *Sefer Hasidim*. The same circles developed a series of esoteric teachings in the cities of Worms and Mainz, particularly under the leadership of members of the Kalonymus family which (as we have seen) had migrated from Lucca in northern Italy to Mainz in the tenth century and acted as communal leaders for the Rhineland communities before and after the First Crusade.

It is not clear whether the Kalonymus family brought mystical teachings with them from Italy or just developed mystical ideas once in the Rhineland. More clearly products of the Rhineland are the series of books written by R. Eleazar b. Yehudah of Worms after 1217, in which he celebrated the total spirituality and transcendence of God, from whose concealed being the visible glory emanates to connect the divine to creation. These books must owe something to the trauma Eleazar had undergone when his wife and daughters had been slaughtered by Crusaders before his eyes, but the metaphysics of his theology were not really coherent. Like others of the Hasidei Ashkenaz he seems to have been more concerned with the achievement of piety through penitence.

It was characteristic of the Hasidei Ashkenaz to emphasize exceptional care and precision in prayer, down to amassing great quantities of esoteric numerological lore as a way to focus on the petitions, which they preferred to learn by heart rather than read so that they could focus solely on the worship itself.[43]

Among the different mystical notions developed by other mystics in the same region at this time, foremost was speculation on the role of the term 'Unique Cherub' as an anthropomorphic designation of the divine Being. This notion was found in a number of anonymous or pseudepigraphic texts and had been cited by R. Elhanan b. Yaakov of London in the early thirteenth century. By the end of this century these ideas were being attributed to Judah the Pious, a cousin and contemporary of Eleazar of Worms. But they are hardly compatible with the mystical teachings espoused by Eleazar and others of the Kalonymus family and must in fact have originated in other groups, perhaps in northern France rather than the Rhineland. It is possible that the asceticism of the Hasidei Ashkenaz, in particular their practice of mortification of the flesh, owes something to Christian influence, especially from the Franciscans, although such asceticism was known in earlier Jewish tradition both in the Second Temple period and in rabbinic culture in talmudic times, and the parallels with Christian asceticism, which are never acknowledged in our sources, may simply reflect an age in which such types of religious self-expression seemed natural.[44]

Christian influence of a very different kind may also explain in part the dualist elements of the distinctive mystical doctrines espoused by an unknown author in northern Spain or Provence who composed, probably at the end of the twelfth century, Sefer haBahir, the 'Book of Brightness'. Sefer haBahir may well have been shaped by the influence of the Cathars, who espoused a strong dualism involving a God of goodness opposed to a God of evil. Catharism became so prevalent in these years in Languedoc that in 1209 it provoked the Albigensian Crusade in which Christians from northern France endeavoured to instil the true faith into Cathar heretics in the south – through slaughter, if necessary. Written in the form of a *midrash* attributed to rabbis of the time of the Mishnah, with many teachings presented in the form of parables, Sefer haBahir discusses the nature of the divine in a series of images, including that of an upside-down tree. The author claimed to record a sequence of utterances by God and assigned a major role (for the first time in Jewish mystical speculation) to a feminine aspect of the divine in the form of the Shekhinah (the 'divine presence'). The noun *Shekhinah* is feminine in form, but it was an innovation in *Sefer haBahir* that this feminine aspect was emphasized by the author.[45]

One has a strong impression that the mystics who produced such works operated either independently of each other or in small groups. They cited each other's works only when it suited them. In contrast to the constraints of Christian theology, or indeed the development of halakhah or philosophical theories within Judaism, mystical speculation was comparatively free. Mutual accusations were certainly made, as we shall see (p. 347), but there was no notion for Jews (as there was for Christians) that a failure to depict correctly the nature of the divine world would inevitably lead to a charge of heresy. In *Sefer haBahir* the origins of evil were said to lie in the divine itself, in the fingers of God's left hand, and the female aspect of the divine world was identified as the source of evil. Similar notions can be found in early Christian Gnostic texts, as well as Cathar doctrines, but neither influence explains the adoption by the author of *Sefer haBahir* of a belief in the transmigration of the soul after death: the notion may have been held by Pharisees back in the period of the Second Temple (see Chapter 6), and it was apparently held by some Jews in the tenth century, since Saadiah as well as his Karaite contemporaries specifically censured the doctrine as 'foolish', but it had not been adopted before within rabbinic circles.[46]

Apparently contemporaneous with the author of *Sefer haBahir* were the theosophical speculations in Provence of the Rabad and his son Isaac the Blind. It was in their time that the term 'kabbalah' first became standard for such speculation. The choice of term (translated literally as 'reception') is significant, since it implied that the doctrines being discovered by intense concentration on the biblical texts and the nature of the universe were in fact already known from antiquity and needed only to be rediscovered: it was precisely their alleged ancient origins that gave them their authority. Flourishing at the same time either in Provence or across the Pyrenees in Castile was a set of mystics whose theosophy was influenced by two other anonymous works, the speculative *Sefer haIyyun* ('The Book of Contemplation'), which described ten (or in some versions thirteen) powers which emanated from the divine, and the ruminations found in *Maayan haHokhma* ('The Spring of Wisdom'), which explained the origins of the world in part through sequences of primal letters. The authors of the quite numerous short mystical treatises that survive from this period were distinguished as much by their independence of thought as by the notions they had in common. The ascription of their books to ancient figures – *Maayan haHokhma* was ascribed to Moses himself – seems to mask real mystical contemplation, much as pseudepigraphy may have disguised real visions in the creation of pseudepigraphic apocalypses in the period of the Second Temple.

The aim of this theosophical kabbalah was theological understanding, reached not, as in philosophical circles (Jewish as well as Christian and Islamic), by logical arguments about the nature of the divine but by deep contemplation of the concealed meanings of ancient texts, especially the Bible. Such contemplation could bring to light the nature of God and his relation to the world as revealed by God himself in the interstices of scripture. This was mysticism as an offshoot of the esoteric scholarly curriculum which constituted rabbinic study, to be combined with that curriculum, and not to be attempted by anyone without sufficient training to enter such elite circles. Kabbalah was to have immense influence on the future of Judaism as lived by Jews at all levels of learning and none, but it began as an adjunct to the talmudic study which was the staple of rabbinic Judaism in the Middle Ages.

The mystics who produced many of these writings are often described by historians as a circle simply because of the similarity of their ideas, but precisely how they related to each other is unknown. We are however on firmer ground in depicting the growth in Girona in north-eastern Spain in the mid-thirteenth century of the first centre of kabbalah in the Iberian peninsula under the leadership of Ezra b. Solomon and of Azriel b. Menahem. Former students of Isaac the Blind, they combined the doctrines of *Sefer haBahir* with Neoplatonic terminology, systematically amalgamating the new symbols of the kabbalah with stories from the Talmud. The Girona mystics, who designated themselves a 'Sacred Association' (*havurah kedoshah*), assumed like other kabbalists that esoteric knowledge must be the preserve of a privileged elite. But they had a decisive effect in the spread of these theosophic ideas through the Torah commentary of their compatriot Nahmanides (see p. 336), in which mystical doctrines were revealed to a wider Jewish readership.[47]

Wholly different from the sedentary speculations of Nahmanides and the Girona mystics was the ecstatic mysticism of their younger contemporary Abraham Abulafia, whose speculations about the divine world stemmed from an adventurous and dramatic life. Born in Saragossa, and brought up in Tudela in Navarre, Abulafia travelled at the age of twenty to the other end of the Mediterranean to seek in the land of Israel the mythical River Sambatyon, only to be thwarted in Acre by the wars between Muslims and Christians in the Holy Land and forced to return to Europe. Travelling via Greece, he stopped off in Italy and began in Verona to study the kabbalah through commentaries on *Sefer Yetsirah*. After a brief return to Spain, where he started to gather around him a select group of disciples, he returned again to Italy, Sicily or Greece in 1273 and began to propagate the notion that the great Maimonides had, in the *Guide for the Perplexed*, really been a kabbalist. A series of short 'Books of Prophecy' attracted a group of scholars to gather round him and in 1280 an inner voice prompted him to travel to Rome to ask Pope Nicholas III to end the sufferings of the Jews; in response to his plea he was sentenced to death by burning, which was averted only because the pope died in August of that year.

By this stage a celebrity, and keenly aware of all he had discovered since 'when I was thirty-one, in the city of Barcelona, God awakened me from my sleep', Abulafia caused a great stir with an announcement that the Messiah was to come in the Jewish year 5050, which corresponded to 1290 of the Common Era, and coincided with his own fiftieth year. Abulafia's views on messianism were complex, but it is highly likely that at times he thought of himself as the Messiah. In any case, the announcement caused uproar, persuading many to prepare to travel to the land of Israel but also provoking condemnation by the leading halakhist in Spain, Shlomo b. Avraham Adret of Barcelona (Rashba), who called Abulafia a charlatan. Reduced to living in exile on the island of Comino near Malta, Abulafia defended himself vigorously in a series of treatises aimed at his critics and a number of mystical works, including a commentary on the Torah and a commentary on *Sefer Yetsirah*.[48]

Abulafia picked up from the Hasidei Ashkenaz of the Rhineland the doctrine of divine emanations, to which (unlike them) he applied the technical term *sefirot* (literally 'enumerations') (see above, p. 282). He enlarged on their techniques of combining letters (*tseruf*), adding up the number equivalent of the letters in words (*gematria*) and taking the letters and words as symbolic of sentences (*notarikon*) in order to discover hidden meanings in scriptural texts. But he also believed that the 'Way of the Divine Name' enabled men to commune directly with God through prophetic power, an enlightened state of consciousness which brought not just knowledge but redemption and enjoyment in the present world of the delights of the world to come. This was a form of practical mysticism quite distinct from the speculation of the theosophists in Girona – which Abulafia himself rejected, as they in turn rejected his teachings. Others, however, adopted his ideas with enthusiasm, as is clear from the numerous manuscripts of his writings which survive.[49]

Abulafia's ecstatic mysticism was based on pseudo-rationality, as is clear from his attempt to foist his ideas on to Maimonides, and in this respect his doctrines were similar to those of Sufism in Islam. In Abulafia's case, this is unlikely to have resulted from direct Islamic influence, but in Egypt the descendants of Maimonides (in particular his son Abraham and grandson Obadiah) advocated quite specifically the adoption of Sufi practices by Jews as a way to attain perfection and union with God:

> Firstly it behoves you to reduce your intercourse with common folk ... Then you must inure yourself to speak little except that which causes you gain in this world and happiness in the hereafter ... Next you must amend your diet as much as you can, decreasing your relish until you become accustomed to partake infrequently of food, so that your thoughts desist therefrom. Strive also to reduce your slumber ... Then train your soul progressively to think of nothing else but Him or that which draws you near to Him until your soul waxes strong enough to help you to obtain the end to which you aspire. Furthermore, at prayer time, purify your intention and be thoroughly mindful of what you utter. Lo, after having attained to this state, so passionate will be your rapture that you shalt not suffer to be separated from Him, even for an instant. And as your bliss increases, so will your passion increase and you will no longer delight in food nor drink nor rest.

Jewish Sufi texts, written in Arabic, belong firmly in the tradition of Islamic Sufism and display much more contact with Muslim mystics such as ibn Arabi than with other branches of Jewish mysticism. We have already seen how the moral teachings of Bahya ibn Pakuda in eleventh-century Spain show traces of Sufi influence.

But, like the reformist teachings of the Hasidei Ashkenaz at the heart of Rhineland Jewish spiritual life in the same period, and indeed as with the absolute poverty espoused by later Christian mystics like St Theresa of Avila, this movement too demonstrated how an intense religiosity among the leaders of a community could lead to ethical and philosophical teachings taking on a distinct mystical tinge. The pious were urged to seek a life as the spiritual heirs of the biblical prophets, especially Elijah, through asceticism, mastery of the passions, and concentration of thought on God, 'attiring themselves in the garment of rags and suchlike garment[s] of the poor resembling the dress of the Sufis in our days, and [also to their assumption of] restriction in food to the point of being content with crumbs and the like ... in order that people might believe concerning them [that they were espousing] the way of the prophets which [embraces] abstinence and contentedness . . .'.[50]

Such, then, was the Jewish background to the Zohar when it first began to circulate at the end of the thirteenth century at around the same time that the teachings of the great Sufi mystic ibn Arabi began to circulate among Spanish Muslims. The Zohar is a curious amalgam of different sorts of material, crammed with mythological imagery, poetry and echoes of Neoplatonic and Aristotelian philosophy, alongside popular superstition, theurgy and mystical psychology:

> The 'soul' is the lowest stirring. It supports the body and nourishes it. The body is bound intimately to the 'soul' and the 'soul' to the body. When the 'soul' has been perfected it becomes a throne on which the 'spirit' may rest, when the 'soul' that is joined to the body is aroused, as Scripture says: 'Till the spirit be poured on us from on high'. When 'soul' and 'spirit' have perfected themselves, they become worthy to receive the 'super-soul', for the 'spirit' acts as a throne on which the 'super-soul' resides. This 'super-soul' stands highest of all, hidden and utterly mysterious. So we find that there is a throne supporting a throne, and a throne for the highest which is over all. When you study these grades of soul you will discover therein the secret of divine Wisdom, for it is always wise to investigate hidden mysteries in this way. Observe that the soul, the lowest stirring, cleaves to the body, just as in a candle flame the dark light at the bottom clings to the wick, from which it cannot be separated and without which it could never be kindled. But when it has been fully kindled on the wick it becomes a throne for the white light above which resides upon that dark light. When both the dark and the white light have been fully kindled, the white light in its turn becomes a throne for a hidden light, for what it is that reposes on that white light can neither be seen nor known. Thus the light is fully formed. And so it is with the man who attains complete perfection, and, as a result, is called 'holy'.

The Zohar insists on the correspondence between the lower and upper worlds, so that actions and prayers by humans have cosmic significance. There is always a danger that evil caused by human sins (including improper thought) may thus cause a disjunction in the *sefirot*, the ten stages of the upper world through which God descends from the Infinite (*Ein Sof*) to the divine manifestation in the Shekhinah, which is both the last of the *sefirot* and the image in heaven of the community of Israel. What matters is harmonious balance in the union of Shekhinah (conceived as female) with the male aspects of the divine, such as the *sefirah* of judgement.[51]

Who wrote the Zohar? The notion that the text is what it purports to be, the product of discussions among the *tannaim* around Shimon bar Yohai in the second century, is belied by the artificiality of the Aramaic and the lack of references to the work before the late thirteenth century. There is now wide acceptance of the hypothesis that the author was in fact the kabbalist Moshe de Leon, who first published the text claiming that it had been copied from an old manuscript which he had obtained from the land of Israel but which no one else ever saw (and which his widow and daughter asserted, after his death, had never existed). Moshe spent his life travelling around Castile and became friendly with other kabbalists, notably Yosef b. Avraham Gikatilla, a follower of the practical mysticism of Avraham Abulafia (in which guise he wrote mystical analyses of the Tetragrammaton and the Hebrew alphabet). Gikatilla moved into a more theosophic form of mystical enquiry in middle age, producing in his *Gates of Light* and *Gates of Justice* particularly clear accounts of the role of the *sefirot* in relation to the Godhead. Moshe himself produced a series of kabbalistic writings in Hebrew, of which a number were dedicated to discussion of the *sefirot*, either in parallel to the composition of the Zohar or to draw attention to it.[52]

The impact of the Zohar on mystics throughout the Jewish world was immediate and it is likely that additions were rapidly made to the text as it circulated after Moshe's death. Attached to the mystical commentary on the inner meaning of scripture are sections which portray, among other matters, the life of Shimon bar Yohai and discussions of physiognomy and chiromancy, and sections in Hebrew rather than Aramaic. Over the course of the next two centuries, kabbalistic circles were founded in Italy, in Greece and in the land of Israel, and the writings of Isaiah b. Joseph of Tabriz in Persia in the 1320s, and of Nathan b. Moses Kilkes in Constantinople in the 1360s, reveal that the kabbalah had spread to the Jews of the east, just as it was adopted in Germany by mystics who combined the Zohar with the traditions of Hasidei Ashkenaz.

In many places in the Jewish world the ideas of the Zohar were mingled with concepts from earlier mystical writings by rabbinic Jews earnestly seeking to understand the place of man and God in the universe and emboldened by the adoption of kabbalistic ideas by many of the greatest authorities in the study of Talmud and halakhah. Despite his strong opposition to Avraham Abulafia, the great talmudist Rashba himself indicated clearly in his writings a great knowledge of kabbalah (as his teacher Nahmanides had done). The many commentaries composed by Adret's own pupils on the mystical part of the commentary by Nahmanides on the Pentateuch reveal the role of his school in transmitting the theosophical kabbalah to later generations by a route separate from the Zohar.[53]

What was the origin of all these ideas? On the one hand it is possible to trace many specific motifs in the developed kabbalah back to Hekhalot mysticism of late antiquity, and the continuing practice of copying manuscripts of these late antique texts from the twelfth century in itself confirms that these traditions were still alive. On the other hand it is possible to trace an explosion of ideas specifically from twelfth- or thirteenth-century Provence and Spain in which esoteric ideas were generated within intense coteries of mystics or hammered out in reaction to the plethora of speculative texts produced over a very short period. It seems clear that such religious outpourings cannot be delineated into a neat history of development. The fecundity of speculation derived precisely from its lack of restrictions. In marked contrast to the strict controls on theological speculation in contemporary Christian circles, and the necessary restraints for rabbis themselves when ruling on halakhah, it was possible to dream with little restraint about the nature of the divine and its secret revelation through the enigmatic words of scripture. The different routes of speculation evidently flourished in parallel.

Mystical speculation was not always easy to combine with the rest of life as a rabbinic Jew, as we have seen most strikingly in the career of Avraham Abulafia: on the one hand, the kabbalah promised everything, but it could also lead into danger. Moses of Burgos, a leading kabbalist in Castile in the thirteenth century and (with his teachers Jacob and Isaac Cohen) an important influence on Moshe de Leon and the composition of the Zohar as well as a repository of traditions that the Zohar omits, asserted uncompromisingly of the philosophers in his time that 'the position attained by their heads reaches only the position of our feet' but also that, despite the effectiveness of the kabbalistic traditions for reciting the divine names, he himself had never tried to put this into practice. There was an evident danger on the one hand that kabbalistic practice might merge into magic, while on the other hand kabbalists might attack specialists in halakhah for lacking real religious intensity: a mystical homily in *Tikkunei Zohar* refers to the Mishnah as 'the burial place of Moses'. What is clear, however, is that neither extreme was standard, so that many halakhists indulged in kabbalistic speculation and no medieval kabbalists believed their mystical insights to absolve themselves and other Jews from the need to follow the halakhah scrupulously. The kabbalists of Provence had led the opposition to the philosophy of Maimonides which ended in the disastrous book burning of 1232, but we have seen that Maimonides' Aristotelianism had not prevented Avraham Abulafia seeing his own prophetic kabbalah as founded on Maimonides' teaching. More positively, the Neoplatonic tradition in Jewish philosophy, which can be traced back to Isaac b. Solomon Israeli in Kairouan in the first half of the tenth century and the citations of Plato by ibn Gabirol in Andalusia in his *Fons Vitae*, had a direct influence on the author of *Sefer haBahir* through the twelfth-century Spanish philosopher Avraham bar Hiyya. The theory of emanations, which was to have a long history in the speculation of kabbalists about the *sefirot*, was an intrinsic element of Neoplatonic thought, and Neoplatonism would play an important role in Christian appropriation of kabbalah in the Renaissance.[54]

The images and concepts of the kabbalah, and especially the Zohar, were gradually adopted in almost all streams of medieval Judaism from the early fourteenth century, even among those who declined themselves to indulge in mystical introspection or theosophical speculation but who accepted the insights of earlier generations as part of the Torah. Individual kabbalists continued to add to the complexity of the kabbalistic system as they struggled with the intractable problem at its core – the relation of God to the material world – while most Jews accepted kabbalist ideas as symbolic images to enhance the liturgy in their prayers.

The popularity of such images attests to a widespread yearning among Jews for a complex theological framework for their practical Judaism in accordance with halakhah, in order to provide a sense of something more numinous and mysterious than the concrete promises and threats in the biblical covenant between God and Israel. It may well have been precisely the prohibition on discussing and analysing kabbalistic notions with those outside the rabbinic elite which lent power and mystique to these ideas among the non-rabbinic laity, so that, however little it was understood by most Jews, the kabbalah became in effect the theological framework for all rabbinic Judaism in the early modern period.

PART IV

Authority and Reaction
(1500–1800)

8. The Jewish World in 1500 CE

RUSS

LITHUANIA

POLAND

Haarlem
Rotterdam • Wittenberg
Antwerp • **GERMAN**
EMPIRE
Lvov • • Dubno

Geneva

Avignon •

CASTILE

Rome •

Bl

Adrianople • Istanbul
Salonica •
OTTOMAN EMP
• Smryna

ANDALUCIA

Naxos

Mediterranean Sea

Dar
Sa
Jerusa

Fez • **MOROCCO**

Cairo •

Northern Italy

• Milan
Verona • Padua
Cremona • • Venice
Mantua
Modena • • Ferrara

Lucca •
• Florence
Livorno •
• Arezzo
Volterra

• Rome

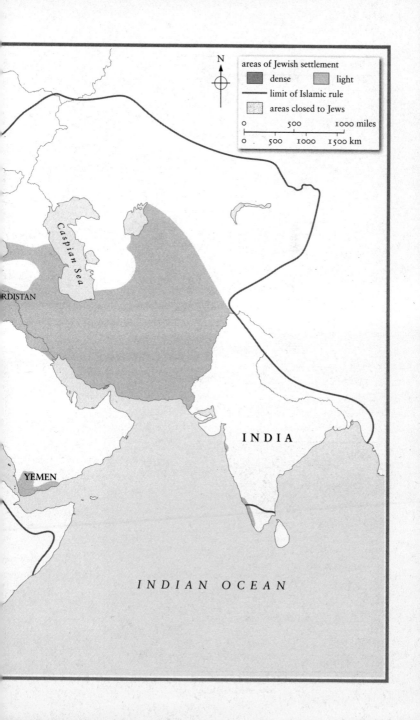

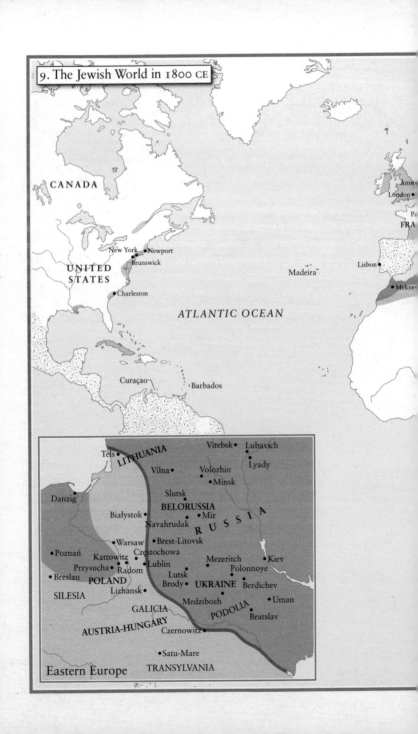

9. The Jewish World in 1800 CE

CANADA

Amst...
London •
Pa...
FRA

New York • Newport
Brunswick
**UNITED
STATES**

Lisbon •
Madeira

• Mekne...

• Charleston

ATLANTIC OCEAN

Curaçao
• Barbados

Eastern Europe

Tels •
LITHUANIA
Vitebsk • Lubavich •
Vilna • Lyady •
Volozhin •
• Minsk

Danzig •
Slutsk •
BELORUSSIA
Białystok •
Navahrudak • Mir •
R U S S I A

• Warsaw • Brest-Litovsk
• Poznań
Kattowitz •
Częstochowa
Przysucha •
• Lublin
Mezeritch •
Kiev •
Radom
Polonnoye •
• Breslau
Lutsk •
POLAND
Brody • **UKRAINE**
Berdichev •
SILESIA
Lizhansk •
Medzibozh
• Uman
GALICIA
PODOLIA
AUSTRIA-HUNGARY
Czernowitz • Bratslav •

• Satu-Mare
TRANSYLVANIA

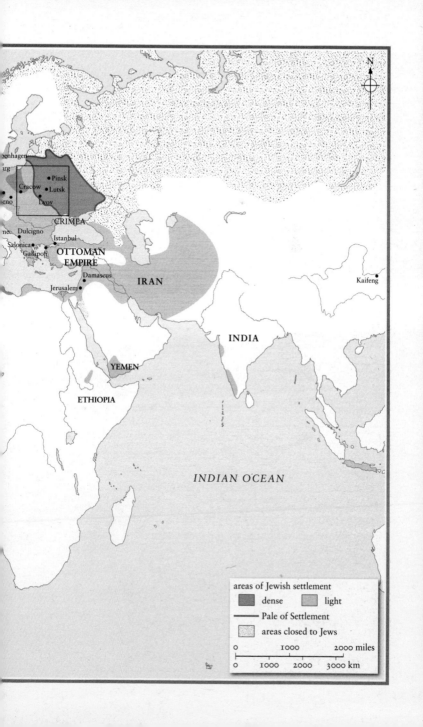

N

Pinsk
Cracow • Lutsk
rno • Lvov
CRIMEA

ne. Dulcigno Istanbul
Salonica •
Gallipoli
OTTOMAN
EMPIRE

Damascus
Jerusalem •

IRAN

Kaifeng

INDIA

YEMEN

ETHIOPIA

INDIAN OCEAN

areas of Jewish settlement
dense   light
— Pale of Settlement
areas closed to Jews

0   1000   2000 miles
0   1000   2000   3000 km

14

The European Renaissance and the New World

In autumn 1523 a Jew calling himself David Reuveni turned up in Venice. Aged about forty, he claimed to be commander-in-chief of the army of the ten lost tribes of Israel, and the brother of Joseph, king of the tribes of Reuben and Gad and the half-tribe of Manasseh. According to what purports to be his diary, Reuveni had travelled in the east before he came to Europe, visiting Alexandria in Egypt, Jerusalem and Safed in the land of Israel, and Damascus before sailing for Italy. On arrival in Venice he persuaded some of the local Jews to help him on a mission to Pope Clement VII in Rome in which he proposed a treaty between the lost tribes of Israel and the Christians against the Muslims. Despite support from the humanist Cardinal Egidio da Viterbo and some wealthy Jews in Rome, Reuveni obtained from the pope only one letter to the king of Portugal and another to the king of Ethiopia, but that was enough for him to be received by the king of Portugal in 1525–7 with all the solemnity of an official ambassador. Success brought suspicion, for Jews in Portugal who had been compelled to adopt Christianity took his arrival as evidence of the imminent arrival of the Messiah, a notion that Reuveni did nothing to try to dispel. When a young Portuguese man of crypto-Jewish parentage named Diego Pires circumcised himself, taking the Hebrew name Solomon Molcho, Reuveni was expelled from the country. Arrested off the Spanish coast, he was imprisoned for two years by the lord of Claremont until a ransom was paid by the Jews of Avignon and Carpentras. Back in Venice in November 1530, he encouraged further messianic hopes, but his notoriety had also aroused enmity among some of the Jews and this was to lead to his downfall.

When Reuveni appeared before the emperor Charles V in the summer of 1532, it was in the company of the Portuguese convert Solomon Molcho, who had spent the intervening seven years in extensive travels in the eastern Mediterranean and in Italy, studying kabbalah in Salonica and seeking signs of the coming redemption. Molcho had become convinced that he was himself the Messiah, demonstrating his conviction by sitting dressed as a beggar for thirty days on a bridge over the Tiber close to the pope's residence to fulfil one of the stories about the Messiah found in the Babylonian Talmud:

> R. Joshua b. Levi met Elijah standing by the entrance of R. Shimon b. Yohai's tomb. He asked him: 'Have I a portion in the world to come?' He replied, 'if this Master desires it.' . . . He then asked him, 'When will the Messiah come?' – 'Go and ask him himself,' was his reply. 'Where is he sitting?' – 'At the entrance of Rome.' And by what sign may I recognise him?' – 'He is sitting among the poor lepers: all of them untie [their bandages] all at once, and rebandage them together, whereas he unties and rebandages each separately, thinking, should I be wanted, I must not be delayed.'

Remarkably, Molcho had succeeded in gaining the protection of the pope, who was particularly impressed when he predicted correctly a flood in Rome and (in January 1531) an earthquake in Portugal. Even when he was condemned by the Inquisition for Judaizing he was saved from execution by the pope's personal intervention. It may be that by the time he faced the emperor in the company of Reuveni in 1532, in Regensburg, Molcho felt he was untouchable. If so, he was wrong: later that year, he was tried and burned at the stake in Mantua. Reuveni was taken to Spain in chains and charged with inciting Portuguese New Christians to convert to Judaism. He died, probably in 1538, while still in prison.[1]

The dramatic careers of Reuveni and Molcho took place against a background of new perspectives opening up to Europeans at the beginning of the sixteenth century. The notion in Christian Europe that Islam was a threat to Christendom was as firmly entrenched as ever since the Ottoman capture of Constantinople in 1453. Ottoman control spread in the sixteenth century south to Syria, Palestine, Egypt and North Africa, west to Hungary and east to Iraq and Yemen. At the same time refugees from Constantinople brought Greek learning to the Latin west and encouraged the rediscovery of lost knowledge that came to be known loosely as the Renaissance. For humanist scholars in all walks of life (including cardinals such as Egidio da Viterbo) there appeared to open up limitless possibilities for new understanding of the world and its relation to the divine. Such hopes were strengthened by the discovery and exploitation of the astonishing resources of the New World across the Atlantic, to which Columbus had sailed in 1492, even as the countries of Europe found themselves convulsed in wars of religion between Catholics and Protestants in which theological difference in the interpretation of Christian creeds and liturgy led to division both between states and within their boundaries, with a degree of bloody violence not previously known in the history of Christianity.

The three centuries from 1500 to 1800 saw the expansion of European civilization across the globe as a result of the discovery of new worlds and general improvements in sea transport which enabled the growth of immensely lucrative intercontinental trade. In 1500, western Europe was still an economic and political backwater in comparison with the Ottoman and Safavid empires of the Middle East. Islam was still being diffused in central and south-east Asia and sub-Saharan Africa, and Christianity was largely confined to Europe. By 1800, Christianity had been spread by European imperialists across the Americas and to trading stations in west Africa and south-east Asia.

The varied forms of Christianity brought by the imperialists to the ends of the world reflected the disunity of Christendom within Europe. Western Europe in the sixteenth century was riven with protest at the perceived inadequacies of the Roman Catholic Church. Almost 40 per cent of the inhabitants of Europe observed a reformed theology in the footsteps of Luther, Zwingli and Calvin. The response of the Catholic hierarchy was both Counter-Reformation, to deal with the worst of the abuses which had brought the Church into disrepute, and the military aid of sympathetic rulers, especially the Holy Roman Emperor. The peace of Münster–Westphalia in 1646, which established for a century the religious and political frontiers of Europe – with most of the inhabitants of France, Bohemia, Austria and Poland Catholic, and northern Europe, including much of Germany, mostly Protestant – came at the end of more than a hundred years of political as well as religious strife. Within Europe, only the Orthodox Christians in the sprawling and expanding territories ruled by the Russian tsars remained immune to this religious turmoil. Russia itself was transformed from an isolated position as a backward country on the edge of Europe in the fifteenth century to become a powerful participant in European politics by the end of the Napoleonic Wars in 1815, fuelled by rapid economic growth in the eighteenth century and territorial expansion to the west into Estonia and Lithuania.

The emerging global economy, from the fur trade in the north which proved so lucrative to Russia to the transatlantic trade and imports from India and China which benefited western Europe, gradually shifted the balance of power within Europe from the end of the fifteenth century. In the Mediterranean world the Italian cities lost their dominance under pressure from the Spanish Habsburgs to the west and the Ottoman Turks to the east; by the early seventeenth century, the Turks held the eastern Mediterranean, leaving Spain in control of the rest. The greatest power and prosperity accrued to the Atlantic powers Spain, Portugal, England and the Dutch Republic, joined belatedly by France in the second half of the seventeenth century during the reign of Louis XIV, whose prosperity was symbolized in the vast palace of Versailles.

This was a connected world within which many Jews moved, setting up new congregations in the midst of existing communities and transplanting long-cherished local traditions to new locations. The Sephardi diaspora from Spain and Portugal was to settle not just in the lands around the Mediterranean and in northern Europe but in the Americas. In eastern Europe steady migration from Germany to Poland from the thirteenth century was much increased during the wars of religion in central Europe of the sixteenth and early seventeenth centuries. The effects of transplantation were mixed, sometimes encouraging those exiled from their homeland to emphasize their difference from the surrounding Jewish society in which they found themselves, sometimes generating a mixture of traditions through intermarriage and other forms of social contact. The former tendency was seen in the adoption of Yiddish, a dialect of German, by Ashkenazi Jews in Poland, setting them apart from the local population. The latter tendency, towards greater uniformity, was promoted by the early adoption by European Jews of printing of religious books, enabling a wider and more rapid geographical dissemination of religious ideas than in the medieval period, as well as a comparative democratization of study through the availability of texts to Jews outside the scholarly rabbinic elite.

Rashi's commentary on the Pentateuch was already in print in 1475, and the first complete printing of the Babylonian Talmud was completed by the Christian printer Daniel Bomberg in Venice in 1523 with the approval of Pope Leo X, making talmudic study easier, particularly with Rashi's commentary printed in the margins of the talmudic text. Printed prayer books became widely available, so that prayer leaders were liable to be called up short by the congregation if they deviated from the words on the page. Hebrew printing in the first half of the sixteenth century was concentrated particularly in Italy, where Gershon Soncino produced the first printed Hebrew Bible, but there were presses in Constantinople and Salonica as well, and also increasingly during the century in northern Europe. In the seventeenth century the role of Amsterdam as a printing centre for general books encouraged a huge output of publications in a wide variety of languages in order to cater for a Jewish market for religious books throughout Europe. Less positive was the increased role of Christian censors, often converts from Judaism, in monitoring the content of Jewish books.[2]

Equally significant as a catalyst of change in the Jewish world was the expulsion of Jews from Spain in 1492 and from Portugal in 1497–8 by the Catholic monarchs Ferdinand and Isabella. The expulsion sent a flood of refugees eastward to the relative tolerance of Ottoman rule. Many settled in Constantinople, Salonica and Adrianople, but others set up congregations in scattered locations in Asia Minor and in Greece, and yet others went to live in Egypt and (in small numbers) in the land of Israel, especially Safed and Jerusalem. By the seventeenth century, some states in Protestant Europe also provided a haven for Jews from Catholic persecution, including Jews who had been living as Christians, and who sought freedom to practise their religion openly. Already around 1590 there was a secret community of conversos in Amsterdam for whom the natural language of religious discourse was not Hebrew or Dutch but Spanish. In 1605 Jews were given permission to build synagogues in Rotterdam and Haarlem, and, although the civic status of Jews differed greatly in the various parts of the Netherlands, they became increasingly integrated into wider society.

The career of one Amsterdam rabbi, Manasseh b. Israel, born in Madeira in 1604 to a family living as Christians and baptized as Manoel Dias Soeiro, was particularly remarkable. Brought to the Netherlands as a child, his theological abilities, and the publicity he gained through the printing press he established in 1626, gained him a reputation among Christians as well as Jews. In 1655, he negotiated with Oliver Cromwell the return of Jews to England, from where they had been banished since 1290. During the voyage of Christopher Columbus in 1492, the first European to set foot on American soil was Luis de Torres, a former Jew, and conversos from Spain and Portugal were quick to settle in the New World. In Brazil in the late seventeenth century many converso communities proclaimed themselves openly as Jews when they came under Dutch rule, only to have to flee north from the Inquisition to the Caribbean and North America when the Dutch parts of Brazil were reconquered by Portuguese settlers in the 1650s. They settled primarily in New Amsterdam (later to be renamed New York). The Touro synagogue in Newport, Rhode Island, the oldest extant Jewish edifice in the United States, was dedicated in 1763, nearly a century after the arrival of Barbados Jews in the town in 1677.[3]

In eastern Europe, the Jewish population of Poland and Lithuania had grown since the thirteenth century under a system of state protection partly through the authority given by the state to local Jewish councils, which encouraged migration east from Germany and settlement in villages in the Ukraine. Already in 1264 a charter known as the Statute of Kalisz had granted Jews in Poland extensive legal rights, including jurisdiction by Jewish courts over Jewish affairs. As a result, the Jewish population expanded greatly from the last quarter of the sixteenth century under the patronage of the Polish–Lithuanian nobility, so that by the early seventeenth century Poland and Lithuania had become the main centres of Ashkenazi culture. This dominance was diminished, but not ended, by the destruction of hundreds of Jewish communities in the Cossack and peasant uprisings against Polish rule in the Ukraine led in 1648–9 by Bogdan Chmielnicki.

The Chmielnicki massacres evoked a mass of liturgical poems and laments and an exodus of Jewish refugees back west towards the Netherlands, where an Ashkenazi population of very different social and economic background and cultural outlook, with Yiddish as their primary Jewish language, thus settled alongside the Sephardi community from Portugal and Spain. The refugees from what is now Ukraine who ended up in small states in Germany brought a distinctive intensity of religious life to the communities in which they settled. Ordinary Jews enjoyed a complex relationship with the court Jews who provided commercial and financial services to autocratic princes throughout the Holy Roman Empire and adjoining states such as Poland and Denmark. Many such Hofjuden did much to help their communities from the court environment in which they operated. For instance, Samuel Oppenheimer, purveyor of military supplies to the army of the Austrian emperor in the late seventeenth century, was a remarkable benefactor of numerous synagogues and academies and wielded immense influence within the Jewish community despite his own lack of learning.[4]

The different trends within Jewish life met during this period in particularly spectacular fashion in Italy, where Jews had flourished in the fourteenth and fifteenth centuries through small-scale money lending to finance the general expansion of the local economy, generally maintaining their civil position despite occasional hostility from Franciscan friars and others. When Jews were exiled from Spain in March 1492, both Sicily and Sardinia were under the rule of Aragon, and in 1503 the

Kingdom of Naples also came under Spanish rule and expelled most of its Jews. In central and northern Italy, by contrast, the popes and the city states, not least the Medici in Florence, welcomed the refugees for the first part of the sixteenth century. But the welcome did not last. As part of the struggle of the Counter-Reformation the pope began to impose restrictions on Jews, and in 1533 Pope Julius III ordered the burning of all copies of the Talmud in Italy on the grounds that it blasphemed Christianity.

From 14 July 1555 Jews were obliged by Pope Paul IV to lock themselves at night into ghettoes. The original ghetto had been established in Venice in 1516 in a quarter near a foundry (*ghetto*) which was declared by the authorities to be the only area of the city where Jews were permitted to settle. By the end of the sixteenth century most cities in Italy had such Jewish quarters, generally locked at night. Sometimes (as in Rome) they were desperately overcrowded and unhealthy, but in other cases the ghetto became a centre for intensive Jewish cultural activity encouraged by the mixture of different sorts of Jews in a confined space. In Venice, for instance, alongside the Italian community which dated back at least to the eleventh century, there were communities from the Levant and from Germany as well as the newcomers from the Iberian peninsula. The Levantine and western Jews, in particular, enjoyed some protection from the Venetian Republic, despite occasional orders of expulsion under pressure from the Inquisition, because of their connections with Jewish communities overseas and their role in the encouragement of trade.[5]

If the social isolation enforced on Italian Jews did not cut them off entirely from the intellectual ferment of the Renaissance, this was in large part because of the fascination of Christian humanist scholars in obtaining knowledge of ancient Hebrew traditions to place alongside the new Greek learning which had been opening up to them since 1453. The search for Hebrew learning was spurred on specifically by the hope of Pico della Mirandola and other Christians in the late fifteenth century that it would be possible to unearth the secrets of the kabbalah, which was thought by Pico to prove the divinity of Christ. The claim stimulated the German humanist Johannes Reuchlin to publish in 1494 the first Latin book on the kabbalah and in 1517 a full treatise *On the Art of the Kabbalah*, which tried to demonstrate the origins of Neoplatonism and the kabbalah in the same mystical doctrines through which the name of Jesus (in the idiosyncratic Hebrew spelling postulated by Reuchlin, the Tetragrammaton with the addition of the letter *shin*, signifying the Logos) had been revealed. The motivation of these Christian kabbalists was not always sympathetic to traditional Judaism. On the contrary, they contrasted the kabbalah as true Judaism to the debased teachings of the Talmud. Part of their aim was to use the kabbalah as a weapon in a challenge to rigid Christian scholasticism.

In the early years much of this Christian kabbalistic learning was derived from Latin translations from the Hebrew by converts to Christianity from Judaism, but some Christian humanists were also drawn into discussion and debates with Jews who remained faithful to their traditions. In 1571 a Jewish doctor named Azariah de' Rossi, caught in Ferrara at the time of a terrible earthquake and sheltering for safety in fields in the outskirts of the city, met a Christian scholar who questioned him about the true meaning of a passage in the Letter of Aristeas, which the Christian assumed (wrongly) must exist in Hebrew as well as in Greek. According to de' Rossi, the results were striking:

> During this frightening time in which, as I said, I was forced to leave the ruins of my home and take up my abode wherever I could, my lot fell in with many peace-loving people south of the river Po. One of our neighbours, a Christian scholar, to pass the time and divert his mind from the distressing earthquake, was enjoying himself by reading the book which I had begun to discuss with him which relates the story of the Translation of our Torah. It was at this time that he came up to greet me and then inquired whether by means of the Hebrew version (for he thought that we Jews possessed the book) I could clarify and elucidate some of the passages he found obscure in the Latin, a language with which he had been conversant for a long time. When I informed him that we had no such thing he was utterly amazed as to how such glory could depart from Israel who could deservedly win great prestige from it . . .[6]

De' Rossi, an astonishingly accomplished and independent scholar, accordingly translated the Letter of Aristeas into Hebrew. In due course this translation became part of de' Rossi's larger work, *The Light of the Eyes*, which was published by him in Mantua in 1574 just a few years before his death. It became part of a remarkable study of Jewish history, chronology, poetry and culture which made use of a great swathe of classical writers, both in Latin (which he read direct from the source) and in Greek (for which he used Latin and Italian translations).

Of particular interest to de' Rossi were the Jewish writings in Greek from the Hellenistic period which had been forgotten in the rabbinic tradition. He devoted himself to an intensive study of Philo (whom he called in Hebrew Yedidiah ha-Alexandroni) and to demonstrating that the Hebrew history of Yosippon constituted in fact an unreliable para-phrase of the Greek text of Josephus as preserved by the Church. In keeping with the spirit of enquiry of humanist scholarship, de' Rossi used evidence from any source he could find, including the writings on Jewish history by the fourth-century Church historian Eusebius and other ancient Christian writings. He even made use of the theology of Thomas Aquinas and other medieval Christian theologians and the Christian kabbalist Pico della Mirandola, whose methods of scholar-ship he admired.

A critical approach to stories in the Talmud was not in itself a novelty in Jewish thought, but de' Rossi's use of non-Jewish sources for the pur-pose was, and publication of *The Light of the Eyes* provoked strong protests. The issue lay not in de' Rossi's religious teachings, which con-formed (as did his personal behaviour) to rabbinic norms of piety. More problematic was the implication of his scholarly enquiry that wisdom from outside the rabbinic tradition could be used not just to amplify and elucidate that tradition in the manner of medieval Jewish philos-ophers in their use of Islamic writings but, far more fundamentally, to challenge that tradition. In 1574, the rabbis of Venice proclaimed a ban against anyone who used the book without special permission from them, and similar bans were prepared not only in many parts of Italy but also in Safed in Palestine. Judah Loew, the Maharal of Prague, devoted a large part of his book *Be'er-haGolah*, published in 1598, to a direct attack on de' Rossi's teachings, even though he was writing some twenty years after de' Rossi had died. For over a century de' Rossi's work was read only surreptitiously – even in Mantua, where the book was printed, it was permitted only to those aged over twenty-five, deemed able to deal with the potential perils of his doctrines. In many respects de' Rossi had trodden carefully by avoiding any criticism of the Bible and by confining himself to technical scholarly issues such as the chronology of ancient Jewish history, using an approach to the sacred text similar to contemporary Christian scholars in the Renaissance. The strength of opposition he evoked is testimony to the awareness of con-temporaries that opening up customary teaching to scrutiny in relation to external literary authorities in this way might prove immensely dan-gerous to those concerned to preserve the integrity of the tradition.[7]

Despite his extensive fame (or notoriety), de' Rossi never held a rabbinic post and he promulgated his ideas as, in essence, a solitary figure – even some of his closer friends deserted him when confronted by the scale of opposition he provoked and his apparently cavalier attitude to established traditions. But others were more successful in infusing aspects of the Renaissance into the intellectual outlook of Italian Jews. In 1587, less than ten years after de' Rossi's death and at the height of controversy over his writings, Judah b. Joseph Moscato, already for nearly twenty years the official preacher in the synagogues of the community in Mantua where de' Rossi had lived and published his book, was nominated chief rabbi to the community.

Moscato's *Nefutsot Yehudah*, a series of fifty-two sermons preached in Mantua and published in Venice in 1589, revealed a religious teacher fully devoted to the aesthetics of Renaissance rhetoric, and in his *Kol Yehudah* (1594), a commentary on Judah Halevi's *Kuzari*, Moscato was an advocate both of medieval Neoplatonists and, more controversially, of Philo. Like de' Rossi, Moscato cited Pico della Mirandola with approval:

> First of all God emanated forth a created intellect as an effect, unitary and perfect; he endowed it with the patterns of all things . . . In the emanation of this effect not only did God create all things but he created them in the most perfect manner. This intellect has been called by the Platonists and other ancient philosophers 'God's son', as is recorded by the sage Pico della Mirandola in a short essay that he wrote on the heavenly and divine love.

The 'God's son' to which Moscato refers is the Logos which Philo postulated as the link between man and the divine. This combination of modern learning with the Jewish medieval philosophical tradition, with occasional references to Italian phrases and contemporary ideas about music and astronomy, a mystical tinge provided by frequent quotations (often unattributed) from the Zohar, and an overall focus on pleasing his audience through the aesthetic qualities of his sermon (both in content and in oral delivery), established among Italian Jews the notion that a homily should be a work of art.[8]

Moscato's sermons are known to have attracted a non-Jewish audience, and it is possible that he preached in Italian as well as Hebrew. It is certain that in the following century the maverick Venetian preacher Leone Modena composed in Italian with the same facility as he wrote in Hebrew, and that he maintained close connections with a wide circle of Christian scholars, publishing, among other works, an account of Jewish customs (*Historia de' riti Ebraici*) for the English ambassador in Venice to present to King James I. According to Leone Modena's autobiography, among the numerous occupations on which he relied for an income to feed his gambling habit was that of a musician. He became *maestro di cappella* of the musical academy established in the ghetto in Venice in the 1630s, and he played a role in encouraging the use in synagogue worship of music composed by his friend Salomone de' Rossi, who introduced the contrapuntal style of Palestrina into the Jewish liturgy. Leone Modena claimed, in his introduction to de' Rossi's settings of Hebrew texts for the festivals, that they had recreated the music of the Temple. But the music reflected more obviously the adoption of aspects of Christian liturgy, much as synagogue architecture imitated aspects of local style, as in the baroque Spanish synagogue at Venice, originally built in the mid-sixteenth century but redesigned in the mid-seventeenth century by the architect of the church of Santa Maria della Salute, and the Huguenot design of the synagogue in Bevis Marks in the city of London built by the Spanish and Portuguese Jewish community in 1702.[9]

Many Jewish communities in the Christian world also embraced contemporary arts and crafts for the enhancement of religious practice in the home as well as the synagogue. For synagogues the greatest attention was paid to the finials placed on the top of the rods holding the two ends of a scroll of the law while the scroll is carried in procession. Such finials (*rimmonim*) were often highly elaborate examples of skilled metalwork. The oldest surviving embroidered curtain used by a community to cover the Torah ark in which the scrolls were housed was made in Italy in the sixteenth century. The custom of commissioning such brocades for the ark and embroidered wrappings for the scrolls themselves was widespread, often providing a means for pious women expert in needlework to express their devotion in a public space but also encouraging in some communities the development of artistic embroidery as a distinctive art form adopted by specialized Jewish male craftsmen.

For rituals in the home Jews considered it a sign of piety, defined as 'glorification of the religious duty' (*hiddur mitzvah*), to indulge in highly wrought metal *kiddush* cups, lamps and spice boxes for celebration of the Sabbath, and special plates for the Passover Seder. These were usually but not always designed and made by Jewish craftsmen. For the images used to illustrate books, now far more widely disseminated than in the medieval period because of the adoption of printing, Christian influence is blatant in (for instance) the frequent reuse in Jewish texts of woodcuts originally created for other purposes. Jews outside Islamic lands seem to have been unconcerned by representations of the human figure even in manuscripts produced for religious purposes. Thus it was common to depict the story of the book of Esther in scrolls used for the celebration of Purim, and highly ornate marriage contracts (*ketubot*) were often decorated with fine illustrations of wedding scenes, sometimes copied widely through engravings.

It is significant that in London the architecture of Bevis Marks was that of non-conformist Christians, since Jews sometimes identified in social terms with minorities within a divided Christian culture. In the Habsburg domains, Jews were careful to be seen as loyal to the Catholic regime, but as the Catholic Church fragmented with challenges to its interpretation of the Bible, Judaism was perceived by some Protestants, including Christian humanists such as Reuchlin and Erasmus, and by the leaders of Reformation within the Church, as a repository of an older scriptural truth. The 'battle of the books' from 1507 to 1521 between Reuchlin and Johannes Pfefferkorn, a Jew who had converted to Christianity in *c.* 1504 in Cologne, placed attitudes to the Talmud at the centre of controversy between reactionary and liberal trends within the Catholic Church. Pfefferkorn, coached by the Dominicans of Cologne, attacked the Talmud and demanded that the emperor Maximilian authorize the confiscation of all Jewish books apart from the Bible. When he was opposed by Reuchlin, the two sides engaged in a pamphlet war of extraordinary vitriol and a great deal of personal abuse on both sides. It was not accidental that Martin Luther's theses were posted in Wittenberg in 1517 at the height of the controversy, in which the obscurantism of elements in the Church had been so effectively revealed by Reuchlin's supporters, who included many of the leading humanists of the day. Both Reuchlin (who intervened to help the Jews of Pforzheim) and Luther originally condemned the persecution of the Jews as well as the confiscation of rabbinic literature. But from the mid-1520s Luther grew more hostile to contemporary Jews, as they failed to accept Christianity even when presented in his enlightened form, and in the three years before his death in 1546 he published a series of pamphlets, starting with *On the Jews and their Lies* in 1543, which urged that the Jews be banished or kept in subjection. Ultimately the Lutheran Church he founded retained as great an abhorrence of Judaism as the Catholicism from which he had broken away. Luther's antagonism may have been influenced by his desire to oppose Judaizing among such Protestant sects as the Sabbatarians, whom he condemned unequivocally.[10]

Luther's younger contemporary, John Calvin, was as vituperative about Jews as Luther was, but he had little contact with real Jews in the theocratic state he set up in Geneva in the 1540s, since Jews had been expelled from the city in 1490. His enthusiasm for the law of the Old Testament was to encourage among his followers and successors both a devotion to Hebrew scholarship for understanding the Bible and an increasing willingness to permit Jews also to turn to scripture for enlightenment in their own way. Thus in Calvinist Holland, Jews were permitted in 1619 to settle with full religious liberty provided they behaved as a religious community like the Calvinists themselves and believed, for instance, that 'there is life after death in which good people will receive their recompense and wicked people their punishment'. It is likely that the punishment of Spinoza by the Jewish community of Amsterdam for his attack on the divine origin of scripture (see below) was prompted by concern as much for the reaction of local Calvinists as for the threat to Jews themselves.[11]

Some trends within Christianity, such as the millenarian impulse which captivated much of Protestant Europe in the mid-seventeenth century, had a direct influence on Jewish life, including, probably, Cromwell's enthusiasm for the return of the Jews to England in the 1650s, (see p. 363). More tenuous, but nonetheless real, was the impact of Christian ideology on Jewish thought, but, as we shall see, it seems implausible to imagine that the enthusiasm shown by followers of Sabbetai Zevi had no connection at all to contemporary parallel movements in the Christian world such as the millenarian expectations of the Fifth Monarchists in England under Cromwell. The most direct influence of Christian ideas was through conversos who imported the assumptions of their Iberian Christian education when they reverted to Judaism: for the Jews of Curaçao, for instance, ties of blood – the *famiya* – were the strongest influence on their religious life throughout the history of the community. Conversos were unusual Jews not least in that they had determined their own religious identity. In many cases, they adjusted only with difficulty to traditional Jewish practices such as the minutiae of the food laws, which they found as hard to stomach as the Catholicism they had rejected, preferring to live secular lives or even to move back and forth between Judaism and Christianity as it suited them for practical reasons.[12]

The version of Judaism adopted by one such Portuguese converso in Amsterdam in the seventeenth century, Uriel Acosta, went hopelessly wrong. Born in Portugal in a Marrano (that is, crypto-Jewish) family, Acosta became sceptical about Christian doctrines after reading the Hebrew Bible and escaped to Amsterdam, only to find that the Judaism to which he converted was not what he had expected. As he explained in his autobiography, his attempts to undermine (as non-biblical) rabbinic tradition, and especially the doctrines of immortality and resurrection, led to his excommunication in 1624 by the Jewish authorities, who were nervous about their status in the city:

> I observed that the customs and ordinances of the modern Jews were quite different from those commanded by Moses. Now if the Law was to be observed according to the letter, as it expressly declares, the Jewish interpreters are not justified in adding to it interpretations quite contrary to the original text. This provoked me to oppose them openly. Nay, I looked upon the open defence of the Law against such innovations as a service to God. The modern rabbis, like their ancestors, are an obstinate and stiff-necked race of men ... This state of affairs led me to write a tract in defence of myself and to prove plainly out of the Law of Moses the vanity and the invalidity of the tradition and ordinances of the Pharisees as well as their conflict with the Law. After I had begun this work (for I consider myself obliged to relate everything clearly and circumstantially), it so happened that I entirely agreed with the opinion of those who confine the rewards and punishments proposed in the Old Testament to this life only and are little concerned with the future life or the immortality of the soul ... The next step they took was to set their children upon me in the streets. They insulted me en masse as I walked along, abusing and railing at me. They cried out, There goes a heretic, there goes an imposter. At other times they assembled before my doors, flung stones at the windows and did everything they could to disturb and annoy me so that I could not live at peace in my own house.

This story of violence and intimidation is all the more striking for taking place in a city which had celebrated an extraordinarily rapid rise to fortune since the beginning of the century by embracing freedom on the grounds that encouraging minority groups like Mennonites, Muslims and indeed Jews was good for business. In Amsterdam, Sephardi Jews could plough the fortunes they had made through trade with fellow Sephardim in the bazaars of North Africa, or across the Atlantic in places like Curaçao, into the building of magnificent private houses and (in 1675) a superb great synagogue in the heart of the Christian city. Amsterdam housed numerous printing presses and a flourishing book trade. But even here, in a place of unparalleled self-confidence, prosperity and freedom, Acosta could not follow his reason as far as it encouraged him to go. He recanted, but in due course he reverted to his opposition to the rabbis, claiming that he was a deist who obeyed a natural law – a position he justified in his autobiography, composed just before his suicide in 1640.[13]

Equally ineffectual in the development of Judaism in his own time, despite his importance in the wider history of European thought as a precursor of the Enlightenment which was to sweep through western Europe in the following century and later Jewish appropriations of his image as the 'first modern Jew', was Uriel Acosta's much younger contemporary Baruch Spinoza. Aged eight when Acosta died, Spinoza came from a Portuguese Marrano family settled in Amsterdam. He had a traditional Jewish education in the Spanish and Portuguese community, gaining outstanding knowledge of the Bible and the Hebrew language. In contrast to Acosta, Spinoza came from a wealthy merchant family and in any case could support himself as a lens-grinder (an occupation which may have contributed to his death from consumption in 1677 at the age of only forty-five). In his *Tractatus Theologico-Politicus*, Spinoza developed a critique not just of Judaism but of all supernatural religion, insisting that everything must be judged by reason, and that miracles are therefore not possible. Accused by his enemies of atheism, Spinoza in fact argued that all nature is governed by the eternal and necessary decrees of God. In his *Ethics*, he concluded that everything in the world is indeed an aspect of God, a form of pantheism which denied any possibility of revelatory knowledge and undermined the basic ingredients of both Jewish and Christian cosmologies. On this basis, study of the Bible must also use the same scientific tools of analysis employed to understand nature. Excommunicated by his own community in Amsterdam at the age of twenty-four after he had denied that the Pentateuch could have been written by Moses, Spinoza lived, as far as he could, a quiet life of contemplation in the Hague away from public affairs, despite the frequent attacks on him, from all sides of Christianity as well as Judaism, for his notorious writings. By the end of his life most of his friends were Christians, although he himself abhorred the prospect of conversion to Christianity and contrived, most unusually in his age, to avoid belonging to any religious group at all.[14]

The pressures to conform were in general less for Jews living in the Islamic empire of the Ottomans. Most impressive was the career of Don Joseph Nasi, born into a wealthy Marrano family in Portugal in *c.* 1524, who left Lisbon for Antwerp as a teenager in 1537, and after many travels around Europe eventually became a close intimate in Constantinople of the sultan Selim III, who ascended to the throne in 1566. Appointed duke of the island of Naxos, Joseph and his equally powerful aunt, Gracia Nasi, obtained concessions in Palestine, repairing the walls of the city of Tiberias and writing to the Jews of Italy to invite them to settle there. But such toleration could never be guaranteed, and, a few decades later but further east, in Persia, the shah Abbas I (1588–1629), the first Muslim ruler in Persia to show an interest in the Hebrew Bible, took against his Jewish subjects for reasons now hard to discover and forced the Jews of his capital Isfahan to accept Islam. They returned openly to their ancestral religion when Abbas I died in 1629, but conversion to Islam was enforced again in 1656 by Abbas II, with the extra imposition on Jews of oaths to break with their Jewish past, and a designation as 'New Muslims' (*Jedid al-Islam*) which in effect recognized their continuing secret devotion to Jewish practices.[15]

The dispersion of Jewish communities to isolated places like the Caribbean, and the presence in some centres (such as Istanbul, Venice and Amsterdam) of Jewish communities with different origins, liturgies and customs, inevitably raised problems of religious authority, only partly offset by the growth of strong lay Jewish communal organizations such as the Council of the Four Lands which administered a huge federation of local and regional Jewish communities in eastern Europe. The more elaborate, complex and powerful such lay organizations became, the less power lay in the hands of the rabbis, particularly in western Europe.[16]

By the beginning of the sixteenth century, the work of a local rabbi had become a profession, employed by the community to carry out standard tasks, from deciding legal cases and dealing with marriages and divorces to preaching in synagogue, giving classes in Mishnah to any interested local Jew each day after morning prayers in the synagogue and teaching Talmud to yeshivah students at a higher level. Appointment continued to be for a fixed period. Ashkenazi congregations valued highly the services of a cantor able to lead the prayers with a pleasant voice and musical skill regardless of his moral or religious standing, let alone his degree of rabbinic knowledge, and although some rabbis fulfilled this role adequately, it was frequently handed over instead to a separate professional. Sephardi rabbis were rather more likely to find themselves asked to undertake the whole range of religious duties required for the smooth running of the congregation.

The whole rabbinic system presupposed an essentially obedient and conformist community such that religious challenges to rabbinic authority were inconceivable from within the community itself, and communities were therefore ill suited to such challenges when they occurred, as we have seen in the cases of Acosta and Spinoza in Amsterdam. This general conformity is all the more remarkable in cities of mixed communities such as Venice, where Jews of different traditions lived tolerantly alongside each other. If a local rabbi had to fear anything, it was the possibility that his contract might not be renewed at the end of its term by the wealthy lay leaders to whom control of congregational finances in practice gave considerable influence, even if in theory they deferred in religious matters to the rabbi's learning and piety. A rabbi might be subject to the approval of a council of sages if they were asked to rule on his behaviour or teachings, but in most of the Jewish world the opinions of such councils had no authority beyond the moral stature of the participating rabbis.

An attempt was made in the first half of the sixteenth century by Yaakov Berab, a Talmud scholar originally from Spain who had settled in Safed after periods as a rabbi in Fez and Egypt, to reintroduce rabbinic ordination, *semikhah*, of the same authority as was believed to have been the case in Palestine in the times of the *amoraim* a thousand years before (Chapter 11). According to the Babylonian Talmud, ordination could be conferred only in the land of Israel and only by those who had themselves been ordained. Maimonides had taken this ruling to imply that, because the chain had been broken since the end of the fourth century, such ordination could be revived only by the unanimous agreement of all the rabbis assembled in the land of Israel. In 1538 Berab declared that this condition had now been met and that the Jewish people would be reunited under one spiritual authority, thus hastening the redemption of Israel. The first rabbi thus to be ordained, with the support of twenty-five rabbis in Safed, was Berab himself. He in turn bestowed ordination on four other rabbis, including his former student the kabbalist Yosef Karo, on whose code of Jewish law there will be more to say in the next chapter. But this attempt to impose unity ended, ironically, in deep acrimony. It elicited the vehement opposition of R. Levi ibn Habib of Jerusalem, who had not been consulted by his colleagues in Safed and wrote an entire treatise to prove the illegality of Berab's actions. Berab had hoped that the practical effects of restored ordination would lead in due course to the re-establishment of a Sanhedrin which could impose fines and require flagellation for sins, but his opponents feared that such innovation would arouse false messianic hopes and that it would be better to await a divine initiative for the Sanhedrin to be re-established. The opposition prevailed, and, after the death of Berab in 1541, the ordination process he had begun gradually lapsed.[17]

Since the authority of a rabbi depended primarily on perceptions of his wisdom and knowledge, rabbinic religious influence was often shared with other, less learned, teachers. A popular preacher (*maggid*) was characteristically appointed alongside a rabbi by Russian and Polish communities from the seventeenth century for the edification of the congregation and could have a more direct effect on the spiritual life of Jews than even the most learned of rabbinic sages, as emerges from the records of his preaching preserved by Judah Leib Pukhovitser in Poland in the second half of the seventeenth century:

> It was our pattern to preach words of ethical rebuke each day, thereby fostering humility. Every Sabbath I would preach novel interpretation of the Torah pertaining to the weekly lesson, based primarily upon the novellae in the works of Alsheikh and those in the *Sefer haGilgulim* attributed to the Ari ... This was followed by ethical content from the Zohar and other ethical writings ... It was also our pattern to admonish about some of the laws that are neglected, in accordance with the talmudic statement ... It is necessary to appoint in every Jewish community a great scholar, advanced in years, one who has feared God from his youth, to reproach the masses and point the way back through repentance ... That scholar must also exert himself to know the sins of those in his community, even if they are not apparent ...

Preaching repentance was an integral part of the job.[18]

For an increasing proportion of Jews in the early modern period, religious edification could come from personal reading. *Ts'enah uReenah*, a popular Yiddish miscellany written in the 1590s in Poland, containing a paraphrase of the Torah readings in the synagogue and the *haftaroth* (readings from the Prophets following the Torah readings in synagogue liturgy), combined with legends, homilies and selections from the biblical commentaries of Rashi and others, was repeatedly reprinted throughout the seventeenth century, making available to those with insufficient Hebrew an insight into the main teachings of Judaism. The book became standard reading for pious Jewish women over the following centuries, with hundreds of reprints. There were also multiple printings from the late sixteenth century of *tehinnus* (a Yiddish word derived from the Hebrew *tehinnot*, 'supplications'), pious prayers, often with a mystical content, written in Yiddish and intended to be recited voluntarily and privately, primarily by women. Also widely available were anthologies addressed specifically to what were seen as women's concerns, such as lighting the Sabbath candles, taking the *hallah* portion from the dough, observing the laws of menstrual purity, pregnancy, child-birth and visiting cemeteries, the observance of festivals, and the making of candles for the synagogue. Many of these books were composed by daughters of rabbis, such as Serl, daughter of the preacher Yaakov b. Wolf Kranz, the famous 'Maggid of Dubno' befriended by the great Vilna Gaon, whose authority will be discussed in the next chapter.

Ashkenazi men often read *Ts'enah u-Re'enah*, despite affecting to despise it as women's literature. Among Sephardim in western Europe and Mediterranean countries, *Me'am Loez*, a Judaeo-Spanish commentary on the Bible, played a similar role in later centuries in popularizing religious ideas for both men and women. Begun by Yaakov Culi in Constantinople in the first quarter of the eighteenth century, *Me'am Loez* is an amalgam of halakhah, *midrash* and kabbalah with legends, proverbs and stories. Only the volume on Genesis was in print by Culi's death in 1732, but the rest of his commentary on the Pentateuch was published posthumously during the next half-century. In the course of the nineteenth century other scholars made their own contributions to what had become a bestseller not least through the appeal of its engaging literary style.[19]

From the popularity of such books it is clear that the impact of printing as an agent of religious change would be hard to overestimate. Already in the sixteenth century the availability of printed copies of the Babylonian Talmud began to encourage new approaches to study in the academies, with intensive argument about each minute detail of the text. The printing of halakhot began to spread norms and expectations far beyond any specific locality. As we shall see in the next chapter, in the sixteenth century Jewish law was codified as never before.

15

New Certainties and New Mysticism

CODIFIERS

It is a religious duty to visit the sick. Relatives and friends may call immediately, and strangers after three days. If, however, a man falls ill suddenly, both parties may call on him immediately. Even an eminent person should visit a humble one, even many times a day, and even if he is of the same age as the invalid. Whoever visits often is considered praiseworthy, provided he does not weary the sick person. Gloss: Some say that an enemy may visit a sick person. However, this does not seem right to me. Rather a man should not visit a sick person or comfort a mourner who is his enemy, lest the latter think that he rejoices at his misfortune, and only be distressed. This seems to me to be the correct view. He who visits the sick may not sit on a bed, or in a chair, or on a stool, but must reverently wrap himself and sit in front of the invalid, for the Shekhinah is above the headboard of his bed. Gloss: This applies only if the invalid lies on the ground so that the person sitting down will be higher than he; but if he lies on the bed, the visitor is permitted to sit on a chair or a stool. This is our custom. One should not visit the sick during the first three hours of the day, for every invalid's illness is less severe in the morning, and so one will not trouble one's self to pray for him. Nor should one visit during the last three hours of the day, for then his illness grows worse and one will despair of praying for him. Gloss: He who visited a sick person and did not pray for him has not fulfilled the religious duty of visiting the sick.

With such admonitions on every aspect of life, however domestic or intimate, the *Shulhan Arukh* ('Laid Table') of Yosef Karo, with the glosses (*Mappah*, or 'Tablecloth') by Moses Isserles, from which these passages are cited, became a standard guide for most Jewish communities almost immediately after their publication in the sixteenth century, with Karo as the guide for Sephardi, and Isserles for Ashkenazi, communities. With great clarity and precision, these sages laid down rules for piety in daily life, interleaving ethical teachings seamlessly with the practical halakhah. They dealt with blessings, prayers, the Sabbath and festivals; dietary laws; laws for mourners, vows, respect for parents and charity; personal status (including marriage and divorce); and Jewish civil law as it was applied in the diaspora. How did their codes come to be so influential?[1]

The remarkable private diary of the Sephardi sage Yosef Karo, entitled *Maggid Mesharim* ('Preacher of Righteousness'), records the nocturnal visits over some fifty years of a *maggid* (meaning in this case a heavenly teacher), a personification of the Mishnah, who urged the sage not just to moral behaviour but to asceticism, rebuking him for drinking too much wine or eating meat, encouraging him to hope for a martyr's death, and exhorting him to study the mysteries of the kabbalah. Hard though it may seem to us to correlate the dry clarity of the *Shulhan Arukh* with a mystical *maggid* who issued his teachings in the form of automated speech which came out of Karo's mouth, it is clear that this *maggid* was also experienced by Karo as an integral part of his religious persona when engaged in the clarification of the halakhah. Intense concentration was required for the *maggid* to come, as Karo acknowledged:

> I rose early as usual in order to recite extracts of the Mishnah. I recited about forty chapters, but as it was still night I went back to sleep and slept until the sun shone on the earth. Then I began to recite. I was grieved that I would perhaps not be visited as usual and continued reciting until it was said to me, 'Be strong and of good courage ... for although you have thought that I had left and forsaken you [this is not so], though it is what you have deserved.'

Karo's authority came not just from his exceptional halakhic knowledge but from a deep, and widely acknowledged, personal piety.[2]

Leaving the Iberian peninsula soon after his birth, Karo had spent much of his youth studying with kabbalists in Greece, under Ottoman rule, moving to Safed in Galilee in 1536 at the age of forty-eight. By this time he had already spent more than a decade working on a commentary on a fourteenth-century code, the *Arba'ah Turim* of Yaakov b. Asher (see Chapter 13), with the explicit aim of sorting out conflicting rules in existing codes and ending the variety of local customs which had grown up. Karo's aim was practical: 'to ensure that there should be one law and one Torah'. The *Arba'ah Turim* commended itself as the basis of his work because it gave the opinions of most previous decisors, unlike the classic code of Maimonides. An added advantage of the *Arba'ah Turim*, in comparison to Maimonides' code, was its omission of laws which were no longer applicable, such as laws about sacrifices, and its inclusion of the views of French and German rabbis who had been ignored by Maimonides – although Karo was at pains to avoid any suggestion that he was intending to overrule Maimonides, whose work in fact he frequently used with full acknowledgement. Karo's commentary, entitled *Beth Yosef* ('House of Joseph'), took twenty years to complete and constitutes an encyclopaedic guide to the development of halakhah from the Talmud to Karo's time, indicating the majority opinion of leading rabbis of previous generations whenever it can be discerned. Karo cited opinions culled from a huge range of rabbinic scholarship, claiming to have consulted no fewer than thirty-two other works. He originally intended to use his own judgement in deciding between authorities, but eventually he decided that this was beyond his abilities, and that instead he would follow whenever possible the views of at least two of the greatest authorities widely accepted in his day – Maimonides, Alfasi and Asher b. Yehiel.

The *Beth Yosef* was not published until 1555, and such a monumental work would be perused only by the exceptionally learned. Its impact on the Jewish world came thus primarily through the authority it gave to the digest of his great work which Karo prepared for 'young students'. The *Shulhan Arukh*, written specifically 'in a succinct manner and with clarity of language', was intended, like Maimonides' code, to enable scholars to give clear decisions and for students to learn halakhah from a young age. The book had all the advantage of Maimonides' code while avoiding the criticism which had plagued Maimonides that he failed to mention dissenting views and the authorities on which his own decisions were based, since users of the *Shulhan Arukh* could find all this information laid out with exemplary precision in the *Beth Yosef*. Just as Martin Luther's translation of the Bible into the vernacular used the mass circulation of books which had become possible through printing for the religious empowerment of Christian laymen, so Karo offered to Jews untrained in rabbinic law a straightforward route to the correct interpretation of the Torah as fashioned through the discussions of rabbinic sages over more than 1,500 years since the time of Hillel and Shammai while the Temple still stood. The *Shulhan Arukh* was an immediate bestseller from the printing of the first edition in Venice in 1564–5. The sixth edition, published in Venice in 1574, was designed in pocket format 'so that it could be carried in one's bosom so that it may be referred to at any time and any place, while resting or travelling'.[3]

The immediate reputation gained by the *Shulhan Arukh* can be gauged from the reaction to its publication by Moses Isserles, a leading Ashkenazi rabbinic authority in Cracow, hundreds of miles from both Safed and Venice. Isserles, known as the Rama, was a scholar from a wealthy family already widely known outside Poland in his mid-twenties. He was engaged on a commentary of his own on the *Arba'ah Turim* of Yaakov b. Asher when he discovered that Karo was completing his commentary in the *Beth Yosef*. So Isserles decided instead to compile, in his *Darkhei Moshe* ('Ways of Moses'), supplementary notes from Ashkenazi scholars to add to Karo's work. When the *Shulhan Arukh* was published, Isserles used the material in *Darkhei Moshe* for his *Mappah*, with glosses to Karo's compilation intended to explain and supplement the text and, in particular, to include the customs of those Ashkenazi scholars ignored by Karo. Such glosses could sometimes subvert the whole burden of Karo's original ruling in particular cases, as in the prohibition against resorting to use of non-Jewish courts:

> Even if the plaintiff possesses a document in which it is written that he may summon the defendant under gentile law – he is still not permitted to summon him before the gentile courts. If the plaintiff handed over the document to the gentile court so that it might summon the defendant under its laws, he is obligated to reimburse the defendant for any loss he caused him, in excess of whatever the defendant is liable to pay under the laws of Israel. Gloss: This whole ruling applies only where one party can compel the other to appear before a Jewish court, but if a debtor proves violent, a creditor may hand over such a document to a gentile court.

Isserles' procedure was helped by the fact that Karo had explicitly laid down in the *Beth Yosef* that if his decision disagreed with Jewish custom in any country, Jews in that country were free to disregard his ruling. The two men were friends, engaging in correspondence on matters of halakhah, with Isserles, a much younger man, scrupulously courteous. The *Mappah* was included in the 1569–71 edition of the *Shulhan Arukh* published in Cracow, only a few years after the first edition of Karo's work in 1564–5 in Venice.[4]

It should not be imagined that the extraordinary popularity of the codifications of Karo and Isserles brought an end to halakhic variety. The whole procedure of codification was strongly attacked in their lifetimes by Hayyim b. Betsalel, who had studied alongside Isserles but became rabbi of Worms and Friedberg and was particularly upset by Isserles' failure to give sufficient weight to German customs. Hayyim laid out a raft of objections to the *Mappah*, beginning with the general principles that it is wrong to oblige a rabbi giving a decision to decide the halakhah according to the views of the majority, that the codes cause neglect of Talmud study and lead to ignorance, and that individual rabbis will lose authority because people will rely on published books. Hayyim noted that, in any case, if Isserles could disagree with Karo, it must in turn be permitted for other rabbis to disagree with Isserles.[5]

Hayyim was correct in both his hopes and his fears. On the one hand, the wide circulation of the *Shulhan Arukh*, with its glosses, in due course led to a democratization of halakhic knowledge, which in turn encouraged observance of the laws through communal peer pressure within Jewish communities in both Sephardi and Ashkenazi worlds. Indeed, with easy access to printed copies of the texts, peer pressure by those able to read the relevant sections of the *Shulhan Arukh* might lead to interference in minutiae of life far beyond observance of halakhah, in areas of life defined by the Talmud, and hence by Karo, as *derekh erets*, 'the way of the land', which stipulated what was decent behaviour. So, for instance, the *Shulhan Arukh* contains a long section on table manners, and another on behaviour when visiting the privy: 'He should be modest when in the privy by not exposing himself until he is seated.' Isserles adds the gloss that 'two men should not be there at the same time and the door should be closed out of modesty.' On the other hand, independent rabbis retained sufficient authority to question the decisions in the codes. Even in Poland, just a generation after the great Isserles, the head of the Lublin academy, Meir b. Gedalyah (known as Maharam), deemed the *Shulhan Arukh* no more than a collection of rulings and reserved his right to make independent decisions.

Numerous communities took advantage of Isserles' comments on the authority of custom, which in general he asserted should be binding even if there is no halakhic source. This approach was somewhat at odds with Isserles' occasional statement that a particular custom is wrong or, 'if I had the power, I would abrogate the custom. For it is based on an error and there is no reason to rely on it.' It was not in any case possible for the codes to cover all eventualities, and local rabbinic leaders inevitably retained a role in deciding particular issues. But it is probably significant that it was the religious leaders of smaller communities who felt the need to assert the right to religious diversity. Thus in the first half of the eighteenth century the great spiritual leader of Moroccan Jewry, Yaakov ibn Zur, decreed that in a small community a single judge (*dayyan*) had as much authority to take decisions as a full court of three judges, and that a ruling handed down in one place could not be challenged in another.[6]

Karo and Isserles were well aware that even quite clear legal stipulations in the Talmud were no longer observed in their day and that it was pointless to object to the way that Jews had responded over the centuries to changed conditions. Thus the Babylonian Talmud explicitly requires workmen to recite only a short form of grace after meals because the time they spend is at the expense of their employer, but Karo ruled that 'nowadays' they should recite the full grace. Conversely, Isserles endorsed the universal practice in his day, when Jews lived among non-Jews, to light Hanukkah lights in the home rather than outside in the street as mandated in the Mishnah. So, too, after the compilation of the *Shulhan Arukh* and *Mappah*, later rabbis felt able to claim that conditions had changed. Thus, R. Joel Sirkes in Poland in the seventeenth century contradicted the ruling of Karo that two males should never be alone together for fear of homosexual acts, noting that 'in our lands, where it is unheard of for anyone to be lax in this matter, there is no need for separation.'[7]

At the same time, some new customs emerged which took hold of the religious imagination of communities and became central to the lives of many Jews, such as the recitation of Kaddish by a mourner. The notion that a mourner should recite this expression of praise of God which had long been used to separate sections of the synagogue service, is not mentioned by Karo in the *Shulhan Arukh*. The practice, which seems to have become common only in the high Middle Ages, was apparently confined at that time to Ashkenazi communities. But Isserles discussed the procedures for the mourner's Kaddish in detail, and it is evident that in Poland the custom was observed with great tenacity:

> One should recite kaddish for a father. Therefore, it is the adopted practice to recite the last kaddish twelve months for a father and mother ... It is the adopted usage to recite kaddish for one's mother although the father is still living ... It is a religious duty to fast on the day that one's father and mother died ... It is customary that when the day on which one's father or mother died arrives, one always recites the mourner's kaddish for them. One who knows how to lead the entire service should do so. However, if

there are other mourners, it is customary that within the seven days of their mourning, they take precedence and he has no rights [regarding] the kaddish at all ... If there is no one present in the synagogue who is in mourning for one's father or mother, that kaddish may be recited by one who has no father and mother on behalf of all the dead of Israel. There are localities where it is customary that other near-of-kin recite kaddish for their relations where [the latter leave] no parental mourners ... In this entire [matter] we follow the accepted custom, provided the custom is fixed in the [particular] city.[8]

In due course the mourner's Kaddish was also to become an integral part of Sephardi culture, along with *yahrzeit*, observance of the anniversary of the death of a relative for whom mourning is required by the lighting of a candle and a role in the public liturgy in the synagogue. Praying for departed close relatives and giving charity on their behalf became a popular custom both in Ashkenazi ritual, where the prayer which opens with Yizkor, 'may he remember', is recited on the three pilgrimage festivals and the Day of Atonement, and in Sephardi synagogues, where each person called to the Torah may recite, or listen to, a memorial prayer for his relatives. The practice was not uncontroversial – in the tenth century, Hai Gaon had specifically opposed it on the grounds that such prayers are valueless since God only takes into account the deeds of an individual in his lifetime – but the offering of memorial prayers, with charitable offerings 'for the repose of the departed souls', became a popular practice, especially in Ashkenazi ritual, where a desire to commemorate martyrs in the Crusades and in the Polish massacres of the seventeenth century led communities to keep death rolls (in Yiddish, *yizker-buch*) so that the names of those without living relatives would also be included in the communal prayers. It is striking that this custom, which came to hold great emotional significance for many ordinary Jews within the synagogue liturgy, seems to have emerged without any specific theological justification or discussion about the status of the souls of the dead for whose benefit these prayers were said: 'May God remember the soul of ... who has gone on to his world, because (without making a vow) I shall give charity on his behalf. As a reward for this, may his soul be bound in the bond of life together with the souls of Abraham, Isaac and Jacob and together with the other righteous men and women in the Garden of Eden.' The popularity of such mourning customs almost certainly owes much to the Catholic Christian world which surrounded Ashkenazi Jews.[9]

The wide circulation of the codes thus had the effect of spreading some customs which had previously been confined, while entrenching some other differences. Among these differences are the distinctive rules of Sephardim and Ashkenazim in the categories of food prohibited on Pesach: Ashkenazim refrain from *kitniot* (legumes and grains, such as rice, peas, lentils, beans and peanuts) which are permitted to Sephardim. The origin of the Ashkenazi restriction is unclear. The best guess is a concern that they might be contaminated with forbidden grain (*hametz*) when stored. But the result of these different customs can be considerable, for it renders the food of even the most pious Sephardi Jews forbidden to an Ashkenazi for the whole of Passover.[10]

Thus the concerns of Hayyim b. Betsalel that the codes of Karo and Isserles would end local variety proved exaggerated. So too did his warning that students would neglect study of the Talmud if all they needed was these handy reference works. In fact the sixteenth and seventeenth centuries witnessed an explosion in yeshivah study in eastern Europe, with major centres in Lublin, Cracow, Prague, Lvov, Brest-Litovsk, Pinsk and Slutsk, and numerous small yeshivot in other communities. Talmud study flourished in Italy (notably Venice and Livorno) and Greece (especially Salonica), and in Constantinople, and in the two main centres in the land of Israel, Jerusalem (where the small Jewish population from the late medieval period had been enlarged by an influx of Sephardim after 1492) and Safed. When the yeshivot in Poland and Lithuania suffered a period of temporary decline after the Chmielnicki massacres in 1648–9, many eastern European scholars migrated to teach in the German communities in Frankfurt am Main, Hamburg, Metz and elsewhere. Others ended up in Hungary, in Eisenstadt and Pressburg (today Bratislava in Slovakia), and in the nineteenth century the communities of central and western Europe developed their own indigenous scholarly traditions, as we shall see (Chapters 17–19).[11]

On the other hand, approaches to Talmud study did change, with far less concern to discover from the ancient texts the halakhah in practice, which was now easily available in the codes. Characteristic of study in these academies, in Ashkenazi countries, was still intensive instruction in the text of the Talmud, with the commentaries of Rashi and others from the medieval French and German tradition. But the method of teaching, *pilpul*, owed something to a humanist stress on intellectual independence, albeit still allied to respect for the traditional sources. *Pilpul* (a word derived from the verb *pilpel*, 'to spice' or 'to season') involved intense oral disputation between the head of the yeshivah and the pupil. It was intended to encourage logical reasoning and an ability to differentiate through casuistic argument even the most minute details in the Talmud. *Pilpul* assumed that every sentence in the Talmud must contain some special meaning which just needed to be teased out by imagination, perception, intuition and hard work, even if this required the splitting of hairs and the subversion of the plain meaning of the text.

It is hard to capture the flavour of such teaching from surviving texts without very extended citation precisely because it is characteristic of the method to pursue every possible trail leading from the original text. One example may suffice. Aryeh Leib b. Asher Gunzberg, head of a yeshivah in Metz in Lithuania from 1765 to his death in 1785 after posts in Minsk and Volozhin, and author of a number of works which have shaped Lithuanian approaches to the study of the Talmud to the present day, proved the correctness of one view of earlier commentaries on the Talmud, and the incorrectness of another, by analysis of two talmudic passages, as follows:

> The Talmud says that the search for and removal of leavened matter on the eve of the Passover is merely a rabbinical prescription; for it is sufficient, according to the commands of the Torah, if merely in words or in thought the owner declares it to be destroyed and equal to the dust. Rashi says that the fact that such a declaration of the owner is sufficient is derived from an expression in Scripture. The tosafot, however, claim that this cannot be derived from the particular expression in Scripture, since the word there means 'to remove' and not 'to declare destroyed'. The mere declaration that it is destroyed is sufficient for the reason that thereby the owner gives up his rights of ownership, and the leavened matter is regarded as having no owner, and as food for which no one is responsible, since at Passover only one's own leavened food may not be kept, while that of strangers may be kept. Although the formula which is sufficient to declare the leavened matter as destroyed is not sufficient to declare one's property as having no owner, yet, as R. Nissim Gerondi, adopting the view of the tosafot, explains, the right of ownership which one has in leavened matter on the eve of Passover, even in the forenoon, is a very slight one; for, beginning with noon, such food may not be enjoyed; hence all rights of ownership become illusory, and, in view of such slight right of ownership, a mere mental renunciation of this right suffices in order that the leavened matter be considered as without an owner. R. Aryeh Leib attempts to prove the correctness of this tosafistic opinion as elaborated by R. Nissim, and to prove at the same time the incorrectness of Rashi's view, from a later

talmudic passage which says that from the hour of noon of the eve [of Passover] to the conclusion of the feast the mere declaration of destruction does not free a person from the responsibility of having leavened matter in the house; for since he is absolutely forbidden to enjoy it, he has no claim to the ownership, which he renounces by such a declaration.

Aryeh Leib's virtuoso reasoning continues through many more steps, citing a number of further talmudic texts, until he feels able to conclude from the method of the talmudic argument that the Tosafistic opinion, represented by R. Nissim, the Ran, who taught in Spain in the mid-fourteenth century, is right and Rashi is wrong. In such a *pilpul*, the topic of discussion and the conclusions reached were less significant for a master of *pilpul* than the display of logical reasoning and ingenuity. Brilliance in argument could all too easily become an end in itself, and young students from the age of thirteen would travel from one yeshivah to another in search of the inspiring instruction which would bring them renown.[12]

Pilpul was not in itself a wholly novel method of study. The term is already found in the Talmuds to describe the penetrating reasoning which straightens out apparent difficulties in the text, and it had been employed too by the Tosafist scholars of France and Germany, and some of their contemporaries in Spain, as they hammered out the apparent contradictions in the talmudic commentaries of Rashi. But the popularity of the method in the Ashkenazi world in the early modern period reached unprecedented heights, with the intuition of the greatest minds seen by some kabbalists as evidence of divine inspiration. The masters of *pilpul* became celebrities, courted for marriage alliances and offered positions of communal leadership as a form of local pride, especially for the yeshivot supported by that community through taxes and grants to poorer students. The medieval yeshivot in Ashkenazi lands had in many cases survived as the more or less private academies of the rabbis who headed them, but from the sixteenth century local communities saw the upkeep of a yeshivah as a religious duty. A resolution of the first assembly of the Council of Lithuanian Jewry in 1622 even obliged every community with a rabbi to maintain a yeshivah of suitable size.[13]

The enthusiasm for *pilpul* did not escape without fierce criticism from within Ashkenazi Jewry, most significantly by Elijah b. Solomon Zalman, the Gaon of Vilna, who was widely recognized in his own lifetime as the most erudite halakhist not only of eighteenth-century Lithuania but of all rabbinic learning since the Middle Ages. The independence and clarity of thought which made Elijah b. Solomon so famous was in part a product of his unusual training. Born in Vilna in 1720, he was a precocious child and so rapidly mastered the standard rabbinic curriculum that from the age of ten he was able to devote himself to direct study of the texts without becoming a student at any particular yeshivah. His reputation spread during his teens and early twenties while he travelled from one Jewish community to another in Poland and Germany, and by the time he returned to Vilna in 1748 he was considered by his home town to be a precious ornament of the city, to be treasured and protected. As a result, the Gaon was able to spend a secluded life devoted to study, supported by a weekly allowance from the Vilna community. He had only a small group of disciples, so his immense influence derived not from any formal position but simply from his reputation as a scholar – none of his voluminous works appeared in print during his lifetime, although a large number of his manuscripts were published by his followers soon after his death in 1797.[14]

Despite a devotion to the study of kabbalah, the Gaon insisted on the supremacy of rational argument and scientific method in the interpretation of the ancient writings, adopting philology and grammar when they help to clarify a complex passage or correct a defective text and seeking to establish talmudic authority for halakhic rulings cited without a talmudic base in the later codes. As his sons insisted in their introduction when they published his commentary on the *Shulhan Arukh*, the student should avoid altogether the casuistic approach of *pilpul*, through which 'transgression increases, iniquity grows, pleasant speech is lost, and truth driven from the congregation of the Lord'. 'Piling up difficulties' for its own sake was to be avoided. For the Gaon, traditional rabbinic scholarship was best preserved by a rational, intellectual, methodical approach to the texts which emphasized the ability of the dedicated individual to penetrate the correct meaning of ancient texts, even, if necessary, by 'correcting' the text, or reconstructing it, to ensure a rational meaning.

The Gaon's lifestyle became an ideal for many east European Jews in the following century. Not all could hope for fame as a child prodigy, but many could opt for a cloistered life removed from communal affairs and dedicated to abstruse study. One of the Gaon's students founded the great Volozhin yeshivah in the nineteenth century where hundreds of students devoted themselves to just such a dream. The city of Vilna, with its medieval town hall and castles and florid baroque architecture in a Baltic landscape, and its hot summers and freezing winters and lakes devoted to ice fishing, became known in the eighteenth century as 'the Jerusalem of Lithuania' through the reputation of the Gaon. The 1795 census recorded 3,613 Jewish poll-tax payers in Vilna and its environs, with Jews a virtual majority in the city and the community established as a pre-eminent centre of Jewish learning.[15]

Nowhere in the Sephardi world developed a comparable reputation for yeshivah learning in the early modern period, and Sephardi yeshivot developed very differently, with study of Bible and *midrash* included in the curriculum. Different again was humanistic study of the variety of Jewish customs (*minhagim*), as by Leone Modena of Venice, or the approach of those in Renaissance Italy who combined the study of Torah with the study of science. Talmud study was in any case impeded in Italy after the Talmud had been banned by the pope in 1559, and systematic instruction in the halakhic codes became common in its place. And students in the yeshivot in Italy, as in the Jewish communities in the Levant under Ottoman rule, could also expect (unlike their fellow students in Ashkenazi lands) formal instruction in the kabbalah, which itself developed greatly in the early modern period, as we shall see.

THE FOLLOWERS OF LURIA

In Meiron in Upper Galilee, against the backdrop of a monumental synagogue of the fourth century CE, crowds of pilgrims gather on Lag BaOmer, to mark the anniversary of the death of Shimon bar Yohai at the reputed site of his grave. It is a time for enthusiastic celebration, with bonfires and dancing, and many small children, since it is traditional for sons to receive their first haircut on the following day, the locks of hair being thrown into the fire. The custom was already well established by the time it is first mentioned in an account by Moses Basola, an Italian rabbi, of his travels in the land of Israel in 1522. Shimon, as we have seen, was believed to be the author of the Zohar, and the Zohar itself relates in the name of Abba that when Shimon bar Yohai died, a voice was heard calling on worshippers to 'ascend and gather' at his tomb to celebrate the anniversary of his death:

> All that day the fire did not leave the house, and no one could get near it. They were unable, because the light and the fire surrounded it the whole day. I threw myself upon the ground and groaned. When the fire had gone I saw that the holy light, the holy of holies, had departed from the world. He was lying on his right side, wrapped in his cloak, and his face was

laughing. Rabbi Eleazar, his son, rose, took his hands and kissed them, and I licked the dust beneath his feet ... Rabbi Hiyya got to his feet, and said, 'Up till now the holy light has taken care of us. Now we can do nothing but attend to his honour.' Rabbi Eleazar and Rabbi Abba rose, and put him in a litter. Who has ever seen disarray like that of the companions? The whole house exuded perfume. They raised him on his bier, and only Rabbi Eleazar and Rabbi Abba occupied themselves with it. The powerful and mighty men of the town came and pleaded with them, and the inhabitants of Meiron cried out all together, for they were afraid that he might not be buried there. When the bier came out of the house, it went up into the air and fire flared out in front of it. They heard a voice, saying, 'Come and assemble for the feast of Rabbi Shimon.'

Upper Galilee was thus a locus of mystical longing, filled with the aura of the sages of the mythical origins of the kabbalah, long before the small town of Safed, a few miles from Meiron, became the cradle of a new form of Jewish mysticism in the mid-sixteenth century. We have already noted Safed as a centre of Jewish learning. It had begun with sporadic Jewish settlement, attested in documents from the Cairo Genizah from the first half of the eleventh century, but the community had only really began to grow with the influx of refugees from Spain after 1492. Ottoman documents reveal over a thousand Jewish households in 1544–5 in the town, with a sizeable Samaritan population alongside them.[16]

This was the town to which Isaac Luria was drawn in 1570, at the age of thirty-six. He died there two years later, on 15 July 1572, from plague, but not before laying the foundations of a whole new form of kabbalah. Isaac b. Solomon Luria was born in 1534 in Jerusalem to a father who had emigrated there from Germany or Poland but died in Isaac's childhood. His Sephardi mother took the boy to Egypt, where he learned and wrote about halakhah and began his studies in mysticism. The profusion of legends which clustered around his life in the recollections of his followers immediately after his early death make it hard to reconstruct precisely the intellectual journey that led him to his mystical insights. A document from the Cairo Genizah in Luria's handwriting shows only that he was engaged in some business relating to grain. Luria's maternal uncle, in whose care he had been raised in Egypt, was a rich tax-farmer and owned the island Jazirat al-Rawda on the Nile near Cairo, and it was said that Luria lived there in seclusion for seven years, writing the commentary on a short portion of the Zohar which is the only work of his to survive. Travel from Egypt to the land of Israel was not difficult at that time, and it is probable that he paid a special visit to Galilee to celebrate Lag BaOmer at Meiron. His pupil Hayyim Vital recorded that Luria brought his small son there together with his whole family, cutting his hair there according to the well-known custom and spending a day of feasting and celebration. At any rate, in 1569 or early 1570, Luria moved to Safed and settled there.[17]

The immediate attraction for Luria seems to have been the prospect of studying with Moshe b. Yaakov Cordovero, who was of Spanish and Portuguese origin and, as the head of the Portuguese yeshivah in Safed, was deeply immersed in the study of kabbalah. In 1548, at the age of twenty-six, Cordovero had written a major book on the notion of the divine, the cosmos, the worship of God and other such major themes of the kabbalah, making eclectic use of the Zohar and the ecstatic kabbalah of Avraham Abulafia. By 1570 he was a major figure in Safed, with a large crowd of disciples. Cordovero's main efforts had been in the production of a coherent speculative system by synthesizing previous ideas, relying on philosophers (especially Maimonides) for a purified concept of God as without attributes. He took from the kabbalah tradition the structure of the *sefirot*, which he saw as both emanations of God and part of God's substance. Cordovero's puzzlement about the relationship of the *sefirot* to the divine will led him to the notion that, in order to be revealed through the *sefirot*, God has to conceal himself: 'revealing is the cause of concealment and concealment is the cause of revealing.'[18]

In some of his Zohar glosses, Luria refers to Cordovero as his teacher, and he was just one of the impressive group of students of kabbalah who had gathered in Safed to benefit from Cordovero's vast knowledge. But when Cordovero died at the end of 1570, Luria became the centre of an academy of his own, with at least thirty disciples, and in the two years before his death he imparted a radical new way of understanding the significance of the kabbalah. Luria taught orally, delivering a flood of ideas to his pupils on how to commune with the souls of the righteous, how to concentrate on the divine names, and how to achieve proper *kavanah*, intensity in mystical meditation. Writing almost nothing, and teaching for so short a period, ensured that Luria's system was by no means coherent. His later influence can be attributed to the conspicuous sanctity of his personal conduct as much as to his religious doctrines, but it is certain that he believed himself to have made new discoveries in the kabbalah (see below), and it is probable that he thought he was a messianic agent, destined to die in the fulfilment of his mission to hasten the redemption of the world.[19]

By the end of the sixteenth century, less than thirty years after Luria's death, he was being called by kabbalists in Italy the Ari, an acronym from the Hebrew for 'the divine Rabbi Isaac'. This elevated status was the product of the wealth of writings which promulgated his teachings after his death. Unconstrained by the evidence of writings by Luria himself, his disciples revealed to the world doctrines which they explicitly stated Luria himself had kept secret and which had survived only in their memories of Luria's discourse until committed to writing after his death. Hagiography of the pious life of the master preceded circulation of his teachings, and since Luria had uttered his ideas in a state of mystical inspiration, those teachings unsurprisingly varied in form.[20]

It does not help in the investigation of Luria's real teachings that his disciples were themselves in many cases powerful personalities with a deep commitment to mysticism, which was their reason for attraction to the charismatic Luria in the first place. Prime among these was Hayyim Vital, probably a native of Safed although his father seems to have come from southern Italy. Vital was a sufficiently restless spirit to have dabbled in alchemy in his early twenties. The period of just under two years which he spent in his late twenties as Luria's leading disciple was to shape the rest of his life. In the years immediately following Luria's death, Vital wrote down the teachings of his master in a book which he called *Ets Hayyim* ('The Tree of Life'), but both he and his son made many alterations to the text over the following years, so that different versions circulated. Other disciples of Luria produced their own competing versions. Striking evidence of the struggle over Luria's heritage was the need for a formal agreement in 1575 by twelve of Luria's disciples to study Luria's theories only from Vital, and not to force Vital to reveal more than he wished (or themselves to reveal these secrets to others). Vital himself moved to Jerusalem in 1577 and eventually to Damascus, where he put together much later in his old age a sort of autobiography, recording his dreams and actions and reflecting on his role as preserver of Luria's insights:

On the New Moon of Adar, in the year 5331 [6 February 1571], he [Luria] told me that while he was in Egypt, he began to gain his inspiration. He was informed there that he should go to the city of Safed, insofar as I, Hayyim, resided there, so as to teach me. And he said to me that the only reason he came to Safed, may it be rebuilt and re-established speedily [following a decline in Jewish population after Jews were expelled in 1583], was on my account. Not only this, but even his current incarnation was for no purpose other than to bring about my perfection. He did not return for himself, as he had no need to do so. He also told me that it was unnecessary for him to teach any other individuals besides me, and when I have learned, there will no longer be any reason for him to remain in the world. He also told me that my soul was superior to many of the exalted angels, and that I could ascend above the firmament of *Aravot* by means of my soul, through my deeds.

It becomes clear from this diary that Vital had been convinced of his own identity as the Messiah even before 1570 when Luria came to Safed.[21]

What, then, was the special nature of Lurianic kabbalah that so aroused his already enthusiastic followers? The main novelty lay in the concentration of speculation not on the nature of the cosmos as it has been created by the eternal Godhead but in the achievement of perfection in the future, not only on the level of the individual (as in earlier kabbalistic thought) but within the whole community of Israel. Where Cordovero had talked about the concealment of the divine, Luria taught that God had withdrawn into himself to allow space for creation. This concept of *tsimtsum* ('contraction') accounted for creation despite the infinite being of God and also for the continued presence of the vessels containing the divine in the world. An impression of the divine remains 'as the fragrance which lingers in the vial after it has been emptied of its perfume'. At the same time, Luria evolved a powerful mythology to explain the presence of evil in the world by positing a catastrophe, before the universe even came into being, in which the vessels containing the divine light that poured out at the moment of creation had shattered, scattering the sparks of light and leaving them captive to the power of evil until they can be raised again by the efforts of Israel. The services of kabbalists are particularly required for this process of setting the world back to rights (*tikkun olam*), through piety and systematic meditation in all aspects of life. The individual soul, too, required *tikkun*, since all souls had originally been contained within the soul of Adam, whose fall constituted the alienation of humanity from God. In the mid-seventeenth century the Portuguese kabbalist Jacob b. Hayyim Zemach asserted that each soul brings on itself its individual exile by its sins which may lead to reincarnation in a lower form of life: 'Know that an individual may at times be perfected by temporarily joining the body of another person and at times he may require reincarnation which is even more painful.' More positively, the concept of *gilgul* ('revolving'), developing notions about the transmigration of souls already found in kabbalistic writings of the twelfth century, gave life a purpose in seeking restoration in the soul of Adam.[22]

The driving force behind Luria's disciples seems to have been messianic hope, for Lurianic doctrines gave a direct role to the kabbalists in bringing about the redemption of Israel. It did not matter for this purpose that knowledge of these doctrines was deliberately confined to the privileged few; on the contrary, Vital and Luria's other disciples appear to have been reluctant to share his teachings at all, and in many accounts of Luria's ideas his central notion of 'contraction' remained unstated or just hinted at even decades after his death. Claiming reluctance to share mystical insights can sometimes be a ploy by mystics to promote and publicize their ideas, and knowledge of the doctrines of specifically Lurianic kabbalah spread more rapidly after the death of Vital in 1620. In the following decades a series of presentations of Luria's thought were printed and widely circulated through the Jewish world.

The practices of the kabbalists, from liturgy to penitential manuals, and their specialized vocabulary, spread even faster than their more complex doctrines. A feeling that the doctrines of the kabbalah were now available to all must have been greatly strengthened by the controversial printing of copies of the Zohar in Mantua (in 1558–60) and Cremona (1559–60), allowing a much wider readership – albeit of texts marred by frequent printing errors, and in a different version from the manuscript of the Zohar used in Safed.[23]

Lurianic doctrines did not appeal to all, and, notwithstanding the spread of Lurianic kabbalistic notions to the extent that Lurianic kabbalah has been described as the default theology of Judaism by the early seventeenth century, there were some who continued throughout the century to favour earlier varieties of the kabbalah. So, for instance, the strong mystical bent of the poems written in the seventeenth century by Shalem Shabbazi, the greatest of the Jewish poets of Yemen, whose compositions dominate the Yemenite liturgy, was based on pre-Lurianic kabbalah. Similarly, although Judah Loew, known as the Maharal of Prague, a prolific scholar of impressively independent temper, was devoted to the dissemination of Jewish mystical teachings to ordinary Jews, the numerous writings he published right up to his death in 1609 owe nothing to Lurianic ideas. Eschewing the technical terminology of the kabbalah despite evident familiarity with such kabbalistic notions as the transcendent nature of the Torah, Loew emphasized the unique metaphysical role of the Jews as the chosen people, inventing new meanings for standard philosophical terminology (such as his assertion that 'Israel' constitutes 'form', while the other nations constitute 'matter') to propagate mystical ideas to a wide readership of non-specialists. Loew was a communal leader as chief rabbi of Moravia and Poznań as well as Prague, and a mathematician and a public figure – the astronomer Tycho Brahe was an acquaintance. It is ironic that both Jews and gentiles in later generations were to remember him most because of a totally unfounded legend that he dabbled in magic and created the Golem of Prague. (According to the legend, which seems to have been transferred to Loew only in the eighteenth century and bears obvious similarities to non-Jewish stories about the creation of artificial men by alchemy, Loew created the golem as a servant but had to reduce it to dust when it proved impossible to control.)[24]

The number of devotees to kabbalistic speculation itself was always quite small, and kabbalists almost without exception combined their mystical studies with study of practical halakhah. We have already seen that Yosef Karo, supreme codifier of rabbinic law, was also a kabbalist. He had studied in Safed from 1536 alongside Moshe Cordovero, the teacher of Luria. So, too, Luria himself was a renowned expert in halakhah, even if, as his disciple Vital recorded, the kabbalah had first call on his attention:

Also in connection with the study of the halakhah in depth, together with his companions, I witnessed my master, of blessed memory, engaging in his halakhic studies until he became weary and covered in perspiration. I asked him why he went to such trouble. He replied that profound application is essential in order to shatter the shells [demonic forces], the difficulties which inhere in every halakhah and which prevent one from understanding that halakhah . . . And my master, of blessed memory, used to say that one whose mind is sufficiently clear, subtle, and keen to reflect on the halakhah for one hour or, in the majority of cases, two hours, it is certainly good that he bothers himself at first with this deep study for one or two hours . . . But one who knows himself to be hampered in his efforts at deep study, so that for him to grasp the meaning of the halakhah he is obliged to expend much time and effort, he does not behave correctly. He is like the man who spends all his time cracking nuts without ever eating the kernels. Far better for such a one to engage in the study of the Torah itself, namely, the laws, the midrashim and the mysteries.[25]

Luria and his followers were generally conservative in upholding traditional ritual, and indeed their tendency to read mystical significance into liturgy strengthened the hold of such practices among the wider Jewish populace. The pervasive legacy of Lurianic kabbalah was less a change in behaviour than a deeper appreciation among ordinary Jews of the significance of their existing religious practices. Luria's preference for, and mystical meditation on, the Sephardi form of the liturgy lent a prestige to this form among Ashkenazi kabbalists. Luria himself was famed for his liturgical poetry, and many of the hymns of the Safed kabbalists, particularly for Sabbath meals, spread the language of kabbalistic symbolism:

> Reveal Yourself, my beloved, and spread over me
> the tabernacle of Your peace.
> Let the earth shine with Your glory,
> let us be overjoyed and rejoice in You.
> Hurry, beloved, for the appointed time has come,
> and be gracious to us as in the times of old.

Some of the practices of the Safed kabbalists remained unique to their community, such as the elaborate procession to inaugurate the Sabbath by going out into the surrounding countryside on Friday evening dressed all in white to welcome the 'Sabbath bride'. This custom was introduced (or renewed) by Shlomo Alkabez, one of the founders of the Safed kabbalist community, who taught, among others, Cordovero. Safed remained a special place, even though the community was to shrink rapidly in numbers towards the end of the century as it declined in prosperity.

Kabbalists referred to Safed as one of the four holy cities of the land of Israel, alongside Hebron (where the biblical patriarchs had been buried), Tiberias (where the Palestinian Talmud had been created) and Jerusalem (where the Temple had once stood). On the other hand, the legacy of Safed belonged to all Jews, and the Sabbath hymn *Lekha Dodi*, 'Come, my Beloved', composed by Alkabez, full of references to the peace and joy of messianic times as a reflection of the peace and joy of the Sabbath, was rapidly adopted throughout the Jewish world:

> To greet the Sabbath, come let us go,
> For of blessing, she is the source.
> From the outset, as of old, ordained:
> Last in deed, first in thought.

> Come, my Beloved, to greet the bride;
> let us welcome the Sabbath.[26]

The popularization of Lurianic kabbalah was not without unintended consequences. One product of a growing belief in the transmigration of souls was the idea that a living person or soul could be impregnated by the spirit of a dead person which has been left disembodied because of the sins of that person during life. Such a *dibbuk* – a Yiddish term first found in the seventeenth century in eastern Europe – was believed to talk through the mouth of the host body. By definition, it was likely to be evil, and rites of exorcism were devised for the expulsion of an evil spirit through the use of a *yihud*, a combination of divine names, conceived as the intimate unification of the male and female manifestations of the divine, as Hayim Vital recounted:

> And following is the procedure, as personally tested by myself. For I would grasp that man's arm and put my hand on the pulse of his left or right arm, since this is where the vestment of the soul is located, and therein it clads itself. And I concentrate upon that soul, clad in the pulse, that he might depart from there by the power of the *yihud*. And while clinging to his hand at the pulse, I recite this verse, normally and backwards, and concentrate upon the following divine Names that issue from the text . . .[27]

Lurianic kabbalah, with its encouraging notion that everyone has a role in redeeming the fallen sparks, became by the end of the early modern period much the most influential type of mysticism both for specialists in kabbalah and for ordinary Jews attracted by the notion that every commandment and every word of every prayer has a hidden mystical meaning and that 'repair of the world' (*tikkun olam*) is a central aim of religious life. There is a correspondence between what is above and what is below. Intensification of prayer was aimed at bringing the redemption by creating harmony in the world of the *sefirot*. Ritual became theurgy. There was also a direct link, as we shall see, from the theology of Lurianic kabbalah to some of the theology devised to support the claims of Sabbetai Zevi.

SABBETAI ZEVI

In April 1665 a charming and learned kabbalist – originally from Smyrna but, now nearly forty years old, for some time past a resident of

Jerusalem and then Cairo, known for unpredictable and sometimes dramatically antinomian behaviour, which involved ostentatious public flouting of religious norms, and notorious for claims, over seventeen years, that he was the Messiah – went to the city of Gaza, at this time ruled by Musa Pasha, the last of the Ridwan dynasty to govern Gaza and Jerusalem on behalf of the Ottoman state, to seek 'peace for his soul' from a certain Abraham Nathan b. Elisha Hayim Ashkenazi. Nathan, a remarkable holy man, had already at the age of twenty established a reputation for his expertise in Lurianic kabbalah, through which he had received visions of angels and deceased souls. The visitor was Sabbetai Zevi. But instead of disabusing him of his fancies, Nathan informed him that he had himself experienced around the time of Purim a prolonged vision, in which he had witnessed the figure of Sabbetai engraved on the divine throne, and that there could be no doubt that Sabbetai was the Messiah. This endorsement by a prophet widely admired among the Jewish population of the land of Israel was to start a tumultuous period of eighteen months in which the equilibrium of Jewish communities from Poland and Russia to Yemen and Kurdistan was shattered, with consequences for generations to come.[28]

The implications took a while to sink in for Sabbetai himself, as he got to know the young man and to appreciate his prophetic expertise. But on 19 May, at the festival of Shavuot, the truth became public in a dramatic scene in the house of Jacob Najara, rabbi to the Gaza community, as Baruch of Arezzo, author of the earliest biography of Sabbetai Zevi, recorded, just over a decade later:

When the Shavuot festival arrived, Master Nathan invited the rabbis of Gaza to spend the night studying Torah with him. About midnight, Master Nathan went into a deep trance. He stood up, walked back and forth in the room, recited the entire tractate *Ketubot* by heart. He ordered one rabbi to sing a certain hymn, then did the same to another. While this was going on, all the rabbis became aware of a pleasant aroma, wonderfully fragrant, like the smell of a field the Lord had blessed. They went looking in the surrounding houses and alleyways for the source of the aroma, but found nothing. All the while [Nathan] was jumping and dancing around the room. He stripped off one piece of clothing after another, until he was down to his undergarment. Then he made a great leap and fell flat on the floor. When the rabbis saw this, they tried to help him to his feet. But they found him lifeless as a corpse. The honourable Rabbi Meir Rofé was present, and he felt his wrist the way physicians do and announced to us that he had no pulse. They laid a cloth over his face, as one does – God protect us! – for the dead. But a short while later they heard a very low voice. They removed the cloth from his face and saw that a voice was emanating from his mouth, though his lips did not move. 'Be careful', [the voice] said, 'of My son, My beloved, My messiah Sabbetai Zevi.' Then it went on: 'Be careful of My son, My beloved, Nathan the prophet.' Thus did the rabbis come to realize that the aroma they smelled had emanated from that same spark of spiritual holiness that had entered into Master Nathan and spoken these words.[29]

When on 31 May Sabbetai Zevi proclaimed himself in public as the Messiah, Najara led his community in acknowledgement. Sabbetai Zevi began immediately to behave in appropriately regal fashion, riding on horseback and appointing his followers to lead the Twelve Tribes of Israel.

The central actor of this drama was a curious personality. Sabbetai's followers referred to periods of depression alternating with 'illumination', when Sabbetai liked to commit 'strange deeds' calculated to shock. The son of a wealthy merchant in Smyrna, he was recognized when young for his talmudic knowledge and began study of the kabbalah as a teenager. He lived in ascetic seclusion in his early twenties, becoming increasingly odd, with claims of an ability to levitate. He failed to consummate either of the marriages into which he entered. Between 1646 and 1650 it became clear that he believed himself destined for higher things; according to later Sabbatian traditions, it was in 1648 that he first decided that he was the Messiah, in the year in which he believed that, according to the Zohar, the dead would be resurrected. By 1651 his behaviour had become too erratic for the local rabbis in Smyrna to tolerate, and he was put under a ban. Expelled for some years from Smyrna, he wandered to Salonica and later to Constantinople, proclaiming from time to time his messianic status and creating scandal by such acts as going through a wedding ceremony with a copy of the Torah. Eventually he travelled in 1662 to Jerusalem, where he was first spotted by the teenage Nathan.[30]

The news from Gaza spread at speed to the other Jews in Palestine. Not all were won over. In Jerusalem, the local rabbi had known Sabbetai Zevi for many years, and a majority opposed him when he arrived at the holy city followed by a large crowd. But some important figures were persuaded, and the rest were cautious, banishing Sabbetai Zevi from their own city but not counteracting the increasingly frenzied messages about the Messiah being promulgated by Nathan. It was hard to stand up to the enthusiasm of Sabbetai Zevi's followers, and Nathan's call on all Israel to repent in order to bring about the imminent redemption was calculated to persuade rabbis to give the movement their support. How could enthusiasts engaged in fasts and other forms of asceticism not be considered pious?

Once allegiance to the new Messiah had been pledged, it was hard to retract, even if the message about the significance of Sabbetai Zevi kept changing with each new revelation to Nathan. In September 1665 Nathan wrote to a leading figure in the Cairo Jewish community to tell him that the time had come for redemption and that any who opposed it would be harmed. In the hidden world the holy sparks were no longer under the control of evil. In the near future Sabbetai Zevi would become king in place of the Ottoman sultan, unleashing a series of events which would include the 'birth pangs of redemption' in which there would be great suffering. In the meantime, all should repent, with fasting and prayer.[31]

Rumours of dramatic events in the Holy Land had reached as far north as England by the summer of 1665, but it was early October by the time that the full story was being told, in suitably embroidered form, throughout Europe. By then Sabbetai Zevi had travelled to Smyrna, his birthplace. He created turmoil in some of the places through which he passed on his way, with many, both male and female, driven to prophesying in what, according to Baruch of Arezzo, became a standard fashion:

> This was the manner of prophesying in those days: people would go into a trance and fall to the ground as though dead, their spirits entirely gone. After about half an hour they would begin to breathe and, without moving their lips, would speak scriptural verses praising God, offering comfort. All would say: 'Sabbetai Zevi is the messiah of the God of Jacob.' Upon recovering, they had no awareness of what they had done or said.

Notable rabbis were caught up in the excitement as much as the ordinary populace.[32]

Nathan had stayed behind in Gaza, although he continued to proclaim the news of the coming redemption. The change in Sabbetai Zevi's message and behaviour in Smyrna at the end of 1665 can only be explained by his own self-belief. After months of ascetic behaviour and pious prayer, he began to contravene the halakhah in public in deliberately conspicuous fashion, as Baruch was to record:

It was after this that [Sabbetai] began to do things that seemed strange. He would pronounce the Sacred Name precisely as it was written. He ate animal fat. He did other things contrary to God and His Torah, and pressed others to do the same wicked deeds ... Then, that Sabbath, he recited petitionary prayers at great length and afterwards went off to the Portuguese synagogue. Many of those who worshipped there did not believe in him, and therefore had barred the synagogue doors. He fell into a terrific rage. He sent for an axe, and, Sabbath though it was, hacked away at the doors until they opened them.

By urging that the law be broken, and especially demanding that his supporters utter aloud the ineffable name of God, Sabbetai Zevi was heralding the messianic age when everything would be changed. But he also flushed out the opposition, thus binding his supporters closer (not least the women whom he called to read the Torah). He announced that the date of redemption would be 15 Sivan 5426, which coincided with 18 June 1666.[33]

By this time, expression of opposition to Sabbetai Zevi's claims was becoming dangerous in Smyrna, even when he shockingly decreed the abolition of the fast of the Tenth of Tevet, a fast ordained within the Bible itself in commemoration of the beginning of the Babylonian siege of Jerusalem which had led to the destruction of the first Temple in 586 BCE. The local Jews began to pray for Sabbetai Zevi as the king of Israel in place of the standard prayer which expressed loyalty to the sultan. He was increasingly addressed as *amirah*, which signified 'Our Lord and King, may his Majesty be exalted'. Jews flooded into Smyrna from all over Turkey to join the celebrations, and on 30 December 1665 Sabbetai, with a huge train, sailed to Constantinople.[34]

Over the two centuries since its capture by the Ottomans in 1453, Constantinople had been transformed into the great Islamic city of Istanbul, in which narrow, twisting streets of wooden houses clustered between great mosques, palaces and bazaars. The holy site of Eyüp stood at the head of the Golden Horn, where the body of the Prophet's standard-bearer killed during the Arab siege of Constantinople in 674–8 had been discovered, and numerous fountains, bridges, schools and other buildings erected by Suleiman the Magnificent and other sultans adorned the capital. But of half a million or so inhabitants only a small majority were Muslims, and the Jews – of whom thousands had settled after the expulsion from Spain in 1492 – were a self-governing community, like the Orthodox Christians, under their own religious authorities (except in criminal cases, which came to the Ottoman courts). Excitement was high both among the Jews and among the (more sceptical) gentiles as Sabbetai Zevi approached, and the Turkish authorities intercepted his boat on 6 February 1666, throwing him into prison. It seems likely that the decision not to put him to death was taken to avoid turning him into a martyr and inflaming Jews throughout the Ottoman realm. He was moved to Gallipoli, and there his prison was in effect transformed by bribery into a protected castle where he held court, receiving emissaries from many parts of the Jewish world:

> So our Lord dwelt in great honour in his 'tower of strength'. God made the superintendent of the tower to be kindly disposed toward him, to such an extent that he became [Sabbetai's] servant. ('I am serving two kings', he used to remark.) Men, women, and children, of our people and of other peoples as well, came from all over the world to see him, talk with him, do obeisance to him, kiss his hands. His fame as messiah had spread everywhere.[35]

Dissenters were excommunicated by the rabbis of Constantinople for seeing fit 'to believe the worst about an angel in human form ... on account of certain acts that on the surface seem peculiar but in truth are marvellous'. In much of the diaspora, Jews fasted, purified themselves and scourged their bodies. Some sold their property to prepare to travel to the Holy Land. In small towns in Germany and in communities in Morocco, Jews waited impatiently for letters from the Holy Land and gathered to hear them read. Poems were written in praise of Sabbetai Zevi and his prophet in countries from Yemen to Amsterdam. Preachers encouraged repentance, and editions of the special prayers mandated by Nathan were published in Amsterdam, Frankfurt, Prague, Mantua and Constantinople.[36]

As the summer of 1666 approached, expectation rose, not least (it seems) for Sabbetai Zevi himself, who declared that the fasts of 17 Tammuz and 9 Av, which commemorated the destruction of the Temple, should be replaced by new festivals: 17 Tammuz became a celebration of the revival of the spirit of Sabbetai Zevi, and 9 Av the celebration of his birthday. In Constantinople the rabbis sought and received divine guidance before agreeing to take so drastic a step:

> When the decree reached Constantinople the people of the city, believers though they were, were in doubt whether to take such a grave step. So their rabbis poured out prayers and petitions before the Lord their God,

begging Him to show them the path they must take and the thing they must do. They all then assembled. They prepared two slips of paper, on one of which was written 'festival' and on the other 'fast'. They put them in a jar; they summoned a boy and told him to pick out one of them and hold his hand high. So he did – and out came 'festival'. Back went the slips of paper into the jar. Again the boy pulled one out – 'festival'. A third time they put the slips into the jar; out came 'festival'.[37]

For all of July and August, Jews waited for the redemption to come at any moment. Then, on 16 September, Sabbetai Zevi was summoned to the presence of the sultan in Adrianople. If the prophecy of Nathan were correct, this should have been the moment when the sultan would hand over his power to the King Messiah. If the expectations of 'the Turks and the uncircumcised' are correctly recorded by Baruch of Arezzo, Sabbetai Zevi should have been killed, and his execution followed by a pogrom of the Jews of Adrianople:

> When the Muslims and Christians of Adrianople heard the king had summoned our Lord, they assumed his head was about to be cut off and all the Jews to be murdered, it having become common knowledge that the king had sentenced the city's Jews to death. They sent emissaries to Constantinople to do that same dreadful deed there. They sharpened their swords and awaited [Sabbetai's] arrival, all ready to work their will upon the Jews.

What actually happened was quite different. The sultan bestowed on Sabbetai Zevi a turban and a new name. Sabbetai Zevi became Aziz Mehmed Effendi, and a Muslim. There was no disguise: he wrote to his brother Elijah in Smyrna just eight days later that 'the Creator has made me into a Muslim . . . created me anew, according to His will.'[38]

Reactions around the Jewish world varied greatly. For those who had never believed in Sabbetai's claims, here was the strongest possible proof of the validity of their doubts, and in November 1666 Joseph Halevi of Livorno wrote to his friend Jacob Sasportas in Hamburg about what had happened to the 'coarse, malignant lunatic whose Jewish name used to be Sabbetai Zevi' and whom 'all Jewry' had invoked as 'our redeemer', instructing Sasportas that he should tell the followers of this redeemer that 'Mehmed their saviour has now returned to his school days, a pupil now of the Muslim religion'. For believers, there was shock, abandonment of hope and, for many, silence. Jewish leaders in Turkey tried to return their community to normality, perhaps in part out of fear of punishment from the Turkish authorities for having encouraged the popular uprising. In Italy, records of the support there had once been for Sabbetai were destroyed, although it would take time for the indignation to die down of those, like Joseph Halevi, who had suffered for opposing the hysteria. It took time also for believers to recover. Glückel of Hameln, who had been a young adult in 1666 and began composing her remarkable memoirs, in Yiddish, in the 1690s primarily as a family chronicle for the benefit of her descendants after the death of her first husband, reported in those memoirs that her father-in-law in Hildesheim had packed his belongings in 1666 to travel to the land of Israel to meet the Messiah, and that it took him three years to bring himself to unpack:

> Many sold their houses and lands and all their possessions, for any day they hoped to be redeemed. My good father-in-law left his home in Hameln, abandoned his house and lands and all his goodly furniture, and moved to Hildesheim. He sent on to us in Hamburg two enormous casks packed with linens and with peas, beans, dried meats, shredded prunes and like stuff, every manner of food that would keep. For the old man expected to sail any moment from Hamburg to the Holy Land. More than a year the casks lay in my house. At length the old folks feared the meat and other edibles would rot; and they wrote us, we should open the casks and remove the foodstuffs, to save the linens from ruin. For three years the casks stood ready, and all this while my father-in-law awaited the signal to depart. But the Most High pleased otherwise.[39]

And there were some – although only a minority of the mass movement of 1665–6 – who continued to believe that Sabbetai Zevi was the Messiah. One such believer was evidently Sabbetai himself, who was observed in 1671 – by the same Jacob Najara who had witnessed in his own house in Gaza the fateful prophecy of Nathan on Pentecost in 1665 – still living as a Jew, despite being a Muslim in the Ottoman court, preaching in synagogues and keeping Jewish customs, albeit in eccentric fashion. Najara himself circumcised a boy aged ten whose father had 'vowed while Amirah was in the Tower of Strength [in Gallipoli] that he would not circumcise his son except in the presence of King Messiah. Amirah thereupon commanded this rabbi [Najara] to circumcise the boy.' At the same time, Sabbetai was in contact with Muslim mystics of the Dervish orders and, according to Najara, enthusiastically encouraged his followers to embrace Islam alongside him:

When Purim was over he went to the home of the sage Rabbi Jacob Alvo, and summoned the rabbi [Najara] along with six other men. In that same courtyard was a janissary barracks; and [Sabbetai] prayed there with the rabbis and welcomed the Sabbath with melody and with great joy, singing aloud . . . When it was daylight he went with his serving-boy to the Portuguese synagogue, where he recited a number of petitionary prayers . . . Afterwards he recited there the *namas* [Muslim prayers], and after that he returned to [Alvo's] house and prayed the morning service [for the Sabbath] . . . Then he went home, bringing with him his bejewelled copy of the Zohar. He arrived at sunset in a state of elation. When the Sabbath was done, early in the night, he declared that all the believers be summoned to him and that everyone who believed in him must take on the turban. About a dozen men and five women agreed to do as he wished.[40]

This was not the view of Nathan of Gaza, who remained convinced of Sabbetai's messianic role but had no desire himself to adopt Islam and warned others to 'stay away from Amirah when he is in a state of illumination because he wants to convert everyone around him to Islam'. Nathan's explanation of Sabbetai's action was theological. In early November 1666 he announced that the mystery would resolve itself in time and set out with a large group of followers from Gaza to meet Sabbetai in Adrianople, gradually evolving as he went the ingenious kabbalistic argument that, now that the Jews had restored the sparks of their own souls by *tikkun*, the Messiah had needed to descend into Islam in order to lift up the holy sparks which were dispersed among the gentiles. Sabbetai had taken upon himself the shame of treachery as the final stage before he would appear in glory. With endorsement from Sabbetai himself, Nathan travelled around Italy and the Balkans spreading this doctrine, and frequent letters between Sabbatian communities in North Africa, Italy and the Balkans had created a powerful sectarian theology by the time that Sabbetai was exiled in January 1673 to Dulcigno in Albania following accusations about his behaviour by both Jews and Muslims.

After the blow of the apostasy, the death of the Messiah on the Day of Atonement in 1676 was less difficult to absorb than might otherwise have been the case. It was clear to the believer Baruch of Arezzo that Sabbetai had not really died:

It became known afterwards that our Lord had journeyed to our Israelite brethren, the ten 'tribes of the Lord' on the far side of the River Sambatyon, there to wed the daughter of Moses our Teacher who lives on among them. If we are deserving, he will return to redeem us immediately after the seven days of his wedding celebrations. But if not, he will delay there until we are deluged by terrible calamities. Only then will he come to avenge us of our enemies and of those who hate us. A certain rabbi from the land of Morea saw our Lord in the town called Malvasia. That very week, [our Lord] told him, he would be on his way to Great Tartary, which is the proper route to the River Sambatyon.

The apparent failure of Sabbetai signalled by his death was explained by claiming that he would reincarnate and complete his work in another body, or that he was away gathering the lost ten tribes, or that he had gone into the spirit world to achieve there the redemption he had completed on earth. Some, like Moshe David Valle (see p. 412), argued that Sabbetai had been the Messiah son of Joseph and would be followed by the Messiah son of David, who would signal the end of time.[41]

Nathan's recognition in 1668 of Sabbetai's status as Messiah had reflected a long-held conviction of Sabbetai himself, which had been confirmed in 1664 when he contracted his third marriage to Sarah, a beautiful but troubled bride of Polish origin. She was described in scornful terms after Sabbetai's conversion by Jacob Sasportas, who had known her in Amsterdam in 1655, as 'a witless girl who used to deliver, to the general amusement, demented speeches about how she was going to be married to King Messiah. She went off to Leghorn [Livorno], where, as Rabbi Joseph HaLevi writes me, she made a practice of going to bed with anyone and everyone.' For Baruch of Arezzo, the significance of the marriage lay only in its confirmation that Sabbetai was the Messiah, relating that her protector in Cairo, Raphael Joseph Chelebi, had 'wanted to marry her to one of his friends and settle great wealth on her'. The two were duly wed, but, according to Baruch, 'he never made love to her until he had set the pure turban on his head.' The marriage had been intended as a prelude to the redemption, not to settled family life.[42]

The impact of Sabbetai across the Jewish world can be explained only by a confluence of causes. Memories of the Chmielnicki massacres in Poland in 1648–9 which had destroyed Sarah's entire family and driven her into exile may help to explain the extraordinary enthusiasm of Polish Jews for Sabbetai's promise of redemption, but such sufferings cannot explain the equal enthusiasm of the Jews of Amsterdam, who were living a Jewish life in comfort and security. It is probable that Christian expectation in England, Holland and Germany that the second coming of Christ would occur in 1666 helped the spread of news about Sabbetai throughout Christian Europe during that year. But Christian millenarianism cannot account for the excitement of Jews in Islamic lands – there is almost no reference to Sabbetai in contemporary Muslim sources, and the gentle treatment meted out to him, compared to the normal policy of brutal suppression of troublemakers, suggests that the Ottoman state could afford to treat the whole episode lightly. Lurianic kabbalah provided Nathan of Gaza with the basis of his theology to explain the descent of the Messiah into the abyss by becoming Muslim in order to bring redemption, but too few Jews in the mid-seventeenth century were familiar with the complexities of Luria's mystical system for them to have seen such dramatic behaviour as self-evidently justified – as is clear from the time taken by Nathan to come up with his theology when the news of Sabbetai's adoption of the turban reached him. Nor can the frustration with the restrictions of a religion based on divine command which irked Spinoza, whose *Tractatus Theologico-Politicus* was published in Amsterdam in 1670, explain the willingness of Jews in Yemen, Turkey and Morocco to cast aside treasured aspects of the Torah in a wild hope that such antinomianism was a sign of a new beginning. Due allowance must be made for mass hysteria, for the impact of ideas spread by the new medium of printing and, as we have seen in the bitter accusations of Joseph Halevi, for the moral blackmail of those who doubted: 'But the reaction of the empty-headed rabble, once they grasped that I [Joseph Halevi] had totally refuted their faith in the prophet and his messiah, was something else again. They waxed mightily indignant and launched against me an unending stream of verbal abuse.'[43]

The aftershocks of the upheavals of 1665 and 1666 rumbled on within many Jewish communities for well over a century. In some rabbinic circles it had long been speculated that the 'Messiah, son of David' would be accompanied by a 'Messiah, son of Joseph', and even before the death of Sabbetai Zevi it was revealed to an uneducated youth in Meknes, in Morocco, called Joseph ibn Tsur, that he was this figure. A contemporary letter from one rabbi to another, dated 5 February 1675, expressed delight at the secret he revealed:

I must inform you, sir, that fresh reports arrive here daily from Meknes concerning this young man, and the interpretations and secret revelations of which he speaks. I could not restrain myself when I realized what was happening. It is essential, said I, that I go see it for myself. So I took the

Zohar and some other books, and travelled there to ask him about certain obscure passages in the Zohar, intending to remain until Passover.
I discovered the young man to be humble and God-fearing, possessor of
every good quality. When I told him, 'I have come to learn from you the
incomprehensible mysteries of the Zohar,' he replied: 'I am astonished at
Your Worship! For my own part, I do not even know Rashi, and I do not
know even a single verse of the Bible beyond what is revealed to me.' . . . I
asked if it were true he is messiah son of Joseph. 'That is what they tell me,'
he answered. Since birth he has had on his arm a mark shaped like a lily,
from the first join of his little finger to his forearm. I came from there, to
make a long story short, in the most excellent spirits. It was clear to us he
was not possessed by a ghost or a demon, God forbid, for his demeanour
was exceedingly calm and rational, and all his conversation was of the
divine Unity. Moreover, he fasts continually. I asked him to perform some
miraculous sign. 'What could be more miraculous', he replied, 'than what
you now see? I once knew nothing even about the Bible, and now I speak
of the ten sefirot and the kabbalistic mysteries. I am not telling you to
anticipate a redemption that is one year away, or two years. Wait two
months only; then you will no longer need to ask questions.

Joseph ibn Tsur died soon after this letter was written, but another contemporary claimant to the role of Messiah, son of Joseph, Abraham Miguel
Cardoso, was to last longer, and leave a greater impression on those who
continued in the hope that Sabbetai's career had religious meaning.[44]

This Cardoso was a converso who had studied Christian theology in
Spain before escaping to Venice in his early twenties and openly profess-
ing his allegiance to Judaism. In 1655 he became a follower of Sabbetai
Zevi, and he was not swayed from his belief by Sabbetai's adoption of
the turban, although he opposed vehemently the conversion of other
Sabbatians to Islam. Defiantly observant of traditional Jewish custom
and opposed to antinomianism, Cardoso aroused opposition nonetheless from other Jews by expounding a new doctrine, related to the
Neoplatonic teachings in his university education, that the God of
Israel, who is the object of worship, is to be distinguished from the First
Cause, which has no relation to created things. He set out this thesis in
a treatise, *Boker Avraham* ('Dawn of Abraham'), which he sent to Sabbetai Zevi in 1673 (although he got no reply). He spent much of the rest
of his life defending it, disparaging the role of the hidden First Cause
and anything within the Sabbatian movement that might smack of the
Catholic dogmas he had left behind in Spain. Frequent travels in Italy,

North Africa and the eastern Mediterranean, over some thirty years, often under compulsion from rabbinic authorities who would not allow him to settle in their midst, and a voluminous correspondence with disciples as far away as Morocco and England, spread his influence in the competition after 1670 to claim to represent truthfully the secret teachings of Sabbetai Zevi, contradicting the kabbalistic system of Nathan of Gaza and others who claimed Sabbetai's legacy.

Different groups of Sabbatians could soon be found in Turkey, Italy and Poland, with wholly different sets of beliefs, as prophets claimed visions of Sabbetai after his death. The greatest division was in attitudes to Islam. Sabbetai Zevi seems to have believed, at least sometimes, that Judaism and Islam were compatible, although it would be unwise to expect him to have been consistent in this attitude any more than in anything else. We have seen that Cardoso knew that Sabbetai had demanded that his believers also enter into Islam, and that some did so, but that Cardoso disapproved strongly, referring with some disdain to 'a man of some importance who had taken on the turban at Sabbetai Zevi's behest'. This man had come to Cardoso in Istanbul on 10 May 1682 to ask if he should remove the turban and return to the Jewish fold. According to Cardoso's reminiscence, he said that he (Cardoso) 'had no competence to issue rulings on this subject, and that they should go and ask the one who had made them wear the turban in the first place' – an impossibility, six years after Sabbetai's death. The following year in Salonica, however, the brother of Sabbetai Zevi's last wife, Jacob Filosof (later known as Jacob Querido), led some 300 local Jewish families into Islam, his authority supported by his sister's claim in 1676 that he had inherited Sabbetai's soul. The new converts were to form the Dönmeh, a distinct group, surviving today, of crypto-Jews who live openly as Muslims but keep many Jewish practices in secret, awaiting the return of the Messiah. In 1999, it was reported that 'one of the elders of the community ... ventures to the shores of the Bosporus, shortly before dawn, and recites [in Ladino (Judaeo-Spanish)] ... "Sabbetai, Sabbetai, we wait for you."' The Dönmeh have retained their separate identity by marrying only among themselves, although early on they split into three groups. Many moved from Salonica to Istanbul in 1924 as part of the population exchanges between Turkey and Greece when the Turkish Republic was founded. One small sect of the Dönmeh, led by a certain Baruchiah Russo (also known as Osman Baba), taught in the early eighteenth century both that Sabbetai Zevi was divine and that the messianic Torah requires a complete reversal of values in which all prohibited sexual activities were to be treated as positive commands. But such views were held by a small minority.[45]

Those Sabbatians who declined to adopt Islam were also, like the Dönmeh, divided in their ideas about the implications of Sabbetai's career for the keeping of the halakhah. Some adopted extreme antinomianism, in some cases explicitly claiming the authority of Baruchiah as 'Santo Señor', but others practised an extreme asceticism, such as the 'holy society of Rabbi Judah Hasid', a group of hundreds of enthusiasts led by Judah Hasid and the Polish rabbi Hayyim Malakh, who went to Jerusalem in 1700 in expectation of the expected advent in 1706 of the Messiah (in the form, although Malakh did not state this openly, of Sabbetai Zevi, returned to life after forty years). Expelled from Jerusalem, Malakh seems to have met Baruchiah in Salonica, and may have been tempted into antinomian views. At any rate, he was denounced in 1710 by the rabbis of Constantinople and, on his return to Poland, formed a radical sect in Podolia (in modern Ukraine and Moldova) from which was to emerge, after his death, the even more extreme Frankist movement.[46]

Jacob Frank was born in 1726 Jacob b. Judah Leib to a middle-class father from Korolówka in Podolia, but was educated (although not to a high level) in Czernowitz. For many years he was resident in Bucharest, where he worked as a dealer in cloth. His studies in the Zohar gave him a certain reputation among Sabbatians and in 1753 he visited Salonica in the company of Sabbatian teachers from the antinomian group of Dönmeh who followed the teachings of Baruchiah. In December 1755 he returned to Poland as a Sabbatian leader. After some twenty-five years in Turkish lands, and speaking Ladino, he was suspected of being a 'Frank', the Yiddish word for a Sephardi, and he adopted 'Frank' as his family name, rapidly gaining a large following across Poland for his teaching of the 'Torah of Emanation', which he presented as a spiritual Torah which permitted transgressions on principle. He himself returned to Turkey, where early in 1757 he became a convert to Islam (like his Dönmeh teachers), leaving the *ma'aminim* ('believers'), as his Sabbatian followers in Galicia, Ukraine and Hungary referred to themselves, to face intense persecution.

The rabbinic authorities in Poland at first just issued a ban against members of the sect, confirmed by the Council of the Four Lands, but then fatefully sought help from the Christian authorities to suppress what they portrayed as a new religion, only for the Sabbatians to claim the protection of the Church from their 'talmudist' persecutors, providing the local bishop with an opportunity to use them as weapons against the rabbinic Jews in his diocese. On 2 August 1756 the Sabbatians presented to the bishop a demand for a public confrontation with the rabbis in which they would argue that their faith was in essence compatible with Christianity. In the ensuing debate, at Kamienice from 20 to 28 June 1757, the Sabbatians proved victorious, and in October and November 1757 huge numbers of copies of the Talmud were burned in the public squares. When the bishop responsible died on 9 November in the middle of these events, the rabbinic Jews recognized divine vengeance and turned on the Sabbatians, so that many fled to Turkey.

Such was the state of mutual antagonism between the 'talmudists' and the 'believers' when Jacob Frank returned to Poland, in December 1758 or early the following year. He revealed himself in Iwanie to his followers as 'the true Jacob' who had come to complete the work of Sabbetai Zevi and Baruchiah by requiring them to adopt Christianity outwardly, as the Dönmeh had done with Islam, in order to keep the true faith in secret. A year later, Frank and many of his followers were duly baptized in Lvov, and Frank and his wife were baptized a second time, under the patronage of the king of Poland, with great pomp in the cathedral in Warsaw on 18 November 1759. The Frankists had requested that they be allowed to continue to live separately from other Christians, and that they be permitted to wear Jewish clothing, to keep their sidelocks, avoid pork, to rest on Saturday as well as Sunday, and to retain use of the Zohar and other works of the kabbalah, but the Church had refused, requiring baptism without preconditions. As a result, the baptism did not end well-founded Christian suspicions about the intentions of the new converts, and in 1760 Frank himself was accused of heresy. Held in captivity for thirteen years, he was treated by his fellows as the 'suffering messiah', holding court from his incarceration in the fortresses of Częstochowa until it was captured by the Russians in August 1772 after the partition of Poland. From 1773 to his death in 1791, Frank lived as a Christian in Brno and then in Offenbach, surrounded by an exotic household and making extravagant claims about the origins of his daughter Eva, believed by some of his followers to be a royal princess of the house of Romanov. The complex mix of Judaism and Christianity he advocated proved impossible to sustain, and the Frankists in Poland merged into wider Christian society.[47]

Against the background of such upheaval it should not surprise that suspicions of Sabbatian sympathies were rife within Jewish communities right across Europe in the first half of the eighteenth century.

In London in 1715, David Nieto, the *haham* (chief rabbi) of the Spanish and Portuguese synagogue, published a vehement accusation of Sabbatianism against his contemporary, Nehemiah Hayon, whose Lurianic doctrines concerning the faces of the deity had been approved by the *haham* in Amsterdam but attacked by his Ashkenazi counterpart in that city. Even more enthusiastic in pursuit of heresy was Moshe Hagiz, a leading kabbalist himself and supporter of rabbinic authority. Hagiz, like Nieto, likewise attacked Nehemiah Hayon between 1713 and 1715, but he also engaged in intense polemics against Yonatan Eybeschütz in the 1720s and against Moshe Hayyim Luzzatto in the 1730s.[48]

In the case of Luzzatto, Hagiz's intervention may be thought successful. Luzzatto was a remarkable mystic and poet, who had experienced a revelation at the age of twenty, in which a *maggid* appeared to him (as had happened to others before, such as Yosef Karo). Among Luzzatto's disciples, Moshe David Valle identified himself as the Messiah, son of David, regarding Sabbetai Zevi as the Messiah, son of Joseph. Luzzatto himself was designated the reincarnation of Moses, and his marriage in 1731 as the union of the male and female elements in the divine world which formed the first element in the messianic process. The suspicions of Sabbatianism voiced by Hagiz were not unreasonable, and the rabbis of Venice forced Luzzatto to migrate to Amsterdam in 1735, ordering his works to be burned. Forbidden by the Venetian court to write kabbalistic works, in Amsterdam Luzzatto produced instead one of the most influential works of Jewish ethics ever written, the *Mesillat Yesharim* ('The Path of the Upright'), which described the path of ethical ascent the individual must climb until sanctity is reached:

> It is fundamentally necessary both for saintliness and for the perfect worship of God to realize clearly what constitutes man's duty in this world, and what goal is worthy of his endeavors throughout all the days of his life. Our sages have taught us that man was created only to find delight in the Lord, and to bask in the radiance of His Presence. But the real place for such happiness is the world to come, which has been created for that very purpose. The present world is only a path to that goal. 'This world', said our Sages, 'is like a vestibule before the world to come.' Therefore has God, blessed be His Name, given us the commandments. For this world is the only place where the commandments can be observed. Man is put here is order to earn with the means at his command the place that has been prepared for him in the world to come.

It is a testimony to the power of Luzzatto's ethical insights that, despite the justified doubts about his Sabbatian sympathies, for students two centuries later in the Lithuanian yeshivot of the Musar movement, which emphasized the teaching of ethics (see Chapter 19), the writings of Luzzatto were compulsory reading.[49]

Whether Hagiz's attack on Eybeschütz was equally justified is less certain. Yonatan Eybeschütz was a talmudic prodigy from Cracow. He headed yeshivot in Prague, Metz and Altona and was widely celebrated for his commentaries on halakhic codes, but he was suspected of Sabbatian tendencies in his kabbalistic practices. His prime opponent was not Hagiz but the local rabbi Yaakov Emden, son of the rabbi of the Ashkenazi community in Amsterdam who had objected so strongly to Nehemiah Hayon earlier in the century. In 1751 Emden accused Eybeschütz of being a secret follower of Sabbetai Zevi, citing the evidence of some amulets written by Eybeschütz which contained Sabbatian formulas. The charge came to the attention of the secular authorities, including the Danish monarch, and a host of rabbis were drawn into supporting one side or the other. In 1753 Eybeschütz was exonerated by the Council of the Four Lands in Poland, and his halakhic works remain in use today – despite the strong suspicions of modern historians that Emden's accusation may have been justified.[50]

Jewish life was never to be the same again after the crisis of Sabbetai Zevi, but passions eventually died down, as proclaimed messiahs came and went. One abiding legacy was the popularization of the language of the Lurianic kabbalah in common liturgy which we have already seen. That in turn was to shape the most lasting movement of the early modern period, Hasidism.

HASIDISM

Towards the end of the eighteenth century, Solomon Maimon, a Polish Jew who had abandoned his Judaism to become an idealist philosopher in Berlin in the intellectual footsteps of Immanuel Kant, described with a sceptical eye the experience of a Sabbath he had attended as a youth a few decades earlier in the court of Dov Ber of Mezeritch, known as the Maggid, in the early 1770s, just before the death of the master:

At last I arrived at M——, and after having rested from my journey I went to the house of the superior under the idea that I could be introduced to him at once. I was told, however, that he could not speak to me at the time, but that I was invited to his table on Sabbath along with the other strangers who had come to visit him; that I should then have the happiness of seeing the saintly man face to face and of hearing the sublimest teachings out of his own mouth; that although this was a public audience, yet, on account of the individual references which I should find made to myself, I might regard it as a special interview. Accordingly on Sabbath I went to this solemn meal, and found there a large number of respectable men who had met here from various quarters. At length the great man appeared in his awe-inspiring form, clothed in white satin. Even his shoes and snuffbox were white, this being among the Cabbalists the colour of grace. He gave to each newcomer his salaam, that is, his greeting. We sat down to table and during the meal a solemn silence reigned. After the meal was over, the superior struck up a solemn inspiriting melody, held his hand for some time upon his brow, and then began to call out, 'Z——of H——, M——of R——,' and so on. Each newcomer was thus called by his own name and the name of his residence, which excited no little astonishment. Each recited, as he was called, some verse of the Holy Scriptures. Thereupon the superior began to deliver a sermon for which the verses recited served as a text, so that although they were disconnected verses taken from different parts of the Holy Scriptures they were combined with as much skill as if they had formed a single whole. What was still more extraordinary, every one of the newcomers believed that he discovered, in that part of the sermon which was founded on his verse, something that had special reference to the facts of his own spiritual life. At this we were of course greatly astonished. It was not long, however, before I began to qualify the high opinion I had formed of this superior and the whole society . . . The whole society also displeased me not a little by their cynical spirit and the excess of their merriment.[51]

Despite the jaundiced view of Maimon, Dov Ber was an inspiring teacher whose students were to carry various versions of his distinctive mystical teachings to much of eastern Europe, so that by the first decade of the nineteenth century, when Europe was facing up to Napoleon, his form of Judaism had taken deep root in the Ukraine, Belorussia and Galicia.

Dov Ber's teachings, or at least the enthusiastic, ecstatic proselytizing of his followers, had also provoked strong opposition by the time of his death. In 1772 the first of a series of bans was issued against them by rabbinic authorities led by the Vilna Gaon in Lithuania. But although such bans succeeded in restricting the enthusiasm of Jews in Lithuania, they had remarkably little success in the rest of eastern Europe. Why in the end did Hasidism such as was witnessed by Solomon Maimon, with its emphasis on the religious experience of the individual *hasid* ('pietist'), succeed in establishing a new form of Judaism accepted by the majority of other Jews, when Sabbetai Zevi and Jacob Frank had failed?

The theology preached by Dov Ber was built on the kabbalah of Luria but emphasized less the intellectual concentration which had characterized elite kabbalist circles than the immersion of the individual in the divine presence through prayer, in which all sense of being is lost and union with the divine is achieved. The true *tsaddik* ('righteous man') is endowed through such devotions, or mindfulness (*da'at*), with a special charisma, enabling him to mediate between believers and God and to work miracles, bringing down the abundance of the divine to the material world. Any ordinary Jew could find a connection with God through allegiance to the *tsaddik* for whom he is by nature suited. This theology opened up new routes for all Jews for personal piety, and also a new and dramatic role for charismatic religious leaders similar to the leading figures of contemporary dissenting Christian sects such as the Doukhobors.[52]

By 1766, when Dov Ber had established the court where he was seen by Solomon Maimon, he was already in his sixties, weakened by a life of extreme asceticism and devotion to kabbalistic study. He was not given to the flamboyant rabble-rousing which had brought a following to Jacob Frank a decade earlier. Nor did he spread the word by intensive publication – his teachings were published only posthumously on the basis of notebook jottings by a disciple, Levi Yitzhak of Berdichev. Levi Yitzhak was a figure about whom tales were told, with many collections of Yiddish stories about his miracles and love for all his fellow Jews (which was said to have included a willingness even to argue with God on their behalf, as Abraham had once argued on behalf of the inhabitants of Sodom and Gomorrah), but Dov Ber was not a powerful personality of this type, meeting only rarely even with his disciples, let alone the wider population.[53]

Behind Dov Ber stood a figure of immense charisma whose life and teachings are shrouded in a mist of myth and hagiography, Israel b. Eliezer, the Baal Shem Tov, known by the initials of his title as the Besht. According to legend, Israel b. Eliezer was born in a small town in Podolia in *c.* 1700 to poor parents. Orphaned at an early age, he made a living as an assistant in a religious school and sexton in a yeshivah and later as a digger of clay in the Carpathian mountains. In the mid-1730s, he discovered that he was a *baal shem*, 'master of the Name [of God]', whose secret knowledge of the Tetragrammaton and other holy names enabled him to work miracles and heal the sick.[54]

Israel b. Eliezer was not the first to discover in himself such remarkable powers. Already in the eleventh century Hai Gaon had recorded 'that they saw a certain man, one of the well-known *baalei shem*, on the eve of the Sabbath in one place, and that at the same time he was seen in another place, several days' journey distant'. The title was given to a number of important talmudic scholars in Germany and Poland from the sixteenth century onwards, but also increasingly to scholars who devoted themselves to kabbalah and gained followers by healing through prayers, amulets and incantations, particularly in the treatment of mental disorders and in exorcisms. Books such as *Mifalot Elohim* ('Works of God'), associated with Yoel Baal Shem and published in 1727, containing formulas used by *ba'alei shem* in their magic and medicine, circulated widely. A younger contemporary of Israel b. Eliezer, Samuel Jacob Hayyim Falk, travelled from Galicia to Westphalia (where he was nearly burned as a sorcerer) to England, where around 1742 he set himself up as a kabbalist in premises on London Bridge, practising alchemy and gaining a wide reputation among the general public, to whom he was known as 'Dr Falk'. Eventually reconciled to the London Jewish community to which he left a large legacy, despite their initial hostility to him on his arrival in the city, he was said to have saved the Great Synagogue from fire through a magical inscription on its doorposts.[55]

Israel b. Eliezer was thus in a long-established tradition as a miraculous healer, but he was also to become a leader and teacher, and the school he established in Medzibozh (in modern Ukraine) in *c.* 1740 attracted crowds seeking spiritual guidance as well as his intercession for their welfare. About his teachings it is possible only to be certain about the general outlines. He himself wrote down none of them, but some of his letters are preserved in the writing of his disciple Yaakov Yosef haCohen of Polonnoye, who also frequently quoted the Baal Shem Tov as 'my teacher' in the first printed hasidic book, published in 1780: 'I heard from my teacher that the primary occupation of Torah and prayer is that one should attach oneself to the inner infinite spiritual light within the letters of the Torah and prayer, and this is what is called study for its own sake.'

The sayings of the Baal Shem Tov recorded by Yaakov Yosef and the later tradition warn against excessive asceticism and fasting, and assert the ability of all to serve God through joy. God is present in all things.

Through concentrated intention (*kavvanah*), prayer can permit the soul to cleave to God, but all human acts relate to the divine if performed in a state of *devekut*, 'attachment'. The same is true of the study of the Torah. All, no matter how unlearned, can open up the divine world by studying the letters of the Torah, even if one does not understand it directly. Such teachings drew upon the ideas and vocabulary of the Lurianic kabbalah, but gave them a new significance. They opened up the possibility of mystical experience to any pious individual prepared to approach the everyday life of Judaism with appropriate devotion and joy. A new mass movement rapidly emerged on the margins of the Jewish community. Podolia and other centres of Hasidism were far away from the great centres of rabbinic learning. Many of the new pietists came from those who felt religiously disenfranchised by the lack of a rabbinic education.[56]

Such democratization of piety was clearly part of its appeal, but the basis of the Baal Shem Tov's fame was undoubtedly the stories about his miracles. Collections of *shevahim* ('praises') of him duly circulated during his lifetime and were published in many different editions in Hebrew and Yiddish in the decades after his death. There were many different stories:

> There was a time when there was no rain. The gentiles took out their idols and carried them around the village according to their custom, but it still did not rain. Once the Besht said to the arrendator [municipal revenue farmer]: 'Send for the Jews in the surrounding area to come here for a *minyan* [a quorum of ten men for prayer].' And he proclaimed a fast. The Besht himself prayed before the ark, and the Jews prolonged the prayer. One gentile asked: 'Why did you remain at prayer so long today? And why was there a great cry among you?' The arrendator told him the truth – that they prayed for rain – and the gentile mocked him sharply, saying, 'We went around with our idols and it did not help. What help will you bring with your prayers?' The arrendator told the words of the gentile to the Besht, who said to him: 'Tell the gentile that it will rain today.' And so it did.

The legendary elements are patent, but, like Dr Falk, the Baal Shem of London, Israel b. Eliezer was widely known in non-Jewish circles. In the Polish tax registers a house near the synagogue in Medzibozh is described in 1742 as 'The Baal Shem in the *kahal* house', in 1758 as 'The Baal Shem' and in 1760 as 'The Baal Shem, the doctor, exempt'. And like Dr Falk, Israel b. Eliezer made no secret of his work as a healer, signing himself proudly as 'Israel Baal Shem of Tłuste'.[57]

The personality of the Baal Shem Tov thus became famous far beyond Podolia and Volhynia where he was active, and he is portrayed in the stories as travelling widely to meet with people of all kinds in small groups or individually. But he did not preach in synagogues, or build an institution, and on his death in 1760 it was unclear how his influence would continue. It is testimony to his extraordinary reputation and charisma that Dov Ber of Mezeritch, who is said to have met the Baal Shem Tov only twice, devoted the rest of his life to promulgating the teachings of his master, who had preached against just the sort of extreme asceticism that Dov Ber had practised for much of his life.

Succession to the aura of the Baal Shem Tov was not immediate, nor without problems. The selection of Dov Ber in 1766 after a hiatus was opposed by Yaakov Yosef of Polonnoye, who had known the master for much longer and could claim to preserve his teachings more accurately. Many who had known the Baal Shem Tov closely declined to join what rapidly became a mass movement, with emissaries sent from Dov Ber's headquarters in Mezeritch to attract others to his teachings. Some of these emissaries were themselves charismatic leaders who developed, over the last quarter of the eighteenth century, distinctive forms of hasidic thought and life, each validated by the reverence accorded to the *tsaddik* at its head. Menahem Mendel of Vitebsk, who became the leading hasidic figure in Belorussia and Lithuania after the death of Dov Ber in 1772, led a large group to the land of Israel in 1777, retaining authority over his followers back home by correspondence.[58]

Shneur Zalman of Lyady established a distinctive form of Hasidism in the north-eastern provinces of Russia. Already known, according to later hasidic hagiography, as a brilliant talmudist before he joined Dov Ber in Mezeritch, he had composed a revision of the *Shulhan Arukh* by the age of twenty-five in 1770. He developed a distinctive mystical theology which incorporated intellectual effort, unlike the intuitive approach to mysticism of the Baal Shem Tov. The Habad system he devised stressed the importance of *Hochma*, *Binah* and *Da'at*, three types of knowledge distinguished in kabbalist thought as 'germinal, developmental and conclusive'; the name 'Habad' is the acronym formed from the three Hebrew words. Through spiritual exercises, meditation and regular study, any man could strive to become a *beinoni*, 'average man'. Such an average man cannot change the world, as the exceptional individuals chosen from birth to be *tsaddikim* can, but they can and should strive towards perfection by controlling evil in the world and thus bringing the divine presence towards harmony and the soul to joy. Shneur Zalman's teachings were less concerned with kabbalist theosophy or theological speculation than a guide to hasidic behaviour. His collected sayings – originally published in 1796, and nowadays best known, from the title page of later editions, as the *Tanya*, which means 'it was taught in a *baraita*' (that is, by a tannaitic rabbi) – became just such a guide, justified within a complete and coherent exposition of the system as a whole.[59]

The pre-eminent role of the *tsaddik* as the source of spiritual illumination for his individual followers engendered a distinctive structure to hasidic communities. The *tsaddik* or *rebbe* presided over a court to which his individual *hasidim* came on pilgrimage to seek blessing and spiritual revitalization. The court was maintained by the *rebbe*'s followers in some considerable affluence, since the *tsaddik* was seen as the link between the *hasid* and heaven. *Hasidim* expected to contribute to these expenses with a suitable payment as *pidyon*, 'redemption' (of the soul). Proximity to the *rebbe*, and participating in the food from the communal table (*der tish*) when he expounded his teachings, generally on Sabbath afternoons, brought the *hasid* as close as he could get to the divine. Any problem could be brought to the *rebbe* for a solution. The process was often formalized, so that the *hasid* would submit his request in writing in a *kvitl*, a small note carefully folded for privacy for the *rebbe*'s perusal. As in any court, the *rebbe*'s closest assistants became from an early stage the most important intermediaries for access to him.[60]

Inevitably, the complete authority of local hasidic leaders, combined with the wide dispersion of Hasidism across eastern Europe and within Hungary by the end of the eighteenth century, led to tension between the courts of *hasidim*. Such tensions were to increase considerably from the 1830s, once the original surge of hasidic enthusiasm was over and the different groups settled into established patterns. Insularization was encouraged by the assumption, already found by the end of the eighteenth century, that the role of *rebbe* was generally to be inherited by a member of the family of the previous *rebbe*. In theological terms, this was explicable by the notion, espoused (as we have seen) by Shneur Zalman of Lyady, that the capacity to be a *tsaddik* is both rare and inherited from birth. A large number of hasidic dynasties, in many cases established in small villages from which their followers took their name, over the course of the nineteenth century evolved fiercely distinctive customs of male dress (especially headwear) and hairstyle, so that they were easily identifiable at least by appearance, even if in theological terms there was little to divide them.

Even within dynasties, personal disagreements between descendants sometimes led to splits. Rivalry could be fierce – as within the family of the Baal Shem Tov himself. In the late 1770s, the young Baruch of Medzibozh, a grandson of the Baal Shem Tov, set up an impressive court in Medzibozh, presenting himself as guardian of the burial place of the great *tsaddik*. As the number of his followers grew, he won recognition from the Russian state. His claims were publicly resisted both by Shneur Zalman of Lyady, whose authority derived from his time as a disciple of Dov Ber, and by Baruch's own nephew, the remarkable Nahman of Bratslav.[61]

Nahman grew up within the court of his uncle and he might reasonably have expected to inherit his role as *rebbe* of what was rapidly becoming a powerful religious movement. But at first he seems to have been deeply conflicted, unable to accept that life in Baruch's court represented genuine Hasidism, while uncertain that he himself had the qualities to become a perfect *tsaddik* and to lead others. A journey to the land of Israel between 1798 and 1799 seems to have transformed his self-confidence, so that at times he came to see himself not only as a *tsaddik* but as the foremost *tsaddik* of his generation, who alone could solve all the problems of the world.

In accordance with this high estimation of his own powers, Nahman required his followers to commit themselves to him even more tightly than the normal link between *rebbe* and *hasid*. By binding their souls to him they could overcome everything in their struggles for perfection. The regime on which he insisted was demanding, requiring intense self-mortification and introspection. His Bratslav followers were instructed to take seriously religious doubts which in other forms of Hasidism would be suppressed as the product of an evil inclination. In keeping with Nahman's unwillingness to accept his uncle's conferral of authority on his successor on the basis of inheritance rather than religious insight, Nahman's son did not succeed him when he died at the early age of thirty-eight. (It may have helped that the son was only four at the time.) Nahman's teachings embraced a search for spiritual perfection through *hitbodedut*, 'self-seclusion', a distinctive meditation practice in which the *hasid* is expected daily to 'break his heart' before God in spontaneous private prayer in his own language in order to establish a personal relationship with the divine and greater self-awareness. Bratslav *hasidim* today still turn to Nahman himself as their *rebbe*, over 200 years after his death in 1810. They visit his grave in Uman in the Ukraine in mass pilgrimage, especially on Rosh haShanah, chanting his name like a spell to aid their meditation: 'Na Nah Nahma Nahman me'Uman'.

Alongside the dynasties, it was still possible in the late eighteenth century, as Hasidism developed, for new charismatic leaders to emerge as the Baal Shem Tov had done. 'The Seer of Lublin', Jacob Isaac Horowitz, who had been a follower of Dov Ber of Mezeritch and of Elimelech of Lizhansk, spread a novel version of Hasidism through Poland and Galicia. A renowned miracle worker, the Seer believed in bringing material comfort to his hasidic followers. He argued that the practical role of the *tsaddik* is to look after his 'children' so that 'the people will be free to worship God'. The Seer himself founded no dynasty, and not all his disciples agreed with the social aspects of his teachings. One of his disciples, Yaakov Yitzhak of Przysucha, known as the Holy Jew, who had served as a spiritual guide in the Seer's court, objected to the Seer's emphasis on material welfare and on magic, and set up a competing hasidic school which emphasized Talmud study and sincerity in worship as part of the quest for individual spiritual perfection by an elite rather than focusing on the needs of ordinary Jews. The response of the Seer was bitter, and the controversy about the correct focus of spiritual endeavour was to divide Polish Hasidism for many years, into the mid-nineteenth century.[62]

The elitism of Yaakov Yitzhak of Przysucha ran counter to the main trend in Hasidism. The attraction of Hasidism for most ordinary Jews in eastern Europe lay precisely in the opportunity for spiritual fulfilment through piety it opened up for the many uneducated village people who felt excluded from the intellectual Judaism of the yeshivot. Prayer in small side rooms (*stieblach*), away from the rest of the population, gave a sense of being special, as did the fervid atmosphere of the court of a *tsaddik*, with crowds of young men in a state of religious enthusiasm. In both the *stiebl* and the court, music and dance played a central role from the start of Hasidism, enlivening a liturgy that many felt had become overburdened with words. Distinctive dress, in particular the girdle to separate the upper part of the body from the lower, marked the dedication of the *hasid* to a holy life, as did the insistence that the knives for the kosher slaughter of animals for consumption be sharpened to a greater degree than was customary among other Jews.

This last issue, the sharpening of the knives, became a charge against the *hasidim* in the often bitter attempts to crush their movement from the early 1770s. The bitterness of the struggle was exacerbated by the lack of Jewish communal authority following the demise of the Council of the Four Lands in 1764, after a decision by the Polish Sejm to establish a new system for collecting the Jewish poll tax without the Council.

The Jews of Poland and Lithuania could no longer look to a central Jewish institution recognized by the state to arbitrate over religious differences as the Council had done in the controversy between Eybeschütz and Emden. The opponents of Hasidism, led for the most part by the great Vilna Gaon, accused the new movement of destroying tradition by downgrading the centrality of Torah study and intellectual endeavour in favour of visions, miracles, enthusiastic prayer and a dangerous reverence for *rebbes* as if they were more than human. It was hard to show that any of these attributes actually contradicted halakhah, so more peripheral matters, such as the knife sharpening and the preference of *hasidim* for the Sephardic prayer forms which had been favoured by Luria, became token charges.[63]

The real issues were political, since the hasidic movement quite deliberately bypassed the established rabbinic authorities, with their supervision of synagogues and the rest of Jewish communal life, which had controlled the Jews in the villages and small towns of Russia, Poland, Lithuania and Ukraine for generations. The hasidic movement attracted such hostility only once it began to appear organized through the authority of Dov Ber, the Maggid of Mezeritch. The wonderworking of the Baal Shem Tov had not been seen as a threat by his rabbinic contemporaries. At worst, he evoked derision. But in 1772 two bans were pronounced against the *hasidim*, and again in 1781 there was a *herem* forbidding Jews 'to do business with them, and to intermarry with them, or to assist at their burial'. A pamphlet published by the *mitnagdim* ('opponents') in 1772 accused the *hasidim* of treating every day like a holiday, of excessive consumption of alcohol and of arrogance in daring to 'enter the rose garden of the kabbalah' while still ignorant of the oral Torah. It is hard to know how much the polemic reflected a real theological anxiety that hasidic thought tended towards a pantheism in which there was no distinction between the sacred and the profane as well as more mundane concerns about the independence from rabbinic control of these Jews from the margins.[64]

In any case, the attacks did not succeed. By 1796, when the opponents of Hasidism issued a *herem* on the publications of Shneur Zalman of Lyady, the *hasidim* were sufficiently influential in Jewish society to issue a *herem* of their own in response, and to seek the support of officials of the Russian state. They had already, as we have seen, achieved a certain amount of recognition from the secular authorities, who may have seen Hasidism as a bulwark against the freethinking encouraged by the Enlightenment. In this case, however, the appeal backfired, since

Shneur Zalman was thrown into prison in 1798 after being formally accused by the rabbi of Pinsk of creating a new sect, and of committing treason by sending money to the land of Israel, which lay within Ottoman territory. The release of Shneur Zalman on 19 Kislev in the same year is still celebrated by Habad *hasidim* as the 'Holiday of Deliverance'.

Solomon Maimon in Berlin claimed in the 1790s that the hasidic revolution had already come and gone:

> This sect was, therefore, in regard to its end and its means, a sort of secret society, which had nearly acquired dominion over the whole nation; and consequently one of the greatest revolutions was to have been expected, if the excesses of some of its members had not laid bare many weak spots, and thus put weapons into the hands of its enemies . . . Men began to find out their weaknesses, to disturb their meetings, and to persecute them everywhere. This was brought about especially by the authority of a celebrated rabbi, Elias of Wilna, who stood in great esteem among the Jews, so that now scarcely any traces of the society can be found scattered here and there.

The claim was premature, for Hasidism was still very much alive. Despite the virulence of polemic between *hasidim* and *mitnagdim*, it is evident that the causes for conflict were much weaker than had been the case with the opposition to Jacob Frank in the 1760s. The *hasidim* did not endorse antinomianism, and many of the *mitnagdim* were also involved in study of the kabbalah, even if the Vilna Gaon, who (according to his disciples) saw visions from heaven every night and wrote a celebrated commentary on the Zohar, preferred to reveal little about his mystical insights to others, relying instead on study and argument as the basis of his kabbalistic as well as his halakhic teachings and Bible commentaries.[65]

In 1774, after the first two bans on *hasidim*, Shneur Zalman had gone to Vilna with his hasidic colleague Menahem Mendel of Vitebsk, in a vain attempt to reach an understanding with the Gaon, only for the Gaon to refuse to meet them. In 1805 the Russian general Kutuzov, impatient with appeals for intervention from different sides in an internal Jewish debate of little interest to the secular government, instituted an inquiry into whether Hasidism was really a sect and required suppression by the state. On deciding that this was not the case, Kutuzov instructed both sides to cease their hostilities and to allow each other to build separate synagogues and choose their own rabbis. When the campaigns of Napoleon in 1812 threatened to do away with this liberal approach and subject the *hasidim* in Russia to centralized rabbinic authority, such as Napoleon had set up in the Paris Sanhedrin in 1806 (as we shall see), the *hasidim* threw their support behind the Russian resistance. The name of Levi Yitzhak b. Meir of Berdichev – another of the surviving pupils of Dov Ber, the Maggid of Mezeritch, who had founded a hasidic movement in central Poland and gained a wide following through his populist use of Yiddish when singing his prayers – headed a list of Jewish contributors to the funds raised by the Russian state as it prepared to face and defeat Napoleon. To both *hasidim* and *mitnagdim*, the threat of Napoleon was far more than political: the forces of the Enlightenment he represented would be a challenge to all east European Jews.[66]

The remarkable success of Hasidism in developing from a movement of religious renewal by small groups of enthusiastic Torah scholars and kabbalists to a mass movement among Jews across eastern Europe must owe much to a loss of trust in communal rabbis as representatives of traditional leadership structures. In part this was because those leaders had come to be identified with the interests of the Polish nobility from whom they increasingly derived their authority, particularly after the abolition of the Council of the Four Lands in Poland in 1764. But there was also a palpable sense of freedom for a young rabbinic student from the margins of Jewish society in his ability to select for himself his *rebbe*, and the religious world to which he would devote his life, on the basis of pious instinct rather than intellectual capacity.

But the same freedom had been available for the followers of Sabbetai Zevi and Jacob Frank, who by contrast were relegated to the margins of Judaism by their fellow Jews far more severely than the *hasidim*. The saving grace for Hasidism in contrast to Frankism was not just the comparatively conservative attitude of *hasidim* to the halakhah but their more circumspect views on messianism. The Baal Shem Tov had envisaged a gradual coming of the kingdom when the preconditions for the coming of the Messiah have all been fulfilled. He did not preach an immediate eschatological expectation. From the time of the Baal Shem Tov, *hasidim* had been accused by their opponents of Sabbatean sympathies, but the charge could not be made to stick. The Baal Shem Tov is said to have lamented the conversion of the Frankists to Christianity in 1759 because 'the *Shekhinah* wails and says that as long as a limb is attached to the body there is hope for its cure, but when it is severed, it cannot be restored – and every Jew is a limb of the *Shekhinah*.' The devotion of the *hasid* to his *rebbe* sufficed as a religious aim, so long as the *rebbe* continued to lead his devotees. Only when the *tsaddik* of an established group died without succession, as when Nahman of Bratslav died in 1811, did hope for his return take on an eschatological character among his followers. Nahman was the first such expected messianic figure within Hasidism but, as we shall see, he was not to be the last.[67]

PART V

The Challenge of the
Modern World

(1750–present)

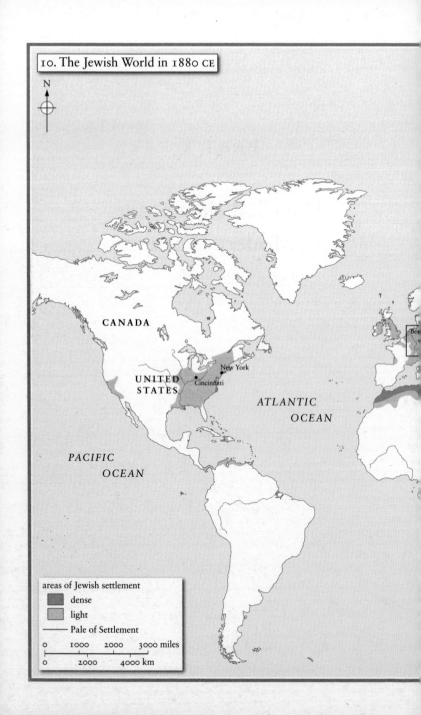

10. The Jewish World in 1880 CE

N

CANADA

UNITED
STATES

New York
Cincinnati

ATLANTIC
OCEAN

PACIFIC
OCEAN

Ber

areas of Jewish settlement

dense

light

— Pale of Settlement

0   1000   2000   3000 miles

0   2000   4000 km

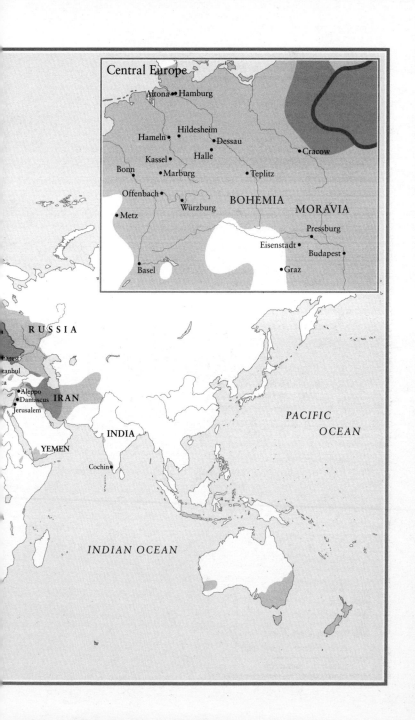

Central Europe

Altona • • Hamburg

Hildesheim
Hameln •   •
        • Dessau
Kassel •   Halle   • Cracow
Bonn •
     • Marburg
Offenbach •   • Teplitz
        •
• Metz   Würzburg   BOHEMIA   MORAVIA

                                Pressburg
                Eisenstadt •   Budapest •
Basel •
        • Graz

RUSSIA

harest
tanbul
a
• Aleppo   IRAN
• Damascus
Jerusalem

YEMEN

INDIA

Cochin •

PACIFIC
OCEAN

INDIAN OCEAN

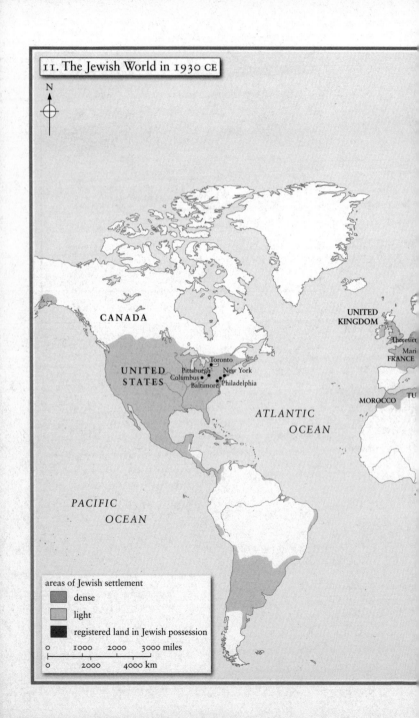

11. The Jewish World in 1930 CE

N

CANADA

UNITED
STATES

Toronto
Pittsburgh • New York
Columbus •
Baltimore • Philadelphia

ATLANTIC
OCEAN

PACIFIC
OCEAN

UNITED
KINGDOM

Theresien
Mari
FRANCE

MOROCCO   TU

areas of Jewish settlement
  dense
  light
  registered land in Jewish possession

0   1000   2000   3000 miles

0   2000   4000 km

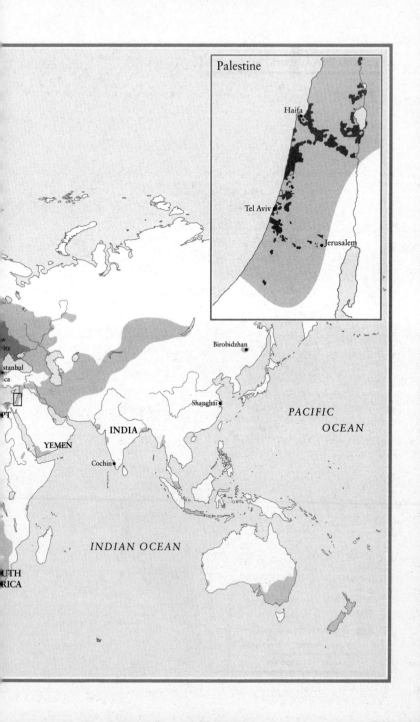

Palestine

Haifa

Tel Aviv

Jerusalem

Birobidzhan

Shanghai

PACIFIC
OCEAN

INDIA

YEMEN

Cochin

INDIAN OCEAN

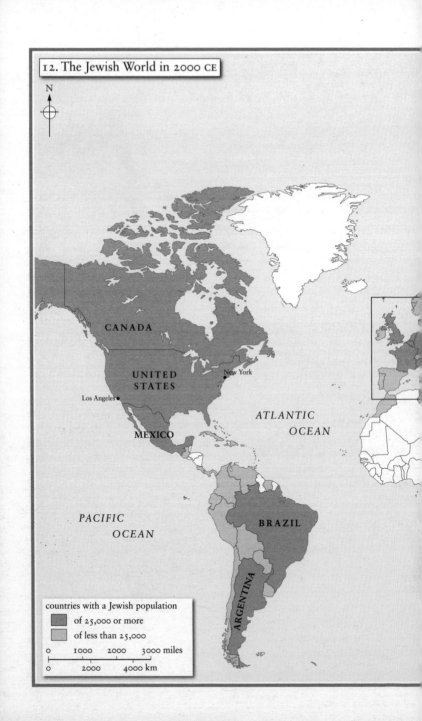

12. The Jewish World in 2000 CE

N

CANADA

UNITED
STATES

New York

Los Angeles

MEXICO

ATLANTIC
OCEAN

PACIFIC
OCEAN

BRAZIL

ARGENTINA

countries with a Jewish population
of 25,000 or more
of less than 25,000

0   1000   2000   3000 miles

0   2000   4000 km

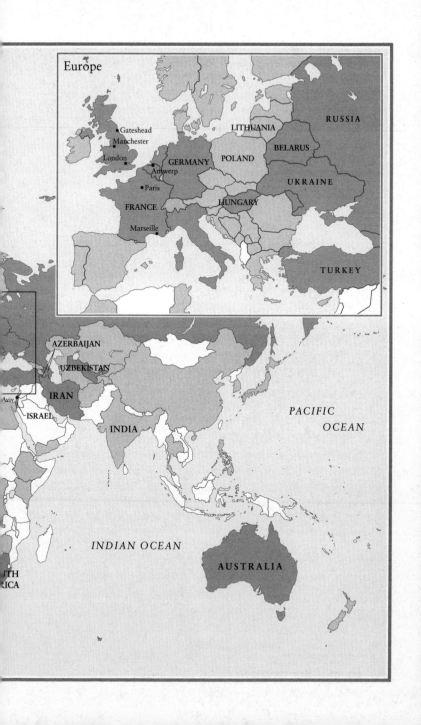

From the Enlightenment to the State of Israel

The standard image of a religious Jew remains for many in the modern world a bearded man in a long black frock coat and wide-brimmed hat, the respectable dress of the bourgeois in Poland, Lithuania and Hungary in the eighteenth and nineteenth centuries. Nor would that image be wholly wrong since, as we shall see in Chapter 19, a section of the Jewish people has elected to attempt preservation of the practices and religious outlook of that period as their way to keep the Torah of Moses. But all Jews, including these preservationists, have experienced extraordinary changes over the two and a half centuries since 1750, and many have adapted their Judaism to reflect these changed circumstances, albeit in different ways.

The main centres of Jewish population in the twenty-first century are the State of Israel and North America (the United States and Canada), with smaller but still sizeable communities in Central and South America (Mexico, Argentina and Brazil), in Australia and South Africa, and in both eastern Europe (especially Russia and Ukraine) and western Europe (especially the United Kingdom, France and, increasingly, Germany). Only small groups of Jews are now to be found in most of central Europe (although there is a substantial community in Hungary), and in the Arab countries of the Middle East and North Africa, and the pockets to be found still in Iran, Syria, Tunisia and Morocco are very isolated. Jews have undergone greater demographic shifts over this period than at any time in their history, for reasons both sociological and political.

The total number of Jews in the world increased greatly in the nineteenth century concurrently with a general population explosion within Europe. In 1800, the eastern European Jewish population was by far the largest. There were some 750,000 Jews in Russia, with a further 450,000 in the parts of Poland ruled by Austria and Prussia. There were some sizeable communities in the main Sephardi centres in North Africa and the Ottoman empire. Only 3,000 or so Jews lived in North America, comprising primarily Sephardic Jews from London and the Netherlands involved in trade and agriculture, who had settled since the establishment of a Jewish community in Charleston, South Carolina, in the late seventeenth century. By 1880, the total number of Jews had grown to over seven and a half million. Of these, some four million were under Russian rule. By comparison, the Jewish population of western Europe and the United States had grown much less, with the exception of New York, where 80,000 Jews had settled: an influx of German and Polish Jews into the thriving city doubled the size of the Jewish population between 1860 and 1880. Mass migration from the east over the following thirty years led to complete upheaval. Between 1881 and 1914 about a third of the Jews of eastern Europe moved to central and western Europe and the United States, partly in fear of persecution and partly for economic betterment. By 1914 immigrant Jews outnumbered the settled Jewish community in Britain by five to one, and 1.3 million Jews (of whom a million were in New York) had settled in the United States. Smaller numbers had moved to Argentina, Brazil, Canada and Palestine, often with the help of charitable organizations funded by wealthy Jews in western Europe to settle their impoverished brethren in agricultural colonies.

Despite massive losses in the Great War of 1914–18, with around 140,000 Jews killed as servicemen (mostly on the Russian side) and many civilians forced to flee by the fighting in eastern Europe and by persecution in the aftermath of the war in Hungary, Poland and Ukraine, the total Jewish population in the world had grown by 1930 to over fifteen million. Of these, half were still in eastern and central Europe, with three million in Poland alone, but the largest concentration of Jews was now in the United States, where some four million had settled, mostly on the eastern seaboard. Successive waves of immigration to Palestine, ruled by the British under a mandate from the League of Nations, had brought the Jewish population to around 160,000.

The rise of Nazism in the 1930s changed dramatically this pattern of migration. Of the half-million Jews who left Europe between 1932 and 1939, including 300,000 German Jews seeking to escape the tightening grip of anti-Jewish laws, nearly half went to Palestine, placing great strains on the Mandate government; in these years immigration to the United States was subject to strict quotas imposed in xenophobic reaction primarily to the economic crisis following the stockmarket crash of 1929. But the suffering of these migrants was insignificant compared to what followed in Europe. Between 1941 and 1945 some six million

European Jews were systematically murdered by the Nazis and their collaborators, wiping out the vast majority of the Jewish populations of Poland (where three million died), Russia (one million), Romania (just under half a million), Hungary (200,000) and Greece (70,000), as well as a large proportion of the Jews of France, Italy, Germany and the Netherlands.

For the first years after 1945 the lives of those European Jews who survived the Holocaust were chaotic, with many housed in refugee camps and unable to return to their homes because of continuing hostility to Jews even after the defeat of Nazi Germany. There were still nearly a quarter of a million European Jews categorized as displaced persons in 1947. Many sought to settle in Palestine but were prevented by the British Mandate authorities, concerned to protect the rights of the indigenous Arab population until, following endorsement by the United Nations General Assembly on 29 November 1947 of the recommendation of a committee that the Mandate should be terminated and Palestine divided into two states, one Jewish and one Arab, the State of Israel declared its independence on 14 May 1948, with free immigration for all Jews.

The foundation of the State of Israel was not accomplished without strong opposition from neighbouring Arab states, and conflict in the Middle East has continued to focus on this issue down to the present day. In the immediate aftermath of 1948 Jewish refugees from Iran, Yemen, Egypt and Morocco flooded into Israel to join both refugees from the war in Europe and idealistic Jews, often young, from the less troubled Jewish communities of the United States, South Africa and the United Kingdom. The Jewish population of Israel has had a continuously shifting profile ever since its foundation, with a major change in the 1970s as a result of immigration from the Soviet Union by Jews (often little acquainted with any Jewish heritage) both escaping discrimination and seeking a better life away from Communism, and in more recent years considerable emigration by native Israelis keen to find a more peaceful and secure life in the United States and elsewhere.[1]

Many Jewish Israelis, including a vocal elite, are defiantly secular, and it may be questioned to what extent the attitude of such secular Israelis to their Jewish heritage, which is sometimes for them essentially a matter only of status within Israeli society in distinguishing them from Arab Israelis (who themselves nowadays usually prefer to be defined as Palestinian Israelis), belongs to a history of Judaism, despite (as we shall see) recent attempts to define the nature of 'Secular Judaism'. The secularization of Jews within diaspora societies creates different demographic problems, since intermarriage with gentiles and assimilation into the host culture raises acute questions as to who is a Jew. For the offspring of mixed marriages, it has become a matter of choice in many societies, and most notably in the United States, whether to describe themselves as Jewish. Many Jews retain a strong cultural affiliation to their heritage without belonging to any synagogue or other religious community, although they may find new forms of engagement in secular organizations. Some may choose to identify as Jewish in one context (perhaps when subjected to some form of antisemitism) but not in another, when alignment with the mainstream culture may be more attractive. Thus estimates of the total Jewish population in the world today vary between twelve and eighteen million, depending on the definition used. Of these, some 5,700,000 are from Israel and 5,275,000 from the United States; compared to these huge centres of Jewish life, the 483,000 Jews in the next most populated country, France, are much less significant. On the other hand, even the very small Jewish communities in Azerbaijan, Belarus, Iran and Turkey may preserve some distinctive forms of Judaism, as do the 1,818 Jews in Tunisia, the 1,500 Jews in China and 15,000 or so Jews in India.[2]

These demographic shifts in Jewish population over the past two centuries have taken place against a backdrop of the transformation of the societies in which Jews have found themselves. Some Jews in the settled communities of Germany, Holland, France and England in the eighteenth century were able to participate in the Age of Enlightenment, which placed faith in the power of human reason alone to reform society and advance knowledge of the world and its purpose – indeed Baruch Spinoza (see Chapter 14) may be seen as one of the philosophers whose questioning of received truths began the Enlightenment, which culminated in the political ideals of the French Revolution and the United States Bill of Rights in the late 1780s. Jews were affected also by the concomitant shift towards secularism, and scepticism about the role to be played by religion in society, as manifest in the breaking of the link between Church and state in some parts of Europe and (at least in theory) in the United States from its foundation. So, too, Jews were affected by the growth of European nationalism in the nineteenth and twentieth centuries. In more recent times, Jews in Europe and Israel and the United States have been learning how to adapt to newer cultural trends, such as gender issues, a greatly increased concern for animal welfare and ecology, and a tendency to promote multiculturalism as a good in itself.

Responses by Jews to these cultural and social changes within the wider society in which they have found themselves in modern times have also been affected by Christian responses, and by changes within Christianity. In many Christian societies since the Enlightenment religious affiliation has been treated by the state as a matter for private choice, and the role of the Church in moulding the policies of the state has been strictly limited either de jure (as in France and the United States since the late eighteenth century) or de facto (as in the many contemporary European countries in which secular voices predominate in the public sphere even where, as in Italy or Ireland, Catholic influence has traditionally been strong). The privatization of religion has left space for a multiplicity of competing Christian denominations and sects, with claims to represent the true form of the faith (sometimes expressed as a fundamental return to origins) balanced by occasional recognition, particularly in recent decades, of the desirability of ecumenism. Wide public debate about the implications of scientific advances for religious faith have covered and recovered essentially the same ground since the mid-nineteenth century, when the evolutionary theories of Darwin were understood by some to contradict the veracity of the Bible. The insights of biblical critics, since the pioneering efforts of Julius Wellhausen in the same era as Darwin, have been taken as evidence for similar doubts on literary and historical grounds. To all these issues have been added in recent years new contentions arising from wider societal change, such as the treatment of women and homosexuals in leadership roles within Christian communities. In many European societies an increase in Muslim populations has prompted reconsideration of questions of faith and toleration, with inevitable impact on Jews as well as Christians: the total number of Muslims in Europe (excluding Turkey) in 2010 was estimated at around forty-four million, constituting 6 per cent of the total population.

In some respects many diaspora Jews now practise their religion in multicultural western societies on much the same terms as Christians do, opting into (or out of) a specific synagogue community in the same way as Christians may opt into a church group – and for similar mixed reasons, from family tradition to social solidarity, convenience of location, the personality of the religious leadership and occasionally (of course) religious conviction. Such freedom of religious association and disassociation may be seen as one of the greatest changes in Jewish religious life over the past two centuries, since, until quite recently, Jews have been marginalized, and sometimes the victims of antisemitism of one kind or another, in most of the societies in which they have lived.

The position of the Jewish population of eastern Europe in the late eighteenth century, when the culture of yeshivot was at its height and Hasidism was beginning to take root, was greatly affected by the expansion of the power of tsarist Russia into Poland from 1772. Jews were largely excluded from Russia itself, and the tsars, who in general imposed strict controls on movement within their territories, established limits to Jewish settlement. The size of what came to be called from the late eighteenth century the 'Pale of Settlement' varied over the next century and a quarter. It included at various times much of modern Lithuania, Belarus, Poland, Moldova and Ukraine as well as parts of western Russia. From the late 1850s rights of residence elsewhere in Russia began to be granted to the richest merchants, and to university graduates, medical professionals and some craftsmen, but such exceptions were ended in 1882, when, after pogroms in southern Russia in 1881 brought to the attention of the state the tensions between Jewish and Russian merchants in the villages, the May Laws also restricted new settlement by Jews in the towns and townlets within the Pale so as to protect the interests of the Russian villagers.

The intense religious life of the *shtetl* (a Yiddish term for a market town inhabited mostly by Jews, such as were common in eastern Europe) came increasingly under threat. For generations Jewish communities had thrived in such small towns, which were originally owned by the Polish nobility and settled by Jews in order to provide services to the surrounding villagers (such as mills, inns and breweries) or to exercise special rights (such as the collection of duties and taxes for the state). The Jews acted as middlemen between the aristocracy and the peasantry as they had done from the late Middle Ages. In these communities, traditional ideals of piety, learning, scholarship, communal justice and charity were fused, against a background of constant graft by each family to ensure an income sufficient to buy chicken or fish for the Sabbath and unleavened bread for Pesach. In the synagogue, where study, assembly and prayer all concentrated, men of learning, substance and status sat near the ark, faced by the established householders, with the ignorant and poor ranged behind and beggars dependent on communal charity by the western wall. At home, according to the idealized stories of the great Yiddish author Shalom Aleichem, the patriarch enjoyed his *Yiddishkeyt* (an evocative Yiddish word meaning 'a Jewish way of life') in the warm glow of his family, centred on the peace of the Sabbath and dignity of the festivals:

> And coming home from the bath, refreshed, invigorated, almost a new man, he dresses for the holiday. He puts on his best gabardine with the new cord, steals a glance at Bath-Sheba in her new dress with the new silk shawl, and finds her still a presentable woman, a good, generous, pious woman … And then with Froike he goes to the synagogue. There greetings fly at him from all sides. 'Well, well! Reb Fishel! How are you? How's the *melamed* ["teacher"]?' 'The *melamed* is still teaching.' 'What's happening in the world?' 'What should happen? It's still the same old world.' 'What's going on in Balta?' 'Balta is still Balta.' Always, every six months, the same formula, exactly the same, word for word. And Nissel the cantor steps up to the lectern to start the evening services … They are home already and the seder is waiting. The wine in the glasses, the horseradish, the eggs, the haroses [a paste made of fruit and nuts, symbolizing the mortar used by the slaves in Egypt], and all the other ritual foods. His 'throne' is ready – two stools with a large pillow spread over them. Any minute now Fishel will become the king, any minute he will seat himself on his royal throne in a white robe, and Bath-Sheba, his queen, with her new silk shawl will sit at his side. Ephraim, the prince, in his new cap and Princess Reizel with her braids will sit facing them.[3]

In practice, Jewish life in eastern Europe was more varied and much less settled than the stereotype suggests, and much of the mass emigration in the late nineteenth century reflected a widespread desire to live in a less traditional environment.

With the Communist revolution of 1917, in which many Jews participated, but many others suffered horrifically (with 200,000 dying in Ukraine alone), the Pale was abolished and Jews migrated en masse to the big cities of Russia, especially Moscow. The attitude of the Communist state to Jews was contradictory. By 1927 Jews formed the third largest national group among members of the Communist party, even though the state vacillated over whether Jews were a nation at all or should just assimilate into wider Soviet society. From the mid-1920s, attempts were made to settle Jews as farmers in Birobidzhan, an extensive but inhospitable region in the eastern Soviet Union on the border with Manchuria. But the projected Soviet Jewish republic never materialized, and Jewish settlers never amounted to more than a quarter of the population there. For all Jews the observance of religious practices was permitted only as an expression of the Jewish national culture, along with Yiddish as a national language. Both were discouraged by the state, particularly during the Black Years from 1948 to 1953, when Stalin campaigned against Jewish nationalism and 'cosmopolitanism'. By 1970 the vast majority of Jews in the Soviet Union had Russian as their mother tongue and knew very little about Judaism, with only the elderly attending those synagogues permitted by the state to remain open for worship. Most of those who gained permission to leave the Soviet Union for Israel in the 1970s and 1980s had to learn their religion on their arrival. Many of them had no interest in religion at all.

The trauma of Soviet Jews under Stalin in the late 1940s had of course been exacerbated beyond measure by the annihilation of many Jewish communities in the western Soviet Union while under German occupation from 1941 to 1945. At first glance it is surprising that this ultimate assault on the Jews stemmed not from the repressive regime in Russia but from what had been considered the more enlightened part of Europe.

The French Revolution, proclaiming equality and fraternity, had opened up the possibility that Jews in western Europe might be freed from the status of a barely tolerated minority, in which they had existed since the end of antiquity, and become full members of the societies in which they lived. But in France itself emancipation for the individual was accompanied by heavy-handed state control of religious life. On the instruction of Napoleon Bonaparte, an Assembly of Jewish Notables, comprising both lay leaders and rabbis, was mustered on 26 July 1806 to transform Jews from a 'nation within a nation' to 'French citizens of the Mosaic faith'. The Assembly responded patriotically, but when it became clear that religious authority would be required to bring the resolutions of the Assembly into effect, Napoleon ordered the convening of a Sanhedrin of seventy-one Jews, mostly but not exclusively rabbis, with a brief to separate the immutable religious laws of Judaism from those which could be safely discarded. The aim was to incorporate into the religious requirements of Judaism services to the French state, including the military, and to require Jews to undergo civil procedures alongside religious ceremonies in marriage and divorce. The Sanhedrin met on 4 February 1807 to undertake this task and its decisions were then used as the framework for the establishment in 1808 of *consistoires* throughout France, with both rabbis and lay participants to regulate Jewish life for the benefit of the state. Their role included the enforcement of military conscription, with the central *consistoires* in Paris under the authority of three *grands rabbins* and two laymen. The system, which is still in operation in France, Belgium and Luxembourg, has not always been used for state interference in Jewish religious affairs. But, with the state maintaining the rabbinical seminary in France from 1830, and the institution of the grand rabbinate from 1845, emancipation may seem to have been purchased in part by the loss of religious autonomy.[4]

Jews in the German communities conquered by Napoleon, such as Frankfurt and the Hanseatic cities, were granted emancipation on French insistence, but despite (or because of) Jewish agitation for civil rights at the Congress of Vienna, the fall of Napoleon produced an antisemitic backlash in many German states, encouraged by a romantic notion of a Christian Teutonic culture in which Jews could play no part unless – and often even if – they renounced their Judaism. In August 1819 a series of rioters, united under the rallying cry 'Hep! Hep!', attacked Jews in Würzburg. The violence, though concentrated in Bavaria, Baden, Halle and Württemberg, where it also involved rural areas, spread to cities as far away as Copenhagen to the north, Danzig and Cracow to the east and Graz to the south. The causes of the riots were partly economic, after famine in rural areas in 1816 had left peasants indebted to Jewish merchants and moneylenders. But there was also resentment at the new freedoms of Jewish financiers, and the houses of the Rothschilds in Frankfurt came under particular attack. The response of the states was to withhold emancipation from the Jews in order to prevent such resentment and disorder, and the following decades witnessed a struggle by German Jews, who were increasingly middle class and drawn to the large cities, especially Berlin, for equal civil and political rights. Jews took part in the revolution of 1848–9, identifying themselves with the wider movement in Germany for the creation of a free, democratic and liberal German state. In the new German Reich established after the Franco-Prussian War of 1870, German Jews became in most respects full citizens, although still with formal limitations on any role in government and, in practice, no access to the highest academic posts in the new universities or to officer posts in the army.[5]

In this latter restriction French society at the end of the nineteenth century remained conspicuously more open than its German counterpart to Jewish participation in the state at the highest levels. Hence the shock to all European Jews at the condemnation to life imprisonment for treason in January 1895 of Alfred Dreyfus, a wealthy assimilated Jew who had become an officer on the French general staff council. Dreyfus was convicted on the basis of forged documents which appeared to show that he had passed a secret military paper to the military attaché in the German embassy in Paris. In the ensuing furore in France among liberal Dreyfusards, who campaigned for his exoneration in part as a way to attack the hold of the Catholic Church on the right wing and the military establishment still smarting from the defeat by Prussia in 1870, it became clear that even the most integrated and assimilated Jew in the most liberal of countries could still become the target of virulent antisemitism, as a pawn in wider social tensions.[6]

The opponents of Dreyfus called themselves the Ligue de la Patrie Française, and nationalist movements in many European countries similarly excluded Jews from the narrative of the nation's history and therefore from a role in its future. Thus Jews in Romania took part in the unsuccessful nationalist revolt against Russia in 1848, but in the following decades they were rarely granted citizenship. Despite the demand by the great powers at the Congress of Berlin in 1878 which finalized Romanian independence, Jews were excluded from the professions (including law and medicine) and from serving as officers in the army, and (from 1893) from attendance at public schools. Many of those who had campaigned for emancipation were driven into exile.[7]

One such exile was Moses Gaster from Bucharest, who had studied at both the University of Breslau and the Jüdisch-Theologische Seminar of Breslau, where he was ordained a rabbi in 1881 at the age of twenty-five, when he was also appointed to a post in the University of Bucharest to teach Romanian language and literature. Expelled from his university post and his native country for his protests against the treatment of Jews, he moved to England, where he was appointed to teach Slavonic literature in the University of Oxford in 1886. A year later he was elected *haham* of the Spanish and Portuguese Jews of England, and by 1907 he was president of the English Zionist Federation. The choice of England as refuge was no accident. Britain was at the height of its imperial power, and Jews had achieved full political emancipation with Lionel de Rothschild, who had been elected to parliament on successive occasions by the City of London since 1847. Unable to take his seat because of the requirement to take a Christian form of oath, Rothschild was finally admitted to the House of Commons in 1858 with permission to take a Jewish form of the oath; in 1885, the year Gaster left Romania, Lionel's son Nathaniel was the first professing Jew to be raised to the peerage. The rabbi of the Great Synagogue in London, who had been informally recognized as chief rabbi of the Ashkenazi Jews of England since the mid-eighteenth century, was in 1845 officially designated by the state as chief rabbi of the United Hebrew Congregations of the British Empire;

rabbis appointed by the lay Jewish leadership to this position have retained considerable prestige within the wider English public down to the present. It would be wrong to assume that there was no anti-semitism in nineteenth-century England, but there was remarkably little hostility on grounds of his origins to Benjamin Disraeli when he became prime minister despite his open pride in his Jewish background, and the cultural hostility which can be discerned in literary depictions of Jews from Shakespeare onwards, and in such social slights as exclusion from golf clubs or antisemitic jokes, cannot compare to the discrimination being suffered by Jews in much of mainland Europe in this period.[8]

The most destructive expression of such discrimination was to be suffered by the Jews of Germany in the twentieth century, when resent-ment at the travails of the nation after war had ended in 1918 and the political chaos of the early 1930s encouraged popular credence of Nazi claims that the Jews were to blame. German Jews were removed from public positions, and deprived of civic rights, at astonishing speed after the rise of Hitler to power in 1933, and with minimal opposition by the general population. What distinguished this form of antisemitism from all previous kinds was not only its virulence, expressed in rhetoric about the extermination of disease which turned out to be intended all too literally, but a racial rather than religious definition of Jewishness, so that anyone of Jewish descent (defined as at least three Jewish grand-parents) was treated as Jewish regardless of religious affiliation. The theoretical origins of racial antisemitism lay in the scientific theories of race and eugenics popular in Europe and the United States in the late nineteenth century. Jews came to be seen as part of an inferior Semitic race which posed a threat to Aryans because of the increased racial inter-mingling enabled by Jewish civic emancipation in many European countries. With the rise of nationalism politicians adopted antisemitic slogans and policies to demonstrate their patriotic fervour across Europe and even in the United States. But it was only in Germany that the rheto-ric led the state to embark on the physical extermination of the Jews.

For many of the countries of Europe in which the Holocaust occurred between 1939 and 1945, it took decades to acknowledge the signifi-cance for wider society of the disappearance of complete populations of Jews. More recently the enormity of what happened has been more widely appreciated, especially in Germany, with numerous museums of Jewish culture, intensive education and huge efforts devoted to research-ing the phenomenon of antisemitism.

In recent times the attitude to Jews of liberal Germans, as of many other Europeans, has been much complicated by perceptions of the role of Israel in the Middle East conflict, where the Israeli state has often been regarded unfavourably as a colonialist proxy of the United States. Local hostility to the few Jews remaining in Arab countries after 1948, when most fled to Israel to escape growing persecution, has also tended to increase as the cause of the Palestinians has been widely adopted in the Islamic world as a paradigm case of the violation of the Dar al-Islam (the region of the world which should be governed by Islamic law). From the Muslim perspective, the licit settlement of Jews as *dhimmi*, a protected minority, within Islamic societies has been subverted by the assertion of Jewish political power in a part of the world that by rights should be ruled by Muslims. The rhetoric of such groups as the Muslim Brotherhood in Egypt has resurrected anti-Jewish material from the Koran and the earliest period of Islam, to create a novel, distinctive and powerful form of Islamic antisemitism which paints a picture of the Jews of Israel and the United States as a worldwide conspiracy, even citing for this purpose the venerable literary forgery of *The Protocols of the Elders of Zion*, which had circulated (and been widely believed) from the late nineteenth century to the 1930s in the European circles which wished to blame Communism on the Jews.[9]

The secular lives of the Jewish communities in which Judaism has evolved over the past two centuries have thus themselves evolved out of all recognition at the same time. Already in the early nineteenth century it was possible for a Jew to attempt to abandon his or her Jewish identity in many European countries and to merge into the wider population. This was indeed common in the deeply acculturated community in Germany, in which many Jews identified with German culture and saw conversion to Christianity as an attractive means to social advancement (which in turn fuelled some of the shock at Nazi legislation which targeted such converts as much as those who had remained within Judaism). Other German Jews, starting with the philosopher Moses Mendelssohn (see Chapter 17), rejected assimilation and instead adapted the values of the Enlightenment to Jewish culture itself, insisting on the importance of a secular education alongside the study of the Talmud. The secular Jewish culture promoted by these *maskilim*, 'enlightened ones', over the nineteenth century in central and eastern Europe took radically different forms, from romantic Hebrew poetry to encouragement of manual labour in arts and craft work and a return to nature, but they all had in common an insistence that the values of the wider secular world were to be embraced rather than rejected.[10]

Among the interests of these *maskilim* in the 1820s was historical research, coinciding in this respect with the concerns of the Jewish scholars in Germany who established the Verein für Kultur und Wissenschaft der Juden in 1819. The members of the Verein had been trained in critical academic studies in German universities and sought to apply the same techniques to the classical Jewish sources without what they saw as the obscurantism of traditional rabbinic approaches or the hostility of Christian scholars. The *Wissenschaft des Judentums* ('Science of Judaism') to which they devoted themselves was intended to present Jewish history in a form which made sense in modern terms, in much the same way as Christian scholars in the same period were undertaking scientific study of the Christian tradition. The movement was immensely productive. Both Isaak Markus Jost and (later in the nineteenth century) Heinrich Graetz wrote vast histories of the Jews, and Leopold Zunz wrote penetrating studies of Jewish homiletic and liturgical history. Nor was the movement confined to Germany: by the end of the nineteenth century, learned Jewish societies similar to the Société des Etudes Juives, established in France in 1880 to bring critical scholarship into the Jewish tradition, were also to be found in England and Hungary.[11]

Alongside such cultural responses to the changing world were the more political ones. Many Jews in the nineteenth century dedicated themselves to different forms of socialism, either within European society as a whole or on a broader world scale (like Karl Marx) or, as in the Bund, with a distinctively Jewish programme. The Bund, the 'General Jewish Workers' Union in Lithuania, Poland and Russia', was founded in Russia in 1897 and devoted to a Jewish socialism allied to a secular, Yiddish-speaking east European Jewish nationalism. The Bundists were deeply opposed to the contemporary emergence of the very different Jewish nationalism urged on the Jews of eastern Europe by Zionists.[12]

Before the late nineteenth century, advocacy of a mass return to the land of Israel was based on religious dogmas such as the messianic expectations of Tzvi Hirsch Kalischer from Poznań, who persuaded the rich philanthropist Sir Moses Montefiore in England, and the Alliance Israélite Universelle in France, to provide practical support in the founding of an agricultural school near Jaffa in 1870. In the 1880s Shmuel Mohilever, rabbi of Białystok, persuaded Baron Edmond de Rothschild in Paris to support agricultural settlements by arguing that God preferred his children to live in their land even without proper observance of the Torah rather than to have them keeping the Torah perfectly in the diaspora. This religious background was not unimportant to the

Hungarian journalist Theodor Herzl, who organized the First Zionist Congress in Basel in 1897, but his plan to establish a national home for the Jewish people in the land of Israel was essentially secular, even if he too turned to rich Jewish financiers (Baron Maurice de Hirsch and the Rothschilds) for help with the project, and indeed gained the support of Mohilever (who was however too ill to attend the Congress, dying the following year). The severely practical and secular aims of the new Zionist movement became starkly apparent in 1903, when Herzl attempted to persuade the Sixth Zionist Congress, also held in Basel, that they should consider a suggestion by the British government that Jews might be settled in an area in east Africa. The proposal had been made more urgent by the flood westwards of eastern European Jewish refugees following reports of a pogrom in Kishinev. The resulting outcry led by those horrified at the idea of a Jewish land elsewhere than Palestine may have in part been responsible for Herzl's death in July 1904 at the age of only forty-four.[13]

Herzl's secular nationalism posed major challenges to traditional Jewish messianic expectations and the longing for a return to Zion embedded in the liturgy. For Jews who prayed daily that God should 'gather our exiles . . . from the four corners of the earth', it was unclear how plans for a political Jewish state played a role in the divine redemption of Israel. As a result, there were sharply conflicting responses to Zionism among religious Jews in the first half of the twentieth century. By the early twenty-first century, religious doubts have not altogether disappeared, but the growing popularity of political Zionism among secular Jews in the first half of the twentieth century, and the eventual foundation of the secular Jewish state in 1948, has encouraged appreciation of the accomplishments of Zionism by most Jews, whether or not they themselves heeded the call to migrate to the land of Israel. Indeed, for many Jews in the latter part of the twentieth century, support for the State of Israel, in what was perceived as its embattled position within a largely hostile Arab Middle East, combined with a vaguely focused desire to commemorate those who died in the Holocaust of 1939–45, has constituted the main bulwark of communal solidarity. Since the 1990s, in particular, a post-Zionist approach has emerged among Jews willing to re-examine the foundational narrative of the State of Israel and to insist on a more central role for the rights and experiences of non-Jews in the national consciousness.

The enormity of the Holocaust (in Hebrew, *Shoah*, meaning 'catastrophe') has ensured a quasi-universal liturgical response by Jews in

treating those who died as martyrs, killed for *kiddush haShem*, 'sanctification of the Name', in the same way as the Jews who died by their own
hands in York in 1190 rather than submit to baptism, or the victims of
the Inquisition in Spain and Portugal. Justification for seeing the six million in this way is not obvious, since although remarkable efforts were
made by some to continue to observe such religious obligations as
prayer, purity and proper burial even in the extreme conditions of the
Warsaw Ghetto, on forced marches and in the camps, many who died
were secular in outlook, and were selected on the basis of racial origin,
not religious faith. It is nevertheless now standard for Ashkenazi Jews to
include references to the six million martyrs in memorial prayers on the
fast of Av, which commemorates the destruction of the First and Second
Temples in Jerusalem, and in the Yizkor prayer (see p. 384):

> O God, full of mercy, Who dwells on high, grant proper rest on the wings
> of the Divine Presence . . . for the souls of . . . the holy and pure ones who
> were killed, murdered, slaughtered, burned, drowned and strangled for the
> sanctification of the Name through the hands of the German oppressors,
> may their name and memory be obliterated.[14]

Most diaspora Jewish communities have also introduced prayers for
the welfare of the State of Israel alongside the loyal prayers for the government of the local state which have been standard in Jewish
communities since the Middle Ages (with rare exceptions – many Jewish communities in Germany did not pray for the Nazi state). Liturgical
changes in synagogue worship have long been a focus for adaptation to
the modern world – and resistance by traditionalists. Many synagogues
in Germany from the early nineteenth century sought to reflect a new
sensibility towards aesthetics and decorum as found in contemporary
Christian worship. Hence an increased emphasis on music, including
the introduction of choral singing and organs by some communities,
and the elimination of much of the complex poetry and the additions
which had accreted to the regular prayers over the preceding millennium, particularly in the wake of Lurianic mysticism. The aim was to
promote a greater focus on the experience of the individual worshipper.
Jews acculturated to appreciation of beauty in the rest of their lives
sought it also in the synagogue.

Synagogue music already enshrined melodies appropriated from gentile sources, both religious and secular, over many centuries, so there
was nothing new in itself in the use of tunes from Beethoven or Verdi to
provide an emotional lift to the prayers. What was novel was the

consciousness of the effort. In the nineteenth century, synagogue liturgy became a public space in which to stake theological claims about the need for Judaism to reform in order to reflect the changed needs of a modern age. There was pressure, often resisted by conservatives, to incorporate sermons in the Christian style into the regular service and to use the vernacular in prayers and sermons. Richer communities erected cathedral-style synagogues in city centres in Europe and America, such as Florence and Budapest and the Neue Synagoge built between 1859 and 1866 on the Oranienburger Strasse in Berlin. Such buildings constituted state-ments of the established place of Jews in these societies, although it is significant that Jews often chose an oriental or some other 'exotic' style of architecture to differentiate their buildings from churches.[15]

Scientific and technological advances laid down many new chal-lenges for living a life according to the halakhah. Arguments about cremation for the disposal of the dead, the use of electricity on the Sab-bath, the permissibility of organ transplants and artificial insemination have at times become fault lines between Jewish religious groups. There has been much debate about the use of machines for various processes required for religious observances. So, for instance, rabbinic debates over the manufacture of *tsitsit* (ceremonial fringes on the corner of a prayer shawl) came down strongly against the use of sewing machines for attaching the fringes to the shawl: since the biblical verse enjoins that 'you shall put fringes on the corners of your garments', most rabbis decreed that such fringes fulfil the commandment only if they have been attached by hand by someone whose intention at the time of sewing was to carry out this particular religious duty. But machines for making *mat-zot* for Passover are widely used after an initially heated debate in 1859 between Solomon Kluger in Brody and Joseph Saul Nathansohn in Lemberg (modern Lviv, in Ukraine), even if handmade (*shemurah*) *mat-zot* are still seen by some as somehow better.[16]

Many of the rabbis guiding Jews in their responses to these challenges have held rather different positions in relation to their communities in western and central Europe and the United States than their predeces-sors before the modern age. From the mid-nineteenth century, most of these communities in the diaspora have been essentially voluntary organizations with rabbis as their employees, on fixed-term contracts. The authority of these rabbis, who are often selected more for their parochial skills than for their rabbinic learning, has generally depended as much on personal qualities as on qualifications. It became common in the nineteenth and twentieth centuries for western European rabbis to wear clerical dress inspired by their Christian colleagues, eschewing traditional Jewish dress, including sidelocks, and emphasizing expertise in university as much as yeshivah learning. For the leaders of these acculturated communities, it was important that the rabbi they hired as spiritual leader should have the qualifications to be addressed as 'Dr' and not just as 'Rabbi'.[17]

The role of rabbis in the State of Israel is more complicated. Problems of modern life, such as rules about abortions and autopsies, inevitably require decision by the state, and the balance of power between parties, in a democratic system using proportional representation, has often given a strong voice in government since 1948 to parties which stand for election on religious platforms. Among the religious decisions of most significance made by the state has been the definition of Jewish status for those who wish to settle in Israel under the Israeli Law of Return, which gives all Jews the right to become Israeli citizens. The state has decided, for instance, that Ethiopian Jews (Falashas) are to be classed as Jews despite the opposition of some rabbinic authorities, and that those immigrants from the Soviet Union who could not demonstrate their Jewish birth because of the paucity of records should nonetheless be treated as Jews if that is what they claim to be. An amendment to the 1950 Law of Return clarified the definition of Jewishness with regard to citizenship (but not in religious matters such as marriage and burial) to include relatives of Jews, since such people had suffered in the Holocaust for being Jewish: 'The rights of a Jew under this Law ... are also vested in a child and a grandchild of a Jew, the spouse of a Jew, the spouse of a child of a Jew and the spouse of a grandchild of a Jew.' There have, however, been limits to this liberality. The amendment also stated that a Jew means a person 'who is not a member of another religion', following the celebrated case in 1962 of Brother Daniel, a Polish Jew who had been hidden by Catholics and baptized as a Christian but still felt himself to be a Jew and wished to settle in Haifa. Judge Silberg, in a landmark verdict in the secular court, stated, in contradiction to the Nazi definition of Jewishness, that 'a Jew who has become a Christian is not deemed a Jew.' The ruling was agreed by orthodox rabbis despite being more stringent than the halakhah.[18]

Nearly 2,000 years of development in the diaspora with little or no political power left Judaism ill prepared to tackle from a religious perspective some of the moral and ethical problems arising from the foundation of a Jewish state. Christians had adapted to the dilemmas incumbent on governments with the conversion of Constantine in the fourth century, and many centuries had been spent in the development of appropriate theology for states that needed at times to impose order on subjects and to oppose enemies by force. The rabbis, accustomed to seeing the state as an external force to be placated and occasionally thwarted, had evolved no such notions. No treatment evolved in rabbinic Judaism equivalent to Christian doctrine about what constitutes a just war. The rabbis in late antiquity and the Middle Ages discussed the rulings in Deuteronomy in terms either of historical reconstruction or of messianic speculation. More concrete issues of the right to proportionate self-defence and the requirement to intervene to help others in peril were confined to discussions in the context of criminal law. In the 1160s, Maimonides had produced a systematic presentation of rabbinic theories of war in a substantial section of the *Mishneh Torah* entitled 'The Laws of Kings and their Wars', but issues such as the acceptability of pre-emptive military action remained quite unclear. When partial emancipation in nineteenth-century Europe gave to some Jews the opportunity of military service, rabbinic opinion was divided on the morality of voluntary enlistment. Similarly, although rabbis have been much involved in the intense debates within Israeli society over the morality of territorial expansion and relations with Palestinians, the arguments have been couched either in terms of the special role of the land of Israel in Judaism or on the basis of general human decency.[19]

Israel was and is a secular political state, but from its foundation a 'Status Quo' was agreed between its first prime minister, David Ben Gurion, and leading rabbis within it. Under this agreement, the Sabbath and Jewish festivals were established as public holidays. All public institutions are required to serve only kosher food, state schools are allotted either to the national secular or the national religious stream, and issues of personal status for Jews, such as marriage and divorce, are subject to the jurisdiction of rabbinic courts recognized by the state. The state recognizes the authority of two chief rabbis, one Ashkenazi and one Sephardi, adopting a practice instituted by the British in 1920 during the Mandate period in imitation of the chief rabbinate of the British Empire (although the authority of the Sephardic chief rabbi, known as the *Rishon leZion*, 'First in Zion', went back further into Ottoman times in the nineteenth century). Elected for a term of ten years by a large electoral assembly of rabbis and representatives of the public, the chief rabbis have generally been sympathetic to the essential aims of the state, with some, like Shlomo Goren, who served as chief rabbi from 1972 to 1983, having a decisive impact on religious aspects of state policy.

Goren had fought in the War of Independence in 1948 and theatrically blew the shofar at the Western Wall of the Temple just after the capture of the Old City of Jerusalem from Jordan in 1967. His authority was important in allowing remarriage by widows of soldiers whose bodies have not been found. He permitted post-mortem examinations of corpses when needed, solved problems involving relations with converts and permitted Jews to pray in some (but not other) areas on the Temple Mount. Goren had previously been Ashkenazi chief rabbi of Tel Aviv, as the state also appoints chief rabbis in each city and town, often providing or subsidizing buildings for use as synagogues in each municipality. Before either of these appointments, Goren had been chief chaplain of the army, in which office he introduced a novel compromise liturgy for the common use of Ashkenazi and Sephardi soldiers.[20]

Compulsory military service for both men and women has provided a unifying focus for most Jewish Israelis from the foundation of the state, intensified by the need for them to be deployed all too frequently in conflict. Since 1963, the state has added a day, within the mourning period (according to the rabbinic calendars) of the counting of the *omer*, of commemoration for fallen Israeli soldiers. The commemoration begins with the nationwide sounding of a siren the previous evening, with a repeat of the siren at 11 o'clock the following morning and the lighting of memorial candles. The Yizkor prayer is recited in public ceremonies and all places of entertainment are closed by law. The day is immediately followed by the celebration of Independence Day on 5 Iyyar: the chief rabbinate decided that the mourning restriction of the *omer* period should be lifted to allow for these celebrations, but by statute enacted by the Knesset, the day of Independence Day is always shifted to Thursday if 5 Iyyar falls on a Friday or Saturday to avoid celebrations leading to desecration of the Sabbath. There has been intensive debate within rabbinic circles on the appropriate liturgy, for which special prayer books have been published similar to those of the major festivals, and to what extent the day should treat the foundation of the state as a miracle like that celebrated on Hanukkah and Purim. Under the leadership of Shlomo Goren, Jerusalem Day, which also falls within the *omer* period (on 28 Iyyar) was instituted as an optional public holiday after the capture of the Old City in 1967, with a public assembly at the Western Wall of the Temple and the Hallel psalms recited in morning prayers along with their accompanying blessings to mark the distinctively religious character of the reclamation of the Temple site for Jewish pilgrims. In April 1951, the Knesset decreed that

28 Nisan should be observed as 'The Day of the Shoah [Holocaust] and the Ghetto Revolt', to commemorate both the Holocaust and the heroic but unsuccessful uprising against the Germans by the Jews of the Warsaw Ghetto in April to May 1943. Ambivalence in the early years of the state about commemoration of the destruction of European Jews rather than of the achievements of those who fought explains the determination to avoid a day of simple mourning, but since the late 1970s special ceremonies, such as the lighting of candles, and new liturgies have been developed to mark what has become known more generally as 'the Day of Holocaust and Heroism'.[21]

Of the festivals, those which have most captured the enthusiasm of secular Israelis are Lag BaOmer, widely celebrated with bonfires and fireworks, Hanukkah (with an emphasis on heroism) and Purim, which is celebrated with carnival processions known as *adlayada*, from the talmudic injunction that a man should revel on Purim *ad dela yada* ('until he does not know' the hero from the villain in the story of Esther (see Chapter 10)). Children wear masks and crowds flood the streets, but, despite the rabbinic injunction to drink wine, drunkenness is not common. The Bible Quiz held on Independence Day was in the early years of the state a national obsession among the secular, to whom this recollection of an essential part of their primary education was both nostalgic and nationalistic. Along with excavation of biblical-period sites, Bible study was much encouraged by Prime Minister David Ben Gurion as an important element in building a sense of national identity linked to both the land and Jewish origins, but without the layers of religious development within Judaism over the intervening two and a half millennia. The quiz continues, but Israeli secular passions have moved on, and a distinctive national Israeli identity of its own has emerged in which the Jewish past from before the twentieth century plays little part. Attempts are being made under the rubric of 'Secular Judaism' to introduce secular Israeli youth to a diaspora Jewish religious heritage which to them feels alien or even, if they view it as leading inexorably to the lifestyle and views of the ultra-religious, obnoxious and threatening.

The establishment of a Jewish identity for secular Jews in multicultural western diaspora societies is more difficult – hence the demographic uncertainties noted at the start of this chapter. Since synagogue communities in many countries rely on private subscription rather than state subvention to ensure the upkeep of buildings and fund the salaries of rabbis, many communities will accept into their membership any who apply, although usually only provided that they can be classified as

Jewish either by birth or by conversion (in both cases, variously defined by different communities) and regardless of religious belief or observance. The issue came unexpectedly into the gaze of the general public in the United Kingdom over a dispute about entry requirements for pupils applying to the Jewish Free School (JFS) in London in 2009. The school, which was popular and oversubscribed, admitted only those children certified as Jewish by the Office of the Chief Rabbi. The law in the United Kingdom permits selection for school entry on religious grounds. Entry to JFS required either that the mother was Jewish by descent or conversion prior to the child's birth (the conventional rabbinic definition) or that the child had converted or had been accepted on a course of conversion. A child was denied entry on the grounds that his mother's conversion to Judaism was not valid because it had not taken place under orthodox auspices. The father appealed to the secular courts, which found that using matrilineal descent as a criterion of Jewish status constitutes race discrimination and is therefore illegal. The practical result is that the United Kingdom Supreme Court has imposed on Jews a religious practice test to establish Jewish identity so as to qualify Jews as a religious group for the purpose of school entry.[22]

For some diaspora Jews, synagogue membership has primarily a social rather than religious function, sometimes with the added incentive of guaranteed burial rights within a Jewish cemetery (although Jewish communities will bury in any case dead Jews of any background, as a religious duty, so long as they are known to be Jewish and, usually, so long as they have not been cremated). It is quite common for Jews to fulfil their religious obligations to a synagogue community by attending prayers twice a year, on Rosh haShanah (the New Year) and on Yom Kippur (the Day of Atonement), much as secularized Christians may attend church only at Christmas and Easter. For such Jews, the touchstone of continuing religious allegiance is the Yom Kippur service, the most solemn part of the liturgical year. The equivalent touchstones for religious life at home are family gatherings for the Seder service on the eve of Pesach and the Sabbath meal on Friday nights. A pair of candlesticks for the Sabbath eve will be seen in many Jewish homes in which no other aspect of Judaism is to be found, and a great deal of nostalgia surrounds these rituals.

It is possible to trace a history of Judaism through the genetic evolution of Jewish food as it is still eaten. For the Ashkenazi world, *hallah* bread, roast chicken (replacing roast goose or brisket), carrot *tzimmes* (a sweetened vegetable stew), potato salad, potato *kugel*, for Friday night; *cholent* (a meat stew left to cook overnight) for Saturday lunch; cold fried fish, pickled herring, sliced cucumbers, smoked salmon, cheesecake for Saturday afternoon and evening. Yemenite Jews leave the *jahnun*, a pastry with a slightly sweet taste, in a slow oven overnight and eat it for Saturday lunch with hardboiled eggs and a spicy sauce. Iraqi, Persian, Libyan, Egyptian and Syrian Jews all have their own distinctive culinary traditions. For Hanukkah, to celebrate the miracle of the oil, Ashkenazim eat deep-fried potato *latkes*, Sephardim eat fritters in syrup or doughnuts, Italian Jews have fried chicken pieces dipped in batter, Moroccans eat couscous with deep-fried chicken. On Purim, Sephardi communities have pastries shaped like Haman's ears dipped in syrup, and Ashkenazim have *hamantaschen*, a three-cornered pastry stuffed with plum jam or poppy seeds. Shavuot is celebrated with cheese *blintzes*, cheesecake and milk puddings. And Pesach, for which so much of the festival concerns the preparation of food without leaven in order to commemorate the exodus from Egypt when the Israelites were required to depart at such speed there was no time for the dough to be left to rise, a huge range of cakes, pancakes, dumplings and fritters using ground almonds, potato flour or *matzah* meal or (in the Arab world) *kibbeh* with ground rice has turned culinary restrictions into a celebration of gastronomic ingenuity.[23]

In many families, recipes for such food, fondly remembered from previous generations, constitute the main link with a religious past which no longer otherwise resonates. But a decline into nostalgia and sentimentality about the world of *Fiddler on the Roof* which was always in part imaginary and has now disappeared is not, as we shall see, the whole story of modern developments within Judaism.

17
Reform

Moses Mendelssohn, the first Jew to retain allegiance to traditional Judaism while simultaneously emerging as one of the leading figures of the European Enlightenment, first became famous in Germany in 1763, when his *Treatise on Metaphysical Evidence* won the essay competition of the Berlin Royal Academy (beating into second place the entry by his older contemporary, Immanuel Kant). Nicknamed 'the German Socrates', Mendelssohn had tried to demonstrate through reason what he saw as the fundamental truths of natural religion – the immortality of the soul, and the existence and providence of God. It was a remarkable achievement at the age of thirty-four for the son of a Torah scribe from Dessau, who had been educated in Talmud and medieval Jewish philosophy. He was self-taught in German, Greek, Latin, French and English, as well as in the writings of John Locke, Christian Wolff and Leibniz.[1]

From the reception accorded to Mendelssohn's work it is clear that in these early years his main readers were not Jews and that the significance of his thought was taken to lie in its underpinning of all religion. But fame brought hostility, and in 1769 the Swiss theologian Johann Caspar Lavater, who had just published his German translation of *La Palingén-ésie philosophique* of Charles Bonnet, challenged Mendelssohn either to refute Bonnet or to accept Christianity. Mendelssohn was not a natural polemicist, but once challenged he felt compelled to respond with an affirmation of his commitment to his ancestral religion on the grounds that, unlike the limitation of salvation to believers within Christianity, Judaism held that salvation is possible for all. This image of Judaism as a religion of tolerance, permitting freedom of conscience, was expressed most forcibly in 1782–3 in his classic work *Jerusalem, or, On Religious Power and Judaism*:

> At least pave the way for a happy posterity toward that height of culture,
> toward that universal tolerance of man for which reason still sighs in vain!

Reward and punish no doctrine, tempt and bribe no one to adopt any religious opinion! Let everyone be permitted to speak as he thinks, to invoke God after his own manner or that of his fathers, and to seek eternal salvation where he thinks he may find it, as long as he does not disturb public felicity and acts honestly toward the civil laws, toward you and his fellow citizens.

Like Spinoza a century earlier, Mendelssohn advocated a separation of religion from the state. The personal interests of disenfranchised Jews in Christian societies coincided neatly with Enlightenment values of individual conscience. For Mendelssohn, as for Spinoza, true religion consists in rational and moral truths available to all. But to Mendelssohn (unlike Spinoza) the special characteristics of Judaism derive from revealed law, whose purpose is to preserve the purity of religious concepts when they are assailed by idolatry. He urged his fellow Jews to appreciate that the issue is as vital now as in the past:

And even today, no wiser advice than this can be given to the House of Jacob. Adapt yourselves to the morals and the constitution of the land to which you have been removed; but hold fast to the religion of your fathers too. Bear both burdens as well as you can! It is true that, on the one hand, the burden of civil life is made heavier for you on account of the religion to which you remain faithful, and, on the other hand, the climate and the times make the observance of your religious laws in some respects more irksome than they are. Nevertheless, persevere, remain unflinchingly at the post which Providence has assigned to you, and endure everything that happens to you as your lawgiver foretold long ago.[2]

The immediate impact of Mendelssohn on German Jewry was less through the specific arguments of his religious philosophy than through his example, as a famous German who remained loyal to his Judaism. His translation of the Torah into German (written in Hebrew characters), with a Hebrew commentary which combined exegesis of the plain sense in the medieval Jewish tradition with aesthetic comments (thus modernizing Bible study in a fashion less revolutionary than Spinoza's critique), was much read. Mendelssohn's continuing publication of Hebrew writings, such as a commentary on Ecclesiastes published in 1768, alongside German philosophical works, and his willingness to use his influence for the benefit of Jewish communities in Germany and Switzerland, combined with his own strict adherence to traditional Jewish religious behaviour to enable all the different strands of Judaism which emerged in Germany in the century after his death to claim him as an inspiration.[3]

It is ironic that the ideas propounded by the Christian philosopher Immanuel Kant, who had been beaten by Mendelssohn in the essay competition in Berlin in 1763, were to have a greater influence than those of Mendelssohn on the future of Judaism. Kant's philosophical innovation was to deny altogether the possibility of knowledge in the areas of metaphysics to which Spinoza and Mendelssohn devoted their reasoning. For Kant, demonstrative knowledge is possible only for the world of sense perception, and the existence of God can therefore only be postulated by reason, as the necessary condition for the possibility of the 'distribution of happiness in exact proportion to morality'. True religion for Kant is ethical religion, an ideal approached most nearly by the idealized, spiritualized, love-based teachings of Christianity.[4]

Kant became a close friend of Mendelssohn, but he followed Spinoza in seeing Judaism as failing to reach the heights required of true religion because it required only external obedience to the laws and not an inner moral conviction, and the attraction of his philosophy to Jews on the route to emancipation resided precisely in the replacement of the Judaism to which they were accustomed by a deeply moral religious commitment free of ritual and communal ties. Hence the devotion to Kant of the wayward former *hasid* Solomon Maimon, whose disillusioned comments about Hasidism were quoted in Chapter 15.

Maimon's *Transcendental Philosophy* took the form of explanatory observations on Kant's *Critique of Pure Reason*, 'just as this system unfolded itself to my mind'. It is remarkable that Maimon had the self-confidence, albeit towards the end of his life, to send the manuscript of his *Transcendental Philosophy* to Kant himself. In the course of his, mostly poverty-stricken, journeys around Europe, Maimon was a rabbinic child prodigy in Sukoviborg in Poland and then a guest of Count Adolf Kalkreuth in his residence near Freistadt in Silesia, before spending some years in the circle of Moses Mendelssohn and eventually being forced to leave Berlin because of his dissolute life. A desperate attempt in Hamburg to persuade a Lutheran pastor to convert him to Christianity failed when Maimon confessed that he did not believe in Christian doctrines. Kant at least is said to have appreciated the insights of his follower, stating that no one else had understood his philosophy as well. Nonetheless, when Maimon died in 1800 he was buried outside the Jewish cemetery, defined as a heretical Jew.[5]

Maimon was not the only Jewish thinker to immerse himself in the exciting new world of Enlightenment philosophy but to have had little impact on the religious lives of fellow Jews in his own time. The Galician *maskil* Nahman Krochmal evolved in the early nineteenth century a distinctive idealist philosophy, based on the ideas of Vico and Herder as well as Kant, Schelling and Hegel, in which he asserted that the monotheistic God of Judaism is the Absolute Spirit in which everything subsists (including the deities of other nations), and that each nation (including the Jews) has a distinctive folk spirit which passes through an organic cycle from birth to destruction. Little known in Krochmal's lifetime, these ideas were disseminated by the members of the *Wissenschaft des Judentums* movement after his death in 1840, with the publication in 1851 of many of his writings in an edition produced by Leopold Zunz. Equally independent was the doctor and poet Salomon Steinheim, a younger contemporary of Krochmal who was born in Germany and (despite moving to Italy) wrote in German. Steinheim attacked fiercely both Christianity and the rationalizing approach to religion advocated by Mendelssohn, insisting both that the truths of revelation are independent of natural reason and that they must be confirmed by philosophy. His notion that religious experience should be subject to the same empirical tests as other areas of human life proved uncongenial both to traditionalists (for whom his philosophy was too rational) and to the spirit of reform which was sweeping through German Jewry by the time of his death in 1866, creating new denominations within Judaism which were to have an impact down to the present day.[6]

In a sermon in 1853, Samuel Holdheim, rabbi of the Reform congregation of Berlin from 1847 until his death in 1860, expressed the central desire of the Reform movement for Jews to use their dispersion among the nations to transcend the specifically national traits of traditional Judaism as the religion just of Israel in relation to God and to bring spiritual illumination to all mankind:

> It is the destiny of Judaism to pour the light of its thoughts, the fire of its sentiments, the fervor of its feelings upon all souls and hearts on earth. Then all of these peoples and nations, each according to its soil and historic characteristics, will, by accepting our teachings, kindle their own lights, which will then shine independently and warm their souls. Judaism shall be the seed-bed of the nations filled with the blessing and promise, but not a fully grown matured tree with roots and trunk, crowned with branches and twigs, with blossoms and fruit – a tree which is merely to be

transplanted into a foreign soil ... This, then, is our task: to maintain Judaism within the Jewish people and at the same time to spread Judaism amongst the nations; to protect the sense of Jewish unity and life and faith without diminishing the sense of unity with all men; to nourish the love for Judaism without diminishing the love of man. We pray that God may give us further strength to search out the way of truth and not to stray from the path of love!

Under Holdheim's leadership, the Berlin community transferred the Sabbath from Saturday to Sunday, and permitted intermarriage between Jews and gentiles, distinguishing between the eternal ethical teachings of Judaism and the transitory ceremonial laws it believed were no longer applicable in the modern age. His was the most radical expression of a movement that for nearly half a century had been seeking a thorough modernization of Jewish worship.[7]

The movement had begun among enlightened upper-class Jews influenced by the universalizing theology of Moses Mendelssohn. In 1808 a wealthy financier called Israel Jacobson, whose suggestion to Napoleon to set up a supreme Jewish council in Paris probably lay behind the establishment of the Paris Sanhedrin in 1807, built a synagogue in Kassel in which sermons were preached in German and the officiant (Jacobson himself) wore the dress of a Protestant cleric. Moving to Berlin after the fall of Napoleon, Jacobson held similar synagogue services in private houses until the orthodox rabbis of the city persuaded the government to ban all private synagogues in 1823. But by that time Jacobson's example had been followed in Hamburg, and the movement had begun to acquire its own momentum.[8]

The New Israelite Temple Association of Hamburg was founded by sixty-six lay Jewish men who dedicated the building on 18 October 1818 with a clear rationale and agenda:

Since public worship has for some time been neglected by so many, because of the ever decreasing knowledge of the language in which alone it has until now been conducted, and also because of many other shortcomings which have crept in at the same time – the undersigned, convinced of the necessity to restore public worship to its deserving dignity and importance, have joined together to follow the example of several Israelite congregations, especially the one in Berlin. They plan to arrange in this city also, for themselves as well as others who think as they do, a dignified and well-ordered ritual according to which the worship service may be conducted on the Sabbath and holy days and on other solemn occasions, and which shall be observed in their own temple, to be erected especially for this purpose.

A new confirmation ceremony, at the age of sixteen, had already been introduced in Kassel in 1810 by Jacobson. The new ceremony, for which the liturgy was fluid, was felt more appropriate to the times than the *bar mitzvah* at the age of thirteen because the child was more genuinely able to take on adult responsibilities at an older age. It was open to girls as well as to boys. By 1844, the need for spiritual reform along these lines was expressed in heartfelt fashion from his final sickbed by the aged Aaron Chorin, rabbi in Arad (then in Hungary):

> The permanent elements of religion must be expressed in terms that appeal to the people and are consonant with the needs of life. If our religion and life appear to conflict with one another this is due either to the defacement of the sanctuary by foreign additions or to the licence of the sinning will which desires to make its unbridled greed and its false tendency authoritative guides for life. If we show ourselves as ready to strip off these unessential additions which often forced themselves upon our noble faith as the spawn of obscure and dark ages, as we are determined to sacrifice our very lives for the upholding of the essential, we will be able to resist successfully with the help of God all wanton, thoughtless and presumptuous attacks which license or ignorance may direct against out sacred cause; the seeming conflict will then disappear and we will have accomplished something lasting for God.[9]

Wide recognition of a need for change did not bring agreement on the limits to be imposed. The early Reform services shortened the synagogue liturgy, used the vernacular for sermons and some prayers, and introduced organs for the accompaniment of the main choral elements of the liturgy, but the changes made by individual congregations were vulnerable to challenge by the local orthodox rabbinic establishment. In June 1844, under the leadership of Abraham Geiger, a leading scholar within the *Wissenschaft des Judentums* movement whose studies of Jewish history and literature in ancient and medieval times were designed to show (correctly, at least in broad terms, as we have seen) how Judaism had always been constantly in a state of evolution, twenty-five rabbis from across Germany who supported religious change were persuaded to meet in Brunswick. Two further conferences followed, in Frankfurt in 1845 and in Breslau in 1846 – but without agreement on such issues of religious practice as the requirement for men to cover the head during prayer, the wearing of *tefillin*, and kosher food laws. There was much discussion about the role of Hebrew in the liturgy (with many wishing to retain an element), unanimous agreement that the traditional prayers for the restoration of sacrifices in the Temple should be omitted, and a majority decision in Frankfurt on 20 July 1845 that 'the messianic idea should retain prominent mention in the prayers, but all petitions for our return to the land of our fathers and for the restoration of a Jewish state should be eliminated', since 'in all contemporary additions to the prayer book our modern concept of the Messiah may clearly be stated, including the confession that our newly gained status as citizens constitutes a partial fulfilment of our messianic hopes.'[10]

There was a close link between these movements for religious reform and the historical concerns of the *Wissenschaft des Judentums* (see Chapter 16). At the heart of both movements was a desire to emphasize the rational aspects of Judaism and Jewish history so that the Jews might see themselves as like other Europeans. Many in the Hamburg congregation had been brought up in homes in which Jewish practices were not much observed, and the search for a rational Judaism paralleled the contemporary adoption of Protestant Christians, in an atmosphere of religious revival particularly in Germany, of a meaningful liberal theology based on biblical criticism.

Both historians and theologians did their best to minimize the mystical traditions of the kabbalah, denigrating or ignoring such practices as unworthy of the lofty religious ideals of an enlightened nation. But in countries independent of the Reform movement in Germany historical scholarship and philosophical speculation sometimes led Jews to somewhat different religious stances. Thus in Italy, Shmuel David Luzzatto (known as Shadal) imbibed the spirit of academic criticism in his learned Bible commentaries, which put to good use his extensive knowledge of Semitic languages, but embraced a romantic 'Judaism of feeling' which he contrasted both to the rationalism of philosophy and to the speculations of the mystics, which he robustly rejected. His younger Italian colleague Eliyahu Benamozegh, rabbi of Leghorn (Livorno), claimed that the kabbalah deserves a status equal to the Bible and the Talmud, and asserted that, since Judaism contains all the universal truths scattered throughout the religions and myths of other peoples, Jews must take a lead in encouraging universal belief in monotheism. Benamozegh, known to some as the Plato of Italian Jewry, was highly esteemed by non-Jewish readers for his attempt to demonstrate the affinities between Judaism and contemporary Italian philosophers and the superiority of

Jewish ethics in comparison to Christian. But his major work in Hebrew, a commentary on the Pentateuch published between 1862 and 1865 which incorporated evidence from comparative philology and archaeology, evoked such strong hostility in parts of the rabbinic world that in Aleppo and Damascus copies were burned in public.[11]

From these modest beginnings the Reform movement in Germany gradually changed the face of Ashkenazi Judaism in central and western Europe over the course of the nineteenth century. Many congregations in Germany liberalized their liturgy, although the Berlin Reformgemeinde, established in 1845, was the only German congregation to worship entirely in the vernacular, with the men bare-headed, and the Sabbath observed on a Sunday. The ideas of Reform were promulgated by rabbis trained in Berlin at the Hochschule für des Wissenschaft des Judentums, which opened in 1872. The Jüdisch-Theologische Seminar founded in Breslau in 1854 at the behest of Abraham Geiger had proved insufficient for this purpose with the less radical Zacharias Frankel as its head. Frankel was sympathetic to Reform but had withdrawn from the Reform synod of 1845 in protest at the proposal to replace Hebrew with German and to end references to sacrifices and the return to Zion, all of which he saw as central to Judaism.

By the 1870s the majority of religious German Jews belonged to communities which had adopted aspects of Reform theology and liturgy to different degrees, and the Reform movement had spread elsewhere. Concurrent with the developments in Frankfurt in the 1840s, many of the Jews of Hungary and Transylvania, who were sufficiently assimilated into wider society to identify with Magyar nationalists, adopted the example of the maverick Aaron Chorin (see above), who had taken a radically independent line since the late 1780s, condemning (in the footsteps of Karo) such ancient folk practices as *kapparot* ('expiations'), which involved swinging a live chicken three times around the head on the eve of Yom Kippur to symbolize the transference of the sins of the individual on to the hapless fowl, which he deemed superstitious and contrary to the spirit of Enlightenment. Chorin supported not only the innovations introduced in Berlin and Hamburg in 1818, but also travel and writing on the Sabbath, and even mixed marriages between Jews and gentiles. The motivations of the Neologists, as they were unofficially known, were complicated by their efforts to avoid divisions such as had opened up within German Judaism and present themselves as the sole representatives of Hungarian Jewry despite the protests of the orthodox. The principle that the Jews should have a unified community was strongly supported by the statesman Baron

József Eötvös, who had fought since the 1840s for the emancipation of the Jews and succeeded in passing an emancipation bill in 1867 upon the formation of an independent Hungarian government in that year. But the National Congress of Hungarian Jewry to which Eötvös helped to organize elections in 1868 to 1869 was an acrimonious affair, with no agreement even on terms of reference. The Neologists defined the Jewish community as 'a society providing for religious needs', whereas the orthodox saw them as 'followers of the Mosaic-rabbinic faith and commands as they are codified in the *Shulhan Arukh*'. When in 1871 the Hungarian parliament bowed to such pressure by allowing the orthodox to set up a separate community at the behest of the Austro-Hungarian Kaiser, the Neologists made great efforts to repair the breach by refraining from drastic reforms in liturgy. Rabbis who graduated from the Budapest Rabbinical Seminary, founded at the behest of the state authorities and with state finances, received an essentially orthodox training, although (as in Breslau) a critical study of the ancient sources was also permitted. Some traditionalist communities which declined to align themselves either with Neology or with orthodoxy, defined themselves accurately but oddly as the Status Quo Ante group. They survived independently, but only in small numbers and without government recognition, until 1928; the merger in 1926 of the Status Quo Ante communities in Slovakia with the Neologists suggests that by this time at least they saw their identity as primarily opposed to orthodoxy.[12]

The Hungarian Neologists had sought to gain control of the religious lives of Hungarian Jews, but they had gone to great lengths to prevent the Reform movement from becoming a schism within Judaism, suppressing in 1852 the younger members of the Pest community who had been trying to establish a Reform synagogue since 1848, and preventing also an attempt to set up a separate Hungarian Reform community in 1884. Very different was the lack of concern about such separation shown by English Jews when the West London Synagogue was founded in 1840. The West London Synagogue was established for singularly pragmatic reasons by those wealthy Jews who had moved away from the City in the east, where the chief rabbi presided over the Great Synagogue, and, against the chief rabbi's wishes, desired a new place of worship closer to their homes. The congregation in London were at first little touched by the debates on the continent. They declared in the words of the dedication sermon that 'our unerring guide has been, and will continue to be, the sacred volume of the scriptures' and that 'in matters relating to public worship, we desire to reject nothing that bears the stamp of Moses.' It helped that the community in the 1840s preserved close family ties with those who remained under the religious auspices of the chief rabbi, and that they refrained from making a radical distinction between the Bible as divinely inspired and the Talmud as merely human.

Reform Judaism in Britain thus became increasingly conservative in the course of the nineteenth century. The general lack of interest in theology and ignorance of the Jewish tradition among English Jews was lamented openly by those who founded the *Jewish Quarterly Review* in 1889. Matters were not much better when publication of the *Review* in London ceased in 1908, to be transferred to the more welcoming environment of the United States. The wealthy Claude Montefiore, who financed and co-edited the *Review*, was a notable exception. A student of Benjamin Jowett at Balliol, he had studied at the Hochschule in Berlin, and in 1902 he founded the radical Jewish Religious Union along with Lily Montagu, who came from a prominent banking family long involved both in British public life as liberal politicians and as leaders of the orthodox United Synagogue. The Union led in turn, in 1911, to the establishment of the Liberal Jewish Synagogue. Montefiore's theology, focusing on the Jewish conception of God and on ethics, stressed the similarities between Judaism and Christianity, and strongly opposed Jewish nationalism, which he saw as compromising Jewish universalist claims. In practical terms, he was in strong agreement on this latter issue with other English Jews of his class and background, including both Lily Montagu's elder brother, the second Baron Swaythling, who remained (like his father) strictly observant but still declared roundly his view that 'Judaism is to me only a religion,' and (of greater practical significance) another brother, the politician Edwin Montagu, who opposed and amended the Balfour Declaration of 1917 from within the British cabinet.[13]

Where Reform Judaism was really to flourish was in the new Jewish world of the United States, where intensive theological debate was rapidly added to institutional formation. The Reformed Society of Israelites was founded in Charleston, South Carolina, in 1825 quite separately from developments in Germany, but the immigrants from central Europe who formed Har Sinai Verein in Baltimore in 1842 and Temple Emanu-El in New York in 1846 brought with them the same debates between radicals, led by David Einhorn, and moderates, led by Isaac Mayer Wise. Einhorn had presided over congregations in Germany and Budapest before taking up a series of posts in the United States from 1855, in his mid-forties, and he sought to institute a theology and forms of worship similar to those in the Berlin Reformgemeinde, unconcerned if such innovations created a split within American Jewry. He championed services on Sunday, organ music and uncovered heads, and believed that ritual elements in Judaism were a hindrance to rational understanding of the real meaning of revelation and that the Talmud was no longer authoritative. His was a complete theology, as can be seen from his prayer book (*Olat Tamid*, published in 1856), which omits reference to the revival of sacrifice, return to Zion and the resurrection of the dead. It was also distinctively German: his last sermon contained a plea for retention of German in Reform congregations in North America. Isaac Mayer Wise had also migrated from Europe, but at a younger age – he was twenty-seven when he arrived in Albany in 1846 – and with a greater concern for Jewish unity and a more distinctively American agenda for a universal faith, based upon monotheism, in which the ideas of Judaism (in which he included the Talmud as well as the Bible) would play a leading role, and which would embrace all sectors of Jewry. His was a rationalistic Judaism, in which an academic lecture each Friday evening played a prominent role, and English was the main language of prayer.[14]

From his base in Cincinnati, Wise had by 1873 organized thirty-four Reform communities in twenty-eight cities into the Union of American Hebrew Congregations. With the support of the Union, Hebrew Union College was founded in 1875 in the basement of a Cincinnati synagogue for the training of American Reform rabbis, with Wise as president. But unification provoked a demand for greater clarity about the principles for which Reform stood, and although Wise presided over the conference of American Reform rabbis who met in Pittsburgh in 1885, most of the decisions expressed in the Pittsburgh Platform which emerged at the end of the conference were far more radical than he himself had wanted, with the spirit of Einhorn (who had died in 1879) prevailing in its eight paragraphs:

> We hold that the modern discoveries of scientific researches in the domains of nature and history are not antagonistic to the doctrines of Judaism ... Today we accept as binding only the moral laws and maintain only such ceremonies as elevate and sanctify our lives, but reject all such as are not adapted to the views and habits of modern civilization ... We hold that all such Mosaic and rabbinical laws as regulate diet, priestly purity and dress originated in ages and under the influence of ideas altogether foreign to our present mental and spiritual state ... We consider ourselves no longer a nation but a religious community, and therefore expect neither a return to Palestine, nor a sacrificial worship under the administration of the sons

of Aaron, nor the restoration of any of the laws concerning the Jewish state ... We reassert the doctrine of Judaism, that the soul of man is immortal ... We reject as ideas not rooted in Judaism the belief both in bodily resurrection and in Gehenna and Eden, as abodes for everlasting punishment or reward ... We deem it our duty to participate in the great task of modern times, to solve on the basis of justice and righteousness the problems presented by the contrasts and evils of the present organization of society.[15]

The Pittsburgh Platform was adopted by the Central Conference of American Rabbis which Wise established in 1889. It is perhaps unsurprising, in light of these declarations of universality, that the CCAR denounced Zionism after the First Zionist Congress in Basel in 1897. But by this time the movement was also starting to be influenced by the huge numbers of Jews coming to the United States from eastern Europe. For many of these immigrants Yiddish was the natural language to express their Jewish identity and the Germanic liberal ethos of earlier decades was irrelevant. For a while, the Reform movement was somewhat knocked off course, although its leaders were loath to lose its ideals, as the president of the CCAR observed in 1908:

I hear it said that since the day of the organization of this Conference the face of the American Jewish universe has greatly changed; that, owing to the arrival of masses of immigrants during the past twenty years our religious situation is altogether different from what it was before. Dismay has seized many. The tide of reactionism has swept them off their feet. The optimistic note of the leaders of the nineteenth century has changed in many quarters to a pessimistic wail. The despairers cry that the progressive tendency that this Conference represents cannot possibly hold its own against the overwhelming odds that spell reactionism, ghettoism, romanticism, neo-nationalism and neo-orthodoxy. In spite of many untoward signs I firmly believe that there is no cause for despair, dismay and disheartenment ... In the process of americanization all the perverted viewpoints that are now distorting the vision of many otherwise excellent people will go the way of all the other extravagant notions wherewith the onward course of civilization has been diverted for a brief spell. Such fads as the glorifying of Yiddish as the national language of the Jews, such vain discussions as to whether there is a Jewish art or no, such empty dreams as the political rehabilitation of the Jewish state ... will all pass as interesting incidents in the strange medley of this period of transition. And that which shall remain will be the great fundamental ideal of the mission of the Jews ... as a people of religion and of Judaism as a religious force through all the world.[16]

In parallel with such declarations by convocations of rabbis in the nineteenth and early twentieth centuries, Reform Judaism spawned a considerable corpus of sophisticated theological literature which applied to Judaism the insights of the greatest German philosophers, especially Kant. It was Hermann Cohen who marked the first determined effort to demonstrate the essential compatibility of ethical idealism as taught by Kant with notions of the nature of Judaism as they were being developed by the Reform movement. The son of a cantor and originally expected to become a rabbi, Cohen was tempted into philosophy at the universities of Breslau and Berlin, receiving a doctorate from the University of Halle at the age of twenty-three in 1865. Just over ten years later he was a full professor in the University of Marburg, where over some forty years he was to develop a distinctive version of Kantian idealism in which he stressed the centrality of the dignity of man, holding that human freedom does not contradict the laws of causality in natural science because ethics and science belong to two different systems which coexist. In Cohen's philosophical system in these Marburg years, there was little need to refer to Judaism. He assumed that religion is necessary for ethics, but his ideas about God were highly abstract: God exists to enable humankind to achieve its ethical ideal by ensuring the continuation of the world, as promised to Noah after the flood. In all his years at Marburg, Cohen directly discussed Judaism only briefly, when required to defend it against the slurs of the antisemitic historian Heinrich von Treitschke (who defined Judaism as the 'national religion of an alien race') and in a lawsuit involving an antisemitic schoolteacher.

It was only in the last six years of his life that Cohen made the forays into Jewish philosophy which were to have such an impact on other Jewish thinkers in the twentieth century. In 1912, at the age of seventy, Cohen finally retired from Marburg and moved to the Reform Hochschule in Berlin, where he devoted himself to the evolution of a new understanding of Judaism, stimulated by a journey to Vilna and Warsaw in 1914 in which he witnessed a kind of Jewish life very different from that he had known in Germany. Cohen transformed his notion of the role of religion in his philosophy of ethics, arguing that, although ethics operate independently within mankind as a whole, it is religion which, since the later Hebrew prophets, has introduced the categories of sin, repentance and salvation to cope with the anguish and guilt of the individual. In his last, and most influential, work, *Die Religion der Vernunft aus den Quellen des Judentums* ('The Religion of Reason out of the Sources of Judaism'), published posthumously in 1919, he expounded a new conception of religion through a selective exegesis of biblical, mid-rashic and liturgical Jewish texts, shifting from his Marburg view that God is a logical postulate of human reason to a dramatically opposite view, that God is a pure being ('I am, that I am'), and that the incomplete world, which is in a state of becoming, is related to God by the Ruah haKodesh ('Holy Spirit'), which is not (as Philo had thought in his concept of the Logos) an independent being but simply an attribute of the 'correlation' between the divine and the human, which exists alongside the correlation between man and man. According to Cohen, man collaborates with God in the work of creation, which will be perfected in the messianic era by the unification of mankind in harmonious community following the model of the Jewish people. For Judaism to provide such a model, it is essential for Jews to follow Jewish tradition and law to some extent, but (as Kant had insisted) the law must be followed freely out of a sense of duty. At the same time, Cohen argued that Judaism is not the only such model: to the degree that other religions foster dignity by their concerns for other humans (the values of fellowship) and for God (the need for atonement), Cohen claimed that they too have a share in reason.[17]

Cohen's last works had been written under the auspices of the Reform Hochschule, and his prestige as a Kantian philosopher lent great weight to his theological ideas within Reform Judaism in the twentieth century, but his philosophical predecessors within the German Reform movement in the nineteenth century had been less inclined to follow Kant than the idealistic philosophies of Schelling and (especially) Hegel, who affirmed the spiritual nature of reality and argued that the progressive self-realization of spirit is unfolded in history and that all history has a religious dimension. The Reform leader Solomon Formstecher recast, in his *Die Religion des Geistes* (1841), Schelling's notion of a world soul manifest in nature, by identifying this world soul with God, arguing however that another manifestation of the world soul is spirit, whose main characteristics are self-consciousness and freedom. The 'religion of the spirit' in his title is the religion of the Jews, which has developed towards greater universalism, a process nearing its culmination with the emancipation of the Jews. Thus Jews needed to prepare themselves for the emergence of the absolute truth of spiritual religion by stripping Judaism of its particularistic elements and its ceremonial law.[18]

Just a year after Formstecher's book had been published, a fellow Reform rabbi, Samuel Hirsch, issued his *Die Religionsphilosophie der Juden* (1842), in which he contrasted Judaism with Christianity, accepting Hegel's notion of the religion of spirit and the possibility of development but subjecting much else in Hegel's philosophy to a profound critique. He rejected Hegel's view that modern German Christendom represented the culmination of the evolution of the perfect absolute spirit, and its corollary that all other religions were mere stations along the way and should now fade into oblivion. Hirsch stressed throughout his book the notion of freedom, arguing that anyone who has discovered the truth of ethical freedom will want to spread it to others, and that this is achieved within Judaism not by missionizing but by Jews becoming witnesses to their faith. The impact of Hirsch's ideas was much enhanced by his public career and his commitment to social justice. After serving as chief rabbi of Luxembourg from 1843 to 1866, he moved to Philadelphia where he presided over the first American conference of rabbis in 1869 and played an important role in the discussions which produced the Pittsburg Platform in 1885 (see above).[19]

The domination of specifically Kantian philosophers within twentieth-century Reform Judaism was thus not inevitable. It owes a great deal to the prestige of Hermann Cohen and to the adoption of his key interpretation of Judaism as 'ethical monotheism' by the towering figure within Reform Judaism in Germany in the first half of the twentieth century, Leo Baeck. Baeck himself had combined study of rabbinics and history with philosophical studies in the universities in Breslau and Berlin before the start of his service as a rabbi (in Oppeln) in 1897. His monumental *Wesen des Judentums* ('The Essence of Judaism'), first published in 1905, was triggered by his objections to Adolf von Harnack's *Wesen des Christentums*, which he attacked in a polemical article in 1901: Baeck argued that a 'classic religion' like Judaism is committed through a 'concrete spirit' to moral action which brings freedom through obeying the commandments, in contrast to the abstract spirit of the 'romantic religion' of Christianity, which brings freedom through grace. As the head of all German Jewry from 1933 following the Nazi decrees against the legal status of German Jews, he acquired unsurpassed moral stature by declining all opportunities to escape until he was deported to the Theresienstadt concentration camp in 1943. In London after 1945, and intermittently in Cincinnati until his death in 1956, he emphasized more than ever that the religious role of the Jewish people is achieved through the fulfilment of ethical duties between man and man.[20]

In 1925, Leo Baeck had bestowed the title of rabbinical teacher on a philosopher of very different temperament and background, the intense theologian Franz Rosenzweig, who had already, in his mid-thirties, been struck down by the paralysis which was to confine him to his home until his death in 1929. This recognition was more an act of friendship and pity than an indication of approval for the distinctive existential philosophy which Rosenzweig had laid out in *Der Stern der Erlösung* ('The Star of Redemption'), which he had published in 1921. Rosenzweig came from a highly assimilated middle-class family in Kassel with only minimal attachment to Judaism, and many of his friends and relatives had converted to Christianity. On the night of 7 July 1913, Rosenzweig himself decided to convert under the influence of one such relative, Eugen Rosenstock-Huessy, who was a Protestant theologian, with the proviso that he would become Christian 'as a Jew'. That autumn he put this resolution to the test by attending services for the Day of Atonement in an orthodox synagogue in Berlin. The notion that the liturgy was what brought him back to his ancestral faith is probably a later myth, but it is certain that soon after this date he 'returned' to Judaism, convinced that all he needed to do was to recover Judaism for himself and for other assimilated Jews like him. The core of *Der Stern der Erlösung* was the collection of postcards sent home from various postings while on military service during the First World War, incorporating ideas about the significance of revelation as a historical and existential reality which had been hammered out in extensive wartime correspondence with Rosenstock. During the war he also found time to go to Berlin for instruction in the Jewish sources about which he felt ill informed. In Berlin he established a close personal friendship with Hermann Cohen and met Martin Buber, with whom he was to work closely in the 1920s.[21]

Der Stern der Erlösung reflects much of this background. The Jews ('the Synagogue', in Rosenzweig's parlance) are portrayed as a meta-historical community of prayer, anticipating, through the cycle of the religious calendar and liturgy, the spiritual redemption and the embodiment of the eschatological promise, a 'fire' complementary to the 'flame' of God's saving light in Christianity. Like Cohen, Rosenzweig saw a role for Christianity, as a partial truth valid for Christians just as Judaism is for Jews, both to be superseded by the absolute truth in the end of days. Crucial to revelation within Judaism is that it is a continuous entry into relationship with man by God through divine love, which evokes a response of love in men which is expressed also in relations between humans. God calls individuals by their 'first and last names', confirming the individual in finite existence and blessing that individual with an encounter with eternity.

Rosenzweig had experienced as a soldier some of what he considered to be the 'authenticity' of the Jews of eastern Europe, and became acutely aware of his own lack of knowledge of the Hebrew sources. So after the war he established in Frankfurt the Freies Jüdisches Lehrhaus ('Free Jewish House of Learning') to enable an acculturated community with insufficient Jewish education to come to grips with the classic Jewish texts in a sympathetic environment which accepted their search for a Jewish identity. The Lehrhaus turned out to be filling a very real need, and not only for the most assimilated German Jews. Among those who joined Rosenzweig in Frankfurt was Martin Buber, with whom he had maintained a friendship since his time in Berlin, and the two of them began together a new translation of the Bible into a strongly Hebraized German which was intended to shock the readers into engaging with the text. The project was unfinished on Rosenzweig's death, and was completed by Buber only in the 1950s.

Martin Buber, unlike Rosenzweig, had received a traditional Jewish education in Lemberg with his grandfather Solomon Buber, a man of independent means who combined an active business life with a devotion to the scholarly publication of midrashic and medieval rabbinic literature. Martin himself abandoned religious observance in his teens, and, after a period immersed in Zionist politics from his early twenties, by the age of twenty-six began the study of Hasidism which was to distinguish him within the Jewish community and be a central component of his life's work. His interest was, in origin, aesthetic, and he began in 1906 with an adaptation in German of the tales of R. Nachman, followed in 1908 by *Die Legende des Baalschem*, but he came also to see in Hasidism the concept of personal piety as the essence of Judaism. There was a direct link from this interest in Hasidism, and his work during the First World War through the Jewish National Committee in Berlin on behalf of the Jews in eastern European countries, to his most influential work *Ich und Du* ('I and Thou'), which was published in 1923 just as he was becoming involved in the Frankfurt Lehrhaus with Rosenzweig. This philosophy of dialogue, much influenced by his reading as a youth of the works of the nineteenth-century Christian philosopher Ludwig Feuerbach, posited that man has two attitudes to the world determined by two relations – 'I–Thou' and 'I–It'. Modern human relations have often sunk to the 'I–It' relation, which is pragmatic and utilitarian. In this relation, a subject dominates and uses an object. New effort, then, is needed to restore the 'I–Thou' relation in which two individuals stand in existential encounter and dialogue with the wholeness and presence of each party. This encounter is most perfectly expressed in the relationship between man and the Eternal Thou, God. God can thus be present in the events of everyday life, wherever there is true dialogue – although the existence of the Eternal Thou cannot be proved, but only recognized by those who are sensitive to it, as in the writings of Hasidism.[22]

Buber's existentialist philosophy bore some similarity to Hermann Cohen's insistence on the importance of correlation, but it was far more personal. The I–Thou encounter, which must be constantly renewed, requires spontaneity in the worshipper, to which God in turn responds spontaneously. Buber therefore saw little place for formal prayer and ritual in religious devotion, leading to a strong disagreement with Rosenzweig, who became increasingly dedicated to practical fulfilment of the *mitzvot* during the illness of the last years of his life. It is an indication of the free spirit of both thinkers that they could remain close colleagues and collaborators in the Lehrhaus despite such fundamental disagreements, and in 1933, four years after Rosenzweig's death and following Buber's dismissal from his post as professor of religion in the University of Frankfurt with the rise of Nazism, Buber headed the Lehrhaus until persecution by the authorities drove him to Palestine and a position in the Hebrew University.

Despite the originality and force of the sophisticated writings of these philosophers from Cohen to Buber, it would be naive to view these works as underpinning the religious lives of many Reform Jews in the twentieth century or now. The thought of Rosenzweig's *Stern der Erlösung* is exceptionally complex, and few ordinary Jews made or make any attempt to get to grips with it. The theology of Martin Buber is less difficult to grasp, and it is ironic, in view of his concern to claim that dialogical encounters are found more in the divine command to Israel to make real the kingship of God in communal life than in any other religion, that in practice his writings have been more influential among Christian theologians than among Jews. For most Jews, the main significance of these thinkers has been their personal demonstration that even the most assimilated Jews can achieve sophisticated insights into their religion through study in adulthood.

The history of developments within Reform Judaism in the twentieth century was less a product of such intellectual influences than the result of cultural and social changes in the lives of increasingly assimilated Jews, especially in the United States, with a growing emphasis on personal autonomy and spirituality. In light of the statement in the sixth paragraph of the Pittsburgh Platform that Judaism is a progressive religion and the designation of the umbrella body for Reform and Liberal Judaism as the World Union for Progressive Judaism (established in London in 1926), it is perhaps unsurprising that change has been dramatic over the past century. One of the most drastic changes has been a complete reversal in attitudes to Zionism. In part, this seems to have been simply in response to the shift in attitude within the American Jewish community as a whole, whose confidence in the right to be as American as all other Americans in a country of immigrants was not shaken by any charge of dual loyalty to another homeland. The liberal rabbi Stephen S. Wise, who founded in 1907 the Free Synagogue in New York, which allowed free speech from the pulpit, combined a call for social justice and racial equality in the United States with a strongly Zionist stance which he promulgated in an independent seminary for training Reform rabbis, the Jewish Institute of Religion, founded in 1922.

By 1937, the beliefs and customs of Reform congregations in the United States had evolved so far since the Pittsburgh Platform of 1885 that a new set of guiding principles was adopted at a convention held in Columbus, Ohio. The convention accepted, among other changes, 'the obligation of all Jewry to aid in the upbuilding of the Jewish homeland by making it not only a haven for the oppressed but also a center of Jewish culture and spiritual life', linking the restoration of Palestine to the establishment of the Kingdom of God. In striking contrast to their predecessors in Pittsburgh, the rabbis in Columbus emphasized Judaism as a 'way of life', and stressed the importance of customs, ceremonies, religious art and music, and the use of Hebrew in worship:

> The perpetuation of Judaism as a living force depends upon religious knowledge and upon the education of each new generation in our rich cultural and spiritual heritage . . . Judaism as a way of life requires in addition to its moral and spiritual demands, the preservation of the Sabbath, festivals and Holy Days, the retention and development of such customs, symbols and ceremonies as possess inspirational value, the cultivation of distinctive forms of religious art and music and the use of Hebrew, together with the vernacular, in our worship and instruction.[23]

Some of the newly enunciated principles came under immediate stress, such as the urge for disarmament, included in Principle 8, which was rapidly overtaken by the call to fight against Nazism in Europe. More change followed through the rest of the twentieth century and continues today. But the embrace of Zionism was maintained: in 1947, the Reform rabbi Abba Hillel Silver was one of the Zionist spokesmen in the United Nations debate on the creation of a Jewish state, and the headquarters of the World Union for Progressive Judaism was moved to Jerusalem in 1973, with a brief to establish schools, synagogues and settlements in many locations in Israel.[24]

In the meantime the Holocaust has engendered intense theological problems for Reform Jews committed to assumptions about human progress. During the war in Europe, the Reform rabbi Judah Magnes, who in 1944 was chancellor of the Hebrew University of Jerusalem, cited a maxim of the hasidic master Levi Yitzhak of Berdichev addressing God: 'I do not ask why I suffer but only do I suffer for your sake.' After the war Martin Buber adapted the biblical notion that God hides himself from the sinner to suggest that God had been temporarily eclipsed: 'On that day they will say, "Have not these troubles come upon us because our God was not in our midst?" On that day I will surely hide my face on account of all the evil they have done by turning to other gods.' But the philosopher Emil Fackenheim, who had trained as a Reform rabbi in Germany before escaping to Canada from a forced-labour camp shortly before 1939 to teach philosophy at the University of Toronto and later at the Hebrew University of Jerusalem, dedicated much of his career to a sophisticated theology of the Holocaust, arguing that the determination of the Jewish people to survive (what he called the '614th commandment') must have its origin in the divine realm. Fackenheim and some other theologians saw the State of Israel as the theological answer to the Holocaust.[25]

After the destruction of German Jewry, the main centre for Jewish theological reflection in the second half of the twentieth century outside the United States and Israel was France, where Emmanuel Levinas, who had come from Lithuania but migrated to France as a teenager in 1923, saw himself, at least from the 1950s, as part of a coterie of assimilated francophone Jewish intellectuals. Levinas was a survivor of the Holocaust, in which much of his family perished, but his major philosophical works were influenced by studying the phenomenology of Husserl and Heidegger in Germany in the late 1920s. Levinas argued strongly that a proper relation with the world involves accepting and respecting the ethical claims inherent in the otherness of other people. In his *lectures talmudiques*, composed for an annual convention of French Jewish intellectuals in an attempt to persuade them to take Jewish sources seriously, the ancient rabbinic texts were used as a platform for an exposition of his philosophical ideas rather than explored in their own right.

Hence, for instance, his interpretation of a puzzling statement in the Talmud that 'when plague [strikes a] town, a man should not walk in the middle of the road, because the Angel of Death walks in the middle of the road, for since he is authorized [to strike], he walks boldly. When there is peace in town, do not walk at the side of the road, for since the Angel of Death is not authorized [to strike], he conceals himself [at the side] as he walks':

> The violence which exterminates: there is no radical difference between peace and war, between war and holocaust ... no radical difference between peace and Auschwitz ... Evil surpasses human responsibility and leaves not a corner intact where reason could collect itself. But perhaps this thesis is precisely a call to man's infinite responsibility ...

Levinas was widely recognized in France as a major philosopher, and he was lauded by some French Jews for having encouraged an intellectual 'return to Judaism', but it is not clear that his writings have in fact been used by many Jews to help to understand their Judaism rather than to get to grips with the complexity of his thought for its own sake.[26]

Discourse about the significance of the Holocaust and the State of Israel has acquired a greater importance in the lives of Reform Jews in the United States than the more abstract theology of the German theologians of the first half of the twentieth century, but the major issues which preoccupy Reform congregations have continued to emerge less from theology than from changes within wider American society. So, for instance, the principle that women have full equality in synagogue ritual and government led eventually to the ordination of a woman rabbi, Sally J. Priesand, in 1972, and in more recent decades to the ordination of gay and lesbian Jews. Ordination of a woman rabbi had already in fact occurred in Germany, where Regina Jonas, who had studied at the Hochschule in Berlin, was ordained by the Union of Liberal Rabbis in December 1935, an ordination endorsed by Leo Baeck in February 1942, but despite serving briefly as a rabbi before being taken away to Theresienstadt, she made little impact on the development of Reform and Liberal Jewry because of her untimely death in Auschwitz at the end of 1944.[27]

The decision of American Reform Jews in 1983 to recognize as Jewish, without any conversion process, the child of a Jewish father and a non-Jewish mother if the child wishes to be Jewish, has opened the way for outreach to the non-Jewish partners of Reform Jews. The National Jewish Population Survey in 2000 found that nearly 40 per cent of those in the United States affiliated to any religious community defined their Judaism as Reform. The principle of patrilineal as well as matrilineal descent has been adopted also by the Reform movement in Britain but not in Canada or in Israel. Reform Judaism has made little headway among native-born Israelis, whose simplistic tendency to divide their society into the ultra-religious on the one side and the purely secular on the other is reinforced by the educational and political systems in the state, which leave little space for other forms of Judaism. Most Reform Jews now living in Israel are immigrants from the diaspora. Reform Judaism has proven more popular among Jews in the former Soviet Union, not least because a good number of them trace their Jewish heritage through their fathers rather than through the maternal line. The enforced lack of Jewish religious education in Soviet times has required many Russian Jews to learn about Judaism from scratch, a process which is facilitated by the provision, through the World Union for Progressive Judaism, of prayer books and other educational materials in the vernacular.[28]

We have seen that in the beginning Reform Jews in the nineteenth century saw themselves as a movement within Judaism as a whole, and that it was only gradually that they began in some places to define themselves as a distinct denomination within the wider body of the religion. Reform Jews have never asserted that the religion of traditionalists is not a valid form of Judaism, even if they have stated at times that the preservation of redundant customs is primitive and stands in the way of true religion. The attitude of traditionalists has been more consistently hostile towards what they see as the betrayal of the essence of Judaism by Reform, and (as we saw in Hungary in the 1860s) they have often appeared puzzled by even the suggestion of compromise. The puzzlement is mutual, for the need to enter the modern age has often seemed obvious to the reformers.

18
Counter-Reform

In 1883 the Reform rabbi Isaac Mayer Wise, who dreamed of a comprehensive union of all American synagogues under his leadership, presided at the ordination of the first rabbis to graduate from the new Hebrew Union College, holding a banquet in Cincinnati to which all sections of the religious community were invited. The meal was a disaster. It began with clams, shrimp, crab, lobster and frog legs in cream sauce, with beef as the main and cheese as the final course. Wise claimed that the menu was simply an error by the caterers, who did not understand kosher food restrictions and had at least avoided pork. But a number of the diners left ostentatiously and a furore erupted over the following months, played out primarily in the Jewish press in the United States.

It was rare for orthodox reaction to Reform to take a violent turn, but we have already noted the burning in Syria of a Bible commentary by Eliyahu Benamozegh some two decades earlier (Chapter 17). In Lemberg, in September 1848, an orthodox Jew named Abraham Ber Pilpel killed the Reform rabbi of the town, Abraham Kohn, by slipping into his kitchen and poisoning the family's soup with arsenic – the first known case since antiquity of religiously motivated murder of one Jew by another. But most opposition – however visceral – took an oral or written form. Some orthodox leaders adopted a more eirenic approach: thus on 27 May 1934 Joseph H. Hertz, chief rabbi of the British Empire, and spokesman for mainstream orthodox Judaism in England, attended the consecration of the new Reform synagogue in London, asserting roundly: 'I am the last person in the world to minimise the significance of religious difference in Jewry. If I have nevertheless decided to be with you this morning, it is because of my conviction that far more calamitous than religious difference in Jewry is religious indifference in Jewry.'

Such an appeal to solidarity among all religious groups in the face of rampant secularism still has a certain force, particularly in Europe. But the divide between orthodox and Reform has hardened greatly in recent decades over issues of Jewish identity, with orthodox refusal to accept the validity of Reform marriages, divorces and conversions. Since the adoption of the patrilineal principle by some Reform communities, many members of Reform congregations would not be considered Jewish according to orthodox halakhah unless they submit to an orthodox conversion. Hence intense disputes over the status of non-orthodox converts to Judaism who wish to settle in Israel under the Law of Return.[1]

MODERN ORTHODOXY

The response by traditionalists to the Reform agenda was swift and blunt from the start. In 1819, *Eleh Divrei haBrit* ('These are the Words of the Covenant'), a volume of responsa by twenty-two leading European rabbis published under the auspices of the Hamburg Rabbinical Court, condemned unequivocally the reforms of the Hamburg Temple, and in 1844 no fewer than 116 rabbis contributed to the diatribe *Shelomei Emunei Yisrael* which asserted, in opposition to the Brunswick Assembly of Reform Rabbis, that 'neither they nor anyone else has the authority to nullify even the least of the religious laws'. From such uncompromising opposition emerged the *haredim*, whose determination to retain the mores of the eighteenth century down to the twenty-first will be examined in Chapter 19 below, but so too did the form of traditional Judaism that came, over the nineteenth century, to define itself as 'orthodox' – although, as Samson Raphael Hirsch, one of the pioneers of orthodoxy (and not to be confused with his younger contemporary Samuel Hirsch, the Reform rabbi and philosopher (see Chapter 17)), observed in 1854, 'it was not the "orthodox" Jews who introduced the word "orthodoxy" into Jewish discussion. It was the modern "progressive" Jews who first applied this name to "old", "backward" Jews as a derogatory term. This name was at first resented by "old" Jews. And rightly so. "Orthodox" Judaism does not know any varieties of Judaism. It conceives Judaism as one and indivisible.'[2]

Samson Raphael Hirsch was born and educated in Hamburg, in the shadow of the intense debates over the establishment of the Reform Temple in the city in 1818, and the form of orthodoxy he espoused (called 'neo-orthodoxy' by some historians, to distinguish it from the Judaism of the *haredim*) can be seen as a direct product of the polemical atmosphere of the city in his youth. In 1821 Hirsch was at *bar mitzvah* age when the Hamburg Community elected as their chief rabbi Isaac Bernays, himself still in his twenties, to combat what they saw as the perils of Reform by modernizing Judaism without the more drastic changes inaugurated by the reformers. It is significant that Reform had been adopted by the Hamburg community sufficiently widely for Bernays to feel the need to call himself not 'rabbi' but *haham* ('sage', in the Sephardi fashion) to indicate the difference between himself and the Reform rabbis. Bernays had combined yeshivah learning in Würzburg with studies at the university, and his sermons in Hamburg, delivered in German (an innovation), preached the need for good citizenship as well as religious observance.[3]

Torah im derekh erets, 'Torah in harmony with secular culture', eventually became the slogan of Hirsch's communities and the ideal of the modern orthodox Judaism which has based itself on his teachings down to the present. In his early twenties, Hirsch (like Bernays before him) went to university to study classical languages, history and philosophy. He struck up a friendship with a slightly younger Jewish student, Abraham Geiger, who, as we have seen, was to become the spiritual leader of German Reform. The two jointly organized a student society in Bonn for the study of Jewish homiletics, and it is salutary to recognize that in the late 1820s the religious options for earnest young men such as these could diverge so dramatically – the friendship cooled only after Geiger published a strong criticism of Hirsch's presentation (in 1836, in perfect German) of the principles of Judaism. The presentation was found in *Neunzehn Briefe über Judentum*, in which Hirsch laid down, in the form of letters between two youths (the perplexed intellectual Benjamin and the reassuring Naphtali), a defence of traditional Judaism within world culture and appropriated the name 'Reform' for an appeal to preserve the essence of tradition:

> Therefore, may our motto be – Reform; let us strive with all our power, with all the good and noble qualities of our character to reach this height of ideal perfection – Reform. Its only object, however, must be the fulfillment of Judaism by Jews in our time, fulfillment of the eternal idea in harmony with the conditions of the time; education, progress to the Torah's height, not, however, lowering the Torah to the level of the age, cutting down the towering summit to the sunken grade of our life. We Jews need to be reformed through Judaism, newly comprehended by the spirit and fulfilled with the utmost energy; but merely to seek greater ease and comfort in life through the destruction of the eternal code set up for all ages by the

God of Eternity, is not and never can be Reform. Judaism seeks to lift us
up to its height, how dare we attempt to drag it down to our level?

Hirsch argued that the Jews, rather than Judaism, were in need of
reform, but not as the reformers imagined it. Jews needed to rise to the
eternal ideals of their religion, even if they are not always comfortable
to live with, and the current troubles relate to the emergence of a 'Judaism that recognises and understands itself'.[4]

Hirsch thus recognized the pressures of modern life as much as his
erstwhile friend Geiger, but chose a wholly different solution. Accom-
modation to secular culture could include a choir in the synagogue
liturgy and preaching in German, but Hebrew must be the sole language
of prayer and alterations to the prayer book should not be lightly undertaken. Crucially, the laws of the Bible and the rabbis must be treated as
the word of God and immutable:

> What kind of thing would Judaism be, if we dared to bring it up to date?
> If the Jew were permitted to bring his Judaism up to date at any time, he
> would no longer have any need for it; it would not be worthwhile any-
> where to speak any longer of Judaism. We should then seize Judaism and
> cast it out among the other misbegotten products of delusion and supersti-
> tion, and hear no more of Judaism and the Jewish religion! . . . Let us not
> deceive ourselves. The whole question is simply this. Is the statement 'And
> God spoke to Moses saying,' with which all the laws of the Jewish Bible
> commence, true or not true? Do we really and truly believe that God, the
> omnipotent and holy, spoke thus to Moses? Are we speaking truth when,
> in the presence of our brethren, we lay our hand upon the Torah Scroll and
> say that God has given us this teaching, his teaching, the teaching of truth,
> and in so doing has planted eternal life in our midst? If this is to be more
> than lip service, more than verbiage and deception, then we must keep this
> Torah and fulfil it without abridgement, without fault-finding, under all
> circumstances and at all times. This word of God must be for us the eternal
> rule, superior to all human judgement, to which at all times we must con-
> form ourselves and all our actions, and, instead of complaining that it is
> no longer suitable to the times, our only complaint must be that the times
> are no longer suitable to it.

Hirsch was treading a difficult middle path between reform and tradition, and his influence depended as much on his personal spirituality,
and his fluency as writer and preacher, as on his specific ideas. The
orthodox community he served in Moravia from 1846 disapproved of

33. (*above*) The system of *sefirot* depicted in 1516 on the cover of a Latin translation of a kabbalistic work, *Sha'arei Orah* ('Gates of Light'), by Yosef b. Avraham Gikatilla. The translator, Paulo Riccio, was a Jewish convert to Christianity.

34. Frontispiece of a Tikkun, a small book of prayers to be recited day and night for the self-proclaimed messiah Sabbetai Zevi. Published in Amsterdam in 1666, the year in which Sabbetai announced that the redemption would come, it shows him enthroned as king and seated at a table with twelve elders.

35. (*above left*) Wine and candle for the havdalah ceremony depicted in a miniature in the Barcelona Haggadah, which dates from the fourteenth century. There was a widespread custom for a child to be given the candle to hold.

36. (*above right*) Spice boxes of pewter and silver made in the eighteenth and nineteenth centuries in Germany and eastern Europe for the havdalah ceremony. Such ritual objects were precious domestic possessions, along with Sabbath candles.

37. Painting by Marco Marcuola (1740–93) of a circumcision in Venice (1780). The baby is held by two men who each wear a *tallit* (prayer shawl). The raised chair on the left of the picture is reserved for the prophet Elijah. The operation on the child is out of sight of the women, who are seated along the wall on the right of the picture.

8. (*above left*) Baruch Spinoza (1632–77), the great philosopher of the Enlightenment, by an unknown Dutch artist from the seventeenth century.

9. (*above right*) Portrait of a Dutch Jew from the same period. His clothes, like those of Spinoza, naturally reflect contemporary Dutch style, but he is also wearing a large *tallit* and carrying a Torah scroll surmounted with *rimmonim* (finials) and a crown.

0. *Megillah* (scroll) of the Book of Esther for use on Purim (eighteenth century; Dutch). Decoration of Purim *megillot* was common. Note the depiction of the signs of the Zodiac in much the same way as in Hammat Tiberias in the fourth century (Plate 17).

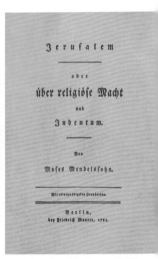

41. (*above left*) The philosopher Moses Mendelssohn (1729–86), painted by Anton Graff in 1771. Mendelssohn appears at first sight as a clean-shaven figure of the Enlightenment, but he has a beard below his chin and jowls.

42. (*above right*) Title page of the first edition (1783) of Mendelssohn's most influential work, *Jerusalem*.

43. An engraving by Louis François Couché (1782–1849) celebrating Napoleon's 'reinstatement of Jewish religion on 30 May 1806'. In practice, this constituted the establishment of an Assembly of Jewish Notables to represent the Jewish community.

44. Wooden *sukkah* (booth) from Fischach, southern Germany, *c.* 1837. The roof has a covering of foliage with fruits hung for decoration. A local painter has depicted on the walls both the village of Fischach and an idealized Jerusalem.

45. (*below*) Lithograph of *Shabbat in the Shtetl* (*c.* 1914) by the Ukrainian artist Issachar Ber Ryback (1897–1935), who travelled the Russian countryside to study Jewish folk life and art. This picture was published in *Shtetl, Mayn khoyever heym: a gedenknish* (1922), Ryback's elegiac depiction of Jewish life in his shtetl before its destruction in the pogroms of 1919.

46. Pair of silver *rimmonim* from the late nineteenth century modelled on a Chinese two-tiered pagoda, with balustrades of cherry-blossom pattern and Chinese roof on the first level, and with hooks for the bells on each level.

47. (*above right*) Painted wooden Torah case from Yemen (nineteenth century). The use of such wooden Torah cases, with the scroll kept upright within the case for reading, is found not only in Yemen but also in some Jewish communities from Iraq, Iran, Afghanistan, Kurdistan, Syria and North Africa.

48. Velour Torah scroll cover with gold braid from twentieth-century North Africa. The Moorish arch in the centre contains a dedicatory Hebrew inscription in honour of a deceased individual. The open right hand (*hamsah*) depicted at the end of the arabesque patterns in each corner and above the arch is a sign of protection against the evil eye common among Christians and Muslims as well as Jews.

49. Mass gathering of Satmar *hasidim* in Brooklyn on the seventy-first anniversary of the escape of their *rebbe*, Yoel Teitelbaum, from Hungary in December 1944.

50. (*left*) Lubavitch student in Brooklyn under a giant portrait of the Lubavitcher *rebbe*, Menahem Mendel Schneerson, 2004.

51. (*above*) Girls help their friend light candles at her *bat mitzvah* celebrations in a Manhattan ballroom, 1998. Rituals for girls to mark their *bat mitzvah* continue to evolve.

52. Carrying new Torah scrolls to a synagogue in Pinner, north-west London, in 1993. Chief Rabbi Jonathan Sacks (*centre*) leads the procession as the spiritual leader of the United Synagogue, the largest union of Orthodox communities in Britain.

53. The ordination of Rabbi Alina Treiger in 2010 by the Abraham Geiger Kolleg in Potsdam was the first rabbinic ordination of a woman in Germany since the Holocaust.

54. Dancing with the Torah on Simhat Torah in Jerusalem in 2013 in celebration of the completion of the annual cycle of reading the Torah.

some of his practices, such as wearing a robe during services, the rejection of casuistry (which held no appeal to someone of his theological bent) and his insistence on study of the Bible, and in 1851 he moved to Frankfurt, where he remained until his death in 1888.[5]

In the 1830s and early 1840s, Hirsch had tried hard to avoid a break with the Reform movement as it threatened to become the mainstream within German Jewry, but in 1844 he wrote to the Reform synod in Brunswick declaring that if they decided to annul the dietary and matrimonial laws he and his followers would have to secede: 'Our covenant of unity will no longer endure and brother shall depart from brother in tears.' In the second half of the nineteenth century, such secession was complicated in Germany by the requirement of the state that all members of a religion must belong within the communal structure of that religion, so that no one uncomfortable within a structure dominated by one type of Judaism could leave except by declaring themselves 'without religion'. It is an indication of the domination of Reform within German Jewry that Hirsch pressed the Prussian authorities from the early 1870s for the right of orthodox Jews 'to leave their local community organization for reasons of conscience', following the example of Hungarian Jews in 1868–9. Likewise it is significant that in July 1876 the *Austrittsgesetz* ('Law of Secession') passed by the Prussian Landstag permitted all orthodox Jews in Germany to join Hirsch's congregation in Frankfurt, along with small orthodox congregations in Berlin and elsewhere, in a separate orthodox *Austrittsgemeinde* ('secession community'). But it is also symptomatic of the desire for Jewish unity that most orthodox Jews preferred to remain within the traditional Jewish communal structure, relying on the good faith of the Reform-minded communal leaders to allow the orthodox to fulfil their religious needs unhampered by interference.[6]

Despite his extensive secular learning and the literary power of his writings, Hirsch rigorously confined his erudition to what might contribute to living a Jewish life. *Menschentum* ('humanity'), as conceived by the classic German philosophers, was for Hirsch merely an intermediate state on the road to the *Israeltum* of the Torah-observant Jew. Hirsch's translations of the Pentateuch and Psalms deliberately adopted an artificial German to demonstrate faithfulness to the original Hebrew. The historical studies of the *Wissenchaft des Judentums* scholars were deemed of no value if they did not contribute to understanding the commandments and (crucially) to carrying them out. 'How many of those who study the *selihot* [penitential prayers] ... still rise early in the morning for *selihot*?' Unsurprisingly, the historian Heinrich Graetz, who had expressed his devotion to Hirsch in the dedication of his *Gnosticismus und Judentum* in 1846 'with sentiments of love and gratitude, to the inspiring defender of historic Judaism, to the unforgettable teacher and loved friend', had drifted away from him by the early 1850s. For Hirsch, all that mattered was the Torah, which had been given to the Jews in the wilderness to show that Jews are a nation even when they lack a land. Exile can be a positive means for Israel to teach the nations 'that God is the source of blessing'. Such insistence during the nineteenth century on the significance of the role of Jews as a nation should seen against the backdrop of the universalist claim of some reformers that Jews were no longer a nation at all (p. 467).[7]

Hirsch's opposition to historical scholarship was probably motivated in part by suspicion that the Jüdisch-Theologische Seminar which opened in 1854 in Breslau would undermine the Torah by training rabbis who would argue that the halakhah derived from rabbis rather than from direct revelation from Mount Sinai. As soon as the Seminar opened, Hirsch challenged its founding spirit and first director, Zacharias Frankel, to state publicly the religious principles which would guide instruction there. When Frankel failed to comply, Hirsch attacked him tenaciously in print, particularly after the publication of Frankel's *Darkhei haMishnah* ('Ways of the Mishnah') in 1859 appeared to confirm his suspicions.

The bitterness of Hirsch's attack on Frankel may be ascribed perhaps to the similarity of their outlooks and the need to differentiate his own orthodoxy from what was to become in Germany the Historical movement and (in the twentieth century) a precedent for the ideology of Conservative Judaism in the United States. Like Hirsch and Geiger, Frankel, who was born in Prague, had studied secular subjects (in Budapest, from 1825 to 1830) as well as the Talmud. As one of the first Bohemian rabbis to preach in German, he was in the vanguard of the modernizers in the 1830s, when he served as the local rabbi of Teplitz. He was thus drawn into the debates of the reformers in the 1840s, but from the start he took an independent line, insisting that the prayer book should be changed only if it continued to reflect the spirit of traditional ritual, including the 'pious wish for the independence of the Jewish people' expressed in the messianic hope despite the loyalty of German Jews to the fatherland. He attended the Reform Conference in Frankfurt in 1845 but withdrew in protest against some of the proposals, notably the gradual phasing out of Hebrew in prayer, but he failed to persuade other rabbis to join him in a counter-synod. Like Hirsch, then, Frankel in the 1850s had been close to the Reform movement as he tried to steer his own 'positivist historical' reforms, even while maintaining to Hirsch and others that he was not deviating from traditional Judaism. When he eventually responded to Hirsch's questioning on the relation of rabbinic tradition to the revelation of Mount Sinai, in a brief article published in 1861 in his journal, the *Monatsschrift für Geschichte und Wissenschaft des Judenthums*, he reaffirmed the significance and antiquity of the rabbinic tradition but asserted that the Mosaic origin of some of the halakhah was yet to be resolved.[8]

Hirschian orthodoxy had a continuous institutional history in Germany down through the 1930s in the *Austrittsgemeinde*, and the refugees from the Nazis who set up Adass Jeshurun ('Congregation of Jeshurun') and Adass Jisroel ('Congregation of Israel') synagogues in New York and Johannesburg respectively preserved his distinctive combination of strict orthodoxy with openness to secular culture. Under the leadership of Hirsch's son-in-law, Salomon Breuer, who succeeded Hirsch in 1888 as rabbi in Frankfurt, the *Austrittsgemeinde* took the initiative of setting up in May 1912 in Kattowitz, in Upper Silesia, Agudat Israel ('Union of Israel', also known simply as the Agudah), which presented itself as a worldwide organization of the orthodox. The embattled German orthodox hoped the Agudah would enlist the support of the great rabbis of the eastern Europe yeshivot in the struggle against Reform, and also against Zionism, which they saw as a secular nationalism inimical to real religion. The move was not supported by all eastern European *haredim*, many of whom preferred to deal with the threat of modernity by ignoring it, and both the east Europeans from Poland and Lithuania and the Hungarian orthodox who joined the organization looked askance at the willingness of the German Jews to accept a great deal of general European culture and practices. However, enough rabbinic leaders from the east participated in 1912, and in three further Great Assemblies, in Vienna in 1923 and 1929, and in Marienbad in 1937, to turn the Agudah into a major lobbying group within Jewish society.[9]

German neo-orthodoxy had developed in so distinctive a fashion that it was easier to see what members of the Agudah opposed than where they agreed, except on the principle that decisions for Jewry should be taken by the authority of rabbis like themselves. The central institution to emerge within the Union was the Moetset Gedolei haTorah, the 'Council of Torah Sages', chosen on the basis of their talmudic learning. On the political issues which arose on the agenda from the start (originally with regard particularly to affairs in Poland, where Agudat Israel formed a political party in 1919), however, great influence was wielded by the democratically elected Great Assembly as well as by the Council it appointed. The participation of universally admired rabbinic sages was crucial to the success of the Agudah. But it also ensured a constant tension, since many of the east European rabbis saw no value whatever in the western culture which the German rabbis had embraced. The Polish and Lithuanian rabbis were little troubled by Reform, which had hardly made any impact on their communities, and the alliance they sought was primarily against the secular Zionists. Following a proposal by Hayyim Soloveitchik, the communal rabbi of Brest-Litovsk (known in Yiddish as Brisk) and widely recognized as the leading talmudist of his day, unity in religious affairs was contrived by agreeing that the different groups should be allowed to maintain their ways of life unaltered. In fact a considerable amount of change proved possible under the auspices of the Agudah, particularly in the status of women. Within the orthodox world, the remarkable Sarah Schenirer, self-taught and from a hasidic family unconcerned with secular education, opened a school in her home in Cracow in 1917 to teach religion to girls so that they would not be required to attend Catholic schools. By 1939 around 200 of her Beth Jacob schools were operating all over eastern Europe under the auspices of Agudat Israel; since 1945, many Beth Jacob schools have opened in the United States and Israel.[10]

Just as the Reform movement came under pressure for its anti-Zionism in the 1930s and 1940s, so too did the Agudah. Isaac Breuer, the son of Salomon, was a leading spokesman of the Agudah from the start, but he became less anti-Zionist after the Balfour Declaration in 1917, and in 1936, when he migrated from Nazi Germany to Palestine, he founded a splinter movement, Poalei Agudat Yisrael, to work for an independent Jewish state 'uniting all the people of Israel under the rule of the Torah, in all aspects of political, economic and spiritual life of the People of Israel in the Land of Israel'. By contrast, Yitzhak, the youngest son of Hayyim Soloveitchik, who succeeded his father as rabbi of Brisk, maintained his father's traditions both of talmudic study and of opposition to secular studies and Zionism. Despite being forced to flee Europe in 1939 and, as a result, resident in Jerusalem for the last twenty years of his life, he aligned himself firmly as a spokesman of the *haredi* community in Israel, declining to take any public position but speaking out in defence of Judaism whenever he believed there to be a threat.[11]

Yitzhak's elder brother, Moshe, and his nephew, Joseph B. Soloveit-chik, took the ethos of Agudat Israel to the United States, where they became leading figures within American orthodoxy. Moshe had avoided secular education like his father, but as head of the Rabbi Isaac Elchanan Theological Seminary in Yeshiva College in New York from 1929 he was open to secular studies and brought the analytic approach to Tal-mud study pioneered by his father to a new, and receptive, orthodox community. The 'Brisker method', which involved the application of abstract, conceptual analysis to the study of Talmud, was felt to encour-age rigorous intellectual creativity without requiring a secular education. It is thus a little surprising – and apparently due to the influence of his mother – that the prodigiously gifted Joseph added a university education to his mastery of Talmud study as taught by his grandfather, receiving a doctorate in Berlin in 1932 for a thesis on the philosophy of Hermann Cohen. It testimony to the abstract nature of the Kantian philosophy espoused by Cohen that Cohen's ideas, which had so strong an influence on Reform Judaism in the first half of the twentieth century (see Chapter 17), could also attract such a pillar of modern orthodox thought.

The combination of philosophical sophistication with outstanding talmudic knowledge and rhetorical gifts gave Joseph B. Soloveitchik an unmatched authority in modern orthodox circles in America from the 1950s to his death in 1993. His philosophical writings on Judaism had as a result a far greater influence within the Jewish community than those of most other Jewish thinkers in the twentieth century. Like Isaac Breuer, and unlike the other members of his family, Soloveitchik advo-cated both the full participation of orthodox Jews in secular culture and wider society and (eventually) support for Zionism, despite the secular nature of the Israeli state. Called by many within modern orthodoxy simply 'the Rav', Soloveitchik was the presiding authority overseeing the ordination of orthodox rabbis through Yeshiva University, to which the Elchanan Theological Seminary is affiliated, trying to equip them with both a talmudic training in the style of European yeshivot and a sensi-tivity to the needs of middle-class American life. Soloveitchik's *Halakhic Man* aims to show that 'the man of halakhah' combines the cognitive drive of scientific man in search for knowledge in this world with the religious yearning to recognize the divine presence through action. His assertion that through the study and practice of halakhah the apparent contradiction between reason and revelation can be overcome, with the interior experience of such *mitzvot* as prayer, repentance, mourning and ritual rejoicing built into the fabric of the *mitzvot* themselves in a productive dialectical tension, has been immensely appealing to those orthodox Jews attempting to combine observance of the commandments with a full integration into contemporary western civilization. Soloveitchik depicted life according to the halakhah, devoted to human productivity, Torah study and repentance, as one of freedom and intellectual creativity, while claiming that the required submission to the inscrutable will of God is inevitable to all who acknowledge the reality of the human condition. The sophistication of his arguments has, at the very least, provided reassurance to those modern orthodox Jews keen to present, to themselves and to others, their lives of *mitzvot* observance as rationally justified in terms of western values. A similar role has been played in more recent times by other modern orthodox theologians such as the former British chief rabbi Jonathan Sacks.[12]

A major task for Soloveitchik was to equip modern orthodox Jews with a reliable guide for living in a western consumer society without breaching the norms of halakhah. His authority was supplemented by that of Moshe Feinstein, who had fled from his post as a rabbi in Belorussia to the United States in 1936 to take up a position as head of a yeshivah in the Lower East Side in New York. In this post, which he held until his death fifty years later, Feinstein issued a stream of responses to queries about the correct religious approach to science, technology and politics and to the gentile world full of consumer goods in which American Jews found themselves, as in this ruling about correct behaviour at the time of Christian holidays:

> It is in itself reprehensible to make a vacation time when they are celebrating their foreign worship – they who have troubled and embittered the nation of Israel for nearly two thousand years and still their hand is outstretched ... In our country, because of the abundant blessing which God, may He be blessed, has bestowed, there is a great desire and appetite for the enjoyments of this world in all the pleasant experiences which they call 'good time', which is also a matter which greatly corrupts a man. It makes him used to desiring things for which there is no need and destroys his character until he becomes an evil beast. At the beginning he seeks [to satisfy] his lusts with some permitted thing ... and when it is impossible [to obtain this] he will not refrain even from the forbidden.[13]

Soloveitchik and Feinstein laid out the pattern for an ideal orthodox life for diaspora Jews in the modern world, but the communal rabbis who have tried to put that pattern into operation know that many in their congregations ignore what they are told to do. Ever since the rise of

Reform in the early nineteenth century, and the growing awareness of Jews that they had other religious options than to obey their communal rabbi, most orthodox leaders acceded, however reluctantly, to what was in effect a double standard. It was common already in Hirsch's community in Hamburg for members of the congregation to do business on the Sabbath. For much of the twentieth century some orthodox Jews insisted on men and women sitting together for prayer in the synagogue despite the opposition of their rabbis, for whom the position, height and nature of the dividing barrier between male and female worshippers sometimes became a totemic issue on which the rabbis had to compromise: in the 1950s, rabbinic graduates of Yeshiva University were encouraged to take up a pulpit with congregations with mixed seating but were expected to ensure a separation within five years of their appointment – not always successfully. In some orthodox synagogues, where the car park will be closed for the Sabbath, the congregation will park their cars in adjoining streets and the rabbi will avoid mentioning the subject in his sermon, on the grounds that it is better to have sinners within the community, where they can still be encouraged (if only by example) to adopt a more religious lifestyle, than to force them out to a different denomination. The policy has, at least until recently, been conspicuously successful in Anglo-Jewry. The United Synagogue, embracing many of the orthodox synagogues in London and some in the provinces under the authority of the British chief rabbi, and established by act of parliament in 1870, claims within its membership about half of English Jews, many of whom observe the halakhah in a fairly relaxed fashion. This does not necessarily imply ignorance on their part – although, following the lead of Maimonides in relation to Karaites, the rabbinic justification for tolerating laxity is that these Jews are like 'infants who have been captured' and thus not responsible for their inability to tread the right path – but rather that contemporary orthodox Jews in the diaspora increasingly see their religion as a way of life derived from a set of textual regulations rather than a way of life imitated from generation to generation.[14]

The position of modern orthodox Jews in Israel is rather different, since living within a majority Jewish society has permitted, at least for some, considerable independence of theological enquiry. So, for instance, the scientist Yeshayahu Leibowitz, who spent his professional life as a professor of chemistry and neurophysiology in the Hebrew University, forged a distinctive conception of Judaism as a theocentric religion which requires believers to serve God simply for the sake of serving him and not for any reward or metaphysical purpose. Arguing that scientific findings are absolute but religion is a matter of choice, Leibowitz defined the halakhah as binding and the ultimate expression of commitment to God, denying any possibility of any specifically Jewish philosophy, theology or mysticism. Uncompromisingly independent, he advocated complete separation between religion and the secular state in Israel after 1948. He fiercely opposed the annexation of territory after the 1967 war in case the increase in Arab population impaired the character of Israel as a state in which the majority of citizens were Jews. He encouraged the full participation of women in learning the Torah (perhaps encouraged by the exceptional reputation of his younger sister Nehama, a scholar and teacher who published, among other works, a commentary on the Bible portion for each Sabbath which reached students all over the world).[15]

Yeshayahu Leibowitz interpreted human atrocities as the product of failings in humanity without theological significance and he therefore saw no need to reflect on any deeper theological meaning in the events of the Holocaust. A similar stance is to be found in much modern orthodox thought. In the United States, Eliezer Berkovits asserted that God was present but unseen in Auschwitz, and that the greatness and power of God were demonstrated precisely by his refusal to intervene. In 1973, in his *Faith after the Holocaust*, Berkovits claimed that, despite the uniqueness of the horror, the Holocaust did not present any novel problem for faith, since Jews have acknowledged since the time of Job that God may withdraw himself to give humans free will to commit acts which may be oppressive. Orthodox theologians have even been able to derive a positive message of redemption from the reality of horror. During the Holocaust itself, R. Isaac Nissenbaum declared in the Warsaw Ghetto the need to sanctify life so far as possible by preserving it rather than seeking martyrdom in death, and the American orthodox rabbi Irving (Yitz) Greenberg, who was born only in 1933 and brought up in the safety of the United States, sees the Holocaust as the end of one stage in the relationship of God and Israel and the beginning of a new stage, with implications for the obligation to perform the commandments. He argued in 1977 both that 'the moral necessity of a world to come . . . arises powerfully out of the encounter with the Holocaust' and that 'if the experience of Auschwitz symbolises that we are cut of from God and hope . . . then the experience of Jerusalem symbolises that God's promises are faithful and his people live on'. Thus Jews have a special responsibility to those who died to work to bring to an end the values which supported genocide.[16]

CONSERVATIVE JUDAISM

The story of 'positivist historical' Judaism begun by Zacharias Frankel at the same time as Hirsch's neo-orthodoxy in the mid-nineteenth century belongs even more than Hirsch to the Jews of the United States. In Germany, the rabbis who graduated from Frankel's Jüdisch-Theologische Seminar in Breslau, where they received a basically orthodox training alongside critical study of the ancient sources in the spirit of the universities, went on to serve either relaxed orthodox communities or, in some cases, Reform congregations. In America, however, Frankel's emphasis on the history and tradition of Israel as the source of law and tradition became the basis of Conservative Judaism under the inspiration of Solomon Schechter in the first decade of the twentieth century.

In 1883, three years before Moses Gaster, after studying in the Breslau Seminar, was to move to England to teach in Oxford and become the *haham* of the orthodox Sephardi community, as we have seen (p. 444), Solomon Schechter, another Romanian, was persuaded by Claude Montefiore, a fellow student at the newly founded Reform Hochschule für die Wissenschaft des Judentums in Berlin, to go to London as Montefiore's tutor in rabbinics. That Montefiore had needed to use his ample means to import such teaching illustrates the dearth of rabbinic learning in the United Kingdom at this time. But Schechter, the son of a Habad *hasid*, rapidly proved himself a remarkably productive critical scholar, and in 1890 he was appointed to a post teaching talmudics at Cambridge. There he became famous for bringing to Cambridge much of the huge archive of manuscripts from the Cairo Genizah which provides such an important source of evidence for Judaism in the Middle Ages.

It was from this scholarly, academic background that Schechter was lured in 1902 – in the same year that his erstwhile employer and pupil Claude Montefiore founded the radical Reform Jewish Religious Union – to head the Jewish Theological Seminary of America, which had been founded fifteen years earlier by the Italian rabbi Sabato Morais. (Morais himself had at one time worked for the Spanish and Portuguese Congregation in London where Gaster became *haham*, and saw the role of the Seminary as the training of rabbis in traditional Judaism precisely in order to counter the lure of radical Reform. One of the eight students in the first class at the Seminary was Joseph H. Hertz, who, as we have seen (p. 479), was later to be chief rabbi of the British Empire.) Schechter's ability to tread a path between orthodoxy and

Reform was bolstered by a strong personal piety, scholarly rigour and a clear vision of the role of the history and future of the people of Israel. Hence his definition of the theology of the historical school within Judaism: 'It is not the mere revealed Bible that is of first importance to the Jew, but the Bible as it repeats itself in history, in other words, as it is interpreted by Tradition.' This traditionalist theology, which allowed for halakhic change in so far as it reflected the current practice of Israel as a whole (however that is to be determined), is strikingly close to the attitude of the Pharisees to ancestral tradition in the period of the Second Temple. It is not accidental that the large study of the Pharisees by Schechter's longest-serving successor as head of the Seminary, Louis Finkelstein (who was connected to the Seminary from his ordination in 1919 to his death in 1991), reveals as much about the preoccupations of twentieth-century Jewish life in America as about the Second Temple group which is its ostensible subject.[17]

Schechter brought to New York a remarkable faculty of European scholars, helped not least by the comparative prosperity of many American Jews in the early twentieth century, and in 1913 he founded the United Synagogue of America, which (nowadays under the less ambitious title 'United Synagogue of Conservative Judaism') coordinates the affairs of Conservative congregations in the United States and Canada. The original title of the organization reflects the hope, which had been paralleled early in 1873 by the Union of American Hebrew Congregations, that this form of Judaism would become standard in the new country of America. For much of the twentieth century this hope seemed not unreasonable. Since the Conservative ideology was of a dynamic tradition shaped by Jews themselves, it allowed for a great deal of religious self-expression in keeping with American ideals of individuality, without either the elaboration of written rule books characteristic of contemporary orthodoxy or the painful extrusion of a consensus on matters of principle characteristic of Reform. Abraham Joshua Heschel, a teacher at the Jewish Theological Seminary from 1946, urged in his influential *God in Search of Man*, published in 1955, that Jews should seek to rediscover fervour and conviction not through rational argument but through existential decisions clarified by reason, to enable themselves to experience awe and reverence, to open their minds to the evocative language of the Torah, and to evoke the mystery of existence through experimenting with the observance of *mitzvot*. Heschel's spiritual and moral approach struck a chord particularly with students at the Seminary in the 1960s.[18]

The self-confidence of Conservative Judaism in America in the mid-twentieth century was bolstered by agreement on the importance of Hebrew and the land of Israel as parts of the national tradition to be conserved. Already in 1905, Schechter wrote about Zionism as 'the great bulwark against assimilation', and in 1913, in the same year that he helped to found the United Synagogue of America, he attended the 11th Zionist Congress in Vienna. But on many other major theological issues Conservative Jews over the past century have simply agreed to disagree. Thus, for instance, views about the theological significance of the Holocaust have varied enormously. Heschel, who had escaped from Berlin in 1939 in his thirties, insisted that the only appropriate response is silence, whereas the philosopher Richard Rubenstein, who was ordained as a Conservative rabbi by the Jewish Theological Seminary in 1952, asserted in *After Auschwitz*, first published in 1966, that 'God really died at Auschwitz' but that the Jewish religious community remains important in giving humans a sense that they are not alone.[19]

Emet ve-Emunah ('Truth and Faith'), the statement of principles produced in 1988 by a Commission on the Philosophy of the Conservative Movement, left open even central issues about the notion of revelation and observance of halakhah:

> The nature of revelation and its meaning for the Jewish people, have been understood in various ways within the Conservative community. We believe that the classical sources of Judaism provide ample precedents for these views of revelation ... Some of us conceive of revelation as the personal encounter between God and human beings ... Others among us conceive of revelation as the continuing discovery, through nature and history, of truths about God and the world. These truths, although always culturally conditioned, are nevertheless seen as God's ultimate purpose for creation. Proponents of this view tend to see revelation as an ongoing process rather than as a specific event ... For many Conservative Jews, Halakhah is indispensable first and foremost because it is what the Jewish community understands God's will to be. Moreover, it is a concrete expression of our ongoing encounter with God. This divine element of Jewish law is understood in varying ways within the Conservative community, but, however it is understood, it is for many the primary rationale for obeying Halakhah, the reason that undergirds all the rest ... We in the Conservative community are committed to carrying on the rabbinic tradition of preserving and enhancing Halakhah by making appropriate changes in it through rabbinic decision ... While change is both a

traditional and a necessary part of Halakhah, we, like our ancestors, are not committed to change for its own sake ... Following the example of our rabbinic predecessors over the ages, however, we consider instituting changes for a variety of reasons. Occasionally the integrity of the law must be maintained by adjusting it to conform to contemporary practice among observant Jews ... Some changes in law are designed to improve the material conditions of the Jewish people or society at large. The goal of others is to foster better relations among Jews or between Jews and the larger community. In some cases changes are necessary to prevent or remove injustice, while in others they constitute a positive program to enhance the quality of Jewish life by elevating its moral standards or deepening its piety.[20]

Underlying the pluralism accepted within the Conservative movement was an evident commitment to integrating Jewish tradition with living in the modern world. This led, for instance, in the 1950s to a positive interpretation of the use of cars on the Sabbath for attending synagogue, in marked contrast to the closure of synagogue car parks considered mandatory by orthodox communities. Hence the statement by the Commission:

Refraining from the use of a motor vehicle is an important aid in the maintenance of the Sabbath spirit of repose. Such restraint aids, moreover, in keeping the members of the family together on the Sabbath. However, where a family resides beyond reasonable walking distance from the synagogue, the use of a motor vehicle for the purpose of synagogue attendance shall in no wise be construed as a violation of the Sabbath but, on the contrary, such attendance shall be deemed an expression of loyalty to our faith.[21]

Such toleration did not prevent schisms within the Conservative movement during the twentieth century. Both Reconstructionism and the Union for Traditional Judaism originated in impassioned debate within the exceptionally talented, knowledgeable and opinionated faculty of the Jewish Theological Seminary. Mordechai Kaplan, the son of an orthodox rabbi and educated in America, was ordained at the Seminary soon after Schechter's arrival, and taught there for over fifty years. The Reconstructionist philosophy he adopted was an offshoot of one aspect of Conservative Judaism as a whole. In 1934 Kaplan produced the defining statement, in *Judaism as a Civilization*, of his contention that the evolution of the religious civilization of the Jewish people as it has adapted to various historical contexts constitutes in itself the nature of Judaism, and that an appropriate response to the modern world is therefore to be embraced rather than endured. Judaism is to be reconstructed and Jewish customs reinterpreted to make them relevant in the modern age. Such an approach, bolstered by a combination of philosophical and sociological argument as well as by the secular cultural Zionism espoused by the Hebrew essayist Asher Ginzberg (known by his pen name 'Ahad Ha'am'), in practice brought Reconstructionists in many aspects of practice and liturgy close to Reform communities and encouraged the popularity in American Jewish suburbia of the notion that a synagogue should be primarily a community centre, with prayer and study as secondary activities. Thus the *Sabbath Prayer Book* edited by Kaplan in 1945 deleted references to the resurrection of the dead and a personal messiah, and even to the Jews as a chosen people. On the other hand, Reconstructionists have retained from their conservative roots a strong emphasis on the need for Hebrew in prayer and for continued practice of rituals which are seen to convey the insights of previous generations (although such rituals may be changed on ethical grounds if the specific historical context of their origins is no longer seen to apply). Kaplan's Society for the Advancement of Judaism, founded in 1922, gave birth in 1955 to the Jewish Reconstructionist Federation and, since 1968, it has funded its own Reconstructionist Rabbinical College in Pennsylvania.[22]

It is not accidental that the Reconstructionist movement responded more rapidly and radically than other forms of Judaism to the changing roles of women. The religious role of women, which had hardly changed since the carving out of a domestic religious role for them in the early rabbinic period, was widely recognized in the twentieth century as a major issue requiring some sort of reform. Services of 'consecration' for girls had been introduced into some orthodox synagogues in England in the nineteenth century, but for Jews aware of female emancipation in wider society and their entry into university education and the professions the continuing ignorance and exclusion of many women came to seem increasingly anachronistic and unacceptable. In 1922 Kaplan was the first to introduce a *bat mitzvah* ritual into the synagogue service, when his own daughter reached the age of maturity (at twelve years and a day), and in the 1940s women were granted full equality in the synagogue rituals in all Reconstructionist congregations. Women were first ordained as Reconstructionist rabbis in 1968, and recognition and inclusion of lesbian, gay, bisexual and transgender Jews has become an integral part of the movement's adaptation to the modern North American world.[23]

Kaplan's Reconstructionism was viewed with suspicion and hostility by others on the faculty at the Jewish Theological Seminary, among them the great Talmud scholar Saul Lieberman, who had trained in yeshivot in Belorussia before coming to the Seminary in 1940 after more than a decade studying and teaching at the new Hebrew University in Jerusalem. Despite their intellectual openness to the historical origins of all aspects of Judaism, most of these teachers were temperamentally inclined to tradition in synagogue liturgy. It was a debate within the Seminary itself in the early 1980s on the ordination of women by the Seminary that led another great talmudist, David Weiss Halivni, to form a separate organization, the Union for Traditional Conservative Judaism, which since 1990 has broken away entirely from the Conservative movement (and dropped 'Conservative' from its name). The Union for Traditional Judaism has opened its own rabbinical school, but it has not, as yet, had a major impact on Conservative congregations in North America, which are, if anything, generally more inclined towards a laxer observance than their rabbis. Indeed, Conservative Judaism of all shades is in something of a crisis as congregants abandon the centre ground it represents, either in hope of a deeper spirituality within one of the orthodox or independent renewal movements, or for the more pluralist Judaism of Reform, or indeed for a wholly secular form of Jewish identity, or none.[24]

In view of the enthusiasm about Zionism within the Conservative movement from the start, it is perhaps ironic that this form of Judaism has never become widespread in the land of Israel, where it is known as Masorti, in part because Masorti leaders were not included in the establishment of the so-called Status Quo which has governed relations between the secular state and rabbinic authorities since 1948. Until recently most Israeli Masorti Jews, like most Israeli Reform Jews, were from families of recent immigrants from the United States, although secular native Israelis have begun increasingly to turn to Masorti, as well as Reform, practices for life rituals such as weddings and funerals. Outreach by the Jewish Theological Seminary to unaffiliated Jews in the former Soviet Union since the 1990s seems to have had little impact. Elsewhere in the diaspora there has been rather more enthusiasm, with a flourishing Conservative rabbinical seminary, the Seminario Rabínico Latinoamericano, founded in 1962 in Buenos Aires in Argentina on the model of the Jewish Theological Seminary in New York.

In the United Kingdom, Louis Jacobs, who, unusually for an English rabbi, had been trained entirely in England (in yeshivot in Manchester and Gateshead, and at London University) and served as rabbi of orthodox synagogues in Manchester and London in the 1940s and 1950s, resigned his teaching post at Jews' College, the only orthodox seminary in the country dedicated to training rabbis for communal service, when his appointment as principal of the College was vetoed in 1961 by the chief rabbi, Israel Brodie, on the grounds of heterodox views in Jacobs' publications. Most important of these (by this stage in Jacobs' life) was *We Have Reason to Believe*, in which Jacobs accepted some of the methods of biblical critics and asserted that the Bible was in part a human composition, notions that would not raise an eyebrow within the Conservative movement. Right up to his death in 2006, Jacobs maintained, adamantly and with great learning, the orthodoxy of his views. But he appeared to have trespassed against what had been identified by Samson Raphael Hirsch as the touchstone of orthodoxy, a belief that the Torah is from heaven, and forgiveness was not forthcoming from the chief rabbi or his erstwhile rabbinical colleagues in the United Synagogue. In 1964 some of his supporters established a new orthodox congregation, the New London Synagogue – outside the auspices of the United Synagogue and the control of the chief rabbi – for Jacobs to serve as rabbi. Jacobs was a respected scholar and the author of books much read even by many of those who disowned him, and he was popular with many lay orthodox Jews within the United Synagogue. He could have continued to present his Judaism as the face of enlightened modern orthodoxy according to local custom (*minhag Anglia*), but he chose instead in the 1980s to affiliate his congregation to the Conservative movement in the United States. The result, however, has not been any mass extension of formal commitment to Conservative Judaism in England, partly because many Jews attached to congregations within the Orthodox United Synagogue in any case practise and believe in a Judaism differentiated from Conservative Judaism only in name.[25]

This has been a European and American story. The intense disputes of reformers and counter-reformers in central and western Europe and the United States in the nineteenth and early twentieth centuries had only faint echoes in the long-established Jewish communities of the Middle East and North Africa. There, as in much of eastern Europe, the main religious response to the challenges of modernity was a reassertion of tradition, as we shall see in the next chapter.

19

Rejection

In the eyes of the *haredim*, those 'fearful of God' or 'anxious' to observe the commandments, as Isaiah had urged his hearers to 'tremble' at God's word and as pious teachers in the time of Ezra had trembled at the divine instruction for Israel to put aside their gentile alliances and disown their offspring, all such attempts to adapt Judaism to modernity over the past two centuries have been profoundly mistaken. The term *haredi* entered modern Hebrew in the nineteenth and early twentieth centuries as a translation of 'orthodox' which was used for (among others) the neo-orthodox followers of Samuel Raphael Hirsch, but over the past half-century it has acquired a more specific connotation in reference to the ultra-orthodox who reject contemporary secular society altogether.[1]

To enter the Meah Shearim neighbourhood in Jerusalem, just to the west of the walls of the Old City, is to step back into the *shtetls* of eastern Europe as imagined by Shalom Aleichem, with Yiddish both spoken and written everywhere; men, even at the height of a Mediterranean summer, in black frock coats and caftans, and a great variety of broad-brimmed fur hats; and women and girls dressed modestly with long sleeves and black stockings. Men and boys wear sidelocks (sometimes tucked behind the ears), and beards are luxuriant. Married women keep their hair covered to all but their husbands by wearing either a scarf or a wig (with a hat when in public). Wigs can be quite glamorous: those manufactured from blonde hair bought in eastern Europe are particularly prized. The market in wigs from the Indian subcontinent is sufficiently large for an attempt by rivals to undermine it by claiming that the hair used might be out of bounds to the religiously scrupulous on the grounds that it might have been given as an offering to a Hindu divinity before it was used for its present purpose. All life is structured around religious ritual, either in the home for the women or in the synagogues and study halls for the men. There is a sense of deep purposefulness, and wariness of visitors and tourists who might disturb this enclave in the modern commercial city – particularly on the Sabbath, when the whole neighbourhood, summoned by sirens to cease work from the appointed time, devotes itself to prayer, Torah study and rest.[2]

Meah Shearim was formed in 1875 by pious Jews from the Old City in search of more salubrious living conditions, but the creation of such ultra-orthodox enclaves has been replicated during the second half of the twentieth century elsewhere in Israel (in places like Bnei Brak, near Tel Aviv) and in the diaspora (in neighbourhoods like Stamford Hill in London, parts of Brooklyn in New York, and areas of Toronto, Antwerp and other cities). In all these places, physical segregation is intended to enable the ultra-orthodox to raise barriers against the influence of television, newspapers, advertising and the rest of popular culture, educating their children in separate schools in which understanding the nature of Torah observance takes priority over everything, and only the most basic skills such as learning to read and write are considered necessary additional accomplishments. Use of the internet has proved a tricky case: it is prevalent among some of the ultra-orthodox, but in a massive rally in 2012 in a baseball stadium in Queens, New York, its general use was condemned.

In these communities, which coexist alongside a western society which is at a high level of sophistication and (they would say) decadence, families maintain solidarity by arranging their marriages, and providing employment and financial help, within the community, so that the outside world does not need to impinge on everyday life. The birth of numerous children is stimulated by observation of the biblical command to be fruitful and multiply, enhanced for some *haredim* by the doctrine that an increased *haredi* population is an appropriate response to the enormity of the Holocaust in which so many of the great centres of Torah learning were destroyed in eastern Europe. The survival of large families (often with ten or more offspring) owes a great deal to advances in medical care and the provision of social services by westernized states (including Israel). The high rate of retention of these children within their communities owes as much to the attractiveness of the lifestyle and the power of ideologies preached as it does to the undoubted barriers faced by *haredim* who seek to venture out of their enclaves into the unfamiliar modern world. Even *haredi* women, whose severely limited schooling has been characterized as 'education for ignorance', and whose premium on modesty ensures near-invisibility in *haredi* public life to the extent that public photographs of women are frowned on and women dancing at weddings are screened off from men, often express themselves satisfied with a role which leaves them supreme in the domestic domain as their menfolk study or work, although economic pressures are pushing an increasing number to seek paid employment, particularly in Israel and the United States.[3]

The *haredim* themselves characterize this way of observing Torah as a preservation of tradition, but in fact it owes a great deal, like so much else in contemporary Judaism, to the reaction to the Enlightenment in the late eighteenth century. Moses Sofer, better known as the Hatam Sofer, came originally from Frankfurt, but his enduring influence on the development of a rigid orthodox response to modernity was the product of his thirty-three years as rabbi of Pressburg, the most important Jewish community of Hungary, a position to which he was appointed in 1806 when already in his mid-forties. Faced in Pressburg by a large minority of enthusiasts for the new enlightened Jewish lifestyle, Sofer threw himself into the conflict with both skill and vigour. He championed a novel and uncompromising application of the talmudic tag that 'that which is new is forbidden according to the Torah', such that any innovation whatsoever can be strictly forbidden just because it is an innovation. It will be apparent from the story of Judaism over the previous centuries that this prohibition of anything new was itself ironically an innovation, but the call to defend tradition had an attractive rhetorical simplicity more often associated with fundamentalism. The Hatam Sofer ensured the spread of his approach by ploughing great effort into the encouragement of educational institutions for Torah study, including his own yeshivah in Pressburg, which had more students than any yeshivah since the time of the Babylonian *geonim*.[4]

The form of Judaism which Moses Sofer thus pronounced as the perfect expression of the Torah of Moses was his perception of the way of life of the Jewish religious elite in Germany and Poland in the middle of the eighteenth century (hence the dress codes of the *haredim* in the modern world). The Hatam Sofer opposed everything to do with the Enlightenment, urging his family in the testament which was to be published after his death in 1839, 'do not ever touch the books of Moses Mendelssohn, and thus shall you never stumble.' The Pressburg yeshivah was to retain its influence under the leadership of his descendants down to the Second World War, and to be refounded in Jerusalem in 1950 by his great-grandson Akiva Sofer. It continues to flourish in the largely *haredi* neighbourhood of Givat Shaul. In 1879 his second son, Shimon, who headed the Mahzikey haDas ('Upholders of the Faith') organization in Cracow, was elected to the Austrian parliament to defend traditional Judaism against the innovators. The testament of the Hatam Sofer to his family laid out in exemplary clarity the lifestyle he wished to enshrine: 'Do not change your name, language, or clothing to imitate the ways of the gentiles. The women should read books in Yiddish, printed in our traditional font and based on the tales of our sages, and nothing else ... Do not say that times have changed, for "we have an old Father", blessed be He, who has not changed and never will change.'[5]

The imposition of such clear laws was enhanced by asserting the absolute authority of Karo's *Shulhan Arukh*. A generation after the Hatam Sofer an abridgement of Karo's work by another rabbi in Hungary, Shlomo Ganzfried, summarized in simple Hebrew, for unlearned but pious Jews, the laws which each individual is required to keep. It proved so popular that it was issued in fourteen editions between its first publication in 1864 and Ganzfried's death in 1886. Ganzfried was much involved, as a communal leader, in a political struggle against the spread of Neologist Judaism in Hungary, but his greatest influence came through this book. The mass printing and dissemination of halakhic works accounts similarly for the influence of many later *haredi* leaders, and many of them have become better known by the title of one of their influential volumes than by their own names. Thus Yisrael Meir haCohen, who was a figure of extraordinary authority in nineteenth-century Lithuania and in the broader ultra-orthodox world but never held any rabbinic post, is known universally by the title of his first book, *Hafets Hayyim* (a legal and ethical treatise on the prohibition of slander), published anonymously in Vilna when he was thirty-five. His authority was projected in particular through mass circulation of his *Mishnah Berurah*, a huge commentary on the first part of Karo's *Shulhan Arukh* intended as a detailed guide to everyday life for those with the same pious outlook as Ganzfried had assumed but greater capacity to delve into minutiae and to countenance variety.

From a small grocery store in the little town of Raduń which his wife managed while he did the book keeping, and then (when business was poor) for many years as a teacher, the Hafets Hayyim produced a string of books on practical observance of the laws and wider issues of morality. In later years he also travelled a great deal, using his personal reputation for piety to raise funds for the maintenance of yeshivot throughout Europe in the financial crisis after the First World War, including the yeshivah that had sprung up in Raduń itself as early as 1869 because of the number of students attracted to study with him. The Hafets Hayyim, who took a leadership role in the Agudah (pp. 485–6), was long-lived, dying in 1933, and his influence overlapped that of a much younger contemporary, Avraham Yeshayahu Karelitz. The career of Karelitz, as a talmudic scholar (known popularly as the Hazon Ish ('Vision of a Man'), from the title of his own anonymous commentary on part of the *Shulhan Arukh*) was similar to that of the Hafets Hayyim in his reliance on his wife's store for economic support. In his mid-fifties he emigrated from Vilna to Bnei Brak in the land of Israel and became the spiritual leader of the *haredi* community – first in Mandate Palestine and then, in the 1940s and early 1950s as the impact of the Holocaust sank in, worldwide.[6]

The authority of the Hazon Ish derived in large part from an explicit refusal to speculate or compromise in the observance of Torah. He detached his followers from other Jews who saw themselves as orthodox with as much vehemence as the Hatam Sofer had opposed Reform and secular ideologies: 'The same way that simplicity and truth are synonymous, thus extremity and greatness are. Extremity is the perfection of the subject. He who partisans Middle-Way and mediocrity, and despises extremity, should find his place among falsifiers or reasonless people ... Naive faith is the sharp response, that clarifies the truth and settles that which is in doubt.' The need to rule on issues to do with everyday living – which for the Hazon Ish after his emigration in 1933 included practical matters for the observation of rulings pertaining specifically to the land of Israel, such as the laws of the sabbatical year – gave these rabbinic leaders a particularly close bond to their followers. The 'great men of the generation', as the *haredim* thought of them, have become de facto political as well as spiritual guides to increasing numbers of yeshivah students, particularly in Israel, over the past half-century.[7]

Yeshivah students provided the massed infantry in support of these quiet, pious authors in the war against secularism and laxity. Devotion to Torah study had been the ideal of rabbinic Judaism, at least for males, for many centuries, as we have seen, but new in the nineteenth century was the practical implementation of this ideal in the proliferation of yeshivot over eastern Europe as large-scale, total institutions in which crowds of young men devoted much of their lives to the study of religious law – and especially the Babylonian Talmud and its commentaries – for its own sake. The first such modern yeshivah was established in Volozhin in 1803 by a disciple of the Vilna Gaon to counter the influence of Hasidism by replacing the casuistry of *pilpul* with study of the true meaning of classical texts. It had 400 students by the second half of the nineteenth century. Some of these students founded,

elsewhere in Lithuania, new yeshivot which established their own distinctive learning traditions and curricula. Thus in 1897 the yeshivah in
Slobodka, a suburb of Kovno (modern Kaunas), had some 200 students.
The yeshivah founded in the town of Tels in 1875 set up a novel structure of four classes based on achievement so that good students could
progress to a higher level. The aim of such educational reform was purely
to enhance learning, since none of these yeshivot saw study primarily
as a route to an examination or certificate of competence, although in
practice many who graduated from the yeshivah became communal rabbis. The point was to preserve and study the tradition for its own sake.
In the 1940s the defiance of students from the yeshivah in Mir in the face
of the destruction of Lithuanian Jewry, when they found refuge from
Nazism after fleeing to Japan through Siberia, was expressed by reprint-
ing classic Jewish texts in Shanghai so that learning should not cease.

For the founders of yeshivot in eastern Europe in the nineteenth century the threat of the Enlightenment was far more distant than in Germany
and Hungary. The more immediate challenge was to garner support in the
wider Jewish community for a lifestyle which might all too easily seem to
reserve real religious experience to an elite intellectual class in contrast to
the mass appeal of Hasidism. Among the most effective responses was the
Musar ('Ethics') movement within the Lithuanian academies initiated in
Vilna by Yisrael Salanter, who combined his work as head of a yeshivah
engaged in traditional studies with a role as sermonizer in instilling ethical conduct among ordinary lay Jews as much as among his students.
Many of his educational techniques in the use of pietistic homilies were
adopted in other Lithuanian yeshivot, as well in the wider Jewish world.[8]

By the time that Salanter founded his own distinctively Musar-
focused yeshivah in Kovno in 1848, the threat of Hasidism to yeshivah
studies had in fact much receded since the height of the struggle by the
mitnagdim in the late eighteenth century under the leadership of the
Vilna Gaon (see Chapter 15). When the organization of Mahzikey
haDas was founded in Cracow in 1879 to combat the inroads of mod-
ernism in Galicia, it could count on mass support from Belz *hasidim*
against a common foe. The opposition of the *hasidim* to the Enlightenment was more a reaction to the hostility of the leaders of the Jewish
modernizers, the *maskilim*, than intrinsic to the nature of Hasidism
itself. The *maskilim* blamed Hasidism for preventing a move of Polish
Jews into western-style education to improve their position in society by
offering a superstitious alternative. Hasidic leaders like Menachem
Mendel Schneerson, a grandson of the founder of the Habad movement

known from his voluminous compendium of Jewish law as the Tsemach Tsedek ('Righteous Scion'), responded in the mid-nineteenth century by justifying punctilious observance of the commandments on the basis of their mystical meaning.[9]

Hasidism was thus transformed, from a revolutionary sectarian movement opposed to the rabbinic establishment in the eighteenth century, to a new role in the nineteenth century in the vanguard of the war waged by the *haredim* in support of conservative rabbinic values. Hasidic communities began to set up their own yeshivot for Torah and Talmud study, to insulate their youth from the harmful influences of the outside world much as the Lithuanian *mitnagdim* had earlier tried to protect themselves against Hasidism. Some hasidic leaders, such as Yitzhak Meir Rothenburg Alter of the Gur *hasidim*, the largest hasidic group in central Poland, became better known for their writings on Jewish law than for their mystical teachings. By 1881, following the great waves of emigration to the west, most *haredi* Jews in the Ukraine, Galicia and central Poland, and many *haredi* Jews in Belorussia, Lithuania and Hungary, followed a hasidic way of life and used hasidic rites of worship. The different hasidic groups fiercely maintained their identities and traditions, and their loyalty to their individual *rebbes* (who continued to develop mystical interpretations of the Torah), but to the wider Jewish world they presented a united front in opposition to secular change. Two crucial issues remained, however, on which consensus among *hasidim*, as among *haredim* in general, was (and still is) rare: attitudes to Zionism, and expectation for the imminent arrival of the Messiah.[10]

The clearest expression of religious opposition to Zionism in the modern *haredi* world was that formulated by Joel Teitelbaum, *rebbe* of the Satmar hasidic sect from Satu-Mare in Hungary (now Romania). In the eyes of the Satmar *hasidim*, the Zionist enterprise is an 'act of Satan' because no attempt should be made to form a Jewish state until the Messiah has come. The existence of the current State of Israel has thus culpably delayed the messianic age and the Holocaust was a divine punishment for Zionists trying to 'force the end'. When Teitelbaum, who was to be the *rebbe* of the Satmar for over fifty years, escaped from Europe in 1944, he brought Hungarian Hasidism to the United States, settling his community in 1947 in Williamsburg in Brooklyn, where they have become a distinct Yiddish-speaking, and wholly unassimilated, enclave in the variegated cultural mix of New York.[11]

The Satmar are extreme in their opposition to the Zionist state, which sometimes extends to a refusal even to countenance the use of spoken

Hebrew, but suspicion of Zionism was normal among the *haredim* of the late nineteenth century because of the fear that secular nationalism based on territory and state would supplant adherence to the Torah. In due course, however, demographic movements in the early twentieth century, with the inclusion of *haredim* in the migration of Jews to Palestine from eastern Europe, and the development of religious expressions of Zionism, encouraged a more complex response, and fierce arguments. We have seen (in Chapter 18) how the establishment in Kattowitz of Agudat Israel in 1912 sought to bring together all those determined to preserve traditional Judaism against the assaults of modernity 'to solve in the spirit of Torah and the commandments the various everyday issues which will arise in the life of the people of Israel', but coexistence within this new organization served only to highlight the differences between the participants, not least in regard to the growing Jewish community in Palestine.

In the forefront of the development of a theology of *haredi* religious Zionism compatible with the practical affairs of Palestinian Jews in the twentieth century was the remarkably independent thought of Abraham Kook. Kook was elected in 1921 as the first Ashkenazi chief rabbi of Palestine, having migrated from Latvia to Palestine in 1904 at the age of thirty-nine to become rabbi of Jaffa. He had received a traditional talmudic education supplemented by independent study of the Bible, philosophy and mysticism, and he had experience as a communal rabbi in eastern Europe, but the theology he developed was original and it proved controversial in both religious and secular circles. Kook regarded the return to the land of Israel as the beginning of divine redemption and urged religious leaders to see their task as the encouragement of a spiritual revival alongside the material revival of Jewish settlement. A deeply mystical thinker, Kook viewed the real world as a unity in which the divine is incarnated, so that the return of the Jews to their land is a link in the process of universal redemption. All Jews in the land of Israel, including the most defiantly secular, have a role to play in the divine scheme. Kook could even claim that attacks by secular idealists on religion should be cherished for their paradoxical religious value, using the Lurianic kabbalistic concept of the 'breaking of the vessels' to assert that 'the great idealists seek an order so noble, so fine and pure, beyond what may be found in the world of reality, and thus they destroy what has been fashioned in conformity to the norms of the world ... The souls inspired by the realm of chaos are greater than the souls whose affinity is with the established order.'[12]

Such tolerance set Kook at variance with other *haredim* – the *rebbe* of Gur (the Yiddish name for Góra Kalwaria) said of him that 'his love for Zion knows no limits, and [therefore] he says that the impure is pure, and welcomes it' – and the meanings Kook ascribed to traditional philosophical and kabbalistic concepts were often radically novel. His thought was so deliberately innovative that he could also have been discussed in the previous chapter as an example, alongside J. B. Soloveitchik (p. 487), of counter-reform. But the central notion of his thought, that the divine intervention in history required to bring about the messianic age could be hastened by Jewish settlement in the land of Israel, had been prefigured over the previous century by religious Zionists in eastern and central Europe, of whom only a few, like Shmuel Mohilever of Białystok (see Chapter 16), had taken practical action in this direction. Zvi Hirsch Kalischer had argued for the restoration of sacrifices in a rebuilt Temple in the land of Israel, from his base as a communal rabbi for fifty years in a large Jewish community in a part of western Poland annexed by Prussia. Yehudah Alkalai, rabbi of a small Sephardi community near Belgrade in the mid-nineteenth century, had put forward practical plans for encouraging the productive economy of settlers in the land of Israel, not least by reviving the notion of the biblical tithe so that one-tenth of the income of each Jew should help to pay for the rebuilding of the land. Alkalai was spurred on originally by kabbalistic speculation that the year 1840 would witness the arrival of the Messiah, but, when this did not happen, he became convinced that Jews were required to take action. Up to 1840 it had been possible to hope for deliverance simply through divine grace. But now deliverance depended on the *teshuva* ('return' or 'repentance') of Israel, which for Alkalai meant return to the land. He himself spent the last four years before his death in 1878 in the land of Israel.[13]

Messianic hope was thus intrinsic to Zionism as it manifested itself among *haredim*, and tension arose most around the question of how much to cooperate with non-religious Jews in the building of a secular Jewish state which would serve a higher religious purpose in due course. Most religious Zionists in the twentieth century lived outside the *haredi* world. The religious Mizrahi movement, formed in Vilna in 1902 but already establishing schools in Palestine combining secular studies with religious education by 1909, and the political party and workers' organization HaPoel HaMizrahi ('The Mizrahi Worker'), which existed alongside it in Palestine from 1922 to promote Torah and labour, placed the Zionist endeavour at the centre of its ideology and worked with secular Jews from the start. It was from former members of its youth movement, Bnei Akiva, that in 1974 emerged the most extreme form of redemptive Zionist orthodoxy, Gush Emunim ('The Bloc of the Faithful'). This group, comprised primarily of young middle-class religious Zionists who felt that the Zionist project had lost its way after the Yom Kippur War in 1973, interpreted the messianic significance of the return of Jews to the land as a prohibition on relinquishing any of the territory overrun by Israeli troops in the Six Day War of 1967 if it lay within 'Judaea and Samaria', the borders of the land which, according to the Bible, had been settled by the children of Israel under the leadership of Joshua in fulfilment of God's promise.[14]

The spiritual leader of Gush Emunim, until his death at the age of ninety-one in 1982, was Zvi Yehudah Kook, the son of Abraham Kook and his successor as head of the influential yeshivah, Merkaz haRav Kook, which his father had established in Jerusalem. Zvi Yehudah regarded himself as custodian of Abraham's legacy after Abraham's death in 1935, and he worked for nearly fifty years on the publication and dissemination of his father's writings. But his own interpretation of these writings was distinctive. His twin beliefs, that Jews have a divinely ordained duty to settle in all the biblical land of Israel and that everything about the secular State of Israel, including its military arm, is intrinsically holy because of its role in the messianic process, were frequently in conflict in the mid-1970s, when members of Gush Emunim were regularly evicted by the Israeli Defence Forces from illegal settlements in the West Bank. Gush Emunim disbanded in 1980 and no longer exists as a separate group largely because its advocacy of settlement in the occupied territories has, since the election of Menachem Begin as prime minister in 1977, in any case been the policy of various governments in Israel – but for political rather than religious reasons, since up to now no Israeli government has been led by a politician openly espousing religious conviction as the basis for policy decisions.

Zvi Yehudah had grown up in Lithuania and remained in contact throughout his life with the east European *haredi* world of yeshivah learning, despite his dramatic forays into the realities of Israel's political disputes. His was a very different background to the distinctively American religious Zionism of Meir (originally Martin David) Kahane, a rabbi from Brooklyn. Kahane had devoted the first part of his public career to vocal opposition to antisemitism in the diaspora, founding the Jewish Defense League in New York in 1968 and organizing mass protests against the persecution of Jews by the Soviet Union when they expressed a desire to emigrate to Israel, before himself migrating from the United States to Israel in 1971. In contrast to Kook and his followers, who advocated (however optimistically) coexistence with the non-Jewish inhabitants of Judaea and Samaria, the Kach party founded by Kahane sought the mass expulsion of Arabs from both Israel and the occupied territories.

Kahane had been trained in Talmud in the *haredi* Mir yeshivah in Brooklyn, but this new ideology derived more from the political atmosphere in right-wing circles in the United States during the Cold War than from local support among *haredim* in Israel and, despite the halakhic strictness adopted by some of his followers, his teachings can be seen, like those of Kook, as a distinctive response to the spread of liberal assumptions in other strands of Judaism in the late twentieth century. His religious outlook, in which Zionist political ideals predominated, might be better described as Zionist religion than as religious Zionism. The yeshivah he opened in 1987 for teaching what he claimed as 'the authentic Jewish idea' was funded by American Jews, and there was a flavour of the Wild West in the establishment of Jewish outposts surrounded by a Palestinian population deemed intrinsically hostile. Within Israel, support for Kach came less from within the *haredi* community than from working-class Sephardi Jews. The *haredim*, including other *haredi* Zionists who were prepared to commit to the state's institutions, were generally unimpressed by Kahane's ostentatious commitment to religious values as demonstrated by his refusal to take the standard oath on his election to the Knesset without adding a verse from Psalms to indicate the priority of Torah over secular laws. His parliamentary speeches were boycotted by other members of the Knesset, and when an amendment to the basic constitutional law of the country was passed in 1985 to disbar racist candidates, Kahane found himself unable to run for election when they were next held, in 1988. The political heat he engendered was demonstrated by the extraordinary size of the crowd which turned out for his funeral in Jerusalem, in November 1990, after he had been shot dead, by an Egyptian American, in a hotel in Manhattan following a speech to *haredim* from Brooklyn.[15]

Kahane's audience had little in common (beyond a conviction that they were devoted to the Torah) with a small group on the fringes of the *haredim*, Neturei Karta ('The Guardians of the City') of Jerusalem, who refuse to recognize the existence, let alone the authority, of the secular State of Israel. Neturei Karta split from the *haredi* confederation of Agudat Israel in 1938, claiming, on the authority of a bon mot in the Palestinian Talmud, that the real protection of a community comes not from its military guards but from 'the scribes and scholars'. Neturei

Karta has taken its anti-Zionism to the extent of sending a delegation to the president of Iran to express support for his implacable opposition to the State of Israel. Other *haredim* have adopted a lesser form of separation, such as the followers of Joseph Hayyim Sonnenfeld, who in 1873, in his mid-twenties, settled in the Old City of Jerusalem and succeeded in avoiding any stay of more than thirty days outside the walls of the Old City until his death nearly sixty years later. A leader of the Hungarian *haredim* in Jerusalem, Sonnenfeld fought fiercely against any mingling of orthodox Jews with others, urging *haredim* to opt out of participation in the institutions set up by secular Zionists and opposing the institution in the 1920s of a chief rabbinate for the land of Israel (even though he was himself close to Abraham Kook). In contrast to Neturei Karta, however, he treated modern Hebrew as his main language, and he was in favour of Jewish settlement in the land of Israel and of efforts to establish good relations with the native Arab population. Sonnenfeld seems to have shared with religious Zionists a belief that the return of Jews to the land preceded the messianic age. The prayer for the State of Israel sanctioned by the Israeli chief rabbinate refers to the state as 'the beginning of the sprouting of our redemption', an eschatological hope generally adopted also in modern orthodox synagogal liturgy in the diaspora.[16]

Such notions of gradual redemption coexist only with difficulty with the messianic fervour around a specific *rebbe* which has on occasion convulsed hasidic groups, often to the dismay of other *haredim*, including other *hasidim*. Immediate eschatological expectations were not intrinsic to hasidic thought, as we have seen, but the conception of the *tsaddik* as spiritual superman, through whom divine grace flows and to whom God has granted control of everything by his prayers, already elevated hasidic *rebbes* far above the level of ordinary humans. The soul of a *tsaddik* is so pure that his prayers can even nullify a divine decision that life should come to an end. In every era, a special saint, the 'righteous of the generation', is born with the potential to become the Messiah if conditions in the world prove right. For hasidic followers of a particular charismatic *rebbe*, the messianic age can thus seem tantalizingly close.

We have seen (in Chapter 15) that, two centuries after the death of Nahman of Bratslav in 1810, the Bratslav *hasidim*, nowadays based in Jerusalem, have revived the practice of mass pilgrimage on Rosh haShanah to his grave in Uman, in the Ukraine, which had been almost entirely suppressed by the authorities during the Communist era. It is believed that shortly before his death he vowed before two witnesses that 'if someone comes to my grave, gives a coin to charity, and says these ten psalms, I will pull him out from the depths of Gehinnom [hell].' Claims among Habad *hasidim* (often called 'Lubavitch' after the village in Smolensk Oblast, now in Russia, which for over a century until 1940 housed their headquarters) of the messianic status of their seventh (and last) *rebbe* have been rather less circumspect. Menahem Mendel Schneerson, who died in 1994, after forty-four years as leader of the movement, was one of the most influential leaders within Judaism in the twentieth century, not just because of the role he played for his hasidic followers, who revered him and attended in great crowds his weekly assemblies, but because of his assertion of a responsibility for all Jews, including the most secular. Astute use of modern methods of mass communication, allied to the willingness of followers enthused by imminent eschatological expectation to settle in places of scant Jewish population in order to plant the seeds of religious observance wherever they could, has raised public awareness of Lubavitch far above that of other hasidic communities. Emissaries from the Rebbe have devoted themselves to the encouragement of Torah observance in France, England, Argentina, Russia and the rest of the former USSR, and Australia, and many other countries, apart from the main centres of Lubavitch settlement in Israel and in the United States – in particular in Crown Heights in New York State, where the Rebbe had his residence. The aim of such emissaries – many of them young couples, with the man ordained as a rabbi in his early twenties (sometimes with only a smattering of the knowledge to be found among other *haredi* rabbis) – is to combat secularism within the Jewish population by engagement with even the least observant in even the most obscure locations. No Jew is considered as too far outside the fold to be enticed by a rabbi in a travelling '*mitzvah* tank' equipped to show Jewish men how to put on *tefillin* or light candles for Hanukkah, or to be reached by the rabbi's wife in the 'Habad House', who will tactfully explain to young women about the lighting of candles on Sabbath and the importance of monthly ritual immersion to ensure that procreation takes place in a state of purity.[17]

In many ways such outreach is as distinctively American, in the footsteps of evangelical Christians, as the bellicosity of Meir Kahane. The Rebbe himself declined even to visit the land of Israel, even though a house identical to his dwelling in 770 Eastern Parkway in New York was constructed for him in Cfar Habad in Israel. Habad Lubavitch is as concerned with Jewish identity in the multicultural context characteristic of Jewish life in the United States as with the life of Jews in Israel. Its aim is not to segregate Jews from the modern world (as sought by other *haredim*), but to reshape that world to incorporate strict observance of the Torah. On university campuses, where since the 1970s Lubavitch has had a particularly high profile, traditional Jewish learning may be packaged as classes, seminars and conferences to avoid any impression that the *haredi* lifestyle requires opting out of modernity, although the Lubavitch rabbi himself will retain the conspicuously hasidic dress of kaftan and girdle.

The prime motivation for the Lubavitch mission has been messianic, as expressed with great clarity by the Rebbe himself on the death of his predecessor in 1950. In the last years of his long life, the Rebbe encouraged his followers with increasing urgency to expect 'Moshiach now'. In an atmosphere of intense anticipation, many of these followers expressed their conviction that the Rebbe himself was the Messiah. The outbreak of the first Gulf War provided further evidence (from an American perspective at least) of the worldwide convulsions expected to precede the last days. In 1993, the Rebbe suffered a debilitating stroke, and some of his followers unearthed medieval texts which declared that the Messiah had to suffer, so his tongue would cleave to his mouth, as in Ezekiel 3:26: 'I will make your tongue cling to the roof of your mouth, so that you shall be speechless.' When the Rebbe passed away in 1994, an ideological split took place in the movement between those who continue to have faith in the Rebbe as the Messiah and who therefore deny that he has died or claim he will return, and those who have reconciled themselves to the apparent evidence that the world was not yet ready for the Messiah to manifest himself, and that further effort in spreading the Torah is required before he will be revealed.[18]

Lubavitch are unique among the *hasidim* in their positive enthusiasm for reaching out to other Jews, and in their interest (inherited from the Rebbe) in the spiritual progress also of gentiles. Most other *haredim* have found it easier to maintain their separatist lifestyle by settling in enclaves in which they can provide mutual support to each other and maintain their practical institutions, from synagogues, schools, yeshivot and ritual baths to shops with kosher provisions, although the renaissance of Lithuanian-style yeshivah learning in the United States owes much to outreach to non-*haredim* by rabbis like Aharon Kotler, founder in 1942 of the huge Lakewood yeshivah in New Jersey. For many of these communities, an *eruv* (literally, 'blending'), a legal device to create a notional boundary within which it is permitted for objects to be carried on the Sabbath as if within a private domain, is a highly significant aspect of life particularly for mothers with babies among their multiple children, who can otherwise find themselves unable to leave their homes for the full twenty-five hours from Friday to Saturday night. These enclaves in the diaspora are mostly in the suburbs of big cities, but occasionally they are clustered around an isolated yeshivah: the Gateshead yeshivah, established in 1929 as one of the numerous branches founded by emissaries of the Novardok yeshivah in Navahrudak (then in the Russian empire and now in Belarus) and dedicated to Talmud learning within the Musar tradition of the Hafets Hayyim, is now the largest in Europe, with hundreds of students, even though the size of the rest of the Jewish community in Gateshead (and even in neighbouring Newcastle) is minimal.[19]

The view of Jewish life in England from within the intense atmosphere of the Gateshead yeshivah inevitably differs from that of modern orthodox Jews in the rest of the United Kingdom. Students from the yeshivah are not encouraged to combine their studies with university education, and any contact which might appear to give legitimacy to non-orthodox forms of Judaism is anathema, as was made very clear to the former British chief rabbi Jonathan Sacks, in the reaction of *haredim* in England to his attendance at a memorial service for a Reform rabbi (and Holocaust survivor) Hugo Gryn in 1997. A similar opposition to any official approval of representatives of Reform and Conservative Judaism is also characteristic of Lubavitch. But in other respects their missionary zeal to attract each individual Jew to greater observance of the commandments encourages a far more welcoming attitude to Jews of varied, or no, beliefs and differing degrees of commitment to Jewish practices, so that, as we have seen, Lubavitch *hasidim* have become communal rabbis in many parts of the Jewish world.

The tolerance of irreligiosity displayed by this particular group of *haredim* is astonishing, but so too has been the willingness of some modern orthodox Jews to accept religious leadership for their non-hasidic communities by Lubavitch rabbis whose central messianic belief about the status of the Rebbe and the imminent end of the world they do not share. The assertion by one wing of the Lubavitch movement after the Rebbe's death in 1994 that the Messiah would return posthumously to complete his mission comes perilously close to beliefs rejected by rabbinic polemicists for nearly 2,000 years in response to Christian claims. Orthodox indifference to such claims about the Rebbe has been characterized by some modern orthodox Jews as a scandal. Some *haredim*, like Aharon Feldman, dean of the Ner Israel yeshivah in Baltimore, have urged publicly that orthodox Jews should avoid praying in Habad synagogues which avow belief in the Rebbe as Messiah, but what is most striking is the extent to which such calls have been ignored, and the willingness of diaspora Jews of widely differing beliefs to worship together and turn a blind eye to the issues which might otherwise drive them apart.[20]

Such mutual tolerance is much less characteristic of some *haredim* in contemporary Israeli society, where the notion that humans are entitled to use force to ensure compliance with the Torah is not uncommon. Cars which enter *haredi* areas of Jerusalem or Bnei Brak on the Sabbath run the risk of being stoned, as do archaeologists who disturb the dead by excavating ancient tombs. Women who enter *haredi* enclaves while 'immodestly' dressed in shorts or with bare arms risk verbal abuse or worse. So do women who demonstrate their right to conduct a women's prayer service while wearing prayer shawls at the Western Wall of the Temple in Jerusalem. In recent years some male *haredim* have tried to impose religious propriety (as they see it) by segregating men and women on buses. Airline travel, in which extended physical proximity to travellers of the opposite sex can be hard to avoid, can provoke intense debates about religious scruples in relation to personal freedom. In December 2011 anti-Zionist *haredi* men in Beit Shemesh, a town to the west of Jerusalem, tried to close down a religious Zionist girls' school by shouting abuse at the pupils, aged from six to twelve, accusing them of being prostitutes. The parents of the frightened girls responded by accompanying their daughters to school with dogs as protection, and the police had to intervene to keep the two sides apart. Such violence is rarely condoned explicitly by the majority of *haredim*, but nor is it condemned.

Intolerance between religious Jews in contemporary Israel is also sometimes directed in the opposite direction, against *haredim*. When *haredim* were granted special privileges such as state financing for full-time yeshivah students by Ben Gurion at the foundation of the state in 1948, their numbers were small, but as their communities have grown dramatically they have come to be seen by some as a drain on the state. The *haredi* lifestyle promotes resentment among many other Israelis in part because of the general refusal of even the most Zionist *haredim* to undertake army service, a duty which provides a peculiarly powerful bonding experience for other Jewish Israelis of differing backgrounds because of the constant tension in which the country has existed since its formation. *Haredi* avoidance of the military owes less to a disinclination to kill in defence of the state than to concern about the mingling of the sexes within the armed forces, the perceived danger of moral corruption, the exposure to secularism and the challenge to religious observance, as well as, in some cases, theological doubts about the legitimacy of the state they would be defending. In response to economic pressures and government incentives, some *haredim* are opting to work in ambulance units or in special army units set up for young *haredim* who are not in yeshivah. But all of them are taught unequivocally that devotion to yeshivah study should be seen as no less valuable than service in the military because of its supreme efficacy in encouraging divine favour towards Israel.

Secular Israeli resentment is stoked still further by *haredi* reliance on the state's social security system to support large families in which the father is too engrossed in yeshivah studies, for much or all of the potentially productive period of his life, to earn a living. The provision of generous government grants to yeshivot – itself a product of political negotiations by the leaders of religious parties over the years – has permitted a growing number of *haredim* to remain as full-time students past their twenties in a fashion that had been possible only for elite pupils in the eastern European yeshivah culture whose traditions the modern Israeli yeshivot claim to maintain. Even with state aid and low expectations among *haredim* for their standard of living, mass yeshivah education lasting a lifetime is very expensive to maintain, and, although few Israeli *haredim* break the taboo of studying in secular universities, some have begun to attend vocational courses to pick up marketable skills in single-sex programmes established by the universities and colleges with government funding specifically for the benefit of *haredi* students, and *haredi* women are much more widely engaged than their menfolk in earning for their families.

The causes of antipathy to *haredim* among diaspora Jews are more oblique. Non-orthodox Jews have sometimes led the opposition to attempts by the orthodox to establish an *eruv*, perhaps because this religious practice involves an incursion into the concerns of the non-Jewish public in a fashion which offends the instinct to keep the practice of Judaism a private matter. The deliberate distinctiveness of *haredim* in the modern world can feel like a threat to those Jews who wish to integrate their practice of Judaism into the wider society in which they live. The arrival in their neighbourhood of a community of 'black hats' may feel like moral pressure to adopt an alien religious life or an inducement to non-Jews to resent the presence of all Jews.

20

Renewal

Tensions between *haredim* who try to ignore or minimize the influence of changes in the western world over the past two centuries and the majority of Jews who have adapted to such changes have increased markedly over the past fifty years as a result of the accelerating pace of change within wider society and the growing power of *haredim* to impose their will on other Jews. Many of the concerns of contemporary Jewish renewal movements have reflected the radical shifts in social and cultural expectations, particularly in relation to the role of women and the norms of sexual relations, in North America since the 1960s, and most of these new trends within Judaism have also originated in the United States, although some have sprung from within Israeli society.

In the mid-1990s, the theologian Arthur Green examined in a public lecture at Hebrew Union College, the seminary for Reform rabbis, the significance of an advertisement in New York's *Jewish Week* inserted by a young woman who described herself as 'DJF, 34, Spiritual, not religious, seeking like-minded JM':

> This young woman should indeed be of interest to us. Allow me to treat her, if you will, as an icon of our age. I think she has a pretty clear idea of what she means by 'spiritual, not religious'. You could meet her, along with a great many other Jews, at a Kripalu Yoga Ashram retreat, where she goes for a weekend of Yoga, massage, a lecture on spiritual teachings, healthy vegetarian food, and conversations with like-minded people. You will not meet her at your synagogue, from which she continues to feel alienated. But she fasts and meditates on Yom Kippur, a day that has some 'special meaning' for her. She reads both Sufi and Hasidic stories. She used to go to Shlomo Carlebach concerts and occasionally lapses into one of his tunes. Passover with her family is still an obnoxious and boisterous, 'totally unspiritual', as she would say, affair. But one year her folks were away on

a cruise, and she got to go to a women's seder. It was a little too verbal and too strident for her tastes, but she'd like to try more of that sort of thing, if it were conveniently available. She read part of *I and Thou* years ago and liked it, but most of her inspiring reading has been by Eastern authors or by Americans who have chosen an Eastern path. The fact is that she really doesn't read very much at all. Being of the video generation, she'd much rather watch tapes of lectures by the Dalai Lama, which she owns, than read his book . . .

The search for spirituality by Jews, mostly in their youth, since the 1960s has led many into eastern religions, especially Buddhism, but others have found a new form of spirituality within Judaism through 'Jewish renewal', an informal movement to capture the spirituality of Hasidism within a largely secular lifestyle, drawing on the writings of Martin Buber and Abraham Joshua Heschel for theological support but inspired by the infectiously melodic, hasidic-inspired music of Shlomo Carlebach and a general revival of interest in klezmer music, with its echoes of the east European *shtetls*.[1]

ALEPH, the 'Alliance for Jewish Renewal', was founded in 1962 by Arthur Green's former teacher, Zalman Schachter-Shalomi, who had been a Habad *hasid* (as had Shlomo Carlebach), with the aim of spreading spirituality to all Jews rather than becoming a new denomination alongside the others which have emerged in modern times. The movement encouraged a quest for *devekut*, 'attachment', or communion with God, as understood in Hasidism, through any spiritual means, from kabbalah and other Jewish resources in midrashic and hasidic traditions, to yoga, Buddhist and Sufi forms of prayer and meditation, using dance, music, storytelling and the visual arts. A distinctively North American phenomenon in origin, with a strong commitment to ecological and peace activism and to social justice, Jewish Renewal has also proved attractive to some secular Israelis seeking spiritual fulfilment without subjection to what they see as the alien world of the religious. The movement has also gained some following, but to a lesser extent, among Jews in South America and Europe.[2]

The search for spiritual experience and expression by young Jews in North America in recent decades reflects of course cultural trends in wider society (especially California), not least in reaction to the materialism of the older generation. Jewish Renewal, with its concentration on personal fulfilment and inspiration (as in Hasidism) by a charismatic leader, allows its followers to decide for themselves how much to pursue elsewhere traditional Jewish notions of community and Torah study. But in the 1960s some of those Jews seeking spiritual renewal in the United States began to meet in *havurot*, gatherings for religious fellowship loosely modelled on a largely imagined notion of such groups in Second Temple times among Pharisees and Essenes. Conceived as loci for worship and study separate from the formality of synagogue worship, *havurot* rapidly became popular in university cities as part of student counter-culture, with experiments in forms of worship and a strict lack of hierarchy, but by the 1980s many synagogue communities in the United States established *havurot* of their own to operate in conjunction with more organized worship.[3]

An important aspect of liberation in the *havurot* from the start was equality of the sexes within each group. Despite the theory within European Reform Judaism in the nineteenth century that Judaism should accentuate personal faith and ethics and that women are entitled to the same rights, and subject to the same religious duties, as men, in practice many Reform Jews were middle class and shared the notions of their Christian compatriots about female domesticity, which fitted well with the traditional role of Jewish women as guardians of the home. In the 1960s, what has become known as 'second-wave' feminism encouraged a great number of women to seek ordination within the Reform movement, in part as a symbol of the genuine commitment of the movement to egalitarianism. We have seen (Chapter 17) that the first woman to be ordained as a Reform rabbi in the United States was Sally Priesand in 1972. She was followed quite rapidly by Jackie Tabick in England in 1975. We have also seen (Chapter 18) that Reconstructionist congregations were quick to follow suit, and that this was the issue within the Conservative movement which led to the breakaway of Traditional Conservative Jews. About half of the students currently studying for ordination as non-orthodox rabbis are women.[4]

Women's ordination has brought far more than simply a widening of opportunities for religious authority. It has encouraged a proliferation of critical feminist scholarship of sacred texts including the Bible and Talmud, and the invention of new religious ceremonies and liturgies to mark events in women's lives, such as a prayer for healing after a miscarriage: 'What is my supplication? Stupid people and new mothers, leave me alone. Deliver me, Lord, of this bitter afterbirth. Open my heart to my husband–lover–friend that we may comfort each other. Open my womb that it may yet bear living fruit.' Most coordinated efforts to place feminist issues on the agenda of Jewish communities have been found in

North America, Israel and Great Britain, but those involved have not always sought the same results, as is evident from lively debate – about everything from feminist funerals to whether Jews should own Christmas trees – in the magazine *Lilith*, published since 1976 and proudly advertised as 'independent, Jewish and frankly feminist'.[5]

For some, what matters is access to all aspects of religious experience in Judaism open to men, as in the appreciation of ritual described by Susan Grossman when first putting on *tefillin* (phylacteries):

> I used to suffer from *tefillin*-phobia. It was an embarrassing condition, one I found difficult to explain to my friends or strangers. They saw me comfortably wrapped in my sky blue *tallit* [prayer shawl] and would ask, 'And do you wear *tefillin* too?' 'No,' I would answer, invariably shrugging my shoulders and looking down ... Everything felt strange and constricting until I began wrapping my fingers with the straps of the yad [the *tefillin* for the arm]. As I wound the straps around my second and ring fingers, I read from the prayer book this excerpt from the prophet Hosea: 'I will betroth you to Myself forever, I will betroth you to Myself in righteousness and in justice, in kindness and in mercy, I will betroth you to Myself in faithfulness and you shall know the Lord.'

In the modern orthodox community, which now includes many women with extensive Jewish learning, women have increasingly since the early 1970s set up their own groups for separate prayer, often meeting on Rosh Hodesh, the New Moon, following a rabbinic legend in *Pirkei de Rabbi Eliezer* that God made the New Moon a special day for women in reward for their refusal to join their husbands in building the golden calf when Moses was on Mount Sinai. It has become common for modern orthodox girls to spend a period studying Jewish texts at a seminary before entering a secular university. The notion that learned women in orthodox circles might be ordained as rabbis with religious authority over men has remained controversial, but Sara Hurwitz, who had served for some time in the orthodox community of the Hebrew Institute of Riverdale in New York as, in effect, assistant rabbi, was given a private ordination and the title *MaHaRat*, 'leader in halakhic, spiritual, and Torah issues'. The title was changed in 2010 to *Rabba* (a feminine form of 'rabbi'), despite opposition by others in the orthodox world. The ordination of women has become the main issue in contention between the 'open orthodoxy' advocated by Avi Weiss, the rabbi who ordained Sara Hurwitz, and more traditional orthodox Jews who prefer to brand the open orthodoxy movement as 'Neo-Conservative'.[6]

For other Jewish feminists, the emancipation of women within Judaism required a full re-evaluation, or even recreation, of the most basic concepts of Judaism. Judith Plaskow has argued for a transformation of Jewish notions of the nature of God, incorporating (or reintegrating) female aspects of the divine. She has urged an integration of women's history into the living memory of the Jewish people, insisting on the need to reflect the female experience in full, including female sexuality, almost totally ignored in traditional Judaism:

> In line with the fundamental feminist insight that sexuality is socially constructed, a Jewish feminist understanding of sexuality begins with the insistence that what goes on in the bedroom can never be isolated from the wider cultural context of which the bedroom is part ... Thus a Jewish feminist approach to sexuality must take sexual mutuality as a task for the whole of life and not just for Friday evening, fitting its commitment to sexual equality into its broader vision of a society based on mutuality and respect for difference.[7]

Parallel since the 1960s to the demand for recognition of the role of women within Judaism has been the demand of lesbians and gays (and bisexual and transgender people) for recognition within a religious system that has traditionally either ignored or condemned their existence. Within modern orthodoxy both the intuitive distaste reflected by Norman Lamm in 1974, who wrote that 'male homosexual acts are treated in the Bible as an "abomination" (Lev 18:22)' because they are *prima facie* disgusting', and the outrage expressed in Moshe Feinstein's claim in 1976 that 'all people, even the wicked, despise homosexuals, and even homosexual partners find each other despicable' have been tempered by the past fifty years of increasingly public acceptance of gay and lesbian relationships in the United States, much of Europe and parts of Israel, so that the standard claim of earlier generations that such sexuality was not to be found among Jews is no longer common. In 1999, Steven Greenberg became the first orthodox rabbi to declare openly that he is homosexual, publishing in 2004 an account of his long struggle to reconcile what he saw as two opposite sides of his identity, and attempting to reinterpret the relevant passages in scripture to allow for the possibility that homosexual love might be acceptable within the Jewish tradition. An implicit response to Greenberg in 2005, by a British Habad rabbi, Chaim Rapoport, eschewed the condemnation of previous generations, asserting the need for orthodox communities to welcome, understand and support gays and lesbians while continuing to insist on the inadmissibility of the sex acts themselves, and Yeshiva University hosted a forum on understanding and acceptance of orthodox homosexuals without any suggestion of condoning homosexuality on halakhic grounds.[8]

Within the Reform and Reconstructionist movements and other constituents of the World Union for Progressive Judaism, such as Liberal Jews in the United Kingdom, recognition of gays and lesbians as full members of the community has been naturally far more rapid and wholehearted. Following the partial decriminalization of male homosexual acts in private in the United Kingdom in 1967 and the era of militant gay liberation in the United States after the Stonewall riots in New York, the World Congress of Gay and Lesbian Jews was founded in 1972, with self-consciously gay and lesbian congregations established in metropolitan areas around the world – many to be attached in due course to the Reform or Reconstructionist movements. The Conservative movement characteristically weighed up the different sides of the argument with great care, as noted in a passage in the 'rabbinic letter' sent by Elliot Dorff to the Rabbinic Assembly in 1996 about the deliberations in 1991 and 1992 of the movement's Law Committee, which was charged with interpreting Jewish law and ethics for the movement as a whole:

> The Committee on Jewish Law and Standards passed four responsa on the issue of homosexual sex. Three rejected it either as a *toevah* (abomination) or as undermining family-centred Judaism or as requiring an impermissible uprooting of a law of the Torah. One maintained that homosexual sex should not be seen as a *toevah* and recommended a commission to study the entire issue of human sexuality. The Committee on Jewish Law and Standards determined that commitment ceremonies should not be performed and that sexually active homosexuals should not be admitted to the Movement's rabbinical and cantorial schools. The fourth responsum qualified both of these last provisions as subject to further research and possible revision. It was left to each synagogue rabbi to determine the extent to which homosexuals could be teachers or youth leaders within the congregation and the extent to which homosexuals would be eligible for positions of synagogue leadership and honors within prayer services.

Ten years after this letter, in 2006 the Conservative movement decided to open up most of their rabbinical training to openly gay and lesbian applicants. For lesbian rabbis like Rebecca Alpert, there has been a real 'transformation of tradition'. Lesbians are well aware that their new role is 'like bread on a seder plate', but the personal and religious dilemmas of the congregants of Beth Simchat Torah in New York, founded in

1973 in Greenwich Village and now the largest gay and lesbian synagogue in the United States, reveal how complicated it is to bring such a
congregation together, but also how synagogue practices have evolved
to reflect both Jewish and gay values, despite the great variety of types
of Judaism (and indeed gay identities) within its membership.[9]

The self-conscious assertion by those who describe themselves as
'queer Jews' of a right to innovate in order to give Judaism its place in
the modern western world does not go as far as those North American
Jews who, since the 1960s, have sought to create a Judaism without
God. Humanistic Jews, whose worldview is based on the autonomous
human rather than the divine, seek like other humanists to use reason as
the basis of ethics but also gather in communities to cultivate Jewish
languages, study Jewish culture and celebrate Jewish holidays and life-
cycle events, sometimes under the leadership of a guide or rabbi. The
International Institute for Secular Humanistic Judaism has provided
training since 1986, and a series of guides for appropriate ceremonies in
the liturgy were devised by Sherwin Wine, originally ordained as a Reform
rabbi but, from 1963, when the first Humanistic Judaism congregation
was founded in Michigan, dedicated to a Judaism without God:

> Humanistic Jews have two important identities. They are Jews, part of the
> Jewish people, members of an ancient kinship group, bound together by a
> social destiny with all other Jews. They are also connected to all other
> humanists whatever their kinship attachments and whatever their ethnic ori-
> gin. For some humanistic Jews, their Jewish identity is the strongest emotional
> bond. For other humanistic Jews, their intellectual and moral commitment to
> humanism is more powerful than their tie to their Jewishness. Both groups
> value their Jewish identity – but in varying degrees. Humanistic Judaism has
> room for both commitments. Humanistic Jews share a Jewish agenda with
> other Jews. Holidays, Israel, anti-Semitism, and the study of Jewish history
> are some of the items on this list of common activity.

Wine insisted that Humanistic Judaism is a positive creed:

> It is very important never to allow others to define you publicly in terms
> of their own attachments. *Humanists* not only *do not* believe in biblical
> creation; they *do* believe in evolution. They not only *do not* believe in the
> efficacy of prayer; they *do* believe in the power of human effort and
> responsibility. They not only *do not* believe in the reality of the supernatu-
> ral; they *do* believe in the natural origin of all experiences . . . Believers tell
> people *first* what they believe, not what they do not believe.

Wine's small congregation in Farmington Hills had originally been Reform in outlook, but as he developed language to reflect their beliefs, Wine came to the realization that the word 'God' could be eliminated from the liturgy, and he concluded (following the logical positivists) that, since it is impossible to prove the existence or non-existence of God, the concept is meaningless. In light of the intense hostility to such a stance from the wider public in the United States, and not just from other Jews, this stance took considerable courage, and only very few Jews have identified themselves with the Humanistic Judaism movement.[10]

The notion of a Humanistic Jew depends to a large extent on the dual origin of Jewish identity in descent as well as in religious affiliation. In the diaspora, a secular Jewish identity without institutional support has seemed to some too difficult to sustain. Agnostic Jews are often more comfortable remaining within religious communities and treating them as a focus of social life, since lack of belief generally goes unchallenged if not thrust on others, as in many parishes of the Church of England. In the mid-twentieth century the eminent Harvard historian of Jewish philosophy Harry A. Wolfson wrote scornfully about 'verbal theists' who would disguise their lack of belief for social and political reasons. A younger contemporary of Wolfson, the socialist Zionist Ben Halpern, accused American Jews of retreating into the bastion of synagogues as a way to make their Jewishness more acceptable to wider American society by treating Jewish identity as if it was only a matter of private religious faith.

In Israel, by contrast, where Jewish identity is stamped on identity cards, secular Jews have been much preoccupied in a battle against religious coercion, and the movement for secular humanistic Judaism has had as a prime aim the encouragement of pluralism, and of dialogue between the secular and the orthodox, within Israeli society. Within the same movement Yaakov Malkin, a professor of aesthetics and rhetoric in Tel Aviv, has promoted the study of Judaism as a secular culture in numerous institutions. Some (such as Alma College in Tel Aviv) have been dedicated specifically to this purpose. In 1988 Malkin produced a credo of the beliefs of secular Jews, characterized by him as 'free':

> What do secular Jews believe? Free Jews – that is, Jews free from the dominion of Halachic religion, free from an exclusive religious interpretation of *mitzvot*, from a religious interpretation of Jewish celebration, traditions and culture, Jews free from one inflexible view of the Bible and post-biblical literature – such Jews believe in: The freedom to choose the ways of realizing

one's Jewishness . . . Free Jews believe in God as the hero of their central book and of other classic works of Jewish literature . . . Free Jews believe in the Bible as a literary and historical anthology . . . Free Jews believe in humanism and democracy as essential to Judaism . . . Free Jews believe in pluralism as fundamental to Jewish identity and culture throughout its history . . . Free Jews believe in openness to other cultures . . . Free Jews believe in holiday celebrations as expressions of unique family and community values . . . Free Jews believe in the uniqueness of the Jews as a nation . . . Free Jews believe that Judaism is part of world culture . . . Free Jews believe in Jewish education as the vanguard of the socialization of all Jewish women and men, of all ages.[11]

PART VI

Epilogue

Waiting for the Messiah?

Until the second half of the twentieth century, the response by European and American Jews to the Enlightenment and more recent developments within western society passed by unnoticed among Jews of North African or Middle Eastern Sephardi background. Most Jews in these regions remained blissfully unaware of the contradictory movements which had emerged from the moral agonizing of German Jews in the first half of the nineteenth century. For these Jews, religion was traditional and unproblematic. Nor, for the most part, did European Jews attempt to disturb their equilibrium. So, for instance, the 'cultural and moral elevation' through which the Alliance Israélite Universelle, founded in 1860, aimed from its headquarters in Paris to improve the social and legal status of the Jews in these regions meant essentially indoctrination not in any particular form of Judaism but in French culture, and the decision of many francophone North African Jews to chose France as their place of refuge rather than Israel in the 1950s was more cultural than religious.

These traditional communities were accustomed to tolerating a wide span of religious observance and took the strains of modernization in their stride. If anything, they saw as a greater threat to their Jewish identity in European society the possibility of Ashkenazi homogenization, leading in reaction to a particular pride in specifically local customs. Hence, for example, the enthusiasm with which the family and community picnics of the Mimouna festival are celebrated on the day after Pesach by Jews of North African origin. The origins and significance of the festival are unknown, and it is popular just because it is distinctive (and enjoyable). Hence even the much assimilated Moroccan Jewish community of Paris has begun to celebrate the Mimouna in recent years.[1]

The Mimouna is also widely observed in Israel under the influence of over a million Israelis of Moroccan origin. But, apart from Moroccans, the State of Israel has also absorbed since 1948 the Jews of Yemen and a mass of Jews from the former Soviet Union, along with many smaller groups with distinctive customs, from the Aramaic-speaking Jewish villagers of Kurdistan to the Bene Israel from the region around Bombay and the Cochin Jews from the Malabar coast in the south of India and Jews from Ethiopia, Iraq, Persia, Libya and elsewhere.

It is salutary to be reminded that the Yemenite Jews, who numbered around 70,000 at the start of the twentieth century but had all migrated to Israel by the 1950s, were hardly affected by any modernizing trends in Europe and North America in the nineteenth and twentieth centuries – just as the messianic movements in Yemen of the nineteenth century (such as that centred in 1862–4 on a certain Judah b. Shalom, who was followed also by some local Zaydi Muslims) had little effect on the Jewish world outside. In the early twentieth century Yihye b. Solomon Kafah, widely acknowledged as the pre-eminent authority within Yemenite Jewry, tried to introduce reforms into the education of the community by setting up a school in 1910 in Sana to encourage Talmud study and enlightenment on the model of the Haskalah in Europe over a century earlier, but he provoked a storm of opposition, especially when he questioned the authorship of the Zohar by Shimon bar Yohai. The community, constituted mostly of poor pedlars and artisans at the bottom of the social pyramid in Yemeni society, had few rights; as late as the 1920s, the state required any Jewish child orphaned as a minor to convert to Islam. About a third of the population emigrated to Israel between 1919 and 1948, with a further 48,000 airlifted there between June 1949 and September 1950. For most Yemenite Jews, their response to the modern world was thus mixed up with a response to immigration to a new society in Israel.[2]

Many traditional rites of these oriental communities have survived transplantation to Israel despite the erosion of their distinctive languages as younger generations adopt Hebrew, and many oriental (*mizrahi*) Jews in Israel maintain a religious lifestyle even if they do not think of themselves as religious. Of the Israelis who define themselves as *shomrei masoret* ('upholders of tradition') rather than as secular or religious, the majority are of oriental origin. Since between a quarter and a half of Israelis assign themselves to this category, it constitutes a significant trend in Israeli society. But within the *haredi* community the self-confident rhetoric of Ashkenazi yeshivah culture has tended to dominate even communities of North African and Iraqi origin. Many Sephardi *haredim* in Israel choose to study in Ashkenazi yeshivot. Even Ovadia Yosef, the former Sephardi chief rabbi of Israel who founded in the 1980s what was to become Shas, a powerful force in Israel's politics established to combat discrimination against non-Ashkenazim and to bolster among Sephardim a sense of pride in their identity, was closely linked politically to the aged Lithuanian rabbi Elazar Shach, who dominated the world of non-hasidic Ashkenazi *haredim* in Israel for the last quarter of the twentieth century. On the other hand, the reputation of Sephardi kabbalists like the Moroccan rabbi Israel Abuhatzeira, known as Baba Sali, who was famed as a miracle-worker through the power of prayer, was recognized also in the Ashkenazi world. The Baba Sali died in 1984, and his tomb in Netivot, a small town close to Gaza, has become a place of pilgrimage.[3]

There is less pressure to conform outside Israel, where Jewish identity of any kind is largely a matter of self-definition, and the grounds for self-definition as a Jew vary greatly, with different degrees of acceptance within the wider Jewish world. It remains the case that most Jews consider themselves Jewish because at least one of their parents was Jewish, but the patrilineal inheritance of, for instance, many of the emigrants from the former Soviet Union who have established sizeable Jewish communities in Germany and Israel is not recognized within orthodox circles.

The inherited Jewish customs of the Ethiopian Beta Israel (see Chapter 9) proved sufficient evidence of Jewish identity for the State of Israel to treat them as Jews and to encourage the migration of much of their community to Israel in the 1990s, but the orthodox rabbinate remains suspicious of them. Claims to Jewishness by a variety of other groups with Judaizing customs in southern Africa, Latin America, India and Japan have been generally treated as exotic but irrelevant within the wider Jewish community. Such claims have proliferated with advances in genetics since the 1970s, with ethnic groups like the Lemba in Zimbabwe and South Africa welcoming DNA testing which suggests the origin of some of their male ancestors in the Middle East. The Lemba, who point to their observance of the Sabbath, male circumcision and food taboos as evidence of their inherited Jewish practices, have sometimes been identified as the lost tribes of Israel, as have the Bnei Menashe in north-east India.

Liberal Jews in the United States, eager to show their anti-racist credentials, have often welcomed such claims from a distance. They have been less welcoming of the claims by Christian groups of black African ancestry in the United States itself, like the Black Hebrew Israelites, to be the only authentic Israelites in contrast to the ethnic claims of ordinary Jews. Christian self-designation as the true Israel goes back, of course, to the early history of the parting of the ways between Judaism and Christianity (see Chapter 7), and a plethora of different black Israelite groups devoted to keeping Jewish practices, with distinctive doctrines and names such as 'Commandment Keepers', sprang up in big American cities in the twentieth century. Numerous members of one such community, the African Hebrew Israelites of Jerusalem, have settled in Israel where, after being denied an automatic right to Israeli citizenship as Jews, they have nonetheless been granted permanent residence and integrated to a considerable extent into Israeli society.

Israelis and most diaspora Jews have proved more suspicious of claims by ethnic Jews converted to Christianity that Jews who accept Jesus as Messiah are not abandoning Judaism but fulfilling it. 'Jews for Jesus', founded in 1973 with an energetic mission to the wider Jewish community, is the most prominent of numerous groups which have promoted Messianic Judaism to Jews since the 1960s. Messianic Jewish congregations have mushroomed in the early twenty-first century, especially in the United States and Israel. Messianic Jews characteristically observe the Sabbath on Saturdays and keep the main Jewish festivals. Many observe Jewish dietary laws – if not from conviction then as a form of outreach to other Jews. They refer to Jesus by his Hebrew name, 'Yeshua'.[4]

This missionary approach of Messianic Jews within the Jewish community is unusual; the only other contemporary Jews with equal missionary enthusiasm are the Lubavitch *hasidim* (see Chapter 19). For much of the time Jewish communities of different outlook operate separately from each other and their clashing criteria for Jewish identity can be ignored. Problems arise most often when it comes to marriage, when doubts about the status of one of the partners can preclude marriage according to orthodox Jewish law. The obstacle generally has nothing to do with the beliefs and practices of either party, although in principle all objections can be circumvented by the lengthy procedure of conversion under the auspices of an orthodox rabbinic court of any individual whose status is in doubt.

Within the orthodox world, even more recalcitrant a problem is the status of a *mamzer* (often roughly, but inaccurately, translated as 'bastard'), as Deuteronomy prohibits the offspring of an adulterous or incestuous union from marrying another Jew; the possibility of acquiring such a status has been greatly increased by the number of Jews remarrying after a civil divorce without undergoing a valid Jewish divorce through the provision of a *get*, a bill of divorce, from the husband to the wife. The problem has been exacerbated both by the disappearance of many in the Holocaust without record of their death and by the difficulty of forcing a recalcitrant husband by social pressure alone to give his wife a bill of divorce, leaving her a 'chained woman' unable to remarry within the orthodox community. The state of limbo in which such women are left is widely recognized as unjust, but solutions have proved hard to find within orthodox halakhic jurisprudence.[5]

Despite the kaleidoscopic variety we have seen within Judaism at all periods in its history, and the occasional bitterness of disputes over such practical issues and (more rarely) over dogma, toleration, albeit often grudging, has emerged as a consistent thread throughout this history. While the Second Temple stood, Jews of different philosophical schools and sects attended the Temple services together, and served as priests, despite intense disagreement about how the rituals should be carried out and about such basic issues of theological doctrine as life after death. Rabbinic literature is replete with stories of rabbis who agreed to disagree. Acceptance of local custom emerged early as a principle in rabbinic thought, and when whole communities were transplanted the right of each congregation to maintain its separate identity was universally recognized. At times, the intervention of secular states intent on imposition of uniformity imposed forbearance from above, but in the multicultural societies in which contemporary Jews now find themselves in Europe and (especially) North America, Jews themselves have sometimes welcomed variety as desirable in itself. The many voices within Judaism are seen by the orthodox theologian David Hartman, a passionate advocate of pluralism who came from New York but was an influential voice in modern orthodox circles in Jerusalem from the 1970s to his death in 2013, as a 'heart of many rooms'.[6]

The unpredictability of the changes within Judaism as a result of the Holocaust and the foundation of the State of Israel during the twentieth century urges caution in predictions about the twenty-first. There are plausible grounds to believe both that adherence to the religion will diminish and that it will grow. A decline in the authority of local religious leaders outside ultra-religious circles has been accompanied, in the age of the internet, by two competing trends. On the one hand, an authoritative view can now be obtained almost instantaneously on almost any topic from rabbinic teachers with access to exceptional halakhic knowledge stored in databases of rabbinic responsa. On the other hand, fora of like-minded Jews have begun to forge new forms of Judaism by cooperation in the democratic space of the worldwide web. Traditional orthodox Judaism in the diaspora, when it is based only on inherited habits and unencumbered either by personal piety or by theological certainties, may vanish in the face of secular temptations in those countries, like the United States, where Jews feel able to merge into the general culture without suffering discrimination, and the most powerful national identity to emerge from Israel over the next few generations may be aggressively secular and uninterested in any Jewish religious heritage. But balancing these demographic changes will be the extraordinary fecundity of *haredi* families determined to fulfil the divine will by adding to the congregation of Israel through breeding, and the high rate of retention within *haredi* communities of those who have known no other way to live their lives.

Even harder to estimate is the attraction of the *haredi* lifestyle for the secular and uncommitted, particularly among the young, who will join the growing ranks of *baalei teshuvah*, 'penitents'. The same search for individual spirituality, particularly since the 1970s, which has spawned renewal movements within Judaism in the United States, has led many Jews dissatisfied with the insufficient religiosity of their upbringing to 'return' to orthodox religious observance. The phenomenon clearly owes much to the encouragement of groups like Lubavitch, with their distinctive messianic zeal, and Aish haTorah ('Fire of the Torah'), which uses websites and a whole range of social media as well as campus chaplains to attract diaspora students at an impressionable age into an appreciation of their orthodox religious heritage. The message preached by Aish from its headquarters, an impressive yeshivah building close to the Western Wall of the Temple in the Old City in Jerusalem, is not sophisticated – its Discovery Seminar makes much of Bible codes reminiscent of the most fundamentalist of contemporary American Christians. The mixture of a New Age search for self-fulfilment and Lithuanian yeshivah traditions taught by its founder, the American rabbi Noah Weinberg (who died in 2009), might seem to categorize Aish as a renewal movement in itself, but that is not how the *baalei teshuvah* see themselves: on the contrary, their hope is to be accepted as full members of whichever orthodox congregation they happen to join. Their 'return' to tradition characteristically starts not with the revelations, miracles and dreams commonly reported by born-again Christians but, more prosaically, with a change in lifestyle and the adoption of practices which differentiate them from their past lives, most often becoming stricter in Sabbath observance and observance of the food laws. The resultant tension with friends and family may serve to validate the significance of their new commitment. Learning the Talmud, as a religious act in itself, becomes part of such observance from the start, despite the obvious difficulties of immersing a student in study of such a difficult text without extensive preparation in Hebrew and Aramaic and biblical studies from childhood. New yeshivot have been set up to cater to those who need to acquire these skills.[7]

The religion to which these Jews 'return' bears little resemblance to the religion ascribed to Moses in the Bible from which it purports to derive. Polygamy has disappeared, as has slavery. The regulations in Leviticus for dealing with mildew on the walls of houses and concerns about divination and soothsaying have long fallen into abeyance, as have the laws of the Jubilee that were devised to ensure social justice among the people of Israel. And just as the requirements of the Torah for relations between individuals have changed to reflect these new social realities, so too have the main ways that Moses is reported to have stipulated for worship of God, through incense, libations, meal offerings and animal sacrifices. None of this is a concern to the *baalei teshuvah* for whom authentic Judaism is located not in the desert of Sinai over 3,000 years ago or in the pilgrimage city of Jerusalem a thousand years later but in the yeshivot and *shtetls* of eastern Europe in the eighteenth and nineteenth centuries. For them, as for most religious Jews, a return to worship as stipulated in the Torah must await the messianic age, and even then its reintroduction will depend on the divine will.

But a few religious Zionist *haredim* are less patient and have begun to plan for the immediate rebuilding of the Temple on its original site, where the Dome of the Rock now stands. The Temple Institute in Jerusalem has been preparing the ritual items required for the Temple service, following closely the descriptions of these objects in the biblical sources as interpreted by rabbinic tradition. The breastplate and the rest of the special uniform of the High Priest, including his crown, are already complete, and much effort has been expended on developing building plans for the reconstruction of the building. Such plans are highly controversial within the *haredi* community, with most rabbis adamantly opposed even to setting foot on the Temple site in case of sacrilege. Up to now any practical plans to reinstate sacrificial worship have in any case been delayed by the inability of the Temple Institute to find a completely red heifer from whose ashes, as stipulated in the book of Numbers, must be derived the purification necessary to enter into the sanctuary (heifers identified as suitable in 1997 and 2002 proved to be insufficiently monochrome).[8]

These are unprecedented times for the Jewish people, with a revived state pulled in different directions by religious as well as political forces and a constant sense of potential catastrophe heightened by memories, still vivid, of the horrors of the Holocaust. Eschatological expectations flourish, even if they express themselves in very different ways. In 2004 a group of seventy-one rabbis made an attempt in a meeting in Tiberias to re-establish the Sanhedrin. The more that religious Zionist settlers come under pressure in the occupied territories, the more they are tempted to appeal not just to past divine promises but to future messianic hopes. Will this indeed be the future of Judaism? Will the violence which in recent decades has begun to characterize religious disputes between Jews, especially in the State of Israel, escalate, or will it subside as it has so often over the past 2,000 years into a grudging acceptance of difference? The historian Josephus, who reckoned he knew the future both as a prophet in his own right and through his readings of the book of Daniel, nonetheless baulked at explaining to his Greek and Roman readers the meaning of Daniel's vision of the four empires, noting that 'I have not thought it proper to relate this, since I am expected to write of what is past and done and not of what is to be . . .' Such reticence in predicting what will happen in the next century is surely wise.[9]

Notes

ABBREVIATIONS AND TRANSLITERATION

Abbreviations follow the conventions in S. Hornblower, A. Spawforth and E. Eidinow, eds., *The Oxford Classical Dictionary*, 4th edn (Oxford, 2012); D. N. Freedman, ed., *The Anchor Bible Dictionary* (New York, 1992), lii–lxxviii, for ancient texts not in *OCD*; H. Danby, *The Mishnah* (Oxford, 1933), 806, for tractates in the Mishnah and Tosefta; A. Berlin, ed., *The Oxford Dictionary of the Jewish Religion*, 2nd edn (New York, 2011), xvii–xviii, for other rabbinic texts; F. Garcia Martinez and E. J. C. Tigchelaar, eds., *The Dead Sea Scrolls Study Edition*, 2 vols. (Leiden, 1997), for Dead Sea scrolls.

Other abbreviations:

AJAJ	*American Jewish Archives Journal*
AJH	*American Jewish History*
AJS	Association for Jewish Studies
b.	ben ('son of')
b.	*Babylonian Talmud*
CP	*Classical Philology*
BAR	*Biblical Archaeology Review*
Heb.	Hebrew
HJS	*Hungarian-Jewish Studies*
HM	*History & Memory*
HTR	*Harvard Theological Review*
HUCA	*Hebrew Union College Annual*
JAS	*Judeo-Arabic Studies*
JBL	*Journal of Biblical Literature*
JJS	*Journal of Jewish Studies*
JJTP	*Journal of Jewish Thought and Philosophy*
JQR	*Jewish Quarterly Review*
JRS	*Journal of Roman Studies*
JSJ	*Journal for the Study of Judaism*
JSQ	*Jewish Studies Quarterly*
JSS	*Jewish Social Studies*

JThS	*Journal of Theological Studies*
KHŻ	*Kwartalnik Historii Żydów*
LBIYB	*Leo Baeck Institute Year Book*
m.	*Mishnah*
MJ	*Modern Judaism*
OH	*Orah Hayyim*
R.	Rabbi
RQ	*Renaissance Quarterly*
SCJ	*Studies in Contemporary Jewry*
Singer–Sacks	S. Singer and J. Sacks, *The Authorised Daily Prayer Book of the United Hebrew Congregations of the Commonwealth*, 4th edn (London, 2006)
SJ	*Studia Judaica*
t.	*Tosefta*
Tur.	*Arba'ah HaTurim*
y.	*Yerushalmi (Palestinian Talmud)*
Yad	*haYad haHazakah*
YD	*Yore De'ah*
ZPE	*Zeitschrift für Papyrologie und Epigraphik*

Quotations from the Hebrew Bible are taken from the New Revised Standard Version, with chapter and verse according to the English text. I have made much use of existing English versions of ancient sources and rabbinic texts when these are available. I have used in particular G. Vermes, *The Complete Dead Sea Scrolls in English* (London, 1997), retaining the use in these translations of { } to indicate text supplied from a different manuscript of the same document, [ ] for hypothetical reconstructions, and ( ) for glosses necessary for fluency (see ibid., p. 93). I have also adopted a number of the translations published in the Loeb Classical Library, especially the translations of Josephus by H. St J. Thackeray and L. H. Feldman, and the translation of the Mishnah in H. Danby, *The Mishnah* (Oxford, 1933). In many cases I have adapted these and other previous translations into more colloquial English.

Numerous systems are in common use for transliteration of Hebrew and other Semitic languages. When a standard English rendering of a name or technical term is in general use, I have adopted this for the sake of simplicity. In other cases, I have used the general transliteration rules in C. Roth, ed., *Encyclopaedia Judaica*, 16 vols. (Jerusalem, 1971), 1:90, except that the letter *het* is not marked with a dot and the letter *tzade* has been transliterated 'ts' to aid pronunciation.

INTRODUCTION: APPROACHING
THE HISTORY OF JUDAISM

1. Exod 19:1, 3-6, 16-19. **2.** Jos. *Ap.* 2.164-5 (theocracy); 2.169-71. **3.** Jos. *AJ* 1.16; *Ap.* 2.154; Hecataeus, ap. Diod. Sic. 40.3.3; Apollonius Molon, ap. Jos.

C. *Ap.* 2. 145; Quint. *Inst.* 3.7.21; Jos. *Ap.* 2.185, 188. **4.** Jos. *Ap.* 2.178, 179-81 (trans. Barclay). **5.** M. Goodman, *Mission and Conversion: Proselytising in the Religious History of the Roman Empire* (Oxford, 1994). **6.** Earlier histories of Judaism: I. Epstein, *Judaism: A Historical Presentation* (Harmondsworth, 1959); S. W. Baron, *A Social and Religious History of the Jews*, 2nd edn (New York, 1952–) (a multi-volume work never completed). **7.** M. L. Satlow, *Creating Judaism: History, Tradition, and Practice* (New York, 2006). **8.** On Phinehas, see Num 25:6-13; on toleration throughout the history of Judaism, see M. Goodman et al., *Toleration within Judaism* (Oxford and Portland, Oreg., 2013).

CHAPTER I: DESERTS, TRIBES AND EMPIRES

1. On Josephus' *Jewish Antiquities* as a whole, see L. H. Feldman in *Flavius Josephus: Translation and Commentary*, vol. 3: *Judaean Antiquities*, Books 1-4 (Leiden, 1999). **2.** On the life of Josephus, see T. Rajak, *Josephus: The Historian and his Society*, 2nd edn (London, 2002). **3.** Jos. *AJ* 1.18 (on Moses); on Abraham: Jos. *AJ* 1.140-53, 155-8, 256, 345. **4.** Jos. *AJ* 2.194-200. **5.** Jos. *AJ* 2. 201-2 (race of the Israelites), 195 (tribes), 210 (Amram); 4.326 (death of Moses); on the name 'Israel': *AJ* 3.133. **6.** Jos. *AJ* 5.125 (giants), 132 (voluptuousness), 348 (Samuel); 6.40 (appointing of king). **7.** On use of different names for Jews: Jos. *AJ* 6.26, 29; on Agag, *AJ* 6.137; on David, *AJ* 6.160. **8.** These elegies are presumably those in 2 Sam 1:19-27; for the narrative about David, see Jos. *AJ* 7. 6-7, 20, 53, 60, 65 (city of David), 68 (515 years). The two half-tribes are Ephraim and Manasseh (see above), so that the total number of the tribes of Israel is twelve (as always in the Bible). **9.** Jos. *AJ* 7.391-4. **10.** On Solomon, Jos. *AJ* 8.42 (wisdom), 55 (Tyrian archives), 211 (80 years); on Rehoboam, Jos. *AJ* 8.221-9, 251-3. **11.** On Shishak, Jos. *AJ* 8.254; on the siege of Samaria, *AJ* 9.277-82; on the Samaritans, *AJ* 9.288-91. **12.** Jos. *AJ* 10.108-44, 184. **13.** On the prophecy of Daniel: Jos. *AJ* 10.232, 243-4; on the fortress in Ecbatana, *AJ* 10. 264-5. **14.** Jos. *AJ* 11.3-5 (Cyrus), 19 (Cuthaeans), 26-7 (Cambyses), 58 (Zerubbabel and Darius). **15.** On the treatment of the last king of Jerusalem: Jos. *AJ* 10.299; on the new constitution: Jos. *AJ* 11.111; on the story of Esther: Jos. *AJ* 11.184-296. **16.** On Alexander: Jos. *AJ* 11.330-33; on the Samaritans: Jos. *AJ* 11.340, 344, 346. **17.** On Ptolemy: Jos. *AJ* 12.4, 7-9; on campaigns by the Seleucids: Jos. *AJ* 12.129-31. **18.** Jos. *AJ* 12.145-6. **19.** On the Hellenizers: Jos. *AJ* 12.240; on the motivation of Antiochus: Jos. *AJ* 12.248-9; on pagan altar and persecutions: Jos. *AJ* 12.253-5. **20.** On Pompey's campaign: Jos. *AJ* 14.63-4; on loss of freedom: Jos. *AJ* 14.77. **21.** On change in high priesthood: Jos. *AJ* 14.75; on accession of Herod: Jos. *AJ* 14.384, 388. **22.** Chronology of Esther story: Jos. *AJ* 11.184; golden-calf narrative: Exod 32:1-35. **23.** Jos. *Ap.* 1.60. **24.** On Solymi: Jos. *Ap.* 1.173-4. **25.** See P. R. Davies, *In Search of Ancient Israel* (London, 1992), on the invention of biblical history; on invented national histories in classical antiquity, see E. J. Bickerman, 'Origines Gentium', *CP* 47 (1952), 65-81. **26.** On the limits of biblical archaeology, see T. W. Davis,

Shifting Sands: The Rise and Fall of Biblical Archaeology (Oxford, 2004); H. G. M. Williamson, ed., *Understanding the History of Ancient Israel* (Oxford, 2007). **27.** On Megiddo, see G. I. Davies, *Megiddo* (Cambridge, 1986); on excavations south of the Temple Mount excavations, see E. Mazar, 'Did I Find King David's Palace?', *BAR* 32 (2006), 16-27, 70; on early Hebrew inscriptions, see G. I. Davies, *Ancient Hebrew Inscriptions*, 2 vols. (Cambridge, 1991-2004); on the campaigns of 701 BCE, see A. Kuhrt, 'Sennacherib's Siege of Jerusalem', in A. K. Bowman, H. M. Cotton, M. Goodman and S. Price, eds., *Representations of Empire: Rome and the Mediterranean World* (Oxford, 2002), 13-33. **28.** On the manipulation of this history by later generations, see M. Z. Brettler, *The Creation of History in Ancient Israel* (London, 1995), 20-47; on the coins, see Y. Meshorer, *A Treasury of Jewish Coins from the Persian Period to Bar Kokhba* (Jerusalem, 2001); on the Elephantine documents, see B. Porten et al., *The Elephantine Papyri in English: Three Millennia of Cross-Cultural Continuity and Change* (Leiden, 1996). **29.** For a concise account of this history, see A. Kuhrt, *The Ancient Near East c. 3000-330 BC*, 2 vols. (London, 1995) and G. Shipley, *The Greek World after Alexander, 323-30 BC* (London, 2000). **30.** On Mesopotamian creation myths, see W. G. Lambert, *Babylonian Creation Myths* (Winona Lake, Ind., 2013); on the partial Romanization of Herodian Jerusalem, see E. Netzer, *The Architecture of Herod, the Great Builder* (Tübingen, 2006). **31.** On the growth of the diaspora before 70 CE, see E. Gruen, *Diaspora: Jews amidst Greeks and Romans* (Cambridge, Mass., 2004); on Asinaeus and Anilaeus, see Jos. *AJ* 18. 314-70; on interventions on behalf of the political rights of diaspora communities, see M. Pucci ben Zeev, *Jewish Rights in the Roman World: The Greek and Roman Documents Quoted by Josephus Flavius* (Tübingen, 1998). **32.** On the variety of names in use, and their significance, see M. Goodman, 'Romans, Jews and Christians on the Names of the Jews', in D. C. Harlow et al., eds., *The 'Other' in Second Temple Judaism* (Grand Rapids, Mich., 2011), 391-401.

CHAPTER 2: THE FORMATION OF THE BIBLE

1. For an introduction to the Bible, see J. Barton, *What is the Bible?* (London, 1991). **2.** On the composition history of the biblical books, see J. A. Soggin, *Introduction to the Old Testament: From its Origins to the Closing of the Alexandrian Canon* (London, 1989). **3.** On redaction criticism in biblical studies, see J. Barton, *Reading the Old Testament: Method in Biblical Study* (London, 1996), 45-60; for a holistic reading of Isaiah, see E. W. Conrad, *Reading Isaiah* (Minneapolis, 1991); on the Qumran Isaiah scroll, see E. Ulrich and P. Flint, *Qumran Cave 1. II: The Isaiah Scrolls*, 2 vols. (Oxford, 2010). **4.** On Mesopotamian bureaucracies, see H. Crawford, *Sumer and the Sumerians* (Cambridge, 2004); on the flood story, see A. Dundes, ed., *The Flood Myth* (Berkeley, 1988); on Hammurabi, see D. Charpin, *Hammurabi of Babylon* (London, 2012). **5.** On hostility to Egypt, see Jer 46:25; for Judaism presented as a counter-religion, see J. Assmann, *Moses the Egyptian* (Cambridge, 1997), 23-54; for speculation on angels in the late biblical period as a reflection of Babylonian and Persian religious influences, see D. S. Russell, *The Method and Message of Jewish Apocalyptic* (Philadephia, 1964), 257-62; on Ecclesiastes: Eccl 1:2; M. Hengel, *Judaism and Hellenism*, 2 vols. (London, 1974), 1.115-28 (Greek influence); R. N. Whybray, *Ecclesiastes* (Sheffield, 1989), 15-30 (dating criteria). **6.** Jos. *Ap.* 1.39-40; on 'the law and the prophets' in the New Testament, see J. Barton, '"The Law and the Prophets": Who are the Prophets?', *Oudtestamentische Studien* 23 (1984), 15; on the Pentateuch at Qumran, see E. Tov, *Hebrew Bible, Greek Bible, and Qumran: Collected Essays* (Tübingen, 2008), 131; on Moses, see Num 12:7-8; Deut 34:10; Num 20:12; Exod 20:1; 34:1; Lev 4:1. **7.** Jos. *Ap.* 1:37-40. **8.** On the concept of canon, see J. Barton, *Oracles of God* (New York, 2007), 1-95. **9.** Jos. *BJ* 2.229-31 (scroll), 289-92 (Caesarea); Jos. *Vit.* 418 (gift); *m. Yad* 3:2; M. Goodman, 'Sacred Scripture and "Defiling the Hands"', in idem, *Judaism in the Roman World* (Leiden, 2007), 69-78; 2 Sam 6:7 (Uzzah); copying rules: *m. Meg.* 1:8; *m. Men.* 3:7; on the rules for the decorative flourishes (*tagin*), see *b. Men.* 29b; on the divine name in Qumran scrolls, see J. P. Siegel, 'The Employment of Paleo-Hebrew Characters for the Divine Names at Qumran in Light of Tannaitic Sources', *HUCA* 42 (1971), 159-72. **10.** On archetypes of texts kept in Jerusalem, see A. van der Kooij, 'Preservation and Promulgation: The Dead Sea Scrolls and the Textual History of the Hebrew Bible', in N. Dávid et al., eds., *The Hebrew Bible in Light of the Dead Sea Scrolls* (Göttingen, 2012), 29-40; on the biblical texts as found in Qumran, see E. Tov, 'The Biblical Texts from the Judaean Desert', in E. D. Herbert and E. Tov, eds., *The Bible as Book* (London, 2002), 139-66; on Ezra as scribe, see Ezra 7:6, 11, 12; on Qumran scribes, see Tov, *Hebrew Bible, Greek Bible, and Qumran*, 112-20; for a discussion of the available evidence for scribes, see C. Schams, *Jewish Scribes in the Second-Temple Period* (Sheffield, 1998); for everyday scribal practice, see H. M. Cotton and A. Yardeni, eds., *Aramaic, Hebrew and Greek Documentary Texts from Nahal Hever and Other Sites* (Oxford, 1997); on 'rendering the hands unclean', see *m. Yad* 3:5; on religious sculpture, see Cic. *Verr.* II.4.2. **11.** On the date of the latest part of the biblical book of Daniel, see L. L. Grabbe, *Judaism from Cyrus to Hadrian* (London, 1994), 226; on the variety of translators of the Septuagint, see J. M. Dines, *The Septuagint* (London, 2004), 13-24; for detailed discussion of the letter of Aristeas, see S. Honigman, *The Septuagint and Homeric Scholarship in Alexandria: A Study in the Narrative of the Letter of Aristeas* (London, 2003); on the Pharos festival, see Philo, *Vita Mos.* II.41; on the translation process, see Let. Aris. 302; Philo, *Vita Mos.* II.36-7. **12.** On the Septuagint as a Christian document, see M. Hengel, *The Septuagint as Christian Scripture: Its Prehistory and the Problem of its Canon* (London, 2002); on the Greek text of the minor prophets in Qumran, see E. Tov, R. A. Kraft and P. J. Parsons, *The Greek Minor Prophets Scroll from Nahal Hever: 8 Hev XII gr* (Oxford, 1990); K. H. Jobes and M. Silva, *Invitation to the Septuagint* (Grand Rapids, Mich., 2000), 171-3; on the Septuagint in the Babylonian Talmud, see *b. Meg.* 9a; on the uses of the *targumim*, see J. Bowker, *The Targums and Rabbinic Literature: An Introduction to Jewish Interpretations of Scripture* (Cambridge, 1969), 23-8; on the revisions of the Septuagint, see A. Salvesen and T. M. Law, eds., *Greek Scripture and the Rabbis* (Leuven, 2012). **13.** On Enoch, see Gen 5: 18-24; on 'Enochic Judaism', see G. Boccaccini, ed., *The Origins of Enochic Judaism* (Turin, 2002). **14.** Temple annals: 1 Kgs 6-8; court histories: 2 Sam 9-20; 1 Kgs 1-2; popular tales: 2 Sam 1-3; Song of Deborah (Judg 5); Amos 5:2; Eccl 1:2. **15.** Ecclesiasticus, Prologue; on Ben Sira in tannaitic texts, see S. Z. Leiman, *The Canonization of Hebrew Scripture: The Talmudic and Midrashic Evidence* (Louisville, Ky, 1976), 92-102; on Song of Songs and Ecclesiastes, see *m. Yad* 3:5; on Ruth and Esther, see *b. Meg.* 7a. **16.** M. Goodman, 'Introduction to the Apocrypha', in idem, ed., *The Apocrypha* (The Oxford Bible Commentary) (Oxford, 2012), 1-13.

CHAPTER 3: WORSHIP

1. Lev 1:3, 8-9. **2.** See Exod 25:1 to 27:21 for the full description of the Tabernacle; reason for the display in Exod 25:2, 8. **3.** On temples in Egypt, Mesopotamia and Canaan, see 'Temples and Sanctuaries', in D. N. Freedman (ed.), *Anchor Bible Dictionary*, 6 vols. (New York, 1992), 6:369-80. **4.** On temples in archaic Greece, see R. A. Tomlinson, *Greek Sanctuaries* (London, 1976); on Solomon's temple, see 1 Kgs 6:21-2, 11-13. **5.** Hag 1:2, 9-10; Ezek 47:1-10. **6.** Mic 6:8; Mal 1:8; Hos 9:1; Jer 7:18, 21-3; on prophets in the Temple, see A. Johnson, *The Cultic Prophet in Ancient Israel* (Cardiff, 1962); J. Barton, 'The Prophets and the Cult', in J. Day (ed.), *Temple and Worship in Biblical Israel* (London, 2005), 111-22; Ps 50:9, 12-13; 50:5; 50:14 (but see Barton, 'The Prophets and the Cult', 116-17). **7.** 1 Kgs 6-8. **8.** On Israelite shrines of the Iron Age period, see W. G. Dever, *Did God Have a Wife? Archaeology and Folk Religion in Ancient Israel* (Grand Rapids, Mich., 2005), 135-75. **9.** Plundering by Rehoboam (1 Kgs 14:25-6); Asa (1 Kgs 15:18-19); Hezekiah (2 Kgs 18:14-16); destruction by Babylonians: Jer 52:12; 2 Kgs 25:13, 16-17; on the ark story, see J. Day, 'Whatever Happened to the Ark of the Covenant?', in idem, *Temple and Worship*, 250-70; on Zerubbabel's Temple: Ezra 1:11; Zech 8:3; Let. Aris. 100-117; cf. C. T. R. Hayward, *The Jewish Temple: A Non-Biblical Sourcebook* (London, 1996). **10.** 1 Macc 1:41-61 (persecution); 4:38, 42-53 (rededication). **11.** See Jos. *AJ* 15.380 on Herod's motive; Jos. *BJ* 5.222 on the gold; on repairs: Jos. *AJ* 20.219; *BJ* 5.190. **12.** Jos. *AJ* 15.391-425; *BJ* 5.184-237; Mishnah *Kodashim, m. Midd.*; Num 28.11. **13.** Impressions of space: Hecataeus in Jos. *Ap.* 1.198; Philo, *Spec Leg* I.74-5, 156; golden chain: Jos. *AJ* 19.294; gilded gate: *m. Yom.* 3:10; tapestries: Jos. *BJ* 5.212-13; golden vine: Jos. *BJ* 5.210; Tac. *Hist.* 5.5; see Goodman, *Judaism in the Roman World* (Leiden, 2007), 49; intense light: Ps. Philo, *L.A.B* 26; Hayward, *Temple*, 15-16. **14.** Quiet: Let. Aris. 92-5; on Psalms in the Temple, see S. Mowinkel, *The Psalms in Israel's Worship*, 2 vols. (Grand Rapids, Mich., 2004); on Hannah, see 1 Sam 1:9-18; on public offerings: Lev 23:12-13, 17, 19. **15.** Exod 23:17; Deut 16:16; on private offerings, see E. P. Sanders, *Judaism: Practice and Belief, 63 BCE–66 CE* (London and Philadelphia, 1992), 112-16, 125-41; on the Passover, see J. B. Segal, *The*

Hebrew Passover from the Earliest Times to AD 70 (London, 1963); Sanders, *Judaism*, 132-8; on Pentecost: *m. Bikk.* 3:2-8. **16.** Deut 16:13, 14-15; *m. Sukk.* 1:1; *m. Taan.* 1:3. **17.** Goodman, 'The Pilgrimage Economy of Jerusalem in the Second Temple Period', in idem, *Judaism in the Roman World*, 59-67; Acts 2:5, 9-11; Philo, *Spec Leg* I.67-8, 69-70. **18.** *m. Sukk.* 5:4; 5:1. **19.** On second tithes, see Deut 14:22-7; Matt 21:12-13; S. Safrai, 'The Temple', in S. Safrai et al., eds., *The Jewish People in the First Century: Historical Geography, Political History, Social, Cultural and Religious Life and Institutions*, 2 vols. (Assen, 1974-6), 2.902-3. **20.** On international pilgrimage, see Goodman, 'Pilgrimage', in idem, *Judaism in the Roman World*, 63-4; on numbers in 65 CE, see Jos. *BJ* 6.420-27; on the first fruits procession, see *m. Bikk.* 3:2-8 (see above, note 15); opposition to the Water-Drawing: *m. Sukk.* 4:9; dancing by King David: 2 Sam 6:14-16; Elephantine papyri: B. Porten, *Archives from Elephantine: The Life of an Ancient Jewish Military Colony* (Berkeley, 1968), 128-33. **21.** Exod 28:1; Lev 21:18-20; on purity of lineage: Jos. *Ap.* 1.35; on prohibition of marriage of priest to a divorced woman, see B. A. Levine, *Leviticus* (Philadelphia, 1989), 143-4; on archives: Jos. *Ap.* 1:30-36. **22.** Sacrifices as 'God's food': Lev 21:6, 8, 17, 21, 22; offerings: Lev 1:2, 14-17; 1:9; 3:1-5; 7:11-15, 29-34. **23.** On the tribe of Levi: Deut 10:8; on Levites in the Second Temple period: L. L. Grabbe, *A History of Jews and Judaism in the Second Temple Period. I. Yehud: A History of the Persian Province of Judah* (London, 2004), 227-30; on *nethinim*, see Neh 3:26; on Levite clothing, Jos. *AJ* 20.216-18. **24.** On intimidation of poor priests: Jos. *AJ* 20.181; on Levites in the time of Nehemiah: Neh 10:37; on priests more generally: Jos. *Ap.* 2.187, 186; on identification of *tsara'at*: Lev 13-14; *m. Neg.*; the priestly blessing: Num 6:22-7. **25.** On the Day of Atonement ritual: Lev 16; *m. Yom.*; on the secular role of High Priests: J. VanderKam, *From Joshua to Caiaphas: High Priests after the Exile* (Minneapolis, 2004); on descent from Zadok: 2 Sam 8:15-18; 1 Kgs 1:38-9, 4:1-4; on Maccabean and later High Priests: Jos. *AJ* 15. 320-22; M. Goodman, *The Ruling Class of Judaea* (Cambridge, 1987), 41; idealized Temple: Ezek 44:15-31. **26.** Christians in Temple court: Acts 2:46-7; on Philo as a pilgrim, see Philo, *Prob* 2.64; A. Kerkeslager, 'Jewish Pilgrimage and Jewish Identity in Hellenistic and Early Roman Egypt', in D. Frankfurter (ed.), *Pilgrimage and Holy Space in Late Antique Egypt* (Leiden, 1998), 107; on tithes, see Sanders, *Judaism*, 146-56; *m. Shek.* 2.4; Exod 30:15; 4Q159, see J. M. Allegro, *Qumran Cave 4, I* (4Q158–4Q186) (Oxford, 1968); Cic. *Flac.* 28. **27.** Jos. *Ap.* 2.193; 1 Kgs 12:26-30; on the excavations at Dan, see Dever, *Did God Have a Wife?*, 139-51; on horned altars, see Dever, *Did God Have a Wife?*, 100, 119-21. **28.** 2 Macc 10:6-7; on 2 Maccabees and the Temple, see R. Doran, *Temple Propaganda: The Purpose and Character of 2 Maccabees* (Washington, DC, 1981); on origins of Hanukkah, see 2 Macc 1:9; on Leontopolis temple: Jos. *AJ* 13.63, 65, 66-7 (pagan site); 13.72 (smaller and poorer); cf. *BJ* 1.33; 7.427; on ancient prophecy, see Isa 19:19, cf. Jos. *AJ* 13.64; *BJ* 7.432; single shrine: Jos. *AJ* 13.65-7; rival to Jerusalem: Jos. *BJ* 7.431; on period of operation, Jos. *BJ* 7.436 refers to 343 years, but this seems to be an error; on closure: Jos. *BJ* 7.433-6; on offerings: *m. Men.* 13:10; search for covert references in G. Bohak, *Joseph and*

Aseneth and the Jewish Temple in Heliopolis (Atlanta, 1996). **29.** J. Macdonald, *Theology of the Samaritans* (London, 1964), 15-21; 2 Kgs 17:24-8. **30.** Ezra 4: 4-5, 24; on the Delos inscriptions, see R. Pummer, *The Samaritans in Flavius Josephus* (Tübingen, 2009), 6, 16-17; M. Kartveit, *The Origin of the Samaritans* (Leiden, 2009), 216-25; comments by Josephus: Jos. *BJ* 1.63; cf. Jos. *AJ* 11.310-11 for the building of the temple, described in the same terms as that in Jerusalem; Jos. *AJ* 9.291; 12.257, 259-60; Mishnah on Samaritans: *m. Ber.* 7:1. **31.** Jos. *Ap.* 2.175, 178, 181. **32.** L. I. Levine, *The Ancient Synagogue: The First Thousand Years*, 2nd edn (New Haven, 2005), 398-404; Philo, *Leg.* 156; Acts 15:21. **33.** J.-B. Frey, ed., *Corpus Inscriptionum Judaicarum*, 2 vols. (Rome and New York, 1936–1975), vol. 2, no. 1404; Jos. *Ap.* 2.187-8; Neh 8:2-3, 8. **34.** On fixed order for reading: *m. Meg.* 3:4; *b. Meg.* 29b. **35.** Acts 13:15; Luke 4:16-21; *m. Meg.* 4:10; *m. Meg.* 1:1-2. **36.** *m. Meg.* 4:4; on the Aramaic translations, see M. Maher, trans., *The Aramaic Bible*, vol.1B. Targum Pseudo-Jonathan: Genesis (Edinburgh, 1992), 79-80. **37.** 1QpHab. 5:1-8. **38.** Jos. *AJ* 2.230-31; Ex. Rab. 1:26, trans. S. M. Lehrman (London, 1939); cf. G. Vermes, *Scripture and Tradition in Judaism*, 2nd edn (Leiden, 1973), 1-10, on the antiquity of many rabbinic exegetical motifs. **39.** On Jubilees, see J. C. VanderKam, *The Book of Jubilees* (Sheffield, 2001); on the Cushite woman: Num 12:1; on Moses as a general: Jos. *AJ* 2.243-53; Artapanus, ap. Eusebius, *Praep. evang.* 9.27; hermeneutical rules: Mechilta de Rabbi Ishmael, *Nezikin* 9 (trans. Alexander). **40.** Term *proseuche*: CIJ II 1440-44, 1449; Josephus in Tiberias: Jos. *Vit.* 276-9, 280, 290-303. **41.** Greek additions to Esther (NRSV Esther 14:3, 19); 4Q509, frag. 3, lines 7-8, in M. Baillet, *Qumrân Grotte 4, III* (4Q482–4Q520) (Oxford, 1982); cf. D. K. Falk, *Daily, Sabbath and Festival Prayers in the Dead Sea Scrolls* (Leiden, 1998); thanksgiving hymn: 1QH, col. 8, lines 16-17; mixed choir: Philo, *Vita Cont* 88. **42.** On the debate between E. Fleischer and S. Reif on whether the rabbinic liturgy started in 70 CE, see *Tarbiz* 59 (1990), 397-441; 60 (1991), 677-88 (Heb.); *m. Ber.* 1:4 on blessings; for Shema, see Deut 6:4-9; 11:13-21; Num 15:37-41 (cf. *m. Ber.* 2:2); on the Nash Papyrus, see M. Greenberg, 'Nash Papyrus', in M. Berenbaum and F. Skolnik, eds., *Encyclopaedia Judaica*, 2nd edn, 22 vols. (Detroit, 2007), 14:783-4; Ten Commandments in Temple: *m. Tam.* 5:1; prohibition of recitation of Ten Commandments: *b. Ber.* 12a; *Shemoneh Esreh*: *m. Ber.* 4:3; on the nineteenth blessing, now the twelfth in the current order, see below, Chapter 10. **43.** *m. Ber.* 5:3; posture for Shema: *m. Ber.* 1:3; Deut 6:7; *m. Ber.* 4:5; *m. Ber.* 5:1; prostration in prayer: *m. Yom.* 6:2; for discussion of postures adopted during prayer see U. Ehrlich, *The Non-Verbal Language of Prayer: A New Approach to Jewish Liturgy* (Tübingen, 2004). **44.** For synagogue inscriptions, see W. Horbury and D. Noy, *Jewish Inscriptions of Graeco-Roman Egypt* (Cambridge, 1992), nos. 22, 24, 25, 27, 117; G. Lüderitz and J. M. Reynolds, *Corpus jüdischer Zeugnisse aus der Cyrenaika* (Wiesbaden, 1983), no. 72; on Passover banquet: Philo, *Spec Leg* II.145, 148; on Seder service: Exod 12:29-39; B. Bokser, *The Origins of the Seder: The Passover Rite and Early Rabbinic Judaism* (Berkeley, 1984), 53-4; on Hanukkah, see 2 Macc 1:9 (above, n. 28); *m. B.K.* 6:6 (candles); *m. Meg.* 3:6 (reading). **45.** On traditional readings at variance with the manuscripts, see E. Tov, *Textual Criticism of the Hebrew Bible*, 3rd edn (Minneapolis, 2012), 54-9; Acts 18:1-17; D. Noy, *Jewish Inscriptions of Western Europe*, 2 vols. (Cambridge, 1993–5), vol. 2, nos. 117, 209, 540, 544, 558, 584; E. Schürer, rev. G. Vermes et al., *History of the Jewish People in the Age of Jesus Christ*, 3 vols. (Edinburgh, 1973-87), 2:434-46; 3:100-101; Jos. *Vit.* 277-98 (Tiberias); Mark 1:21-9; 3:1-7; Jos. *BJ* 2.285-90 (Caesarea). **46.** Philo, *Leg.* 134; Jos. *BJ* 7.45; Philo, *Quod Omn* 81 (Essenes); Jos. *BJ* 2.291 (Caesarea). **47.** For a different view, see D. D. Binder, *Into the Temple Courts: The Place of the Synagogues in the Second Temple Period* (Atlanta, 1999), 226, 336-41, and P. Flesher, 'Palestinian Synagogues before 70 C.E.: A Review of the Evidence', in D. Urman and P. V. M. Flesher (eds.), *Ancient Synagogues: Historical Analysis and Archaeological Discovery* (Leiden, 1995), 27-39.

CHAPTER 4: THE TORAH OF MOSES: JUDAISM IN THE BIBLE

1. Plutarch, *Quaest. conv.* 4.6.2; for the Jewish formula, see Exod 3:15-16. **2.** Gen 1:1; on biblical notions of God, see M. Mills, *Images of God in the Old Testament* (London, 1998); intangible and invisible: Exod 33:19-22; images: Ps 29:10; Gen 1:26-8; 5:1-3; 9:6; Deut 33:2; Ps 84:10-11. **3.** YHVH: 2 Kgs 8:27-9; *m. Yom.* 6.2 (only in Holy of Holies): E. Tov, *Scribal Practices and Approaches Reflected in the Texts Found in the Judean Desert* (Leiden, 2004), 218; origins: Exod 3:13-14; B. Porten, *Archives from Elephantine: The Life of an Ancient Jewish Military Colony* (Berkeley, 1968), 105-6; Gen 14:22. **4.** Exod 15:11; Judg 2:11-12 (following other gods); Isa 45:6; Deut 33:2; Josh 5:14-15; Satan: Zech 3:1-2; Job 2:6-7; Wisdom: Prov 8:22, 29-31. **5.** On relations to natural bodies: Ezek 8:16 (on sun worship in Jerusalem Temple); Job 9:7; Josh 10:12-13; 2 Kgs 20:11; Isa 40:22 ('like grasshoppers'); Exod 34:6-7 (proclamation of qualities). **6.** Ps 136 (kindness); warrior: Ps 74:14; Isa 42:13; on fear of the Lord: Prov 2:1-6; 9.10; 14:26-7; 15:33; 19:23. **7.** Exod 19:7-8; 32:1, 23; 35; Deut 30:16-19; for curses: Deut 28:20, with a full and chilling list in Deut 28:16-65; Deut 30:11-14. **8.** Ecstatic behaviour: 1 Sam 10:10; impelled to speak: Amos 3:8; Jer 20:7-9; visions: Ezek 1:1; Amos 8:1-3; Zech 1:7-13; eschaton: Joel 2:28 (Hebrew 3:1); Urim and Thummim: 1 Sam 23:10-11; Jos. *AJ* 3.218; *m. Sot.* 9:12. **9.** Exile as divine judgement: Lev 26:3-45; hardening of Pharaoh's heart: Exod 4:21; 7:1-5; 14:1-4; promise to Noah: Gen 9:8-16; Israel as light to the nations: Isa 42:6-7; last days: Isa 2:2-4; Zech 8:20-23; Nineveh: Jonah 3; Ruth 4:13-17; 1:16; Ezra on foreign wives: Ezra 10:2-14. **10.** Exod 20:12-17 (Ten Commandments); charity: Deut 15:11 (RSV); Isa 58:7; Lev 19:9-10; Deut 24:19; Ruth 2; Deut 24:17, 19-20, 22 (remembering slavery in Egypt). **11.** Exod 21:23-5; Deut 25:11-12; Deut 22:28-9; Lev 20:10; Deut 21:18-21; Exod 21:16; 22:1-4 (Hebrew 21:37–22:3); on biblical criminal law, see R. Westbrook and B. Wells, *Everyday Law in Biblical Israel: An Introduction* (Louisville, Ky, 2009); Lev 25:35-7 (no interest on loans); Deut 23:19-20 (loans to foreigners); Lev 25:9-10

(Jubilee). **12.** Marriage to brother's widow: Deut 25:5-6, 8-9 (ceremony for refusal); divorce: Deut 24:1; Num 5:14-31 (abridged), on the 'water of bitterness'; Gen 1:28 (procreation); slaves: Exod 21:20, 26-7; Deut 23:15-16; slaves on Sabbath: Exod 20:10; 23:12; Deut 5:14; slaves at Passover: Exod 12:44. **13.** Jos. *Ap.* 2.185 (Barclay); Elijah and Ahab (1 Kgs 18:18); holiness: Lev 19:2; first born: Exod 13:11-13; Deut 15:19-23 (animals); Num 18:15-18 (Israelites). **14.** Food laws: Lev 11:1-23; 17:10-14; 19:26 (avoidance of blood); emissions: Lev 12-15; on biblical notions of purity, see J. Klawans, *Impurity and Sin in Ancient Judaism* (New York, 2000), 20-42; menstruation: Lev 15:19-30; 18:19. **15.** Num 15:37-41 (fringes); prohibition on mix of wool and linen: Lev 19:19; Deut 22:11; prohibition on hairstyles and tattoos: Lev 19:27-8. **16.** Gen 17:9-12, 14; Lev 19:23-5 (trees). **17.** Lev 18:22-3; Gen 1:27-8; 38:9-10 (Onan). **18.** Doorposts: Deut 6:6, 9; R. de Vaux and J. T. Milik, *Qumrân Grotte 4, II* (Oxford, 1977), 80-85; Y. B. Cohn, *Tangled Up in Text: Tefillin and the Ancient World* (Providence, RI, 2008), 55-79, 93-8; Sabbath: Exod 16:23; 31: 12-17; 20:8-10. **19.** Lev 20:22, 23; 25:3-4 (land to rest); Gen 12:7 (land promised to Abraham); covenant with Abraham: Gen 15:1, 5, 7, 18. **20.** Holy land: Zech 2:12; Deut 11:12 (RSV); Gen 12:5 (Land of Canaan); boundaries of land: Gen 15:18; 2 Sam 24:2; Num 34:3-12. **21.** On languages: Gen 1:5, 8, 10 (Hebrew); Dan 2:4-7:28 (Aramaic); on the status of the Hebrew language in Second Temple Judaism, see S. Schwartz, 'Language, Power and Identity in Ancient Palestine', *Past and Present* 148 (1995), 3-47. **22.** Festivals: Lev 23:40; Deut 12:12; 16:11; Day of Atonement; Lev 23:26-8; Ezek 33:11 (atonement in general); Exod 34:7 (sins of the fathers); Dan 12:2 (punishment after death); Lev 16:21 (confession). **23.** Atonement rituals: Deut 21:1-8 (unresolved murder); individual repentance: Ps 130:3-4; Ps 51:17. **24.** Isa 2:3-4; Gen 9:10; Joel 1:2-12; 2:31-2. **25.** Ps 6:6 (Sheol); Jer 1:4.

CHAPTER 5: JEWS IN A GRAECO-ROMAN WORLD

1. 2 Macc 4:9. Contrasting explanations of the origins of the revolt of the Maccabees in V. A. Tcherikover, *Hellenistic Civilization and the Jews* (Philadelphia, 1959); E. Bickerman, *The God of the Maccabees: Studies on the Meaning and Origin of the Maccabean Revolt* (Leiden, 1979); D. Gera, *Judaea and Mediterranean Politics, 219-161 BCE* (Leiden, 1998). **2.** 2 Macc 4:24. **3.** 1 Macc 1: 20-23. **4.** 2 Macc 5:15; Dan 11:29-31. **5.** 1 Macc 1:41-3; Jos. *AJ* 12.257-64 (Samaritans). **6.** 2 Macc 6:7, 10. **7.** 1 Macc 2:44. **8.** 1 Macc 4:52, 56, 59. **9.** Discussion of these political issues in J. Sievers, *The Hasmoneans and their Supporters: From Mattathias to the Death of John Hyrcanus I* (Atlanta, 1990). **10.** Hints: Jos. *AJ* 12.414, 434; explicit statement: Jos. *AJ* 20.237. **11.** 1 Macc 10: 18-21 (letter); 1 Macc 14:28 (assembly); declaration: 1 Macc 14:35, 41; tablets: 1 Macc 14:48-9. **12.** Jos. *AJ* 13.257-8 (Idumaeans). **13.** On the coins of John Hyrcanus, see Y. Meshorer, *A Treasury of Jewish Coins* (Jerusalem, 2001); Aristobulus: Jos. *AJ* 13.301; Ituraeans: Jos. *AJ* 13.319 (citing Strabo); appointment of Alexander Jannaeus: Jos. *AJ* 13.320.   **14.** On Alexandra Jannaea, see T. Ilan, *Jewish Women in Greco-Roman Palestine* (Peabody, Mass., 1995); eadem, *Silencing the Queen: The Literary Histories of Shelamzion and Other Jewish Women* (Tübingen, 2006); on relation to Pharisees and selection of Hyrcanus, see Jos. *AJ* 13.408.   **15.** 'Philhellene': Jos. *AJ* 13.318; Philo the epic poet in Eusebius, *Praep. evang.* 9.20, 24, 37; Ezekiel the Tragedian in H. Jacobson, *The Exagoge of Ezekiel* (Cambridge, 1983).   **16.** On Eupolemus, see B. Z. Wacholder, *Eupolemus: A Study of Judaeo-Greek Literature* (Cincinnati, 1974); 1 Macc 8:17-32; on Justus: Jos. *Vit.* 40.   **17.** On Jewish Greek literature in general, see M. Goodman, 'Jewish Literature Composed in Greek', in E. Schürer, rev. G. Vermes et al., *The History of the Jewish People in the Age of Jesus Christ*, 3 vols. (Edinburgh, 1973-87), 3:470-704; on notions about wisdom in Qumran in relation to Hellenistic conceptions of the sage, see H. Najman et al., *Tracing Sapiential Traditions in Ancient Judaism* (Leiden, 2016).   **18.** Jos. *AJ* 14.66.   **19.** Jos. *AJ* 14.34-6, 41, 65-7.   **20.** For a detailed narrative of ensuing events, see Schürer, *History*, vol. 1.   **21.** Jos. *AJ* 14.403. On the conversion of the Idumaeans in the time of John Hyrcanus, see note 12 above.   **22.** On 'the day of Herod', see Persius, *Sat.* 5.180; on Herod's rule in general, see P. Richardson, *Herod: King of the Jews and Friend of the Romans* (Columbus, SC, 1996).   **23.** A fuller account of Jewish history in this period in M. Goodman, *Rome and Jerusalem: The Clash of Ancient Civilizations* (London, 2007).   **24.** On Agrippa I, see D. R. Schwartz, *Agrippa I: The Last King of Judaea* (Tübingen, 1990); on Agrippa II, see M. Goodman, 'The Shaping of Memory: Josephus on Agrippa II in Jerusalem', in G. J. Brooke and R. Smithuis, eds., *Jewish Education from Antiquity to the Middle Ages* (Leiden, 2017), 85-94.   **25.** M. Goodman, 'Coinage and Identity: The Jewish Evidence', in C. Howgego, V. Heuchert and A. Burnett, eds., *Coinage and Identity in the Roman Provinces* (Oxford, 2005), 163-6.   **26.** Jos. *BJ* 4.155-7 (trans. Hammond).   **27.** For Josephus on governors, see Jos. *BJ* 2.266-79; for causes of the revolt in general, see M. Goodman, *The Ruling Class of Judaea* (Cambridge, 1987).   **28.** On the Fourth Philosophy, see Jos. *AJ.* 18.11, 23 (and below, Chapter 6); on the messianic oracle, see Jos. *BJ* 6.312 (and below, Chapter 8); on Simon son of Gioras, see Jos. *BJ* 7.29.   **29.** On defeat of Cestius Gallus, see Jos. *BJ* 2.499; for detailed accounts of the revolt, see J. Price, *Jerusalem under Siege: The Collapse of the Jewish State, 66-70 C.E.* (Leiden, 1992); S. Mason, *A History of the Jewish War: AD 66-74* (Cambridge, 2016).   **30.** On Titus' reluctance to destroy the Temple, see Jos. *BJ* 6.236-43, 256.   **31.** On the expectation that a High Priest should consult a *synhedrion*, see Jos. *AJ* 20.197-203; on the trial of Paul, see Acts 23:1-9.   **32.** On Claudius' edict, see Jos. *AJ* 19.288; for Philo's embassy, see Philo, *Gaium*.   **33.** On crowd problems at festivals, see Jos. *BJ* 6.422; on 66 CE, see Jos. *BJ* 2.449-50.   **34.** On 'peace and prosperity' in 62 CE, see Jos. *BJ* 6.300.

CHAPTER 6: 'JEWISH DOCTRINE TAKES THREE FORMS'

1. Jos. *BJ* 2.119; Jos. *AJ* 18.9, 23 (Fourth Philosophy); Jos. *AJ* 18.11 (antiquity); comparison to Greek philosophies: Jos. *Vit.* 12 (Stoics); Jos. *AJ* 15.371 (Pythagoraeans); A. I. Baumgarten, *The Flourishing of Jewish Sects in the Maccabean Era: An Interpretation* (London, 1997). **2.** For perceptions of Jews by pagans, see M. Stern, *Greek and Latin Authors on Jews and Judaism*, 3 vols. (Jerusalem, 1974-86); on common Judaism as sufficient for most Jews, see E. P. Sanders, *Judaism: Practice and Belief, 63 BCE–66 CE* (London and Philadelphia, 1992). **3.** On Josephus' spiritual odyssey, see Jos. *Vit.* 10; on Pharisees and proselytes, see Matt 23:15; on Jewish mission more generally, see M. Goodman, *Mission and Conversion* (Oxford, 1994); on Jewish population and Bar Hebraeus, see B. McGing, 'Population and Proselytism: How Many Jews Were There in the Ancient World?', in J. R. Bartlett, ed., *Jews in the Hellenistic and Roman Cities* (London, 2002), 88-106; for the story of the conversion of the royal family of Adiabene, see Jos. *AJ* 20.17-96; on famine relief: Jos. *AJ* 20.49, 51, 101; in Mishnah: *m. Yom.* 3:10. **4.** On *Seder Olam*, see Ch. Milikowsky, 'Seder Olam', in S. Safrai et al., eds., *The Literature of the Sages*, 2 parts (Assen, 1987-2006), 2: 231-7; on *Megillat Ta'anit*, see V. Noam, 'Megillat Taanit: The Scroll of Fasting', ibid., 339-62; *m. Ab.* 1:2-12. **5.** Matt 23:13, 16, 17, 33 (woes); 23:2, 27 (tombs); E. B. Pusey, *Our Pharisaism: A Sermon* (London, 1868). **6.** Jos. *Vit.* 9-12 (Josephus); Paul: Phil 3:5, 8; Acts 22:3; 5:34; 26:4-5; 23:6. **7.** A. I. Baumgarten, 'The Name of the Pharisees', *JBL* 102 (1983), 411-28; on the meaning of *perushim*, see D. Flusser, *Judaism of the Second Temple Period*, 2 vols. (Grand Rapids, Mich., 2007), 1:97-8; J. Bowker, *Jesus and the Pharisees* (Cambridge, 1973). **8.** Gal 1:13 (Paul's earlier life in Judaism); Phil 3:6 ('blameless'); Jos. *Vit.* 12 (Stoicism); on Nicolaus, see D. R. Schwartz, 'Josephus and Nicolaus on the Pharisees', *JSJ* 14 (1983), 157-71. **9.** Jos. *BJ* 2.163; *AJ* 18.14; *BJ* 2.162 ('accuracy'); *Vit.* 191 (Simon son of Gamaliel); Acts 22:3 (Paul). **10.** Matt 23:25 (purity); Jos. *BJ* 2.123, 129 (Essenes on purity); Matt 22:23 (tithing); Mark 2:23-4, 27 (Sabbath); Jos. *BJ* 2.147 (Essene Sabbath); *m. Yad* 4:6-7. **11.** Oaths: Matt 23:16-22; Jos. *AJ* 17.41-2; influence: Jos. *AJ* 18.15; *AJ* 13.298 (contrast to Sadducees); 17.42 (6,000); 17.41 (women of Herod's court); 18.12 (avoidance of luxury); Matt 23: 6-7 (self-promotion). **12.** Jos. *AJ* 13.297; Mark 7:5 (cf. also Matt 15:2); Hippolytus, *Haer.* 9.28.3; cf. A. I. Baumgarten, 'The Pharisaic Paradosis', *HTR* 80 (1987), 63-77; Jos. *AJ* 13.297 (traditions not written down); Philo, *Spec Leg* IV. 149-50. **13.** M. Goodman, 'A Note on Josephus, the Pharisees and Ancestral Tradition', in idem, *Judaism in the Roman World* (Leiden, 2007), 117-21. **14.** Jos. *BJ* 2.166; *AJ* 18.12, 15 (influence); Matt 23:5; controversies with Sadducees: Jos. *AJ* 13.298; *m. Yad* 4:7. **15.** Matt 23:3 (objection to practice, not doctrine); Mark 7:9-13 (on *korban*). **16.** Gamaliel: Acts 22:3; 5:33, 35-40; *m. Gitt.* 4:2 (divorce); *m. R.Sh.* 2:5 (Sabbath walk); *m. Sot.* 9:15; Simon son of Gamaliel: Jos. *Vit.* 191; *m. Ker.* 1:7. **17.** *m. Yad* 4:6 (Yohanan ben Zakkai); Alexander Jannaeus: E. Schürer, rev. G. Vermes et al., *The History of the Jewish*

People in the Age of Jesus Christ, 3 vols. (Edinburgh, 1973–86), 1:222-4; *b. Ber.* 48a. **18.** J. M. Lieu, 'Epiphanius on the Scribes and Pharisees', *JThS* 39 (1988), 509-24. **19.** Josephus on Sadducees: Jos. *BJ* 2.166; *AJ* 18.17; 20.199; 13.298; for the standard picture of the Sadducees, see Schürer, *History*, 2:404-14; revisionist view in M. Goodman, 'The Place of the Sadducees in First-Century Judaism', in idem, *Judaism in the Roman World*, 123-35. **20.** On the name 'Sadducee', see Goodman, 'The Place of the Sadducees', 125-6; earlier reference: Jos. *AJ* 13.171. **21.** Ananus: Jos. *BJ* 2.197; *AJ* 20.197-203. **22.** Jos. *Vit.* 10 (Josephus as Sadducee); Jos. *AJ* 13.291-6 (John Hyrcanus); Ananus: Jos. *BJ* 2.562-3 (in 66); Jos. *BJ* 4.319-21 (eulogy after death). **23.** Life after death and angels: Acts 23:8; Jos. *BJ* 2.165; Acts 23:8 may refer only to angels in the resurrection, cf. D. Daube, 'On Acts 23: Sadducees and Angels', *JBL* 109 (1990), 493-7; unbroken stream of liquid: *m. Yad* 4:7; red heifer: *m. Par.* 3:7. **24.** Jos. *AJ* 13.292 (written regulations only); *omer*: Lev 23:15-16; *m. Men.* 10:3 (on Boethusians). **25.** J. Barr, *Fundamentalism*, 2nd edn (London, 1981). **26.** Jos. *BJ* 2.165. **27.** Jos. *AJ* 13.173 (Sadducees); Jos. *AJ* 10.277-8 (Epicureans). **28.** Jos. *AJ* 13.298 (no following); Jos. *AJ* 18.17 (nothing achieved). **29.** Jos. *AJ* 18.17; *AJ* 13.298; Rabban Gamaliel: *m. Erub.* 6:7; Simon b. Gamaliel and Ananus: Jos. *Vit.* 193. **30.** Sadducees as disputatious: Jos. *AJ* 18.16; *BJ* 2.166; political group: *BJ* 1.288-98; Boethus: *AJ* 15.320-22; on Sadducees and priests, see J. Le Moyne, *Les Sadducéens* (Paris, 1972); Acts 4:1; 5:17. **31.** M. Goodman, 'Sadducees and Essenes after 70', in idem, *Judaism in the Roman World*, 153-62. **32.** Philo, *Quod Omn* 88, 81; Jos. *AJ* 15.371-9 (Pythagoreans); Pliny *HN* 5.73.2; Synesius, *Dio* 3.2. **33.** Philo, *Quod Omn* 82; Jos. *BJ* 1.78; *AJ* 13.311; Hegesippus, ap. Eusebius, *Hist. eccl.* 4.22.7; Philo, *Quod Omn* 75 (related to *hosiotes*); Philo, *Quod Omn* 91 (gloss of *hosioi*); Semitic etymologies: G. Vermes, 'The Etymology of "Essenes"', *RQ* 2 (1960), 427-43. **34.** Philo, *Hypo* 12; *Quod Omn* 79; Jos. *AJ* 18.21. **35.** Philo, *Quod Omn* 75; Jos. *AJ* 18.20. **36.** Jos. *AJ* 15.371 (reference to the description in the *Jewish War*); Jos. *BJ* 2.119-22, 124-7 (trans. Mason). **37.** Jos. *BJ* 2.128-33; 137-9; 141;145-6;143-4 (trans. Mason). **38.** Jos. *BJ* 2.128; 136; 147; 123 (avoidance of oil); 159 (toilet habits). **39.** Judas the Essene: Jos. *BJ* 1.78; *AJ* 13.311-15; Manaemus: Jos. *AJ* 15.373-9. **40.** Jos. *BJ* 2.160; Philo, *Hypo* 14-17; Pliny, *HN* 5.73. **41.** Philo, *Quod Omn* 82; immortality of soul: Jos. *BJ* 2.154-5, 156-8; fate: Jos. *AJ* 13.172; 18.18. **42.** Four thousand: Philo, *Quod Omn* 75; Jos. *AJ* 18.20; Dead Sea community: Pliny, *HN* 5.70; Dio, ap. Synesius, *Dio* 3.2; widespread: Philo, *Hypo* 1; Philo, *Quod Omn* 76; Jos. *BJ* 2.124, 125 (journeys); 5.145 (gate of the Essenes). **43.** On Essenes and Temple, compare the Greek and Latin versions of Jos. *AJ* 18.19, with discussion in J. M. Baumgarten, 'The Essenes and the Temple', in idem, *Studies in Qumran Law* (Leiden, 1977), 57-74; A. I. Baumgarten, 'Josephus on Essene Sacrifice', *JJS* 45 (1994), 169-83; Philo on Essenes and sacrifice: Philo, *Quod Omn* 75, with discussion in J. E. Taylor, *The Essenes, the Scrolls and the Dead Sea* (Oxford, 2015), 30. **44.** Philo, *Vita Cont* 2. 22-4, 27-8, 29. **45.** Philo, *Vita Cont* 35 ('live upon air'); 37 (diet); 65 (Shavuot); 66 (hands outstretched); 75 (banquet); 78 (allegories); 83-5, 88-9 (hymns). **46.** Jos. *BJ* 2.161 (Essene women); Philo on women generally: Philo, *Hypo* 14; women among

Therapeutae: *Vita Cont* 32-3; 68; cf. J. E. Taylor, *Jewish Women Philosophers of First-Century Alexandria: Philo's 'Therapeutae' Reconsidered* (Oxford, 2006). **47.** Philo, *Vita Cont* 21; John the Essene: Jos. *BJ* 2.567; 3.11, 19; Essenes and martyrdom: Jos. *BJ* 2.151-3. **48.** Pliny, *HN* 5.73; Philo, *Hypo* 3; Jos. *BJ* 2.120, 160; on Essenes after 70 CE, see Chapter 9. **49.** Origins of Essenes: Jos. *AJ* 13.171; Pliny, *HN* 5.73; origins of Fourth Philosophy: Jos. *BJ* 2.118; Jos. *AJ* 18.9. **50.** Jos. *AJ* 18.23; theocracy: Jos. *Ap.* 2. 165; on objections to a king rather than judges, see 1 Sam 8:7. **51.** Descriptions of Fourth Philosophy: Jos. *BJ* 2.118; *AJ* 18.4-10, 23-5; Judas from Galilee: Jos. *BJ* 2.118; *AJ* 18.23; Judas from Gamala: Jos. *AJ* 18.4, 10; nothing like other philosophies: Jos. *BJ* 2.118; like Pharisees: Jos. *AJ* 18.23; Judas as leader: Jos. *AJ* 18.23. **52.** Jos. *AJ* 18.25 (led to disaster). **53.** Jos. *BJ* 7.253-4 (Masada), 418 (*sicarii* in Egypt); 2.254-5 (defined as terrorists); on descendants of Judas, see M. Hengel, *The Zealots: Investigation into the Jewish Freedom Movement in the Period from Herod I until 70 AD* (Edinburgh, 1989). **54.** Jos. *BJ* 4.161 (name of Zealots); 197-201 (warfare); on the rebel armies as split, see Tac. *Hist.* 5.12.3-4. **55.** Jos. *BJ* 4. 560-63. **56.** Eleazar b. Simon: Jos. *BJ* 2.564, 565; Jos. *BJ* 4.153-7 (new High Priest appointed). **57.** Luke 6:15; Pinchas: Num 25:1-15; Ben Sira 48:1-2; 1 Macc 2:26; zeal as praiseworthy: John 2:17; Gal 1:13-14; *m. Sanh.* 9:6. **58.** Menachem: Jos. *BJ* 2.433, 434, 442, 444, 445; Eleazar b. Yair: Jos. *BJ* 2.447; Zealots distinguished from *sicarii*: Jos. *BJ* 7.262-73. **59.** Jos. *AJ* 18.8-9, 25; Acts 5:37. **60.** Jos. *BJ* 5.99-104; *b. Yom.* 9b ('causeless hatred'); M. Hadas-Lebel, *Jerusalem against Rome* (Paris, 2006) (hatred of Rome). **61.** For these arguments, see M. Goodman, 'A Note on the Qumran Sectarians, the Essenes and Josephus', in idem, *Judaism in the Roman World*, 137-43. **62.** Songs of Sabbath Sacrifice: 4Q403, frag. 1, col. 1, lines 30-34. **63.** Introduction to the Dead Sea scrolls in J. VanderKam and P. Flint, *The Meaning of the Dead Sea Scrolls* (London, 2005); on Qumran, see J. Magness, *The Archaeology of Qumran and the Dead Sea Scrolls* (Grand Rapids, Mich., 2002). **64.** Passages cited: 1QS, col. 1, lines 1-20; col. 9, line 21. **65.** On the self-designation of the community, see Schürer, *History*, 2:575, n. 4; text cited: 1QS, col. 8, lines 5-10. **66.** 1QS, col. 6, lines 7-10, 24-7. **67.** CD-A, col. 6 line 19 (new covenant); col. 16, line 10 (women); col. 9, line 11 (property); col. 11, line 11 (manservants and maidservants); col. 12, line 1 (sexual relations); col. 12, lines 6-11 (gentiles); col. 13, line 15 (commerce). **68.** 4Q270, frag. 7, col. 1, lines 13-14; hybrid text: 4Q265. **69.** Priest at meals: 1QS, col. 6, lines 2-5; teaching: CD, col. 13, lines 2-3; Guardian: CD, col. 13, lines 7-9 (cf. 1QS, col. 6, line 12); initiation: 1QS, col. 1, lines 16-24; Shavuot: Jub. 6:17-22. **70.** On the War Scroll, see J. Duhaime, *The War Texts: 1QM and Related Manuscripts* (London, 2004); Temple Scroll: 11Q19, col. 51, lines 15-16; hymns: IQH (Hodayot). **71.** On the Qumran commentary on Habakkuk (*Pesher Habakkuk*): on Hab 1:5, 1QpHab, col. 2, lines 1-10; 1QpHab, col. 5, lines 9-12, on Hab 1:3; CD BII, col. 19, line 33–col. 20, line 8. **72.** CD BII, col. 20, lines 8-19. **73.** 4Q416, frag. 2, col. 3, lines 12-13; 1QS, col. 11, lines 8-9; on the dual Messiah, see J. J. Collins, *The Scepter and the Star: The Messiahs of the Dead Sea Scrolls and Other Ancient Literature* (Grand Rapids, Mich., 2010).

74. On 4QMMT, see J. Kampen and M. J. Bernstein, eds., *Reading 4QMMT: New Perspectives on Qumran Law and History* (Atlanta, 1996); on calendars, see Schürer, *History*, 2:582; S. Stern, 'Qumran Calendar', in idem, ed., *Sects and Sectarianism in Jewish History* (Leiden, 2011), 39-62; wicked priest: 1QpHab, col. 11, lines 14-18, on Hab 2:15 (break with community); col. 12, lines 2-10, on Hab 2:17 (future sufferings). **75.** Community as atonement sacrifice: 1QS, col. 8, line 6; on the Temple Scroll, see J. Maier, *Die Tempelrolle vom Toten Meer und das 'Neue Jerusalem'* (Munich, 1997); on MMT, see e.g. 4Q395, lines 3-9; see, in general, M. Goodman, 'The Qumran Sectarians and the Temple in Jerusalem', in C. Hempel, ed., *The Dead Sea Scrolls: Texts and Contexts* (Leiden, 2010), 263-73. **76.** Criticism of sacrifices: Amos 5:21-4; Isa 1:11-15; CD-A, col. 11, lines 18-21; objection to Temple tax: 4Q159, frag. 1, line 7. **77.** 1QS, col. 5, lines 1-2; 4QMMTC (4Q397, frags. 14-21, line 7); P. S. Alexander and G. Vermes, *Qumran Cave 4. XIX. Serekh ha-Yahad and Two Related Texts* (Oxford, 1998) (sons of Zadok); for attempts to wring more history from these allusions to specific individuals, see H. Eshel, *The Dead Sea Scrolls and the Hasmonean State* (Grand Rapids, Mich., 2008). **78.** Wicked Priest on Day of Atonement: 1QpHab, col. 11, lines 4-8; destruction of enemies: 1QpHab, col. 10, lines 2-5; col. 13, lines 1-3. **79.** 1QSa, col. 2, lines 20-21; col. 1, lines 1-3; this rule was included in the same scroll as the Community Rule from Cave 1. **80.** 1QS, col. 5, lines 1-6.

CHAPTER 7: THE LIMITS OF VARIETY

1. Philo, *Migr* 89, 91-2. **2.** On the name *talmid hakham*, see E. Schürer, rev. G. Vermes et al., *The History of the Jewish People in the Age of Jesus Christ*, 3 vols. (Edinburgh, 1973–86), 2:333, n. 44; *m. Ab.* 1:1-4, 6, 10, 12, 16. **3.** *m. Ab.* 1:7 (maxim attributed to Nittai); on the development of legends about rabbis of this period and the impossibility of writing their biographies, see J. Neusner, *Development of a Legend: Stories on the Traditions Concerning Yohanan ben Zakkai* (Leiden, 1970); *m. Hag.* 2:2. **4.** *m. Ber.* 8:1-4, 7; *m. Eduy.* 4:8 **5.** *m. Eduy.* 1:12 (House of Hillel changed mind); *m. Eduy.* 1:1; H. W. Guggenheimer, ed., *The Jerusalem Talmud: First Order. Zeraim; Tractate Berakhot* (Berlin and New York, 2000), 116. **6.** J. Neusner, *Rabbinic Traditions about the Pharisees before 70*, 3 vols. (Leiden, 1971); B. T. Viviano, *Study as Worship: Aboth and the New Testament* (Leiden, 1978); Schürer, *History*, 2:333; *t. Dem.* 2:13 (memorization). **7.** On names of sages, see *m. Ab.* 5:22 (Ben Bag-Bag), 23 (Ben He-He); on Jewish names in this period, see T. Ilan, *Lexicon of Jewish Names in Late Antiquity*, Part 1 (Tübingen, 2002). **8.** Matt 23:7 (Jesus addressed as 'rabbi'). **9.** On the Chamber of Hewn Stone, see *m. Sanh.* 11:2; *Sifre to Deuteronomy* 152 (Finkelstein). **10.** On nazirites: Num 6:1-21; S. Chepey, *Nazirites in Late Second Temple Judaism* (Leiden, 2005). **11.** Acts 18:18-21, cf. 21:23-4; Jos. *BJ* 2.313 (Berenice); *m. Naz.* 3:6. **12.** *t. Dem.* 2:2. **13.** *m. Ter.* 4:3 (heave-offering amount); Deut 12:17; *m. Maas.* 1:1 (products liable to tithes), 2 (ripening); *t. Dem.* 2:2 (trustworthy on tithes). **14.** *t. Dem.* 2:14 (formal statement); lapsed *haver*: *t. Dem.* 2:9; 3:4. **15.** *t. Dem.* 2:12 (probation period); *t. Dem.* 2:15 (maternal grandfather); 3:9 (trans. Neusner, adapted). **16.** *t. Dem.* 2:13. **17.** *t. Dem.* 2:17 (daughter and wife of *haver*); 3:9 ('serpent'); *t. A. Zar.* 3:10 (Gamaliel). **18.** *m. Kidd.* 1:9; *b. B.B* 75a (*haverim* as scholars). **19.** Philo, *Spec Leg* I.134. **20.** On Philo's life and family, see S. Sandmel, *Philo of Alexandria: An Introduction* (New York, 1979); on pilgrimage: Philo, *Provid II.* 64; on embassy: E. M. Smallwood, *Philonis Alexandrini Legatio ad Gaium*, 2nd edn (Leiden, 1970). **21.** Eusebius, *Hist. eccl.* 2.4.2 (trans. Runia); see D. T. Runia, *Philo in Early Christian Literature: A Survey* (Assen, 1993), 212-34. **22.** Philo, *Op* 8 (on Moses as philosopher); Philo, *Spec Leg* IV.105-9. **23.** Philo, *Vita Mos* 74, 76; Philo, *Dec* 20. **24.** Philo, *Mut* 15; D. T. Runia, *Philo of Alexandria and the Timaeus of Plato* (Leiden, 1986); A. Kamesar, ed., *The Cambridge Companion to Philo* (Cambridge, 2009). **25.** Wis 16:12; Philo, *Heres* 230-31 (trans. Colson); *Op* 24 (Logos as mind of God); *Somn II* 188, with 183 (Logos between man and God). **26.** Philo, *Migr* 1-3. **27.** Philo, *Quaes Gen I-IV* 2.57; M. Niehoff, *Jewish Exegesis and Homeric Scholarship in Alexandria* (Cambridge, 2011); Philo, *Leg All* II.19-22 (Adam); *Vita Mos* 2.40. **28.** S. Belkin, *Philo and the Oral Law* (Cambridge, Mass., 1940) (on Philo and rabbinic tradition); M. Niehoff, *Philo on Jewish Identity and Culture* (Tübingen, 2001) (on laws as a whole); on Aristobulus: C. R. Holladay, *Fragments from Hellenistic Jewish Authors*, 4 vols. (Chico, Calif., 1987-96), 3:153-5, 136-7, 185; Schürer, *History*, 3:582. **29.** Philo, *De Abrahamo* 99 (Colson); on other allegorists, see Philo, *De Posteritate Caini* 41-2; *Migr* 89 (extreme allegorists). **30.** Jos. *AJ* 19.259-60 (Josephus on Philo); Philo, *Vita Mos* 1.1-2; use of Philo's writings by Josephus: Jos. *AJ* 18.18-21 (Essenes); Jos. *AJ* 18.234-19.274 (Rome in time of Caligula). **31.** Pork: Philo, *Leg.* 361-2; *Spec Leg* IV.100-101 (pork as delicious); M. Goodman, 'Philo as a Philosopher in Rome', in B. Decharneux and S. Inowlocki, eds., *Philon d'Alexandrie: Un Penseur à l'intersection des cultures gréco-romaine, orientale, juive et chrétienne* (Turnhout, 2011), 37-45. **32.** J. Gutmann, ed., *The Dura-Europos Synagogue: A Re-evaluation (1932-1992)* (Atlanta, 1992) on the Dura-Europos Synagogue; Philo in rabbinic commentary: *Ber. Rab.* 1:1; Philo, *Op* 16; J. Weinberg, trans., *Azariah de' Rossi: The Light of the Eyes* (New Haven, 2001); see below, Chapter 14. **33.** Jos. *AJ* 18.63-4. **34.** Roman sources: Tac. *Ann.* 15.44; Pliny, *Ep.* 10.96; rabbinic sources: P. Schäfer, M. Meerson and Y. Deutsch, eds., *Toledot Yeshu ('The Life Story of Jesus') Revisited* (Tübingen, 2011). **35.** On disputes about the authenticity of this passage, see A. Whealey, *Josephus on Jesus: The Testimonium Flavianum Controversy from Late Antiquity to Modern Times* (New York and Oxford, 2003). **36.** E. P. Sanders, *Jesus and Judaism* (London, 1988). **37.** Acts 5:34-9 (Gamaliel); Jesus on Temple worship: Matt 5:23-4. **38.** Acts 10:9-15. **39.** Mark 11:15-17 ('cleansing of the Temple'); Mark 13:1-2 (prophecy). **40.** Matt 5:21-2; Mark 10:5-9 (Jesus on divorce). **41.** Mark 14:55-64 (blasphemy charge); 15:26 ('King of the Jews'); G. Vermes, *Jesus: Nativity, Passion, Resurrection* (London, 2010). **42.** 1 Cor 1:1; 2 Cor 1:3; 'son of God': Rom 1:4. **43.** John 11:1-44 (Lazarus); G. Vermes, *Resurrection: History and Myth* (London, 2008). **44.** On early Christian beliefs, see P. Fredriksen, *From Jesus to*

Christ: The Origins of the New Testament Images of Christ, 2nd edn (New Haven, 2000). **45.** Mark 16:5, 7 (young man in white robe); Acts 2:29-36 (Peter's speech at Shavuot); Acts 2:5 (international pilgrims). **46.** Stephen: Acts 7:57-8, 2-56; 8:1 (general persecution); 21:27-30 (Christians preaching in Temple); Jos. *AJ* 20.200 (James, brother of Jesus); Jos. *BJ* 6.300-309 (Jesus b. Ananias); see below, Chapter 8. **47.** Phil 3:4-6; Rom 11:1; 1 Cor 11:21-2, 24; E. P. Sanders, *Paul, the Law and the Jewish People* (Philadelphia, 1983), 192 (punishment implies inclusion); on Tiberius Julius Alexander: Jos. *AJ* 20.100. **48.** Acts 22:24-9; on disputes about Acts as a historical source, see M. Hengel, *Acts and the History of Earliest Christianity* (Philadelphia, 1979). **49.** Acts 22:3 ('sat at feet of Gamaliel'); Gal 1:14 ('advanced in Judaism'); J. Norton (on biblical texts in Paul); persecutor of Christians: 1 Cor 15:9; Gal 1:13; Acts 9:1-2 (authority from High Priest); 1 Cor 9:1 (vision of 'Jesus, our Lord'). **50.** Acts 9:3-9, cf. 22:15-16; 26:4-15; 2 Cor 12:2-4. **51.** Gal 1:16 (proclaiming Jesus among the gentiles); on Paul's mission, see E. P. Sanders, *Paul* (Oxford, 1991); 1 Cor 9:20 ('as a Jew to Jews'); Gal 2:21-2. **52.** Acts 15:9-21 (meeting in Jerusalem); 21:23-6 (Paul describing himself as Pharisee); Rom 9:3-5; 11:25, 28-9 ('all Israel will be saved'); Gal 2:15-16 (faith needed for salvation); Gal 2:11-14; law is good for Jews: Rom 7:12; 3:30-31. **53.** Phil 2:5-11; on Christ worship and mediator figures, see L. Hurtado, *One God, One Lord: Early Christian Devotion and Ancient Jewish Monotheism*, 3rd edn (London, 2015); W. Horbury, *Jewish Messianism and the Cult of Christ* (London, 1998); 1 Cor 15:3 (death of Jesus as a sacrifice); Gal 4:4-5 ('adoption as children'); Rom 6:3 ('baptized into Christ'); Rom 12:5 ('one body in Christ'); on 'putting on' Christ, see Gal 3:26-7; 1 Cor 8:5-6 ('one God ... and one Lord'). **54.** Silversmiths in Ephesus: Acts 19:23-41; see M. Goodman, 'The Persecution of Paul by Diaspora Jews', in idem, *Judaism in the Roman World* (Leiden, 2009), 145-52. **55.** Isa 60:8-12 (on last days); Gal 2:7 ('gospel for the uncircumcised'); 2 Cor 3:13-14. **56.** On evidence for Jewish Christians, see A. F. J. Klijn and G. J. Reinink, *Patristic Evidence for Jewish-Christian Sects* (Leiden, 1973); for problems in interpretation of this evidence, see M. S. Taylor, *Anti-Judaism and Early Christian Identity: A Critique of the Scholarly Consensus* (Leiden, 1995). **57.** On the history of 'Jews for Jesus', see D. H. Stern, *Messianic Judaism: A Modern Movement with an Ancient Past* (Jerusalem, 2007). **58.** On the parting of the ways, see M. Goodman, 'Modeling the "Parting of the Ways"', in idem, *Judaism in the Roman World*, 175-85.

CHAPTER 8: PREOCCUPATIONS AND EXPECTATIONS

1. Ps 51:9; Isa 4:4; unbroken stream of liquid: MMT, 11.55-8; *m. Yad* 4:7. On the significance of purity and pollution language in this period, see J. Klawans, *Impurity and Sin in Ancient Judaism* (New York, 2000). **2.** Lev 11:44-5; Jub. 22:17; 30:10; gentile oil: Jos. *Vit.* 74-6; M. Goodman, 'Kosher Olive Oil in Antiquity', in idem, *Judaism in the Roman World* (Leiden, 2007), 187-203; on milk and meat: Exod 23:19; 34:24; Deut 14:21; *m. Hull.* 8:1; Philo, *Virt* 144;

D. Kraemer, *Jewish Eating and Identity through the Ages* (New York, 2007), 35-7, 50 (on the taboo as rabbinic); IQS 5.13; Jos. *BJ* 2.149 (Essenes); Matt 23:26 (Pharisees). **3.** On ritual baths (*mikvaot*), see R. Reich, 'The Hot Bath-house Balneum, the Miqweh and the Jewish Community in the Second Temple Period', *JJS* 39 (1998), 102-7; Jos. *BJ* 2.129 (Essenes); M. Simon, *Jewish Sects at the Time of Jesus*, trans. J. H. Farley (Philadelphia, 1967) (Hemerobaptists); Jos. *AJ* 18.117 (John the Baptist). **4.** Jos. *AJ* 16. 168 (privilege not to appear in court on a Sabbath); Philo, *Migr* 89-93 (extreme allegorists); Jos. *BJ* 2.147 (Essenes); Sabbath journey: *m. Shab.* 23:4; *m. Erub.* 4:3; cordoned-off space and Sadducees: *m. Erub.* 6:2; Maccabees on Sabbath: 1 Macc 1:43; 2:35-8, 40-41. **5.** Jos. *AJ* 14.63; Asinaeus: Jos. *AJ* 18.322, 233. **6.** Sabbath in Jubilees: Jub. 2:17-32; 50: 6-13; on the calendar in Jubilees, see L. Ravid, 'The Book of Jubilees and its Calendar – A Reexamination', *Dead Sea Discoveries* 10 (2003), 371-94; S. Stern, *Calendar and Community: A History of the Jewish Calendar, 2nd Century BCE– 10th Century CE* (Oxford, 2001); *1 En.* 72:2-3; 4Q 208-11; J. Ben Dov, *Qumran Calendar* (Leiden, 2008); lunar time reckoning: Ben Sira 43:7; *m. R.Sh.* 2:8. **7.** False swearing: Exod 20:7; sacrifice for failing to keep oath: Lev 5:4-13; Num 30:3-5 (oaths by wife or daughter); Ben Sira 23:9-11; avoidance of oaths: Philo, *Spec Leg* II.1-38; *Dec* 82-95; Jos. *BJ* 2.135, 139-42 (initiation oath of Essenes); Jesus on oaths: Matt 5:33-7; 23:16-21 (attack on Pharisees). **8.** Jos. *Vit.* 11; John the Baptist: Mark 1:6; Luke 7:33; Matt 11:18-19. **9.** Tac. *Hist.* 5.4.3; Jos. *Ap.* 2.282; *m. Taan.* 2:6. **10.** *m. Taan.* 3:8 (Honi); on Judith: Judith 8:6, 8; 13: 6-20; on Esther and Susanna, see A. Brenner, ed., *A Feminist Companion to Esther, Judith and Susanna* (Sheffield, 1995). **11.** Ezek 13:18-20; Exod 22:18; Hanina b. Dosa: *b. Ber.* 34b, cf. *m. Ber.* 5:5; *m. Sot.* 9:15; Ps. Philo, *L.A.B* 34 (Aod); Jos. *AJ* 8.45-9 (Solomon); Acts 19:11-20. **12.** Bible on demons: Deut 32:17; 1 Sam 16:23; 18:10; *1 En.* 10:15; 15:19; 1QM 1:13-14; Jub. 1:20; 15:33 (Mastema); Jub. 10:1-5. **13.** Jos. *BJ* 6:310; 2.163 (Sadducees); *m. Ab.* 3:16. **14.** 4Q405, frag. 20, col. 2 to frags. 21-2, lines 7-9. **15.** 1QM, col. 17, lines 6-8 (angels in eschatological battle); angelic hierarchies: Jub. 2:17-18; 3 Macc 6:16-21 (elephants); Wis. 7:24-6; 8:1-4 (personified wisdom). **16.** Apocalypse of Abraham 10:4; Dan 10:1-2, 4-9; 10:3 (preparation for vision); Rev 1:10-16. **17.** Jos. *Ap.* 1.41; *t. Sot.* 13:2; Jos. *BJ* 6.301 (Jesus son of Ananias); Jos. *BJ* 3.352 (Josephus as prophet): *BJ* 6.285 (pseudo-prophet); Luke 4:24. **18.** Testament of Abraham A. 11-13; J. J. Collins, *Apocalypticism in the Dead Sea Scrolls* (London and New York, 1997); Philo on the end time: Philo, *Praem* 164-5, 169; *Ps. Sol* 17.4, 26. **19.** Theudas: Jos. *AJ* 20.97-8; Acts 5:36-9; the Egyptian: Jos. *AJ* 20.170. **20.** Jos. *BJ* 6.312 ('ambiguous oracle'); 6.313 (Vespasian); 3.400-402 (on Josephus' prophecy); Jos. *AJ* 18.64 (on Christians). **21.** 1QM, col. 16, line 11–col. 17, line 9. **22.** Elijah: Mal 3:23-4 (Heb.); 4:5-6 (Engl.); the Prophet: 1QS, col. 9, lines 9-11; Deut 18:15; Elijah and prophet: John 1:20-21. **23.** *Ps. Sol* 17: 41-2 (earthly king); supernatural Messiah: *1 En.* 48:3; 49:2-4; 1QS 9:10 (messiahs in Dead Sea scrolls); Jos. *BJ* 7.29 (Simon son of Gioras); 1 Cor 1:1. **24.** *1 En.* 22:2, 11; 2 Macc 7:23; Jub. 23:31; Dan 12:3; Wis 9:15; 15:8. **25.** P. van der Horst, *Ancient Jewish Epitaphs* (Kampen, 1991); disputes on life after death: Jos.

BJ 2.154, 156, 163, 166; Matt 22:28; Acts 23:6.   **26.** J. E. Wright, *The Early History of Heaven* (New York, 1999); Luke 23:43; Garden of Eden: *Test. Abrahami* 20:14.   **27.** Jos. *Ap.* 2.218, 219, 232-3; 1.43.   **28.** 2 Macc 7:1-5.   **29.** W. H. C. Frend, *Martyrdom and Persecution in the Early Church: A Study of a Conflict from the Maccabees to Donatus* (Oxford, 1965); on binding of Isaac: Jos. *AJ* 1. 227-31, 232; see G. Vermes, 'Redemption and Genesis xxii – The Binding of Isaac and the Sacrifice of Jesus', in idem, *Scripture and Tradition: Haggadic Studies*, 2nd edn (Leiden, 1973), 193-227.   **30.** Jos. *BJ* 2.195-7.

CHAPTER 9: FROM PAGAN ROME TO ISLAM AND MEDIEVAL CHRISTENDOM

1. M. Goodman, *Rome and Jerusalem: The Clash of Ancient Civilizations* (London, 2007), 445-63; M. Goodman, 'The Roman State and Jewish Diaspora Communities in the Antonine Age', in Y. Furstenberg, ed., *Jewish and Christian Communal Identities in the Roman World* (Leiden, 2016), 75-83.   **2.** Jos. *AJ* 10. 203-10, on Dan 2:31-45 (on Daniel prophecy); on Jewish hopes for retribution on Rome, see M. Hadas-Lebel, *Jerusalem against Rome* (Leuven, 2006).   **3.** For the history of this period, see S. Schwartz, *Imperialism and Jewish Society: 200 B.C.E. TO 640 C.E.* (Princeton, 2001).   **4.** On Byzantine Jewry, see R. Bonfil et al., eds., *Jews in Byzantium: Dialectics of Minority and Majority Cultures* (Leiden, 2012).   **5.** On the Khazars, see D. M. Dunlop, *The History of the Jewish Khazars* (Princeton, 1954); on Benjamin of Tudela, see N. M. Adler, *The Itinerary of Benjamin of Tudela: Critical Text, Translation and Commentary* (London, 1907).   **6.** J. Neusner, *A History of the Jews of Babylonia*, vol. 2 (Leiden, 1966), p. 18 (Kartir inscription).   **7.** For the history of Jews in Iraq in the early Islamic centuries, see N. Stillman, *The Jews of Arab Lands: A History and Source Book* (Philadelphia, 1979).   **8.** On Meshulam of Volterra, see A. Yaari, *Masa' Meshulam mi Volterah beErets Yisrael* (Jerusalem, 1948).   **9.** On the mass conversion in Minorca, see S. Bradbury, ed., *Severus of Minorca: Letter on the Conversion of the Jews* (Oxford, 1996).   **10.** On the history of Jews in medieval Spain, see Y. Baer, *A History of the Jews in Christian Spain*, 2nd edn, 2 vols. (Philadelphia, 1992).   **11.** *C. Th.* 16.8.3 (Jews in Cologne); on Jews in the Crusades, see R. Chazan, *In the Year 1096: The First Crusade and the Jews* (Philadelphia, 1996).   **12.** On the blood libel, see Y. Yuval, *Two Nations in your Womb: Perceptions of Jews and Christians in the Middle Ages* (Berkeley, 2006), 135-203; E. M. Rose, *The Murder of William of Norwich* (New York, 2015); on the Jews of medieval England, see P. Skinner, ed., *The Jews in Medieval Britain: Historical, Literary, and Archaeological Perspectives* (Woodbridge, 2003).   **13.** On Yemen: L. Y. Tobi, *The Jews of Yemen: Studies in their History and Culture* (Leiden, 1999); on India, see N. Katz, *Who are the Jews of India?* (Berkeley, 2000); on China, see J. D. Paper, *The Theology of the Chinese Jews, 1000-1850* (Waterloo, Ont., 2012); on Ethiopia, see S. Kaplan, *The Beta Israel (Falasha) in Ethiopia: From Earliest Times to the Twentieth Century* (New York and London,

1992). **14.** On the significance of the material from the Cairo Genizah, see S. C. Reif, *A Jewish Archive from Old Cairo* (Richmond, Surrey, 2000).

CHAPTER 10: JUDAISM WITHOUT A TEMPLE

1. 4 Ezra 11:44-6; on 4 *Ezra*, see M. E. Stone, *Fourth Ezra* (Minneapolis, 1990). **2.** On Tiberius Julius Alexander, see V. A. Burr, *Tiberius Julius Alexander* (Bonn, 1955); on reactions to 70 CE in general, see D. R. Schwarz and Z. Weiss, eds., *Was 70 CE a Watershed in Jewish History?* (Leiden, 2012). **3.** M. Goodman, 'Sadducees and Essenes after 70 CE', in idem, *Judaism in a Roman World* (Leiden, 2007), 153-62; for Josephus on the destruction of the Temple, see M. Goodman, *Rome and Jerusalem: The Clash of Ancient Civilizations* (London, 2007), 440-49. **4.** Jos. *Ap.* 2.193-6 (trans. Barclay). **5.** On the Temple Mount, see Y. Z. Eliav, *God's Mountain: The Temple Mount in Time, Place, and Memory* (Baltimore, 2005). **6.** Menander of Laodicea, *Epideictica* (in Spengel, *Rhet. Graec.*, vol. 3, p. 366). **7.** For Bar Kokhba coins, see L. Mildenberg, *The Coins of the Bar Kokhba War* (Aarau, 1984); on the significance of references to priests and Temple in mosaics in late antique Palestine, see S. Fine, 'Between Liturgy and Social History: Priestly Power in Late Antique Palestinian Synagogues?', in idem, *Art, History and the Historiography of Judaism in Roman Antiquity* (Leiden, 2013), 181-93; Maimonides on sacrifices: *Guide for the Perplexed* 3.32. **8.** For the daily prayer for restoration of the Temple, see Singer–Sacks, 86, 88. **9.** *m. R.Sh.* 4:1, 3-4. **10.** *b. Meg.* 29a on the 'small sanctuary' (cf. Ezek 11:16); on medieval liturgical art, see C. Roth, 'Art', in idem, ed., *Encyclopaedia Judaica*, 16 vols. (Jerusalem, 1971), 3:522-3. **11.** Singer–Sacks, 438 (prayer in the Additional Service for Shabbat describing Sabbath sacrifices); *b. Ber.* 28b-29a (tradition about standardization); Isa 6:3 (in *kedushah*). **12.** On *piyyut*, see J. Yahalom, *Poetry and Society in Jewish Galilee of Late Antiquity* (Tel Aviv, 1999) (Heb.); on late antique and medieval synagogue music, see A. Z. Idelsohn, *Jewish Music: Its Historical Development* (New York, 1992); on posture and dance within Jewish forms of worship, see above, Chapter 3. **13.** On the work of the masoretes, see I. Yeivin, *Introduction to the Tiberian Masorah*, trans. E. J. Revell (Missoula, Mont., 1980); on the *targumim*, see D. R. G. Beattie and M. J. McNamara, eds., *The Aramaic Bible: Targums in the Historic Context* (Dublin, 1992); for *Pesikta* text, see W. Braude and I. Kapstein, trans., *Pesikta de Rab Kahana* (London, 1975), Piska 25.1 (adapted). **14.** On women in medieval synagogues, see A. Grossman, *Pious and Rebellious: Jewish Women in Medieval Europe* (Waltham, Mass., 2004), 180-88. **15.** On medieval *mikvaot*, see *Mikwe: Geschichte und Architektur jüdischer Ritualbäder in Deutschland* (Frankfurt am Main, 1992); S. D. Gruber, 'Archaeological Remains of Ashkenazic Jewry in Europe: A New Source of Pride and History', in L. V. Rutgers, ed., *What Athens Has to Do with Jerusalem* (Leuven, 2002), 267-301. **16.** *m. Shek.* 1:1 (community responsibility); *b. Sanh.* 47a (burial next to righteous person desirable); on Beth Shearim burials, see Z. Weiss, 'Social Aspects of Burial in Beth She'arim:

Archaeological Finds and Talmudic Sources', in L. I. Levine, ed., *The Galilee in Late Antiquity* (New York, 1992), 357–71; T. Ilan, 'Kever Israel: Since When Do Jews Bury their Dead Separately and What Did They Do Beforehand?', in H. Eshel et al., eds., *Halakhah in Light of Epigraphy* (Göttingen, 2010), 241-54; M. Maier, *The Jewish Cemetery of Worms* (Worms, 1992). **17.** *m. Shab.* 2:6-7. **18.** Singer–Sacks, 302 (Sabbath blessing), 610 (havdalah). **19.** Ch. Raphael, *A Feast of History: The Drama of Passover through the Ages* (London, 1972), 27 [230]; on observance of the holidays for two days instead of one, see S. Zeitlin, *Studies in the Early History of Judaism* (New York, 1973), 223-33. **20.** *m. R.Sh.* 1:2. On the development of festival liturgical practices, see A. P. Bloch, *The Biblical and Historical Background of the Jewish Holy Days* (New York, 1978). **21.** On the complex history of the Kol Nidrei declaration, and rabbinic objections to it, see I. Elbogen, *Jewish Liturgy: A Comprehensive History* (Philadelphia, 1993), 128, 311; on Sukkot, see J. L. Rubenstein, *The History of Sukkot in the Second Temple and Rabbinic Periods* (Atlanta, 1995); on the Hanukkah oil miracle, see *b. Shab.* 21b; on both Hanukkah and Purim, see T. Gaster, *Purim and Hanukkah: In Custom and Tradition* (New York, 1950); on domestic liturgical objects, see A. Kanof, *Jewish Ceremonial Art and Religious Observance* (New York, 1969). **22.** *m. A. Zar.* 1:1, 3; J. Gutmann, ed., *The Dura-Europos Synagogue: A Re-evaluation (1932–1992)* (Atlanta, 1992); A Hachlili, *Ancient Jewish Art and Archaeology in the Land of Israel* (Leiden, 1988); J. Elsner, 'Reflections on Late Antique Jewish Art and Early Christian Art', *JRS* 93 (2003), 114-28. **23.** In general, see M. Goodman, 'Palestinian Rabbis and the Conversion of Constantine to Christianity', in P. Schafer and C. Hezser, eds., *The Talmud Yerushalmi and Greco-Roman Culture*, vol. 2 (Tübingen, 2000), 1-9; on Isaiah passage: Justin, *Dialogue with Trypho*, 66-7; Isaiah 7:14; Matt.1:22-3; on competing claims to be the 'true Israel': Justin, *Dialogue with Trypho*, 123; *Song of Songs Rabbah* 7:3; M. Hirshman, *A Rivalry of Genius: Jewish and Christian Biblical Interpretation in Late Antiquity* (New York, 1996), 15-16. **24.** On the disputations, see H. Maccoby, *Judaism on Trial: Jewish–Christian Disputations in the Middle Ages* (London, 1993); for response by Nahmanides, see 119-20. **25.** On Jewish society as based on Christian models, see S. Schwartz, *Imperialism and Jewish Society: 200 BCE to 640 CE* (Princeton, 2004); on polygamy, see Z. Falk, *Matrimonial Law in the Middle Ages* (London, 1966), 1-34; on martyrdom of Akiva: *b. Ber.* 61b. **26.** R. Chazan, *God, Humanity, and History: The Hebrew First Crusade Narratives* (Berkeley and London, 2000). **27.** On Saadiah and disputations, see R. Brody, *The Geonim of Babylonia and the Shaping of Medieval Jewish Culture* (New Haven, 1998), 97-8, 235-48; Maimonides in *Teshuvot Rambam* (1958), no. 149; on the influence of Islamic scholasticism on medieval Judaism, see S. Stroumsa, *Maimonides in his World: Portrait of a Mediterranean Thinker* (Princeton, 2009). **28.** M. Hyamson, trans., *Duties of the Heart by R. Bachya ben Joseph ibn Paquda*, 2 vols. (New York, 1970), vol. 2, p. 295 (Bahya); M. Adler, ed. and trans., *The Itineraries of Benjamin of Tudela* (London, 1907), 44-5 (pilgrimage stories).

CHAPTER II: RABBIS IN THE EAST

1. *b. Men.* 29b. **2.** On rabbinic texts in late antiquity, see F. Millar, E. Ben Eliyahu and Y. Cohn, *Handbook of Jewish Literature from Late Antiquity, 135–700 CE* (Oxford, 2012); citation from Shiur Qomah from M. S. Cohen, *The Shi'ur Qomah: Texts and Recensions* (Tübingen, 1985), 135-7. **3.** On the responsa, including the prayer book of Rav Amram, see R. Brody, *The Geonim of Babylonia and the Shaping of Medieval Jewish Culture* (New Haven, 1998), 185-201; on Sherira, see R. Brody, 'The Epistle of Sherira Gaon', in M. Goodman and P. Alexander, eds., *Rabbinic Texts and the History of Late-Roman Palestine* (Oxford, 2010), 253-64. **4.** D. Goodblatt, *Rabbinic Instruction in Sasanian Babylonia* (Leiden, 1975), 161 (*kallah*); on the title *gaon*, see Brody, *The Geonim of Babylonia*, 49. **5.** On the final editing of the Babylonian Talmud, see L. Jacobs, *The Talmudic Argument* (Cambridge, 1984); R. Kalmin, 'The Formation and Character of the Babylonian Talmud', in S. T. Katz, ed., *The Cambridge History of Judaism*, vol. 4: *The Late Roman-Rabbinic Period* (Cambridge, 2006), 840-76; D. Weiss Halivni, *The Formation of the Babylonian Talmud* (Oxford, 2013). **6.** On Babylonian local patriotism among rabbis, see I. M. Gafni, *Land, Center and Diaspora: Jewish Constructs in Late Antiquity* (Sheffield, 1997), 96-117; on definitions of the land of Israel, see *Sifre to Deuteronomy* 51; P. S. Alexander, 'Geography and the Bible', *Anchor Bible Dictionary* (New York, 1992), 2:986-7. **7.** On Yohanan ben Zakkai: *m. R.Sh.* 4:1; J. Neusner, *Development of a Legend: Studies in the Traditions Concerning Yohanan ben Zakkai* (Leiden, 1970); C. Hezser, *The Social Structures of the Rabbinic Movement in Roman Palestine* (Tübingen, 1997) (disciple circles); procedures: *m. Sanh.* 4:3-4 (like Sanhedrin); *t. Sanh.* 7:2 (voting). **8.** A. Oppenheimer, 'Jewish Lydda in the Roman Era', *HUCA* 59 (1988), 115-36; Ch. Raphael, *A Feast of History* (London, 1972), 28 [229]. **9.** N. R. M. de Lange, *Origen and the Jews* (Cambridge, 1976). **10.** On the patriarchs, see M. Goodman, *State and Society in Roman Galilee*, 2nd edn (London, 2000), 111-18; A. Applebaum, *The Dynasty of the Jewish Patriarchs* (Tübingen, 2013). **11.** *b. Sanh.* 14a (Judah b. Baba); *b. Sanh.* 5b (ordination); *y. Sanh.* 1:3, 19a (appointment of judges); D. Goodblatt, *Rabbinic Instruction in Sasanian Babylonia* (Leiden, 1975); *b. Sanh.* 5a (Rav). **12.** On Kairouan, see M. Ben-Sasson, 'The Emergence of the Qayrawan Jewish Community and its Importance as a Maghrebi Community', *JAS* (1997), 1-13; on Moses ben Hanokh, see G. D. Cohen, 'The Story of the Four Captives', *Proceedings of the American Academy for Jewish Research* 29 (1960–61), 55-75; G. D. Cohen, ed., *A Critical Edition with a Translation and Notes of the Book of Tradition (Sefer haQabbalah)* (London, 1967), 63-5. **13.** For the letter found in the Cairo Genizah, see S. Schechter, 'Geniza Specimens: A Letter of Chushiel', *JQR* 11 (1899), 643-50. **14.** On the Kalonymus family, see W. Transier, 'Speyer: The Jewish Community in the Middle Ages', in Christoph Cluse, ed., *The Jews of Europe in the Middle Ages (Tenth to Fifteenth Centuries)* (Speyer, 2002), 435-45; on rabbinic Judaism in Italy in the early medieval period, see R. Bonfil, *History and*

Folklore in a Medieval Jewish Chronicle (Leiden, 2009), 45-127. **15.** On the *herem bet din*, see I. Levitats in C. Roth, ed., *Encyclopaedia Judaica*, 16 vols. (Jerusalem, 1971), 8.355-6; on polygamy within Judaism, see A. Grossman, *Pious and Rebellious: Jewish Women in Medieval Europe* (Waltham, Mass., 2004), 68-101. **16.** Sifra, Baraita de Rabbi Ishmael, Perek I. 1-8, in J. Neusner, trans., *Sifra: An Analytical Translation*, vol. 7 (Atlanta, 1988), 61-3; Mekilta d'R. Ishmael, *Nezikin* 14.26-31 (in J. Lauterbach, ed., *Mekilta de Rabbi Ishmael*, 3 vols. (Philadelphia, 1935), 3.110); *b. B.K.* 83b; *b. Makk.* 23b-24a. **17.** *b. Pes.* 10b (trans. Epstein) (on mouse). **18.** Pesik. Rab. Kah 4:7 (in W. Braude and I. Kapstein, trans., *Pesikta de Rab Kahana* (London, 1975), 82-3); *b. B.B* 21a (on education). **19.** *b. B.M.* 59b (carob tree); Houses disputes: *m. Yeb.* 1:4; *b. Erub.* 3b; Elijah: *y. Yeb.* 12:1 (12c); *b. Yeb.* 102a. **20.** *m. Ab.* 2:10; 5:16; 5:15 (four types of sages); 5:13 (four types of charity); on the rabbinic concept of *teshuvah*, see E. E. Urbach, *The Sages: Their Concepts and Beliefs* (Jerusalem, 1975), 462-71. **21.** Singer-Sacks, 462; on Lag BaOmer: *b. Yeb.* 62b. **22.** On *Sefer Zerubbabel*, see D. Biale, 'Counter-History and Jewish Polemics against Christianity: The "Sefer Toldot Yeshu" and the "Sefer Zerubavel"', *JSS* 6.1 (1999), 130-45; see J. C. Reeves, *Trajectories in Near Eastern Apocalyptic: A Postrabbinic Jewish Apocalypse Reader* (Atlanta, 2005). **23.** *m. Hag.* 2:1; *y. Hag.* 2:1 (77a-c), trans. Neusner, adapted; Philip Alexander, *The Mystical Texts* (London, 2006) argues for a continuous mystical tradition from Second Temple times; P. Schäfer, *The Origins of Jewish Mysticism* (Princeton, 2009), argues for discontinuity. **24.** *b. Shab.* 33b (Shimon bar Yohai); *Sefer Yetsirah* 7 (in A. P. Hayman, *Sefer Yesira: Edition, Translation and Text-Critical Commentary* (Tübingen, 2004), 76); *b. Shab.* 156a (astrology); *b. Ber.* 55a, 56b (dream interpretation). **25.** On the Sepphoris synagogue mosaics, see Z. Weiss and E. Netzer, *Promise and Redemption: A Synagogue Mosaic from Sepphoris* (Jerusalem, 1996); on Hammat Tiberias, see M. Dothan, *Hammat Tiberias: Early Synagogues and the Hellenistic and Roman Remains* (Jerusalem, 1983); on magic bowls, see S. Shaked, J. N. Ford and S. Bayhro, *Aramaic Bowl Spells: Jewish Babylonian Aramaic Bowls* (Leiden, 2013); on local influence on rabbis in Sasanian Babylonia, see C. Bakhos and M. R. Shayegan, eds., *The Talmud in its Iranian Context* (Tübingen, 2010). **26.** *m. Pes.* 4:1; cf. *m. Sukk.* 3:11; on Pirqoi ben Baboi, see R. Brody, *The Geonim of Babylonia and the Shaping of Medieval Jewish Culture* (New Haven and London, 1998), 113-17. **27.** On solipsism, see S. Stern, *Jewish Identity in Rabbinic Judaism in Late Antiquity* (Leiden, 1994); *b. Pes.* 49a-49b. **28.** *C. Th.* 16.8.13; S. Schwartz, 'The Patriarchs and the Diaspora', *JJS* 50 (1999), 208-22; D. Noy, *Jewish Inscriptions of Western Europe*, 2 vols. (Cambridge, 1993-5), 1:39, no. 22 (Abba Maris); S. J. D. Cohen, 'Epigraphical Rabbis', *JQR* 72 (1981), 1-17; H. Lapin, 'Epigraphical Rabbis: A Reconsideration', *JQR* 101 (2011), 311-46. **29.** M. Goodman, 'The Function of Minim in Early Rabbinic Judaism', in idem, *Judaism in the Roman World* (Leiden, 2007), 163-73; *t. Hull.* 2:22-3 (Neusner) (Eleazar b. Dama); *b. Ber.* 28b (Simeon ha-Pakuli); Justin Martyr, *Dialogue with Trypho* 16.4; on this blessing, see especially R. Kimelman, 'Birkat ha-Minim and the Lack of Evidence for Anti-Christian Jewish Prayer in Late Antiquity', in E. P. Sanders,

A. I. Baumgarten and A. Mendelson, eds., *Jewish and Christian Self-Definition*, vol. 2 (London, 1981), 226-44. **30.** *m. Sanh.* 10:1; *t. Sanh.* 12:9-10. **31.** Samaritans: *m. Ber.* 7:1; *m. Shebi.* 8:10; *b. Hull.* 6a; on Samaritans in late antiquity, see H. Sivan, *Palestine in Late Antiquity* (Oxford, 2008). **32.** On Hiwi al-Balkhi, see M. Zucker, 'Hiwi HaBalkhi', *Proceedings of the American Academy for Jewish Research* 40 (1972), 1-7.

CHAPTER 12: JUDAISM BEYOND THE RABBIS

1. R. L. Wilken, *John Chrysostom and the Jews* (Berkeley, 1983); N. de Lange, *Greek Jewish Texts from the Cairo Genizah* (Tübingen, 1996). **2.** Greek used by Jews in Rome: D. Noy, *Jewish Inscriptions of Western Europe*, 2 vols. (Cambridge, 1993–5), vol. 2; L. V. Rutgers, *Jews of Late Ancient Rome* (Leiden, 2000); synagogue officials: E. Schürer, rev. G. Vermes et al., *The History of the Jewish People in the Age of Jesus Christ*, 3 vols. (Edinburgh, 1973–86), 3:98ff; *disarchon*: CIJ I (2nd edn) 397, 2989, 391; D. Barthélémy, *Les Devanciers d'Aquila* (Paris, 1963) (Greek biblical texts at Qumran); Jerome, *Ep.* 57.11. **3.** Justinian, *Novella* 146. **4.** Irenaeus 3.21.1, in Eusebius, *Hist. eccl.* 5.8.10; *y. Meg.* 1:11, 71c; N. de Lange, *Greek Jewish Texts from the Cairo Genizah* (Tübingen, 1996); J. Krivoruchko, 'The Constantinople Pentateuch within the Context of Septuagint Studies', *Congress of the International Organization for Septuagint and Cognate Studies* (Paris, 2008), 255-76; N. de Lange, *Japhhet in the Tents of Shem: Greek Bible Translations in Byzantine Judaism* (Tübingen, 2015). **5.** G. M. A. Hanfmann, *Sardis from Prehistoric to Roman Times* (Cambridge, 1983); M. Goodman, 'Jews and Judaism in the Mediterranean Diaspora in the Late-Roman Period: The Limitations of the Evidence', in idem, *Judaism in the Roman World* (Leiden, 2007), 233-59; *t. Sukk.* 4:6; L. I. Levine, *The Ancient Synagogue: The First Thousand Years*, 2nd edn (New Haven, 2005), 91-6. **6.** Levine, *Ancient Synagogue*, 299-302. **7.** C. Kraeling, *Excavations at Dura-Europos: The Synagogue* (New Haven, 1979); Levine, *Ancient Synagogue*, 257. **8.** On midrashic echoes in Dura painting, see S. Fine, *Art and Judaism in the Greco-Roman World* (Cambridge, 2005), 173. **9.** D. Noy and H. Bloedhorn, eds., *Inscriptiones Judaicae Orientis*, vol. 3 (Tübingen, 2003), p. 94 (syr. 55) (Thaumasis); Levine, *Ancient Synagogue*, 260 (inscriptions); L. Roth-Gerson, *Jews of Syria as Reflected in the Greek Inscriptions* (Jerusalem, 2001), 54, 57 (Iliasos) (Heb.); Levine, *Ancient Synagogue*, 288. **10.** Catacomb inscriptions: Levine, *Ancient Synagogue*, 284, n. 74; Philo, *Leg.* 155 (Jews in Trastevere in time of Augustus); catacomb practice: Noy, *Jewish Inscriptions of Western Europe*, vol. 1 (Rome); M. Williams, 'The Organisation of Jewish Burials in Ancient Rome in the Light of Evidence from Palestine and the Diaspora', *ZPE* 101 (1994), 165-82; Rutgers, *Jews of Late Ancient Rome*, 92-9 (gold-inlaid glass); Noy, *Jewish Inscriptions of Western Europe*, vol. 1, no. 13 (Mindius Faustus); G. Hermansen, *Ostia: Aspects of Roman City Life* (Edmonton, 1982), 55-89; P. Richardson, 'An Architectural Case for Synagogues as Associations', in B. Olsson and M. Zetterholm, eds., *The*

Ancient Synagogue from its Origins until 200 C.E. (Stockholm, 2003), 90-117. **11.** On images and their meanings: Levine, *Ancient Synagogue*, 232-5, 232 (David as Orpheus); Aphrodisias inscription: J. Reynolds and R. Tannenbaum, *Jews and God-Fearers at Aphrodisias* (Cambridge, 1987), with redating in A. Chaniotis, 'The Jews of Aphrodisias: New Evidence and Old Problems', *Scripta Classica Israelica* 21 (2002), 209-42; for attitudes to converts, see M. Goodman, *Mission and Conversion* (Oxford, 1994). **12.** J. Kloppenborg and S. G. Wilson, eds., *Voluntary Associations in the Graeco-Roman World* (London, 1996); *Cod. Iust.* 1.9.4 ('place of religion'); *Cod. Theod.* 16.8.2 (Constantine), cf. A. Linder, *Jews in Roman Imperial Legislation* (Detroit, 1987), 134; Procopius, *Anecdota* 28.16-18 (trans. Dewing). **13.** J. Dunbabin, *Mosaics of Roman North Africa* (Oxford, 1978), 194-5 (Naru); R. Hachlili, *Ancient Jewish Art and Archeology in the Diaspora* (Leiden, 1998), 408 (Juliana); Noy, *Jewish Inscriptions of Western Europe*, vol. 2, no. 181 (Elche); Rutgers, *Jews in Late Ancient Rome*, 211-52 (*Collatio*). **14.** On Stobi inscription, see Levine, *Ancient Synagogue*, 270-71; see also works cited above, Chapter 11, n. 28. **15.** *Cod. Theod.* 2.1.10 (judicial powers of patriarchs); 16.8.11 ('illustrious patriarchs'); 16.8.17 (taxes); 16.8.22 (demotion of Gamaliel); 16.8.29 (confiscation of taxes and the end of the patriarchate). **16.** Noy, *Jewish Inscriptions of Western Europe*, 1:76-82; M. Williams, 'The Jews of Early Byzantine Venosa', *JJS* 50 (1999), 38-52. **17.** On Yossipon, see S. Dönitz, 'Historiography among Byzantine Jews: The Case of "Sefer Yosippon"', in R. Bonfil et al., eds., *Jews in Byzantium: Dialectics of Minority and Majority Cultures* (Leiden, 2012), 951-68; on Ahimaaz, see N. de Lange, *Japhet in the Tents of Shem: Greek Bible Translations in Byzantine Judaism* (Tübingen, 2016), 83; Greek in Hebrew letters: N. de Lange, *Greek Jewish Texts from the Cairo Genizah* (Tübingen, 1996); Oxford Bodleian Ms. 1144; for Jewish Greek customs, see D. Goldschmidt, *Mehkarei Tefillah uPiyyut* (Jerusalem, 1980), 122-52. **18.** N. de Lange, 'A Jewish Greek Version of the Book of Jonah', *Bulletin of Judaeo-Greek Studies* 16 (1995), 29-31; G. Corrazol, 'Gli ebrei a Candia nei secoli XIV-XVI' (PhD dissertation, EPHE, Paris, and University of Bologna, 2015), 20 (on Bodleian manuscript Opp. Add. Oct. 19 and the correspondence of Elijah Capsali, head of the Candia community, with Katzenellenbogen). **19.** See M. Polliack, ed., *Karaite Judaism: A Guide to its History and Literary Sources* (Leiden, 2004). **20.** Citation of Pseudo-Saadiah in L. Nemoy, *Karaite Anthology* (New Haven, 1952), 4; al-Kirkisani, cited in ibid., 3. **21.** Y. Erder, 'The Doctrine of Abu 'Isa al-Isfahani and its Sources', *Jerusalem Studies in Arabic and Islam* 20 (1996), 162-99; citation of al-Kirkisani from D. Cohn-Sherbok, *The Jewish Messiah* (Edinburgh, 1997), 95; N. Schur, *History of the Karaites* (Frankfurt am Main, 1992). **22.** Anan b. David in Nemoy, *Karaite Anthology*, 16-17, 17-18. **23.** Y. Erder, 'The Karaites and the Second Temple Sects', in Polliack, ed., *Karaite Judaism*, 119-43; Nemoy, *Karaite Anthology*, 11-20; xvii (parallels to Shiites). **24.** al-Nahawandi in Nemoy, *Karaite Anthology*, 29. **25.** On al-Kumisi, see S. Poznanski, 'Daniel ben Moses al-Kumisi', in I. Singer, ed., *The Jewish Encyclopedia*, 12 vols. (New York, 1901–6), 4:432-4; on the growth of Karaite traditions, see Schur, *History of the Karaites*; al-Kirkisani 1.19.6

(in B. Chiesa and W. Lockwood, *Ya'qub al-Qirqisani on Jewish Sects and Christianity* (Frankfurt am Main, 1984), 156). **26.** On the Ukbarites, see N. Schur, *The Karaite Encyclopaedia* (Frankfurt am Main, 1995), 287; for Malik al-Ramli and al-Kumisi, see D. Frank, 'May Karaites Eat Chicken? Indeterminacy in Sectarian Halakhic Exegesis', in N. B. Dohrmann and D. Stern, eds., *Jewish Biblical Interpretation and Cultural Exchange: Comparative Exegesis in Context* (Philadelphia, 2008), 124-38. **27.** On the Karaites and Hanukkah, see Schur, *The Karaite Encyclopaedia*, 126; for Karaite rules on Sabbath and dietary laws, see Schur, *History of the Karaites*, 52-3; Basyatchi in Nemoy, *Karaite Anthology*, 250, 252. **28.** On Karaites as missionary in the tenth century, see Schur, *History of the Karaites*, 44-5. **29.** I. Davidson, *Saadia's Polemic against Hiwi al-Balkhi* (New York, 1915), 43, 53. **30.** J. Kraemer, *Maimonides: The Life and Works of One of Civilization's Greatest Minds* (New York, 2008), 274-5; on Karaite–Rabbanite relations: Bodl. MsHeb. a.3.42, II.33, 35-7, in J. Olszowy-Schlanger, *Karaite Marriage: Documents from the Cairo Geniza* (Leiden, 1998), 476-7, text no. 56; Cambridge Genizah Taylor-Schechter T-S 20.45 recto (letter); M. Rustow, *Heresy and the Politics of the Community: The Jews of the Fatimid Caliphate* (Ithaca, NY, 2008), 239-65 (on close relations between Karaites and Rabbanites); on Shemariah b. Elijah, see A. Arend, ed., *Elef HaMagen* (Jerusalem, 2000). **31.** On Karaism and Islam, see F. Astren, 'Islamic Contexts of Medieval Karaism', in Polliack, ed., *Karaite Judaism*, 145-78. **32.** On Firkovich, see T. Harvianen, 'Abraham Firkovich', in Polliack, ed., *Karaite Judaism*, 875-92. **33.** On Karaites in nineteenth-century Russia, see P. Miller, 'The Karaites of Czarist Russia, 1780-1918', in Polliack, ed., *Karaite Judaism*, 819-26; on Karaites during the Holocaust, see Schur, *History of the Karaites*, 123-5; on Karaites in contemporary Israel, see E. T. Semi, 'From Egypt to Israel: The Birth of a Karaite *'Edah* in Israel', in Polliack, ed., *Karaite Judaism*, 431-50; on the demography of contemporary Karaite settlement, see Schur, *History of the Karaites*, 148-50; al-Kumisi in Nemoy, *Karaite Anthology*, 36.

CHAPTER 13: RABBIS IN THE WEST

1. S. Schwarzfuchs, *A Concise History of the Rabbinate* (Oxford, 1993), 38-9. **2.** M. Perani, *Talmudic and Midrashic Fragments from the Italian Genizah* (Florence, 2004), on the 'Italian Genizah'; S. Emanuel, 'The "European Genizah" and its Contribution to Jewish Studies', *Henoch* 19.3 (1997), 313-40. **3.** On Hananel b. Hushiel and Nissim b. Yaakov, see T. Fishman, *Becoming the People of the Talmud* (Philadelphia, 2011), 68-71; on Rashi and his influence, see A. Grossman, *Rashi* (Oxford, 2012). **4.** R. Brody, *The Geonim of Babylonia and the Shaping of Medieval Jewish Culture* (New Haven, 1998), 198; Sefer ha-Qabbalah 62-3 in G. D. Cohen, ed., *A Critical Edition of the Book of Tradition (Sefer ha-Qabbalah)* (London, 1967), 66 (on the *Book of Tradition*); on Meir b. Baruch, see I. A. Agus, *Rabbi Meir of Rothenburg* (Philadelphia, 1947). **5.** On

Alfasi, see G. Blidstein, 'Alfasi, Yitsaq ben Yaaqov', in M. Eliade, ed., *Encyclopedia of Religion*, 16 vols. (New York, 1987), vol. 1, pp. 203-4; on Hefets, see B. Halper (ed.), *A Volume of the Book of Precepts, by Hefes b. Yasliah* (Philadelphia, 1915, 1972). **6.** On Eleazer b. Yehudah, see A. Reiner, 'From Rabbenu Tam to R. Isaac of Vienna: The Hegemony of the French Talmudic School in the Twelfth Century', in C. Cluse, ed., *The Jews of Europe in the Middle Ages (Tenth to Fifteenth Centuries)* (Turnhout, 2004), 273-82; on the Tosafists in general, see H. Soloveitchik, 'The Printed Page of the Talmud: The Commentaries and their Authors', in S. L. Mintz and G. M. Goldstein, eds., *Printing the Talmud: From Bomberg to Schottenstein* (New York, 2006), 37-42; on the Rosh and Yaakov b. Asher, see I. M. Ta-Shma, *Creativity and Tradition* (Cambridge, Mass., 2006), 111-26. **7.** Jacob of Marvège, *Responsa*, ed., R. Margoliot (Jerusalem, 1956/7), 52 (in L. Jacobs, *The Jewish Mystics* (London, 1990), 76-7); on later acceptance of some of his rulings, see L. Jacobs, *A Tree of Life: Diversity, Flexibility, and Creativity in Jewish Law*, 2nd edn (London and Portland, Oreg., 2000), 62. **8.** On geographical dispersion, see N. de Lange, *Atlas of the Jewish World* (Oxford and New York, 1984), 99. **9.** On Rashi's Bible commentary, see Grossman, *Rashi*; citation from Rashi on Gen 3:8; on medieval Bible interpretation, see J. D. McAuliffe, B. D. Walfish and J. W. Goering, eds., *With Reverence for the Word: Medieval Scriptural Exegesis in Judaism, Christianity and Islam* (Oxford, 2003); M. Fishbane and J. Weinberg, eds., *Midrash Unbound: Transformations and Innovations* (Oxford, 2013). **10.** Rashi on Exod 20:22. **11.** On the relation of Rashi to non-Jewish culture in his time, see C. Pearl, *Rashi* (London, 1988); on Rashi as commentator on the Talmud, see Grossman, *Rashi*, 133-48. **12.** On the formulas used by the Tosafists to present their ideas, see H. Soloveitchik, 'The Printed Page of the Talmud: The Commentaries and their Authors', 39; on use of new manuscript readings by the Tosafists, see T. Fishman, *Becoming the People of the Talmud* (Philadelphia, 2011), 146-7; E. E. Urbach, *Ba'alei haTosafot*, 4th edn (Jerusalem, 1980), 528-9; on Rabbenu Tam, see Soloveitchik, 'The Printed Page of the Talmud: The Commentaries and their Authors', 39-40. **13.** On the *tefillin* rules of Rabbenu Tam, see Y. Cohn, 'Were Tefillin Phylacteries?', *JJS* 59 (2008), 39-61; R. Ilai in *b. Kidd.* 40a; cf. Jacobs, *Tree of Life*, 41. **14.** On hand washing: *b. Ber.* 53b; *b. Hul.* 105a, with Tosafists ad loc. (see Jacobs, *Tree of Life*, 112); on dancing and clapping: *m. Betz.* 5:2; Tosafists to *b. Betz.* 30a (see Jacobs, *Tree of Life*, 113); on *sha'atnez*: Deut 22:11; Rosh, cited in Jacobs, *Tree of Life*, 141 (on night-time Shema while light); 111-12 (Isserlin); on Evening Service: Rambam, *Yad, Tefillah* 1:8, in M. Hyamson, ed., *Mishneh Torah: The Book of Adoration by Maimonides* (Jerusalem, 1974), 99a. **15.** Jacobs, *Tree of Life*, 139 (snake); on Avraham b. Natan, see Isaac Rephael, *Sefer HaManhig leRabbi Avraham ben Natan HaYerchi* (Jerusalem, 1978); on the development of local liturgical variation in this period, see I. Elbogen, *Jewish Liturgy: A Comprehensive History* (Philadelphia, 1993); H. J. Zimmels, *Ashkenazim and Sephardim* (Farnborough, 1958); on *tashlich*: A. C. Feuer and N. Scherman, *Tashlich* (New York, 1980); S. Steiman, *Custom and*

Survival (New York, 1963). **16.** On local 'Purims', see E. Horowitz, *Reckless Rites: Purim and the Legacy of Jewish Violence* (Princeton, 2006), ch. 10, with 293-301 on Narbonne; tombs of saints: J. W. Meri, *The Cult of Saints among Muslims and Jews in Medieval Syria* (Oxford, 2002), 221 (on Sahl); on head covering: *b. Kidd.* 51a; Isaac b. Jacob ha-Kohen Alfasi (the Rif), *Kidd.* 217b; R. Yitzak b. Moshe, *Or Zaru'a, Hilkhot Shabbat* (Zhitomir, 1862), II 43. **17.** T. Alexander-Frizer, *The Pious Sinner* (Tübingen, 1991), 24 (story from *Sefer Hasidim*); on the Hasidei Ashkenaz in general, see I. Marcus, *Piety and Society: The Jewish Pietists of Medieval Germany* (Leiden, 1981); Bahya in M. Hyamson, trans., *Duties of the Heart by R. Bachya ben Joseph ibn Paquda*, 2 vols. (New York, 1970), vol. 2, p. 303, citing Isa 45:18. **18.** E. N. Adler, *Jewish Travellers* (London, 1930) (on Eldad the Danite); Rosh, *Responsa* 17:8 (on Cordoba). **19.** Rabbenu Tam on need for unanimity: M. Elon, *The Principles of Jewish Law* (Jerusalem, 1975), 163-5; L. Finkelstein, *Jewish Self-Government in the Middle Ages* (New York, 1974), 49-55; on Rabbenu Tam's controversy with Meshullam, see T. Fishman, *Becoming the People of the Talmud* (Philadelphia, 2011), 144-7; I. Twersky, *Rabad of Posquières* (Cambridge, Mass., 1962), 131 (Rabad on Maimonides). **20.** H. A. Wolfson, *The Philosophy of the Kalam* (Cambridge, 1976); Saadiah Gaon, *The Book of Beliefs and Opinions*, Introduction, Section 6. 1-3 (trans. Alexander); on Saadiah in general, see R. Brody, *Sa'adyah Gaon* (Oxford, 2013). **21.** S. Stroumsa, *Dawud ibn Marwan Al-Muqammis's Twenty Chapters* (Leiden, 1989), 158, 160; on Bahya, see C. Sirat, *A History of Jewish Philosophy in the Middle Ages* (Cambridge, 1990), 81-3. **22.** On the philosophical works of ibn Gabirol, see Sirat, *History of Jewish Philosophy*, 68-81; philosophical aims: S. Wise, *The Improvement of the Moral Qualities* (New York, 1901), 50; poetry: R. Loewe, *Ibn Gabirol* (London, 1989), 119. **23.** On the golden age of Hebrew religious poetry in Spain, see P. Cole, *The Dream of the Poem* (Princeton, 2007); on the *Kuzari*, see N. D. Korobkin, *The Kuzari: In Defense of the Despised Faith*, 2nd edn (New York, 2009). **24.** Judah Halevi, *Kuzari* 5:14 (trans. Alexander). **25.** M. R. Menocal, *The Ornament of the World* (Boston, 2002) (*convivencia*); S. Stroumsa, *Maimonides in his World: Portrait of a Mediterranean Thinker* (Princeton, 2009), 6 (intellectual openness). **26.** H. A. Davidson, *Moses Maimonides: The Man and his Works* (New York, 2005); M. Halbertal, *Maimonides: Life and Thought* (Princeton, 2013). **27.** Stroumsa, *Maimonides*, 8-9; on the death of Maimonides' brother: S. D. Goitein, *Letters of Medieval Jewish Traders* (Princeton, 1973), 207. **28.** Maimonides, *Guide* 2.13.1, in Moses Maimonides, *The Guide of the Perplexed*, trans. S. Pines (Chicago, 1963), 281; on Maimonides as a philosopher, see D. H. Frank and O. Leaman, eds., *The Cambridge Companion to Medieval Jewish Philosophy* (Cambridge, 2003). **29.** Maimonides, *Letter on Astrology*, p. 235, cited by M. M. Kellner, *Maimonides on the 'Decline of the Generations' and the Nature of Rabbinic Authority* (Albany, NY, 1996), 56 (reason required in halakha); *m. Sanh.* 10:1-4; Maimonides, *Commentary on the Mishnah*, Sanhedrin 10 (Helek) 1-21 (trans. Alexander). **30.** On Maimonides and Islam, see Stroumsa, *Maimonides*, 9-10; Singer–Sacks, 308 (*Yigdal*). **31.** L. D. Stitskin, trans. and ed., *Letters of Maimonides* (New York,

1977). **32.** Ezek 17:3 ('Great Eagle'); J. Finkl, 'Maimonides' Treatise on Resurrection', 1941; parallels in Christian world: D. J. Silver, *Maimonidean Criticism and Controversy, 1180-1240* (Leiden, 1965). **33.** Y. Brill, ed., *Kitab alrasa'il: meturgam be-Ivrit* (Paris, 1871), p. 14 (trans. Ben-Sasson) (Abulafia). **34.** On Nahmanides' letter to the rabbis of northern France, see C. B. Chavel, *Ramban (Nachmanides: Writings and Discourses)* (New York, 1978). **35.** On the disputation in Paris, see H. Maccoby, *Judaism on Trial* (London, 1982), 153. **36.** On the ban in 1305, see H. Dimitrovsky, ed., *Teshuvot haRashba*, 2 vols. (Jerusalem, 1990), vol. 2, *Perek* 99, lines 13-16, 23-4 (trans. L. and D. Cohn-Sherbok); on the letter of Yosef Caspi, see F. Kohler, ed., *Letters of Jewry* (London, 1978), pp. 268-9. **37.** G. Freudenthal, ed., *Studies on Gersonides* (Leiden, 1992). **38.** H. A. Wolfson, *Crescas' Critique of Aristotle* (Cambridge, 1929); J. T. Robinson, 'Hasdai Crescas and Anti-Aristotelianism', *The Cambridge Companion to Medieval Jewish Philosophy* (Cambridge, 2003), 391-413; M. Waxman, *The Philosophy of Don Hisdas Crescas* (New York, 1920). **39.** On the Tortosa disputes, see H. Maccoby, *Judaism on Trial* (London, 1982), 82-94; on lists of principles, see L. Jacobs, *Principles of the Jewish Faith* (London, 1964), 20-23. **40.** On Arama, see H. J. Pollak, ed., *Isaac Arama, Akedat Yitzhak* (New York, 1849), f. 19b (trans. Pearl); C. Pearl, *The Medieval Jewish Mind: The Religious Philosophy of Isaac Arama* (London, 1971). **41.** On the architecture of medieval synagogues, see C. H. Krinsky, *Synagogues of Europe: Architecture, History, Meaning* (New York, 1985); R. Krautheimer, *Mittelalterliche Synagogen* (Berlin, 1927). **42.** *Zohar, BeHa'alotkha* 3.152a (trans. Alexander); G. Scholem, *Major Trends in Jewish Mysticism* (New York, 1946); Y. Liebes, *Studies in the Zohar* (Albany, NY, 1993). **43.** T. Fishman, 'Rhineland Pietist Approaches to Prayer and the Textualization of Rabbinic Culture in Medieval Northern Europe', *JSQ* 11 (2004), 331. **44.** On Eleazar b. Yehudah, see J. Dan, *Kabbalah: A Very Short Introduction* (Oxford, 2006), 20; on the roots of rabbinic asceticism, see E. Diamond, *Holy Men and Hunger Artists: Fasting and Asceticism in Rabbinic Culture* (New York, 2004). **45.** On the Albigensian Crusade and the Cathars, see M. G. Pegg, *A Most Holy War: The Albigensian Crusade and the Battle for Christendom* (Oxford, 2008); on *Sefer haBahir*, see D. Abrams, *The Book Bahir* (Los Angeles, 1994). **46.** On the notion of transmigration of souls in *Sefer haBahir*, see *Sefer haBahir*, Part I, 195, in L. L. Bronner, *Journey to Heaven: Exploring Jewish Views of the Afterlife* (Jerusalem, 2011), 136. **47.** On Azriel of Girona, see M. Idel, *Kabbalah* (Oxford, 1988). **48.** On Abraham Abulafia, see M. Idel, *The Mystical Experience in Abraham Abulafia* (Albany, NY, 1988). **49.** On Abulafia's ideas in relation to other contemporary streams of kabbalah, see M. Idel, *Messianic Mysticism* (New Haven, 1998), 58-125. **50.** P. B. Fenton, *The Treatise of the Pool by Obadyah* (London, 1981), 102, 93; S. Rosenblatt, *The High Ways to Perfection of Abraham Maimonides*, vol. 2 (New York, 1938), p. 321 (on Sufi behaviour). **51.** *Zohar, hekh.* 1.83b (trans. Alexander); D. C. Matt, *The Zohar* (Stanford, 2003-9). **52.** On Gikatilla, see J. Gikatilla, *Gates of Light: Sha'are Orah* (San Francisco, 1994); on Moshe de Leon, see I. Tishby, *The Wisdom of the Zohar*, 3 vols. (Oxford, 1989), 1:13-17. **53.** On

Adret, see J. Perles, *R. Salomo b. Abraham b. Adereth* (Breslau, 1863). **54.** On Avraham bar Hiyya, see I. I. Efros, 'Studies in Pre-Tibbonian Philosophical Terminology: I. Abraham Bar Hiyya, the Prince', *JQR* 17.2 (1926), 129-64.

CHAPTER 14: THE EUROPEAN
RENAISSANCE AND THE NEW WORLD

1. On the careers of David Reuveni and Solomon Molcho, see M. Benmelech, 'History, Politics, and Messianism: David Ha-Reuveni's Origin and Mission', *AJS Review* 35.1 (2011), 35-60; the talmudic passage is in *b. Sanh.* 98a. **2.** For an overview of this period, D. Ruderman, *Early Modern Jewry: A New Cultural History* (Princeton, 2010). **3.** On the demographic impact of the expulsions from Spain and Portugal, see J. S. Gerber, *The Jews of Spain: A History of the Sephardic Experience* (New York, 1994); on Sephardi Jews in the Netherlands in the seventeenth century, see M. Bodian, *Hebrews of the Portuguese Nation: Conversos and Community in Early Modern Amsterdam* (Bloomington, Ind., 2009); D. Swetchinski, *Reluctant Cosmopolitans: The Portuguese Jews of Seventeenth-Century Amsterdam* (London, 2004); on Manasseh ben Israel, see Y. Kaplan, H. Méchoulan and R. Popkin, eds., *Menasseh ben Israel and his World* (Leiden, 1989); D. S. Katz, *Philo-Semitism and the Readmission of the Jews to England, 1603-1655* (Oxford, 1992); on Jewish settlement in the United States, see E. Faber, *A Time for Planting: The First Migration, 1654-1820* (Baltimore, 1995); J. Sarna, *American Judaism* (New Haven, 2004), 1-30; H. R. Diner, *The Jews of the United States, 1654-2000* (New Haven, 2004); J. Israel, 'The Jews of Dutch America', in P. Bernardini and N. Fiering, eds., *The Jews and the Expansion of Europe to the West, 1450-1800* (New York, 2001), 335–49. **4.** On the Chmielnicki massacres, see J. Raba, *Between Remembrance and Denial: The Fate of the Jews in the Wars of the Polish Commonwealth during the Mid-Seventeenth Century as Shown in Contemporary Writings and Historical Research* (Boulder, Colo., 1995); on the Ashkenazi influx into the Netherlands in the seventeenth century, see M. Shulvass, *From East to West: The Westward Migration of Jews from Eastern Europe during the Seventeenth and Eighteenth Centuries* (Detroit, 1971); Y. Kaplan, 'Amsterdam and Ashkenazic Migration in the Seventeenth Century', *Studia Rosenthaliana* 23 (1989), 22-44; S. Stern, *Court Jew* (Philadelphia, 1950); M. Breuer, 'The Court Jews', in M. A. Meyer, ed., *German-Jewish History in Modern Times* (New York, 1996), 104-26. **5.** On the Jews of Venice in the sixteenth century, see R. C. Davis and B. Ravid, eds., *The Jews of Early Modern Venice* (Baltimore, 2001). **6.** J. Reuchlin, *On the Art of the Kabbalah*, trans. M. and S. Goodman (London, 1982); on Christian Hebraism, see F. E. Manuel, *The Broken Staff: Judaism through Christian Eyes* (Cambridge, Mass., 1992); A. Coudert and J. S. Shoulson, eds., *Hebraica Veritas?: Christian Hebraists and the Study of Judaism in Early Modern Europe* (Philadelphia, 2004); J. Weinberg, trans., *The Light of the Eyes: Azariah de' Rossi* (New Haven, 2001), 31. **7.** For restrictions on reading de' Rossi, see Weinberg, *The Light of the Eyes*, xx-xxii.

8. Judah Moscato, *Sefer Nefutsot Yehudah* (Venice, 1871), 21b (trans. S. Feldman); on Moscato, see G. Veltri and G. Miletto, *Rabbi Judah Moscato and the Jewish Intellectual World of Mantua in the 16th–17th Centuries* (Leiden, 2012). **9.** On Leone Modena, see M. Cohen, trans. and ed., *The Autobiography of a Seventeenth-Century Venetian Rabbi: Leon Modena's Life of Judah* (Princeton, 1988); T. Fishman, *Shaking the Pillars of Exile: 'Voice of a Fool', an Early Modern Jewish Critique of Rabbinic Culture* (Stanford, 1997); Y. Dweck, *The Scandal of Kabbalah: Leon Modena, Jewish Mysticism, Early Modern Venice* (Princeton, 2011); on Salomone de' Rossi, see D. Harrán, *Salamone Rossi, Jewish Musician in Late Renaissance Mantua* (Oxford, 1999); Leone Modena in Salomone de' Rossi, *Hashirim asher leShlomo* (1622-3); on the architecture of Bevis Marks synagogue, see S. Kadish, '"Sha'ar ha-Shamayim": London's Bevis Marks Synagogue and the Sephardi Architectural Heritage', in A. Cohen-Mushlin and H. H. Thies, eds., *Jewish Architecture in Europe* (Petersberg, 2010), 229-42. **10.** On the battle of the books, see M. Brod, *Johannes Reuchlin and sein Kampf* (Stuttgart, 1908); D. Price, *Johannes Reuchlin and the Campaign to Destroy Jewish Books* (Oxford, 2010); on Luther and the Jews, see T. Kaufmann in D. Bell and S. G. Burnett, eds., *Jews, Judaism, and the Reformation in Sixteenth-Century Germany* (Leiden, 2006), 69-104. **11.** On Calvin and the Jews, see A. Detmers in Bell and Burnett, eds., *Jews, Judaism, and the Reformation in Sixteenth-Century Germany*, 197-217; M. Satlow, *Creating Judaism: History, Tradition, Practice* (New York, 2006), 256 (requirement to believe in afterlife); on Calvinists in Amsterdam in the time of Spinoza, see S. Nadler, 'The Excommunication of Spinoza: Trouble and Toleration in the "Dutch Jerusalem"', *Shofar* 19.4 (2001), 40-52. **12.** On Christian millenarianism in the seventeenth century, see vols. 2–4 in R. Popkin et al., eds., *Millenarianism and Messianism in Early Modern European Culture*, 4 vols. (Dordrecht, 2001); on the Jews of Curaçao, see C. R. Kaiser, 'Islets of Toleration among the Jews of Curacao', in M. Goodman et al., *Toleration within Judaism* (Oxford and Portland, Oreg., 2013), 130-60; on conversos, see Ruderman, *Early Modern Jewry*, 100-103; Y. Kaplan, 'Bom Judesmo: The Western Sephardic Diaspora', in D. Biale, ed., *Cultures of the Jews: A New History* (New York, 2002), 639-69. **13.** Uriel Acosta in L. Schwartz (ed.), *Memoirs of my People* (New York, 1963), 86-7. **14.** D. B. Schwartz, *The First Modern Jew: Spinoza and the History of an Image* (Princeton, 2012); B. Spinoza, *Tractatus Theologico-Politicus*, trans. S. Shirley (Leiden, 2001), 110; S. Nadler, *Spinoza: A Life* (Cambridge, 2001); R. Goldstein, *Betraying Spinoza* (New York, 2006). **15.** On Jews in the Ottoman world in the sixteenth and seventeenth centuries, see A. Levy, ed., *The Jews of the Ottoman Empire* (Princeton, 1994). **16.** Ruderman, *Early Modern Jewry*, 57-9. **17.** On ordination, see S. Schwarzfuchs, *A Concise History of the Rabbinate* (Oxford, 1993), ch. 3; Maimonides, *Yad*, Hilkhot Sanhedrin 4:11; J. Katz, 'The Dispute between Jacob Berab and Levi ben Habib over Renewing Ordination', in J. Dan, ed., *Binah: Studies in Jewish History, Thought and Culture*, 3 vols. (Westport, Conn., and London, 1989–94), vol. 1, 119-41. **18.** M. Saperstein, *Jewish Preaching, 1200-1800: An Anthology* (New Haven, 1989), 412-13. **19.** On the printing of books for Jewish women, see E. Fram, *My Dear Daughter: Rabbi Benjamin Slonik and the Education of Jewish Women in Sixteenth-Century Poland* (Cincinnati, 2007); on *tehinnot*, see C. Weissler, *Voices of the Matriarchs: Listening to the Prayers of Early Modern Jewish Women* (Boston, 1998); on *Me'am Loez*, see M. Molho, *Le Meam-Loez: Encyclopédie populaire du sephardisme levantin* (Salonica, 1945).

CHAPTER 15: NEW CERTAINTIES AND NEW MYSTICISM

1. *Shulhan Arukh*, YD, 335:1-4, 9   2. *Maggid Meysharim*, p. 57b; J. Karo, *Sefer Maggid Meysharim* (Jerusalem, 1990), 23 (p. 403), translated in R. J. Z. Werblowsky, *Joseph Karo: Lawyer and Mystic* (Philadelphia, 1977), 260.   3. On the production and reception of the *Shulhan Arukh*, see I. Twersky, 'The Shulhan 'Arukh: Enduring Code of Jewish Law', *Judaism* 16 (Philadelphia, 1967), 141-58.   4. *Shulhan Arukh*, Hoshen Mishpat 26.4; on Isserles, see A. Siev, *HaRama: Rabbi Moshe Isserles* (Jerusalem, 1956) (Heb.).   5. On Hayyim b. Betsalel and the attack on Karo and Isserles, see E. Reiner, 'The Rise of an Urban Community: Some Insights on the Transition from the Medieval Ashkenazi to the 16th Century Jewish Community in Poland', *KHŻ* 207 (2003), 363-72.   6. *Shulhan Arukh*, OH 3:2 (trans. Jacobs) (on privy); on Maharam, see S. M. Chones, *Sefer Toledot haPosekim* (New York, 1945–6), 366-71; on Isserles' recognition of local custom, see L. Jacobs, *A Tree of Life: Diversity, Flexibility, and Creativity in Jewish Law*, 2nd edn (London and Portland, Oreg., 2000), 211-15.   7. Responses to changed conditions for workmen: *b. Ber.* 16a; *Shulhan Arukh*, OH 191:2; cf. Jacobs, *Tree of Life*, 150; on Hanukkah lights: *m. B.K* 6:6; *Shulhan Arukh*, OH 671:7; on homosexuality: *Bah* to *Tur.* EH 24; cf. Jacobs, *Tree of Life*, 136-7.   8. Isserles, YD 376:4 (trans. Denburg) in *Laws of Mourning*, 242-6.   9. On *yahrzeit*, see M. Lamm, *The Jewish Way in Death and Mourning* (New York, 1988); on Yizkor, see A. Z. Idelsohn, *Jewish Liturgy and its Development* (New York, 1967), 230f., 293.   10. On *kitniot*, see I. M. Ta-Shma, *Minhag Ashkenaz haKadmon: Heker veIyun* (Jerusalem, 1992), 271-82.   11. On the spread of yeshivot in the sixteenth and seventeenth centuries, see E. Fram, *Ideals Face Reality: Jewish Law and Life in Poland, 1550-1655* (Cincinnati, 1997), 5-6.   12. The example is excerpted and adapted from the article on *pilpul* by Alexander Kisch in I. Singer, ed., *The Jewish Encyclopaedia*, 12 vols. (New York, 1901–6), 10:42.   13. *b. B.B* 14b (term *pilpul*).   14. On the Vilna Gaon, see E. Stern, *The Genius: Elijah of Vilna and the Making of Modern Judaism* (New Haven, 2014).   15. I. Cohen, *History of Jews in Vilna* (Philadelphia, 1943).   16. A. David, *In Zion and Jerusalem: The Itinerary of Rabbi Moses Basola (1521-1523)* (Jerusalem, 1999); *Zohar, Devarim* 296b in I. Tishby, *The Wisdom of the Zohar*, 3 vols. (Oxford, 1989), 1:164-5; on Jewish settlement in Safed, see A. David, 'Demographic Changes in the Safed Jewish Community in the Sixteenth Century', in R. Dan, ed., *Occident and Orient: A Tribute to the Memory of A. Scheiber* (Leiden, 1988); A. Cohen and B. Lewis, *Population and Revenue in the Towns of Palestine in the Sixteenth Century* (Princeton, 1978).   17. L. Fine, *Physician*

of the Soul, Healer of the Cosmos: Isaac Luria and his Kabbalistic Fellowship (Stanford, 2003). **18.** On Moshe Cordovero, see B. Sack, *The Kabbalah of Rabbi Moshe Cordovero* (Jerusalem, 1995) (Heb.). **19.** On Luria, see especially Fine, *Physician of the Soul.* **20.** On the transmission of Luria's teachings, see R. Meroz, 'Faithful Transmission versus Innovation: Luria and his Disciples', in P. Schäfer and J. Dan, eds., *Gershom Scholem's Major Trends in Jewish Mysticism Fifty Years After* (Tübingen, 1993), 257-74. **21.** Fine, *Physician of the Soul*, 340-50 (on the formal agreement between Vital and other disciples of Luria); H. Vital, *Sefer haHezyonot*, ed. A. Eshkoli (Jerusalem, 1954), 154, trans. Fine (in Fine, *Physician of the Soul*, 337). **22.** Fine, *Physician of the Soul*, 128-31 (*tsimtsum*); 187-258 (*tikkun olam*); Jacob ben Hayyim Zemah, *Nagid uMetsaveh* (trans. L. and D. Cohn-Sherbok, *A Short Reader in Judaism* (Oxford, 1996), 110). **23.** On the printings of the Zohar in sixteenth-century Italy, see I. Zinberg, *Italian Jewry in the Renaissance Era* (New York, 1974), 121. **24.** On Shalem Shabbazi, see A. Afag'in, *Aba Sholem Shabbazi Ne'im Zemirot Yisrael* (Rosh HaAyin, 1994); on the Maharal, see B. L. Sherwin, *Mystical Theology and Social Dissent: The Life and Works of Judah Loew of Prague* (London, 1982). **25.** Vital, *Sha'ar haMitsvot*, Va'ethanan, 79, cited in Jacobs, *Tree of Life*, 69-70. **26.** Singer–Sacks, 257 ('Beloved of the soul'); on the greeting of the Sabbath by Safed kabbalists, see Fine, *Physician of the Soul*, 248-50; Singer–Sacks, 267 ('Come, my Beloved'). **27.** H. Vital, *Sha'ar Ruah haKodesh* (Tel Aviv, 1963), 88-9, cited in G. Nigal, *Magic, Mysticism and Hasidism* (London, 1994), 118; on spirit possession, see J. H. Chajes, *Between Worlds: Dybbuks, Exorcists, and Early Modern Judaism* (Philadelphia, 2003). **28.** G. Scholem, *Sabbatai Sevi: The Mystical Messiah, 1626–76* (London, 1973), 206 (meeting with Nathan). **29.** Baruch of Arezzo, *Memorial* 5, cited in D. J. Halperin, *Sabbatai Zevi: Testimonies to a Fallen Messiah* (Oxford and Portland, Oreg., 2007), 35-6. **30.** Scholem, *Sabbatai Sevi* remains the principal account of Sabbetai's career and influence. **31.** Ibid., 207-13. **32.** Barukh of Arezzo, *Memorial* 8, cited in Halperin, *Sabbatai Zevi*, p. 41; on the role of prophets in spreading the Sabbatian message, see M. Goldish, *The Sabbatean Prophet* (Cambridge, Mass., 2004). **33.** Barukh of Arezzo, *Memorial* 7, cited in Halperin, *Sabbatai Zevi*, 38-9. **34.** Scholem, *Sabbatai Sevi*, 417-33. **35.** Barukh of Arezzo, *Memorial* 11, cited in Halperin, *Sabbatai Zevi*, 47. **36.** Barukh of Arezzo, *Memorial* 12, cited in Halperin, *Sabbatai Zevi*, 49 (Constantinople); Scholem, *Sabbatai Sevi*, 461-602. **37.** Barukh of Arezzo, *Memorial* 15, cited in Halperin, *Sabbatai Zevi*, 57. **38.** Barukh of Arezzo, *Memorial* 16, cited in Halperin, *Sabbatai Zevi*, 61; letter by Sabbetai cited in Halperin, *Sabbatai Zevi*, 10. **39.** Joseph Halevi, cited in Halperin, *Sabbatai Zevi*, 107, 112; M. Loewenthal, trans., *The Memoirs of Glückel of Hameln* (New York, 1977), 46-7. **40.** Jacob Najara, *Chronicle*, cited in Halperin, *Sabbatai Zevi*, 135, 130-31. **41.** Nathan of Gaza, cited in Halperin, *Sabbatai Zevi*, 11; on redemption through sin, see Scholem, *Sabbatai Sevi*, 802-15; G. Scholem, *Major Trends in Jewish Mysticism* (New York, 1971), 78-141; Barukh of Arezzo, *Memorial* 26, cited in Halperin, *Sabbatai Zevi*, 88. **42.** Jacob Sasportas, cited in Halperin, *Sabbatai Zevi*, 6; Barukh of Arezzo, *Memorial* 3, cited in Halperin, *Sabbatai Zevi*, 33. **43.** On Nathan's reaction, see Halperin, *Sabbatai Zevi*, 17; M. Idel, '"One from a Town, Two from a Clan" – The Diffusion of Lurianic Kabbala and Sabbateanism: A Re-examination', *Jewish History* 7.2 (1993), 79-104; for suggestions of antinomianism as a motivation, see Halperin, *Sabbatai Zevi*, 17-19; Joseph Halevi, *Letters*, cited in Halperin, *Sabbatai Zevi*, 108; on the power of mass media, see M. Goldish, *The Sabbatean Prophets* (Cambridge, Mass., and London, 2004). **44.** Barukh of Arezzo, *Memorial* 28, cited in Halperin, *Sabbatai Zevi*, 93-4. **45.** On Cardoso in 1682, see Halperin, *Sabbatai Zevi*, 186; on the Dönmeh in the modern world, see M. D. Baer, *The Dönme: Jewish Converts, Muslim Revolutionaries, and Secular Turks* (Stanford, 2010). **46.** On the ascetic followers of 'Rabbi Judah Hasid', see Meir Benayahu, 'The Holy Society of Judah Hasid and its Immigration to the Land of Israel', *Sefunot* 3-4 (1959-60), 133-4 (Heb.). **47.** P. Maciejko, *The Mixed Multitude: Jacob Frank and the Frankist Movement, 1755-1816* (Philadelphia, 2011). **48.** On the polemics of Moshe Hagiz, see E. Carlebach, *The Pursuit of Heresy: Rabbi Moses Hagiz and the Sabbatian Controversies* (New York, 1990). **49.** Moses Hayyim Luzzatto, *Mesillat Yesharim*, ed. M. Kaplan (Jerusalem, 1948), 11-12. **50.** On Eybeschütz and Emden, see J. J. Schacter, 'Rabbi Jacob Emden, Life and Major Works' (PhD dissertation, Harvard University, 1988), 370-498. **51.** *Solomon Maimon: An Autobiography*, trans. J. Clark Murray (Urbana, Ill., 2001), 167-9. **52.** On the role of the *tsaddik*, see A. Rapoport-Albert, 'God and the Zaddik as the Two Focal Points of Hasidic Worship', in G. D. Hundert, ed., *Essential Papers on Hasidism* (New York, 1991), 299-330; I. Etkes, 'The Zaddik: The Interrelationship between Religious Doctrine and Social Organization', in A. Rapoport-Albert, ed., *Hasidism Reappraised* (London, 1996), 159-67. **53.** S. Dressner, *Levi Yitzhak* (New York, 1974). **54.** M. Rosman, *Founder of Hasidism: A Quest for the Historical Ba'al Shem Tov* (Berkeley, 1996); I. Etkes, *The Besht: Magician, Mystic, and Leader* (Waltham, Mass., 2005). **55.** On *ba'alei shem* in the sixteenth through eighteenth centuries, see Etkes, *The Besht*, 7-45; on *Mifalot Elohim* of Yoel Ba'al Shem, see ibid., 33-42; on Falk, see C. Roth, *Essays and Portraits in Anglo-Jewish History* (Philadelphia, 1962), 139-64. M. K. Schuchard, 'Dr. Samuel Jacob Falk: A Sabbatian Adventurer in the Masonic Underground', in M. Goldish and R. Popkin, eds., *Jewish Messianism in the Early Modern World* (Dordrecht, 2001), 203-26. **56.** *Toledot Ya'akov Yosef*, 'Vayetse', 89, cited in R. Elior, *The Mystical Origins of Hasidism* (Oxford, 2006), 58; *Toledot Yaakov Yosef*, 25. **57.** For different historiographical approaches to the social dimensions of the founding of Hasidism, see S. Ettinger, 'The Hasidic Movement – Reality and Ideals', in G. D. Hundert, ed., *Essential Papers on Hasidism* (New York, 1991), 226-43; M. J. Rosman, 'Social Conflicts in Międzybóz in the Generation of the Besht', in Rapoport-Albert, ed., *Hasidism Reappraised*, 51-62; G. Dynner, *Men of Silk: The Hasidic Conquest of Polish Jewish Society* (Oxford, 2006); *Shiv[h]ei haBesht* 21, in D. Ben-Amos and J. R. Mintz, *In Praise of Baal Shem Tov* (New York, 1984), 35-6; M. Rosman, *Founder of Hasidism: A Quest for the Historical Ba'al Shem Tov* (Berkeley, 1996), 165. **58.** Rapoport-Albert (ed.), *Hasidism Reappraised*, 80-94, 268-87. **59.** On Shneur

Zalman of Lyady, see R. Elior, *The Paradoxical Ascent to God: The Kabbalistic Theosophy of Habad Hasidism*, trans. J. M. Green (Albany, NY, 1993). **60.** On the functioning of a hasidic court, see I. Etkes, 'The Early Hasidic Court', in E. Lederhendler and J. Wertheimer, eds., *Text and Context: Essays in Modern Jewish History and Historiography in Honor of Ismar Schorsch* (New York, 2005), 157-86. **61.** On Nahman of Bratslav, see A. Green, *Tormented Master: A Life of Rabbi Nachman of Bratslav* (Philadelphia, 1979). **62.** On the image and memory of the Seer of Lublin, see D. Assaf, 'One Event, Two Interpretations: The Fall of the Seer of Lublin in the Hasidic Memory and Maskilic Satire', *Polin* 15 (2002), 187–202. **63.** On the bans against the *hasidim* in 1772 and after, see M. L. Wilensky, 'Hasidic–Mitnaggedic Polemics in the Jewish Communities of Eastern Europe: The Hostile Phase', in G. D. Hundert, ed., *Essential Papers on Hasidism* (New York, 1991), 244-71. **64.** For the opponents of Hasidism, see E. J. Schochet, *The Hasidic Movement and the Gaon of Vilna* (Lanham, Md, 1993); A. Nadler, *The Faith of the Mithnagdim: Rabbinic Responses to Hasidic Rapture* (Baltimore, 1997), 29-49; on accusations of Hasidism as tending towards pantheism, see Nadler, *The Faith of the Mithnagdim*, 11-28. **65.** *Solomon Maimon: An Autobiography*, 174-5. **66.** On attempts by the Russian state to end hostilities, see J. D. Klier, *Russia Gathers her Jews* (DeKalb, Ill., 1986), 142; on Levi Isaac ben Meir of Berdichev, see Y. Petrovsky-Shtern, 'The Drama of Berdichev: Levi Yitshak and his Town', *Polin* 17 (2004), 83–95. **67.** *Shivhei haBesht* 21, in Ben-Amos and Mintz, *In Praise of Baal Shem Tov*; on the relationship between Hasidism and messianism, see G. Scholem, *The Messianic Idea in Judaism: And Other Essays on Jewish Spirituality* (London, 1971), 176-202.

CHAPTER 16: FROM THE ENLIGHTENMENT TO THE STATE OF ISRAEL

1. On the demographic changes to Jewish populations in the modern period, see 'Appendix: The Demography of Modern Jewish History', in P. Mendes-Flohr and J. Reinharz, eds., *The Jew in the Modern World: A Documentary History*, 2nd edn (New York and Oxford, 1995), 701–21. **2.** On the problems in establishing the size of current Jewish populations, see S. DellaPergola, 'World Jewish Population 2010', *Current Jewish Population Reports* (Cincinnati, 2010), Number 2, pp. 8-11. **3.** Shalom Aleichem, *The Old Country*, trans. F. and J. Butwin (London, 1973), pp. 76-7. **4.** S. Schwarzfuchs, *Napoleon, the Jews and the Sanhedrin* (London, 1979). **5.** On Jews in Germany in the nineteenth century, see M. Meyer, *The Origins of the Modern Jew* (Detroit, 1979); D. Sorkin, *The Transformation of German Jewry 1780-1840* (New York, 1987). **6.** R. Harris, *The Man on Devil's Island: Alfred Dreyfus and the Affair that Divided France* (London, 2010). **7.** On Jews in Romania in the nineteenth century, see C. Iancu and L. Rotman, *The History of the Jews of Romania*, vol. 2 (Bucharest, 2005). **8.** On the British chief rabbinate, see M. Freud-Kandel, *Orthodox Judaism in Britain since 1913: An Ideology Forsaken* (London, 2006); on English antisemitism:

A. Julius, *Trials of the Diaspora: A History of Anti-Semitism in England* (Oxford, 2012).   **9.** On Islamic antisemitism, see R. Wistrich, *A Lethal Obsession: Anti-Semitism from Antiquity to the Global Jihad* (New York, 2010); on the *Protocols*, see B. Segel, *A Lie and a Libel: A History of the Protocols of the Elders of Zion* (Lincoln, Nebr., 1995).   **10.** On the history of the Jewish Enlightenment, see S. Feiner, *Haskalah and History: The Emergence of a Modern Jewish Historical Consciousness* (Oxford, 2002).   **11.** On the history of the *Wissenschaft des Judentums*, see I. Schorsch, 'Breakthrough into the Past: The Verein für Cultur und Wissenschaft der Juden', *LBIYB* 33 (1988), 3-28.   **12.** On the Bund, see N. Levin, *While Messiah Tarried: Jewish Socialist Movements, 1871-1917* (New York, 1977); on 'Zionist' ideas in the nineteenth century before Herzl, see A. Hertzberg, ed., *The Zionist Idea* (New York, 1997), 101-98.   **13.** For the history of Zionism, see W. Laqueur, *A History of Zionism* (London, 2003); on post-Zionism, see D. Penslar, *Israel in History: The Jewish State in Comparative Perspective* (London, 2007).   **14.** S. Huberband, *Kiddush Hashem* (Hoboken, NJ, 1987); Yizkor prayer in A. Gold et al., eds., *The Complete Art Scroll Machzor: Pesach* (New York, 1990), 993.   **15.** I. Elbogen, *Jewish Liturgy: A Comprehensive History* (Philadelphia, 1993); on synagogue architecture in the nineteenth and twentieth centuries, see C. Krinsky, *Synagogues of Europe: Architecture, History, Meaning* (New York, 1985) and D. Stolzman and H. Stolzman, eds., *Synagogue Architecture in America: Faith, Spirit and Identity* (Philadelphia, 2004).   **16.** L. Jacobs, *A Tree of Life: Diversity, Flexibility, and Creativity in Jewish Law*, 2nd edn (Oxford and Portland, Oreg., 1984), 157-9.   **17.** For an early example of an orthodox rabbi seeking an academic doctorate to acquire status within his community, see D. H. Ellenson, *Rabbi Esriel Hildesheimer and the Creation of Modern Jewish Orthodoxy* (Tuscaloosa, Alas., and London, 1990), 14-15 (on Hildesheimer in 1843).   **18.** On Jewish identity in modern Israel, see N. Rothenberg and E. Schweid, eds., *Jewish Identity in Modern Israel* (Jerusalem, 2004); The Law of Return, amended 1970, sections 4A and 4B; on the Brother Daniel case, see N. Tec, *In the Lion's Den: The Life of Oswald Rufeisen* (New York, 2008).   **19.** On Judaism and modern warfare, see L. Jacobs, *What Does Judaism Say about . . . ?* (Jerusalem, 1973), 228-30 (on lack of treatment of 'just war' theory); A. Ravitzky, 'Prohibited Wars in the Jewish Tradition'; and M. Walzer, 'War and Peace in the Jewish Tradition', in T. Nardin, ed., *The Ethics of War and Peace* (Princeton, 1998).   **20.** On Goren, see S. Freedman, *Rabbi Shlomo Goren: Torah Sage and General* (New York, 2006).   **21.** On Holocaust Day (Yom HaShoah), see J. Young, 'When a Day Remembers: A Performative History of Yom Ha-Shoah', *HM* 2.2 (1990), 54-75.   **22.** On the JFS case, see R on the application of E) v Governing Body of JFS and others (2009), UKSC 15; J. Weiler, 'Discrimination and Identity in London: The Jewish Free School Case', *Jewish Review of Books* (Spring, 2010).   **23.** C. Rosen, *The Book of Jewish Food* (London, 1997).

CHAPTER 17: REFORM

1. A. Arkush, *Mendelssohn* (Albany, NY, 2004); D. Sorkin, 'The Case for Comparison: Moses Mendelssohn and the Religious Enlightenment', *MJ* 14.2 (1994), 121-38. **2.** M. Mendelssohn, *Jerusalem, or, On Religious Power and Judaism*, trans. A. Arkush (Hanover, 1983), 139, 133. **3.** On Mendelssohn and his influence, see S. Feiner, *Moses Mendelssohn: Sage of Modernity* (New Haven, 2010). **4.** On Kant and Judaism, see N. Rotenstreich, *Jews and German Philosophy: The Polemics of Emancipation* (New York, 1984). **5.** *Solomon Maimon: An Autobiography*, trans. J. Clark Murray (Urbana, Ill., 2001), 280; A. Socher, *The Radical Enlightenment of Solomon Maimon: Judaism, Heresy and Philosophy* (Stanford, 2006). **6.** J. M. Harris, *Nachman Krochmal: Guiding the Perplexed of the Modern Age* (New York, 1991); on Salomon Steinheim, see J. Guttman, *Philosophies of Judaism* (Philadelphia, 1964), 344-9. **7.** W. G. Plaut, *The Rise of Reform Judaism* (New York, 1963), 138-9; on Holdheim, see C. Wiese, ed., *Redefining Judaism in an Age of Emancipation: Comparative Perspectives on Samuel Holdheim* (Leiden, 2007). **8.** On Israel Jacobson, see J. R. Marcus, *Israel Jacobson: The Founder of the Reform Movement in Judaism* (Cincinnati, 1972). **9.** Plaut, *The Rise of Reform Judaism*, 31; on the confirmation ceremony, see D. Resnik, 'Confirmation Education from the Old World to the New: A 150 Year Follow-Up', *MJ* 31.2 (2011), 213-28; Chorin cited in D. Philipson, *The Reform Movement in Judaism*, ed. S. B. Freehov (rev. edn, New York, 1967), 442, n. 1.2. **10.** On Geiger, see M. Wiener, *Abraham Geiger and Liberal Judaism: The Challenge of the Nineteenth Century* (Philadelphia, 1962); on the Frankfurt conference decisions, see Philipson, *The Reform Movement*, 143-224, and M. Meyer, *Response to Modernity: A History of the Reform Movement in Judaism* (Detroit, 1995), 133ff. **11.** On Luzzatto (Shadal), see N. H. Rosenbloom, *Luzzatto's Ethico-Psychological Interpretation of Judaism* (New York, 1965); Y. Harel, 'The Edict to Destroy Em la-Miqra', Aleppo 1865', *HUCA* 64 (1993), 36 (Heb.) **12.** On reform in Hungary and Transylvania, see M. Carmilly-Weinberger, 'The Jewish Reform Movement in Transylvania and Banat: Rabbi Aaron Chorin', *SJ* 5 (1996), 13-60; on the emancipation bill in Hungary in 1867, see R. Patai, *The Jews of Hungary: History, Culture, Psychology* (Detroit, 1996), 230-40; on the Neologists, see N. Katzburg, 'The Jewish Congress of Hungary, 1868-1869', *HJS* 2 (1969), 1-33; M. Carmilly-Weinberger, ed., *The Rabbinical Seminary of Budapest, 1877-1977* (New York, 1986); on the Status Quo Ante group, see H. Lupovitch, 'Between Orthodox Judaism and Neology: The Origins of the Status Quo Movement', *JSS* 9.2 (2003), 123-53. **13.** A. Kershen and J. Romain, *Tradition and Change: A History of Reform Judaism in Britain 1840–1995* (New York, 1995). **14.** On the religious world of Jews in the United States, see the superb survey in J. D. Sarna, *American Judaism: A History* (New Haven and London, 2004); on Einhorn, see G. Greenberg, 'Mendelssohn in America: David Einhorn's Radical Reform Judaism', *LBIYB* 27 (1982), 281-94; on Wise, see S. Temkin, *Isaac Mayer Wise* (London, 1992).

15. Pittsburgh Platform, paragraphs 2, 3, 4, 5, 7, 8; see W. Jacob, *The Changing World of Reform Judaism* (Pittsburgh, 1985). **16.** On the Central Conference of American Rabbis, see Meyer, *Response*, passim; D. Philipson, 'Message of the President', Proceedings of the Nineteenth Annual Congregation of the Central Conference of American Rabbis, *Yearbook of the Central Conference of American Rabbis*, 18 (Baltimore, 1908), 145-6. **17.** H. Cohen, *Der Begriff der Religion in System der Philosophie* (Giessen, 1915); J. Melber, *Hermann Cohen's Philosophy of Judaism* (New York, 1968); J. Lyden, 'Hermann Cohen's Relationship to Christian Thought', *JJTP* 3.2 (1994), 279-301. **18.** On Formstecher, see Guttmann, *Philosophies of Judaism*, 308-13. **19.** On Samuel Hirsch, see N. Rotensteich, *Jewish Philosophy in Modern Times* (New York, 1968), 120-36. **20.** A. Friedlander, *Leo Baeck* (London, 1973); L. Baker, *Days of Sorrow and Pain: Leo Baeck and the Berlin Jews* (New York, 1978). **21.** On Rosenzweig, see N. Glatzer, *Franz Rosenzweig: His Life and Thought* (Indianapolis, 1998) and P. Mendes-Flohr, ed., *The Philosophy of Franz Rosenzweig* (London, 1988). **22.** P. Vermes, *Buber* (London, 1988). **23.** On the impact of adult education on assimilated German Jews, see N. H. Roemer, *Jewish Scholarship and Culture in Nineteenth-Century Germany: Between History and Faith* (Madison, Wis., 2005); on American Reform, see M. I. Urofsky, *The Voice that Spoke for Justice: The Life and Times of Stephen S. Wise* (Albany, NY, 1982); D. Polish, *Renew our Days: The Zionist Issue in Reform Judaism* (Jerusalem, 1976); Columbus Platform, paragraphs 16, 18. **24.** On Abba Hillel Silver, see M. Raider, *Abba Hillel Silver and American Zionism* (London, 1997). **25.** Judah Magnes cited in 'Holocaust Theology', in A. Berlin and M. Grossman, eds., *The Oxford Dictionary of the Jewish Religion*, 2nd edn (New York and Oxford, 2011); on Holocaust theology, see S. Katz, ed., *The Impact of the Holocaust on Jewish Theology* (New York, 2007); M. Buber, *The Eclipse of God* (London, 1952); on Emil Fackenheim, see S. Portnoff et al., *Emil L. Fackenheim: Philosopher, Theologian, Jew* (Leiden, 2008). **26.** E. Levinas, *Talmudic Readings*, 440; on Levinas, see E. Levinas, *The Levinas Reader*, ed. S. Hand (Oxford, 1989); A. Herzog, 'Benny Levy versus Emmanuel Levinas on "Being Jewish"', *MJ* 26 (2006), 15–30. **27.** On Regina Jonas, see K. von Kellenbach, '"God Does Not Oppress Any Human Being": The Life and Thought of Rabbi Regina Jonas', *LBIYB* 39 (1994), 213-25; E. Klapheck, *Fräulein Rabbiner Jonas: The Story of the First Woman Rabbi* (San Francisco, 2004). **28.** *National Jewish Population Survey 2000-2001* (2003); on the World Union for Progressive Judaism, see Meyer, *Response*, 335-53; on contemporary developments within Reform Judaism, see W. G. Plaut, *The Growth of Reform Judaism: American and European Sources: 50th Anniversary Edition, with Select Documents, 1975-2008* (Philadelphia and Lincoln, Nebr., 2015).

CHAPTER 18: COUNTER-REFORM

1. On the banquet, see L. Sussman, 'The Myth of the Trefa Banquet: American Culinary Culture and the Radicalization of Food Policy in American Reform Judaism', *AJAJ* 57 (2005), 29-52; M. Stanislawski, *A Murder in Lemberg:*

Politics, Religion and Violence in Modern Jewish History (Princeton, 2007); J. H. Hertz, cited in A. Kershen and J. Romain, eds., *Tradition and Change* (London, 1995), 159; on the conversion issue in relations between Reform and orthodox, see E. Tabory, '"The Legitimacy of Reform Judaism: The Impact of Israel on the United States', in D. Kaplan, ed., *Contemporary Debates in American Reform Judaism: Conflicting Visions* (London, 2001), 221-34. **2.** On *Eleh Divrei haBrit*, see P. Mendes-Flohr and J. Reinharz, eds., *The Jew in the Modern World: A Documentary History*, 2nd edn (New York and Oxford, 1995), 167-9; S. R. Hirsch, 'Religion Allied to Progress', cited in ibid., 197-202. **3.** On Bernays, see S. Poppel, 'The Politics of Religious Leadership: The Rabbinate in 19th-Century Hamburg', *LBIYB* 28 (1983), 439-70. **4.** Seventeenth Letter in S. R. Hirsch, *The Nineteen Letters of Ben Uziel*, trans. B. Drachman (New York, 1899), 170-71. **5.** S. R. Hirsch, *Judaism Eternal: Selected Essays from the Writings*, trans. I. Grunfeld, 2 vols. (London, 1956), 2:215-16. **6.** On the *Austrittsgemeinden* in the nineteenth century, see R. Liberles, *Religious Conflict in Social Context: The Resurgence of Orthodox Judaism in Frankfurt am Main, 1838-1877* (New York, 1985), 210-26. **7.** H. Graetz, *Gnosticismus und Judentum* (Krotoschin, 1846); on the relationship of Graetz with Hirsch, see I. Grunfeld in Hirsch, *Judaism Eternal*, 1:xxxvii, xliv. **8.** On Zacharias Frankel, see I. Schorsch, 'Zacharias Frankel and the European Origins of Conservative Judaism', *Judaism* 30.3 (1981), 344-54. **9.** On Salomon Breuer, see J. Breuer, 'Rav Dr. Salomon Breuer: His Life and Times', in *The Living Hirschian Legacy* (New York, 1989), 25-44. **10.** On Agudat Israel in the early twentieth century, see G. Bacon, *The Politics of Tradition: Agudath Yisrael in Poland, 1916-1939* (Jerusalem, 1996); on Hayyim Soloveitchik, see N. Solomon, *The Analytic Movement: Hayyim Soloveitchik and his Circle* (Atlanta, 1993); on the Beth Jacob schools, see J. Grunfeld-Rosenbaum, *Sara Schenirer* (New York, 1968). **11.** On Isaac Breuer, see M. Morgenstern, *From Frankfurt to Jerusalem: Isaac Breuer and the History of the Secession Dispute in Modern Jewish Orthodoxy* (Leiden, 2002); on Yitzhak Soloveitchik, see S. Meller, *The Brisker Rav: The Life and Times of Maran Hagaon Harav Yitzchok Ze'ev Halevi Soloveichik* (Jerusalem, 2007). **12.** On Joseph B. Soloveitchik, see R. Ziegler, *Majesty and Humility: The Thought of Rabbi Joseph B. Soloveitchik* (New York, 2012). **13.** Moshe Feinstein, cited in I. Robinson, '"Because of our Many Sins": The Contemporary Jewish World as Reflected in the Responsa of Moshe Feinstein', *Judaism* 35 (1986), 42. **14.** A. Ferziger, *Exclusion and Hierarchy: Orthodoxy, Non-Observance and the Emergence of Modern Jewish Identity* (Philadelphia, 2005); C. Kaiser, 'Sitting on Fences: The Toleration of Compromise and Mixed Seating in Orthodox Synagogues in the USA', in M. Goodman et al., *Toleration within Judaism* (Oxford and Portland, Oreg., 2013), ch. 10; H. Soloveitchik, 'Rupture and Reconstruction in the Transformation of Contemporary Orthodoxy', *Tradition* 28.4 (1994), 69-130; on the development of modern orthodoxy into a structured movement, see Z. Eleff, *Modern Orthodox Judaism: A Documentary History* (Philadelphia and Lincoln, Nebr., 2016). **15.** Y. Leibovitz, *Judaism, Human Values and the Jewish State* (Cambridge, Mass., 1992), with introduction by E. Goldman. **16.** On Eliezer

Berkovits, see C. Raffel, 'Eliezer Berkovits', in S. Katz, ed., *Interpreters of Judaism in the Late Twentieth Century* (Washington, DC, 1993), 1-15; on the declaration in the Warsaw Ghetto, see G. Bacon, 'Birthpangs of the Messiah: The Reflections of Two Polish Rabbis on their Era', *SCJ* 7 (1991), 86-99; I. Greenberg, 'Cloud of Smoke, Pillar of Fire: Judaism, Christianity, and Modernity after the Holocaust', in E. Fleischner, ed., *Auschwitz: Beginning of a New Era? Reflections on the Holocaust* (New York, 1977), 30, 33. **17.** On Sabato Morais, see A. Kiron, 'Dust and Ashes: The Funeral and Forgetting of Sabato Morais', *AJH* 84.3 (1996), 155-88; S. Schechter, *Studies in Judaism* (London, 1896), xvii–xviii; L. Finkelstein, *The Pharisees*, 2 vols. (Philadelphia, 1936–66). **18.** See N. Bentwich, *Solomon Schechter: A Biography* (Cambridge, 1938); E. K. Kaplan, *Holiness in Words: Heschel's Poetics of Piety* (Albany, NY, 1996). **19.** J. Hellig, 'Richard Rubenstein', in Katz, ed., *Interpreters of Judaism in the Late Twentieth Century*, 249-64. **20.** R. Gordis, ed., *Emet ve-Emunah: Statement of Principles of Conservative Judaism* (New York, 1988), 19-22. **21.** M. Waxman, *Tradition and Change* (New York, 1958), 361. **22.** On the history of Reconstructionist Judaism, see J. Gurock and J. Schacter, *A Modern Heretic and a Traditional Community: Mordecai M. Kaplan, Orthodoxy, and American Judaism* (New York, 1996); on the synagogue as community centre, see D. Kaufman, *Shul with a Pool: The 'Synagogue-Center' in American Jewish History* (Hanover, 1999). **23.** R. T. Alpert and J. J. Staub, *Exploring Judaism: A Reconstructionist Approach* (New York, 2000). **24.** On the contemporary state of Conservative Judaism, see E. Cosgrove, 'Conservative Judaism's "Consistent Inconsistencies"', *Conservative Judaism* 59.3 (2007), 3-26. **25.** L. Jacobs, *We Have Reason to Believe* (London, 1957; 3rd edn, 1965); on the history of Jewish ideas about 'Torah from Heaven', see N. Solomon, *Torah from Heaven: The Reconstruction of Faith* (Oxford, 2012).

CHAPTER 19: REJECTION

1. Isa 66:5; Ezra 10:3; S. C. Heilman, *Defenders of the Faith: Life among the Ultra-Orthodox* (New York, 1992). **2.** On the Indian wig scandal, see D. Wakin, 'Rabbis' Rules and Indian Wigs Stir Crisis in Orthodox Brooklyn', *New York Times*, 14 May 2004. **3.** On the role of women in *haredi* society, see T. El-Or, *Educated and Ignorant* (Boulder, Colo., 1994); N. Stadler, *Yeshiva Fundamentalism: Piety, Gender and Resistance in the Ultra-Orthodox World* (New York, 2009), 117-34. **4.** On the Hatam Sofer, see P. Mendes-Flohr and J. Reinharz, *The Jew in the Modern World: A Documentary History*, 2nd edn (New York and Oxford, 1995), 172; Y. D. Shulman, *The Chasam Sofer: The Story of Rabbi Moshe Sofer* (Lakewood, NJ, 1992). **5.** Shulman, *The Chasam Sofer*, 25. **6.** On Ganzfried, see J. Katz, 'The Changing Position and Outlook of Halachists in Early Modernity', in L. Landman, ed., *Scholars and Scholarship* (New York, 1990), 93-106; on the Hafets Hayyim, see M. M. Yashar, *Saint and Sage: Hafetz Hayim* (New York, 1937); on the *Mishnah Berurah*, see S. Fishbane, *The Method and Meaning of the Mishnah Berurah* (Hoboken, NJ, 1991); on Karelitz, see S. Finkelman, *The Chazon Ish: The Life and Ideals of Rabbi Yeshayah Karelitz*

(New York, 1989). **7.** Finkelman, *The Chazon Ish*, 218. **8.** I. Etkes, *Rabbi Israel Salanter and the Musar Movement: Seeking the Torah of Truth* (Jerusalem, 1993). **9.** L. S. Dawidowicz, ed., *The Golden Tradition: Jewish Life and Thought in Eastern Europe* (New York, 1989), 192-200. **10.** On the Gur *hasidim*, see A. Y. Bromberg, *Rebbes of Ger: Sfar Emes and Imrei Emes* (Brooklyn, NY, 1987). **11.** J. R. Mintz, *Hasidic People: A Place in the New World* (Cambridge, Mass., 1992). **12.** A. I. Kook, *The Light of Penitence . . .* (London, 1978), 256; see Y. Mirsky, *Rav Kook: Mystic in a Time of Revolution* (New Haven, 2014). **13.** J. Agus, *High Priest of Rebirth: The Life, Times and Thought of Abraham Isaac Kuk* (New York, 1972); M. Weiss, *Rabbi Zvi Hirsch Kalischer, Founder of Modern and Religious Zionism* (New York, 1969); on Alkalai, see J. Katz, 'The Forerunners of Zionism and the Jewish National Movement', in idem, *Jewish Emancipation and Self-Emancipation* (Philadelphia, 1986), 89-115. **14.** On Gush Emunim, see M. Keige, *Settling in the Hearts: Jewish Fundamentalism in the Occupied Territories* (Detroit, 2009). **15.** On Meir Kahane, see R. Friedman, *The False Prophet: Meir Kahane – from FBI Informant to Knesset Member* (London, 1990). **16.** On Neturei Karta, see I. Domb, *The Transformation: The Case of the Neturei Karta* (London, 1989). **17.** A. Kaplan, *Rabbi Nahman's Wisdom* (New York, 1973), p. 275, no. 141 (with reference to slightly different versions); cf. A. Green, *Tormented Master: A Life of Rabbi Nachman of Bratslav* (Philadelphia, 1979); on the contemporary Lubavitch movement, see S. Fishkoff, *The Rebbe's Army: Inside the World of Chabad-Lubavitch* (New York, 2005). **18.** S. Hellman and M. Friedman, *The Rebbe: The Life and Afterlife of Menachem Mendel Schneerson* (Princeton, 2010). **19.** A. S. Ferziger, 'From Lubavitch to Lakewood: The Chabadization of American Orthodoxy', *MJ* 33 (2013), 101-24; M. Dansky, *Gateshead: Its Community, its Personalities, its Institutions* (Jerusalem, 1992). **20.** D. Berger, *The Rebbe, the Messiah, and the Scandal of Orthodox Indifference* (London, 2001).

CHAPTER 20: RENEWAL

1. A. Green, 'Judaism for the Post-Modern Era', The Samuel H. Goldenson Lecture, Hebrew Union College, 12 December 1994; on Jewish Buddhists, see J. Linzer, *Torah and Dharma: Jewish Seekers in Eastern Religions* (Oxford, 1996). **2.** Z. Schachter-Shalomi, *Jewish with Feeling* (Woodstock, Vt, 2005). **3.** R.-E. Prell, *Prayer & Community: The Havurah in American Judaism* (Detroit, 1989). **4.** P. S. Nadell, *Women Who Would be Rabbis: A History of Women's Ordination, 1889-1985* (Boston, 1998). **5.** Prayer cited from M. Feld, *A Spiritual Life: A Jewish Feminist Journey* (Albany, NY, 1999), 58. **6.** S. C. Grossman, in E. M. Umansky and D. Ashton, eds., *Four Centuries of Jewish Women's Spirituality: A Source Book* (Boston, 1992), 279-80 (on *tefillin*); S. Berrin, ed., *Celebrating the New Moon: A Rosh Chodesh Anthology* (Northvale, NJ, 1996); C. Kaiser in M. Goodman et al., *Toleration within Judaism* (Oxford and Portland, Oreg., 2013), ch. 11; A. Weiss, 'Open Orthodoxy! A Modern Orthodox Rabbi's Creed', *Judaism* 46 (1997), 409-26. **7.** J. Plaskow, *Standing Again at Sinai: Judaism from a Feminist Perspective* (New York, 1991), 198. **8.** N. Lamm,

'Judaism and the Modern Attitude to Homosexuality', in *Encyclopaedia Judaica Year Book* (Jerusalem, 1974); M. Feinstein, *Iggerot Moshe, Orach Hayyim*, vol. 4, no. 115 (New York, 1976); S. Greenberg, *Wrestling with God and Men* (Madison, Wis., 2005); C. Rapoport, *Judaism and Homosexuality* (London, 2005). **9.** E. Dorff, '*This is my Beloved, This is my Friend*': *A Rabbinic Letter on Intimate Relations* (New York, 1996), 38-40; R. Alpert, *Like Bread on the Seder Plate: Jewish Lesbians and the Transformation of Tradition* (New York, 1997); M. Shokeid, *A Gay Synagogue in New York* (New York, 1995). **10.** D. Schneer and C. Aviv, eds., *Queer Jews* (London, 2002); on Humanistic Judaism, see S. Wine, *Judaism beyond God* (Hoboken, NJ, 1995), 217, 228; D. Cohn-Sherbok et al., eds., *A Life of Courage: Sherwin Wine and Humanistic Judaism* (Farmington Hills, Mich., 2003). **11.** H. A. Wolfson, 'Sermotta', in idem, *Religious Philosophies: A Group of Essays* (Cambridge, Mass., 1961), 270-71; B. Halpern, *The American Dream: A Zionist Analysis* (New York, 1956), 144; Y. Malkin, *What Do Secular Jews Believe?* (Tel Aviv, 1998), 11-16.

CHAPTER 21: WAITING FOR THE MESSIAH?

1. On the Alliance Israélite Universelle, see M. Laskier, *The Alliance Israélite Universelle and the Jewish Communities of Morocco, 1862–1962* (Albany, NY, 1983), and A. Rodrigue, *French Jews, Turkish Jews: The Alliance Israélite Universelle and the Politics of Jewish Schooling in Turkey, 1860-1925* (Bloomington, Ind., 1990). **2.** On messianic movements in Yemen in the nineteenth century, see B. Z. Eraqi Klorman, *The Jews of Yemen in the Nineteenth Century: A Portrait of a Messianic Community* (Leiden, 1993); for Yemenite Jews in the twentieth century, see H. Lewis, *After the Eagles Landed: The Yemenites of Israel* (Boulder, Colo., 1989); T. Parfitt, *The Road to Redemption: The Jews of the Yemen, 1900-1950* (Leiden, 1996). **3.** C. S. Liebman and Y. Yadgar, 'Beyond the Religious–Secular Dichotomy: *Masortim* in Israel', in Z. Gitelman, ed., *Religion or Ethnicity? Jewish Identities in Evolution* (New Brunswick, 2009), 171-92. **4.** T. Parfitt and E. Semi, *The Beta Israel in Ethiopia and Israel: Studies on the Ethiopian Jews* (Richmond, Surrey, 1998); T. Parfitt and E. Trevisan Semi, *Judaising Movements* (London, 2002); J. E. Landing, *Black Judaism: Story of an American Movement* (Durham, NC, 2002); D. H. Stern, *Messianic Judaism: A Modern Movement with an Ancient Past* (Jerusalem, 2007) (see above, Chapter 7). **5.** Deut 23:3; S. Riskin, *A Jewish Woman's Right to Divorce* (New York, 2006). **6.** D. Hartman, *A Heart of Many Rooms* (Woodstock, Vt, 2001). **7.** M. H. Danzger, *Returning to Tradition* (New Haven, 1989); L. Davidman, *Tradition in a Rootless World* (Berkeley, 1991). **8.** On the Temple Institute, see J. Goldberg, 'Jerusalem Endgames', *New York Times Magazine*, 3 October 1998. **9.** N. Shragai, 'Present-day Sanhedrin', *Haaretz*, 28 February 2007; Jos. *AJ* 10.210.

Further Reading

The classic survey by S. W. Baron, *A Social and Religious History of the Jews*, 2nd edn (New York, 1952–) is hugely informative and remains very readable, but it was left incomplete (at 18 volumes, with two separate index volumes) on the author's death in 1989. W. D. Davies et al., eds., *The Cambridge History of Judaism* (Cambridge, 1984–), which currently stands at 4 volumes, covers the millennium from the Persian period to the late Roman-rabbinic period.

Of general histories of the Jews, the most accessible brief accounts can be found in N. de Lange, *Atlas of the Jewish World* (Oxford and New York, 1984) and M. Gilbert, *The Routledge Atlas of Jewish History*, 6th edn (London, 2003). S. Grayzel, *A History of the Jews: From the Babylonian Exile to the Present*, 2nd edn (New York, 1968) is now very out of date, but many of the contributions in H. H. Ben-Sasson, ed., *A History of the Jewish People* (London, 1976) continue to be valuable. P. Johnson, *History of the Jews* (London, 1987) is enthusiastic and engaging. S. Schama, *The Story of the Jews* (London, 2013–) is being published in three volumes and provides a more substantial narrative, but it still will not displace the superb multi-authored narrative in D. Biale, ed., *Cultures of the Jews: A New History* (New York, 2002), which emphasizes the variety of Jewish experiences in different places and periods.

For the history of the development of Judaism in the biblical period, see A. Rainer, *A History of Israelite Religion in the Old Testament Period*, 2 vols. (Louisville, Ky, 1994). On the late Second Temple period and its aftermath, S. J. D. Cohen, *From the Maccabees to the Mishnah*, 3rd edn (Louisville, Ky, 2014) provides a clear guide. S. Schwartz, *Imperialism and Jewish Society, 200 B.C.E. to 640 C.E.* (Princeton, 2001) is primarily concerned to promote a distinctive and stimulating (if controversial) thesis about the impact of Christianity in the Roman world on the development of Judaism, but in the process gives readers an excellent account of the variety of Jewish religious life in the Roman world before Islam. For the thought world of the rabbinic sages in the talmudic period, E. E. Urbach, *The Sages, their Concepts and Beliefs*, 2 vols. (Jerusalem, 1975) remains valuable despite its outdated methodology in describing the development of these concepts and beliefs from tannaitic to amoraic times. For the rabbinic society in Babylonia in which these ideas took shape, the most accessible recent accounts in English are the relevant chapters in S. T. Katz, ed., *The Cambridge History of Judaism*, vol. 4: *The Late Roman-Rabbinic Period* (Cambridge, 2006).

R. Brody, *The Geonim of Babylonia and the Shaping of Medieval Jewish Culture* (New Haven and London, 1998) provides a clear and scholarly description of rabbinic Judaism in the last centuries of the first millennium CE. The substantial collection of essays in M. Polliack, ed., *Karaite Judaism: A Guide to its History and Literary Sources* (Leiden, 2004) is the best introduction to this aspect of Judaism beyond the rabbis. For Greek Judaism in the Middle Ages, see A. Sharf, *Byzantine Jewry from Justinian to the Fourth Crusade* (London, 1971).

Most books on medieval Judaism focus on specific rabbis or religious movements, but S. Stroumsa, *Maimonides in his World: Portrait of a Mediterranean Thinker* (Princeton, 2009) has a wider scope. D. H. Frank and O. Leaman, eds., *The Cambridge Companion to Medieval Jewish Philosophy* (Cambridge, 2003) contains essays on the philosophical approach to Judaism taken by medieval Jews from the ninth to the sixteenth century under the influence of Islam and Christianity. L. Jacobs, *A Tree of Life: Diversity, Flexibility, and Creativity in Jewish Law*, 2nd edn (London and Portland, Oreg., 2000) is a classic study, packed with erudition and insights, which covers more than just the medieval period. The illuminating presentation of complex medieval and later texts in D. R. Blumenthal, *Understanding Jewish Mysticism: A Source Reader*, 2 vols. (New York, 1978–82) encourages sympathetic understanding of mystical trends while precluding simple explanations. On early modern Judaism, the best survey is by D. Ruderman, *Early Modern Jewry: A New Cultural History* (Princeton, 2010). D. Abulafia, *The Great Sea: A Human History of the Mediterranean* (London, 2011) provides much detail and colour on Jewish Communities across the Mediterranean in the medieval and early modern periods. For a clear introduction to the issues which have shaped Judaism in the modern period, see the collection of essays in N. de Lange and M. Freud-Kandel, eds., *Modern Judaism: An Oxford Guide* (Oxford, 2005).

Many short introductions to contemporary Judaism are available and all provide some historical background. Among the best are N. de Lange, *Judaism*, 2nd edn (Oxford, 2003); idem, *An Introduction to Judaism*, 2nd edn (Cambridge, 2010); O. Leaman, *Judaism: An Introduction* (London, 2011); N. Solomon, *Judaism: A Very Short Introduction*, 2nd edn (Oxford, 2014). Of reference works, C. Roth, ed., *Encyclopaedia Judaica*, 16 vols. (Jerusalem, 1971) is pre-eminent and has not been wholly displaced by the second edition, edited in 22 volumes by M. Berenbaum and F. Skolnik (Detroit, 2007), which is much less widely available. I. Singer, ed., *The Jewish Encyclopedia*, 12 vols. (New York, 1901–6) is now over a century old and therefore lacking in any coverage of the twentieth century, but the whole work is freely available on the internet, and many of the entries on earlier Judaism remain useful.

Among other valuable reference works, see L. Jacobs, *The Jewish Religion: A Companion* (Oxford, 1995), N. de Lange, *The Penguin Dictionary of Judaism* (London, 2008) and A. Berlin and M. Grossman, eds., *The Oxford Dictionary of the Jewish Religion*, 2nd edn (New York and Oxford, 2011).

Index

ALLEN LANE
an imprint of
PENGUIN BOOKS

Also Published

Sunil Amrith, *Unruly Waters: How Mountain Rivers and Monsoons Have Shaped South Asia's History*

Christopher Harding, *Japan Story: In Search of a Nation, 1850 to the Present*

Timothy Day, *I Saw Eternity the Other Night: King's College, Cambridge, and an English Singing Style*

Richard Abels, *Aethelred the Unready: The Failed King*

Eric Kaufmann, *Whiteshift: Populism, Immigration and the Future of White Majorities*

Alan Greenspan and Adrian Wooldridge, *Capitalism in America: A History*

Philip Hensher, *The Penguin Book of the Contemporary British Short Story*

Paul Collier, *The Future of Capitalism: Facing the New Anxieties*

Andrew Roberts, *Churchill: Walking With Destiny*

Tim Flannery, *Europe: A Natural History*